MUSIC
FOR
THE VOICE

MUSIC

FOR

THE VOICE

A Descriptive List of Concert and Teaching Material

by

SERGIUS KAGEN

Volume III of the series

The Field of Music

edited by Ernest Hutcheson, *President Emeritus*
of the Juilliard School of Music

RINEHART & COMPANY, INC.

NEW YORK · TORONTO

To the memory of

MARCELLA SEMBRICH

who first introduced me to most of

the music listed in this volume

CONTENTS

IV

OPERATIC EXCERPTS

1. For Soprano:

2. For Mezzo-soprano or Alto:

3. For Tenor:

4. For Bass and Baritone:

ACKNOWLEDGMENTS

The compilation of this volume, particularly at a time when practically no foreign publications were available in the United States, was a complex task. It was further complicated by the fact that most of our libraries possess rather incomplete collections of songs, especially those of minor composers.

I tender my sincerest thanks to Mr. Ernest Hutcheson, without whose invaluable advice and unfailing interest, this volume would never have been written; to Madame Eva Gauthier, Madame Povla Frijsh, Miss Florence Kimball and Mr. George Fergusson, among many others, for allowing me the use of their collections of vocal music and for giving me much necessary information; to Misses Burnette Bradley, Audrey Goodman, and Mary Williamson Hooker, and Messrs. Norman Farrow and Robert Harmon for their patient and diligent co-operation in the necessary research and clerical work involved in collecting and classifying the material, and to Miss Ruth Neal for her valuable help in preparing the list of folk songs. I also am much indebted to Miss Gwendolyn Mackillop of the Juilliard School of Music Library, to Dr. George S. Dickinson of Vassar College, to G. Schirmer, Inc. (especially to Mr. Lester Hodges, who was kind enough to put the stock of the Schirmer store at my disposal, and to Mr. David Green who located the copies which I needed), and to Mr. M. C. Platte of G. Ricordi and Company.

PREFACE

Any descriptive work ought to state with utmost exactitude its aim and scope. It seems only fair that the author and the reader should agree from the outset on what the work in question is or is not.

The aim of this book is to provide the singer, the teacher, the coach, and the amateur in the search of suitable material with a handy guide listing as many composers of vocal solo music as seems practicable and as many examples of each composer's work as seems advisable for the purpose of giving the reader an opportunity to form a fair idea of this composer's vocal music.

Any and every serious student of vocal music will no doubt know most of the compositions listed in this guide. Yet, for many a singer and teacher this guide may prove to be valuable; it may remind one of a composer or a song that had slipped one's memory; it may - and I hope it will - stimulate the reader to acquaint himself with the unlisted compositions of the composers mentioned here and - this being one of the main purposes of this guide - will assist him in selecting material for his type of voice, or for his students.

This guide is not in any way intended as a work of musicology. Vocal literature is so vast that any guide to it, claiming any degree of completeness, would become through sheer volume almost totally useless for any practical purpose. If one considers that a complete list of Bach soli for bass alone would comprise some three hundred entries, and that Handel, Gluck, Piccini, Grétry, Scarlatti, to name but a very few, would not be far behind in their output, one can easily realize that the perusal of such a list would leave the reader only bewildered.

Again, many a good song or aria has been written by some composer who otherwise has not succeeded in attaining any distinction in his art. The number of such solitary successful efforts must be legion. To try to list them all would, again, seem utterly useless.

The selection of solo excerpts from sacred works has been limited to only those examples which have by now become a part of standard concert repertoire, such as excerpts from the sacred works of Purcell, Handel, Bach, Haydn, Mozart, Mendelssohn, etc. Thus, the entire and very considerable field of sacred music, as such, has not been considered in preparation of this volume, and this volume contains no special section devoted to sacred music. The excerpts included are to be found appended to the lists of the songs of the respective composers.

The selection of nineteenth century operatic excerpts has been deliberately limited to the most celebrated airs only. No attempt was made to include the multitude of effective airs and solo excerpts of minor operatic composers, since such an attempt would obviously lead to an enormously extended list of doubtful practical value. A few widely known airs of minor composers, however, have been included, in instances when such airs are easily available. Twentieth century opera is barely represented in this volume since for the most part it lacks well-defined solo pieces suitable for separate performance with pianoforte accompaniment.

No attempt has been made to list examples of the song literature before the seventeenth century, since that music, in the opinion of this writer, does not lend itself too well to performance with pianoforte accompaniment and is for the most part not easily available in modern reprints.

The bibliographical references found in this volume are simply intended for practical use in the United States only, since practically all of the material that happens to be in the public domain is available in a multitude of editions. It must be mentioned that during the war a great number of copyright transfers took place, and that at present the music publishing, importing and exporting business is in a rather chaotic state, here and abroad, so that much of the music listed in this volume may be temporarily out of print or published by publishers other than those mentioned in this volume.

Another consideration presented itself. This guide being primarily intended for use in America, songs and airs in Russian, Eastern European and Scandinavian languages which have no adequate English translations had perforce to be omitted. The same consideration had to govern the selection of folk songs. It seemed best to exclude all but Irish, Scottish, English and American examples.

It seems necessary also to remind the readers of this volume that because of the staggeringly large amount of vocal music, the so-called "standard repertoire" of a singer varies considerably, depending on the country in which the singer lives. A standard repertoire of an instrumentalist is essentially much more stable and more easily defined than that of a vocalist. This volume is primarily devoted to the repertoire at present used in the United States, a repertoire in many respects quite different from that used in Great Britain, not to mention France, Italy or Germany.

To reiterate: this guide does not claim to furnish anything approaching a complete list of all the compositions for solo voice, even by the most celebrated composers. If one is particularly interested in the vocal compositions of some particular composer, one can find the desired information in any of the reliable biographies, music dictionaries, and such works, or obtain it from the catalogues of a good musical library.

This guide is not intended to remind one of the justly or unjustly forgotten works of the celebrated composers, or to remind one of the perhaps very excellent works of composers now totally forgotten.

It is a practical guide, a bare outline, accompanied by a few critical notes and practical performance suggestions, and even as such will no doubt be criticized severely for innumerable omissions, committed wittingly or unwittingly, as well as for the inclusion of numerous entries and their evaluation. But the process of selection and evaluation, in so far as any art is concerned, is unfortunately a largely personal matter.

However, should this guide prove to be of help in stimulating anyone's interest in exploring the realm of music for voice, and should it prove itself useful to a singer attempting to lay the foundation for a repertoire, its purpose will have been accomplished.

I know that many errors will be discovered in this book. I have striven to keep their number as low as possible and I shall be glad to have my attention drawn to such errors so that, should there be another edition, they may be corrected.

HOW TO USE THIS BOOK

This book is not an encyclopedia of vocal music. Please read the preface.

This book is divided into the following main sections:

(1) Songs and Airs before the Nineteenth Century
(2) Songs: Nineteenth and Twentieth Centuries
(3) Folk Songs
(4) Operatic Excerpts (mainly Nineteenth Century).

As noted in the preface, no special section is devoted to excerpts from sacred works. Whenever such excerpts are included they are to be found attached to the song lists of the respective composers.

For the sake of convenience in listing the songs and airs of Bach, Handel, Gluck, Haydn and Mozart, all the material included of each of these five masters is listed in a separate section.

Concert arias are listed in song lists of the respective composers. Arias from dramatic cantatas, such as "L'Enfant Prodigue" by Debussy, are listed with operatic excerpts.

The composers in each section are listed alphabetically. Under the names of the composers all titles are listed alphabetically, in their original languages, with the exception of Russian, Scandinavian and miscellaneous songs and airs which are listed in English translations. In listing the operatic excerpts in the section "Songs and Airs before the Nineteenth Century", the first words of a recitative (when a recitative is listed) are listed first, the first words of the air are listed below and the title of the opera is given in parentheses, below the first words of the air. Thus, an air by Cimarosa, for instance, is listed as follows: Recitative: Cara, son tutto vostro
Air: Brillar mi sento il core
(Il Matrimonio Segreto)

In listing operatic excerpts from the works of the Nineteenth and Twentieth Centuries, however, and in listing excerpts from the operas and oratorios by Handel and Mozart, the title of the opera is given first, the recitative and/or air being listed below it, thus:

Le Nozze di Figaro
Recitative: Giunse al fin il momento
Air: Deh vieni non tardar

or

Carmen
Votre toast

As mentioned before, the opera titles are listed by composers.

In listing song titles it seemed advisable sometimes to give the first line of the text in parentheses, when there are two or more songs by the same composer possessing the same title, but different texts (as in the case of many songs by Schubert, for instance). Sometimes an identifying subtitle given by the composer is listed in parentheses.

The following system is used to indicate the pitches:

C - B   c - b   c1 - b1 c2 - b2   c3 - f3

Thus, for instance, a compass of G-f1 would mean:

a compass of d-bb1:

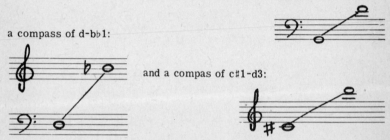

and a compas of c#1-d3:

In cases where the composer has inserted optional notes, such notes are indicated in parenthesis. For instance, the compass (a) c'-g^2 (c3) is a-c3, but both a and c3 are optional.

The tessitura is given approximately only, since to establish the tessitura of any vocal piece with precision is obviously an impossibility. When (H) or (L) is added to the pitches of the tessitura it indicates that it was impossible to establish with certainty the original key of the song in question and either a high copy (H) or a low copy (L) was used for the listing. When no pitches are indicated in the tessitura column, the tessitura and the compass seemed identical to this writer. The entries in the Type of Voice are primarily suggestions and are to be considered as such by the reader, since it is obvious that any singer who has acquired a more than adequate command of his instrument could, theoretically at least, perform any song, provided it was transposed to suit his voice. In instances when "All voices" is indicated the necessity of such transposition is of course taken for granted. It does not mean, however, that the song is available in transposed editions. The suggestions "Men's voices" and "Women's voices" are as a rule prompted by considerations of the text. It is obvious that such suggestions are largely a matter of personal preference.

In many instances where operatic material is listed, especially in airs intended for soprano, the type of voice for which this writer considers the air most suitable is given first and the type of voice for which the air may be suitable in his opinion is given in parentheses, such as lyric soprano (coloratura soprano) or dramatic soprano (Lyric soprano). When only "Soprano" is indicated, it means that in the opinion of this writer the air is suitable for all types of soprano voices. The same procedure is adopted in listing tenor airs.

In some instances, when the composer writes in a manner suitable to all varieties of any type of voice (as Bach and Handel) the Type of Voice column is omitted. Also in instances when the composer favors some special type of voice (as, for example, Mozart, Wagner and Gluck in their tenor airs), a note prefacing the list discusses the type of voice for which the airs may be most suitable, and the Type of Voice column is again omitted.

In the Remarks column a short description of the characteristics of the song or air is attempted, limited for the most part to its tempo, the character of its vocal line, and its general mood. No critical comment is included, although some obvious performance demands and performance suggestions are from time to time discussed.

"See" followed by the name or names of composers indicates that the same text has been set to music under the same title by the composer or composers mentioned.

In describing operatic airs the terms "Andante, Allegro" and an "Andante, Allegro Air" are often used. They denote a two-movement aria form much in fashion during the second half of the eighteenth and the first half of the nineteenth century. Airs written according to such a pattern consist of a sustained, lyrical slow movement and a brilliant, often very florid final allegro, intended for a display piece. Practically all airs of, for instance, Bellini or Donizetti follow this pattern.

The term "Compound Air" denotes a rather free aria form where several contrasting movements are manipulated according to the demands of the text. An excellent example of a compound air is the "Divinités du Styx" (Alceste) by Gluck. The term "Scena" denotes a very extended recitative, containing independent melodic material. It often seems impossible to establish a clearly defined distinction between a recitative and a scena.

Bibliographical indications are given last in parentheses. As a rule the publisher's name is given; in some instances, however (as in the Songs and Airs before the Nineteenth Century section), a general bibliography is attached, with a list of abbreviations used, and such abbreviations, usually the names of arrangers or editors of collections instead of publishers, are indicated in parentheses. In instances when songs are available in many excellent editions, the editions are discussed in the prefatory note and no bibliographical material is included in the Remarks column.

"Generally available" in parentheses indicates that there are so many separate editions of the song or air that to single out one of them in preference to the others seemed unfair.

The name of the publisher in parentheses indicates that the song or air is available separately in that edition.

"Score" followed by the publisher's name indicates that the most authentic and the most easily obtainable version of the air is to be found in the complete piano score of the opera or oratorio, in the edition indicated.

Whenever possible, biographical data has been included. In some instances, however, it has been omitted since it was not obtainable in standard reference works, and this writer did not have the inclination nor the necessary equipment to embark on such researches, which in most cases seemed fruitless as well as unnecessary. No biographical data is included in the section dealing with contemporary British and American songs.

I

SONGS AND AIRS

BEFORE THE NINETEENTH CENTURY

SONGS AND AIRS BEFORE THE NINETEENTH CENTURY

The few songs and solo excerpts from the larger vocal works of the seventeenth and eighteenth century composers, listed below, represent but a pitifully small fraction of an extraordinarily extensive literature.

The reasons that limited the listing of this material to so few, standard examples are as follows:

(1) The sheer bulk of the material of this period is so vast that a thoroughly representative list of such music would occupy a larger space than is presently allotted to the entire volume.

(2) Most of the material, at present little known, is as yet available only in editions which are for the most part difficult to obtain.

(3) Each school and mode or manner of composing that arose during those two centuries possesses a certain general uniformity of style, form and texture. This uniformity seems to overshadow the individual characteristics of the minor composers who wrote in the manner of any of such respective schools, at least in so far as the average well-informed performer of today and not an expert musicologist is concerned.

Thus even this scant list can be considered as being to a certain degree representative of the vocal music of the period.

Most of the music for solo voice written before the end of the eighteenth century is published today in the form of various arrangements. This is due to the fact that most such music, in its original form, lacks a written-out piano accompaniment, being either scored for orchestra or confined to the figured or unfigured bass.

Many of these arrangements, admirable as they may be, are nevertheless singularly lacking in much textual information which seems to be desirable. Songs and airs have been frequently transposed in such arrangements, yet the original key is rarely indicated; a translation has often been substituted for the original text, yet no mention of this fact is made. Whole sections of the original are sometimes omitted, yet no indication of the fact that a cut has been made is present; sometimes a recitative of one air is summarily attached to the set musical piece of another; sometimes the editor's own cadenzas are incorporated into the supposedly original melodic line; once in a while one may even encounter a vocal ensemble piece arranged as a solo, though no mention of this fact is made by the arranger. The harmonization of some arrangements is sometimes stylistically indefensible, abounding in chromaticisms, cross relations and chordal progressions unknown or studiously avoided by the composers of the period. In view of all this it seemed best to list only examples found in the most reliable collections available, and to omit most of the multitude of arrangements published singly, and often anonymously, by many publishers.

An overwhelmingly large percentage of the songs and airs listed below is of operatic origin. Yet when an opera ceases to be performed as a stage work and the few airs extracted from it survive only as music, the type of voice for which the air was originally intended by the composer becomes a consideration of little practical import. Since this question is still further complicated by the fact that singing as now practiced differs greatly in one respect from singing as it was practiced during the seventeenth and eighteenth centuries, nothing less than the most extensive and exhaustive research could establish with any amount of certitude the precise type of voice for which some particular air was originally intended. The difference mentioned above lies, of course, in the seventeenth and eighteenth century practice of employing castrati, falsetto singers (not to be confused with the former), as well as boy singers for the singing of alto and soprano parts. This practice, however, was not so prevalent as to exclude the employment of female voices completely. The current practice of considering the old operatic airs as songs, and of singing them in whatever key happens to be most suitable for the individual type of voice, seems therefore fully justified. The procedure adopted by this writer in compiling the following lists is as follows:

In listing airs excerpted from the operas of Mozart, the most frequently performed operas of Gluck, and oratorios and cantatas by Handel, Bach and Haydn, the type of voice is indicated as precisely as his knowledge of the subject permits.

In listing airs excerpted from the now-forgotten operas of the period it seemed best to dispense with precise indications of the type of voice whenever the text and the general character of the vocal line seemed to allow it.

Whenever possible, the title of the opera is listed in parentheses under the title of the air. The arrangement and the edition which this writer considers preferable is indicated in the Remarks column. The material, with few exceptions, is listed by language groups, though the national origin of the composer is thus often disregarded. The airs and songs of Handel, Bach, Gluck, Mozart and Haydn are listed in separate sections. It is hoped that by arranging the material in this way a number of unnecessary duplications and confusing cross references have been avoided.

Generally speaking, the Italian vocal music of the seventeenth and eighteenth centuries is now most widely known among singers, due no doubt to the use of much of it for teaching purposes.

The French vocal music of the period is as yet neither widely known nor much appreciated outside of France. This seems a great pity, since in so far as the average present-day English-speaking singer is concerned, his repertoire of music written before the nineteenth century is very limited and, as noticed above, consists largely of Italian airs long since familiar to every singing student. It is sincerely hoped that the perusal of some of the examples of French music of the seventeenth and eighteenth centuries listed below will encourage the readers of this volume to delve further into this extraordinarily rich and rewarding literature.

Much of what applies to the French vocal music of this period applies equally to the English songs and airs, especially those of the seventeenth century. It seems incomprehensible that so little of this music is used in teaching, for instance, in the United States, and that so little of it is performed.

The German composers of this period, who wrote in German with the exception of Mozart and the towering genius of J. S. Bach, whose music transcends all limitations of time and style, have contributed relatively little to vocal literature. It seemed advisable to list but a few examples of minor German masters, since their music is largely of only historical interest, and since most of it is for all practical purposes unavailable now.

A few songs and airs of Spanish composers of the period can be found in the section devoted to Spanish songs. They are listed under Joaquin Nin, who arranged them.

SONGS AND AIRS IN ENGLISH BEFORE THE NINETEENTH CENTURY

Bibliography

The name found in parentheses in the Remarks column indicates one of the following collections:

Bantock: One Hundred Songs of England, edited by Bantock, published by Ditson.

Dolmetsch Selected English Songs and Dialogues, edited by Dolmetsch, published by Boosey.

Duncan: The Minstrelsy of England, Vo. II edited by Duncan, published by Augener.

Fellowes: Forty Elizabethan Songs, edited by Fellowes, published by Stainer and Bell.

Hatton and Fanning: Songs of England, edited by Hatton and Fanning, published by Boosey.

Keel: Elizabethan Love Songs, edited by Keel, published by Boosey.

Moffat: The Minstrelsy of England, edited by Moffat, published by Bayley and Ferguson.

Potter: Reliquary of English Song, edited by Potter, published by Schirmer.

Wilson: Old English Melodies, edited by Wilson, published by Boosey.

ANONYMOUS

TITLE	COMP.	TESS.	TYPE	REMARKS
Ah! Willow	bb-c2	d1-bb1	All voices	Slow, sustained. (Wilson)
Come, let's be merry	bb-eb2 (f2)	f1-c2	Not too suitable for very light high voices	Spirited, gay. (Wilson)
Drink to me only with thine eyes	f1-f2	f1-c2	All voices	Sustained. (generally available)
False Phillis	a-d2 (e2)	d1-b1	Men's voices	Animated, graceful, humorous. (Wilson)
Have you seen but a whyte lillie grow	e1-f2	f1-d2	All voices	Sustained, delicate. (Dolmetsch)
Ralph's ramble to London	c1-e2	e1-c2	Most suitable for men's voices	Animated. Demands facile articulation. Humorous. (Wilson)
The happy lover	bb-eb2	eb1-c2	Most suitable for men's voices	Sustained, graceful. Demands some flexibility. (Wilson)
The slighted swain	c1-d2	e1-c2	All voices	A graceful, humorous minuet. (Wilson)

MICHAEL ARNE
(1740-1786)

TITLE	COMP.	TESS.	TYPE	REMARKS
Lass with the delicate air	b-g2	g1-e2	Not too suitable for very low voices	Light and graceful. Demands some flexibility and lightness of tone. (generally available)
The topsails shiver in the wind	ab-f1	eb-eb1	Baritone	Vigorous. Demands some flexibility. (Moffat)
This cold flinty heart	d#1-g#2	g#1-e2	Soprano	Graceful. Demands some flexibility. (Duncan)

DR. THOMAS AUGUSTINE ARNE
(1710-1778)

Many, if not most of the astonishingly large number of songs and airs by Dr. Arne are now almost totally forgotten, since only a few are obtainable in modern reprints.

Although one could hardly consider Dr. Arne a composer of great importance, practically all of his vocal music possesses a certain distinctive charm and grace and seems to have lost little, if any of its effectiveness. Like all the minor eighteenth century composers Arne was an expert craftsman who fashioned his music in accordance with the conventional pattern of his day, a pattern largely dominated by the dance forms of his time, such as the minuet, the gavotte, etc.

Musically his songs present no problem, being unabashedly simple in their harmonic and rhythmic scheme. His treatment of the vocal line, however, though invariably effective and considerate of the singer, demands often a more than elementary technical proficiency.

In the opinion of this writer his songs and airs could be most successfully used as teaching material designed to acquaint the present-day English-speaking singer with the stylistic problems of the vocal music of the eighteenth century.

TITLE	COMP.	TESS.	TYPE	REMARKS
Bacchus god of mirth and wine	A-e1	d-d1	Bass or baritone	A vigorous, animated, drinking song. (Barrett, Twenty Songs of Arne, (Novello)
Blow, blow, thou winter wind	c1-f2	f1-d2	All voices	Sustained. Demands some flexibility. (Potter)
By dimpled brook (Comus)	d1-g2	g1-e2	All voices	Graceful, sustained. (Potter)
By the gaily circling glass	B♭-e♭1	f-c1	Bass or baritone	Animated, vigorous. (Barrett, Twenty Songs of Arne, Novello)
Cast, my love, thine eyes around	d1-g2	g1-e2	Most suitable for high voices	Graceful, sustained. Demands some flexibility. (Duncan)
Decrepit winter limps away	d1-e♭2	e♭1-c2	All voices	Animated, graceful, spirited. Demands facile articulation. (Moffat)
Despairing beside a clear stream	c1-f2	f1-e2	High or medium voices	Sustained, graceful. Demands some flexibility. (Barrett, Twenty Songs of Arne, Novello)
Fresh and strong the breeze is blowing	a1-e2		All voices	Sustained. (Barrett, Twenty Songs of Arne, Novello)
Honest lover	d1-f♯2	g1-d2	All voices	Sustained. (A saraband) (Duncan)
In infancy	c1-f2	f1-d2	Women's voices	Sustained. Has some florid passages. (Barrett, Twenty Songs of Arne, Novello)

TITLE	COMP.	TESS.	TYPE	REMARKS
My dog and my gun	c1-f2	e1-c2	Men's voices	A gay, spirited song in praise of hunting. Demands some flexibility. (Duncan)
Now Phoebus sinketh in the west (Comus)	A-e1 (f1)	c-c1	Bass or baritone	Recitative and a spirited air. Demands some flexibility. A transposed edition for tenor can be found in Hatton and Fanning. (Potter)
Peggy	eb-g2	g1-f2	Most suitable for men's voices, excepting bass	Graceful. Demands some flexibility. (Potter)
Phillis, we don't grieve	d1-g2	g1-e2	Not too suitable for very low voices	Graceful. Demands some flexibility. (Potter)
Preach me not your musty rules (Comus)	d1-g2	d1-d2 (H)	Men's voices	Spirited, vigorous. Demands some flexibility. (Arranged by Samuel Endicott. R. D. Row Music Co.)
Sally	d1-g2	f1-eb2	Not too suitable for very low voices	Graceful. Demands some flexibility. (Potter)
Strephon on the hill	e1-f2	f1-d2	Women's voices	Graceful, light. Demands some flexibility. (Moffat)
Sweet Nan of the vale	d1-f2	f1-eb2	Not too suitable for very low voices	Graceful. (Moffat)
Tell me where is fancy bred	b-g2	g1-eb2 (H)	All voices	Animated, graceful. Demands some flexibility. (Bantock)
The arch denial	c1-f2	f1-c2	All voices	Animated, light, humorous. (Moffat)
The echoing horn	f1-g2	f1-eb2	Men's voices	A spirited, vigorous hunting song. Demands facile articulation and some flexibility. (Duncan)
The faithful lover	d#1-g2	g1-e2	Not too suitable for very low voices	Sustained. Demands some flexibility. (Potter)
The maiden's complaint	e1-gb2	g1-eb2	Women's voices	Recitative and a sustained air. Demands some flexibility. (Moffat)

TITLE	COMP.	TESS.	TYPE	REMARKS
The plague of love	d1-g2	g1-eb2	All voices	Sustained, graceful. Demands some flexibility. (Wilson)
The shepherd	d#1-e2	f#1-d2	Most suitable for men's voices	Slow. Demands some flexibility. (Barrett, Twenty Songs of Arne, Novello)
The soldier tired of war's alarms	c#1-b2	f#1-a2	Soprano. Most suitable for high voices	A spirited, in parts florid display piece. Could be sung by a high baritone, tenor, or mezzo-soprano if transposed. (Hatton and Fanning)
The sycamore shade	bb-f2	f1-eb2	Alto or mezzo-soprano	Sustained, graceful. Demands some flexibility. A trifle long. (Barrett, Twenty Songs of Arne, Novello)
Under the greenwood tree	c1-f#2	f#1-d2	All voices	Spirited, light. (Potter)
Water parted from the sea	eb1-g2	f1-eb2	All voices	Sustained. Demands some flexibility. (Potter)
We all love a pretty girl under the rose	c1-f2	eb1-c2	All voices	Light, animated, humorous. Demands facile articulation. (Hatton and Fanning)
When daisies pied	d1-eb2	f1-eb2	Not too suitable for very low voices	Graceful, delicate. Demands some flexibility. (Moffat)
When forced from dear Hebe to go	d1-f2	f1-d2	Men's voices	Sustained. (Hatton and Fanning)
Where the bee sucks	c1-f2	f1-d2	Not too suitable for very low voices	Graceful, animated. Demands some flexibility. (Bantock)
Why so pale and wan?	a-e2	d1-d2	Not too suitable for light high voices	Rather vigorous, gently humorous. (Duncan)

DR. SAMUEL ARNOLD
(1740-1802)

Amo, amas, I love a lass	g1-g2	g1-e2	Men's voices	Spirited, humorous. (Duncan)

JOHN ATTEY
(d. 1640?)

On a time	b-e2	e1-b1	Not too suitable for light high voices	Sustained, graceful. (Keel)

TITLE	COMP.	TESS.	TYPE	REMARKS
Sweet was the song	e1-a2	a1-f2	Most suitable for light soprano	Delicate, sustained. Demands some flexibility. A Christmas lullaby. (Keel)

THOMAS ATTWOOD
(1765-1838)

TITLE	COMP.	TESS.	TYPE	REMARKS
At early dawn	e1-f♯2	a1-e2	Not too suitable for very low voices	Animated, graceful. Demands some flexibility. (Potter)

JOHN BARTLET
(Early 17th Century)

TITLE	COMP.	TESS.	TYPE	REMARKS
A pretty, pretty ducke	f1-g2	a1-f2	Most suitable for light soprano	Animated, graceful. Gently humorous. (Keel)
If there be anyone	f1-f2	a1-f2	Not too suitable for very low voices	Graceful. (Keel)
I heard of late	d1-g2	g1-e2	Not too suitable for very low voices	Graceful, sustained. (Keel)
What thing is love	e1-f♯2	a1-e2	Most suitable for men's voices	Animated, graceful. Gently humorous. (Keel)
When from my love I lookte	e1-g2	g1-e2	Most suitable for men's voices	Graceful. (Keel)
Whither runneth my sweetheart?	d1-g2	g1-e2	Most suitable for high voices	Animated, light. Demands facile articulation. (Keel)
Who doth behold my mistress' face?	a1-f♯2		Most suit- for men's voices	Light, graceful. (Keel)

THOMAS H. BAYLY
(1797-1839)

TITLE	COMP.	TESS.	TYPE	REMARKS
I'd be a butterfly	g1-c3	b1-g2	Light soprano	Graceful. Has florid cadenzas by La Forge. (Arranged by La Forge, Fischer)
Long, long ago	eb1-f2	ab1-eb2 (H)	All voices	Sustained. (generally available)
We met	d1-f2	d1-b1	Women's voices	Sustained. (Hatton and Fanning)

JOHN BENET
(1570-1615)

Title	Comp.	Tess.	Type	Remarks
My mistress is as fair as fine	c1-c2		Men's voices	Sustained. (Duncan)
Weep, O mine eyes	d1-e2	g1-d2	All voices	Slow and sustained. A Transcription of a four-part madrigal. (Bantock)

SIR HENRY R. BISHOP
(1786-1855)

The inclusion of songs by Bishop in this section was primarily prompted by stylistic considerations. Bishop's pleasing and effective songs could hardly be classed as belonging to the nineteenth century, since harmonically and melodically they are written in a manner which most probably must have seemed "old-fashioned" to the listners of his day. Of no great consequence, most of his song which have survived did so mainly as florid display pieces for coloratura soprano.

Title	Comp.	Tess.	Type	Remarks
Bid me discourse	b-a2	g1-g2	Soprano	A brilliant, somewhat florid display song. (Hatton and Fanning)
Echo song	d1-c3 (eb3)	g1-g2	Coloratura soprano	A florid display piece (Arr. by La Forge, Schirmer)
Home, sweet home	e1-e2		All voices	Sustained. (generally available)
Lo, here the gentle lark	e1-c3	f1-g2	Coloratura soprano or light soprano	Animated, brilliant display song. Has florid cadenzas. Flute obbligato (Generally available)
Love has eyes	f1-g2	bb1-f2	Most suitable for women's voices	Light, animated. Demands facile articulation. (Generally available)
Pretty mocking bird	d1-ab2	g1-f2	Coloratura or light soprano	Animated, has florid cadenzas. Demands facile articulation. (Hatton and Fanning)
Rest, my child	f1-f2		Women's voices	Sustained, subdued. (Duncan)
Should he upbraid	d1-d3	g1-e2	Light soprano	Light and spirited. Demands some flexibility. For a shortened version see the Liebling edition published by Schirmer.
Tell me, my heart	d1-ab2	g1-f2	Light soprano	A sustained introduction and an animated and rather florid andantino. (Hatton and Fanning)

JOHN BLOW
(1648-1708)

Title	Comp.	Tess.	Type	Remarks
It is not that I love you less	d1-g2	g1-e2	Men's voices	Sustained. (Bantock)

TITLE	COMP.	TESS.	TYPE	REMARKS
Since the spring comes on	d1-g#2	d1-d2	Most suitable for men's voices	Graceful. (Duncan)
Tell me no more	d1-g2	e1-e2 (H)	All voices	Animated, graceful. Demands some flexibility (Bantock)
The self-banished	c1-f2	f1-d2	All voices	Sustained. (Potter)

DR. BOYCE
(1710-1779)

TITLE	COMP.	TESS.	TYPE	REMARKS
Tell me no more I am deceived	d1-ab2	g1-e2	Men's voices	Animated, graceful.
The sword within the scabbard keep (from Dryden's "Secular Masque")	bb-eb2	eb1-c2	Medium or low voices	Animated, vigorous. (Arr. by G. E. P. Arkwright. Oxford)

THOMAS BROWN
(18th Century?)

TITLE	COMP.	TESS.	TYPE	REMARKS
Shepherd! thy demeanor vary	e1-c3	a1-f2	Light soprano	Animated, light. Has florid passages. (Wilson)

WILLIAM BYRD
(1542-1623)

TITLE	COMP.	TESS.	TYPE	REMARKS
I thought that love had been a boy	e1-g2	g1-e2 (H)	All voices	Delicate, sustained. A transcription of a madrigal. (Bantock)
My mind to me a kingdom is	bb-eb2	eb1-bb1	All voices	Sustained. (Moffat)
O mistress mine	g1-g2	g1-e2 (H)	Most suitable for men's voices	Sustained. (Bantock)

THOMAS CAMPIAN
(1567-1620)
(See prefatory note to John Dowland)

TITLE	COMP.	TESS.	TYPE	REMARKS
Beauty is but painted hell	e1-f#2	g#1-e2	All voices	Sustained (Keel)
Breake now my heart and die	e1-g2	f#1-e2	Men's voices	Graceful, sustained. (Keel)
Come, you pretty false eyed wanton	g#1-f#2	a1-e2	Men's voices	Spirited, light. (Keel)
Every dame affects good fame	e1-g2	a1-f2	Most suitable for men's voices	Graceful, humorous. (Keel)
Fair, if you expect admiring	b-c#2	e1-b1 (L)	Men's voices	Animated, graceful. (Fellowes)
Follow thy fair sun	c#1-c#2		Men's voices Most	Sustained, somber. (Fellowes)

- 12 -

TITLE	COMP.	TESS.	TYPE	REMARKS
Follow your saint	d1-d2		Most suitable for men's voices	Sustained. (Fellowes)
Here she her sacred bower adornes	d1-d2		Men's voices	Animated, graceful. Demands some flexibility. (Keel)
Her rosie cheeks	e1-f#2	g#1-e2	Men's voices	Sustained. Demands some flexibility. Graceful. (Keel)
Jack and Joan	f1-d2		All voices	Spirited. (Fellowes)
Move now with measured sound	e1-e2	g1-e2	All voices	Sustained. (Duncan)
My sweetest Lesbia	c1-d2	e1-c2	Men's voices	Sustained. (Fellowes)
Never weather beaten sail	d1-e2	g1-d2	All voices	Sustained. A religious song taken from Divine and Moral Songs. Originally written for four parts. (Bantock)
Now hath Flora robb'd her bow'rs	d1-e2	g1-d2	All voices	Sustained. (Duncan)
O deare, that I with thee might live	f#1-f#2	b1-f#2	Most suitable for men's voices	Sustained. (Keel)
Oft have I sighed for him	f1-f2	g1-db2	Women's voices	Sustained, somber. (Keel)
Shall I come, sweet love, to thee	f1-f2 (H)		Most suitable for men's voices	Sustained. Originally for two voices with lute accompaniment. (Bantock)
The cypress curtain of the night	d1-c2		All voices, excepting a very light soprano	Slow, sustained, somber. (Fellowes)
There is a garden in her face	d1-e2	g1-d2	Most suitable for men's voices	Sustained. (Bantock)
Thrice tosse these oaken ashes in the air	e1-g2	g1-e2	All voices	Sustained. A magic incantation to break love's spell. (Keel)
The peaceful westerne winde	f1-g2	bb1-f2	Most suitable for men's voices	Sustained. (Keel)
When to her lute Corinna sings	b-d2	e1-b1 (L)	Most suitable for men's voices	Sustained, somewhat declamatory. (Fellowes)

TITLE	COMP.	TESS.	TYPE	REMARKS

HENRY CAREY
(1690-1743)

TITLE	COMP.	TESS.	TYPE	REMARKS
A pastoral	c1-g2 (a2)	g1-e2	Soprano	Animated, florid, graceful. (Wilson)
Divinest fair	d1-g2	g1-e2	Most suitable for men's voices	Sustained, graceful. (Duncan)
Here's to thee, my boy	b♭-e♭2	e♭1-e♭2	Men's voices, except a very light tenor.	A spirited vigorous, somewhat rowdy drinking song. Demands some flexibility. (Moffat)
The plausible lover	d1-g2	g1-e2	Most suitable for light high voices.	Graceful, delicate. Delicate. Demands considerable flexibility and a good command of high pp. (Potter)

JEREMIAH CLARK
(1659-1707)

TITLE	COMP.	TESS.	TYPE	REMARKS
The bonny grey-eyed morn	c1-g2	g1-e2	All voices	Graceful. Demands some flexibility. (Duncan)

WILLIAM CORKINE
(Early 17th Century)

TITLE	COMP.	TESS.	TYPE	REMARKS
Deare, though your mind	b-d2	e1-c2	Most suitable for men's voices	Animated, graceful. (Keel)
Down, down, proud mind	a-d2	d1-d2 (L)	Not too suitable for very light voices	Very sustained, grave. (Fellowes)
Shall a smile or a guileful glance	g1-g2	g1-e2	Most suitable for men's voices	Graceful. (Keel)
Sweete cupid, ripen her desire	d1-d2		Men's voices	Animated, graceful. (Keel)

WILLIAM CROFT
(1678-1727)

TITLE	COMP.	TESS.	TYPE	REMARKS
Musidora	d1-g2 (a2)	g1-e2	Most suitable for high voices	Sustained. (Duncan)

JOHN DAVY
(1763-1824)

TITLE	COMP.	TESS.	TYPE	REMARKS
Just like love is yonder rose	f1-g2	g1-e2	Not too suitable for very low voices	Graceful. Requires some flexibility. (Duncan)

WILLIAM de FESCH
(1700-1758)

Daphne	d1-e2	f#1-d2	All voices	Graceful, humorous. (Potter)

For other songs and airs see under "Italian" in this section (Page 32).

CHARLES DIBDIN
(1745-1814)

Blow high, blow low	G-c1	Bb-bb	Bass	A vigorous sailor's song. (Potter)
Jolly young waterman	d1-e2	g1-d2	Men's voices	Animated. Demands facile articulation. (Bantock)
The tinker's song	db1-f2	db1-db2	Men's voices	Spirited, vigorous, humorous. (Wilson)
The wily fox	a-g2	e1-e2	Men's voices	A spirited hunting song. Demands facile articulation. (Duncan)

JOHN DOWLAND
(1563-1626)

The songs of John Dowland, Thomas Campian, and a number of lesser known Elizabethan composers for one or more voices with lute accompaniment, have been made popularly available only comparatively recently, mainly in the admirable transcriptions of Frederick Keel and Dr. Edmund H. Fellowes.

Every singer, especially in the English-speaking countries, ought to be thoroughly familiar with these remarkable songs. None of them are vocally taxing, their compass rarely exceeding a tenth and for the most part being confined to an octave or a ninth. Stylistically, however, they may present a number of difficulties to those who are used to the more flamboyant manner of delivery considered desirable in certain types of nineteenth century vocal music.

A competent performance of these songs would seem to demand above all a considerable degree of rhythmic precision, as well as a certain amount of understatement in the delivery of the text. Under no circumstances, however, should the search for such precision and simplicity terminate in superficial pedantry, for these songs are by no means "quaint" examples of the music of the past. Unless the present-day singer can accept these songs as an artistically valid combination of poetry and music it would be best for him not to attempt to perform them.

Those who are particularly interested in English song of the seventeenth century are referred to the monumental collection by Dr. Fellowes, comprising some five hundred titles and published in twenty-three issues by Stainer and Bell under the title The English School of Lutenist Song-Writers.

TITLE	COMP.	TESS.	TYPE	REMARKS
A shepherd in a shade	d1-d2		All voices	Animated, graceful. (Keel)
Awake, sweet love	e1-f2	a1-f2	Most suitable for men's voices	Animated, graceful. (Potter)
Away with these self-loving lads	e1-f#2	g#1-e2	Most suitable for men's voices	Animated, graceful. (Keel)
Come again	d1-e2	g1-d2	All voices	Graceful, animated. (Bantock)
Come away	g#1-g2	b1-e2	Not too suitable for very low voices	Graceful, light. (Keel)
Deare, if you change	c1-d2	g1-d2	All voices	Sustained. (Keel)
Farewell, unkind, farewell	g#1-f#2	a1-e2	All voices	Sustained. (Keel)
Fine knacks for ladies	d1-eb2		Most suitable for men's voices	An animated, somewhat vigorous "peddler's song."
Flow, my tears	c1-d2	d1-bb1	All voices, excepting very light soprano	Slow, sustained, somber. (Fellowes)
Flow not so fast, ye fountains	e1-e2	g#1-d2	All voices	Very sustained, somber. (Keel)
If my complaint could passions move	d#1-d2		All voices	Sustained. (Fellowes)
I saw my lady weep	e1-e2	g1-d2	Men's voices	Slow, sustained, somber (Fellowes)
Now, o now, I needs must part	e1-e2		All voices	Sustained, graceful. An arrangement a four-part madrigal. (Bantock)
Say, love, if ever thou didst find	f#1-d2		Most suitable for men's voices	Animated, graceful. (Fellowes)
Shall I sue, shall I seeke for grace?	f#1-f#2	f#1-e2	Most suitable for men's voices	Light, graceful. Demands facile articulation. (Keel)
Sleep, wayward thoughts	eb1-c2		Most suitable for men's voices	Sustained. (Fellowes)
Sorrow, sorrow, stay	f#1-f#2	a#1-e2	All voices	Slow, somber, somewhat declamatory. (Keel)
Stay, time, awhile thy flying	g1-f2		All voices	Graceful, sustained. (Keel)
Weep you no more, sad fountains	e#1-f#2	a1-e2	All voices	Slow, sustained. (Keel)

TITLE	COMP.	TESS.	TYPE	REMARKS
What if I never speede?	f#1-g2	b1-f#2	Most suitable for men's voices	Animated, graceful. (Keel)
Woeful heart with griefe oppressed	c1-eb2	eb1-c2	Not too suitable for very high voices	Slow, sustained, somber. (Keel)

JOHN ECCLES
(1650-1735)

The avowal	e1-g2	g1-e2	Men's voices	Graceful, sustained. (Duncan)

THOMAS FORD
(1580-1648)

Come, Phillis	e#1-e2	f#1-d2	Most suitable for men's voices	Sustained, graceful. (Keel)
Faire, sweet, cruell	c1-eb2	e1-c2	All voices	Somewhat declamatory. Not fast. (Fellowes)
Not full twelve years	a-e2	e1-c2	Not too suitable for very light high voices	Sustained, slow, somber. Demands some flexibility. (Fellowes)
Now I see thy looks were feigned	b-d2	e1-b1	Men's voices	Sustained, not slow. (Fellowes)
Passing by	d1-e2	g1-d2	Men's voices	Sustained. (Duncan
Since first I saw your face	f1-f2	f1-c2	Most suitable for men's voices	Sustained. (Bantock)
What then is love, sings Corydon	c1-d2		All voices	Sustained, not slow. (Fellowes)

JOHN ERNEST GALLIARD
(1687-1749)

The early horn	c1-g2	f1-f2	Men's voices	Recitative and a spirited, rather florid hunting song. (Potter)
The lover's message	d1-e2	f#1-d2	All voices	Sustained, graceful. (Potter)

ORLANDO GIBBONS
(1583-1615)

The silver swan	f1-g2	bb1-f2 (H)	All voices	Slow and sustained. A transcription of a five-part madrigal. One of Gibbon's few secular songs. (Bantock)

TITLE	COMP.	TESS.	TYPE	REMARKS
Like as a huntsman	f1-f2		Most suitable for men's voices	Animated. Demands some flexibility. (Duncan)
Orpheus with his lute	f1-g2	f1-e2	Most suitable for high voices	Animated. Demands flexibility. (Duncan)
The nymph that undoes me	f1-f2		Men's voices	Graceful. (Duncan)

JAMES HOOK
(1746-1827)

TITLE	COMP.	TESS.	TYPE	REMARKS
Bright Phoebus	eb1-f2	ab1-eb2	Men's voices	A spirited hunting song. Demands considerable flexibility. (Neitzel, Gems of Antiquity, J. Church Co.)
Lass of Richmond Hill	c1-f2	f1-d2	Most suitable for men's voices	Graceful. (Bantock)
Love's call	db1-eb2	f1-db2	Men's voices	Graceful, sustained. (Duncan)
Mary of Allendale	eb1-ab2	g1-eb2	Most suitable for high voices	Sustained. Demands good command of high pp. (Wilson)
Softly waft, ye southern breezes	e1-g2	a1-f#2	Soprano	Animated, graceful. Demands some flexibility. (Potter)
The sweet little girl that I love	f1-a2	a1-f2	Most suitable for tenor	Sustained, graceful. Demands good command of high pp. (Wilson)

FRANCIS HOPKINSON
(1737-1791)

The songs of Francis Hopkinson, one of the first American composers, have lately attained a considerable popularity. Pleasant and tuneful, these songs are as typical of the period as any of Dr. Arne, though perhaps not as skillfully executed.

TITLE	COMP.	TESS.	TYPE	REMARKS
Beneath a weeping willows shade	d1-g2	g1-d2	All voices	Graceful. Demands some flexibility.
Come, fair Rosina	e1-f#2	a1-d2	All voices	Graceful, sustained.
My days have been so wondrous free	eb1-g2 (ab2)	ab1-eb2 (H)	All voices	Graceful.
My generous heart disdains	d1-g2	g1-d2	Most suitable for men's voices	Graceful, gently humorous. A trifle long.
O'er the hills	c#1-g2	f#1-d2	All voices	Spirited, vigorous hunting song. Demands some flexibility.

TITLE	COMP.	TESS.	TYPE	REMARKS
The traveler be-nighted	d1-g2	f1-d2	All voices	Sustained, graceful.

All songs arranged by H. V. Milligan, Arthur Schmidt edition.

TITLE	COMP.	TESS.	TYPE	REMARKS
Ode from Ossian's poems	d1-a2	e1-e2	High voices	A short solo Cantata in several contrasting movements. Demands some flexibility. (Arr. by Carl Deis. Schirmer)

CHARLES EDWARD HORN
(1786-1849)

TITLE	COMP.	TESS.	TYPE	REMARKS
Cherry ripe	d1-g2	g1-eb2	Not too suitable for very low voices	Animated, graceful. Demands some flexibility. (Generally available)
I've been roaming	c#1-f#2	f#1-d2	Women's voices	Animated, graceful. Demands facile articulation. (Bantock)
The deep, deep sea	a-g2	f#1-d2	Most suitable for men's voices	Sustained, graceful. (Hatton and Fanning)

SAMUEL HOWARD
(1710-1782)

TITLE	COMP.	TESS.	TYPE	REMARKS
The diffident lover	f#1-g2	g1-e2	Not too suitable for very low voices	Sustained, delicate. Demands some flexibility. (Potter)

TOBIAS HUME
(d. 1648)

TITLE	COMP.	TESS.	TYPE	REMARKS
Fain would I change that note	bb-eb2	eb1-c2	All voices, except a very light soprano	Sustained. (Keel)

PELHAM HUMPHREY
(1647-1674)

TITLE	COMP.	TESS.	TYPE	REMARKS
I pass all my hours	e1-f2	g#1-e2	Most suitable for men's voices	Sustained. (Bantock)
O the sad day	c1-g2	f1-eb2	All voices	Sustained, somewhat declamatory. (Bantock)
Wherever I am	c#1-f2	f#1-eb2	Men's voices	Graceful. (Moffat)

WILLIAM JACKSON
(1730-1803)

TITLE	COMP.	TESS.	TYPE	REMARKS
To fairest Delia's grassy tomb	g1-g2	g1-eb2 (H)	Most suitable for men's voices	Sustained. (Bantock)
What shepherd or nymph of the grove?	c1-g2	g1-eb2 (H)	Most suitable for men's voices	Sustained. Demands some flexibility. (Bantock)
Ye shepherds, give ear to my lay	d1-g2	a1-f2	Not too suitable for very low voices	Sustained, graceful. (Moffat)

ROBERT JOHNSON
(d. about 1634)

TITLE	COMP.	TESS.	TYPE	REMARKS
As I walked forth one summer day	c1-f2	f1-c2	Not too suitable for very light, high voices	Slow and sustained. (Bantock)
Dear, do not your fair beauty wrong	c1-g2	f1-e2 (H)	All voices	Sustained. (Bantock)

ROBERT JONES
(Early 17th Century)

TITLE	COMP.	TESS.	TYPE	REMARKS
Go to bed, sweet muse	c1-eb2	f1-c2	All voices	Animated, humorous. (Keel)
In Sherwood lived stout Robin Hood	bb-eb2	eb1-c2	All voices	Spirited. (Fellowes)
Love is a bable	a-d2	d1-d2 (L)	Most suitable for men's voices	Animated, humorous. (Fellowes)
Love's god is a boy	c1-c2		All voices	Animated, humorous. Demands in parts facile articulation. (Fellowes)
My love bound me with a kisse	e1-e2	e1-b1	Men's voices	Sustained. (Moffat)
Now what is love	c1-c2	f1-c2	All voices	Animated, gently humorous. (Fellowes)
Sweet Kate	d1-d2	e1-c2	All voices	A humorous dialogue between Kate and her lover. Demands some flexibility. (Keel)
What if I seek for love	c#1-e2	f#1-c#2	All voices	Not fast. Demands rather facile articulation. (Keel)
What if I speede	e1-g2	a1-e2	Not too suitable for very low voices	Animated, gay. (Keel)

TITLE	COMP.	TESS.	TYPE	REMARKS

HENRY LAWES
(1595-1662)

TITLE	COMP.	TESS.	TYPE	REMARKS
Amarantha sweet and fair	f1-f2		Men's voices	Sustained. (Duncan)
About the sweet bag of a bee	g1-f2		All voices	Sustained. (Potter)
Ask me why I send you here	f1-f2		All voices	Sustained. (Duncan)
Beauty and love	c#1-e2	f#1-c#2	All voices	Graceful. (Potter)
Bid me but live	g1-f2		All voices	Graceful, sustained. (Bantock)
Chloris, yourself you so excel	c1-e2	e1-c2	Men's voices	Graceful, sustained. (Duncan)
Come, lovely Phillis	d1-d2		Men's voices	Graceful. (Potter)
How happy art thou	c1-e2	g1-c2	Men's voices	Spirited. (Potter)
I am confirmed a woman can	c1-e2	g1-c2	Most suitable for men's voices	Animated, humorous. (Dolmetsch)
I do confess thou'rt smooth and fair	d1-d2	g1-d2	All voices	Sustained. (Potter)
I prithee, send me back my heart	eb1-eb2	g1-c2	All voices	Sustained. (Moffat)
If the quick spirit of your eye	f#1-f#2	g1-d2	Men's voices	Graceful, animated. (Potter)
The angler's song	f1-f2		Most suitable for men's voices	Spirited. Words by Izaak Walton. (Dolmetsch)
Tavola	c#1-e2	d1-d2	All voices	Lawes wrote this song as a satire upon the Italian songs of his day. The text is the Index of a volume of Italian songs and madrigals. (Bridge, Seventeenth Century Songs, Novello)
The nightingale	c#2-c#2	e1-b1 (L)	All voices	Sustained, delicate. (J. Woodside, Seven Centuries of Solo Song Vol. II, Boston Music Co.)
To a lady weeping	e1-d2		All voices	Sustained. (Moffat)
Unfading beauty	g1-f2		All voices	Sustained. (Duncan)
While I listen to thy voice	d1-eb2	g1-d2	Men's voices	Sustained. (Neitzel, Gems of Antiquity. J. Church Co.)

WILLIAM LAWES
(d. 1645)

TITLE	COMP.	TESS.	TYPE	REMARKS
Gather ye rosebuds while you may	g1-e2		All voices	Sustained, graceful. (Potter)

TITLE	COMP.	TESS.	TYPE	REMARKS

RICHARD LEVERIDGE
(1670-1758)

TITLE	COMP.	TESS.	TYPE	REMARKS
Black eyed Susan	d1-f#2	f#1-d2	Women's voices	A narrative song. The tune has become as popular as a folk song. (Bantock)
Jilted	f1-g2	a1-f2	Not too suitable for very low voices	Graceful. Demands some flexibility. (Duncan)
Send back my long-strayed eyes to me	d1-f2	e1-e2	All voices	Sustained. One of Leveridge's most appealing songs. (Duncan)
Sweet are the charms of her I love	d1-f2	g1-eb2	Men's voices	Sustained, graceful. Demands some flexibility. (Moffat)
The beggar's song	(g) a-d2	d1-b1	Men's voices, excepting a very light tenor	Spirited, vigorous. (Wilson)
The fairies (Now the hungry lions roar)	e1-g2	g1-e2	All voices	Animated. (Duncan)
The maid's resolution	d1-f#2	f#1-e2	Women's voices	Graceful, sustained. The words are of an amusingly moral character. (Potter)
The sweet rosy morning	eb1-eb2		Men's voices	A spirited hunting song. Demands facile articulation. (Moffat)
When dull care	b-e2 (g2)	d1-c2	Men's voices	A spirited, vigorous drinking song. (Wilson)

THOMAS LINLEY
(1732-1795)

TITLE	COMP.	TESS.	TYPE	REMARKS
Here's to the maiden of bashful fifteen	d1-d2	d1-b1	Men's voices	A spirited toast to women of all ages. Demands facile articulation. (Bantock)
Lawn, as white as driven snow	b-e2	e1-c2	Medium or low voices	A spirited setting of Autolycus' song from The Winter's Tale. (Neitzel, Gems of Antiquity. J. Church Co.)
No flower that blows	e1-f#2	a1-e2	All voices	Sustained, delicate. (Potter)
O, bid your faithful Ariel fly	b-g#2	d1-d2	High voices	Animated. Quite florid in parts. (Hatton and Fanning)
Primroses deck the bank's green side	b-e2	e1-c#2	Most suitable for men's voices	Sustained, graceful. Demands some flexibility. (Hatton and Fanning)

TITLE	COMP.	TESS.	TYPE	REMARKS
Still the lark finds repose	e1-f#2	g1-f#2	Not too suitable for very low voices	Graceful and sustained. (Duncan)
While the foaming billows roll	bb-eb2 (ab)	eb1-c2	Men's voices	A vigorous, patriotic sea song. (Wilson)

MATTHEW LOCKE
(1630-1677)

TITLE	COMP.	TESS.	TYPE	REMARKS
My lodging, it is on the cold ground	c1-eb2	f1-c2	Women's voices	Sustained. (Bantock)
The delights of the bottle	d1-e2		Men's voices	A spirited drinking song. (Duncan)

THOMAS MORLEY
(1557-1603)

TITLE	COMP.	TESS.	TYPE	REMARKS
Flora, wilt thou torment me?	d1-g2	g1-e2	Most suitable for men's voices	Animated, graceful. A transcription of a two-part canzonet. (Keel)
It was a lover and his lass	f1-f2 (H)		All voices	Light, animated. Demands facile articulation. (Bantock)
Now is the month of maying	d1-d2 (H)			Animated. (Bantock)
Sweet nymph, come to thy lover	b-e2	e1-b1	Most suitable for men's voices	Animated, graceful. Demands some flexibility. A transcription of a two-part canzonet. (Keel)
When lo! by breake of morning	a-e2	d1-d2	Most suitable for men's voices	Animated, graceful. A transcription of a two-part canzonet. (Keel)

GEORGE MUNRO
(18th Century)

TITLE	COMP.	TESS.	TYPE	REMARKS
My lovely Celia	d1-g2	g1-d2	All voices	Sustained, graceful. Demands good command of high pp. and some flexibility. (Wilson)

JAMES OSWALD
(1712-1769)

TITLE	COMP.	TESS.	TYPE	REMARKS
Peace, the fairest child of heaven	d1-g2	f1-eb2	All voices	Sustained. Demands some flexibility. (Potter)

FRANCIS PILKINGTON
(1562-1638)

TITLE	COMP.	TESS.	TYPE	REMARKS
Diaphenia	d1-d2		Men's voices	Graceful, sustained. (Keel)

TITLE	COMP.	TESS.	TYPE	REMARKS
Downe-a-downe	f1-f2	bb1-f2	Not too suitable for very low voices	Graceful. (Keel)
Rest, sweet nymphs	e1-d2		All voices	Sustained and subdued. (Fellowes)
Underneath a cypress tree	eb1-eb2	f1-c2	All voices	Sustained. (Keel)

DANIEL PURCELL
(1663-1717)

TITLE	COMP.	TESS.	TYPE	REMARKS
Phillis, talk no more of passion	d1-f2	a1-d2	All voices	Graceful. Demands some flexibility. (Potter)

HENRY PURCELL
(1658-1695)

Purcell's name, generally speaking, seems to be much more familiar than his music to the majority of performers and music lovers of today. In this respect the somewhat paradoxical nature of his fame is rather similar to that of Rameau and Lully.

One of the greatest seventeenth century composers, Purcell wrote in a remarkably individual manner. His songs and airs are perhaps among the most striking examples of his style of writing. Never unnecessarily florid, powerfully descriptive in the delineation of the mood and character of the text, impeccable in prosody, his songs and airs are nevertheless often marred, at least for the present-day performer and listener, by their undistinguished and antiquated texts. Musically, however, Purcell's songs and airs are so extraordinarily powerful that the limitations of his poetic material seem to vanish during the actual performance.

Purcell's songs and airs demand from the vocalist a peculiarly delicate balance between dramatic delivery and the impeccably clear delineation of the musical line. In singing Purcell the vocalist should always remember that the florid passages are never intended for mere display, but serve as an intensification of the dramatic context, and are for the most part strikingly descriptive of the word upon which they occur. One must also remember that Purcell's bass line is melodically almost as important as his vocal line. This writer believes that many a scholarly and well-intentioned editor of Purcell's songs and airs, which were originally written for bass (figured or unfigured) and voice, has obscured the magnificently eloquent bass line by overloading the accompaniment with too many independent inner parts. Purcell was very fond of the basso ostinato, and in certain editions the recurrence of the bass figure in some of his songs is almost inaudible in the maze of unnecessarily elaborate added counterpoint in the inner voices.

Purcell, when not writing for alto or bass often favors very high tessituras. In most of the available present-day editions his soprano or tenor songs are transposed, sometimes as much as a fourth lower than the original. The original keys can be easily ascertained by consulting the Purcell Society edition.

TITLE	COMP.	TESS.	TYPE	REMARKS
Address to Britain (King Arthur)	d1-f#2	g1-e2	All voices	Sustained and graceful. This air of Venus was originally written for (Cont.)

TITLE	COMP.	TESS.	TYPE	REMARKS
Address to Britain (King Arthur) (Cont.)	d1-f♯2	g1-e2	All voices	soprano, compass-f1-a2 but is now transposed in most modern editions. (Augener)
Ah, Belinda, I am prest with torment (Dido and Aeneas)	c1-f2	g1-eb2	Soprano or mezzo soprano	Sustained. (Score, Oxford)
Ah! cruel ruthless fate	bb-f2	eb1-eb2	All voices	Rather slow and sustained (Duncan)
Ah! how pleasant 'tis to love	e1-e2	g♯1-d2	All voices	Graceful, sustained. (Arr. by Moffat, Forsyth Bros.)
Ah, how sweet it is to love (Tyrannick love)	f♯1-g2	a1-eb2	All voices	Not fast, graceful. Demands some flexibility. Originally written for soprano. (Augener)
Ah, me, too many deaths	d1-f2	g1-e2	Women's voices	Rather slow; in parts quite florid. (Duncan)
Ah what pains	d1-g2	g1-f2	High voices	Sustained. Demands some flexibility. (Somervell, Seventeen Songs by Purcell, Novello)
Anacreon's defeat (This poet sings)	G-e1	c-c1	Bass or baritone	A short solo cantata in three contrasting movements. Demands in parts considerable flexibility. (Somervell, Seventeen Songs by Purcell, Novello)
An evening hymn (Now that the sun hath veiled his light)	d1-g2	g1-e2	All voices except a very light soprano	Very sustained sacred song on a ground bass. Demands some flexibility. (Arr. by Harvey Grace, Novello)
April who till now has mourn'd	e1-f2	a1-e2	Not too suitable for very low voices	Animated, graceful. Has florid passages. (Moffat, Six Songs by Purcell, (Bailey and Ferguson)
Arise, ye subterranean winds (The Tempest)	E-d1	c-c1	Bass	Animated, vigorous, florid. (Potter)
Ask me to love no more	d1-g2	g1-eb2	Soprano	Graceful. Demands some flexibility. (Moffat, Six Songs by Purcell. Bailey and Ferguson)
Cease, o my sad soul	g1-g2	g1-eb2	All voices	Slow, sustained. (Potter)
Come unto these yellow sands (The Tempest)	c1-g2	e1-c2	All voices	Animated. Demands some flexibility. (Ariel's song) (Augener)
Crown the year	f♯1-f2	g1-d2	All voices	Sustained. Demands some flexibility. (Augener)

TITLE	COMP.	TESS.	TYPE	REMARKS
Fly swift, ye hours	B-e1	e-d1	Baritone	Vigorous, animated, quite florid. The final section is slow and sustained. Rather long. (Somervell, Fifteen Songs by Purcell, Novello)
From rosy bow'rs	d1-g2	g1-f2	Soprano	A rather long cantata-like song describing the phases of madness of a "lady distracted by love." The phases are as follows: " sullenly mad, mirthfully mad, melancholy madness, fantastically mad, stark mad." Has some florid passages. Interpretatively, as well as stylistically, not easy. (Augener)
Full fathom five thy father lies (The Tempest)	c1-f2 (g2)	e1-d2	All voices, except a light soprano	Vigorous, spirited. Demands some flexibility. (Ariel's song) (Augener)
Had I but love	g1-g2	g1-e2	Not too suitable for very low voices	Sustained. (Duncan)
Hark! how all things in one sound rejoice	d1-f2	g1-d2	All voices	Spirited, quite florid. (Moffat, Six Songs by Purcell. Bailey and Ferguson)
Hark! the echoing air a triumph sings (Fairy Queen)	c1-f2	f1-eb2	All voices	Spirited, florid. (Moffat, Six Songs by Purcell, Bailey and Ferguson)
Hence with your trifling deity (Timon of Athens)	F-eb1	c-c1	Bass	Vigorous, spirited. Has florid passages. (Potter)
How blest are shepherds (King Arthur)	d1-g2	g1-e2	All voices	Animated, graceful. (Augener)
How delightful's the life	d1-f#2	g1-e2	All voices	Graceful. Demands some flexibility. (Somervell, Seventeen Songs by Purcell, Novello)
I attempt from love's sickness to fly (The Indian Queen)	d1-f2	ab1-eb2	All voices	Graceful. Demands some flexibility. Originally written for tenor. (Generally available)
I envy not a monarch's fate	c#1-e2	e1-c#2	Men's voices	Graceful. Demands some flexibility. (Somervell, Fifteen Songs by Purcell, Novello)

TITLE	COMP.	TESS.	TYPE	REMARKS
I fain would be free	e1-g2	g1-e2	All voices	Graceful, humorous. (Somervell, Seventeen Songs by Purcell, Novello)
If music be the food of love	d1-g2	g1-eb2	All voices	Sustained. Demands some flexibility. (Somervell, Seventeen Songs by Purcell, Novello)
I'll sail upon the Dog-star (A fool's preferment)	c1-g2	f1-d2	Men's voices	Vigorous, spirited; in parts florid. (Generally available)
In Cloris all soft charms agree	bb-eb2	eb1-c2	All voices	Graceful, sustained. (Somervell, Fifteen Songs by Purcell, Novello)
I saw that you were grown so high	c1-eb2	g1-c2	All voices	Sustained. (Moffat, Six Songs by Purcell, Forsyth Bros.)
Kind fortune smiles (The Tempest)	c1-f2	c1-c2	All voices, except a light soprano	Animated, has florid passages. (Ariel's song) (Augener)
Let each gallant heart	c1-g2	g1-e2	All voices	Sustained, graceful. Demands some flexibility. (Somervell, Seventeen Songs by Purcell, Novello)
Let us dance, let us sing (Dioclesian)	d1-f#2	g1-d2	All voices	Animated. Demands considerable flexibility. (Potter)
Mad Bess (Bess of Bedlam)	c1-g2	e1-e2	Women's voices	A dramatic, cantata-like song with many recitatives. Interpretatively and stylistically not easy. Compare with Purcell's "From Rosy Bow'rs." (Bantock)
More love or more disdain I crave	b-e2	e1-c#2	All voices	Sustained. Has alternating sections in 4/4 and 3/4 rhythms. (Moffat, Six Songs by Purcell, Forsyth Bros.)
Music for awhile	bb-eb2	g1-d2	All voices	Sustained. Has florid passages. (Edited by Dawson Freer, Ashdown)
My heart, whenever you appear	d1-f2	f1-d2	Men's voices	Sustained. Demands some flexibility. (Somervell, Fifteen Songs by Purcell, Novello)
Next winter comes slowly (The Fairy Queen)	G-d1	d-bb	Bass	Slow, sustained. Demands some flexibility. (Potter)
Not all my torments	b-f2	e1-d2	All voices	A free, recitative-like, florid, rather slow song. Perhaps one of Purcell's most remarkable songs. (Somervell, Fifteen Songs by Purcell, Novello)

TITLE	COMP.	TESS.	TYPE	REMARKS
No watch, dear Celia	d1-e2	e1-d2	Most suitable for men's voices	Delicate, graceful. Has florid passages. (Somervell, Fifteen Songs by Purcell, Novello)
Nymphs and shepherds (The Libertine)	d1-g2	g1-d2	All voices	Animated, light, graceful. Has florid passages. (Generally available)
O! fair Cedaria	bb-f2	eb1-eb2	Most suitable for men's voices	A very sustained ground bass song, preceded and followed by a recitative which demands some flexibility. (Somervell, Fifteen Songs by Purcell, Novello)
Phillis, I can ne'er forgive it	c#1-e2	e1-e2	Men's voices	Sustained. (Moffat)
Since from my dear (The Prophetess)	d1-f2	g1-e2	All voices	Sustained. Demands some flexibility. (Augener)
Solitude	a-e2	e1-d2	Low voices	A slow, sustained, ground bass song. Quite long. (Somervell, Fifteen Songs by Purcell, Novello)
Strike the viol	e1-f2	g1-e2	All voices	Not fast. Demands considerable flexibility. (Moffat)
Stript of their green our groves appear	e1-g2 (a2)	g1-e2	Not too suitable for very low voices	Graceful. Demands considerable flexibility. (Augener)
Sweet, be no longer sad	f#1-f2	a1-d2	Most suitable for men's voices	Sustained. (Somervell, Fifteen Songs by Purcell, Novello)
Sweet tyranness	e1-f2	g1-e2	Men's voices	Sustained. (Somervell, Fifteen Songs by Purcell, Novello)
Sylvia, now your scorn give over	e1-e2	f#1-d2	Men's voices	Graceful, gently humorous.(Arr. by Moffat. Forsyth Bros.)
The airy violin (Ode on St. Cecilia's day)	g-bb1	b-g1	Alto	Graceful. Demands some flexibility. Has a very low tessitura. (Score, Novello)
The fife and all the harmony of war (Ode on St. Cecilia's day)	a-d1	d1-a1	Alto	Spirited, vigorous. Demands some flexibility. Has a very low tessitura. (Score, Novello)
The knotting song	f1-g2	g1-e2	All voices	Graceful. Demands some flexibility. (Generally available)
The message	c#1-e2	f#1-c#2	Most suitable for men's voices	Sustained. Demands some flexibility. (Moffat)

TITLE	COMP.	TESS.	TYPE	REMARKS
The Myrtle shade	f#1-e2 (g2)	g1-c2	All voices	A graceful minuet. (Arr. by T. F. Dunhill. Curwen)
The pale and purple Rose	g#-c2	c1-a2	Medium or low voices	Animated. Demands some flexibility. (Augener)
The storm	d1-g2	g1-e2	Men's voices	A vigorous mariner's song. (Augener)
Thou tunest this world (Ode on St. Cecilia's day)	f1-g2	bb1-g2	Soprano	Graceful, not fast. Demands flexibility. Although a solo with chorus, this song could be sung as a solo piece. (Score, Novello)
Recitative: Thy hand, Belinda Air: When I am laid in earth (Dido and Aeneas)	c#1-g2	g1-d2	Women's voices, except a light soprano	Slow and very sustained. The most authentic version of this celebrated air is to be found in the complete score of Dido and Aeneas published by the Oxford University Press.
'Tis nature's voice (Ode on St. Cecilia's day)	f-bb1	bb-g1	Alto	Slow, very florid. Has an extraordinarily low tessitura (Score, Novello)
Turn then thine eyes	c1-f2	g1-eb2	Not suitable for very heavy voices	Animated, florid, graceful. (Somervell, Fifteen Songs by Purcell, Novello)
What shall I do to show how much I love her? (Dioclesian)	eb1-g2	g1-eb2	Most suitable for men's voices	Graceful. (Augener)
When I a lover pale do see	c1-g2	f1-d2	All voices	Graceful, gently humorous. (Bridge, Seventeenth Century Songs. Novello)
When I have often heard (The Fairy Queen)	c1-g2	f1-f2	Women's voices	Animated. (Potter)
Whilst I with grief did on you look	b-e2	e1-c2	Most suitable for baritone or bass	A recitative-like slow, florid introduction, and a spirited rather florid air. (Moffat, Six Songs by Purcell, Bailey and Ferguson)
Wondrous machine (Ode on St. Cecilia's day)	B-e1	e-c1	Bass	Slow, sustained. Demands in parts considerable flexibility. (Score, Novello)
Ye twice ten hundred Deities (The Indian Queen)	G-eb1	d-d1	Bass or baritone	Recitative and a spirited air, with a slow, sustained final section. In parts florid. (Hatton and Fanring)

TITLE	COMP.	TESS.	TYPE	REMARKS

PHILIP ROSSETER
(1575-1623)

TITLE	COMP.	TESS.	TYPE	REMARKS
If I urge my kind desires	f#1-e2		Men's voices	Animated, graceful. (Keel)
If she forsake me	d1-e2	g1-e2	Men's voices	Animated, graceful. (Bantock)
What then is love but mourning	d1-c2		Men's voices	Sustained. (Fellowes)
When Laura smiles	d1-e2	g1-d2	All voices	Animated, graceful. (Keel) (Also Fellowes)

WILLIAM SHIELD
(1748-1829)

TITLE	COMP.	TESS.	TYPE	REMARKS
Eve around the huge oak	bb-g2	eb1-bb1	Men's voices	Animated. (Neitzel, Gems of Antiquity, J. Church Co.)

RICHARD J. S. STEVENS
(1757-1837)

TITLE	COMP.	TESS.	TYPE	REMARKS
Sigh no more, ladies	d1-e2 (g2)	g1-d2	All voices	Animated. Demands some flexibility. (Generally available)

STEPHEN STORACE
(1763-1796)

TITLE	COMP.	TESS.	TYPE	REMARKS
A sailor loved a lass	c1-eb2 (f2)	c1-bb1	All voices except a very light soprano	Animated, humorous. (Wilson)
Peaceful slumbering	bb-f2	f1-d2	Most suitable for women's voices	Sustained, subdued. (Potter)
The pretty creature	c1-d2 (f2)	e1-c2	Most suitable for men's voices	Animated, light. Demands facile articulation. (Wilson)
The summer heat's bestowing	e1-b2	a1-f#2	Soprano	Sustained. (Neitzel, Gems of Antiquity, J. Church Co.)

THOMAS WEELKES
(1575-1623)

TITLE	COMP.	TESS.	TYPE	REMARKS
Cease sorrows now	d#1-g2	f#1-e2 (H)	All voices	Grave and sustained. (Bantock)

JOHN WELDON
(1676-1736)

TITLE	COMP.	TESS.	TYPE	REMARKS
Celia, let not pride undo you	b-e2	d1-d2	All voices	Animated, graceful. Demands some flexibility. Humorous. (Potter)

TITLE	COMP.	TESS.	TYPE	REMARKS
Prithee, Celia	d1-f#2	d1-d2	All voices	Graceful. Demands some flexibility. (Potter)

JOHN WILBYE
(1574-1638)

TITLE	COMP.	TESS.	TYPE	REMARKS
Flora gave me fairest flowers	f1-g2	a1-f2 (H)	Most suitable for men's voices	Animated, graceful . A transcription of a five part madrigal. (Bantock)

JOHN WILSON
(1595-1674)

TITLE	COMP.	TESS.	TYPE	REMARKS
In the merry month of May	d1-e2	f#1-d2	All voices	Animated, graceful. Demands some flexibility. (Moffat)

ANTHONY YOUNG
(18th Century)

TITLE	COMP.	TESS.	TYPE	REMARKS
Phillis has such charming graces	e1-gb2	bb1-f2	Most suitable for high voices	Graceful, sustained. Demands some flexibility. (Wilson)

SONGS AND AIRS IN ITALIAN BEFORE THE NINETEENTH CENTURY
Bibliography

The name found in parentheses in the remarks column indicates one of the following collections:

Echos de l' Italie: <u>Echos de l'Italie,</u> Vol. VI edited by Viardot-Garcia, published by Durand, Paris.

Floridia: <u>Early Italian Songs and Airs,</u> 2 vols. edited by Floridia, published by Ditson. (Available in high and low keys. An excellent collection; somewhat marred by overelaborate pianoforte parts.)

Gevaert: <u>Les Gloires de l'Italie</u>, edited by Gevaert, published by Heugel, Paris.

Krehbiel: <u>Voices from the Golden Age</u>, edited by Krehbiel, published by Schirmer.

Landshoff: <u>Alte Meister des Bel Canto</u>, 2 vols. edited by Landshoff, published by Peters.

Parisotti, Schirmer: <u>Italian Anthology</u>, 2 vols. edited by Parisotti, published by Schirmer. (Almost all songs and airs in this admirable collection as well as in the one published by Ricordi are transposed to suit the medium voices.)

Parisotti, Ricordi: <u>Arie Antiche</u>, 3 vols. edited by Parisotti, published by Ricordi. (All songs and airs of this and the above collection published by Schirmer are also available separately in Ricordi edition.)

Zanon: <u>Arias by old Italian Masters,</u> 2 vols. edited by Zanon, published by Boston Music Co.

See also the catalogues of Ricordi, Ashdown, and Oxford University Press for many other excellent transcriptions and arrangements, as well as <u>Mâitres du Chant,</u> edited by Prunières, published by Heugel, Paris.

TITLE	COMP.	TESS.	TYPE	REMARKS
ANTONIO MARIA ABBATINI (1595-1677)				
Quanto è bello il mio diletto	g1-g2	b1-e2	Soprano	Not fast, rather florid. Has a sustained middle section. (Landshoff)
PANCRAZIO ANIELLO (Late 18th Century)				
Lo so che pria mi moro	a-c♯2	d1-b1	Medium or low voices	A rather slow, sustained Siciliana. (Zanon)
ANONYMOUS				
"Lamento" Chi sa le mie pene (Neapolitan school eighteenth century)	b-f2	eb1-eb2	Medium or low voices	Slow, sustained. (Gevaert, Répertoire Classique du chant Français. Lemoine, Paris)
ATTILIO ARIOSTI (1666-1740?)				
Vuoi, che parta! (Lucio Vero)	e1-g♯2	a1-f♯2	Soprano	Slower; in parts quite florid. (Landshoff)

- 32 -

TITLE	COMP.	TESS.	TYPE	REMARKS

EMANUELE D'ASTORGA
(1680-1756)

TITLE	COMP.	TESS.	TYPE	REMARKS
Auretta vezzosa	b-e2	e1-c2	Medium or low voices	Graceful. Demands some flexibility. (Echos de l'Italie
L'immago tua	f1-g2	bb1-f2	Most suitable for light, high voices	Animated, graceful, somewhat florid. (Echos de l'Italie)
Morir vogl'io	d1-e2	f#1-d2	Most suitable for medium or low voices	Slow and sustained. (Floridia; also Neitzel, Gems of Antiquity. J. Church Co.)
Ti parlo	d1-g2	g1-eb2	Soprano	Recitative and a graceful air. Demands some flexibility. (Echos de l'Italie)
Vo cercando in queste valli	d1-g2	g1-e2 (H)	All voices	Light and delicate. (Floridia)

JOHANN CHRISTIAN BACH
(1735-1782)

TITLE	COMP.	TESS.	TYPE	REMARKS
Non è ver (Caratacco)	f1-bb2	bb1-g2	Soprano	Not fast, quite florid. (Landshoff)

(See also **J. C. Bach 12 Konzert und Opern Arien**, edited by Landshoff, published by Peters.)

GIOVANNI BATTISTA BASSANI
(1657-1716)

TITLE	COMP.	TESS.	TYPE	REMARKS
Dormi, bella, dormi tu?	eb1-f2	eb1-eb2	Most suitable for men's voices	A graceful, sustained air. Has rapid sections. (Parisotti, Schirmer)
Posate, dormite	eb1-f2	bb1-eb2	All voices	Recitative and a sustained cavatina. Demands good command of pp. The tessitura is somewhat high. (Parisotti, Schirmer)
Seguita a piangere	d1-f2	f1-db2	Most suitable for medium voices	Recitative and a graceful arietta, interrupted by several recitative passages. Demands some flexibility. (Parisotti, Schirmer)

DOMENICO BELLI
(Early 17th Century)

TITLE	COMP.	TESS.	TYPE	REMARKS
Di vostri occhi le facelle	bb-f2	f1-d2	Most suitable for medium voices	Light, animated. Demands very facile articulation. (Gevaert)

TITLE	COMP.	TESS.	TYPE	REMARKS

ANDREA BERNASCONI
(1712-1784)

TITLE	COMP.	TESS.	TYPE	REMARKS
Se non ti mora allato (Adriano)	c♯1-e2	g1-d2	Mezzo-soprano or alto	Sustained. Demands some flexibility. A little long. (Krehbiel)

FRANCESCO BIANCHI
(1752-1811)

TITLE	COMP.	TESS.	TYPE	REMARKS
La mia virtù non ceve (L'Orfano della China)	c1-f2	f1-c2	Mezzo-soprano or alto	Recitative and a dramatic air. Has some florid passages. (Krehbiel)
Tu seconda i voti miei (L'Orfano della China)	d1-e2	f♯1-c♯2	Medium or low voices	Recitative and a slow, sustained air. (Krehbiel)

GIOVANNI BATTISTA BONONCINI
(1672-1755)

TITLE	COMP.	TESS.	TYPE	REMARKS
Ben che speranza	b1-e2	g1-d2	Low or medium voices	Vigorous, rhythmical. (Echos de l'Italie)
Deh lascia o core (Astianatte)	b-g2	e1-e2	Mezzo-soprano or dramatic soprano	Slow. Has florid passages. (Gevaert)
Deh più a me non v'ascondete	eb1-f2	ab1-eb2	All voices	Delicate. Demands some flexibility. (Parisotti, Schirmer; also Floridia)
L'esperto nocchiero (Astarte)	d1-g2	g1-e2 (H)	All voices	Spirited. Has some florid passages. (Floridia)
Per la gloria d'adorarvi	d1-f2	g1-d2	All voices	Sustained. (Parisotti, Schirmer; also Floridia)
Pietà, mio caro bene	d1-g2	a1-e2 (H)	All voices	Slow and very sustained. (Floridia)
Piu non ti voglio credere	d1-ab2	bb1-ab2	Soprano	Spirited. Demands facile articulation. The tessitura is quite high, the ab2 being used very frequently. The violin obbligato part can be easily played by the pianist. (Landshoff)
Se mai vien tocca	d1-f2	g1-d2 (H)	Not too suitable for very light voices	Sustained. Demands some flexibility. (Floridia)
Si che fedele	eb1-g2	g1-f2	Light soprano	Graceful. Demands facile articulation and some flexibility. (Echos de l'Italie)

TITLE	COMP.	TESS.	TYPE	REMARKS

DOMENICO BRUNI
(Late 18th Century)

TITLE	COMP.	TESS.	TYPE	REMARKS
La vezzosa pastorella	c1-g2	f1-d2	Not too suitable for very low voices	Graceful, light, animated. Demands flexibility. (Zanon)
Se meritar potessi	eb1-g2	g1-eb2	Most suitable for high voices	Graceful. Demands flexibility. (Zanon)

FRANCESCA CACCINI
(1570-1630)

TITLE	COMP.	TESS.	TYPE	REMARKS
Per la più vaga	g1-f2	g1-e2	High voices	Graceful. Demands some flexibility. (Landshoff)

GUILIO CACCINI
(1558-1615)

TITLE	COMP.	TESS.	TYPE	REMARKS
Amarilli, mia bella	d1-e2	g1-d2	All voices	Slow and very sustained. (Parisotti, Schirmer; also Floridia)
Amor ch'attendi?	f#1-e2	g1-d2	All voices	Sustained. (Parisotti, Ricordi)
Fere selvaggie	e1-e2	g1-d2 (H)	Not too suitable for very light high voices	Majestic, very sustained. (Floridia)
Non piango e non sospiro (Euridice)	d1-d2	e1-bb1	Medium or low voices	Grave and sustained. (Krehbiel)
Occhi immortali	d1-c2	eb1-bb1 (L)	All voices	Slow and sustained. (J. Woodside, Seven Centuries of Solo Song, Vol. I, Boston Music Co.)
Tu, ch'hai le penne, amore	f#1-d2	g1-c2	Not too suitable for very high light voices	Slow and sustained. (Parisotti, Ricordi)

ANTONIO CALDARA
(1670-1736)

TITLE	COMP.	TESS.	TYPE	REMARKS
Alma nel core	a1-f#2	b1-e2 (H)	All voices	A graceful minuet. Demands lightness of tone. (Floridia)
Come raggio di sol	c#1-e2	e1-c2	Most suitable for medium or low voices	Slow and very sustained. (Parisotti, Schirmer; also Floridia)
Mirti, faggi	b-c2	e1-b1	Low or medium voices	Slow. Demands some flexibility. (Landshoff)

TITLE	COMP.	TESS.	TYPE	REMARKS
Sebben crudele	d1-e2	g1-d2	All voices	Sustained. (Parisotti, Schirmer)
Selve amiche, ombrose piante	e1-e2	a1-d2	All voices	Sustained. Demands so some flexibility. (Parisotti, Schirmer; also Floridia)
Vaghe luci	bb-c2	c1-ab1	Low or medium voices	Slow. The violin obbligato part can be easily played by the pianist. (Landshoff)

RINALDO DA CAPUA
(1715-1780)

TITLE	COMP.	TESS.	TYPE	REMARKS
Dal sen del caro sposo (Vologeso)	d1-a2	a1-f#2	Soprano	A very sustained air. Has short spirited sections. The tessitura is somewhat high. (Krehbiel)
Nell orror di notte oscura (Vologeso)	bb-bb2	g1-g2	Soprano	Recitative and a florid, brilliant air. (Krehbiel)

GIACOMO CARISSIMI
1604-1674)

TITLE	COMP.	TESS.	TYPE	REMARKS
Ah, morire!	d1-f2	a1-e2 (H)	All voices	Slow and sustained. Demands some flexibility. (Floridia)
Così volete, così sarà	d1-a2	g1-eb2	Soprano	Sustained. The middle section is animated and florid. (Landshoff)
Deh, contentatevi	e1-g2	ab1-eb2 (H)	All voices	Very sustained. (Floridia)
Filli, non t'amo più	d#1-f#2	a1-e2 (H)	Men's voices	Spirited. Demands some flexibility.(Floridia)
La mia fede altrai giurata	f#1-ab2	g1-d2	High voices	Not fast, rather sustained. (Landshoff)
No, no, mio core	d1-g2	g1-e2 (H)	All voices	Sustained. (Floridia)
No, no, non si spèri	f-g1	g-eb1	Alto or bass	Slow, sustained. Has some florid passages. (Landshoff; also Floridia)
Piangete aure	d1-f2	f1-e2	Not suitable for very light high voices	A short cantata; somewhat declamatory in parts. Dramatic. (Echos de l'Italie)
Piangete ohimè, anime innamorate	b-e2	e1-c#2	Not suitable for very light high voices	Slow and sustained. (Parisotti, Ricordi)
Soccorretemi	c1-g2	eb1-eb2	High voices except a very light soprano	Sustained. Somewhat declamatory. Has some florid passages and some recitatives. Somewhat long. (Landshoff)
Vittoria, mio core	c1-f2	f1-d2	All voices	Spirited. Has florid passages. (Parisotti, Schirmer; also Floridia)

TITLE	COMP.	TESS.	TYPE	REMARKS

PIETRO FRANCESCO CAVALLI
(1602-1676)

TITLE	COMP.	TESS.	TYPE	REMARKS
Affè mi fate ridere	d1-f2	g1-d2	High or medium voices	Spirited, gay. Demands facile articulation and some flexibility. (Parisotti, Ricordi)
Beato chi può (Serse)	A-d1	d-b	Bass or baritone (also suitable for alto)	Sustained. Has some florid passages. (Gevaert)
Chi si pasce (Eritrea)	f1-f2	g1-d2	High or medium voices	Spirited. Demands some flexibility. (Echos de l'Italie)
Delizie contente, che l'alma beate (Giasone)	f1-eb2	g1-c2	All voices	Graceful. (Parisotti, Schirmer)
Dell'antro magico (Giasone)	c1-g2	e1-e2	Dramatic soprano or mezzo-soprano	Vigorous, dramatic, majestic. (Gevaert; also Neitzel, Gems of Antiquity. J. Church Co)
Dolce amor, bendato dio	d1-g2	a1-e2 (H)	Not too suitable for very heavy low voices	Delicate and graceful. (Floridia)
Donzelle fuggite	e1-g2	g1-e2 (H)	All voices	Rapid and light. Demands facile articulation. (Floridia)
Gran pazzia (Eritrea)	e1-f♯2	g♯1-e2	High voices except a very light soprano	Vigorous. Demands some flexibility. (Echos de l'Italie)
In amor (Eritrea)	c1-g2	f1-f2	Most suitable for light soprano	Graceful. Demands some flexibility. Two very florid variations by Lorenzo Pagans are attached. (Echos de l'Italie)
Troppo soavi i gusti	g1-g2	ab1-eb2 (H)	All voices	Very sustained, but has rapid parlato passages. (Floridia)

CARLO F. CESARINI
(1660-1720)

TITLE	COMP.	TESS.	TYPE	REMARKS
Recitative: Filli, Filli nol niego Air: Compatite me, sono infermo	f♯1-ab2	ab1-f2	Soprano or tenor	Recitative and a sustained air. Has a florid passage. (Landshoff)

MARCANTONIO CESTI
(1618-1669)

Recitative:

Title	Comp.	Tess.	Type	Remarks
Addio Corindo Air: Vieni Alidoro	f1-g2	g1-f2	Soprano	Slow, sustained. Has florid passages. (Landshoff)
Ah, quanto è vero (Il pomo d'Oro)	a1-a2	c1-f2 (H)	All voices	Very sustained. (Floridia)
Che angoscia, che affanno (Il pomo d'Oro)	e1-f2	a1-e2 (H)	All voices	Very sustained. (Floridia)
E dove t'aggiri (Il pomo d' Oro)	d#1-f2	a1-e2 (H)	Most suitable for medium or low voices	Very slow and sustained. (Sarabande) (Floridia)
Intorno all'idol mio	d1-f2	g1-d2	All voices	Sustained, graceful. (Parisotti, Schirmer)
O del ben che acquisterò (Il pomo d'Oro)	e1-g2	a1-f2 (H)	Most suitable for men's voices	Very sustained. (Floridia)
Tu mancavi a tormentarti	c1-g2	g1-d2	All voices	Sustained. Has an animated middle section which demands some flexibility. (Gevaert; also Parisotti, Schirmer)

LUIGI CHERUBINI
(1760-1842)

Recitative:

Title	Comp.	Tess.	Type	Remarks
Ahi! che forse ai miei di Air: Ahi, sola quand'io vivea (Demofonte)	db1-gb2	f1-db2	Soprano or high mezzo-soprano	Recitative and a sustained air. (Parisotti, Ricordi)
Ave Maria	e1-a2	f1-f2	Soprano or tenor	Very sustained. Demands in parts some flexibility. (Schirmer)

For other songs and airs see under "French" in this section (page 59).

DOMENICO CIMAROSA
(1749-1801)

Title	Comp.	Tess.	Type	Remarks
Ah, tornar la bella aurora (La Vergine del Sole)	c#1-c3	g#1-g2	Soprano	An andante, allegro air. In parts quite florid. (Landshoff)
Bel nume che adoro	d1-eb2	g1-eb2	High voices	Sustained. (Parisotti, Ricordi)

TITLE	COMP.	TESS.	TYPE	REMARKS
Recitative: Cara, son tutto vostro Air: Brillar mi sento il core (Il Matrimonio Segreto)	f-a1	a-f1	Lyric tenor	Spirited, in parts quite florid. (Parisotti, Ricordi)
È vero che in casa io sono padrone (Il Matrimonio Segreto)	e1-a2	a1-f2	Soprano or mezzo-soprano	Animated. Demands facile articulation and some flexibility. In the opera assigned to contralto. The tessitura, however, seems somewhat high for this type of voice. (Parisotti, Ricordi)
Recitative: Misero Bernardone Air: Maritati poverelli (Gianina e Bernardone)	Ab-f1	f-d1	Baritone	A buffo scena, andante, allegro. Demands in parts facile articulation. (Gevaert)
Nel lasciarti (Olimpiade)	bb-bb2	f1-eb2	Mezzo-soprano or dramatic soprano	An andante, allegro aria. Demands some flexibility. (Parisotti, Ricordi)
Perdonate signor mio (Il Matrimonio Segreto)	d#1-a2	a1-f#2	Coloratura soprano (lyric soprano)	Spirited. Demands facile articulation and considerable flexibility. (Score, Ricordi)
Pria che spunti in cielo (Il Matrimonio Segreto)	eb-bb1	bb-g1	Lyric tenor	An andante, allegro aria. Demands some flexibility and facile articulation. (Score, Ricordi)
Quel soave e bel diletto	b-g2	e1-d2	High voices	Slow. Has florid passages. (Parisotti, Ricordi)
Resta in pace, idolo mio	bb-f2	f1-eb2	Soprano or mezzo-soprano	Sustained. Demands some flexibility. (Parisotti, Ricordi)
Se son vendicata (Il Matrimonio Segreto)	d#1-a2	a1-e2	Sorpano	A spirited andante, allegro aria. In parts very florid; demands facile articulation. (Score, Ricordi)
Udite tutti, udite (Il Matrimonio Segreto)	A-e1	d-d1	Bass or baritone	A spirited buffo aria. Demands facile articulation. (Score, Ricordi)
Vedrai la forte (Don Calandrino)	B-f#1	f#-d1	Baritone	A very spirited compound buffo aria. Demands in parts very facile articulation. (Gevaert)

GIOACCHINO COCCHI
(1720-1804)

TITLE	COMP.	TESS.	TYPE	REMARKS
Gli sbirri già l'aspettano (La Scaltra Governatrice)	B-d1	c-c1	Bass or baritone	A spirited buffo air. Demands facile articulation. (Gevaert)

WILLIAM DEFESCH
(1700-1758)

TITLE	COMP.	TESS.	TYPE	REMARKS
Tu fai la superbetta	d#1-c#3	f#1-f#2	Coloratura soprano	A theme and two florid brilliant variations. (Arr. by Estelle Liebling. Schirmer)

For other songs and airs see the section Songs and Airs in English before the Nineteenth Century.
See also Alfred Moffat collection Old Mastersongs, 17th and 18th Centuries (Augener)

FRANCESCO DURANTE
(1684-1755)

TITLE	COMP.	TESS.	TYPE	REMARKS
Danza, danza fanciulla gentile	bb-f2	f1-db2	Most suitable for men's voices	Spirited and light. Demands facile articulation and some flexibility. (Parisotti, Schirmer; also Floridia)
Vergin tutto amor	c1-eb2	g1-d2	Not too suitable for very light high voices	Very sustained. (Parisotti, Schirmer; also Floridia)

ANDREA FALCONIERI
(15.. -16..)

TITLE	COMP.	TESS.	TYPE	REMARKS
Bella porta di rubini	e1-eb2	f1-c2	All voices	Sustained, graceful. Demands some flexibility. (Parisotti, Ricordi; also Floridia)
Non più d'amore	eb1-f2	ab1-eb2 (H)	All voices	Spirited. Demands facile articulation. The accompaniment is somewhat elaborate. (Floridia)
Nudo arciero	db1-ab2	ab1-f2 (H)	All voices	Spirited. Demands facile articulation. The accompaniment is quite elaborate. (Floridia)
O bellissimi capelli	d1-f2	g1-d2 (H)	Most suitable for men's voices	Graceful. (Parisotti, Ricordi; also Floridia)

TITLE	COMP.	TESS.	TYPE	REMARKS
Occhietti amati	d1-f2	f1-d2	Most suitable for men's voices	Sustained. Demands some flexibility. (Parisotti, Ricordi; also Floridia)
Segui, segui dolente core	d1-f#2	f#1-d2	All voices	Graceful, not fast. (Parisotti, Ricordi)
Vezzosette e care	c#1-e2	e1-c#2	All voices	Light and graceful. (Gavotte) Demands facile articulation. (Parisotti, Schirmer)

GIOVANNI BATTISTA FASOLO
(16.. -16..)

TITLE	COMP.	TESS.	TYPE	REMARKS
Cangia, cangia tue voglie	c1-g2	e1-d2	All voices	Graceful. Demands some flexibility. (Parisotti, Schirmer)
Lungi, lungi è amor da me	d1-f2	f1-d2	All voices	Sustained. (Parisotti, Ricordi)

RUGGIERO FEDELI
(16.. -1722)

TITLE	COMP.	TESS.	TYPE	REMARKS
Il mio core non è con me	f1-f2	g1-c2 (H)	All voices	Graceful. (Floridia)

GIROLAMO FRESCOBALDI
(1583-1645)

TITLE	COMP.	TESS.	TYPE	REMARKS
Se l'aura spira	d#1-f#2	g#1-d#2	All voices	Delicate, sustained. Demands good command of pp. (Floridia)

BERNARDO GAFFI
(Early 17th Century)

TITLE	COMP.	TESS.	TYPE	REMARKS
Luci vezzose	f1-g2	bb1-f2 (H)	All voices	A graceful minuet. (Floridia)

MARCO ZANOBI DA GAGLIANO
(1575-1642)

TITLE	COMP.	TESS.	TYPE	REMARKS
Chi da' lacci d'amor (Dafne)	d1-d2	f1-c2	Soprano or mezzo-soprano	Graceful and delicate. Has some florid passages. (Krehbiel)
Dormi amore (La Flora)	e1-g2	a1-d2 (H)	All voices	Delicate and sustained. Demands good command of pp. (Floridia)
Valli profonde (Il Dannato)	c-f#1	d-d1	Baritone or alto	Sustained. Has some florid passages. (Gevaert)

TITLE	COMP.	TESS.	TYPE	REMARKS

BALDASSARE GALUPPI
(1706-1785)

TITLE	COMP.	TESS.	TYPE	REMARKS
E ingrato, lo veggio (Adriano in Siria)	b-d2	g1-d2	Mezzo-soprano or alto	Spirited. Has florid passages. (Krehbiel)
La pastorella al prato (Il Filosofo di Campagna)	e1-g2	g1-e2	High voices	A graceful pastoral. (Echos de l'Italie)
Prigioniera, abbandonata (Adriano in Siria)	d1-a2	b1-g2	Soprano	Florid. Most suitable for lyric or coloratura soprano (Krehbiel)
Son io semplice fanciulla (L'Inimico delle Donne)	d1-ab2	g1-eb2	Light soprano	Graceful, quite florid. (Gevaert)
Son troppo vezzose (Enrico)	c-g1	f-d1	Tenor	Graceful. Demands some flexibility. (Krehbiel, Songs from the Operas, Tenor. Ditson)

FRANCESCO GASPARINI
(1665-1737)

TITLE	COMP.	TESS.	TYPE	REMARKS
Augellin vago e canoro	d1-f2	f#1-d2	High voices	Andante and a spirited allegro; the spirited allegro has a florid passage. (Parisotti, Ricordi)
Caro laccio, dolce nodo	eb1-eb2	f1-c2	All voices	Graceful. Demands lightness of tone. (Parisotti, Schirmer)
Lasciar d'amarti	eb1-f2	ab1-eb2	All voices	Graceful, sustained. (Parisotti, Schirmer, also Floridia)

GIUSEPPE GIORDANI
(1744-1798)

TITLE	COMP.	TESS.	TYPE	REMARKS
Caro mio ben	d1-f2	g1-eb2	All voices	Very sustained. (Parisotti, Schirmer; also Floridia)

CARL H. GRAUN
(1701-1759)

TITLE	COMP.	TESS.	TYPE	REMARKS
Recitative: Disperata Porcia Air, Quanto dolce	f1-c3	bb1-g2	Soprano	Recitative and a slow, rather sustained air. Has florid passages. (Landshoff)

For other songs and airs see under "German" in this section (page 81).

TITLE	COMP.	TESS.	TYPE	REMARKS

JOHANN A. HASSE
(1699-1783)

TITLE	COMP.	TESS.	TYPE	REMARKS
Agnus Dei (Mass in d minor) (Latin text)	c#1-d2	e1-b1	Alto	Sustained. Has florid passages (Alt Arien. Breitkopf und Härtel)
La tua virtù mi dice	d1-f2	g1-d2	Soprano	Graceful. Demands some flexibility. (Landshoff)
Padre, perdona (Demofoonte)	b-f#2	e1-e2	Mezzo-soprano (dramatic soprano)	Sustained. Demands some flexibility. The middle section is a spirited allegro. (Gevaert)
Ritornerai fra poco	d1-a2	g1-g2	Most suitable for light soprano	Animated, graceful. Rather florid. (Schirmer)
Salve Regina (Latin text)	a-e2	b-b1	Alto	Slow, ustained. Demands some flexibility. (Alt Arien. Breitkopf und Härtel)

See also J. A. Hasse, Ausgewählte Geistliche Gesänge, edited by O. Schmidt, published by Breitkopf und Härtel.

NICCOLO JOMMELLI
(1714-1774)

TITLE	COMP.	TESS.	TYPE	REMARKS
Recitative: Bella mia fiamma, addio Air: Resta o cara (Cerere placata)	d1-g2 (bb2)	eb1-eb2	Lyric soprano (dramatic soprano)	Scena, andante, allegro. Demands in parts considerable flexibility. (Gevaert)
Chi vuol comprar la bella calandrina	b-g2	g1-e2	Most suitable for high voices	Light. Demands some flexibility. (Parisotti, Schirmer)

GAETANO LATILLA
(1713-1789)

TITLE	COMP.	TESS.	TYPE	REMARKS
Fra degno ed amore (Siroë)	e1-a2	a1-e2	Soprano	Majestic. Has florid passages. (Krehbiel)
Sgombra dall'anima (Siroë)	d1-a2	a1-eb2	Soprano	Light and graceful. Demands some flexibility. (Krehbiel)

GIOVANNI LEGRENZI
(1626-1690)

TITLE	COMP.	TESS.	TYPE	REMARKS
Che fiero costume	d1-g2	g1-eb2	All voices	Demands facile articulation. Rapid. (Parisotti, Schirmer; also Floridia)

TITLE	COMP.	TESS.	TYPE	REMARKS
Farci pazzo	c1-g2	g1-f2	High voices	Animated, light. Demands some flexibility and facile articulation. (Gevaert)
Non mi dir di palesar	c#1-f2	e1-e2	High or medium voices	Sustained. Rhythmically quite interesting. (Landshoff)

LEONARDO LEO
(1694-1744)

TITLE	COMP.	TESS.	TYPE	REMARKS
Ahi,che la pena mia	d1-g2	a1-f2	High voices	A graceful Siciliana. Demands some flexibility. Has a vigorous middle section. (Gevaert)
Dirti, ben mio, vorrei (Alessandro in Persia)	eb1-f2	eb1-eb2	Soprano	Sustained, graceful. (Schirmer)
Dunque si sforza (La morte d'Abel)	bb-f2 (f)	d1-d2	Low voices	Vigorous, grave. Demands some flexibility. (Echos de l'Italie)
Recitative: Io vado Air: Se cerca, se dice (Olimpiade)	bb-eb2	c1-c2	Medium or low voices	Recitative and a spirited vigorous air. (Landshoff)
Se mai senti (La Clemenza di Tito)	d1-g2	g1-d2 (H)	All voices	Sustained. Demands some flexibility. Originally written for alto, b-e2. (Gevaert; also Floridia)

ARCANGELO DEL LEUTO
(15..-16..)

TITLE	COMP.	TESS.	TYPE	REMARKS
Dimmi, amor	c1-f2	e1-c2	All voices	Sustained. (Parisotti, Schirmer)

CARLO AMBROGIO LONATI
(1650-1710)

TITLE	COMP.	TESS.	TYPE	REMARKS
Tu paristi idolo amato	d1-ab2	g1-f2	High voices	Sustained. (Landshoff)

ANTONIO LOTTI
(1667-1740)

TITLE	COMP.	TESS.	TYPE	REMARKS
Pur dicesti, o bocca bella	d1-f#2	a1-d2	All voices	Light and delicate. Demands some flexibility. (Parisotti, Schirmer)

S. DE LUCA
(Early 16th Century)

TITLE	COMP.	TESS.	TYPE	REMARKS
Non posso disperar	d1-f#2	g1-d2	All voices	Graceful. Demands facile articulation. (Parisotti, Schirmer)

FRANCESCO DE MAJO
(1740--1770)

TITLE	COMP.	TESS.	TYPE	REMARKS
Recitative: Accresca pietoso Air: Se il labbro si lagra (Ifigenia in Tauride)	e1-a2	a1-f2	Soprano	Recitative, andante, allegro. (Landshoff)

FRANCESCO MANCINI
(1679-1739)

TITLE	COMP.	TESS.	TYPE	REMARKS
Dir ch'io t'ami	d#1-g2	a1-e2 (H)	Most suit- able for men's voices	Vigorous. (Floridia)

BENEDETTO MARCELLO
(1686-1739)

TITLE	COMP.	TESS.	TYPE	REMARKS
Il mio bel foco	c1-g2 (a)	f1-d2	Not too suitable for very light high voices	Recitative and animated air. (Parisotti, Schirmer; also Floridia)
Didone	bb-c3	d1-g2	Dramatic soprano (Lyric soprano)	A long cantata (22 pages) arranged by Respighi. Has several contrast- ing movements inter- rupted by recitative passages. Demands in parts considerable flex- ibility as well as consid- erable dramatic intensity. (Ricordi)
Non m'è grave morir per amore	c1-e2	g1-d2	All voices	Recitative and a grace- ful aria. (Parisotti, Schirmer)

NICOLA MATTEIS
(1650-1700)

TITLE	COMP.	TESS.	TYPE	REMARKS
Caro volto pallidet- to	e1-g2	g1-eb2	High voices	Rapid, light. Demands facile articulation. (Landshoff)

GIOVANNI BATTISTA MAZZAFERRATA
(16..-1691)

TITLE	COMP.	TESS.	TYPE	REMARKS
Presto, presto io m'innamoro	e1-g2	g1-eb2	All voices	Light and rapid. (Floridia)

DOMENICO MAZZOCCHI
(1590?-1650?)

TITLE	COMP.	TESS.	TYPE	REMARKS
Piu non sia, che m'innamori	e1-f2	g1-e2	High or medium voices	Graceful. Demands some flexibility. (Land-shoff)

ANTONIO MAZZONI
(1718-17..)

Io veggio in lonta-nanza (Demetrio)	c1-g2	f1-f2	Dramatic soprano (lyric so-prano)	Spirited and florid. (Krehbiel)

CLAUDIO MONTEVERDE
(1567-1643)

Monteverde, one of the first composers to write in the monodic style, could be considered one of the inventors of vocal solo music as we know it today.

His airs and songs are strangely "modern," not in their harmonic idiom but in their treatment of the vocal line, which is fashioned not as a self-contained melodic pattern but primarily as a musical intensification of speech. In so far as musical form is concerned, Monteverde wrote as freely as any late romantic composer, and much more freely than most twentieth century composers, though naturally within the frame of the stylistic conventions of his time.

The singer wishing to do justice to a Monteverde air would do well to train himself to recite the text as such, by memory, for Monteverde's music is shaped and dominated by the text to a greater degree, perhaps, than any other vocal music written before the latter part of the nineteenth century.

As a rule Monteverde's airs and songs are sustained and do not contain any florid passages of the type encountered in the operatic soli of his successors, and are best suited to rather heavy voices.

Editions: Complete edition of Monteverde's works, under the editor-ship of Malipiero, was being prepared by the Universal Edi-tion (fourteen volumes had appeared by 1933).
Combattimento di Clorinda e Tancredo. Published by Ricordi.
Incoronazione di Poppea (French text only). Edited by d'Indy, published by Rouart Lerolle.

Ahi, troppo è duro (Il Balletto delle Ingrate)	d1-f2	a1-d2 (H)	Not too suitable for light high voices	Grave and declamatory, very sustained. (Floridia)
Con che soavità	d1-e2	f1-d2	Medium or low voices	Sustained. Has some florid passages. (Land-shoff)
Ecco pur ch'a voi ritorno (Orfeo)	f1-d2	g1-c2	Medium or low voices	Very sustained. (Krehbiel)

TITLE	COMP.	TESS.	TYPE	REMARKS
Lasciatemi morire (Ariana)	f1-f2	g1-db2	Medium or low voices	Grave and declamatory, very sustained. (Parisotti, Schirmer; also Floridia)
In un fiorito prato (Orfeo)	c1-e2	d1-c2	Not suitable for high light voices	Slow, declamatory. (Parisotti, Ricordi)
Si dolce è' L tormento	b-d2	e1-b1 (L)	All voices	Graceful, sustained. (J. Woodside, Seven Centuries of Solo Song, Boston Music Co.)
Tu se' morta (Orfeo)	c1-e2	f1-d2	Medium or low voices	Grave and declamatory, very sustained. (Krehbiel)

FERNANDO ORLANDI
(1777-1848)

TITLE	COMP.	TESS.	TYPE	REMARKS
Degli angelletti al canto (Il Podesta di Chioggia)	c1-d2	g1-c2	Mezzo-soprano or alto	Graceful. Demands some flexibility. (Krehbiel)

GIOVANNI MARIA ORLANDINI
(1690-1745)

TITLE	COMP.	TESS.	TYPE	REMARKS
Caro, son tua così (Temistocle)	c#1-e2	e1-c#2	Mezzo-soprano or alto	Graceful. (Krehbiel)

FERDINANDO PAER
(1771-1839)

TITLE	COMP.	TESS.	TYPE	REMARKS
Ecco de' miei trascorsi (Agnese)	d1-f2	f1-e2	Soprano or light mezzo-soprano	Animated, graceful. (Schirmer)

For other songs and airs see under "French" in this section (page 59).

GIOVANNI PAESIELLO
(1741-1816)

TITLE	COMP.	TESS.	TYPE	REMARKS
Chi vuol la Zingarella	c1-f2	d1-c2	Women's voices	Light and somewhat humorous. Demands facile articulation. (Parisotti, Schirmer)
Recitative: Dove, ahi dove son io? Air: Mentre ti lascio o figlia (La Disfatta di Dario)	c-bb1	bb-f1	Lyric tenor	A scena, andante, allegro. In parts very florid. (Gevaert)
Il mio ben quando verrà	c1-a2	a1-f2	Soprano	Delicate. Demands good flexibility. (Parisotti, Schirmer)

TITLE	COMP.	TESS.	TYPE	REMARKS
Nel cor più non mi sento (La Moli- nara)	d1-f2	f1-d2	Light soprano	Graceful and light. (Parisotti, Schirmer; also Floridia, a tone higher in this collection)

For other songs and airs see under "French in this section (page 59).

PIETRO DOMENICO PARADIES
(1710-1792)

TITLE	COMP.	TESS.	TYPE	REMARKS
M'ha preso alla sua ragna	eb1-f2	ab1-eb2	High or medium voices	Light and animated. De- mands facile articula- tion and flexibility. (Pari- sotti, Schirmer)
Quel ruscelletto	d1-a2	g1-g2	Soprano	Graceful, florid. (Arr. by La Forge. Carl Fischer)

BERNARDO PASQUINI
(1637-1710)

TITLE	COMP.	TESS.	TYPE	REMARKS
Quanto è folle quell' amante	c1-f2	f1-d2	Soprano	Light, animated. Demands facile articulation. Has florid passages. (Land- shoff)

GIOVANNI BATTISTA PERGOLESI
(1710-1736)

TITLE	COMP.	TESS.	TYPE	REMARKS
A Serpina penserete (La Serva Padrona)	d1-g2	a1-f2	Light so- prano	Light and gently humor- ous. Has rapid sections demanding facile articula- tion. (Score, Ricordi)
Bella mia (Il Maestro di Musica)	c-e1 (G)	d-d1	Bass, bass baritone	Sustained, graceful. De- mands some flexibility. (Schirmer, Operatic Anthology)
Confusa, smarrita, spiegarti vorrei (Catone)	c1-f2	f1-d2	Mezzo- soprano or alto	Spirited and dramatic. (Krehbiel)
Dite ch'ogni momento	f1-g2	a1-f2	Not too suitable for very low voices	Sustained, graceful. De- mands some flexibility. (Zanon)
Gemo in un punto e fremo (L'Olimpi- ade)	a-b2	a1-f#2	Dramatic soprano	Spirited. Demands some flexibility. (Krehbiel)
Recitative: Io vado Air: Se cerca e dice: L'amico dov'è? (L'Olimpiade)	db1-gb2 (bb2)	ab1-f2	Soprano	Recitative and a com- pound aria, (andante allegro repeated). De- mands some flexibility. (Gevaert; also Parisotti, Ricordi)
Mentre dormi, amor fomenti	f1-a2	f1-f2	Soprano	Not fast, quite florid. (Landshoff)

TITLE	COMP.	TESS.	TYPE	REMARKS
Ogni pena più spietata	b-e2	e1-c2	Most suitable for medium or high voices	Graceful. Demands some flexibility. (Parisotti, Schirmer)
Se al labbro mio non credi (L'Olimpiade)	a-eb2	f1-c2	Alto or mezzo-soprano	Sustained and slow. Has some florid passages. (Krehbiel)
Sempre in contrasti con te si sta (La Serva Padrona)	F-f1	c-d1	Bass or bass baritone	Very animated buffo air. Has a florid passage. Demands facile articulation. (Ricordi)
Se tu m'ami	bb-f2	g1-eb2	Women's voices	Graceful, delicate. (Parisotti, Schirmer)
Son imbrogliato io già (La Serva Padrona)	Eb-eb1	Bb-c1	Bass or bass baritone	A very animated buffo air. Demands facile articulation. (Ricordi)
Stizzoso, mio stizzoso (La Serva Padrona)	e1-a2	a1-f#2	Soprano	Light and humorous. (Parisotti, Schirmer; transposed one-half tone lower)
Tre giorni	e1-f2	ab1-eb2 (H)	Men's voices	The authorship of this famous air is not definitely established. Exists in many arrangements, sometimes named "Nina." Very sustained. (Floridia)

AIRS FROM THE "STABAT MATER"
(The score is generally available)

TITLE	COMP.	TESS.	TYPE	REMARKS
Cujus animam gementem	f1-ab2	bb1-g2	Soprano	Animated, graceful.
Fac ut portem	c1-eb2	eb1-c2	Alto or mezzo-soprano	Slow. Has florid passages.
Pia mater, fons amoris	b-eb2	c1-bb1	Alto or mezzo-soprano	Sustained. Demands some flexibility.
Quae moerebat	d1-f2	eb1-c2	Alto or mezzo-soprano	Animated. Demands some flexibility
Vidit suum dulcem natum	f1-ab2	g1-f2	Soprano	Sustained. Demands some flexibility.

JACOPO PERI
(1561-1633)

TITLE	COMP.	TESS.	TYPE	REMARKS
Funeste piaggie (Euridice)	d1-d2	g1-d2	Baritone (mezzo-soprano or alto)	Majestic and sustained. (Krehbiel)
Gioite al canto mio (Euridice)	f#1-e2	g1-d2 (H)	Not suitable for light voices	Majestic and sustained. (Parisotti, Ricordi; also Floridia)

TITLE	COMP.	TESS.	TYPE	REMARKS
Nel puro ardor (Euridice)	g1-e2	a1-d2 (H)	All voices	Very sustained. (Floridia)

JACOPO A. PERTI
(1661-1756)

TITLE	COMP.	TESS.	TYPE	REMARKS
Begli occhi, io non mi pento	d1-g2	a1-eb2 (H)	All voices	Light and animated. (Floridia)
Io son zittella	e1-g2	g1-e2	Soprano	Very animated, light. (Landshoff)

NICOLA PICCINI
(1728-1800)

Piccini, primarily remembered now as Gluck's Parisian rival, seems to have suffered the fate of most of his contemporaries, namely, polite neglect. Hardly any of the songs and airs from his eighty or more operas are now available in reprints, and of those available only a few are still encountered occasionally on concert programs. Of these the "Se il ciel mi divide" from "Alessandro nelle Indie" is perhaps most widely known, having been included in the Parisotti collection as well as in the Gevaert "Les Gloires de l'Italie."

TITLE	COMP.	TESS.	TYPE	REMARKS
Giammai provai (La Donna Vana)	f#1-g2	g1-e2	Not too suitable for very low voices	Graceful, delicate tempo di minuetto. (Zanon)
Non sarei si sventurata	g1-b2	a1-f#2	Soprano	Animated. Demands considerable flexibility. (Landshoff)
Se il ciel mi divide (Alessandro nelle Indie)	c#1-g2	f1-d2	Mezzo-soprano or dramatic soprano	Scena and a spirited air. Transposed a third lower than the original. A cut from bar 3, page 149, to bar 8, page 143, is recommended. (Parisotti, Schirmer). This air in the original key can be found in Gevaert's Les Gloires de l'Italie (Heugel). See Vinci.

For other songs and airs see under "French" in this section (page 59).

NICCOLO PORPORA
(1686-1766)

TITLE	COMP.	TESS.	TYPE	REMARKS
Già la Notte	d1-g2	g1-e2	Soprano or light tenor	Slow, has florid passages. See also "Già la Notte" by Viardot(an arrangement of a movement from a Haydn string quartet). (Echos de l'Italie)

TITLE	COMP.	TESS.	TYPE	REMARKS
Recitative: Lascia, lascia una volta Air: Non più fra sassi	d1-g2	g1-e2	Soprano or light tenor	Recitative and an animated, graceful, rather florid air. A trifle long. (Echos de l'Italie)
So ben, che le speranze	d1-a2	g1-e2	Soprano	Animated. Demands some flexibility. (Landshoff)

FRANCESCO PROVENZALE
(1640-1700)

TITLE	COMP.	TESS.	TYPE	REMARKS
Deh, rendetemi	f1-f2	a1-eb2 (H)	Most suitable for medium or low voices	Delicate. Demands good command of pp. (Floridia) This air in the original key (a sixth lower) can be found in the Landshoff collection "Alte Meister des Bel Canto," Peters.

PAOLO QUAGLIATI
(15..-16..)

TITLE	COMP.	TESS.	TYPE	REMARKS
Apra il suo verde seno		g1-e2 (H)	All voices	Delicate and graceful. The accompaniment is somewhat elaborate. (Floridia) A simpler version can be found in Landshoff.

VINCENZO RIGHINI
(1756-1812)

TITLE	COMP.	TESS.	TYPE	REMARKS
Amor, che cieco sei (La Gerusalema liberata)	c1-f2	f1-c2	Soprano or mezzo-soprano	Graceful. Demands some flexibility. (Krehbiel)
Recitative: O ammirabile, o bella gelosia Air: Al nome tuo temuto (La Selva Incantata)	E-d1	c-c1	Bass	Sustained. Demands some flexibility. (Schirmer Operatic Anthology)

RAFUELLO RONTANI
(15..-16..)

TITLE	COMP.	TESS.	TYPE	REMARKS
Caldi sospiri	g1-f2	a1-eb2	All voices	Sustained. Demands some flexibility. (Parisotti, Ricordi)
Or ch'io non segno più	eb1-gb2	eb1-eb2 (H)	All voices	Light and animated. Somewhat humorous. Demands facile articulation. (Floridia)
Se bel rio	f1-f2	a1-d2	All voices	Graceful. Demands lightness of tone (Parisotti, Schirmer; also Floridia)

TITLE	COMP.	TESS.	TYPE	REMARKS

SALVATOR ROSA
(1615-1673)

TITLE	COMP.	TESS.	TYPE	REMARKS
Selve, voi che le speranza	d1-g2	g1-d2	All voices	Very sustained. (Floridia)
Star vicino	f1-g2	bb1-f2 (H)	Most suitable for men's voices	Demands good command of pp. and some flexibility. (Floridia)
Vado ben spesso	f1-f2	g1-d2 (H)	Most suitable for men's voices	Graceful and rhythmic. (Liszt made a piano transcription of this tune, "Canzonetta di Salvator Rosa.") (Floridia) This song is attributed to either Salvator Rosa or Giovanni Battista Bononcini.

LUIGI ROSSI
(1598-1653)

TITLE	COMP.	TESS.	TYPE	REMARKS
Ah, rendimi (Mitrane)	g-f#2	b-b1	Mezzo-soprano or alto	An andante, allegro air. Rather vigorous. (Schirmer, Operatic Anthology)
Che sventura	e1-g2	g1-e2	High voices	Not fast. Demands some flexibility. (Landshoff)
Fanciulla son io	f1-g2	bb1-f2	Light soprano	Animated, graceful. Demands facile articulation. Has florid passages. The verse beginning "Tuo strale dorato" could be omitted. (Neitzel, Gems of Antiquity, J. Church Co.)
Gelosia, che a poco a poco (Cantata)	c1-g2	eb1-eb2	Mezzo-soprano (Dramatic soprano) or tenor	Has several contrasting movements. In parts very florid. (Gevaert)
Non la volete intendere	f1-g2	g1-f2	High voices	Sustained; has a slower middle section. (Landshoff)
Se mi toglie ria sventura	f1-g2	g1-eb2	Soprano	Sustained. Demands good command of high pp. Has some florid passages. (Landshoff)

ANTONIO SACCHINI
(1734-1786)

TITLE	COMP.	TESS.	TYPE	REMARKS
Recitative: Deh calma, o cara Air: Cara, ascondi a me quel pianto (Motezuma)	b-g#2 (a2)	f#1-e2	Dramatic soprano (lyric soprano) or tenor	Recitative and a sustained air. In parts florid. (Gevaert)

TITLE	COMP.	TESS.	TYPE	REMARKS
Se mai più sarò (Alessandro nell' Indie)	d#1-a2	g#1-e2	High voices	Sustained. Has some florid passages. (Gevaert, reprinted by Schirmer)

For other songs and airs see under "French" in this section (page 59).

DOMENICO SARRI
(1678-1745)

TITLE	COMP.	TESS.	TYPE	REMARKS
Non ha ragione ingrato	e1-f2	f1-e2	Soprano	Not fast, graceful. Demands some flexibility. (Landshoff)
Sen corre l'agneletta	c1-f2	f1-c2	All voices	Graceful. Demands lightness of tone and some flexibility. (Parisotti, Schirmer)

GIUSEPPE SARTI
(1729-1802)

TITLE	COMP.	TESS.	TYPE	REMARKS
Mia speranza io pur vorrei	b-b2 (a)	e1-e2	Dramatic soprano (lyric soprano)	An andante, allegro aria. Demands some flexibility. (Gevaert)
S'inganna chi crede (Medoro)	f#1-a2	g#1-e2	Soprano or tenor	Graceful. Demands some flexibility. (Zanon)

ANTONIO SARTORIO
(1620-1681)

TITLE	COMP.	TESS.	TYPE	REMARKS
Oh, che umore stravagante	c1-e2	e1-c2	Most suitable for men's voices	Very spirited. Demands some flexibility and facile articulation. (Parisotti, Ricordi)

ALESSANDRO SCARLATTI
(1658-1725)

The few airs and songs of Alessandro Scarlatti available in modern reprints are too well known to every singer to need any sort of comment. Beautifully written for the voice, extraordinarily perfect in the elegance of their form, powerfully characteristic in the musical delineation of their poetic content, they have long been used as teaching material, no doubt because of their comparative harmonic simplicity. Yet if one considers that Scarlatti wrote some 115 operas, 200 masses, and a great number of miscellaneous vocal works, one wonders why, in view of the obvious popularity of the few of his airs available in modern reprints, no publisher has found it advisable to issue a comprehensive anthology of Scarlatti's songs and airs.

Scarlatti's vocal music, like that of Rameau and Purcell, seems, with a few exceptions, to have suffered the same polite neglect justly accorded to the work of their lesser contemporaries. It seems a pity that these three great composers are not as yet fully appreciated, and that their music is largely looked upon as a sort of relic of olden times, instead of being treated as music which is as magnificently alive today as it was when first conceived.

TITLE	COMP.	TESS.	TYPE	REMARKS
All' acquisto di gloria (Tigrane)	c1-g2	f1-d2	Medium or low voices	Spirited. Has florid passages. (Parisotti, Schirmer)
Caldo sangue (Il Sedecia, Re di Gerusalemene) (Oratorio)	f#1-a2	a1-f#2	Soprano	Slow and sustained. Demands some flexibility. (Landshoff)
Chi vuole innamorarsi	f#1-g2	a1-e2 (H)	Most suitable for high voices	Light and rapid. Demands facile articulation. (Floridia)
Già il sole dal Gange	eb1-f2	ab1-eb2	Not too suitable for very light high voices	Vigorous and spirited. (Parisotti, Schirmer)
Già mai	d1-g2	g1-eb2	High voices	A graceful, sustained Siciliana. (Echos de l'Italie)
La fortuna è un pronto ardir	d2-d2 (L)	e1-c#2 (L)	All voices	Graceful. Demands some flexibility. (J. Woodside, Seven Centuries of Solo Song, Boston Music Co.)
Non dar più pene, o caro (La Rosaura)	e1-f#2	a1-e2	Soprano	Light and animated. The violin obbligato can be easily incorporated into the piano part. (Krehbiel)
Non vogl'io se non vederti	f#1-e2	g1-d2 (H)	All voices	A minuet. Demands lightness of tone. (Floridia)
O cessate di piagarmi	d#1-d2	g1-c2	All voices	Very sustained. (Parisotti, Schirmer; also Floridia)
Povera pellegrina	f1-f2	ab1-eb2	Soprano	A graceful, sustained siciliana. (Gevaert)
Recitative: Qual mia colpa Air: Se delitto è l'adorarti	c1-f2	g1-eb2	All voices	Sustained. (Parisotti, Ricordi)
Rugiadose, odorose	f1-g2	bb1-eb2 (H)	All voices	Light and animated. Demands facile articulation and lightness of tone. Exists in many arrangements. Sometimes named "Le Violette" or "Violette." (Floridia)
Se Florindo è fedele	eb1-eb2	ab1-db2	Women's voices	Light and delicate. (Parisotti, Schirmer)
Sento nel core	e1-f2	g1-eb2	All voices	Slow and sustained. (Parisotti, Schirmer)
Se tu della mia morte	c1-eb2	f1-db2	All voices	Sustained. (Parisotti, Schirmer)
Son tutta duolo	d1-eb2	g1-d2	Most suitable for medium or low voices	Grave and declamatory. (Parisotti, Schirmer)

TITLE	COMP.	TESS.	TYPE	REMARKS
Su, venite a consiglio	d1-f#2	g1-d2	Not too suitable for very light high voices	An amusing, spirited dialogue between the composer and his thoughts. Demands facile articulation. (Parisotti, Schirmer)
Toglietemi la vita ancor	c#1-eb2	f#1-d2	Not too suitable for very light high voices	Somewhat declamatory, not fast. (Parisotti, Ricordi)
Un cor da voi ferito (La Rosaura)	b-b1	e1-b1	Alto or mezzo-soprano	Very sustained. (Krehbiel)

DOMENICO SCARLATTI
(1685-1757)

TITLE	COMP.	TESS.	TYPE	REMARKS
Consolati e spera	bb-e2	f1-d2	Not too suitable for very light high voices	Sustained. (Parisotti, Schirmer)
Dire non voglio	d1-a2	f#1-e2	High voices	Spirited, vigorous. Demands some flexibility. A trifle long. (Oxford University Press)
Qual farfaletta amante	f#1-ab2	g1-g2 (H)	Not too suitable for very low voices	Animated, graceful. Demands some flexibility. (Ascherberg, Hopwood and Crew, London)
Sono amante e	d1-g2	g1-f2	High voices	Sustained. Demands some flexibility. (Oxford University Press)
Tuo mi chiami	e1-g2	g1-e2	High voices	Sustained. Has some florid passages. (Oxford University Press)
Vorresti, si vorresti	e1-a2	g#1-f#2	High voices	Sustained. Has a vigorous, animated middle section. (Oxford University Press)

GAETANO MARIA SCHIASSI
(16..-1754)

TITLE	COMP.	TESS.	TYPE	REMARKS
Digli, ch'io son fedele (Alessandro nell'Indie)	c1-d2	e1-b1	Alto or mezzo-soprano	Majestic. Demands some flexibility. (Krehbiel)

ANTONIO SECCHI
(1761-1833)

TITLE	COMP.	TESS.	TYPE	REMARKS
Lungi dal caro bene	c1-a2	a1-f2 (H)	All voices	Very sustained. The authorship of this famous air has not been definitely established. (Cont.)

TITLE	COMP.	TESS.	TYPE	REMARKS
Lungi dal caro bene (Cont.)	c1-a2	a1-fe (H)	All voices	Another very effective arrangement by Bruno Huehn (Schirmer). (Floridia)

AGOSTINO STEFFANI
(1654-1748)

TITLE	COMP.	TESS.	TYPE	REMARKS
Sei si caro (Marco Aurelio)	d#1-f2	a1-e2 (H)	Women's voices	Slow and sustained. Demands flexibility. (Floridia)

ALESSANDRO STRADELLA
(1645?-1682)

TITLE	COMP.	TESS.	TYPE	REMARKS
Col mio sangue comprenderei (Il Floridoro)	eb1-ab2	g1-eb2 (H)	All voices	Slow and very sustained. (Floridia)
Così, amor, mi fai languir	f1-g2	a1-f2 (H)	All voices	Sustained. (Floridia)
Per pietà (Il Floridoro)	f1-ab2	ab1-eb2 (H)	All voices	Very sustained. (Floridia)
Pietà signore	c1-f2	g1-eb2 (H)	Not suitable for very light voices	Very sustained. (Floridia)
Ragion sempre addita	d1-g2	e1-e2	All voices	Spirited. Demands facile articulation. Has florid passages. (Parisotti, Schirmer)
Se amor m'annoda il piede	bb-f2	f1-d2	Most suitable for medium voices	A short cantata. (Parisotti, Schirmer)
Se nel ben sempre incostante	d1-e2	g1-d2	All voices	Sustained, graceful. (Parisotti, Ricordi)
So ben che mi saettano	c1-a2	g1-f2	Soprano	Animated, graceful. Demands facile articulation. (Landshoff)

BARBARA STROZZI
(1583-1660)

TITLE	COMP.	TESS.	TYPE	REMARKS
Amor dormiglione	f1-g2	ab1-f2 (H)	Not too suitable for very light high voices	Spirited. (Floridia)

FRANCESCO SUPRIANI
(attributed to)
(16..-17..)

TITLE	COMP.	TESS.	TYPE	REMARKS
Potrà lasciare il rio	e1-g#2	b1-f#2 (H)	All voices	Delicate. (Floridia)

TITLE	COMP.	TESS.	TYPE	REMARKS

ANTON FRANCESCO TENAGLIA
(1600-16..)

TITLE	COMP.	TESS.	TYPE	REMARKS
Begli occhi, mercè	c#1-e2	e1-c2	Not too suitable for very light high voices	Sustained. Demands some flexibility. (Parisotti, Ricordi)
Quando sarà quel di	d1-d2	g1-c2	Most suitable for medium voices	Light and animated. (Parisotti, Schirmer)

GIUSEPPE TORELLI
(d. 1708)

TITLE	COMP.	TESS.	TYPE	REMARKS
Tu lo sai	c#1-f#2 (g#2)	a1-e2 (H)	All voices	Very sustained. (Floridia)

TOMMASO TRAETTA
(1727-1779)

TITLE	COMP.	TESS.	TYPE	REMARKS
Dovrei...ma no...	b-f2	e1-d2	Soprano or mezzo-soprano	Sustained, somewhat declamatory. (Parisotti, Ricordi)
Ombra cara, amorosa	b-g2	g1-e2	Not too suitable for very light high voices	Scena and aria. Dramatic.(Parisotti, Schirmer; also Floridia)

FRANCESCO MARIA VERACINI
(1685-1750)

TITLE	COMP.	TESS.	TYPE	REMARKS
Pastorale	c1-g2 (a2)	a1-f2	Soprano	Light and delicate. Demands some flexibility and a good command of high pp. Arr. by A. L., Boosey)

LEONARDO VINCI
(1690-1730)

TITLE	COMP.	TESS.	TYPE	REMARKS
Deh respirar lasciatemi (Artasere)	d1-g2	g1-eb2	Soprano	Sustained. Demands some flexibility. (Gevaert)
Se il ciel mi divide (Alessandro nelle Indie)	eb1-ab2	ab1-f2	Soprano	Animated. Demands some flexibility. (Gevaert) See Piccini.
Sentirsi dire	c1-e2	e1-d2	Medium or low voices	Very spirited. Demands some flexibility. (Parisotti, Ricordi)
Si bella mercede	c1-f2	f1-d2	High voices	Animated. Demands some flexibility. (Parisotti, Ricordi)

TITLE	COMP.	TESS.	TYPE	REMARKS
Teco, si, vengo anch'io	d1-f2	f1-eb2	High voices	Graceful. Has some florid passages. (Parisotti, Ricordi)
Vedovella afflitta e sola	c1-d2	e1-c2	Mezzo-soprano or alto	Animated. Demands facile articulation. (Parisotti, Ricordi)
Vo solcando un mar crudele (Artaserse)	d1-a2	f#1-e2	Soprano	Spirited, florid. (Schirmer)

FILIPPO VITALI
(15..-16..)

TITLE	COMP.	TESS.	TYPE	REMARKS
Pastorella ove t'ascondi	d1-d2	g1-c2	All voices	Sustained, graceful. (Gevaert)

ANTONIO VIVALDI
(1675-1740)

TITLE	COMP.	TESS.	TYPE	REMARKS
Un certo non so che	c1-f2	e1-c2	Most suitable for medium voices	Sustained. Demands some flexibility. (Parisotti, Schirmer; also Floridia)

DIONIGI ZAMPERELLI
(17..-17..)

TITLE	COMP.	TESS.	TYPE	REMARKS
So che godendo vai (Catone)	a-f2	eb1-c2	Mezzo-soprano or alto	Majestic and sustained. (Krehbiel)

Bibliography

The name found in parentheses in the remarks column indicates one of the following collections:

Echos de France: Echos de France, 3 vols. edited anonymously, published by Durand. (Not overly accurate)

Gevaert: Répertoire classique du chant Français, 25 vols. edited by Gevaert, published by Lemoine, Paris. One of the most comprehensive, accurate and well-edited collections available. Each song or air is also available separately in the Lemoine edition.

Grovlez: Les plus beaux airs de l'Opéra François, 8 vols. (2 for each type of voice), edited by Grovlez, published by Chester, London.

See also Maîtres du Chant, edited by Prunières, published by Heugel, Paris. Echos du temps passé, 3 vols. edited by Weckerlin, published by Durand.

TITLE	COMP.	TESS.	TYPE	REMARKS
PIERRE BERTON **(1727-1780)**				
Oui, c'est demain que l'hyménée (Montano et Sté- phanie)	g1-ab2	ab1-eb2	Soprano	An andante, allegro air. Demands flexibility. (Gevaert)
FELICE BLANGINI **(1781-1841)**				
Il est parti	b-f2	eb1-eb2	Women's voices	Sustained. (Parisotti, Arie Antiche. Ricordi)
C'est une misère que nos jeunes gens	b-e2	e1-c2	Women's voices	A graceful humorous arietta. (Parisotti, Arie Antiche. Ricordi)
FRANCOIS BOÏELDIEU **(1775-1834)**				
Ah! quel plaisir d'être soldat (La Dame Blanche)	f-c2	a-f♯1	Tenor	Spirited, martial air. Rather long. (Gevaert)
Essayons, s'il se peut, de parler son langage (Les Voitures Versées)	a-bb2	eb1-f2	Coloratura soprano or lyric so- prano	A very florid, comic bravura aria. Requires good command of med- ium and low voice, as the singer is required to mockingly imitate a man. (Gevaert)
Il me semble (Beniowsky)	e1-b2	g1-e2	Soprano	Scena and an andante, allegro air. (Gevaert)
Recitative: Maintenant obser- vons Air: Viens, gentille dame (La Dame Blanche)	d-c2	bb-g1	Lyric tenor	A graceful compound aria, in parts quite flor- id. (Krehbiel, Songs from the Operas. Ditson)

TITLE	COMP.	TESS.	TYPE	REMARKS
Oui, je saurai combattre et plaire (Bayard à Mézières)	c#-a1	f#f#1	Dramatic tenor	Robust, vigorous character air. Demands considerable flexibility. (Gevaert)
Recitative: Qu'à mes ordres ici Air: C'est la Princesse de Navarre (Jean de Paris)	Bb-f1	eb-c1	Baritone	A spirited buffo air. (Krehbiel, Songs from the Operas. Ditson)

LOUIS T. BOURGEOIS
(1676-1750)

TITLE	COMP.	TESS.	TYPE	REMARKS
Paisible nuit (Les Amours Déguisés)	g1-a1	a1-g1	Lyric tenor or soprano	Slow and very sustained. The final section more animated. Very high tessitura. (Grovlez)

FRANCOIS BOUVARD
(1683-1760)

TITLE	COMP.	TESS.	TYPE	REMARKS
Ruisseau dont le bruit charmant (Cassandre)	g#-a1	a-f#1	Lyric tenor (or soprano)	Slow, sustained. (Grovlez)

ANDRE CAMPRA
(1660-1744)

TITLE	COMP.	TESS.	TYPE	REMARKS
Air Italien (Ad un cuore) (Italian text) (L'Europe Galante)	d1-f2	a1-f2	Soprano or mezzo-soprano	Delicate. Demands some flexibility. The tessitura is somewhat high for mezzo-soprano. (Grovlez)
Charmant Papillon (Les Fêtes Vénitiennes)	d1-g2	g1-eb2	Soprano	Light, florid. (Generally available)
Recitative: Irène, paraissez Air: Rassurez votre coeur timide (Les Fêtes Vénitiennes)	c-d1	e-c1	Bass or baritone	Graceful. (Grovlez)
Naissez brillantes fleurs (Les Fêtes Vénitiennes)	f-a1	c1-g1	Lyric tenor (or soprano)	Animated, graceful. Has florid passages. Very high tessitura. (Grovlez)
Seuls confidents de mes peines (Iphigénie)	d#1-f#2	g#1-e2	Soprano or mezzo-soprano	Very sustained. The tessitura is somewhat high. (Grovlez)
Venez, venez, fières beautés (Les Fêtes Vénitiennes)	eb1-ab2	c1-g2	Light soprano	Recitative and a florid air. (Grovlez)

CHARLES CATEL
(1773-1830)

TITLE	COMP.	TESS.	TYPE	REMARKS
Recitative: Du doute ou je vous vois Air: Pleurez, mais chantez ma victoire (Les Bayadères)	e1-a2	a1-f♯2	Dramatic soprano or lyric soprano	Recitative and an andante, allegro air. (Gevaert)
J'avais cru que ces dieux (Semiramis)	d1-b♭2	g1-e♭2	Soprano	Recitative and a dramatic, vigorous air. (Grovlez)

MARC ANTOINE CHARPENTIER
(1634-1704)

TITLE	COMP.	TESS.	TYPE	REMARKS
Quel prix de mon amour (Médée)	e1-f2	a1-e2	Mezzo-soprano or soprano	Slow and very sustained. (Grovlez)
Que d'horreurs, que de maux (Médée)	d1-g2	f♯1-e2	Mezzo-soprano or soprano	Declamatory and dramatic. (Grovlez)

LUIGI CHERUBINI
(1760-1842)

TITLE	COMP.	TESS.	TYPE	REMARKS
Guide mes pas (Les Deux Journées)	e♭-e♭1	g-d1	Baritone	Animated, rather vigorous. (Krehbiehl, Songs from the Operas. Ditson)
Jeunes filles aux regards doux (Anacréon)	e♭1-b♭2	g1-f2	Soprano	Rather animated, the vocal line sustained. (Gevaert)
Loin de celui (Rondo intercalé dans l'Italiana in Londra de Cimarosa)	e♭1-a♭2	a♭1-g♭2	Soprano	Sustained. Demands some flexibility. (Gevaert)
Recitative: Suspendez à ces murs Air: J' ai vu disparaître (Les Abencérages)	f♯-a1	a-f1	Dramatic tenor	Recitative and an andante, allegro air. Has dramatic climaxes. (Gevaert)
Vous voyez de vos fils (Médée)	d♭1-a♭2	f1-f2	Dramatic soprano	Slow, sustained. Demands some flexibility. The final section, declamatory and dramatic. (Gevaert)

For other songs and airs see under "Italian" in this section (page 32).

TITLE	COMP.	TESS.	TYPE	REMARKS

PASCAL COLASSE
(1640-1709)

Tristes honneurs, gloire cruelle, (Thétis et Pélée) — d1-f2 — f1-d2 — Mezzo-soprano or soprano — Slow and sustained. (Grovlez)

See also under Lully et Colasse.

NICOLAS DALAYRAC
(1753-1809)

Recitative: Cent esclaves ornaient / Air: Ah! que mon âme était ravie (Gulistan) — d-c2 — g-f♯1 — Lyric tenor (or soprano) — Recitative. Andante, allegro. Has some florid passages. (Grovlez)

D'un époux chéri — d1-g2 — g1-d2 — Soprano — Graceful arietta in contrasting tempi. Demands lightness of tone and some flexibility. (Echos de France.)

Hélas! c'est près de vous (Sargines) — f-b♭1 — g-g1 — Tenor — Sustained. (Gevaert)

O ma Georgette — c1-f2 — e1-c2 — Men's voices — Sustained. (Echos de France.)

Quand le bien aimé reviendra — d1-e2 — e1-b1 — Women's voices — Graceful, light. (Echos de France; also Parisotti, Ricordi)

ANTOINE DAUVERGNE
(1713-1797)

D'un amant inconstant (Les Troqueurs) — f1-b♭2 — a1-f2 — Light soprano — Spirited, light. Demands considerable flexibility. (Gevaert)

J'ai cru faire un bon coup (Les Troqueurs) — A-e1 — f♯-d1 — Bass baritone or baritone — Recitative and a spirited air. (Grovlez)

HENRI DESMARETS
(1659-1741)

Qu'un triste éloignement (Vénus et Adonis) — d♯1-a2 — g1-e2 — Soprano — Delicate, sustained. Demands in parts considerable flexibility and a good command of p. (Grovlez)

ANDRÉ CARDINAL DESTOUCHES
(1672-1749)

Brillez dans ces beaux lieux   n- (Les Eléments) — e♭1-g2 — g1-e♭2 — Soprano — Majestic sustained. Has florid passages. (Grovlez)

TITLE	COMP.	TESS.	TYPE	REMARKS
Le feu qu'en ce temple (Les Eléments)	A-e1	d-d1	Bass or baritone	An andante, allegro air. Vigorous. Has florid passages. (Grovlez)

FRANCOIS DEVIENNE
(1760-1803)

TITLE	COMP.	TESS.	TYPE	REMARKS
Dans l'asile de l'innocence	d1-f2	f1-d2	High or medium voices	Sustained, graceful. (Echos de France.)

EGIDIO R. DUNI
(1709-1775)

TITLE	COMP.	TESS.	TYPE	REMARKS
Ah! que l'amour est chose jolie	c1-a2	e1-e2	Soprano (or tenor)	Sustained, graceful. (Echos de France.) Durand)
Les temps passé (Les Moissonneurs)	d1-g2	g1-e2	Soprano	Animated, graceful. (Gevaert)

FRANCOIS GOSSEC
(1734-1829)

TITLE	COMP.	TESS.	TYPE	REMARKS
Ah! faut-il me venger (Thésée)	f#1-a2	g1-g2	Dramatic soprano	A compound, rather sustained air interrupted by recitative passages. (Gevaert)
Dors, mon enfant (Rosine)	c#1-f#2	a1-d2	Mezzo-soprano or soprano	Slow, sustained. Demands good command of pp. (Grovlez)
Doux repos, innocente paix (Thésée)	eb1-bb2	g1-g2	Soprano	A compound dramatic air. Demands flexibility. (Gevaert)
Ne verrais-je paraître (Thésée)	f1-bb2	g1-g2	Dramatic soprano	Sustained. (Gevaert)
Songe: Aux douceurs du sommeil (Sabinus)	A-f#1 (g1)	e-d1	Bass baritone or baritone	A scena and a compound air with a spirited final allegro. (Gevaert)
Un tendre engagement va plus loin (Thésée)	f1-bb2	f1-f2	Dramatic soprano	Recitative and a rather vigorous, dramatic compound air. (Gevaert)

ANDRE GRETRY
(1741-1813)

Grétry, in his time one of the most popular and elegant of the French opera composers, was extremely prolific, even when judged by the severe standards of his time. Much of his music is now forgotten and unavailable, yet judging by the few songs and airs available in modern reprints, one wonders why the publishers of today have not found it advisable to make a comprehensive anthology of his songs and airs.

Grétry's humor, his beautifully conceived vocal line, always considerate of the singer, his melodic gift, and his unfailingly felicitous, though perhaps not invariably powerful or individual manner of expression ought to make him a most popular representative of the late eighteenth century French vocal music.

He seems to have favored the high voices, seldom writing anything for bass or alto, and being especially fond of high baritone, tenor and light soprano voices.

SOPRANO

TITLE	COMP.	TESS.	TYPE	REMARKS
Ah, quel tourment! (Le Huron)	c1-a2	g1-f2	Soprano or mezzo-soprano	A scena and an andante, allegro air. (Gevaert)
Ah! si parfois (L'Ami de la Maison)	e1-b2	f#1-f#2	Lyric soprano (coloratura soprano)	Delicate, sustained. In parts quite florid. (Gevaert)
Recitative: C'est ici que le beau Céphale Air: Naissantes fleurs (Céphale et Procris)	d1-a2	g1-e2	Lyric soprano (coloratura soprano)	Graceful, sustained, delicate. Demands some flexibility. (Gevaert)
Cher objet (Aucassin et Nicolette)	cb1-ab2	ab1-f2	Soprano	Sustained; has a rapid middle section. (Gevaert)
En conscience (La Fausse Magie)	c1-a2	f1-e2	Lyric soprano (coloratura soprano)	A spirited buffo arietta. Demands facile articulation and some flexibility. (Gevaert)
Eprise d'un feu (Anacréon chez Polycrate)	g1-c3	bb1-g2	Lyric soprano	A sustained larghetto and a spirited allegro. Demands some flexibility. (Grovlez)
Il est certains barbons (Le Tableau Parlant)	c1-g2	g1-e2	Lyric soprano (colaratura soprano)	A spirited subrette air; Demands facile articulation and some flexibility. (Gevaert)
Il va venir (Sylvain)	b-bb2	g1-f2	Soprano	A sustained, subdued andante and a spirited allegro. (Gevaert)
Je crains de lui (Richard Coeur de Lion)	e1-ab2	f1-db2	Lyric soprano (coloratura soprano	Animated, graceful. (Gevaert)
Je ne fais semblant de rien (L'Ami de la Maison)	c#1-a2	g1-e2	Lyric soprano (coloratura soprano)	Delicate and light. (Gevaert)
Je ne le dis qu'à vous (La Fausse Magie)	eb1-ab2	eb1-eb2	Lyric soprano (coloratura soprano)	Not fast. Very florid. (Gevaert)
Je ne sais pas si ma soeur (Sylvain)	eb1-bb2	f1-f2	Lyric soprano (Coloratura soprano)	Animated, delicate air. Demands flexibility. (Gevaert)

TITLE	COMP.	TESS.	TYPE	REMARKS
La fauvette avec ses petits (Zémire et Azor)	d1-b2	g1-g2	Coloratura soprano	A spirited, brilliant, florid air. The middle section is sustained and delicate. (Gevaert)
O douce nuit (L'Amant Jaloux)	eb1-bb2	f1-f2	Soprano	Sustained compound air. (Gevaert)
Oui, mes amis, la bienfaisance (Pierre-le-Grand)	eb1-ab2	ab1-eb2	Soprano or mezzo- soprano	An andante, allegro air. (Gevaert)
Plus de dépit (Les Deux Avares)	c1-bb2	ab1-f2	Lyric soprano (coloratura soprano)	Graceful, delicate, sus- tained. Has some flor- id passages. (Schirmer, Operatic Anthology)
Rose chérie (Zémire et Azor)	c1-a2	g1-e2	Lyric soprano (coloratura soprano)	Sustained, delicate. De- mands good command of high pp. (Gevaert)

ALTO

TITLE	COMP.	TESS.	TYPE	REMARKS
A quels maux tu me livres (L'Amitié à l'Epreuve)	b-e2	e1-c#2	Alto or mezzo - soprano	Very sustained. This charming cantilena, or- iginally written for so- prano, is transposed a fourth lower in the Gev- aert edition to make it suitable for alto."The classic French reper- toire has but a very few arias suitable for this type of voice." (Gevaert)
Ah, quel tourment! (Le Huron)	c1-a2	g1-f2	Soprano or mezzo-so- prano	A scena and an andante, allegro air. (Gevaert)
Du destin qui m'opprime (Le Jugement de Midas)	a-f2	d1-d2	Alto or Mezzo- soprano	Sustained. Demands some flexibility. Orig- inally written for tenor; transposed a minor third lower in the Gev- aert edition. (Gevaert)
Oui, mes amis, la bienfaisance (Pierre-le-Grand)	eb1-ab2	ab1-eb2	Soprano or mezzo-so- prano	An andante, allegro air. (Gevaert)

TENOR

TITLE	COMP.	TESS.	TYPE	REMARKS
Ah! Quel tourment (Zémire et Azor)	d-gb1	f-f1	Tenor	Sustained. Demands some flexibility. (Gevaert)
Assuré de ton in- nocence (Le Comte d'Albert)	e-a1	a-f1	Tenor	Sustained. (Gevaert)
Certain coucou, cer- tain hibou. (Le Jugement de Midas)	c-a1	g-f1	Lyric ten- or (or so- prano)	Light, graceful, humor- ous, in parts quite flor- id. (Grovlez)

TITLE	COMP.	TESS.	TYPE	REMARKS
Doux charme de la vie (Le Jugement de Midas)	e-ab1	ab-f1	Tenor	Graceful, sustained air. (Gevaert)
Du moment qu'on aime (Zémire et Azor)	d♯-g1	g♯-e1	Lyric tenor	Sustained, graceful. Demands some flexibility. (Schirmer, Operatic Anthology)
Par une grâce touchante (Le Jugement de Midas)	f-g1	a-f1	Lyric tenor	Andante, allegro air. Demands considerable flexibility and good command of high pianissimo. (Gevaert)
Qu'il est cruel d'aimer (Les Evénements Imprévus)	f-ab1 (d)	ab-f1	Tenor	Grave, sustained. (Gevaert)
Si l'univers entier m'oublie (Richard Coeur de Lion)	f-bb1 (Ab)	bb-f1	Dramatic tenor	Rather animated. Has florid passages and dramatic climaxes. Demands an extensive range. (Gevaert)
Tandis que tout sommeille (L' Amant Jaloux)	f♯-g1	bb-g1	Lyric tenor	Delicate, light serenade. Demands good command of pp. and rather facile articulation. (Schirmer, Operatic Anthology)

BARITONE

TITLE	COMP.	TESS.	TYPE	REMARKS
Adieu, Marton, adieu, Lisette (L'Epreuve Villageoise)	e-f♯1	g-e1	Baritone	Animated, light, humorous. Demands some flexibility. (Gevaert)
Ah, ma femme! Qu'avez vous fait? (Lucille)	Ab-gb1	eb-eb1	Baritone	Slow, sustained, somewhat declamatory. In parts demands considerable dramatic intensity. (Gevaert)
Déesse des beaux jours (Céphale et Procris)	B-g1	d-d1	Baritone	Graceful, sustained. Demands some flexibility. (Gevaert)
De ma barque légère (Anacréon)	c♯-d♯1 (f♯1)	e♯-c♯1	Baritone (bass-baritone)	Light, graceful. (Gevaert)
Quand l'âge vient l'Amour nous laisse (La Fausse Magie)	A-f♯1 (g1)	d-d1	Baritone	Sustained, graceful. Demands some flexibility. (Gevaert)
Laisse en paix le dieu des combats (Chanson Bachique) (Anacréon)	B-e1	e-d1	Baritone (bass-baritone)	Spirited, vigorous. Demands some flexibility. (Gevaert)
Le pauvre enfant ne savait pas (Zémire et Azor)	c-f1	d-c1	Baritone	Sustained. In parts demands considerable dramatic intensity. Orig-(Cont.)

TITLE	COMP.	TESS.	TYPE	REMARKS
Le pauvre enfant ne savait pas (Zémire et Azor) (Cont.)	c-f1	d-c1	Baritone	inally written for tenor. In this edition transposed a minor third lower than the original. (Gevaert)
Nièces, neveux (Les Deux Avares)	A-g1	e-d1	Baritone	A comic, spirited air. (Gevaert)
O fortune ennemie (Anacréon chez Polycrate)	Bb-eb1	f♯-d1	Baritone (bass-baritone)	Vigorous and spirited. (Grovlez)
O Richard, ô mon roi (Richard Coeur de Lion)	Bb-g1	f-d1	Baritone	An andante, allegro air. Demands some flexibility. Originally written for tenor. (Schirmer, Operatic Anthology.)
Songe enchanteur (Anacréon)	A-f♯1	d-d1	Baritone	Slow, sustained. (Gevaert)

NICCOLO ISOUARD
(1775-1818)

TITLE	COMP.	TESS.	TYPE	REMARKS
Ah! Pour moi quelle peine extrême (Jeannot et Colin)	c1-c3	f1-f2	Dramatic soprano or lyric soprano	Andante, allegro air. Very spirited and dramatic. (Gevaert)
Dieu puissant! (Michel-Ange)	f1-c3	g1-f2	Soprano	Rather animated, sustained. Interrupted by a recitative passage. (Gevaert)
Scena and rondo: Non, je ne veux pas chanter (Le Billet de Loterie)	d1-c3 (eb3)	f1-f2	Coloratura soprano	Brilliant, spirited. Very florid. A little long. Was once a celebrated bravura piece. (Gevaert)

JEAN MARIE LECLAIR
(1697-1764)

TITLE	COMP.	TESS.	TYPE	REMARKS
Chantez, chantez l'amour (Scylla et Glaucus)	f-bb1	a-f1	Lyric tenor (or soprano)	Animated, in parts very florid. Very high tessitura.(Grovlez)
Serments trompeurs (Scylla et Glaucus)	eb1-f2	f1-db2	Mezzo-soprano or alto	Slow, grave. Demands some flexibility. (Grovlez)

JEAN F. LESUEUR
(1760-1837)

TITLE	COMP.	TESS.	TYPE	REMARKS
Hélas! Sans m'entendre (Ossian ou les Bardes)	c1-e2	e1-c2	Mezzo-soprano or alto	Dramatic. Somewhat declamatory, vigorous. (Grovlez)

JEAN BAPTISTE LULLY
(1632-1687)

Most of the songs and airs of Lully are but rarely performed at present. It may be that the severe simplicity of his style seems too bare and forbidding to the majority of present-day singers. It may, however, be that the difficulty of procuring most of Lully's music in modern reprints is primarily responsible for this neglect, since the few readily available airs like "Bois Epais" are frequently performed. In the opinion of this writer, Lully's music is as remarkably alive today as it was some three hundred years ago. Nobly declamatory in style and devoid of any unnecessary embellishments, Lully's songs and airs seem to be most suitable for rather heavy voices and are, superficially at least, rather similar to Monteverde in the character of their vocal line.

A collection of Airs by Lully edited by Hettich, is published by Rouart Lerolle.

TITLE	COMP.	TESS.	TYPE	REMARKS
Ah! faut-il me venger (Thésée)	d1-f2	g1-d2	Soprano	Short, grave, sustained. (Gevaert)
Ah! Quel tourment (Roland)	f-ab1	ab-f1	Tenor	Sustained, rather grave air. (Gevaert)
Ah! Si la liberté (Armide)	e1-g2	a1-f2	Soprano	Majestic. (Grovlez)
Allez, éloignez-vous (Armide)	f-ab1	f-f1	Tenor	Short, sustained arioso. (Gevaert)
Allez remplir ma place (Armide)	f-ab1	ab-eb1	Tenoi	A recitative with a spirited main section. (Gevaert)
Amour, que veux-tu de moi (Amadis)	b-d2	e1-c2	Alto or mezzo-soprano	Very sustained. (Schirmer, Operatic Anthology)
Amour, vois quels maux (Cadmus et Hermione)	f1-f2	g1-eb2	Soprano or mezzo-soprano	Grave, sustained. (Gevaert)
Belle Hermione (Cadmus et Hermione)	c#-e1	e-d1	Baritone or bass	Slow and sustained. One of Lully's most remarkable airs. (Gevaert)
Bois épais (Amadis)	d1-f2	f1-c2	Originally written for tenor. Now sung by all voices; most suitable for medium or low voices	Very sustained. Perhaps Lully's most famous air. (Krehbiel, Songs from the Operas, Alto. Ditson; also arranged by A. L., published by Boosey)
Dans un piège fatal (Amadis)	Bb-eb1	eb-d1	Bass or baritone	Sustained, majestic. (Grovlez)
Dormons tous! (Atys)	g1-a2	a1-g2	Lyric tenor (or soprano)	Very sustained. Very high tessitura. (Grovlez)
Fermez-vous pour jamais (Amadis)	d1-g2	f1-d2	Soprano or mezzo-soprano	Grave and very sustained. (Gevaert)
Il faut passer tôt ou tard (Alceste)	G-d1	c-c1	Bass or bass-baritone	Rather animated compound air. (Gevaert)
Le héros que j' attends (Alceste)	e1-f2		Soprano or mezzo-soprano	Sustained. (Gevaert)
Pauvres amants (Le Sicilien)	g-à1	b-f#1	Lyric tenor (or soprano)	Graceful, sustained. Demands some flexibility. (Grovlez)

TITLE	COMP.	TESS.	TYPE	REMARKS
Plus j'observe ces lieux (Armide)	f#-a1	a-g#1	Lyric tenor (or soprano)	Slow, sustained. Very high tessitura. (Grovlez)
Que rien ne trouble ici (Thésée)	G-d1	c-c1	Bass or bass-baritone	An andante, allegro air. Has some florid passages. (Grovlez)
Que soupirer d'amour est une douce chose (Le Carnaval)	e1-f#2	g1-d2	Soprano or mezzo-soprano	Animated, graceful. (Gevaert)
Que vois-je, ô spectacle effroyable (Amadis)	e1-g2	g1-eb2	Soprano or mezzo-soprano	A rather dramatic recitative and a sustained air. (Gevaert)
Réponds, charmante nuit (Le Carnaval)	e1-f#2	g1-d2	Soprano or mezzo-soprano	Very sustained. (Gevaert) This text is an extravagant mixture of French, Spanish and Italian.
Revenez, revenez amours (Thésée)	d1-f2	g1-d2	Soprano	Sustained, graceful. Has a few declamatory passages. (Grovlez)

LULLY ET COLASSE

TITLE	COMP.	TESS.	TYPE	REMARKS
Amour, tu m as soumise encor (Les Saisons)	f#1-g2	a1-e2	Soprano	Sustained, delicate. Has florid passages. (Gevaert)
Charmants ruisseaux (Les Saisons)	f-g1	bb-g1	Tenor	Graceful, sustained. (Gevaert)
L'affreuse discorde (Les Saisons)	f#-a1	b-g1	Tenor	Animated. (Gevaert)
Le doux printemps (Les Saisons)	c-eb1	f-c1	Bass or baritone	Short recitative and a sustained air. (Gevaert)
Me plaindrai-je toujours, Amour (Les Saisons)	d1-g2	f1-f2	Soprano	Sustained, graceful air. Demands flexibility. (Gevaert)
Mon retour des mortels (Les Saisons)	G-d1	c-c1	Bass or baritone	Animated, vigorous air. (Gevaert)
Que mon destin est déplorable (Les Saisons)	B-e1	e-d1	Bass or baritone	Sustained. Demands some flexibility. (Gevaert)
Tout cède à vos doux appas (Les Saisons)	f1-ab2	ab1-f2	Soprano	Sustained, graceful. (Schirmer, Operatic Anthology)

GIOVANNI MARTINI
(1741-1816)

TITLE	COMP.	TESS.	TYPE	REMARKS
Plaisir d'amour	bb-eb2	eb1-c2	All voices	Very sustained. (Parisotti, Italian Anthology. Schirmer)

ETIENNE MÉHUL
(1763-1817)

TITLE	COMP.	TESS.	TYPE	REMARKS
Ah, lorsque la mort trop cruelle (Joseph)	f#1-e2		Soprano (mezzo-soprano	Graceful, animated. Vocally not taxing. (Score, Peters)

TITLE	COMP.	TESS.	TYPE	REMARKS
A peine au sortir de l'enfance (Joseph)	g-f1	g-e1	Tenor	Sustained. Vocally not taxing. (Score, Peters)
Femme sensible, entends-tu? (Ariodant)	eb-eb1	ab-db1	Baritone	Very sustained. (Schirmer, Operatic Anthology)
Recitative: Mais que dis-je? Air: O des amants le plus fidèle (Ariodant)	g♯-a2	d1-e2	Mezzo-soprano (dramatic soprano)	Recitative, andante, allegro. In parts very dramatic. (Gevaert; also Krehbiel, Songs from the Operas, Ditson)
Sur le sort de son fils (Stratonice)	B-f1	f-d1	Baritone	Recitative, andante, allegro. (Grovlez)
Recitative: Vainement Pharaon Air: Champs paternels (Joseph)	d♯-a1	a-e1	Tenor	Recitative, andante, allegro. (Schirmer, Operatic Anthology)
Versez tous vos chagrins (Stratonice)	e-ab1	g-f1	Tenor	Short recitative and an andante, allegro air. (Gevaert)

JEAN JOSEPH MONDONVILLE
(1711-1772)

TITLE	COMP.	TESS.	TYPE	REMARKS
Sur les pâles humains (Titon et l'Aurore)	G-f1	d-bb	Bass-baritone or baritone	Rapid and vigorous. Demands considerable flexibility. (Grovlez)
Venez, venez sous ce riant feuillage (Titon et l'Aurore)	e1-b2	a1-f♯2	Coloratura soprano or lyric soprano	Animated, delicate, florid. (Grovlez)

PIERRE A. MONSIGNY
(1729-1817)

TITLE	COMP.	TESS.	TYPE	REMARKS
Adieu, chère Louise (Le Déserteur)	d-f1	g-eb1	Baritone	Slow and very sustained. (Schirmer Operatic Anthology)
C'est ici que Rose respire (Rose et Colas)	f-g1	g-e1	Tenor	Very sustained, delicate. (Gevaert)
Il m'eût été si doux de t'embrasser (Le Déserteur)	B-e1	e-d1	Baritone	Sustained, somewhat declamatory. In parts demands considerable dramatic intensity. (Gevaert)
Il regardait mon bouquet (Le Roi et le Fermier)	d♯1-g♯2	f♯1-f♯2	Light soprano	A delicate buffo arietta. Demands very facile articulation. (Schirmer, Operatic Anthology)

TITLE	COMP.	TESS.	TYPE	REMARKS
Je ne déserterai jamais (Le Déserteur)	c-f1	f-d1	Baritone	Spirited, vigorous. Demands some flexibility. (Gevaert)
L'art surpasse ici la nature (La Belle Arsène)	eb1-c3	ab1-f2	Light soprano or coloratura soprano	Sustained. Has some florid cadenzas. (Gevaert)
Un jeune coeur (Les Aveux Indiscrets)	d1-a2	a1-f#2	Light soprano	Graceful. Demands considerable flexibility and a good command of staccato. (Grovlez)

MICHEL MONTECLAIR
(1666-1737)

TITLE	COMP.	TESS.	TYPE	REMARKS
Qu'ai je entendu! (Jephté)	e1-f2	f1-d2	Mezzo-soprano	Sustained, stately. Somewhat declamatory. (Grovlez)
Quel funeste appareil (Jephté)	B-eb1	d-c1	Bass or baritone	Sustained, majestic. Somewhat declamatory. (Grovlez)

JEAN J. MOURET
(1682-1738)

TITLE	COMP.	TESS.	TYPE	REMARKS
Doux plaisirs (Pirithoüs)	c1-f2	eb1-c2	Mezzo-soprano or alto	Graceful, delicate. Demands good command of p. (Grovlez)

FERDINANDO PAËR
(1771-1839)

TITLE	COMP.	TESS.	TYPE	REMARKS
Hélas! C'est près de vous	d1-f2	g1-e2	Most suitable for men's voices	Sustained, graceful. (Echos de France)
Si l'hymen a quelque douceur	d1-g2	g1-d2	High voices	Graceful. (Echos de France)

For other songs and airs see under "Italian" in this section (page 32).

GIOVANNI PAESIELLO
(1741-1816)

TITLE	COMP.	TESS.	TYPE	REMARKS
Recitative: De l'aurore au couchant Air: Déserts écartés (Proserpine)	bb-bb2	eb1-eb2	Dramatic soprano or high mezzo-soprano	Very sustained. Demands some flexibility. (Gevaert)

For other songs and airs see under "Italian" in this section (page 32).

TITLE	COMP.	TESS.	TYPE	REMARKS

ANDRE D. PHILIDOR
(1647-1730)

TITLE	COMP.	TESS.	TYPE	REMARKS
Belle Ernelinde (Ernelinde)	c-e1 (G)	d-d1	Bass or bass-bari-tone	Majestic, not slow. Demands some flexibility. (Gevaert)
Dans la magie (Le Sorcier)	c-g1	f-f1	Tenor	A compound air. Has alternate sections of mock majesty and graceful gaiety. (Gevaert)
Né dans un camp (Ernelinde)	c-g1	f-d1	Baritone	Sustained, rhythmical. Has some florid passages. (Grovlez)
Non, cher objet que j'adore (Melide or Le Navigateur)	d-ab1	ab-g1	Tenor	A dramatic scena and air. (Gevaert)
O toi qui ne peux m'entendre (Tom Jones)	eb1-bb2	g1-e2	Soprano	Scena and an andante, allegro air. Demands flexibility. (Gevaert)
Quand pour le grand voyage (Le Maréchal-ferrant)	d-a1	a-f#1	Tenor	Animated, delicate air. Demands facile articulation. (Gevaert)

NICOLA PICCINI
(1728-1800)

TITLE	COMP.	TESS.	TYPE	REMARKS
Recitative: Amants qui vous plaignez Air: Brûle d'une flamme (Atys)	c-ab1	g-f1	Tenor	Subdued recitative and graceful air. Demands flexibility. (Gevaert)
J'ai mérité qu'on me punisse (Atys)	g-ab1	ab-f1	Dramatic tenor	Spirited. Has dramatic climaxes. Demands flexibility. (Gevaert)
Je mourrai (Roland)	d#1-f#2	f#1-e2	Not too suitable for very light high voices	Sustained. (Echos de France)
Recitative: Je t'aime plus que moi Air: Oreste, au nom de la patrie (Iphigénie en Tauride)	c-d1 (f1)	e-c1	Bass-bari-tone or bass	Sustained. (Gevaert)
L'amour fait verser trop de pleurs (Atys)	g-a1	a-f#1	Tenor	Delicate. Has animated sections. Demands some flexibility. (Gevaert)

Recitative: O funeste amitié Air: Quel trouble agite non cöeur? (Atys)	e-b♭1	c1-a1	Dramatic tenor	Dramatic and spirited. Demands flexibility. Very high tessitura. (Gevaert)
O nuit, déesse du mystère (Le Faux Lord)	b-e2	g1-d2	Mezzo- soprano or alto	Sustained. Has dramatic climaxes. (Parisotti, Italian Anthology. Schirmer)
Recitative: Qu'ai-je donc fait, cruel Air: Ah! Prends pitié de ma faiblesse (Didon)	c1-a♭2	f1-f2	Dramatic soprano or lyric soprano	Sustained. Has dramatic climaxes. (Gevaert)

For other songs and airs see under "Italian" in this section (page 32).

JEAN PHILIPPE RAMEAU
(1683-1764)

Rameau's name is unfortunately much more widely known among the present-day singers than his music. In the opinion of this writer the neglect of Rameau's music coupled with the veneration accorted to his name is as inexplicable as it is unjustified; for not much of the early eighteenth century vocal music can equal Rameau's in vitality, elegance and simplicity. Of course, when one considers that no piano score edition of his vocal works was available until Durand published one under the editorship of Saint-Saëns one realizes that this neglect is not solely attributable to lack of interest on the part, of singers.

However, Rameau's airs are still but rarely encountered on the concert programs of today and are still for the most part rather difficult to obtain.

Rameau's airs, although in no way difficult musically, present a number of rather complex stylistic problems for the present-day singer; one of such problems, that of proper declamation of the text, seems to demand not only a considerable knowledge of French prosody but also of the French dramatic conventions of the period. Another is the problem of a rhythmically satisfactory performance of short embellishments in which Rameau's music abounds.

In the opinion of this writer it would often seem more practical and satisfactory to dispense with such embellishments unless one can learn to perform them gracefully, casually and in a rhythmically impeccable fashion.

As in the case of most of the eighteenth century vocal music a knowledge of classical mythology would add greatly to the understanding of Rameau's texts.

Editions:
Complete works, piano score, Durand.
Collection of Airs, edited by Saint-Saëns, published by Durand
Most authentic reprints of excerpts from operas and cantatas are to be found in the following collections:
Gevaert: Répertoire classique du chant Français. Lemoine, Paris.
Grovlez: Les plus beaux airs de l'Opéra François, Chester, London.
Prunières: Maîtres du chant. Heugel, Paris.

TITLE	COMP.	TESS.	TYPE	REMARKS
A l'amour rendez les armes (Hippolyte et Aricie)	d1-f2	f1-d2	All voices	A graceful gavotte, (Durand Collection, also Echos de France)
Accourez riante jeunesse (Les Fêtes d'Hébé)	d1-f2	g1-e2	Soprano	Animated, graceful, has florid passages. (Gevaert)
Amour quand du destin (Les Indes Galantes)	e1-g2	a1-f2	Soprano	Delicate, sustained, demands some flexibility. (Durand Collection)
Arrachez de mon coeur (Dardanus)	c1-d2	f#1-d2	Medium or low voices	Sustained. (Echos de France)
Aux langueurs d'Apollon (Platée)	d1-a2	e1-e2	Soprano	Animated, rather florid. (Gevaert)
Chassons de nos plaisirs (Acanthe et Céphise)	e1-f2	g1-d2	Soprano(or tenor)	Sustained, graceful. (Spicker, Operatic Anthology, Schirmer)
Dans ces doux asiles (Castor et Pollux)	c1-f2	d1-d2	High or medium voices	A graceful, delicate menuet. (Gevaert) The original is a third higher, a solo with chorus. Known as "Menuet Chanté")
Recitative: Vous excitez la plus sincère ardeur Air: Et vous, jeune beauté (La Princesse de Navarre)	e1-g2	a1-f#2	Soprano	Graceful, demands some flexibility. Rather high tessitura. (Durand Collection)
Recitative: Ah! que me faites-vous entendre? Air: Il faut que l'amour (Les Indes Galantes)	a-e2	d1-d2	Medium or low voices	A graceful menuet, demands some flexibility. (Durand Collection)
La Musette (Excerpt from a solo cantata)	c1-eb2	e1-c2 (L)	All voices	Recitative and a graceful air. (J. Woodside "Seven Centuries of Solo Song" Boston Music Co.)
Le grillon	c1-f2	f1-e2	High or medium voices	Sustained, graceful. An arrangement of a Rameau melody with words by Béranger (1780-1857) (Echos de France)
Les plaisirs et les jeux (Zoroastre)	c#1-e2	g1-e2	Soprano	Rather slow, sustained. Demands some flexibility. (Gevaert)
Recitative: Voici les tristes lieux Air: Monstre affreux	F-f1	c-d1	Bass or baritone	Very sustained, vigorous and majestic. (Spicker, Operatic Anthology, Schirmer)

TITLE	COMP.	TESS.	TYPE	REMARKS
Nature, amour, qui partagez mon coeur (Castor et Pollux)	d-e1	e-d1	Bass or baritone	Sustained. (Grovlez)
O jour affreux (Dardanus)	e1-g2	f1-f2	Soprano	Grave, sustained air. (Gevaert) In the Durand Collection transposed a tone lower, suitable for lower voices.
O mort, n'exerce pas ta rigueur (Les Fêtes d'Hébé)	e1-g2	a1-f2	Soprano	Slow, sustained, grave. (Durand Collection)
Papillon inconstant (Les Indes Galantes)	f#1-b2	b1-f#2	Light soprano	Animated, graceful, quite florid. (Durand Collection)
Permettez, astre du jour (Les Indes Galantes)	c#1-e2	f#1-d2	Medium or low voices	Graceful, light. (Durand Collection)
Recitative: Les oiseaux d'alentour Air: Pourquoi leur envier (L'Impatience)	c1-f2	f1-d2	All voices	Graceful. (Durand Collection)
Puisque Pluton est inflexible (Hippolyte et Aricie)	bb-eb2	eb1-c2	Medium or low voices	Rather vigorous, stately. (Durand Collection)
Puissant Maître des flots (Hippolyte et Aricie)	B-e1	f#-d1	Bass or baritone	Slow, very sustained. (Grovlez)
Recitative: Ciel! Tandis qu'au sommeil Air: Quand le silence (Diane et Actéon)	d1-f2	f1-d2	All voices	A rather extended recitative and a graceful, sustained air. (Durand Collection)
Ranimez vos flambeaux (Les Indes Galantes)	d1-g2	a1-g2	Soprano	Animated, graceful, in parts quite florid. (Durand Collection)
Rossignols amoureux (Hippolyte et Aricie)	e1-a2	a1-f#2	Light soprano	Slow, delicate. Has many florid passages. (Grovlez) In the Gevaert edition transposed a half tone lower and provided with some cadenzas. This edition also reprinted by Ditson. In the Durand Collection transposed a tone lower.
Séjour de l'éternelle le paix (Castor et Pollux)	c1-f2	f1-d2	All voices	Slow, sustained, graceful air. Has a recitative in the middle section. (Durand Collection) The original is a fourth higher, for light soprano or tenor.

TITLE	COMP.	TESS.	TYPE	REMARKS
Soleil! On a détruit tes superbes asiles (Les Indes Galantes)	Ab-eb1	eb-db	Bass or baritone	A declamatory, majestic, compound air. Demands some flexibility. A trifle long. Known as "Invocation et Hymne au Soleil" (Gevaert)
Sur les ombres fugitives (Castor et Pollux)	e1-a2	b1-f#2	Light soprano	A somewhat florid gavotte (Durand Collection)
Tristes apprêts (Castor et Pollux)	eb1-g2	g1-eb2	Soprano or tenor	Very sustained. (Grovlez) In the Durand Collection transposed to suit medium voices.
Troubles cruels (Dardanus)	c1-bb2	f1-f2	Most suitable for light soprano	An andante, allegro air. Most of this air is quite spirited and florid. (Gevaert)
Tu veux avoir la préférence (Les Fêtes d'Hébé)	g#-a1	a-f1	Lyric tenor (or soprano	Graceful, sustained. (Grovlez)
Vents furieux (La Princesse de Navarre)	d1-bb2	g1-g2	Soprano	Animated, quite florid, rather vigorous. Has a short sustained, slow middle section. (Durand Collection)
Recitative: Les nymphes de Diane Air: Vole, lance tes traits! (Zéphyre)	e1-bb2	a1-f2	Most suitable for light soprano	Animated, graceful, quite florid. (Durand Collection)

JEAN FERRY REBEL
(1669-1747)

TITLE	COMP.	TESS.	TYPE	REMARKS
Souffrirai-je toujours (Ulysse)	c1-f2	f1-db2	Mezzo-soprano or alto	Slow, sustained, somewhat declamatory. (Grovlez)
Volez, zéphirs amoureux	c#1-e2		All voices	An animated "Tambourin". Demands rather facile articulation. (Echo du Temps Passé, Durand)

JEAN JACQUES ROUSSEAU
(1712-1778)

TITLE	COMP.	TESS.	TYPE	REMARKS
Je vais revoir ma charmante maîtresse (Le Devin du Village)	d-bb1	g-g1	Lyric tenor	Graceful. Has a very high tessitura. (Grovlez)
Le Rosier	g1-e2		All voices	Sustained, graceful. (Echos du Temps Passé, Durand)
Que le jour me dure	g1-b1		All voices	Sustained. A song on three notes. (Echos de France)

ANTONIO SACCHINI
(1734-1786)

TITLE	COMP.	TESS.	TYPE	REMARKS
Recitative: Appesanti par l'âge Air: Dieux! ce n'est pas pour moi (Oedipe à Colone)	eb1-ab2	f1-f2	Dramatic soprano (lyric soprano)	An andante, allegro air. (Gevaert)
Recitative: Douce et modeste Evelina Air: Justes dieux que j'implore (Evelina)	A-eb1	d-d1	Bass or bass-baritone	Animated, majestic. (Gevaert)
Recitative: D'un penchant si fatal Air: Arrachez de mon coeur (Dardanus)	d1-ab2	g1-eb2	Dramatic soprano (lyric soprano)	Slow and sustained, majestic. Demands in parts some flexibility. (Gevaert)
Recitative: J'aime la sombre horreur Air: O ma patrie! (Evelina)	Bb-f1	e-d1	Bass or bass-baritone	Very sustained, majestic. (Gevaert)
Recitative: Je tombe à vos genoux Air: C'est votre bonté que j'implore (Chimène)	f1-ab2	ab1-f2	Dramatic soprano (lyric soprano	Sustained. Demands some flexibility. (Gevaert)
Jour heureux (Dardanus)	f-g2 (bb2)	bb-f1	Tenor	Sustained. Demands in parts some flexibility. (Schirmer, Operatic Anthology)
Juge mieux un frère qui t'aime (Evelina)	eb-g1	ab-eb1	Tenor	Graceful air. Demands some flexibility. (Gevaert)
Recitative: Mon fils, tu ne l'es plus Air: Elle m'a prodigué sa tendresse (Oedipe à Colone)	Bb-eb1	d-c1	Bass, bass-baritone	Very sustained, majestic. (Gevaert)
Tout mon bonheur (Oedipe à Colone)	eb1-ab2	ab1-f2	Soprano	Slow and sustained. (Gevaert)

For other songs and airs see under "Italian" in this section (page 32).

TITLE	COMP.	TESS.	TYPE	REMARKS

GASPARO SPONTINI
(1774-1851)

TITLE	COMP.	TESS.	TYPE	REMARKS
Recitative: Cruels! Déli- vrez-moi de ces apprêts Air: Hélas! Si de ma faible vie (Fernando Cortez)	d1-g2	g1-eb2	Dramatic soprano (lyric soprano)	Sustained. (Gevaert)
Dans le sein d'un ami (La Vestale)	d-f1	g-eb1	Baritone	Sustained. Demands some flexibility. Has high tessitura. (Peters, Anthology)
Recitative: Dieux secourez Cassandre Air: O saintes lois (Olympie)	f1-a2 (c3)	a1-f2	Dramatic soprano (lyric soprano)	A majestic andante, al- legro air. (Gevaert)
Il faut hélas! Bien peu de chose	c1-f2	f1-d2	Women's voices	Graceful. Demands some flexibility. (Pari- sotti, Ricordi)
O des infortunés (La Vestale)	c#1-f#2	f#1-d2	Dramatic soprano or mezzo- soprano	Very slow, sustained. Vocally not taxing. (Gevaert)
O patrie, ô lieux pleins de charmes (Fernando Cortez)	e-f#1	f#-e1	Baritone	An andante, allegro air. In parts very vigorous and dramatic. High tes- situra. (Peters, Anthol- ogy)
O toi, dont l'univers (Hymne au soleil) (Milton)	db-f1	db-ab1	Baritone	Very sustained. De- mands some flexibility. (Gevaert)
Toi, que je laisse sur la terre (La Vestale)	db1-f2	f1-eb2	Dramatic soprano or lyric soprano	Slow, very sustained. Demands some flexibil- ity. (Gevaert)
Toi que j'implore avec ferveur (often sung in the Italian version: Tu che invoco con orrore) (La Vest- ale)	eb1-bb2	g1-g2	Dramatic soprano	A sustained andante, a dramatic scena, and a vigorous allegro. De- mands some flexibility. (Gevaert)

APPENDIX

BERGERETTES

The so-called "bergerettes," or French popular songs, of the seventeenth and eighteenth centuries occupy a rather unique position, since they
are neither folk songs nor traditional airs in the proper sense of this word.

Composed and sung for the most part for and by the upper strata of French p
prerevolutionary society, they could be perhaps best defined as old popular
songs, which have survied because of the extraordinary charm and grace
of their tunes and words.

Musically and vocally these songs present no problems even to an untrained singer. Sytlistically, however, they demand great elegance and an
extraordinarily fluent command of the language. Their great popularity
now is largely due to the efforts of J. B. Weckerlin, who has collected and
admirably arranged a great number of such songs (Echos du Temps Passe,
3 vols. Durand). A rather representative collection of his arrangements is
available in the Ditson and Schirmer edition. The short list below is limited
to the bergerettes available in American reprints.

See also, among many other excellent collections, those by Yvette Guil-
bert (Augener) and Perilhou (Heugel).

TITLE	COMP.	TESS.	TYPE	REMARKS
Aminte	c1-d2	e1-c2	Most suitable for men's voices	Delicate. Demands light, facile articulation.
Bergère légère	d1-e2	f#1-d2	All voices	Delicate. Demands lightness of tone.
Chantons les amours de Jean	d1-e2 (g2)	g1-d2	All voices	Spirited. Demands facile articulation.
Chaque chose a son temps	c1-c2	f1-b♭1	All voices	Light.
Je connais un berger discret	e♭1-f2	g1-e♭2	All voices	Light
Jeunes fillettes	g1-e2	a1-e2	All voices	Light and spirited. Demands some flexibility.
L'amour s'envole	e1-g2	g1-d2	Not too suitable for very heavy, low voices	Demands some flexibility.
La Mère Bontemps	d1-d2	g1-d2	Women's voices	Light. Demands facile articulation.
Lisette	e1-g2	g1-d2	All voices	Delicate.
Maman, dites-moi	e1-f#2	g1-d2	Women's voices	Light. Demands facile articulation.
Menuet d'Exaudet (Cet étang)	d1-g2	f#1-c2	All voices	Delicate. Demands good sense of rhythm.
Nanette	e1-g2	g1-d2	All voices	Light
Non, je ne crois pas	e1-e2	f1-c2	Women's voices	Light
Non, je n'irai plus au bois	e1-f2 (a2)	a1-e2	Women's voices	Light
O ma tendre musette	g#1-e2	d1-d2	All voices	Delicate. Has a delightful accompaniment.
Par un matin	f1-d2	g1-c2	All voices	Light
Philis plus avare que tendre	d1-d2	g1-c2	All voices	Sustained, delicate.
Que ne suis-je la fougère	f#1-e♭2	g1-d2	All voices	Sustained, delicate.

TITLE	COMP.	TESS.	TYPE	REMARKS
Trop aimable Sylvie	d1-e2	g1-c2	Most suitable for men's voices	Delicate. Demands facile articulation.
Venez, agréable printemps	c1-f2	f1-c2	All voices	Demands facile articulation.

MARIE ANTOINETTE

TITLE	COMP.	TESS.	TYPE	REMARKS
Chanson de Marie Antoinette	d#1-g#2	e1-e2	Soprano	Graceful, light. This melody is supposedly by Marie Antoinette, the queen of France; arranged by Myron Jacobson. (Fischer)

SONGS AND AIRS IN GERMAN BEFORE THE NINETEENTH CENTURY
Bibliography

The name found in parentheses in the Remarks column indicates one of the following collections:

Reimann: Das deutsche Lied, 4 vols. edited by Reimann, published by Simrock.

Reimann, Das geistliche Lied: Das deutsche geistliche Lied, 6 vols. edited by Reimann, published by Simrock.

Moser: Alte Meister des deutschen Liedes, edited by Moser, published by Peters.

TITLE	COMP.	TESS.	TYPE	REMARKS
JOHANN GEORG AHLE **(1651-1706)**				
Brünstiges Verlangen einer Seele	e1-e2	e1-c2	Not suitable for high light voices	Slow and very sustained. Religious text. (Reimann)
JOHANN RUDOLF AHLE **(1625-1673)**				
Auf die Zukunft unseres Heilandes	c1-f2	e1-c2	Not too suitable for very light high voices	A sacred dialogue between the Herald and the Soul in contrasting moods and tempi. (Reimann)
CARL PHILIPP EMANUEL BACH **(1714-1788)**				
Das Gebet	c1-ab2	f1-f2	High voices	Sustained, in parts florid. (Reimann)
Der Frühling	e1-f#2	g#1-e2	High or medium voices	Graceful, rather florid. (Reimann, Das geistliche Lied)
Der gestirnte Himmel	e1-f#2	g#1-e2	High or medium voices	Graceful. Demands some flexibility. (Reimann, Das geistliche Lied)
Der Phönix	d1-eb2	f1-d2	All voices	Sustained. In a manner of a minuet. (Reimann)
Der Tag des Weltgerichts	d1-eb2	g1-d2	Heavy voices	Majestic, vigorous, dramatic. (Reimann, Das geistliche Lied)
Die Himmel rühmen des Ewigen Ehre	c#1-g#2	e1-e2	Most suitable for heavy voices	Very sustained, majestic, vigorous. Religious text. (Reimann, Das geistliche Lied)
Gottes Grösse in der Natur	d1-f2	a1-f2	High or medium voices	Graceful. Demands some flexibility. Religious text. (Reimann, Das geistliche Lied)
Jesus in Gethsemane	e1-eb2	f#1-d2	Medium or low voices	Slow, somewhat declamatory, grave. Religious text. (Reimann, Das geistliche Lied)

TITLE	COMP.	TESS.	TYPE	REMARKS
Passionslied	d1-g2	g1-eb2	Most suitable for high or medium voices	Sustained, somber. Religious text. (Reimann, Das geistliche Lied)

See also C. Ph. E. Bach, Geistliche Lieder, edited by Roth, published by Peters.

W. FRIEDEMANN BACH
(1710-1784)

TITLE	COMP.	TESS.	TYPE	REMARKS
Kein Hälmlein wächst auf Erden	bb-eb2	eb1-c2	Most suitable for medium or low voices	Very sustained. (Neitzel, Gems of Antiquity. J. Church Co.)

GEORG BÖHM
(1661-1733)

TITLE	COMP.	TESS.	TYPE	REMARKS
Mein Freund ist mein (from Cantata, Mein Freund ist mein)	a-c2	c1-b1	Alto	Sustained. Demands some flexibility. (Breitkopf & Härtel, Collection of Arias for Alto)

DAVID CORNER
(16..-16..)

TITLE	COMP.	TESS.	TYPE	REMARKS
Ein neues andächtiges Kindelwiegen	f1-eb2		All voices	Sustained, delicate, graceful. Religious text. (Reimann, Das geistliche Lied)

JOHANN GEORG EBELING
(1637-1676)

TITLE	COMP.	TESS.	TYPE	REMARKS
Ich steh an deiner Krippe hier	eb1-f2	g1-d2	All voices	Sustained. Religious text. (Reimann, Das geistliche Lied)

JOHANN WOLFGANG FRANCK
(1641-17..)

TITLE	COMP.	TESS.	TYPE	REMARKS
Auf, auf! zu Gottes Lob	g1-g2	g1-e2	High voices	Animated, vigorous. Has a sustained majestic ending. Religious text. (Reimann, Das geistliche Lied)
Die bitt're Leidenszeit	c1-g2	g1-eb2	High voices	Sustained. Religious text. (Reimann, Das geistliche Lied)
Jesus neight sein Haupt und stirbt	e1-e2		All voices	Slow and sustained. For the most part very subdued. Religious text. (Reimann, Das geistliche Lied)

TITLE	COMP.	TESS.	TYPE	REMARKS
Mein Gott, ich bin bereit	c1-g2	g1-eb2	High voices	Very slow and sustained. Religious text. (Reimann, Das geistliche Lied)
Wie seh' ich dich, mein Jesu, bluten	e1-f#2		All voices	Slow. Rather florid. Religious text. (Reimann, Das geistliche Lied)

MELCHIOR FRANCK
(1573-1639)

TITLE	COMP.	TESS.	TYPE	REMARKS
Ach, treuer Gott, Herr Jesu Christ	a1-f2		All voices	Sustained. Religious text. (Reimann, Das geistliche Lied)
Kommt ihr Gespielen	eb1-eb2		All voices	Animated, gay. (Reimann)

CARL HEINRICH GRAUN
(1703-1759)

Der Tod Jesu (An Oratorio)
(Score, Peters)

TITLE	COMP.	TESS.	TYPE	REMARKS
Recitative: Ach mein Immannel Air: Ein Gebet um neue Stärke	e1-a2	g1-e2	Lyric soprano (coloratura soprano)	A rather extended recitative and a graceful, in parts quite florid air.
Recitative: Gethsemane! Wen hören deine Mauern Air: Du Held!	eb1-bb2	bb1-f2	Lyric soprano (coloratura soprano)	A rather extended recitative and an animated, quite florid air. Has a sustained middle section.
Recitative: Jerusalem, voll Mordlust Air: So stehet ein Berg Gottes	Bb-f#1	e-e1	Baritone	A dramatic scena and a vigorous, animated aria. Has florid passages.
Recitative: Nun klingen Waffen Air: Ihr Weichgeschaff'-nen Seelen	e-ab1	a-gb1	Tenor	A rather extended recitative and a slow, sustained, in parts quite florid air, which has a rapid middle section.
Recitative: Wer ist der Heilige Air: Singt dem göttlichen Propheten	eb1-c3	a1-g2	Lyric soprano (coloratura soprano)	Animated, brilliant, in parts very florid air. This air, with English words "Lo! the heaven descended Prophet" is published by Novello.
Schäfer und Schäferin	d#1-e2	e1-c#2	All voices	A delicate, graceful dialogue with a sprightly final section. (Reimann)

For other songs and airs see under "Italian" in this section (page 32).

TITLE	COMP.	TESS.	TYPE	REMARKS

HANS LEO HASSLER
(1564-1612)

TITLE	COMP.	TESS.	TYPE	REMARKS
Gagliarda	f#1-f2	a1-e2	All voices	Vigorous, spirited. (Reimann)
Mein G'müth ist mir verwirret	e1-e2	f#1-d2	All voices	Slow, sustained. Originally written for five voices. (Reimann)
Tanzlied	d#1-e2	f#1-d2	All voices	Light and delicate. The final section is sustained. (Reimann)

JOHANN A. HILLER
(1728-1804)

TITLE	COMP.	TESS.	TYPE	REMARKS
Aeol	c1-f2	g1-e2	Not too suitable for very light, high voices	Spirited, humorous, vigorous. Demands facile articulation. (Reimann)

F. H. HIMMEL
(1765-1814)

TITLE	COMP.	TESS.	TYPE	REMARKS
Der Lockvogel	f1-f2	g1-d2	All voices	Light, gently humorous. Demands some flexibility. (Reimann)
Der Rosenstock	c1-g2	a1-e2	All voices	Delicate, sustained. Demands some flexibility. (Reimann)
Die Gewalt des Blickes	eb1-gb2	g1-eb2	Most suitable for men's voices	Animated. (Reimann)
Die Sendung	eb1-eb2	f1-c2	Women's voices	Sustained. (Reimann)

GEORG JOSEPH
(16..-17..)

TITLE	COMP.	TESS.	TYPE	REMARKS
Die Psyche jubilirt über die Auferstehung Jesu Christi	d1-e2	g1-d2	Not too suitable for very light voices	Animated, rather vigorous. Religious text. (Reimann, Das geistliche Lied)

REINHARD KEISER
(1673-1734)

TITLE	COMP.	TESS.	TYPE	REMARKS
Von dem Landleben	c1-g2	f#1-d2	Soprano	A short cantata, "arietta," recitative, and a spirited aria. Has florid passages. (Reimann)

TITLE	COMP. TESS.	TYPE	REMARKS

JOHANN PH. KIRNBERGER
(1721-1783)

TITLE	COMP.	TESS.	TYPE	REMARKS
Schön sind Rosen	c1-f2	f1-d2	All voices	Delicate. Demands some flexibility.(Reimann)

BERNHARD KLEIN
(1793-1832)

TITLE	COMP.	TESS.	TYPE	REMARKS
Ein Seufzer	g1-e2		All voices, except a very light soprano	Animated. (Reimann)
Heil'ge Nacht	d#1-e2	f#1-c#2	Medium or low voices	Slow, very sustained. (Reimann)

ADAM KRIEGER
(1634-1666)

TITLE	COMP.	TESS.	TYPE	REMARKS
Der hat gesiegt, den Got vergnügt	c1-bb1		Medium or low voices	Sustained. Religious text. (Reimann, Das geistliche Lied)

JOHANN LÖHNER
(16..-17..)

TITLE	COMP.	TESS.	TYPE	REMARKS
O Ewigkeit	d#1-f#2	f#1-d2	Not too suitable for very light,high voices	Sustained. Somewhat declamatory. Religious text. (Reimann, Das geistliche Lied)

CHRISTIAN GOTTLOB NEEFE
(1748-1798)

TITLE	COMP.	TESS.	TYPE	REMARKS
Die frühen Gräber	c1-g2	d1-bb1	Not too suitable for very light voices	Slow and very sustained. (Reimann)
Die Wassernymphe	c#1-e2	e1-e2	All voices	Animated, delicate. Demands some flexibility. (Moser)
Serenade	c1-f2	ab1-db2	Most suitable for men's voices	A song in contrasting moods and tempi. Demands some flexibility. (Moser)

VALENTIN RATHGEBER
(1682-1750)

TITLE	COMP.	TESS.	TYPE	REMARKS
Von der edlen Musik	c1-e2	d1-d2	All voices	A minuet in praise of music. (Moser)

JOHANN FR. REICHARDT
(1752-1814)

TITLE	COMP.	TESS.	TYPE	REMARKS
Das Lösegeld	e1-f2	a1-e2	All voices	Gently humorous. Somewhat declamatory. (Reimann)

TITLE	COMP.	TESS.	TYPE	REMARKS
Lied an die Nacht	bb-f2	eb1-bb1	Most suitable for medium or low voices	Slow and sustained. (Reimann)
Mailied	c#1-e2	d1-d2	All voices	Animated, gay. (Moser)
Rhapsodie	bb-f2	eb1-eb2	Medium or low voices	Sustained, majestic. See Alto Rhapsody by Brahms (for alto, male chorus and orchestra). (Moser)

LUISE REICHARDT
(1778-1825)

TITLE	COMP.	TESS.	TYPE	REMARKS
Wenn die Rosen blühen (In the time of Roses)	f#-g2	a1-e2	All voices	Sustained, subdued, delicate. (Ditson)

FRIEDRICH W. RUST
(1739-1796)

TITLE	COMP.	TESS.	TYPE	REMARKS
An die Nachtigall	c1-d2	d1-c2	Not too suitable for very light, high voices	Very sustained. (Reimann)

J. A. P. SCHULZE
(1747-1800)

TITLE	COMP.	TESS.	TYPE	REMARKS
Der Schmetterling	e1-f#2 (a)	a1-e2	All voices	Light. Demands facile articulation. (Reimann)
Die Mutter bei der Wiege	f1-d2		Women's voices	Delicate, sustained, gently humorous. (Reimann)
Frühlingsliebe	c1-f2	f1-d2	All voices	Delicate, sustained. (Reimann)
Liebeszauber	e1-f#2	a1-e2	All voices	Light, animated. Demands facile articulatior and some flexibility. (Reimann)
Sagt, wo sind die Veilchen hin?	bb-eb2	eb1-eb2	All voices except a very light soprano	Delicate, sustained. (Reimann)
Ständchen	d1-g2	g1-d2	Not too suitable for very low voices	A light, graceful waltz song. (Reimann)

HEINRICH SCHÜTZ
(1585-1672)

TITLE	COMP.	TESS.	TYPE	REMARKS
Aus dem 119ten Psalm	c1-d2	f1-c2	All voices	Sustained. Religious text. (Reimann)

TITLE	COMP.	TESS.	TYPE	REMARKS

GEORG P. TELEMANN
(1681-1767)

TITLE	COMP.	TESS.	TYPE	REMARKS
Die rechte Stim- mung	f1-f2		All voices	Humorous. Demands some flexibility. (Reimann)

See also a collection of Telemann's songs and airs published by Peters.

CARL F. ZELTER
(1758-1832)

TITLE	COMP.	TESS.	TYPE	REMARKS
Der Arme Thoms	c1-f2	f1-db2	All voices	Sustained. (Reimann)
Félicité passée (French Text)	c1-g2	a1-f2	All voices	Sustained. The poem is by J. J. Rousseau. (Reimann)
Geistergrass	bb-c2 (f)	c1-g1	Low voices	Slow and very sustained. (Reimann)
Ständchen	e1-f#2	a1-e2	Most suitable for high voices	Light and delicate. Demands some flexibility and a good sense of rhythm. (Reimann)

JOHANN R. ZUMSTEEG
(1760-1802)

TITLE	COMP.	TESS.	TYPE	REMARKS
Una	eb1-d2	f1-bb1	Most suitable for medium or low voices	Slow, sustained, somewhat dramatic. (Reimann)

JOHANN SEBASTIAN BACH
(1685-1750)

It seems unnecessary, as well as impossible, to try to evaluate the vocal music of Bach in a short prefatory note. A few practical suggestions pertaining to matters of performance may, however, be of some value.

1. Although not popularly considered so, Bach's airs are for the most part not vocal solo pieces, but chamber music with a vocal part, since he very frequently employs an obbligato part or parts of equal importance with the vocal line. The transference of such an obbligato line, possessing its own distinctive sonority (such as oboe, flute, or a string instrument), into the pianoforte "accompaniment" is for the most part a musically unsatisfactory and even reprehensible practice. Some Bach airs lose so much by this procedure as to become almost unintelligible.

In Bach's airs the vocal line as such is seldom paramount in importance, as it is for instance in his songs, or in the airs of Gluck and Handel. The singer must learn to accompany the instrumental passages, when this is necessary. Often this is forgotten, and the resulting emphasis on a contrapuntal detail contained in the vocal part is responsible for the harsh and unintelligible effects which would never arise were the vocal part considered in the proper perspective - as one of the active melodic parts and not as the only melodic part.

2. The available pianoforte reductions of the instrumental part of Bach's airs seem to be overloaded with contrapuntal detail, added by the arrangers and not found in the original obbligato and figured bass parts. These obscure the melodic expressiveness of the vocal line, the obbligato line, and the bass line.

For concert performance of Bach's airs, when pianoforte is employed as the only instrument and some of the available pianoforte reductions is used, the pianist would do well to allow the original obbligato part and the bass line to stand out at the expense of many a contrapuntal passage in the middle voices, often of doubtful authenticity. The best way to attain the desired balance would be to compare the pianoforte arrangement with the original score, and to reduce the pianoforte part to the absolute minimum, so that the bass and the obbligato part stand out as melodically important parts.

3. One must bear in mind the fact that Bach's soprano and alto airs were originally intended for boy singers or male falsetto singers (not to be confused with castrati).

4. Most singers, especially tenors and soprani, would do well to sing Bach airs a half tone lower than the original, since much of the available evidence seems to prove almost conclusively that the pitch in Bach's time was considerably lower than the present-day 440 or 442 a. Unless the vocal line can be negotiated without strain in its original key, there seems to be no reason, aesthetic or otherwise, to disregard this now almost conclusively established difference in pitch.

5. The often enormously long florid passages vocalized on one vowel do not have to be sung on one breath. A tied note, such as ♩♪♪♪ or ♪♪♪♪ , offers an excellent opportunity for the intake of breath without disturbance to the melodic line or to the rhythmic pattern. The now often-encountered practice of rushing through such passages at top speed and minimum volume for the sake of preserving them on one breath seems to me to be pedantic and harmful to the music, even if it may afford some slight gratification to the performer by offering him an opportunity to display the excellence of his breath control Only in instances where taking a phrase on one breath does not in any way affect the tempo, the volume, and the melodic expressiveness of the phrase in question is such a practice artistically valid. As soon as singing a phrase in one breath becomes a problem and the singer has to exert himself in every possible way to keep up this self-imposed race against time, it seems better

to break the phrase vocally (which can be easily done without breaking it musically), instead of keeping it intact at the cost of impairing the tone quality and the steady rhythm.

6. Although a metronomically rigid, totally inflexible rhythm is undesirable in performing Bach's music, as in performing any music, a nineteenth century romantic rubato is even less desirable.

One must not forget that Bach frequently employed strict dance forms such as the minuet, gavotte and sarabande in his airs, and that such dance forms demand a precise accentuation and a steady tempo.

7. The present-day singer is apt to forget that the manner of dramatic delivery of the text of Bach's airs is very different from the one employed by the nineteenth century composers, or even Gluck or Mozart.

Bach, in his own way, is perhaps as conscious of the dramatic possibilities of his texts as Wagner, but he uses entirely different means to achieve the desired effect. The text never dominates his music, though it most definitely influences its pattern and is as important, in so far as the entire mood of an air is concerned, as the text is in a song by Hugo Wolf. The means of expression, however, remain at all times purely musical, and never enter the province of acting as opposed to singing. The stylistically untenable violence and "expressive declamation" so often employed by present-day singers in performing Bach's airs is as repulsive as the suppression of any normal emotional reaction toward the text accorded to Bach's vocal music by those who seem to believe it to be nothing more than a contrapuntal vocalise.

8. One of the most frequently encountered malpractices in singing Bach is the practice of over-phrasing, as well as of overloading each phrase with too many dynamic shadings. One must remember that in doing so the singer may easily disturb and sacrifice the line and the mood of a large phrase, which in some instances is of considerable duration (often as long as sixteen bars). This of course by no means implies that Bach should be sung with no dynamic shadings whatsoever.

9. Bach's airs make very severe demands upon the musicianship of the vocalist, since Bach hardly ever uses any doubling of the vocal line for the purpose of helping the singer (as Gluck, for instance, almost invariably does). Since Bach's music is chromatic to a degree not encountered in vocal music until the latter half of the nineteenth century, and since more than one melodic line is almost constantly employed, the singer would do well to acquaint himself thoroughly with the obbligato parts before attempting to sing his own part.

10. In closing I want to remind the reader that the da capo aria form which Bach used often can sometimes be cut down to fit the present-day requirements of length, by substituting the instrumental ritornel for the entire recapitulation, or by singing the da capo section and omitting the ritornel. The desirability of such cuts is questionable, however, since by shortening one of the three sections the architecture of the piece as a whole is undoubtedly endangered.

The selection of Bach airs for this list was extraordinarily difficult, since hardly one Bach air seems to be superior to another. In selecting the following list the airs available in piano scores have been favored.

The name (or names) in parentheses in the Remarks column indicates one of the following collections:

Prout, Augener: Bach Songs and Airs, 2 vols. for each voice, edited by Dr. Prout, published by Augener.

Straube, Peters: Bach Arien, 1 vol. for each type of voice, edited by K. Straube, published by Peters. (This edition, though accurate, abounds in a variety of expression marks by Straube which are of questionable value.)

Whittaker, Oxford: The Oxford Series of Bach Arias, edited by W. G. Whittaker, published by Oxford University Press (English texts only, available separately).

When no bibliographical reference is given, the Breitkopf & Härtel or the
Peters edition of the complete piano score is meant.
All of Bach's 214 cantatas are published in piano score edition by Breitkopf
& Härtel and by Peters.
Piano scores of cantatas published by Novello: Nos. 1, 4, 6, 8, 11, 12, 17,
21, 25, 27, 28, 34, 38, 39, 41, 43, 50, 61, 63, 65, 68, 70, 79, 81, 93, 95,
104, 106, 112, 115, 116, 119, 140, 149, 180, 189. (English texts only)
Piano scores of cantatas published by Schirmer: Nos. 11, 19, 21, 45, 65,
78, 80, 93, 102, 106, 146, 180, 192, 198.
Some cantatas published by Oxford University Press and a few other pub-
lishers.
Larger works generally available.
Songs: Breitkopf & Härtel.
Airs from the cantatas, with pianoforte and obbligato instruments, are
published by the "Neue Bach Gesellschaft," Breitkopf & Härtel. (This
is no doubt the most practical of all modern editions of Bach airs.)
Number of Miniature scores of cantatas reprinted by Broude Bros., New
York: Nos: 1, 4, 6, 11, 12, 19, 21, 31, 34, 39, 46, 50, 51, 56, 60, 65, 78,
79, 80, 85, 104, 105, 106, 140, 161, 176, 182, 211, 212.
A collection of Bach airs (English texts only) is published by Novello
in 4 vols. one for each type of voice. The identifying numbers of cantatas
are unfortunately omitted in this collection.
A number of Bach airs are to be found in the Breitkopf & Härtel Arien
Album as well as in the Arien Album published by Peters and the Arien
Album published by Universal Edition.
Since Bach wrote within a rather uniform compass and tessitura for
each of the four main types of voice, and since the character of each air,
as described in the Remarks column, seems sufficient to indicate the type
of voice for which the air is possibly best suited, it seemed best to dispense
with the Type of Voice Column in the following lists.

AIRS FROM CANTATAS AND ORATORIOS

SOPRANO

TITLE:AIR	TITLE:WORK	COMP.	TESS.	REMARKS
Auch mit gedämpften, schwachen Stimmen	Cantata 36 Schwingt freudig euch empor	d1-g2	f♯1-e2	Not fast. Has a florid middle section. (Straube, Peters)
Blute nur (Bleed and break)	Matthäus Passion (St. Matthew Passion)	e1-g2	g1-e2	Sustained. Demands some flexibility. (Score generally available)
Die Armen will der Herr umarmen	Cantata 186 Ärge dich, o Seele, nicht	d1-g2	g1-e♭2	Sustained. (Straube, Peters)
Die Seele ruht in Jesu Händen	Cantata 127 Herr Jesu Christ, wahr'r Mensch und Gott	c1-a♭2	g1-e♭2	Slow, sustained. Demands some flexibility. (Straube, Peters; also Prout, Augener)

TITLE:AIR	TITLE:WORK	COMP.	TESS.	REMARKS
Ei! Wie schmeckt der Kaffee süsse	Cantata 211 (Kaffee Cantata) Schweiget stille plaudert nicht	d1-a2	a1-f2	Graceful, gently humorous. Demands flexibility. Best for light voices.
Recitative: Er hat uns allen wohlgetan (To all men Jesus good hath done) Air: Aus Liebe will mein Heiland sterben (In love my Saviour now is dying)	Matthäus Passion (St. Matthew Passion)	e1-a2	a1-f2	Very slow. Has florid passages. Best for light voices. (Score generally available)
Es ist und bleibt der Christen Trost	Cantata 44 Sie werden euch in den Bann thun	d1-a2	g1-eb2	Animated and florid. (Straube, Peters)
Flösst, mein Heiland, flösst dein Namen (Ah! my Saviour)	Weihnachts Oratorium (Christmas Oratorio)	d1-g2	g1-e2	Graceful. Demands some flexibility. This air is not too suitable for concert performance because of the occasional chorus entrances. (Score generally available)
Gedenk'an uns mit deiner Liebe	Cantata 29 Wir danken dir, Gott, wir danken dir	f#1-a2	a1-f#2	Graceful, sustained. Demands some flexibility. (Prout, Augener)
Gottes Engel weichen nie	Cantata 149 Man singet mit Freuden vom Sieg	c#1-a2	g1-e2	Delicate, graceful. (Straube, Peters; also Prout, Augener)
Gottlob! Gottlob!	Cantata 28 Gottlob, nun geht das Jahr zu Ende	d1-a2	g1-f2	Spirited, has florid passages.

TITLE:AIR	TITLE:WORK	COMP.	TESS.	REMARKS
Gott versorget alles Leben	Cantata 187 Es wartet alles auf dich	d1-ab2	f1-f2	Slow, somewhat florid. Has a graceful middle section.
Heil und Segen	Cantata 120 Gott, man Lobet dich in der Stille	d1-g2	g1-e2	Slow, very sustained. Demands some flexibility. (Straube, Peters)
Herr, deine Güte reicht (Lord, wide as heaven above)	Cantata 17 Wer Dank opfert, der preiset mich	e1-g#2	f#1-e2	Animated, spirited. Demands flexibility. (Whittaker, Oxford)
Herr, der du stark und mächtig bist	Cantata 10 Meine Seel' erhebt den Herren	c1-a2	g1-g2	Vigorous, very spirited, florid. Best for rather heavy voices.
Höchster, Höchster	Cantata 51 Jauchzet Gott in allen Landen	e1-a2	g1-e2	Not fast, sustained. Has florid passages.
Höchster, Tröster	Cantata 183 Sie Werden euch in den Bann thun	d1-a2	g1-f2	Graceful and florid. Best for light voices.
Hört, ihr Augen, auf zu weinen	Cantata 98 Was Gott thut das ist wohlgetan	c1-ab2	g1-eb2	Not fast. Demands considerable flexibility. (Straube, Peters)
Hört, ihr Völker	Cantata 76 Die Himmel erzählen die Ehre Gottes	d1-g2	g1-e2	Graceful. Demands flexibility.
Ich esse mit Freuden	Cantata 84 Ich bin vergnügt mit meinem Glücke	d1-a2	g1-e2	Animated and graceful' Best for light voices.
Ich folge dir gleichfalls	Johannes Passion (St. John's Passion)	d1-ab2	a1-f2	Animated, florid. (Score generally available)
Ich nehme mein Leiden	Cantata 75 Die Elenden sollen essen	c1-a2	f1-e2	Graceful and delicate. Has rapid florid passages. (Prout, Augener)

TITLE:AIR	TITLE:WORK	COMP.	TESS.	REMARKS
Ich säe meine Zähren	Cantata 146 Wir müssen durch viel Trübsal	c1-g2	a1-e2	Not fast. Has florid passages. (Straube, Peters)
Ich wünschte mir den Tod	Cantata 57 Selig ist der Mann	c1-ab2	g1-eb2	Slow and sustained, grave. (Prout, Augener)
Ihm hab'ich mich ergeben	Cantata 97 In allen meinen Thaten	c1-g2	e1-c2	Animated and graceful. Has florid passages.
Jauchzet Gott in allen Landen	Cantata 51 Jauchzet Gott in allen Landen	e1-c3	a1-f2	Animated, brilliant, florid.
Komm in mein Herzenshaus	Cantata 80 Ein feste Burg ist unser Gott	e1-a2	a1-f#2	Not fast, florid. (Prout, Augener)
Lass der Spötter Zungen schmähen	Cantata 70 Wachet, betet	d1-a2	g1-e2	Not fast. Demands some flexibility.
Lass uns, o höchster Gott	Cantata 41 Jesu nun sei gepreiset	d1-a2	a1-f#2	Graceful. Has some florid passages. (Straube, Peters; also Prout, Augener)
Meinem Hirten bleib' ich treu	Cantata 92 Ich hab in Gottes Herz und Sinn	d1-a2	g1-e2	Graceful. (Straube, Peters)
Mein gläubiges Herze (My heart ever faithful)	Cantata 68 Also hat Gott die Welt geliebt	f1-a2	a1-f2	Animated. Demands some flexibility. This famous air exists also in many transposed editions, and is sometimes sung by alti. (Generally available)
Recitative: Mein Gott, wie lang', ach lange? Air: Wirf, mein Herze, wirf dich noch	Cantata 155 Mein Gott, wie lang'	c1-a2	f1-f2	A sustained recitative (has a florid final passage) and a vigorous, majestic air, which demands some flexibility. (Prout, Augener)

TITLE:AIR	TITLE:WORK	COMP.	TESS.	REMARKS
Mein Jesus will es thun	Cantata 72 Alles nur nach Gottes willen	d1-a2	f1-e2	Animated, graceful. Has some florid passages. (Straube, Peters)
Mein Seelen-schatz ist Gottes Wort!	Cantata 18 Gleich wie der Regen und Schnee vom Himmel fällt	eb1-ab2	g1-eb2	Animated. Demands flexibility. (Prout, Augener)
Nur ein Wink von seinen Händen (Naught against the pow'r He wieldeth)	Weihnachts Oratorium (Christmas Oratorio)	c#1-a2	a1-f#2	Not fast. Demands considerable flexibility. (Score generally available)
Öffne dich, mein ganzes Herze	Cantata 61 Nun komm, du Heiden Heiland	d1-g2	g1-d2	Rather slow, sustained.
Patron das macht der Wind	Phoebus und Pan	d-a2	g1-e2	Spirited, humorous. Demands facile articulation and some flexibility. Schirmer has published a transposed edition of this air one tone lower than the original. (Prout, Augener)
Quia respexit (Latin text)	Magnificat in D Major	d1-f#2	g1-e2	Slow. Has florid passages. (Score, Novello)
Ruhet hie, matte Sinne	Cantata 210 O holder Tag	d#1-a2	g#1-e2	Sustained. Demands some flexibility. (Prout, Augener)
Schafe können sicher weiden	Geburtstags-cantate Was mir behagt ist nur die muntre Jagd	f1-ab2	bb1-f2	Sustained, delicate. Published by Galaxy a whole tone lower than the original; edited by W. Kramer; by Fischer (in the original key); edited by LaForge.
Sei Lob und Preis mit Ehren	Cantata 51 Jauchzet Gott in allen Landen	c1-c3	g1-e2	First part a sustained solo choral; second part animated and very florid.

TITLE:AIR	TITLE:WORK	COMP.	TESS.	REMARKS
Seufzer, Tränen, Kummer, Not	Cantata 21 Ich hatte viel Bekümmernis	d1-ab2	g1-f2	Slow, sustained, subdued. Demands good command of high pp. (Score generally available)
Stein, der über alle Schätze	Cantata 152 Tritt auf die. Glaubensbahn	d1-g2	g1-e2	Slow and sustained. (Straube, Peters)
Süsser Trost, mein Jesus kömmt	Cantata 151 Süsser Trost mein Jesus kömmt	f#1-a2	a1-f#2	Very sustained, delicate. Has a more animated florid middle section. (Straube, Peters; also Prout, Augener)
Was die Welt in sich hält (Little worth is found on earth)	Cantata 64 Sehet! welch eine Liebe hat uns der Vater erzeiget	d1-g2	f#1-f#2	Slow and sustained. (Whittaker, Oxford)
Wie lieblich klingt es in den Ohren	Cantata 133 Ich freue mich in dir	e1-a2	a#1-g2	Not fast. Demands some flexibility. (Straube, Peters)
Recitative: Wiewohl mein Herz (Althrough my heart) Air: Ich will dir mein Herze schenken (Lord, to thee my heart I proffer)	Matthäus Passion (St. Matthew Passion)	c1-g2	e1-e2	Animated. Demands considerable flexibility. (Score generally available)
Wir beten zu dem Tempel an	Cantata 51 Jauchzet Gott in allen Landen	e1-a2	g1-e2	Slow. Has florid passages.
Wie Zittern und wanken	Cantata 105 Herr, gehe nicht ins Gericht	c1-ab2	g1-f2	Rather animated. Has. florid passages.
Zerfliesse, mein Herze	Johannes Passion (St. John's Passion)	c1-ab2	ab1-g2	Slow, quite florid. (Score generally available)

TITLE:AIR	TITLE:WORK	COMP.	TESS.	REMARKS
Ach, schläfrige Seele-wie?	Cantata 115 Mache dich, mein Geist, bereit	a-d2	c1-c2	Sustained. Has a rapid middle section. Florid. (Prout, Augener)
Recitative: Ach Golgotha (Ah Golgotha) Air: Sehet, Jesus hat die Hand (Look ye Jesus waiting stands)	Matthäus Passion (St. Matthew Passion)	g-eb2	eb1-db2	Slow. Demands considerable flexibility. (Score generally available)
Ach Herr! Was ist ein Menschenkind?	Cantata 110 Unser Mund, sei voll Lachens	c#1-d#2	e1-c#2	Sustained. Demands some flexibility. (Prout, Augener)
Ach, lege das Sodom der sündlichen Glieder	Cantata 48 Ich elender Mensch, wer wird mich erlösen	bb-eb2	eb1-c2	Not fast, graceful. Demands flexibility.
Agnus Dei (Latin text)	Mass in B Minor	a-eb2	d1-bb1	Very slow and sustained (Score generally available)
Bereite dich Zion (Prepare thyself, Zion)	Weihnachts Oratorium (Christmas Oratorio)	b-e2	e1-c2	Animated. Has florid passages (Score generally available)
Doch Jesus will	Cantata 46 Schauet doch und sehet, ob irgend ein Schmerz sei	g-eb2	d1-c2	Not fast. Demands flexibility.
Du Herr, du krönst allein	Cantata 187 Es wartet Alles auf dich	bb-eb2	e1-c2	Graceful. Has florid passages. (Prout, Augener) A simplified version of "Domine Fili unigenite" from Mass in G Minor.
Recitative: Du lieber Heiland du (O blessed Saviour) Air: Buss und Reu (Grief and pain)	Matthäus Passion (St. Matthew Passion)	b-e2	f#-d2	Sustained. Demands some flexibility. (Score generally available)

TITLE:AIR	TITLE:WORK	COMP.	TESS.	REMARKS
Du machst, o Tod	Cantata 114 Ach, lieben Christen, seid getrost	bb-eb2	eb1-c2	Animated, rather vigorous. Demands flexibility. (Prout, Augener; also Straube, Peters)
Ein unbarmherziges Gerichte	Cantata 89 Was soll ich aus dir machen, Ephraim?	bb-e2	e1-c2	Animated and vigorous.
Erbarme dich mein Gott (Have mercy, Lord, on me)	Matthäus Passion (St. Matthew Passion)	c#1-e2	f#1-d2	Slow, very sustained. Demands some flexibility. (Score generally available)
Recitative: Erbarm' es Gott (O gracious God) Air: Können Tränen meiner Wangen (If my tears be unavailing)	Matthäus Passion (St. Matthew Passion)	c1-eb2	g1-d2	Not slow. Demands considerable flexibility. (Score generally available)
Es ist vollbracht (It is finished)	Johannes Passion (St. John's Passion)	b-d2	d1-b1	Very slow, sustained, grave. Has a spirited, somewhat florid middle section. (Score generally available)
Esurientes implevit bonis (Latin text)	Magnificat in D Major	g#-d2	d#1-b1	Not fast, graceful, florid. (Score, Novello)
Et exultavit spiritus meus (Latin text)	Magnificat in D Major	c#1-f#2	e1-d2	Animated. Has florid passages. (Score, Novello)
Geist und Seele wird verwirret	Cantata 35 Geist und Seele wird verwirret	b-e2	e1-d2	Slow. Has florid passages.
Gelobet sei der Herr	Cantata 129 Gelobet sei der Herr, mein Gott	c#1-e2	e1-c2	Not slow, graceful. Has florid passages. (Prout, Augener)

TITLE:AIR	TITLE:WORK	COMP.	TESS.	REMARKS
Getrost, getrost! (Be glad)	Cantata 133 Ich freue mich in dir	a-e2	e1-c#2	Spirited. In parts quite florid. (Whittaker, Oxford)
Gott hat Alles wohlgemacht	Cantata 35 Geist und Seele wird verwirret	c1-e2	e1-c2	Rather vigorous. In parts quite florid.
Gott ist unser Sonn' und Schild	Cantata 79 Gott der Herr ist Sonn' und Schild	c#1-e2	e1-d2	Spirited. Has florid passages. (Prout, Augener)
Gott man lobet dich, in der Stille	Cantata 120 Gott man Lobet dich	a-e2	e1-d2	Slow, sustained. In parts very florid. (Straube, Peters)
Halleluja, Stärk und und Macht	Cantata 29 Wir danken dir Gott, wir danken dir	a-e2	d1-b1	Vigorous, spirited, quite florid.
Herr, was du willst soll mir gefallen	Cantata 156 Ich steh' mit einem Fuss im Grabe	f-e2	d1-d2	Vigorous, animated. Has florid passages. (Prout, Augener)
Leget euch dem Heiland unter (Lowly bend before the Saviour)	Cantata 182 Himmels- könig sei wilkommen	a-d2	d1-b1	Slow, sustained. Demands some flexibility. (Whittaker, Oxford)
Hochgelobter Gottesohn	Cantata 6 Bleib bei uns, denn es will Abend werden	bb-eb2	eb1-c2	Not fast. Rather florid.
Ich sehe schon im Geist	Cantata 43 Gott fähret auf mit Jauchzen	b-e2	e1-c2	Graceful. Has florid passages.
Ich will dich all mein Leben lang	Cantata 117 Sei Lob und Ehr	a-e2	e1-c#2	Animated. Demands some flexibility.
Ich wünsche mir bei Gott zu leben	Cantata 35 Geist und Seele wird verwirret	c1-e2	d1-c2	Rather animated. In parts quite florid.

TITLE:AIR	TITLE:WORK	COMP.	TESS.	REMARKS
In deine Hände	Cantata 106 Gottes Zeit ist die allerbeste Zeit	bb-eb2	f1-db2	Slow, sustained.
In Jesu Demuth kann ich Trost	Cantata 151 Süsser Trost mein Jesus kömmt	a-e2	e1-c2	Not slow. Demands flexibility. (Prout, Augener)
Jesu, lass dich finden	Cantata 154 Mein liebster Jesus ist verloren	b-d#2	e1-b1	Subdued, graceful. Demands some flexibility. (Prout, Augener)
Jesus schläft	Cantata 81 Jesus schläft was soll ich hoffen?	a-d2	b-b1	Sustained, subdued. (Prout, Augener)
Komm, leite mich	Cantata 175 Er rufet seinen Schafen mit Namen	b-e2	e1-b1	Not fast, sustained. (Straube, Peters)
Kommt, ihr angefocht'-nen Sünder	Cantata 30 Freue dich erlöste Schaar	a-e2	e1-c2	Not fast. Demands flexibility. Has interesting syncopated rhythm. (Straube, Peters)
Laudamus te (Latin text)	Mass in B Minor	c#1-e2	e1-c#2	Not fast, florid. Can be sung by soprani also, except a very light high voice. (Score generally available)
Leg ich mich späte nieder	Cantata 97 In allen meinen Thaten	b-eb2	eb1-c2	Grave. Demands some flexibility. (Straube, Peters)
Liebt, ihr Christen, in der That	Cantata 76 Die Himmel erzählen die Ehre Gottes	b-d2	e1-c2	Grave and sustained.
Mein Jesu, ziehe mich nach dir	Cantata 22 Jesus nahm zu sich die Zwölfe	bb-eb2	g1-c2	Flowing and subdued, graceful. (Straube, Peters)
Menschen, glaubt doch dieser Gnade	Cantata 7 Christ unser Herr zum Jordan kam	b-e2	d#1-c2	Very vigorous, dramatic. Has some florid passages. (Prout, Augener)

TITLE:AIR	TITLE:WORK	COMP.	TESS.	REMARKS
Mund und Herze steht dir offen	Cantata 148 Bringet dem Herrn Ehre seines Namens!	b-e2	f#1-d2	Graceful. Demands flexibility. (Prout, Eugener)
Murre nicht, lieber Christ	Cantata 144 Nimm, was dein ist, und gehe hin	a-d2	b-b1	Not slow, sustained, graceful. (Prout, Augener)
Nichts kann mich erretten	Cantata 74 Wer mich liebet, der wird mein Wort halten	g-e2	d1-c2	Animated and vigorous. Has florid passages. (Prout, Augener)
O Mensch, errette deine Seele	Cantata 20 O Ewigkeit, du Donnerwort	c#1-e2	f1-c2	Slow, grave. Demands some flexibility.
Recitative: O sel'ger Christ Arioso: Herr, so du willt Air: Mit Allem was ich hab und bin	Cantata 72 Alles nur nach Gottes willen	bb-e2	e1-c2	Recitative, and a sustained arioso, followed by spirited air requiring great flexibility. (Straube, Peters)
Recitative: O Wort, das Geist und Seel erschreckt Air: Vergib, o Vater	Cantata 87 Bisher habt ihr nichts gebeten	bb-e2	d1-c2	Slow, sustained. Demands flexibility.
Qui sedes (Latin text)	Mass in B Minor	c#1-e2	e1-c#2	Gently animated. Has florid passages. (Score generally available)
Schlafe, mein Liebster (Slumber, beloved)	Weihnachts Oratorium (Christmas Oratorio)	a-e2	e1-c2	Slow, very sustained. Has florid passages. (Score generally available)
Schläfert aller Sorgen Kummer	Cantata 197 Gott ist unsere Zuversicht	a-e2	e1-c#2	Very sustained. Has a spirited, florid middle section.

TITLE:AIR	TITLE:WORK	COMP.	TESS.	REMARKS
Schlage doch gewünschte Stunde	Cantata 53 (for alto solo) Schlage doch, gewünschte Stunde	b-e2	e-c#2	Very sustained, grave. (Prout, Augener)
Schliesse, mein Herze, dies selige Wunder (Keep, o my spirit)	Weihnachts Oratorium (Christmas Oratorio)	b-e2	e1-d2	Sustained, rather vigorous. (Score generally available)
Vergnügte Ruh, beliebte Seelenlust	Cantata 170 Vergnügte Ruh, beliebte Seelenlust	b-e2	e1-d2	Sustained. Demands some flexibility.
Von den Stricken meiner Sünden	Johannes Passion (St. John's Passion)	bb-eb2	d1-c2	Not fast. Demands flexibility. (Score generally available)
Von der Welt verlang' ich nichts (Of this world I ask for nought)	Cantata 64 Sehet! welch eine Liebe hat uns der Vater erzeiget	b-e2	e1-c2	Not fast, graceful. Demands flexibility. (Whittaker, Oxford)
Wann kommt der Tag	Cantata 70 Wachet, betet, seid bereit	a-d2	d1-b1	Sustained. Has some florid passages.
Was Gott thut	Cantata 100 Was Gott thut, das ist wohlgethan	a-e2	d1-a1	Animated and graceful. Demands some flexibility. (Prout, Augener)
Weh! der Seele	Cantata 102 Herr, deine Augen sehen nach dem Glauben	b-eb2	f1-c2	Sustained, grave. Demands some flexibility. (Straube, Peters)
Wer Gott bekennt	Cantata 45 Es ist dir gesagt, Mensch, was gut ist	b#-d#2	e1-c#2	Not fast, grave. Has florid passages.
Wer Sünde tut	Cantata 54 (for alto solo) Widerstehe doch der Sünde	f-c2	c1-g1	Not fast, grave. Has florid passages.

TITLE:AIR	TITLE:WORK	COMP.	TESS.	REMARKS
Widerstehe doch der Sünde	Cantata 54 (for alto solo) Widerstehe doch der Sünde	f-bb1	c1-f1	Rather slow and sustained, grave. (Prout, Augener)
Wie furchtsam wankten meine Schritte	Cantata 33 Allein zu dir Herr Jesu Christ	a-d2	d-b1	Not fast. Demands flexibility. (Straube, Peters)
Wohl euch, ihr aus- erwählten Seelen	Cantata 34 O Ewiges Feuer	b-e2	e1-c#2	Sustained. Demands some flexibility. (Straube, Peters)
Wo Zwei und Drei versam- melt sind in Jesu theurem Namen	Cantata 42 Am Abend aber desselbi- gen Sabbaths	b-e2	e1-c2	Not fast. Has florid passages. (Straube, Peters)

TITLE:AIR	TITLE:WORK	COMP.	TESS.	REMARKS
Ach, mein Sinn	Johannes Passion (St. John's Passion)	e-a1	a-f#1	Sustained. (Score generally available)
Ach, schlage doch bald	Cantata 95 Christus, der ist mein Leben	d-b1	a-f#1 (g1)	Not fast. Demands flexibility. (Straube, Peters; in the Prout collection this air is transposed one tone lower)
Adam muss in uns verwesen (He who would in Christ be living)	Cantata 31 Der Himmel lacht, die Erde jubiliret	c-g1	g-e1	Animated, very short. (Whittaker, Oxford)
Auf, auf, Gläubige	Cantata 134 Ein Herz, das seinen Jesum	d-bb1	f-f1	Vigorous. Has florid passages. (Straube, Peters)
Bäche von gesalznen Zähren	Cantata 21 Ich hatte viel Bekümmernis	c-g1	ab-eb1	Slow, rather florid. (Prout, Augener)
Benedictus	Mass in B Minor	e-a1	a-f#1	Sustained. Demands flexibility. (Score generally available)
Bewundert, o Menschen	Cantata 62 Nun komm, der Heiden Heiland	c-a1	a-f1	Animated and florid.
Deposuit potentes (Latin text)	Magnificat in D	c#-a1	f#-d1	Animated, quite florid. (Score, Novello)
Die schäumenden Wellen	Cantata 81 Jesus schläft, was soll ich hoffen?	d-a1	a-f1	Spirited. Has rapid florid passages. Has several recitative passages interrupting the set musical piece. (Prout, Augener)
Die Welt kann ihre Lust und Freud'	Cantata 94 Was frag' ich nach der Welt	c#-b1	f-f1	Animated, rather florid. (Prout, Augener)
Erbarme dich	Cantata 55 Ich armer Mensch, ich Sünden Knecht	f-bb1	a-f1	Not fast. For the most part sustained. Demands flexibility.

TITLE:AIR	TITLE:WORK	COMP.	TESS.	REMARKS
Erfreue dich Seele	Cantata 21 Ich hatte viel Bekümmernis	c-a1	a-f1	Very spirited. Demands considerable flexibility.
Erwage, wie sein blut- gefärbter Rücken	Johannes Pas- sion (St. John's passion)	e-a1	g-f1	Slow. Has florid passages. (Score generally available)
Ewigkeit, du machst mir bange	Cantata 20 O Ewigkeit, du Donnerwort	c-ab1	g-eb1	Slow grave. Has a florid middle section. (Straube, Peters)
Frohe Hirten, eilt (Haste, ye shepherds)	Weihnachts Oratorium (Christmas Oratorio)	d-a1	g-e1	Graceful, florid (Score, generally available)
Gott, dem der Erdenkreis zu Klein	Cantata 91 Gelobet seist du, Jesus Christ	e-a1	g-e1	Spirited, somewhat declam- atory. Demands flexibility.
Handle nicht nach deinen Rechten	Cantata 101 Nimm von uns, Herr, du treuer Gott	d-ab1	g-e1	Not fast; rather sustained. Demands flexibility.
Hasse nur, hasse mich recht	Cantata 76 Die, Himmel erzählen die Ehre Gottes	c-g1	g-e1	Dramatic and vigorous. Has florid passages. Best for heavy voices; could be sung by a high baritone.
Hebt euer Haupt empor	Cantata 70 Wachet, betet, seid bereit allezeit	c-g1	g-e1	Animated. Demands some flexibility. (Prout, Augener)
Ich traue seiner Gnaden	Cantata 97 In allen meinen Thaten	d-ab1	g-eb1	Sustained and grave. Has florid passages.
Ich weiss dass mein Erlöser lebet	Cantata 160 Ich weiss dass mein Erlöser lebet	d-g1	g-e1	Not fast, rather sustained. Demands in parts some flexibility. (Prout, Augener)
Ich will leiden	Cantata 87 Bisher habt ihr nichts gebeten in meinem Namen	f-bb1	g-g1	Rather slow. Demands some flexibility. (Straube, Peters; also Prout, Augener)
Ich will nur dir zu Ehren leben	Weihnachts Oratorium	c-g1	f-d1	Animated, florid.

TITLE:AIR	TITLE:WORK	COMP.	TESS.	REMARKS
('Tis thee I would be praising)	(Christmas Oratorio)			(Score generally available)
Ihr Menschen rühmet Gottes Liebe	Cantata 167 Ihr Menschen rühmet Gottes Liebe	d-a1	g-f1	Animated. Has florid passages. (Straube, Peters)
Ja tausendmal	Cantata 43 Gott fähret auf mit Jauchzen	d-a1	f#-i#1	Very animated, spirited, and florid.
Jesu lass durch Wohl und Weh (Jesu, paths of weal and woe)	Cantata 182 Himmelskönig sei wilkommen	d-g1	f#-e1	For the most part sustained. Has two florid passages. (Whittaker, Oxford)
Jesus Christus, Gottessohn	Cantata 4 Christ lag in Todesbanden	d#-f#1	e-e1	Very spirited. The vocal line consists of a sustained chorale melody, except the final phrase which is florid. (Prout, Augener)
Kann ich nur Jesum mir zum Freunde machen (If my Lord Jesus)	Cantata 105 Herr, gehe nicht ins Gericht	d-ab1	f-eb1	Not fast. Demands flexibility. (Whittaker, Oxford)
Komm, Jesu	Cantata 61 Nun komm, der Heiden Heiland	c-f1	f-d1	Subdued and graceful.
Kommt, eilet!	Cantata 74 Wer mich liebet, der wird mein Wort halten	d-a1	a-f#1	Rapid and very florid.
Man halte nur ein wenig stille	Cantata 93 Wer nur den lieben Gott lasst walten	d-bb1	a-f1	Sustained. Has a florid closing passage. (Straube, Peters)
Mein alles in Allem, mein ewiges Gut (O treasure of treasures)	Cantata 22 Jesus nahm zu sich die Zwölfe	d-g1	f-d1	Graceful. In parts demands considerable flexibility. (Whittaker, Oxford)
Meine Seufzer, meine Thränen	Cantata 13 Meine Seufzer, meine Thränen	d-ab1	g-e1	Sustained, grave. Has one florid passage. (Straube, Peters)

TITLE:AIR	TITLE:WORK	COMP.	TESS.	REMARKS
Mein Jesus is erstanden	Cantata 67 Halt' im Gedächtnis Jesum Christ	e-a1	(b-f♯1) b-g♯1	Spirited. Demands flexibility. The tessitura is very high. (Prout, Augener)
Recitative: Mein Jesus schweigt (He holds his peace) Air: Geduld, geduld, wenn mich falsche Zungen stechen (Be still, be still)	Matthäus Passion (St. Matthew Passion)	e-a1	a-f1	Slow, quite florid. (Score generally available)
Mein Jesus soll mein Alles sein	Cantata 75 Die Elenden sollen essen	d-g1	g-e1	Animated and graceful. (Straube, Peters)
Mein liebster Jesus ist verloren	Cantata 154 Mein liebster Jesus ist verloren	f♯-a1	a-f♯1	Sustained. (Prout, Augener)
Nimm mich dir zu eigen hin	Cantata 65 Sie werden aus Saba alle kommen	d-a1	g-e1	Animated. Has florid passages. (Prout, Augener)
Nun mögt ihr stolzen Feinde schrecken (Ye foes of man)	Weihnachts Oratorium (Christmas Oratorio)	d-a1	a-f♯1	Rather vigorous. Demands some flexibility. (Score generally available)
O Seelenparadies	Cantata 172 Erschallet, ihr Lieder	c-g1	g-e1	Sustained. Has some florid passages. (Prout, Augener)
Sanfte soll mein Todeskummer	Oster Oratorium	c♯-a1	f-f1	Slow, sustained, subdued. Demands some flexibility. (Straube, Peters; also Prout, Augener)
Seht, was die Liebe thut	Cantata 85 Ich bin ein guter Hird	d-b♭1	a-g1	Not fast; sustained and graceful. (Straube, Peters; also Prout, Augener)
Stürmt, nur stürmt	Cantata 153 Schau lieber Gott wie meine Feind'	e-a1	g-f1	Vigorous, florid. (Straube, Peters)

TITLE:AIR	TITLE:WORK	COMP.	TESS.	REMARKS
Tröste mir Jesu mein Gemüte	Cantata 135 Ach Herr, mich armen Sünder	c-a1	g-f1	For the most part sustained. Has a few florid passages. (Prout, Augener)
Was des Höchsten Glanz erfüllt	Cantata 194 Höchst-erwünschtes Freudenfest	d-g1	f-f1	Not fast; rather florid. Originally written in bass clef, for high baritone. (Prout, Augener)
Recitative: Was Gott den Vätern alter Zeit Arioso: Sein Same musste sich so sehr	Cantata 10 Meine Seel' erhebt den Herren	d-g1	a-g1	Recitative and a short sustained arioso.
Welch' Übermass der Güte schenkst du mir	Cantata 17 Wer Dank opfert, der preiset mich	d-a1	g-e1	Animated. Has florid passages. (Straube, Peters; also Prout, Augener)
Recitative: Welt, deine Lust Air: Mein Verlangen	Cantata 161 Komm, du süsse Todesstunde	c-g1	f-e1	Very sustained. (Straube, Peters)

TITLE:AIR	TITLE:WORK	COMP.	TESS.	REMARKS
Ach, soll nicht dieser grosse Tag	Cantata 70 Wachet, betet, seid bereit allezeit	G-f1	c-c1	Majestic. Closes with a florid passage.
Recitative: Ach unser Wille bleibt verkehrt Air: Herr, so du willt	Cantata 73 Herr, wie du willt, so schick's mit mir	G-eb1	eb-d1	Recitative and a sustained, grave air. (Prout, Augener)
Ächzen und erbärmlich Weinen	Cantata 13 Meine Seufzer, meine Thränen	G-eb1	eb-c1	Sustained. In parts demands some flexibility.
Am Abend, da es kühle war	Matthäus Passion (St. Matthew Passion)	G-eb1	c-c1	A sustained arioso. (Score generally available)
An irdische Schätze	Cantata 26 Ach wie flüchtig, ach wie nichtig	G-e1	d-b	Rather animated. Has florid passages. (Straube, Peters)
Auf, auf mit hellem Schall	Cantata 128 Auf Christi Himmelfahrt allein	F#-e1	d-d1	Animated, vigorous. Has florid passages. The final section is a short recitative followed by the instrumental ritornel. (Prout, Augener)
Beglückte Herde	Cantata 104 Du Hirte, Israel, höre	F#-d1	B-b	Rather subdued, graceful. Requires flexibility. (Prout, Augener; also Straube, Peters)
Betrachte meine Seel'	Johannes Passion (St. John's Passion)	Bb-eb1	eb-db1	Slow, sustained. (Score generally available)
Darum sollt ihr nicht sorgen	Cantata 187 Es wartet alles auf dich	c-eb1 (G)	f-d1	Vigorous, animated. (Prout, Augener)
Das Brausen von den rauhen Winden	Cantata 92 Ich hab' in Gottes Herz und Sinn	A-e1	c-c1	Rapid and very florid.

TITLE:AIR	TITLE:WORK	COMP.	TESS.	REMARKS
Dein Geburtstag ist erschienen	Cantata 142 Uns ist ein Kind geboren	E-d1	e-c1	Sustained. Demands some flexibility. (Galaxy)
Dein Wetter zog sich auf von Weitem	Cantata 46 Schauet doch und sehet, ob irgend ein Schmerz sei	Bb-e1	eb-c1	Majestic. Has very florid passages. (Straube, Peters)
Recitative: Der Heiland fällt vor seinem Vater nieder (The Saviour low before his Father bending) Air: Gerne will ich mich bequemen (Gladly would I be 'enduring)	Matthäus Passion (St. Matthew Passion)	G-eb1	d-c1	Sustained. Demands some flexibility.
Doch weichet ihr tollen vergeblichen Sorgen	Cantata 8 Liebster Gott, wann werd' ich sterben	A-e1	e-d1	Animated, graceful, quite florid. (Prout, Augener)
Eilt, ihr angefocht'nen Seelen	Johannes Passion (St. John's Passion)	G-e1	c-c1	Animated, florid. (With chorus, but could be sung as a solo piece) (Score generally available)
Endlich, endlich	Cantata 56 Ich will den Kreuzstab gerne tragen	G-e1	c-c1	Spirited and florid.
Erleuch auch meine finstre Sinnen (O Lord, my darkened Heart enlighten)	Weihnachts Oratorium (Christmas Oratorio)	b-e1	e-d1	Not fast. Has many florid passages. (Score generally available)
Es ist vollbracht	Cantata 159 Sehet, wir geh'n hinauf	G-eb1	d-d1	Sustained. Has some florid passages. (Prout, Augener)
Et in Spiritum Sanctum	Mass in B Minor	A-e1	e-c#1	Not fast. Demands some flexibility. The tessitura is somewhat high. (Score generally available)

TITLE:AIR	TITLE:WORK	COMP.	TESS.	REMARKS
Fürst des Lebens, starker Streiter (Prince eternal)	Cantata 31 Der Himmel lacht, die Erde jubiliret	G-d1	c-a	Not fast, florid. (Whittaker, Oxford)
Gebt mir meinen Jesum wieder (Bring him back is all my prayer)	Matthäus Passion (St. Matthew Passion)	G-e1	d-c1	Not slow. Has florid passages. (Score generally available)
Gewaltige stösst Gott vom Stuhl hinunter	Cantata 10 Meine Seel' erhebt den Herren	F-eb1	c-c1	Animated, vigorous, dramatic. Has florid passages.
Grosser Herr, und starker König (Mighty Lord and King all glorious)	Weihnachts Oratorium (Christmas Oratorio)	A-e1	e-d1	Vigorous. Demands some flexibility. (Score generally available)
Gute Nacht du Weltgetümmel	Cantata 27 Wer weiss wie nahe mir mein Ende	G-eb1	d-c1	Grave, sustained. Has florid passages. (Straube, Peters; also Prout, Augener)
Hat man nicht mit seinen Kindern	Cantata 211 Kaffee Cantata (Schweiget stille, plandert nicht)	B-e1	d-d1	Animated, humorous. Demands facile articulation and some flexibility. (Prout, Augener)
Heiligste Dreieinigkeit	Cantata 172 Erschallet ihr Lieder	G-d1	c-c1	Majestic. Demands some flexibility. (Prout, Augener)
Hier, in meines Vaters Stätte	Cantata 32 Liebster Jesu, mein Verlangen	G-e1	e-c1	Slow and sustained. Demands some flexibility. (Prout, Augener)
Hier,is das rechte Osterlamm	Cantata 4 Christ lag in Todesbanden	E-e1	e-b	Slow, grave, and sustained. Has a very majestic, vigorous ending.
Höllische Schlange, wird dir nicht bange	Cantata 40 Dazu ist erschienen der Sohn Gottes	G-e1	d-c1	Vigorous. (Straube, Peters)

TITLE:AIR	TITLE:WORK	COMP.	TESS.	REMARKS
Ich freue mich auf meinen Tod	Cantata 82 Ich habe genug	G-eb1	B-b	Very animated. Has florid passages.
Ich habe genug	Cantata 82 Ich habe genug	G-eb1	f-c1	Sustained, grave. Demands some flexibility. (Straube, Peters)
Ich will den Krentzstab	Cantata 56 Ich will den Krenzstab gerne tragen	G-e1	e-c1	Fairly sustained. Demands some flexibility. (Prout, Augener)
Arioso: Ihr Kleingläubigen Air: Schweig, schweig	Cantata 81 Jesus schläft, was soll ich hoffen?	G-e1	c-c1	Grave arioso followed by fast vigorous air. (Prout, Augener; also Straube, Peters)
Recitative: Ja! freilich will in mir (In truth, to bear the cross) Air: Komm süsses Kreuz (Come, healing cross)	Matthäus Passion (St. Matthew Passion)	A-e1	d-d1	Slow, quite florid. (Score generally available)
Ja, ja, ich kann die Feinde schlagen	Cantata 57 Selig ist der Mann	G-eb1	e-c1	Animated, vigorous. Demands flexibility. (Prout, Augener)
Johannis freudenvolles Springen (John filled with joy)	Cantata 121 Christum wir sollen loben schon	G-e1	c-c1	Spirited, quite florid. (Whittaker, Oxford)
Lasset dem Höchsten	Cantata 66 Erfreut euch, ihr Herzen!	A-e1	d-c1	Vigorous, animated. Has florid passages. (Straube, Peters)
Mache dich mein Herze rein (Make thee clean my heart from sin)	Matthäus Passion (St. Matthew Passion)	A-eb1	c-c1	Sustained. Demands some flexibility. (Score generally available)
Meinen Jesum lass' ich nicht (Never Jesus will I leave)	Cantata 98 Was Gott thut, das ist wohlgetan	A-eb1	eb-c1	Animated, rather vigorous. Demands considerable flexibility. (Whittaker, Oxford)

TITLE:AIR	TITLE:WORK	COMP.	TESS.	REMARKS
Mein Erlöser und Erhalter	Cantata 69 Lobe den Herrn, mein Seele	A-e1	e-b	Rather grave and sustained. Has some floric passages.
Merke mein Herze beständig nur dies	Cantata 145 So du mit deinem Munde	A-e1	d-d1	Animated. In parts quite florid. (Prout, Augener)
Mit Verlangen	Phoebus und Pan	B-f#1	e-e1	Sustained. Has florid passages. (Prout, Augener)
O Menschen, die ihr täglich sündigt (We mortals)	Cantata 122 Das Neugebor'ne Kindelein	c-eb1 (G)	c-c1	Vigorous. Has florid passages. (Whittaker, Oxford)
Quia fecit mihi magna (Latin text)	Magnificat in D Major	G#-d#1	c#-c#1	Not fast, quite florid. (Score, Novello)
Quoniam tu solus sanctus (Latin text)	Mass in B Minor	G#-e1	B-b	Slow. Has florid passages. (Score generally available)
Schlummert ein	Cantata 82 Ich habe genug	Bb-eb1	c-c1	Rather slow, sustained, and subdued. (Prout, Augener)
Selig ist der Mann	Cantata 57 Selig ist der Mann	G-eb1	e-c1	Slow and very sustained. Has one florid passage.
Seligster Erquikkungs-tag	Cantata 70 Wachet, betet, seid bereit allezeit	G-d1	c-c1	Slow and rather sustained at the beginning and end. Rapid and florid middle section. (Prout, Augener; also Straube, Peters)
Recitative: Siehe, siehe, ich komme Air: Starkes Lieben (Great they Love, Lord)	Cantata 182 Himmelskönig, sei Wilkommen	E-c1	c-b	Not fast. Demands flexibility. (Whittaker, Oxford)
So löschet im Eifer	Cantata 90 Es reifet euch ein schrecklich Ende	Bb-eb1	d-b	Vigorous and majestic. Demands flexibility

TITLE:AIR	TITLE:WORK	COMP.	TESS.	REMARKS
Tag und Nacht	Cantata 71 Gott ist mein König	F-e1	c-c1	Slow, sustained. Has a florid middle section.
Verachtest du den Reichthum seiner Gnade	Cantata 102 Herr, deine Augen sehen nach dem Glauben	G-eb1	eb-c1	Spirited. (Prout, Augener)
Verstumme, Höllenheer	Cantata 5 Wo soll ich fliehen hin	A-e1	d-d1	Animated, vigorous. Demands some flexibility. (Prout, Augener)
Wacht auf ihr Adern und ihr Glieder	Cantata 110 Unser Mund sei voll Lachen	F♯-e1	d-d1	Vigorous. In parts quite florid. (Prout, Augener)
Wacht Auf	Cantata 20 O Ewigkeit, du Donnerwort	G-e1	c-d1	Majestic, vigorous. Has florid passages. (Prout, Augener)
Wahrlich, ich sage euch	Cantata 86 Wahrlich, ich sage euch	G-d1	d-b	Majestic, rather vigorous.
Was Gott thut	Cantata 100 Was Gott thut, das ist wohlgethan	A-e1	e-c1	Animated. Has florid passages.
Weicht all', ihr Übeltäter	Cantata 135 Ach Herr, mich armen Sünder·	A-e1	d-d1	Animated, vigorous. Has rather unusual florid passages. (Prout, Augener)
Wie will ich lustig lachen (How jovial is my laughter)	Cantata 205 Der Zufrieden- gestellte Aeolus	F♯-f♯1	e-e1	Spirited, vigorous, florid. In the Oxford edition, trans- posed one tone lower. (Whittaker, Oxford)

SONGS

Edition: Breitkopf & Härtel

TITLE	COMP.	TESS.	TYPE	REMARKS
Bist du bei mir	d1-ab2	ab1-f2	All voices	Sustained. (Generally available)
Dir, dir Jehova	f1-g2	a1-eb2	Not too suitable for very light voices	Majestic, vigorous.
Es ist vollbracht	d1-f#2	f#1-d2	All voices	Sustained, grave.
Komm, süsser Tod	c1-g2	g1-eb2	Not too suitable for very light voices	Slow and sustained, grave. (Generally available)
Liebster Herr Jesu	g1-f2	a1-d2	All voices	Sustained.
Meine Seele, lass es gehen	f1-ab2	ab1-g2	All voices	Slow and sustained.
So oft ich meine Tabakspfeife	d1-f2	g1-d2	Most suitable for men's voices	Humorous, sustained.
Vergiss mein nicht	d#1-g2	a1-f2	All voices	Very slow and sustained, grave.
Willst du dein Herz mir schenken	d1-g2	g1-eb2	All voices	Sustained. Demands in parts considerable flexibility.

GEORGE FREDERICK HANDEL
(1685-1759)

Handel's songs and airs are perhaps more frequently performed now than the vocal music of any of his contemporaries, including Bach. One of the main reasons for this popularity, aside from the magnificent nature of Handel's music, is the fact that Handel's manner of writing for the voice is so extraordinarily considerate of the singer. Even his most difficult display pieces, written for the famed vocal virtuosi of his time and demanding optimum vocal endowment as well as a maximum of control, are never vocally awkward. His idiom is largely diatonic in character, and is thus extremely well suited to the human voice, as well as easily comprehended by the listener. Employing the flatteringly vocal manner of writing of his Italian contemporaries, and as aware of the limitations and possibilities of each type of voice as any servile hack composer of his period, Handel, with a truly miraculous sense of balance, perhaps not possessed by any composer save Mozart, nonetheless never permitted this manner or this awareness to influence the content of his vocal music.

Thus it is not surprising that Handel's songs and airs are seemingly as satisfying to the singer and the listener of today as they were to the singer and the listener of some two hundred years ago.

Since Handel wrote magnificently for all types of voice, from bass to coloratura soprano, and since he wrote in every conceivable manner, from extremely florid display pieces to sustained airs of inconceivable majesty and nobility, it would seem superfluous to attempt to formulate any general suggestions pertaining to the performance of his vocal music. Every singer at any stage of development, will be able to find at least a few of Handel's songs and airs suitable to his type of voice and singing.

As most of Handel's Italian operas are now forgotten, being dramatically too static for present-day audiences, the airs extracted from them can now be easily performed by voices other than those for which they were originally intended. The peculiarly apt and adroit manner of writing for the voice in which Handel excelled makes many of his Italian tenor airs suitable for performance by soprano voices, and many of his bass and baritone airs suitable for performance by alto and mezzo-soprano voices, as well as vice versa. Naturally the characteristics of each individual air and voice will have to be taken into account when considering such a procedure. It would also seem advisable to mention the fact that many of his airs are suitable for all types of voices, if transposed.

The number of editions in which Handel's Italian airs are available is so great that anything approaching a bibliographical survey even in a most limited sense of the word would comprise several hundred entries.

The editions mentioned below are by no means the only ones in which the airs listed can be obtained. In the opinion of this writer, however, the editions referred to in the list below are either the most accurate or the most easily available.

The inclusion of Dresel and Robert Franz collections, which are at present unavailable due to the disrupted state of German music publishing business seemed warranted, since these collections rank among the best and will no doubt be soon available, either in American reprints or in their original form.

The famous English oratorios are of course generally available in piano scores in a variety of editions. The mention of publishers in the lists devoted to airs with English text is intended only as a matter of convenience, since, for all practical purposes nearly all of these airs could be classed generally available.

The name or names in parentheses in the Remarks column indicates one of the following collections:

Bibliography

Best, Boosey: <u>Fifty Arias by Handel,</u> edited by Best, published by Boosey.

Breitkopf & Härtel: <u>Händel Arien,</u> published by Breitkopf & Härtel.

J. Church Co.: <u>Oratorio Songs,</u> published by J. Church Co.

Dresel, Brockhaus: <u>Händel Arien für Sopran</u> and Händel Arien für Alt, edited by Dresel, published by Brockhaus, Leipzig.

Franz, Kistner: <u>Händel Arien,</u> edited by Robert Franz, published by Kistner, Leipzig.

Handel Renaissance, refers to <u>Händel Renaissance,</u> edited by Günther, published by Bote & Bock, Berlin.

Prout, Ditson: <u>Handel Songs and Airs</u>, 2 vols. edited by Dr. Prout, published by Ditson (available separately).

Whittaker, Oxford: <u>Arias from Handel's Italian Operas</u>, edited by Whittaker published by Oxford University Press (available separately).

Wolff, Music Press: <u>Eight Handel Arias for Bass</u>, edited by E. V. Wolff, published by Music Press, Inc., New York. (These airs, although printed in bass clef, are also suitable for alto.)

There are numerous other collections. Most of the famous airs are now available in a variety of editions in transposed keys, to suit almost all types of voice (see the catalogues of Ashdown, Ltd., and Augener, London). An excellent collection of Handel's airs with English text only, edited by Ford, is now published by Boosey in seven volumes, each containing airs for one type of voice only, such as dramatic soprano, light soprano, bass, baritone, and so on.

Since Handel wrote within a rather uniform compass and tessitura for each of the four main types of voice, and since the character of each air, as described in the Remarks column seems sufficient to indicate the type of voice for which the air is possibly best suited, it seemed best to dispense with the Type of Voice column in the following lists. Note: The title of the Opera or Oratorio is placed above the title of the air.

ITALIAN TEXT - SOPRANO

TITLE	COMP.	TESS.	REMARKS
Admeto Luci care	eb1-g2	g1-eb2	Slow, Sustained. (Prout, Ditson)
Admeto Quanto godrà	e1-g2	a1-f2	Spirited. Has florid passages. (Best, Boosey)
Admeto Spera, si	c1-g2	f1-db2	Not fast. Demands some flexibility. (Best, Boosey)
Agrippina Recitative: Ah che sperar mi resta Air: Ingannata una sol volta	e1-a2	e1-e2	Sustained. (Dresel, Brockhaus)
Agrippina Bel piacere	db1-gb2	gb1-eb2	Graceful. Demands lightness of tone and some flexibility. Has a very interesting rhythmic pattern. (Arr. by F. Bibb. Schirmer)

TITLE	COMP.	TESS.	REMARKS
Agrippina Ogni vento	d1-g2	f#1-d2	Spirited. Demands some flexibility. (Best, Boosey)
Alcina Ah! Mio cor	f1-ab2	bb1-g2	Sustained, somewhat declamatory. Has a spirited middle section. This air is published in the Parisotti collection, transposed a fourth lower, with the middle section omitted. (Best, Boosey)
Alcina Mi restano le lagrime	e#1-a2	a1-f#2	Sustained, graceful. Most suitable for a light voice. (Best, Boosey)
Alessandro Recitative: Ne trionfa d'Alessandro Air: Lusinghe più care	d1-g2	g1-d2	Florid, spirited. (Generally available)
Amadigi Gioje, venite in sen	eb1-ab2	g1-eb2	A graceful, rather slow siciliana. Has florid passages. (Whittaker, Oxford)
Atalanta Riportai, gloriosa palma	e1-a2	a1-e2	Spirited, vigorous. Has florid passages. (Best, Boosey)
Deidamia Se pensi amor tu solo	f#1-a2	b1-g2	Animated. Has florid passages. Best for light voice. (Best, Boosey)
Flavio Quanto dolci	f#1-a2	a1-f#2	Graceful, sustained. Has some florid passages. (Dresel, Brockhaus)
Floridante Amor comanda	f1-bb2	bb1-f2	Animated. In parts florid. (Handel Renaissance)
Giulio Cesare Da tempeste	d#1-a2	e1-e2	Spirited. Quite florid. (Best, Boosey)
Giulio Cesare Recitative: E pur così in un giorno Air: Piangerò la sorte mia	e1-a2	g#-e1	A very sustained air with a spirited, florid middle section. (Best, Boosey)

Giulio Cesare
Se pietà di me non senti — e1-a2 — a1-f#2 — Slow, sustained. Demands some flexibility. Optional for tenor. (Arr. by S. Endicott, R.D.Row, Inc.)

Giulio Cesare
V'adoro, pupille saette d'amore — f1-g2 — a1-f2 — Slow, sustained. Demands in parts some flexibility. (Best, Boosey)

Ottone
Affanni del pensier — eb1-ab2 — ab1-eb2 — Slow, graceful, sustained. Demands some flexibility. Parisotti collection. (Best, Boosey)

Ottone
Recitative:
  Ben a ragion — d#1-f#2 — — Sustained. Optional for alto.
Air: — (g#2) — — (Arr. by F. Bibb. Schirmer)
  Vieni o figlio

Ottone
O grati orrori — f1-a2 — g1-f2 — Scena and graceful air. Demands some flexibility. (Arr. by Wintter Watts. Ricordi)

Partenope
Qual farfaletta — e1-a2 — a1-f#2 — Animated, graceful. Quite florid. Best for light voice. (Generally available)

Radamisto
Quel nave smarrita — c#1-g2 — f#1-d2 — Slow, rather vigorous. Demands some flexibility. (Best, Boosey; also Prout, Ditson)

Radamisto
Sommi Dei — g1-a2 — g1-e2 — Majestic, declamatory, grave. Best for dramatic soprano. See also the arrangement by F. Bibb (Schirmer), published in high and low keys. (Best, Boosey)

Rinaldo
Recitative:
  Armida, dispietata — f1-g2 — a1-f2 — Very sustained. Best for dramatic
Air: — — — soprano. Optional for alto.
  Lascia ch'io pianga — — — (Prout, Ditson)

Rinaldo
Vò far guerra — d1-g2 — f#1-d2 — Spirited, vigorous. Has florid passages. Optional for tenor. (Best, Boosey)

Rodelinda
Ho perduta il caro sposo — eb1-ab2 — g1-eb2 — Slow and sustained. Demands some flexibility. (Whittaker, Oxford)

TITLE	COMP.	TESS.	REMARKS
Rodelinda L'empio rigor del fato	d1-bb2	bb1-g2	Animated, spirited. Has florid passages. Best for light voice. (Whittaker, Oxford)
Rodelinda Mio caro bene	f#1-a2	a1-e2	Animated, spirited. Has florid passages. Best for light voice. (Whittaker, Oxford)
Rodelinda Morrai sì	d#1-g#2	g#1-e2	Vigorous, spirited. Has florid passages. (Best Boosey)
Rodelinda Ombre, piante	f#1-a2	b1-f#2	Slow, sustained. Demands some flexibility. (Whittaker, Oxford)
Rodelinda Ritorna, oh caro	g1-a2	a1-e2	Sustained. (Whittaker, Oxford)
Rodelinda Spietati Io vi giurai	f1-ab2	a1-f2	Spirited. Demands some flexibility. (Best, Boosey)
Rodrigo Begl'occhi del mio ben	d1-g2	g1-eb2	Graceful. (Dresel, Brockhaus)
Rodrigo Il dolce foco mio	f1-a2	a1-f2	Graceful. Has florid passages. (Dresel, Brockhaus)
Scipione Dimmi cara	eb1-ab2	g1-eb2 (H)	Slow, sustained. Optional for tenor. (Handel Renaissance)
Serse Recitative: Aspide sono; Air: Nè men con L'ombre	e1-a2	g#1-e2	Graceful, not fast. Demands some flexibility. (Whittaker, Oxford)
Serse Caro voi siete all'alma	e1-a2	a1-e2	Sustained, graceful. (Whittaker, Oxford)
Serse Dirà che amor per me	f1-a2	a1-e2	Animated, graceful. Demands facile articulation and some flexibility. (Whittaker, Oxford)
Serse Và godendo vezzoso e bello	e1-a2	a1-e2	Animated, graceful, florid. Best for light voice. (Whittaker, Oxford)

TITLE	COMP.	TESS.	REMARKS
Siroe Ch'io mai vi possa	d#1-g2	g1-e2	Animated. Has florid passages. (Ashdown)
Siroe Mi lagnero tacendo	f-a2	a1-f2	Graceful, sustained. (Best, Boosey)

Siroe
Recitative:
  Si diversi
  sembianti;
Air:
  Non vi piacque
	e1-g#2	g#1-e2	Slow, somewhat florid. (Best, Boosey)

Siroe Torrente cresciuto	e1-g#2	f#1-e2	Animated, rather vigorous and florid. Has a sustained middle section. (Dresel, Brockhaus)

Sosarme
Recitative:
  Rasserena, o
  madre;
Air:
  Rend'il sereno al
  ciglio
	f#1-g#2	g#1-e2	Slow, sustained. (Best, Boosey)

Tamerlano Cor di padre	d1-a2	g1-e2	Slow, grave, somewhat declamatory. Demands some flexibility. (Whittaker, Oxford)
Tamerlano Deh! Lasciatemi il nemico	e#1-g#2	a1-e2	Slow, sustained. Demands some flexibility. (Whittaker, Oxford)
Tamerlano Par che mi nasca in seno	e1-g2	g1-e2	Sustained, graceful. Demands some flexibility. (Whittaker, Oxford)
Teseo Vieni, torna idol mio	d1-f2	a1-d2	Not fast; graceful. (Whittaker, Oxford)
Tolomeo Voi dolce aurette al cor	d1-g2	g1-e2	Graceful. Demands some flexibility. Best for light voice. (Arr. by Frank Bibb. Schirmer)

ALTO OR MEZZO-SOPRANO

Admeto Cangiò d'aspetto	a-d2	d1-b1	Animated, graceful. Has florid passages. (Best, Boosey)

TITLE	COMP.	TESS.	REMARKS
Alcina La bocca vaga	b-e2	e1-c#2	Graceful. (Breitkopf & Härtel)
Alcina Verdi prati	c#1-e2	e1-c#2	Slow and very sustained. (Prout, Ditson)
Amadigi Ah! Spietato!	b-d2	e1-c2	Very Sustained. Optional for baritone. (Generally available)
Amadigi Recitative: D'un sventurato amante; Air; Pena tiranna	c1-eb2	e1-c2	Vigorous, majestic. (Breitkopf & Härtel)
Amadigi O rendetemi il mio bene	c#1-eb2	f1-d2	Slow, grave. Optional for baritone. (Whittaker, Oxford)
Amadigi Tu mia speranza	b-d2	d1-b1	Animated. Demands some flexi- bility. (Prout, Ditson)
Arminio Vado a morir	d1-eb2	eb1-bb1	Slow, sustained, grave. Optional for baritone. (Whittaker, Oxford)
Atalanta Ben'io sento l'ingrata	b-db2	d1-c2	Not fast; vigorous. Has florid passages. (Whittaker, Oxford)
Atalanta Come alla tortorella	b-e2	e1-c#2	Sustained, somewhat subdued. Demands some flexibility. (Whittaker, Oxford)
Atalanta Soffri in pace	bb-eb2	eb1-c2	Sustained, graceful. Has florid passages. (Whittaker, Oxford)
Berenice No! Soffrir non può il mio amore	c1-e2		Sustained. Demands some flexi- bility. Optional for bass. (Wolff, Music Press)
Berenice Si tra i ceppi	b-d2	c1-c2	Spirited. Has florid passages. Optional for bass. (Prout, Ditson)
Ezio Quanto mai felici siete	c#1-d2	e1-b1	Animated. Has florid passages. (Best, Boosey)

TITLE	COMP.	TESS.	REMARKS
Ezio Vi fida lo sposo	bb-c2	d1-bb1	Sustained. (Franz, Kistner)
Faramondo Sento che un giusto sdegno	bb-f2	eb1-c2	Animated. Has florid passages. (Whittaker, Oxford)
Flavio Chi può mirare	g-eb2	c1-c2	Animated. Demands some flexi- bility. (Breitkopf & Härtel)
Flavio L'armellin' vita non cura	b-e2	e1-c#2	Animated. Demands considerable flexibility. (Best, Boosey)
Flavio O Amor! Nel mio penar	bb-db2	db1-bb1	Very sustained. (Breitkopf & Härtel)
Floridante Alma mia	c#1-e2	d1-d2	Sustained, graceful. Optional for baritone. (Wolff, Music Press)
Floridante Se dolce m'era già	b-eb2	eb1-c2	Graceful. Demands some flexi- bility. (Breitkopf & Härtel)
Lotario Già mi sembra	a-e2	e1-c2	Vigorous, spirited. Demands some flexibility. (Prout, Ditson)
Lotario Per salvarti idol mio	b-d2	d#1-b1	Not fast; sustained. Has florid passages. (Best, Boosey)
Muzio Scevola Pupille sdegnose	c#1-d2	e1-c#2	Not fast; sustained. Has florid passages. (Franz, Kistner)
Muzio Scevola Volate più dei venti	a-f2	f1-d2	Animated, vigorous. Demands some flexibility. Has slow sus- tained middle section. Optional for bass. (Wolff, Music Press)
Orlando Vaghe pupille, no non piangete	a-d2	d1-bb1	In three sections: allegretto, larghetto on a basso ostinato, and a somewhat florid allegro. (Best, Boosey)
Ottone Ah! Tu non sai	c1-d2	e1-c2	Slow, graceful, delicate. (Breitkopf & Härtel)

TITLE	COMP.	TESS.	REMARKS

Ottone
Recitative:
Ben a ragion   d#1-f#2   Sustained. Optional for soprano.
Air: (g#2)   (Arr. by F. Bibb. (Schirmer)
Vieni o figlio

Ottone
Recitative:
Io son tradito;   c1-f2   eb1-db2   Animated, vigorous. In parts
Air: quite florid. (Franz, Kistner)
Un disprezzato
affetto

Ottone
Io sperai trovar   b-c#2   e1-b1   Vigorous, majestic. Demands
riposo   some flexibility. (Franz, Kistner)

Partenope
Furibondo spira il   b-e2   e1-d2   Rapid, florid, vigorous. Optional
vento   for baritone. (Franz, Kistner)

Poro
Che vive amante   c1-d2   e1-c2   Animated, graceful. (Ashdown)

Poro
È prezzo leggiero   a-d2   d1-c2   Spirited. Has florid passages.
                    (eb2)   (Prout, Ditson)

Poro
Son confusa   a-d2   d1-c2   Graceful and sustained.
pastorella   (Franz, Kistner)

Radamisto
Giacchè morir non   bb-eb2   eb1-c2   Animated, vigorous. Demands
posso   some flexibility. (Franz, Kistner)

Radamisto
Ombra cara   c1-e2   d1-b1   Very sustained. Optional for tenor,
                                   a minor third higher, though Prout
                                   collection lists it as for alto.
                                   (Prout, Ditson)

Radamisto
Perfido, di a   bb-eb2   eb-c2   Animated, vigorous. Has florid
quell'empio   passages. Optional for bass.
                                   (Wolff, Music Press)

Radamisto
Quando mai   db1-eb2   eb1-c2   Slow, sustained. Demands some
spietata   flexibility. (Best, Boosey)

Rinaldo
Recitative:
Armida, dispietata; f1-g2   a1-f2   Very sustained. Optional for dra-
Air: matic soprano. (Generally available)
Lascia ch'io pianga

TITLE	COMP.	TESS.	REMARKS
Rinaldo Cara sposa	b-e2	e1-c2	A very sustained andante; middle section is an allegro which demands facile articulation. (Prout, Ditson)
Rodelinda Con rauco mormorio	bb-d1	eb1-c2	Graceful, sustained. Optional for baritone. (Prout, Ditson)
Rodelinda Confusa si miri l'infida consorte	b-d2	e1-b1	Animated, vigorous. Has florid passages. (Franz, Kistner)
Rodelinda Recitative: Pompe vane di morte; Air: Dove sei?	b-e2	e1-b1	An extended recitative and a slow sustained air. (Best, Boosey; also Prout, Ditson, without recitative)
Rodelinda Scacciata dal suo nido	bb-eb2	eb1-c2	Animated. In parts quite florid. Optional for bass. (Wolff, Music Press)
Scipione Recitative: Nulla temer; Air: Generoso, chi sol brama	b-d#2	e1-b1	Recitative and a sustained air. Demands some flexibility. (Schirmer)
Scipione Ombra cara	c1-e2	d1-c2	Very sustained. (Dresel, Brockhaus)
Scipione Parto, fuggo	c1-db2	eb1-c2	Vigorous, animated. Demands some flexibility. (Dresel, Brockhaus)
Scipione Pensa, oh bella	a-d2	c1-c2	Graceful, rather florid. Optional for baritone. (Whittaker, Oxford)
Scipione Recitative: Quando timor costate; Air: Son pellegrino	b-d2	e1-c#2	Not fast. Has florid passages. (Breitkopf & Härtel)
Scipione Se mormora	b-e2	e1-c#2	Sustained. Demands some flexibility. (Dresel, Brockhaus)

TITLE	COMP.	TESS.	REMARKS
Scipione Tutta raccolta ancor	a-f2	e1-c2	Grave, sustained. Optional for bass. (Ashdown) Also now widely known as "Hear Me, Ye Winds and Waves" with an added recitative from Julius Caesar. (Boosey)
Serse Non so se sia la speme	d1-e2	e1-c2	Slow. Demands some flexibility. (Best, Boosey)
Siroe La sorte mia tiranna	c1-d2	eb1-c2	Not fast; vigorous. Has some florid passages. (Dresel, Brockhaus)
Siroe Recitative: Son stanco ingiusti numi; Air: Deggio morire, o stelle	bb-eb2	f1-db2	Slow, grave. (Breitkopf, Härtel)
Sosarme Si, si minaccia, e vinta	b-e2	e1-c2	Animated, quite forid. (Franz, Kistner)
Tamerlano Recitative: Che farò! Air: Bell'Asteria	a-d2	d1-b1	Sustained, slow. Demands some flexibility. (Breitkopf & Härtel)
Teseo Più non cerca libertà	c1-d2	f1-c2	Animated, graceful. Demands some flexibility. (Breitkopf & Härtel)
Teseo Ricordati, oh bella	b-d2	d1-b1	Not show. Demands some flexibility. Optional for baritone. (Whittaker, Oxford)
Tolomeo Recitative: Inumano fratel; Air: Stille amare	bb-db2	f1-c2	A dramatic recitative and a very sustained, grave air. (Franz, Kistner) Optional for bass. (Wolff, Music Press)

TENOR

TITLE	COMP.	TESS.	REMARKS
Alcina Semplicetto! A donna credi?	e-g1	g-f1	Spirited, graceful. Has florid passages. Prout, Ditson)

TITLE	COMP.	TESS.	REMARKS
Atalanta Dì ad Irene	d-ab	g-eb1	Spirited. Has florid passages. (Prout, Ditson)
Atalanta Lascia ch'io parta solo	e-bb1	g-f1	Sustained. Has florid passages. (Whittaker, Oxford)
Atalanta M'allontano	d-g1	f-eb1	Not fast. Has florid passages. (Whittaker, Oxford)
Atalanta S'è tuo piacer ch'io mora	e-a1	f#-d1	Sustained. (Whittaker, Oxford)
Deidamia Due bell'alme	f-bb1	a-f1	Sustained. (Best, Boosey)
Giulio Cesare Se pietà di me non senti	e1-a2	a1-f#2	Slow, sustained. Demands some flexibility. Optional for soprano. (Arr. by S. Endicott. R.D.Row,Inc.)
Radamisto Cara sposa, amato bene	e-f#1	f#-e1	Slow, sustained. (Best, Boosey)
Radamisto Ombra cara	eb-g1	f-d1	Very sustained. (Best Boosey) Optional for alto, a minor third lower, in Prout collection.(Ditson)
Rinaldo Vò far guerra	d-g1	f#-d1	Spirited, vigorous. Has florid passages. Optional for soprano. (Best, Boosey)

Rodelinda
Recitative:
  Fatto inferno;
Air:
  Pastorello d'un
  povero Armento
	d-g1	g-d1	Sustained, graceful.
			(Whittaker, Oxford)

Rodelinda Prigioniera, ho l'alma in pena	e-a1	g#-e1	Animated. Has florid passages. (Best, Boosey)
Rodrigo Allor che sorge astro lucente	d-g1	f#-d1	Sustained. Demands some flexi- bility. (Best, Boosey)
Scipione Dimmi,cara	eb-ab1	g-eb1 (H)	Slow and sustained. Optional for soprano. (Handel Renais- sance, Bote & Bock)

TITLE	COMP.	TESS.	REMARKS
Serse Recitative: Frondi tenere e belle Air: Ombra mai fu	c1-f2	f1-d2	Very slow and sustained. Optional for all voices except very light soprano. (Generally available)
Serse Quella che tutta fè	d-g1	g-d1	Slow, sustained. (Whittaker, Oxford)
Tamerlano A sui piedi padre	d-g1 (a#) (a1)	e-e1	Vigorous, sustained. (Whittaker, Oxford)
Tamerlano Recitative: E il soffrirete; Air: Empio, per farti guerra	c-a1	f-eb1	Animated, vigorous, dramatic. Has some florid passages. (Whittaker, Oxford)
Tamerlano Forte e lieto a morte andrei	d-a1	g-f#1	Not fast; vigorous. Has florid passages. (Whittaker, Oxford)
Tamerlano No, il tuo sdegno mi placo	c#-g1	a-e1	Vigorous. Has florid passages. (Whittaker, Oxford)
Tamerlano Recitative: Si figlia, io moro; Air: Figlia mia, non pianger, no	eb-ab1	g-eb1	Declamatory, dramatic. (Whittaker, Oxford)

BARITONE OR BASS

TITLE	COMP.	TESS.	REMARKS
Admeto Signor lo credi a me	A-e1	d-c1	Animated, vigorous. Has florid passages. (Best, Boosey)
Agrippina Io di Roma il Giove sono	G-e1	d-c1	Vigorous. Has florid passages. (Best, Boosey)
Agrippina Se ben nemica sorte; Col raggio placido	G-eb1	c-c1	Vigorous, spirited. Has florid passages. (Schirmer)
Amadigi Ah! Spietato!	B-d1	e-c1	Very sustained. Optional for alto. (Generally available)

TITLE	COMP.	TESS.	REMARKS

Amadigi
Recitative:
D'un sventurato
  amante;
Air:
  Pena tiranna
	c-eb1	e-c1	Sustained. Optional for alto.
			(Prout, Ditson)

Amadigi O rendetemi il mio bene	c#-eb1	f-d1	Slow, grave. Optional for alto. (Whittaker, Oxford)
Ariodante Al sen ti stringo e parto	G#-e1	c#-c#1	Sustained, graceful. (Prout, Ditson)
Arminio Vado a morir	d-eb1	eb-bb	Slow, sustained, grave. Optional for alto. (Whittaker, Oxford)
Berenice Recitative: Nò, soffrir non può Air: Il mio amore	c-e1		Sustained. Demands some flexi- bility. Optional for alto. (Wolff, Music Press)
Berenice Si tra i ceppi	B-d1	c-c1	Spirited. Has florid passages. Optional for alto. (Prout, Ditson)
Deidamia Nel riposo e nel contento	G-d1	Bb-c1	Slow, sustained, subdued. Demands some flexibility. (Prout, Ditson)
Ezio Nasce al bosco	A-f1 (F)	c-c1	Vigorous, stately. Has florid passages. (Ashdown)
Ezio Se un bell'ardire	G-e1	c-c1	Vigorous, spirited. Has florid passages. (Prout, Ditson)
Ezio Tutta raccolta ancor	d-f1	g-c1	Vigorous, short. (Bass Arias, Peters)
Floridante Alma mia	C#-e1	d-d1	Sustained, graceful. Optional for alto. (Wolff, Music Press)
Floridante Finchè lo strale	Bb-f1	eb-eb1	Vigorous, spirited. Has florid passages. (Best, Boosey)
Floridante Non lasciar	Bb-f1	eb-eb1	Spirited, vigorous. Has florid passages. (Prout, Ditson)

TITLE	COMP.	TESS.	REMARKS
Giulio Cesare Dal fulgor di questa spada	B♭-f1	d-d1	Spirited, vigorous, quite florid. (Prout, Ditson)
Muzio Scevola Volate piu dei venti	A-f1	f-d1	Animated, vigorous, with a slow sustained middle section. Demands some flexibility. Optional for alto. (Wolff, Music Press)
Orlando Lascia amor	A-e♭1	d-d1	Vigorous. Has florid passages. (Ashdown)
Orlando Sorge infausta	G-e♭1	e♭-c1	Vigorous, spirited. Has florid passages. (Prout, Ditson)
Ottone Del minacciar del vento	A-f1	d-d1	Vigorous, spirited. Has florid passages. (Best, Boosey)
Partenope Furibondo spira il vento	B-e1	e-d1	Rapid, florid, vigorous. Optional for alto. (Franz, Kistner)
Radamisto Perfido, di a quell'empio	B♭-e♭1	e♭-c1	Animated, vigorous. Has florid passages. Optional for alto. (Wolff, Music Press)
Riccardo Nel mondo e nell'abisso	G-f1	d♭-e♭1	Vigorous, animated. Has florid passages. (Best, Boosey)
Rinaldo Il tricerbero umiliato	A-f1	c-c1	Vigorous, spirited. Has florid passages. (Best, Boosey)
Rodelinda Con rauco mormorio	B♭-d1	d-b♭	A sustained siciliana. Optional for alto. (Whittaker, Oxford)
Rodelinda Confusa si miri	B-d1	c#-c#1	Animated, vigorous. Has florid passages. (Whittaker, Oxford)
Rodelinda Di cupido impiego	B♭-f1	e♭-e♭1	Spirited, vigorous. Has florid passages. (Whittaker, Oxford)
Rodelinda Scacciata dal suo nido	B♭-e♭1	e♭-c1	Animated. In parts quite florid. Optional for alto. (Wolff, Music Press)

TITLE	COMP.	TESS.	REMARKS
Scipione Pensa, oh bella	A-d1	c-c1	Graceful, rather florid. Optional for alto. (Whittaker, Oxford)
Scipione Tutta raccolta ancor	A-f1	e-c1	Grave, sustained. Optional for alto. (Ashdown) Also now widely known as "Hear Me, Ye Winds and Waves" with an added recitative from Julius Caesar. (Boosey)
Serse Del mio caro Bacco amabile	G-e1	e-c1	A spirited drinking song. Demands some flexibility. (Best, Boosey)
Siroe Gelido, in ogni vena	E-f#1	f#-c#1	Slow, sustained. (Best, Boosey)
Teseo Ricordati, oh bella	B-d1	d-b	Not slow. Demands some flexibility. Optional for alto. (Whittaker, Oxford)
Tolomeo Recitative: Inumano fratel; Air: Stille amare	Bb-db1	eb-c1	A dramatic recitative and a very sustained, grave air. Optional for alto. (Wolff, Music Press)

ENGLISH TEXT- SOPRANO

TITLE	COMP.	TESS.	REMARKS
Acis and Galatea As when the dove laments her love	d1-g2	a1-f2	Graceful, delicate. Demands some flexibility and good command of pp. (Generally available)
Acis and Galatea Would you gain the tender creature	e1-g2	a1-f2	Animated, graceful. Optional for tenor. (Prout, Ditson)
Alexander Balus Recitative: Calm thou my soul Air: Convey me to some peaceful shore	d#1-f#2	f#1-d#2	Sustained. (Prout, Ditson)
Alexander Balus Here amid the shady woods	d1-f2	f1-e2	Sustained, graceful. (Prout, Ditson)
Alexander Balus Subtle love, with fancy viewing	e1-f#2	f#1-e2	Not fast; quite florid. (Schirmer)

TITLE	COMP.	TESS.	REMARKS
Athalia Will God, whose mercies ever flow	f1-a♭2	g1-f2	Sustained. Demands some flexibility. (Prout, Ditson)
Esther Hallelujah	e1-a2	g1-f2	Rapid and very florid. The La Forge edition published by Fischer is transposed a whole tone higher for coloratura soprano.
Hercules My father! Ah, methinks I see	c1-f2	f1-e♭2	Slow, sustained, somewhat declamatory. Suitable for either dramatic or lyric soprano. (Prout, Ditson)
Hercules Recitative: O Hercules! Why art thou absent Air: The world when day's career is run	c1-g2	f#1-d2	Slow, sustained. Demands some flexibility. (Score generally available)
Jephtha Recitative: Deeper and deeper still Air: Waft her, angels, to the skies	d1-a2	g1-g2	A scena and a rather slow, somewhat florid air. Optional for tenor. (Prout, Ditson)
Jephtha Farewell ye limpid spring and floods	d#1-g2	f#1-e2	Sustained. (Prout, Ditson)
Jephtha The smiling dawn of happier days	c1-a♭2	g1-e♭2	Animated, graceful. Demands some flexibility. (Dresel, Brockhaus)
Joseph What's sweeter than a new-blown rose?	e1-a2	g1-f2	Animated, graceful. Has florid passages. (J. Church Co.)
Joshua Hark! 'Tis the linnet	d1-g2	f#1-e2	Animated, graceful, rather florid. (J. Church Co.)
Joshua O had I Jubal's lyre	d#1-f#2	g#1-e2	Spirited; quit florid. (Generally available)
Judas Maccabaeus Come, ever smiling liberty	e1-a2	a1-e2.	Graceful. Demands some flexibility. (Generally available)

Judas Maccabaeus
Recitative:

O let eternal honours crown his name Air: From mighty kings he took the spoil	d1-a2	g#1-e2	Florid; not fast. The middle section is spirited. (Generally available)

Judas Maccabaeus

Pious orgies	d1-g2	g1-e2	Slow, sustained. Originally written for bass (Bb-eb1; eb-c1) (Generally available)

Judas Maccabaeus

So shall the lute and harp awake	d1-g2	g1-eb2	Spirited, light, florid. (Generally available)

Judas Maccabaeus
Recitative:

To heaven's almighty King we kneel Air: O liberty! Thou choicest treasure	d#1-f#2	f#1-e2	Slow, sustained. Demands some flexibility. Optional for mezzo- soprano. Usually sung by tenor. (Generally available)

Judas Maccabaeus

Wise men, flatt'ring, may deceive you	d1-a2	f1-f2	Graceful, sustained. (Generally available)

L'Allegro

But o, sad virgin	d#1-a2	f#1-f#2	Slow, in parts very florid. Demands good command of short trills. Best for light voice. (Novello)

L'Allegro

Come, come, thou goddess fair and free	f1-bb2	a1-f2	Animated. Demands some flexi- bility. (Score, Novello)

L'Allegro

Hide me from day's garish eye	f1-ab2	ab1-f2	Slow, sustained, subdued. (Prout, Ditson)

L'Allegro

Let me wander not unseen	d1-g2	a1-f2	A graceful, sustained, subdued siciliana. Optional for tenor. Often sung together with "Or Let the Merry Bells Ring Round" from L'Allegro, which air is in the same key and follows nicely as a sort of contrasting movement. (Prout, Ditson)

TITLE	COMP.	TESS.	REMARKS
L'Allegro Oft on a plat of rising ground	f1-g2	a1-f2	Slow, sustained. Demands some flexibility. (Prout, Ditson)
L'Allegro Or let the merry bells ring round	d1-a2	a1-e2	Animated, spirited. Demands some flexibility. Optional for tenor. See: L'Allegro, "Let Me Wander Not Unseen." (Prout, Ditson)
L'Allegro Sweet bird that shun'st the noise of folly	d1-a2	a1-f#2	Slow, delicate. In parts very florid. Best for light voice. (Novello)
Messiah Come unto Him	f1-g2	a1-f2	Slow, sustained, rather subdued. (Generally available)
Messiah How beautiful are the feet of them	f1-g2	g1-eb2	Slow, sustained, delicate. (Score generally available)
Messiah I know that my Redeemer liveth	e1-g#2	g#-e2	Slow, very sustained. (Generally available)
Messiah If God be with us who can be against us	eb1-ab2	g1-f2	Slow, sustained. Has florid passages. (Generally available)
Messiah Rejoice greatly	eb1-ab2	g1-eb2	Animated, florid. The middle section is sustained. (Generally available)
Ode for St. Cecilia's Day The soft complaining flute	d1-g2	a#1-f#2	Sustained. Has florid passages. Best for light voice. (Schirmer)
Samson Let the bright Seraphim	d1-a2	a1-f#2	Rather vigorous, quite florid. (J. Church Co.)
Saul Fell rage and black despair	e1-a2	f#1-e2	Sustained. (Prout, Ditson)
Saul Oh God-like youth	f1-ab2	a1-f2	Sustained. Demands some flexibility. (J. Church Co.)

TITLE	COMP.	TESS.	REMARKS
Semele O sleep, why dost thou leave me	d#1-g#2	e1-e2	Slow and sustained. Demands some flexibility. Optional for tenor. (Generally available)
Solomon With thee th'unsheltered moor I'd tread	d1-g2	f#1-d2	Very sustained. (Prout, Ditson)
Susanna Ask if yon damask rose	d1-g2	g1-eb2	Animated, graceful. Optional for tenor. (Neitzel, Gems of Antiquity. J. Church Co.)
Susanna Recitative: I know the pangs Air: Beneath the cypress' gloomy shade	d1-f2	f1-d2	Recitative and a sustained, graceful siciliana. (Schirmer)
Susanna If guiltless blood be your intent	c#1-g2	f1-e2	Spirited. Has florid passages. Middle section is very sustained. Suitable for either dramatic or lyric voice. (Prout, Ditson)
Susanna Recitative: Lead me to some cool retreat Air: Crystal streams in murmurs flowing	d1-g2	f#1-d2	Not fast. Demands considerable flexibility. (Schirmer)
Theodora Recitative: O worse than death indeed Air: Angels ever bright and fair	d1-f2	f1-d2	Very sustained. Suitable for either dramatic or lyric soprano. (Generally available)

ALTO OR MEZZO-SOPRANO

TITLE	COMP.	TESS.	REMARKS
Athalia Recitative: O Judah, chosen seed Air: O Lord, whom we adore	bb-c2	d1-bb1	Slow, sustained. (Schirmer)

TITLE	COMP.	TESS.	REMARKS
Belshazzar			
Great God! who yet but darkly known	c1-d2	e1-c2	Very sustained. (Prout, Ditson)
Belschazzar			
O sacred oracles of truth	bb-eb2	c1-c2	Slow, rather sustained. (Prout, Ditson)
Belshazzar			
Recitative: Rejoice, my countrymen Air: Thus saith the Lord to Cyrus	a-d2	d1-b1	Recitative and a majestic arioso. Demands some flexibility. (Prout, Ditson)
Deborah			
All dangers disdaining	a-d2	d1-d2	Spirited, vigorous. Has florid passages. (Breitkopf & Härtel)
Deborah			
Impious mortal	bb-eb2	eb1-c2	Grave, slow. Demands some flexibility. (Dresel, Brockhaus)
Deborah			
In the battle fame pursuing	b-d2 (a)	d1-b1	Not fast; rather florid. (Prout, Ditson)
Hercules			
The smiling hours, a joyful train	bb-d2	d1-c2	Animated, graceful, florid. (Schirmer)
Israel in Egypt			
Thou shalt bring them in	b-e2	e1-b1	Sustained. Demands some flexibility. (Score generally available)
Jephtha			
Recitative: 'Twill be a painful separation Air: In gentle murmurs will I mourn	b-e2	e1-c2	Slow, sustained. Demands some flexibility. (J. Church Co.)
Joseph			
The peasant tastes the sweets of life	a-d2	e1-c2	A graceful, sustained pastorale. The middle section is florid and more robust. (J. Church Co.)
Joshua			
Recitative: But who is he? Air: Awful, pleasing being, say	b-e2	d#-b1	Sustained. Demands some flexibility. (Schirmer)

Joshua
Recitative:

| Now give the army breath | c1-f2 | e1-c2 | A spirited gavotte. Demands some flexibility. (Prout, Ditson) |

Air:
Heroes when with glory burning

Judas Maccabaeus

| Father of heaven | c1-eb2 | e1-c2 | Slow, sustained. Demands some flexibility. (Schirmer) |

Judas Maccabaeus
Recitative:

| To heaven's almighty King we kneel | d#1-f#2 | f#1-e2 | Slow, sustained. Demands some flexibility. Optional for soprano or tenor. (Generally available) |

Air:
O liberty, thou choicest treasure

Messiah
Recitative:

| Behold! A virgin shall conceive | a-b1 | d1-a1 | Spirited, vigorous. Has florid passages. (Generally available) |

Air:
O thou that tellest good tidings to Zion

Messiah

| He was despised | bb-bb1 | d1-ab1 | Slow, grave, sustained. Somewhat declamatory. (Generally available) |

Messiah
Recitative:

| Then shall the eyes of the blind be opened | c1-d2 | e1-c2 | Slow, sustained, rather subdued. (Generally available) |

Air:
He shall feed his flock

Samson

| Return, o God of hosts | bb-eb2 | eb1-c2 | Slow and sustained. (Schirmer) |

Samson

| Ye sons of Israel, now lament | bb-db2 | eb1-c2 | Slow, sustained. (Generally available) |

Saul

| Brave Jonathan his bow ne'er drew | b-e2 | d1-d2 | Very sustained. (Breitkopf & Härtel) |

TITLE	COMP.	TESS.	REMARKS
Saul			
O Lord, whose mercies numberless	bb-d2	c1-bb1	Slow, very sustained. (Prout, Ditson)
Semele			
Hence, Iris, hence away	bb-eb2	eb1-c2	Spirited, vigorous. Has florid passages. (Breitkopf & Härtel)
Semele			
Hymen, haste! Thy torch prepare	a-c2	bb-bb1	Spirited. Has florid passages. (Prout, Ditson)
Solomon			
What though I trace	c#1-e2	e1-c#2	Slow and sustained. Optional for heavy soprano voice. (Prout, Ditson)
Susanna Recitative: A love like mine Air: When first I saw my lovely maid	c1-e2	e1-d2	Recitative and sustained, graceful air. (Schirmer)
Susanna			
The parent bird in search of food	b-e2	e1-d2	Slow, graceful. Demands some flexibility. (Dresel, Brockhaus)
Theodora			
As with rosy steps the morn	c1-e2	e1-c2	Slow, rather sustained. Demands some flexibility. (Prout, Ditson)
Theodora			
Defend her, Heaven	d#1-f#2	e1-e2	Very sustained. Demands some flexibility. Optional for baritone. (Arr. by L. Lebell, Stainer & Bell)
Theodora			
Lord, to thee each night and day	c#1-e2	e1-d2	Slow, sustained. The middle section is animated and has florid passages. (Prout, Ditson)

TENOR

TITLE	COMP.	TESS.	REMARKS
Acis and Galatea			
Love in her eyes sits playing	f-ab1	bb-g1	Graceful, sustained. Demands some flexibility. (Prout, Ditson)
Acis and Galatea			
Would you gain the tender creature	e-g1	a-f1	Animated, graceful. Optional for soprano. (Prout, Ditson)
Athalia			
Gentle airs, melodious strains	e-f#1	g#-e1	Slow, quite florid. (Prout, Ditson)

TITLE	COMP.	TESS.	REMARKS

Chandos Anthem
Recitative:
  O come let us
   sing
Air:
  O come let us
  worship
	e-a1	g-f1	Slow, sustained. Demands flexibility. (Prout, Ditson)

Esther O beauteous queen	e-g1	a-f1	Sustained. (Prout, Ditson)

Esther
Recitative:
  O God, who from
  the suckling's
  mouth;
Air:
  Sing songs of
  praise
	f-a1	a-f1	Sustained. (Randegger, Novello)

Hercules From celestial seats descending	c-g1	f-f1	A sustained siciliana. (Schirmer)
Israel in Egypt The enemy said	d-a1	g-e1	Spirited; quite florid. (Randegger, Novello)

Jephtha
Recitative:
  Deeper and deeper
  still
Air:
  Waft her, angels,
  to the skies
	d-a1	g-g1	A scena and a rather slow, somewhat florid air. Optional for soprano. (Prout, Ditson)

Judas Maccabaeus
Recitative:
  Ambition! If e'er
  honour was thine
  aim
Air:
  No, unhallowed
  desire
	.f-g1	g-e1	Spirited. In parts quite florid. (Score generally available)

Judas Maccabaeus
Recitative:
  O Judas! May those
  noble views
Air:
  'Tis liberty
	e-g#1	e-e1	Not fast. Has florid passages. (Score generally available)

Judas Maccabaeus So rapid thy course is	B-g1	d-d1	Spirited. Demands considerable flexibility. (Score generally available)

TITLE	COMP. TESS.		REMARKS

Judas Maccabaeus
Sound an alarm   d-a1   a-e1   Spirited, vigorous. Has florid passages. (Generally available)

Judas Maccabaeus
Recitative:
  Thanks to my   d-g1   g-f1   Vigorous. Demands considerable
   brethren   flexibility. (Generally available)
Air:
  How vain is man
  who boasts

Judas Maccabaeus
Recitative:
  'Tis well, my   d-a1   a-f#1   Spirited, vigorous. Has florid
   friends   passages. (Score generally
Air:
  Call forth thy   available)
  powers

Judas Maccabaeus
Recitative:
  To heaven's   d#-f#1   f#-e1   Slow, sustained. Demands some
   almighty King   flexibility. Optional for soprano
   we kneel   or mezzo-soprano. (Generally
Air:
  O liberty thou   available)
  choicest treasure

Judas Maccabaeus
With honour let   d-a1   a-e1   Not fast. In parts quite florid.
  desert be crowned   (Score generally available)

L'Allegro
Come and trip it   eb-ab1   g-eb1   Graceful, animated. Has florid passages. An air with chorus, but can be sung as a solo. (Novello)

L'Allegro
Recitative:
  Hence, loathed   f#-g1   a-e1   Very animated, spirited. Demands
   melancholy   some flexibility. (Novello)
Air:
  Mirth, admit me
  of thy crew

L'Allegro
Let me wander not   d-g1   a-f1   A graceful, sustained, subdued
  unseen   siciliana. Often sung together with "Or Let the Merry Bells Ring Round" from L'Allegro, which air is in the same key and follows nicely as a sort of contrasting movement. Optional for soprano. (Prout, Ditson)

TITLE	COMP.	TESS.	REMARKS
L'Allegro Or let the merry bells ring round	d–a1	a–e1	Animated, spirited. Demands some flexibility. Optional for soprano. See L'Allegro, "Let Me Wander Not Unseen." (Prout, Ditson)

Messiah
Recitative:
  Comfort ye my people
Air:
  Every valley shall be exalted
	d#–g#1	e–e1	A sustained accompanied recitative (arioso) and a rather spirited, florid air. (Generally available)

Messiah
Recitative:
  He was cut off
Air:
  But Thou didst not leave his soul in hell
	e–g1	f#–e1	Slow, sustained. (Score generally available)

Messiah
Recitative:
  He that dwelleth
Air:
  Thou shalt break them
	e–a1	a–e1	Vigorous. Has florid passages. (Score generally available)

Messiah
Recitative:
  Thy rebuke hath broken his heart
Air:
  Behold and see
	d#–g1	g–e1	Slow, sustained. (Score generally available)

Occasional Oratorio Jehovah! To my words give ear	d#–f#1	f#–e1	Sustained. (Schirmer)
Occasional Oratorio Then will I Jehovah's praise	e–f#1	e–e1	Spirited. Demands some flexibility. (Prout, Ditson)

Samson
Recitative:
  My grief for this
Air:
  Why does the God of Israel sleep
	d–ab1	f–f1	Spirited. Has many florid passages. (Schirmer)

Samson Thus when the sun	d–g1	f–d1	Sustained. Demands some flexibility. (Prout, Ditson)

TITLE	COMP.	TESS.	REMARKS
Samson Total eclipse	e-g1	g-e1	Slow, somewhat declamatory. (Prout, Ditson)
Saul Sin not, o King	d-f1	f-eb1	Slow and sustained. (Prout, Ditson)
Semele O sleep, why dost thou leave me	d#-g#1	e-e1	Slow and sustained. Demands some flexibility. Optional for soprano. (Generally available)
Semele Where 'er you walk	f-g1	g-d1	Slow, sustained. Demands some flexibility. (Generally available)
Susanna Ask if yon damask rose	d-g1	g-eb1	Animated and graceful. Optional for soprano (Neitzel, Gems of Antiquity J. Church Co.)

Susanna
Recitative:
  Tyrannic love
Air:
  Ye verdant hills
	d-f#1	f#-d1	A scena and a sustained air. (Schirmer)

BASS OR BARITONE

TITLE	COMP.	TESS.	REMARKS

Acis and Galatea
Recitative:
  I rage, I melt, I burn
Air:
  O ruddier than the cherry
	F-f1	Bb-d1	Spirited, vigorous. Has florid passages. (Prout, Ditson)

Alexander's Feast Bacchus, ever fair and young	c-f1	f-d1	Very sustained. (Bass Arias, Peters)
Alexander's Feast Revenge, Timotheus cries	G-e1	d-d1	Animated, vigorous. Has florid passages. The slow middle section of this rather long da capo air, "Behold a Ghastly Band," as well as the allegro are sometimes sung separately. (Prout, Ditson)
Deborah Tears such as tender fathers shed	Bb-eb1	eb-bb	Slow, sustained. (Prout, Ditson)

TITLE	COMP.	TESS.	REMARKS
Dettinger Te Deum			
Vouchsafe, o Lord	d-d#1	e-c#1	Slow, majestic, very sustained. (Score, Peters)
Dettinger Te Deum			
When Thou tookest upon Thee	d#-e1	e-c#1	Slow, sustained. Demands some flexibility. (Score, Peters)
Esther			
Recitative:			
I'll hear no more	G-eb1	d-d1	Vigorous. (Randegger, Novello)
Air:			
Pluck root and branch			
Esther			
Turn not, o queen,, thy face away	c-d1	d-c1	Slow and sustained. (Prout, Ditson)
Jephtha			
Recitative:			
It must be so	A-eb1	c-c1	Spirited, vigorous. Demands
Air:			some flexibility. (Randegger,
Pour forth no more unheeded prayers			Novello)
Joshua			
See the raging flames arise	A-e1	d-d1	Spirited, vigorous. Has florid passages. (Prout, Ditson)
Joshua			
Shall I in Mamre's fertile plain	G-eb1	eb-c1	Slow, sustained. (Prout, Ditson)
Judas Maccabaeus			
Recitative:			
Be comforted	A-e1	c-c1	Spirited, vigorous, florid.
Air:			(Score, generally available)
The Lord worketh wonders			
Judas Maccabaeus			
Recitative:			
Enough! To heaven we leave the rest	G-e1	d-c1	Sustained. (Score generally available)
Air:			
With pious hearts			
Judas Maccabaeus			
Recitative:			
I feel the Deity within	B-e1	c-c1	Spirited, vigorous. Demands some flexibility. (Generally available)
Air:			
Arm, arm, ye brave			

TITLE	COMP.	TESS.	REMARKS
L'Allegro Come with native lustre shine	c-eb1	e-c1	Stately, sustained. Has some florid passages. (Score, Novello)

L'Allegro
Recitative:
  If I give thee
  honour due
Air:
  Mirth, admit me
  of thy crew
	Ab-eb1	eb-eb1	A spirited hunting song. Has
			florid passages in which the voice
			imitates the call of a horn.
			(Score, Novello)

Messiah
Recitative:
  Behold, I tell you
  a mystery
Air:
  The trumpet
  shall sound
	A-e1	f#-d1	Very vigorous. Has florid passages.
			(Generally available)

Messiah
Recitative:
  For behold,
  darkness shall
  cover the earth
Air:
  The people that
  walked in dark-
  ness
	G-e1
	(F#)
		B-b	Slow, somber. Demands some
			flexibility. (Generally available)

Messiah Thou art gone up on high	B-e1	e-d1	Vigorous, animated. Has florid passages. (Score generally avail- able)

Messiah
Recitative:
  Thus saith the Lord
Air:
  But who may abide
  the day of His
  coming
	G-e1	d-d1	The recitative is florid. The air
			consists of two repeated contrast-
			ing sections - a sustained larghetto
			and a vigorous presto which has
			florid passages. (Generally avail-
			able)

Messiah Why do the nations so furiously rage together	B-e1	c-c1	Vigorous, very animated. Has florid passages. (Generally available)

Occasional Oratorio
Recitative:
  Humbled with fear
Air:
  His sceptre is the
  rod of righteousness
	G#-e1	c#-d1	Vigorous, spirited. Has many
			florid passages. (Schirmer)

TITLE	COMP.	TESS.	REMARKS
The Passion My Father, look upon my anguish	Bb-eb1	d-c1	Slow and sustained. Has a recitative for middle section. (Schirmer)
Samson Honour and arms	G-eb1	Bb-d1	Vigorous, spirited. Has florid passages. (Generally available)
Samson How willing my paternal love	B-e1	B-b	Slow and sustained. Demands some flexibility. (Prout, Ditson)
Samson Thy glorious deeds inspired my tongue	Bb-f1	d-d1	Spirited. Has many florid passages. The middle section is slow and sustained. (Prout, Ditson)
Semele Leave me, loathsome light	A-d1	d-b	Very sustained. (Prout, Ditson)
The Triumph of Time and Truth False, destructive ways of pleasure	Ab-f1	eb-d1	Spirited, quite florid. (Prout, Ditson)
The Triumph of Time and Truth Loathsome urns, disclose your treasure	Bb-db1	c-c1	Sustained. (Prout, Ditson)
Theodora Defend her, heaven	d-f#1	e-e1	Very sustained. Demands some flexibility. Optional for alto or mezzo-soprano. (Arr. by L. Lebell, Stainer & Bell)

MISCELLANEOUS AIRS

TITLE	COMP.	TESS.	TYPE	REMARKS
Alcina Ah! Mio cor (Italian text)	c1-eb2	f1-d2	Not suitable for very light high voices	Grave, somewhat declamatory (Parisotti, Italian anthology, Schirmer)
Almira (Handel's first opera) Zweier Augen Majestät (German text)	Bb-eb1	eb-c1	Bass or alto	Sustained. Demands some flexibility. (Wolff, Music Press)
Atalanta Care selve (Italian text)	F#1-a2	A1-f#2 (H)	All voices, except bass	Slow, very sustained. Arr. by A. L. (Boosey)

TITLE	COMP.	TESS.	TYPE	REMARKS
Dank sei Dir, Herr (German text)	e1-g2	g1-e2 (H)	Not suitable for light, high voices	Very sustained, majestic. Of questionable authenticity. (Boston Music Co.)
Ottone Affanni del pensier (Italian text)	c1-eb2	f1-c2	Most suitable for medium or low voices	A sustained, graceful siciliana. (Parisotti, Italian Anthology Schirmer)
Pack clouds away	b-e2	e1-c#2 (L)	All voices	Animated, graceful. Demands some flexibility. (Arr. by Henry Coleman. Paterson, Glasgow)
La Passione (The Passion) Chi sprezzando il sommo bene (Italian text)	eb1-f2	eb1-eb2	Not suitable for light high voices	Slow and very sustained. Available only in Italian translation. (Parisotti, Ricordi)
Rinaldo Recitative: Armida dispietata; Air: Lascia ch'io pianga (Italian text)	f1-g2	a1-f2	All voices, except a very light soprano	Very sustained. (Prout, Ditson)
Serse Recitative: Frondi tenere e belle; Air: Ombra mai fu (Italian text)	c1-f2	f1-d2	All voices, except a very light soprano	Very slow and sustained. Originally written for tenor. (Generally available)
Silent worship	e1-f#2	a1-e2 (H)	Most suitable for men's voices	Spirited, graceful. An arrangement, by A. Somervell, of "Non lo diro col labbro," from Ptolemy, provided with an excellent English text. (Curwen)

CHRISTOPH WILLIBALD GLUCK
(1714-1787)

Gluck's revolt against the stultifying conventions of the eighteenth century Italian opera led him to abandon one of the salient features of the 18th century operatic form, the florid da capo aria, designed almost solely to provide the singer with a suitable vehicle for the exhibition of his virtuosity. This allowed Gluck to experiment widely with the form of his vocal soli. His airs are for the most part of compound form; that is, they consist of two or more movements manipulated freely in accordance with the demands of the text. However, his airs often conform to a strict dance form such as the minuet, gavotte or sarabande, which apparently did not seem dramatically restrictive to him.

In studying Gluck's airs one would do well to acquaint oneself thoroughly with the respective libretti of his operas and their classical archetypes. The easiest and most enjoyable way of doing the latter would be to consult a standard work on mythology, such as Bulfinch's Mythology (available in many inexpensive reprints) and to have a classical dictionary handy (such as the one published in the Everyman's Library series).

As a musical dramatist Gluck is perhaps nearer to Wagner than to any eighteenth century composer. One of the essential attainments he demands of the singer is the ability to recite texts with the proper dramatic inflection. As a sort of standard procedure that may be most helpful in studying his airs, the singer should endeavor to learn to recite their texts by memory before attempting to sing them. Through such a comparison of the spoken sentence with the musical phrase the singer may be able to realize more fully the extraordinary dramatic impact that underlies and directs the flow of Gluck's melodic line.

Stylistically Gluck's airs are quite complex. The eighteenth century conception of the classical drama differed greatly from ours, abounding in peculiar anachronisms which seem strangely out of place to the present-day actor and singer whose conception of the classical drama has been greatly influenced by the intervening one hundred fifty years of exhaustive historical and archaeological research. Yet notwithstanding his inadequate historical knowledge, Gluck, in his music, seems to have approximated the spirit of the classical drama better than anyone before or after him.

Gluck's important soprano airs are for the most part best suited to rather heavy dramatic voices, and if transposed a tone lower than the original are excellently suited to the high dramatic mezzo-soprano type of voice. His smaller dance-form airs are, however, very suitable for light soprano voices. In his mature period Gluck seems to have written no airs designed specifically for coloratura soprano.

His alto and mezzo-soprano airs are few, the most famous of these being of course the Orfeo airs. Gevaert in his splendid Répertoire Classique du Chant Français has transposed several dramatic soprano airs to suit the lower voices, a perfectly justified and sensible procedure in the opinion of this writer.

Gluck's tenor and baritone airs often seem to lie too high for present-day singers. Since there are indications that the pitch in Gluck's time was considerably lower than the present 440-442 a, it seems only sensible to recommend the transposition of these airs in preference to the comparative oblivion to which they are now subject, due no doubt largely to their forbiddingly high tessitura.

Editions: Orfeo, Alceste, Iphigénie en Tauride, Iphigénie en Aulide, and Armide are generally available in piano scores.

Excerpted airs from these and other operas can be found in most authentic form in Gevaert, Répertoire Classique du Chant Français, Lemoine, Paris; and the Breitkopf & Härtel collections of arias for soprano, alto, tenor and bass. A few celebrated airs are generally available in a variety of editions. In the following list the name Gevaert indicates Répertoire Classique du Chant, edited by Gevaert, published by Lemoine.

FRENCH TEXT
SOPRANO

TITLE	COMP.	TESS.	TYPE	REMARKS
Adieu! Conservez dans votre âme (Iphigénie en Aulide)	d1-ab2	f1-eb2	Soprano	Slow, sustained, short. Vocally not too taxing. (Score, Novello)
Ah! Si la liberté (Armide)	e1-g2	g1-e2	Dramatic soprano (lyric soprano)	Sustained. In the Gevaert edition, this aria is transposed a whole tone lower.
Amour, sors pour jamais (Armide)	f1-g2	g#1-eb2	Dramatic soprano (mezzo-soprano)	Animated, vigorous. (Score, Peters)
Armez vous d'un noble courage (Iphigénie en Aulide)	d1-a2	f1-d2	Dramatic soprano (mezzo-soprano)	Animated, vigorous, dramatic. (Score, Novello)
Recitative: Cette nuit, j'ai revu le palais de mon père Air: O toi, qui prolongeas mes jours (Iphigénie en Tauride)	f1-a2	a1-f#2	Dramatic soprano (lyric soprano)	A very extended, interpretatively taxing scena and a sustained air. (Gevaert)
Recitative: Dérobez-moi Air: Ah! Malgré moi (Alceste)	eb1-a2	g1-f2	Dramatic soprano	Recitative, andante, allegro. Vigorous, majestic, dramatic. (Spicker, Operatic Anthology. Schirmer)
Recitative: Dieux puissants, que j'atteste! Air: Jupiter, lance ta foudre (Iphigénie en Aulide)	d1-g2	g1-e2	Dramatic soprano or mezzo-soprano	A very dramatic scena and an animated vigorous dramatic air. (Score, Novello)

TITLE	COMP.	TESS.	TYPE	REMARKS
Divinités du Styx (Alceste)	c1-bb2	f1-f2	Dramatic soprano	A majestic, vigorous compound air. Sometimes sung by mezzo-soprani transposed a third lower. (Generally available)
Recitative: Enfin il est en ma puissance Air: Venez, secondez mes désirs (Armide)	d1-a2 (b2)	g1-f#2	Dramatic soprano	A dramatic scena, a graceful andantino, and a sustained, rather vigorous andante. (Gevaert)
Recitative: Grands dieux soutenez mon courage Air: Ah, divinités implacables (Alceste)	d1-a2	f1-f2	Dramatic soprano	A very dramatic scena and a sustained air. (Gevaert)
Recitative: Hélas, c'est mon coeur que je crains! Air: De mes plus doux regards (Armide)	f1-g2	a1-f2	Soprano	Short, sustained. (Score, Peters)
Recitative: Hélas! dans ce malheur extrême Air: Grands dieux! Du destin qui m'accable (Alceste)	e1-bb2	f1-f2	Dramatic soprano (lyric soprano)	An andante, allegro air. Majestic, dramatic. (Reprinted by Schirmer from the Gevaert Edition)
Heureux guerriers, volez à la victoire (Iphigénie en Aulide)	g1-a2	a1-e2	Lyric soprano (dramatic soprano)	Graceful, minuetlike air. (Score, Novello)
Il faut de mon destin subir la loi (Iphigénie en Aulide)	bb-g2	f1-eb2	Soprano or mezzo-soprano	Short, sustained. (Score, Novello)
Recitative: Il m'aime? quel amour! Air: Venez, venez, haine implacable (Armide)	f1-a2	a1-f2	Dramatic soprano	Scena and a vigorous dramatic air. (Score, Peters)
Iphigénie, hélas! vous a trop fait connaître (Iphigénie en Aulide)	f#1-f#2	g#1-d2	Soprano	Short, sustained. Vocally not taxing. (Score, Novello)

TITLE	COMP.	TESS.	TYPE	REMARKS
Jamais dans ces beaux lieux (Armide)	f1-f2	a1-f2	Soprano	Short, graceful, sustained. (Score, Peters)
Recitative: Je cède à vos désirs Air: D'une image hélas! trop chérie (Iphigénie en Tauride)	f1-g2	g1-eb2	Soprano	Recitative and a sustained, graceful air. (Score, Novello)
Jeunes coeurs! tout vous est favorable (Armide)	d1-e2	g1-d2	Soprano (mezzo-soprano)	Short, graceful. Vocally not taxing. (Score, Peters)
La chaîne de l'Hymen m'étonne (Armide)	e1-f#2	g#1-e2	Soprano	Sustained, graceful. Vocally not taxing. (Score, Peters)
Recitative: L'ai-je bien entendu? Air: Hélas! mon coeur sensible et tendre (Iphigénie en Aulide)	f1-g2	g1-f2	Dramatic soprano	Recitative and a dramatic, compound air. (Gevaert)
Recitative: Les dieux ont entendu Air: Je n'ai jamais chéri la vie (Alceste)	c#1-a2	a1-e2	Dramatic soprano (lyric soprano)	Sustained. (Gevaert)
Le perfide Renaud me fuit (Armide)	g1-a2	a1-f2	Dramatic soprano	A very dramatic scena. (Score, Peters)
Les voeux dont ce peuple (Iphigénie en Aulide)	d1-ab2	g1-e2	Soprano	Short, sustained, vocally not taxing. (Gevaert)
Recitative: Non, cet affreux devoir Air: Je t'implore et je tremble (Iphigénie en Tauride)	d#1-a2	a1-e2	Dramatic soprano (lyric soprano)	Animated, dramatic, majestic. (Score, Novello)
O malheureuse Iphigénie (Iphigénie en Tauride)	b-a2	g1-g2	Dramatic soprano	Very sustained, majestic. Not slow. (Gevaert)
On s'étonnerait moins (Armide)	f#1-a2	a1-f#2	Light soprano	Graceful, delicate. (Score, Peters)
Recitative: Où suis-je? Air: Non! ce n'est pas un sacrifice (Alceste)	f#1-a2	a1-f#2	Dramatic soprano (lyric soprano)	A scena and a sustained, majestic air. (Gevaert)

TITLE	COMP. TESS.	TYPE	REMARKS

TITLE	COMP.	TESS.	TYPE	REMARKS
Que j'aime à voir (Iphigénie·en Aulide)	g1-e2		Soprano or mezzo-soprano	Very short, sustained. Vocally not taxing. (Gevaert)
Recitative: Seigneur! j'embrasse vos genoux Air: Par son père cruel à la mort condamnée (Iphigénie en Aulide)	e1-g2	f#1-d2	Dramatic soprano (mezzo-soprano	Recitative and a sustained air. (Score, Novello)
Si je dois m'engager (Armide)	f#1-g2	a1-e2	Soprano	Short, sustained, majestic. (Score, Peters)
Son front est couronne (Iphigénie en Aulide)	d1-f#2	g#1-d2	Soprano	Very short, sustained, vocally not taxing. (Score, Novello)
Vivez, vivez pour Oreste (Iphigénie en Aulide)	e1-e2	g1-d2	Soprano	Short, sustained. Vocally not taxing. (Gevaert)
Voici la charmante retraite (Armide)	f1-f2	g1-d2	Soprano	Short, graceful. Vocally not taxing. (Score, Peters)
Recitative: Vous essayez en vain de bannir mes alarmes Air: Par la crainte et par l'espérance (Iphigénie en Aulide)	d1-a2	f1-f2	Dramatic soprano (lyric soprano)	Recitative and a vigorous, sustained dramatic air. (Score, Novello)
Vous troublez-vous (Armide)	g1-ab2	bb1-f2	Soprano	Short, sustained, graceful. (Score, Peters)

MEZZO-SOPRANO OR ALTO

TITLE	COMP.	TESS.	TYPE	REMARKS
Amour, sors pour jamais (Armide)	f1-g2	g#1-eb2	Mezzo-soprano or alto	Animated, vigorous. (Score, Peters)
Armez-vous d'un noble courage (Iphigénie en Aulide)	bb-g2	eb1-eb2	Mezzo-soprano or alto	Animated, vigorous, dramatic. Transposed into this key in the Gevaert edition.
Recitative: Dieux puissants que j'atteste! Air: Jupiter, lance ta foudre (Iphigénie en Aulide)	d1-g2	g1-e2	Mezzo-soprano or dramatic soprano	A very dramatic scena and an animated, vigorous dramatic air. (Gevaert)
Il faut de mon destin subir la loi (Iphigénie en Aulide)	bb-g2	f1-eb2	Mezzo-soprano or soprano	Short, sustained. (Score, Novello)

TITLE	COMP.	TESS.	TYPE	REMARKS
Je n'ai jamais chéri la vie (Alceste)	a-f2	d1-d2	Alto	Sustained, grave. Originally written for soprano. This aria is transposed into this key in the Gevaert edition.
Jeunes coeurs! tout vous est favorable (Armide)	d1-e2	g1-d2	Mezzo-soprano or soprano	Short, graceful. Vocally not taxing. (Score, Peters)
Que j'aime à voir (Iphigénie en Aulide)	g1-e2		Mezzo-soprano or soprano	Very short, sustained. Vocally not taxing. (Score, Novello)
Recitative: Seigneur! J'embrasse vos genoux Air: Par son père cruel, à la mort condamnée (Iphigénie en Aulide)	c1-eb2	d1-d2	Mezzo-soprano or alto	Recitative and a sustained air. Originally written for soprano transposed into this key in the Gevaert edition.

TENOR

Since practically all of the Gluck tenor airs listed below are most suitable for rather heavy type of voice, it seemed best to dispense with the Type of Voice column here.

TITLE	COMP.	TESS.	REMARKS
Ah, mon ami (Iphigénie en Tauride)	a-ab1	bb-eb1	Animated. The vocal line sustained. (Score, Novello)
Allez éloignez-vous de moi (Armide)	g-a1	b-g1	Sustained, short. Score, Peters)
De l'amitié touchante (Echo et Narcisse)	f-ab1	ab-f1	Scena, sustained air, and closing scena. (Gevaert)
Recitative: Divinité des eaux Air: Je ne puis m'ouvrir ta froide demeure (Echo et Narcisse)	f#-g1	g#f1	An extended scena and a sustained air. (Gevaert)
Divinité des grandes âmes (Iphigénie en Tauride)	g-a1	b-e1	Animated, majestic. (Score, Novello)
Recitative: Eh bien! obéissez, barbares! Air: Calchas, d'un trait mortel blessé (Iphigénie en Aulide)	g#-b1	b-g1	Animated, vigorous, dramatic. (Score, Novello)

TITLE	COMP.	TESS.	TYPE	REMARKS
Recitative:				
O moment délicieux	e-a1	a-e1		Animated. (Score, Peters)
Air:				
Bannis la crainte et les alarmes (Alceste)				
Par ma voix (Echo et Narcisse)	f-g1	g-eb1		Recitative and sustained, dramatic air with a florid closing passage. (Gevaert)
Plus j'observe ces lieux (Armide)	g-a1	b-f#1		Sustained. The tessitura is very high. (Score, Peters)
Recitative:				
Quel Langage accablant	f#-a1	a-e1		Sustained, graceful. (Score, Novello)
Air:				
Unis dès la plus tendre enfance (Iphigénie en Tauride)				
Recitative:				
S'il était vrai	g#-b1	a-f1		Recitative and a sustained, majestic air. (Score, Novello)
Air:				
Cruelle, non, jamais votre insensible coeur (Iphigénie en Aulide)				
Recitative:				
Tu veux mourir	e-a1	a-f1		A scena and a sustained, dramatic air with a vigorous, rapid middle section. (Score, Peters)
Air:				
Barbare, non, sans toi je ne puis vivre (Alceste)				
Viens! Du froid de la mort (Echo et Narcisse)	f-ab1	g-eb1		Recitative and sustained arioso. Demands some flexibility. (Gevaert)
Recitative:				
Vivre sans toi, moi, vivre sans Alceste?	f-a1	ab-f1		Recitative and sustained dramatic air. (Score, Peters)
Air:				
Alceste, au nom des Dieux, sois sensible (Alceste)				

BARITONE

TITLE	COMP.	TESS.	TYPE	REMARKS
Recitative:				
Armide, que le sang qui m'unit avec vous	c-eb1	f-d1	Baritone	Recitative, andante, allegro. (Gevaert)
Air:				
Je vois de près la mort (Armide)				

TITLE	COMP.	TESS.	TYPE	REMARKS
Recitative:				
Au pouvoir de la mort je saurai la ravir	d#-e1	e-d1	Baritone (bass-baritone)	Animated, vigorous. (Score, Peters)
Air:				
C'est en vain que l'enfer compte sur sa victime (Alceste)				
Caron t'appelle, entends sa voix! (Alceste)	c#-e1 (f#1)	e-d1	Bass (bass-baritone)	Animated, very vigorous. (Score, Peters)
C'est un torrent (Les pélerins de la Mecque)	c#-f1	f-d1	Baritone	A spirited allegro and a graceful andante. (Gevaert)
Recitative:				
Dans ta fureur enfin j'ai lu mon triomphe!	B-e1	e-c#1	Bass-baritone or bass	Recitative and a sustained air. The Gevaert edition does not have the original Italian text. (Gevaert)
Air:				
Et cet instant suprême (Ezio)				
Recitative:				
Diane impitoyable	c-e1	f#-d1	Baritone	A sustained, majestic scena and a compound air, ending in a recitative. (Gevaert)
Air:				
Brillant auteur de la lumière				
Iphigénie en aulide)				
Recitative:				
Dieux! protecteurs de ces affreux rivages	d-f#1	a-d1	Baritone	A short scena and a sustained majestic air. (Score, Novello)
Air:				
Le calme rentre dans mon coeur (Iphigénie en Tauride)				
Hector et les Troyens (Iphigénie en Aulide)	B-e1	e-e1	Baritone	Short, vigorous. (Score, Novello)
Recitative:				
Je t'ai donné la mort	f#-f#1	a-e1	Baritone	Animated, vigorous, dramatic. (Score, Novello)
Air:				
Dieux! qui me poursuivez (Iphigénie en Tauride)				
Recitative:				
Le ciel par d'éclatants miracles	e#-g1	a-e1	High baritone	Recitative and a sustained, dramatic air. Transposed a third lower in the Gevaert edition; also reprinted in the Spicker, Operatic
Air:				
De noirs pressentiments				

TITLE	COMP.	TESS.	TYPE	REMARKS
Cont'd				
De noirs pressentiments (Iphigénie en Tauride)				Anthology, Bass. (Schirmer)
Peuvent-ils ordonner qu'un père (Iphigénie en Aulide)	d-f1	g-d1	Baritone	Sustained, vigorous, dramatic. (Gevaert)
Pour vous, quand il vous plaît (Armide)	e-f1	g#-e1	Baritone	Animated, rather vigorous. (Score, Peters)
Recitative: Tes destins sont remplis! Air: Déjà la mort s'apprête (Alceste)	c-f1	eb-eb1	Baritone (bass-baritone)	Majestic, sustained, vigorous. (Score, Peters)
Recitative: Tu décides son sort Air: O toi, l'objet le plus aimable (Iphigénie en Aulide)	c-f#1	e-d1	Baritone	A very long scena (which could be omitted if so desired) and a majestic, dramatic compound air. (Gevaert)

ITALIAN TEXT

TITLE	COMP.	TESS.	TYPE	REMARKS
Recitative: Ahimè! Dove trascorsi Air: Che farò senza Euridice (Orfeo)	b-f2	e1-c2	Alto	A dramatic recitative and a very sustained air. (Generally available)
An, non chiamarmi ingrato (Telemacco)	eb-ab1	ab-eb1	Tenor (or soprano)	Sustained, graceful. (Krehbiel, Songs from the Operas. Ditson)
Ah, ritorna (Il trionfo di Clelia)	d1-b2	g1-f2	Soprano	A graceful minuet. Demands some flexibility. (Landshoff, Alte Meister, Peters)
Che puro ciel! (Orfeo)	c1-e2	d1-c2	Alto	A sustained "quasi recitative"; somewhat declamatory. (Score generally available)
Chiamo il mio ben cosî (Orfeo)	a-eb2	c1-c2	Alto	A short, sustained air which is repeated three times with two interpolated recitatives. (Score generally available)
Deh placatevi con me (Orfeo)	bb-eb2	eb1-c2	Alto	Air with chorus. Sustained, rather vigorous. (Score generally available)

TITLE	COMP.	TESS.	TYPE	REMARKS
Di questa cetra (Parnasso Confuso)	d1-g2	g1-d2	Soprano	Graceful. Demands lightness of tone. (Gevaert)
È quest' asilo ameno e grato (Orfeo)	e1-a2	g1-f2	Soprano	A graceful, delicate sustained air with chorus. (Score generally available)
Recitative: Ferma crudele, ferma Air: Prenditi, il figlio (Le Donne Chinese)	a#-d2 (f#2)	d1-c#2	Alto	Vigorous, dramatic, spirited. (Breitkopf & Härtel, Alt Arien, volume II)
Gli squardi trattieni (Orfeo)	d1-g2	g1-e2	Soprano	Graceful. (Score generally available)
Numi offesi (Aristeo)	e1-d2 (a)	e1-c2	Alto	Very sustained, slow. (Breitkopf & Härtel, Alt Arien, vol. II)
O del mio dolce ardor (Elena e Paride)	b-f#2	f#1-d2	All voices	Very sustained. (Parisotti, Italian Anthology. Schirmer) Originally written for soprano.
Oscura il sol le stelle (Semiramide)	g-c2	c1-c2	Alto	Majestic, sustained. (Breitkopf & Härtel, Alt Arien, vol. II)
Recitative: Qual vita è questa mai Air: Che fiero momento, che barbara sorte (Orfeo)	d#1-ab2	g1-eb2	Dramatic soprano (lyric soprano)	Recitative and a vigorous, animated, dramatic air.
Spiagge amate (Elena e Paride)	d1-g2	f1-eb2	All voices	Very sustained. (Ricordi) Originally written for soprano.
Tradita, sprezzata, che piango? (Semiramide)	bb-eb2	d1-d2	Alto	Vigorous, dramatic. (Breitkopf & Härtel, Alt Arien, vol. II)
Vieni, che poi sereno (Semiramide)	b-e2	g1-d2	All voices	A graceful minuet. Originally written for alto. (Krehbiel, Songs from the Operas. Ditson) A transposed edition, a minor third higher, for soprano or tenor. (Schirmer)

FRANZ JOSEPH HAYDN
(1732-1809)

Most of Haydn's best vocal music is to be found in his oratorios. His songs, as those of Mozart, charming and pleasant as they are, can hardly be called in any way representative of his style of writing for the voice. The canzonettas to English texts, among them the delightful "Mermaid's song," as well as the more widely known "My mother bids me bind my hair," "The spirit's song," and "She never told her love" are perhaps the most representative and rewarding among his few songs.

Editions: Peters
Augener
Novello
Numerous reprints of single songs by many American publishers

TITLE	COMP.	TESS.	TYPE	REMARKS
Eine sehr gewöhn-liche Geschichte	d1-e2	g1-d2	All voices	Light and humorous. Demands facile articulation.
Der erste Kuss	d1-g2	g1-eb2	Not too suitable for very low voices	Graceful, sustained. Demands some flexibility.
Jeder meint, der Gegenstand	e1-f2	f1-d2	All voices	Light, delicate
Liebes Mädchen, hör mir zu	e1-e2	f#1-c#2	Most suitable for men's voices	Delicate.
Lob der Faulheit	c1-f#2	g1-e2	All voices	A mock-serious hymn in praise of laziness.
My mother bids me bind my hair	e1-e2	a1-e2	Women's voices	Light, delicate.
Sailor's song	e-f#1	a-e1	Men's voices	A spirited, rollicking song extolling the British Navy.
She never told her love	d1-f2	ab1-eb2	All voices except a very light soprano	Slow and grave.
O tuneful voice	b-g2	f1-eb2	All voices	A beautiful cantilena, unfortunately marred by poor English prosody. The German translation may be preferable.
Pensi a me (Italian text)	c#1-g2	g1-e2	All voices	A slow arietta
The mermaid's song	c1-g2	e1-d2	Soprano or mezzo-soprano	Light, spirited. Demands some flexibility and an accomplished pianist.
The spirit's song	b-gb2	f1-db2	Medium or low voices	Slow and somber.

TITLE	COMP.	TESS.	TYPE	REMARKS
The wanderer	d1-eb2	f1-d2	Medium or low voices	Slow and sustained.
Un tetto umil (Italian text)	d#1-g#2	e1-e2	All voices	A delicate, sustained arietta.

AIRS FROM THE ORATORIOS
(The scores of "The Creation" and "The Seasons" are generally available)

TITLE	COMP.	TESS.	TYPE	REMARKS
Recitative: And God created man Air: In native worth (The Creation)	f#-a1	g-e1	Tenor	Sustained, graceful. Demands some flexibility.
Recitative: And God said: Let the earth bring forth grass Air: With Verdure clad (The Creation)	e1-bb2	a1-f2	Soprano	Graceful. Has florid passages.
Recitative: And God said: Let the earth bring forth the living creature Air: Now heav'n in fullest glory shone (The Creation)	F-d1	d-c#1	Bass	An extended recitative, and a vigorous, majestic air. Demands some flexibility.
Recitative: And God said: Let the waters Air: Rolling and foaming billows (The Creation)	G-f1	d-d1	Bass or baritone	Rapid, vigorous, demands some flexibility. The vocal line is sustained. The final section is subdued.
Recitative: And God said: Let the waters Air: On mighty pens (The Creation)	e1-bb2	g1-f2	Soprano	Graceful. Has florid passages.
Air: The marvelous work behold amazed (The Creation)	c1-c3	g1-f2	Soprano	A spirited solo with choral accompaniment. May be used as a solo excerpt. Demands some flexibility.
Recitative: A crystal pavement lies the lake Air: The trav'ler stands perplexed (The Seasons)	d-b1	e-e1	Tenor	Fast. Has some florid passages.

TITLE	COMP.	TESS.	TYPE	REMARKS
Recitative: At last the boun- teous sun Air: With joy the impat- ient husbandman (The Seasons)	B#-e1	c-c1	Bass	Graceful. Demands some flexibility.
From out the fold the shepherd drives (The Seasons)	Bb-f1	f-c1	Bass	Sustained, graceful. Has florid passages.
Light and life de- jected languish (The Seasons)	c1-f2	e1-c2	Soprano	A short, slow and sustain-ed air. Also suitable for mezzo-soprano or alto.
Recitative: Lo! where the plenteous harvest wav'd Air: Behold, along the dewy grass (The Seasons)	G-f1	c-d1	Bass	Vigorous, spirited. Has some florid passages and some very wide leaps.
Recitative: O welcome now Air: O, how pleasing to the senses (The Seasons)	bb-bb2	a1-f2	Soprano	An extended recitative and an andante, allegro air. Demands consider-able flexibility.
Recitative: 'Tis noon, and now intense the sun Air: Distressful nature fainting sinks (The Seasons)	b#-f#1	e-e1	Tenor	Slow and sustained. Not suitable for light high voices.

OPERATIC AIRS
Der Apotheker
(German text. Score published by Gutmann)

TITLE	COMP.	TESS.	TYPE	REMARKS
Diese Püppchen	G#-d1	e-b	Bass	A rapid buffo air. De-mands extremely facile articulation.
Es Kam ein Pascha aus Türkenland	d1-g#2	e1-e2	Mezzo-so-prano or soprano	Graceful, comic nar-rative. Demands con-siderable flexibility.
Sitzt Einem hier im Kopf das Weh'	d#-a1	e-e1	Tenor	Spirited comic air. Has florid passages.
Wie Schleier seh' ich's nieder- schweben	c-bb2	f1-e2	Soprano	Sustained.
Wo Liebesgötter lachten	b-g2	f1-e2	Mezzo-so-prano or soprano	Rapid comic air. De-mands considerable flexibility and facile articulation

Orfeo
(Italian Text)

TITLE	COMP.	TESS.	TYPE	REMARKS
Recitative:				
Dov'è l'amato bene	d1-g♭2 (a♭2)	e♭1-e♭2	Lyric soprano (Dramatic soprano)	Recitative and a sustained aria. Vocally not taxing. (Schirmer, Operatic Anthology)
Air: Del mio core				
Il pensier sta negli oggetti	B-e1	e-c♯1	Baritone	Sustained. (Schirmer, Operatic Anthology)

WOLFGANG AMADEUS MOZART
(1756-1791)

OPERATIC AIRS:
The operatic airs of Mozart often follow a pattern of a recitative (sometimes so extended as to reach the proportions of a dramatic "scena"), a sustained cantabile movement and a more or less florid, spirited allegro. For the most part Mozart avoids the older da capo aria form. Yet perhaps fully as often he abandons the andante, allegro form in favor of a more unified single-movement song form, as for instance in the "Porgi Amor" (Nozze di Figaro) or "Finche han dal vino" (Don Giovanni).

Vocally, Mozart arias, although magnificently written for the voice, are for the most part quite difficult, demanding considerable flexibility, excellent breath control and a good command of dynamics. Sometimes they demand a voice possessing a very extensive range, but only in a few instances does Mozart demand a voice of unusual power.

His concert arias are extraordinarily difficult display pieces. Seldom performed now because of their difficulty, they would seem to be of considerable value to any virtuoso vocalist's repertoire, especially to the repertoire of a coloratura soprano. In the opinion of this writer, the tenor concert arias, as well as the tenor airs from Idomeneo and La Clemenza di Tito, can now be performed effectively by soprani, or in some instances by high mezzo-soprani, since these two works have not been performed as stage works for nearly a hundred years, and the association between the air and the character of the drama is now, for all practical purposes, forgotten.

In studying Mozart's airs one should bear in mind the fact that, as a musical dramatist, Mozart is unique and perhaps unequaled. One can safely say that Mozart never wrote a piece of vocal music in which the text and the music were not in complete and miraculous accord; even his use of florid passages, which to many a present-day singer may imply a nondramatic approach to the problem of setting words to music, is emotionally significant, naturally within the stylistic frame of his time.

To appreciate the dramatic expressiveness of a florid air of Mozart, one should compare it with a florid air of a composer like Galuppi, for instance, who, like most composers of the period, wrote delightful florid passages without being able to endow them with much, if any, emotional significance.

A singer who is trying to learn a Mozart air would do well to study the libretto of the entire opera - a procedure which of course is always helpful, but which would add little to his appreciation of an air by composers like Cesti, Bononcini, or even Händel in some instances.

The soprano airs of Mozart are, generally speaking, written for the following types of voices: the rather heavy lyric soprano (Spinto), the light soubrette soprano and the coloratura soprano. In some instances (the Queen of the Night airs in Zauberflöte, some Constanza airs in the Entführung, and the Fiordiligi airs in Cosî fan Tutte, as well as in his concert arias) Mozart writes for a voice of an unusually wide range and power; these airs are not recommended for the student, as the problems of both range and volume could hardly be mastered if the instrument itself is not adequate to the demands made upon it.

Mozart wrote hardly any airs for alto and only a few for mezzo-soprano. Most of his mezzo-soprano airs can easily be sung by heavy dramatic soprano voices, for which his soprano airs may be too high in tessitura.

His tenor airs are, practically without exception, written for a rather light lyric voice, and demand considerable facility in florid work. The tessitura is for the most part rather high and would seem to be too taxing for a heavy voice.

There are not many airs of Mozart suitable for high baritone; most of his baritone airs are best suited for heavier bass-baritone voices. His bass airs, with the exception of the two Sarastro airs in Zauberflöte and the Concert Aria, are almost always of the buffo character.

TITLE	COMP.	TESS.	TYPE	REMARKS

OPERATIC AIRS - SOPRANO

TITLE	COMP.	TESS.	TYPE	REMARKS
Così fan Tutte E amore un ladron-cello	f1-g2	bb1-f2	Soprano	Light and rapid. Gently humorous. Demands some flexibility and facile articulation. (Score generally available)
Così fan Tutte Recitative: Ei parte, senti, ah no... Air: Per pietà ben mio perdona	a-b2	e1-e2	Dramatic soprano (lyric soprano)	Recitative, andante, allegro. Has florid passages. Demands a voice of very extensive range, possessing a well-developed lower register. (Score generally available)
Così fan Tutte In uomini, in soldati	c1-a2	f1-f2	Soprano	Animated, light. Gently humorous. Demands facile articulation. (Score generally available)
Così fan Tutte Recitative: Temerari, sortite fuori Air: Come scoglio	a-c3	f1-f2	Dramatic soprano (lyric soprano)	Recitative and a vigorous, spirited air. Has many florid passages. Demands a voice of unusually extensive range. (Score generally available)
Così fan Tutte Una donna a quindici anni	d1-b2	g1-e2	Soprano	Light, humorous, animated. Demands facile articulation. (Score generally available)
Der Schauspiel-direktor Bester Jüngling (German text)	eb1-bb2	g1-g2	Soprano	An andante, allegro air. Has florid passages. (Score, Peters)
Der Schauspiel-direktor, Da Schlägt die Abschiedsstunde (German text)	f#1-d3	bb1-g2	Coloratura soprano	An andante, allegro air. In parts very florid. (Score, Peters)
Die Entführung aus dem Serail Ach ich liebte (German text)	f1-d3	bb1-f2	Coloratura soprano	An andante, allegro air. In parts very florid. (Score, generally available)

TITLE	COMP.	TESS.	TYPE	REMARKS
Die Entführung aus dem Serail				
Durch Zärtlichkeit	e1-e3	a1-f#2	Lyric soprano (coloratura soprano)	Graceful, gently humorous. Has florid passages. (Score generally available)
Die Entführung aus dem Serail				
Martern aller Arten (German text)	b-d3	a1-a2	Coloratura soprano	Dramatic, spirited, brilliant and florid. Demands a rather unusual coloratura voice, having good command of forte and of medium register. (Score generally available)
Die Entführung aus dem Serail				
Welcher Kummer herrscht in meiner Seele (German text)	f#1-bb2	g1-g2	Lyric soprano (coloratura soprano)	Slow, very sustained. Demands some flexibility. (Score generally available)
Die Entführung aus dem Serail				
Welche Wonne, welch Lust (German text)	g1-a2	b1-g2	Lyric soprano (coloratura soprano)	Rapid, light. Demands facile articulation. (Score generally available)
Don Giovanni				
Ah, fuggi il traditor	f#1-a2	a1-f#2	Dramatic soprano (lyric soprano)	Dramatic, spirited. Has florid passages. (Score generally available)
Don Giovanni				
Batti, batti o bel Masetto	c1-bb2	f1-f2	Soprano	A graceful andante, allegro aria. Has florid passages. Gently humorous. Graceful. (Generally available)
Don Giovanni Recitative: Crudele? An no, mio bene Air: Non mi dir	e1-bb2	g1-g2	Dramatic soprano (lyric soprano)	Recitative, andante, allegro. Has florid passages. (Generally available)
Don Giovanni Or sai chi l'onore	f1-a2	a1-g2	Dramatic soprano (lyric soprano)	Dramatic, vigorous. (Score generally available)
Don Giovanni Vedrai carino	g1-g2	g1-e2	Soprano	Graceful. Vocally not taxing. (Generally available)
Don Giovanni Recitative: Un quali eccessi, o Numi Air: Mi tradi quel alma ingrata	d1-bb2	bb1-g2	Dramatic soprano (lyric soprano)	Recitative and an animated florid aria. (Generally available)

TITLE	COMP.	TESS.	TYPE	REMARKS
Idomeneo Recitative: Chi mai del mio provo Air: Idol mio, se ritroso	g1-a2	g1-f#2	Soprano	Recitative and sustained air. Has florid passages. (Score, Peters)
Idomeneo Recitative: Estinto è Idomeneo Air: Tutte nel cor vi sento	c1-a2	a1-f2	Dramatic soprano (high mezzo-soprano)	An extended recitative and a spirited, vigorous, dramatic air. (Score, Peters)
Idomeneo Recitative: O smania! O furie! Air: D'Oreste, d'Ajace!!	eb1-c3	g1-g2	Dramatic soprano (lyric soprano)	Recitative and dramatic, spirited, vigorous air. (Score, Peters)
Idomeneo Recitative: Qundo avran' fine o mai Air: Padre! Germani!	e1-ab2	g1-g2	Soprano	Sustained. Demands some flexibility. (Score, Peters)
Idomeneo Se il padre perdei	eb1-bb2	g1-eb2	Soprano	Slow. Demands considerable flexibility. (Score, Peters)
Idomeneo Recitative: Solitudini amiche Air: Zeffiretti lusinghieri	e#1-a2	g#1-e2	Soprano	Recitative and a sustained graceful air. In parts quite florid. (Score, Peters)
Il Re Pastore L'amerò, sarò costante	eb1-bb2	bb1-f2	Soprano	Sustained, graceful. Demands some flexibility. The Lauterbach arrangement, with violin obbligato, provided with an elaborate cadenza, is often used in concert. (Schweers & Haake, Bremen)
La Clemenza di Tito Deh per questo istante solo	c#1-f#2	a1-e2	Soprano or mezzo-soprano	An andante, allegro air. Demands some flexibility. (Score, Peters)
La Clemenza di Tito Deh' se piacer mi vuoi	b-b2	g1-d2	Dramatic soprano or high mezzo-soprano	An andante, allegro air. Quite florid. (Score, Peters)
La Clemenza di Tito Recitative: Ecco il punto Air: Non più di fiori	c1-a2 (g)	f1-f2	Dramatic soprano or mezzo-soprano	Scena, andante, allegro. Demands some flexibility. (Spicker, Operatic Anthology. Schirmer)

TITLE	COMP.	TESS.	TYPE	REMARKS
La Clemenza di Tito Parto, parto, ma tu, ben mio	c1-bb2	g1-eb2	Soprano or mezzo-soprano	An andante, allegro air. Has florid passages. (Score, Peters)
La Clemenza di Tito Saltro che lacrime	f#1-a2	a1-f#2	Lyric soprano (coloratura soprano)	A graceful minuet. (Score, Peters)
La Clemenza di Tito Torna di Tito a lato	d-g1	g-d1	Soprano or mezzo-soprano	Graceful. Demands some flexibility. (Score, Peters)
La Clemenza di Tito Tu fosti tradito	e1-a2	g1-f2	Soprano	Sustained. Demands some flexibility. (Score, Peters)
Le Nozze di Figaro Al desio	b-a2	f1-f2	Dramatic soprano (high mezzo-soprano)	Andante, allegro. Has florid passages. An alternate air for the role of the Countess; never used in stage performances of the opera now. (Score generally available)
Le Nozze di Figaro Recitative: Giunse al fin il momento Air: Deh vieni non tardar	c1-a2 (a)	f1-f2	Soprano	Recitative and a sustained delicate air. In bar fifteen of the andante, the bb and a are often sung as bb1, a1. (Generally available)
Le Nozze di Figaro Recitative: E Susanna non vien Air: Dove sono	d1-a2	g1-f2	Dramatic soprano (lyric soprano)	Recitative, a very sustained andante, and a spirited allegro. (Generally available)
Le Nozze di Figaro L'ho perduta, me meschina	f1-f2	ab1-e2	Soprano	Short and sustained. Vocally not taxing. (Score generally available)
Le Nozze di Figaro Non so più	eb1-g2	g1-eb2	Soprano (mezzo-soprano)	Rapid, light. Demands very facile articulation. (Generally available)
Le Nozze di Figaro Porgi amor	d1-ab2	bb1-f2	Dramatic soprano (lyric soprano)	Slow, very sustained. (Generally available)

TITLE	COMP.	TESS.	TYPE	REMARKS
Le Nozze di Figaro				
Un moto di gioia	b-g2	g1-d2	Soprano	Light, animated. Vocally not taxing. An alternate arietta for the role of Susanna, never used in stage performances of the opera now. (Score generally available)
Le Nozze di Figaro				
Venite, inginocchiatevi	d1-g2	g1-e2	Soprano	Gently humorous. Vocally not too taxing. (Score generally available)
Le Nozze di Figaro				
Voi che sapete	c1-f2	f1-eb2	Soprano (mezzo-soprano)	Sustained, graceful. Vocally not taxing. (Generally available)
Zauberflöte				
Ach ich fühl's (German text)	c#1-bb2	g1-g2	Most suitable for lyric soprano	Very sustained, slow. Demands in parts some flexibility. (Generally available)
Zauberflöte				
Der Hölle Rache (German text)	f1-f3	a1-a2	Coloratura soprano	Dramatic, brilliant, florid allegro. Demands a rather unusual coloratura voice, possessing good command of forte and of medium register. (Generally available)
Zauberflöte Recitative: O zittre nicht mein lieber Sohn Air: Zum Leiden bin ich auserkoren (German text)	d1-f3	bb1-g2	Coloratura soprano	Recitative, andante, allegro. Florid. Demands a rather unusual coloratura voice, possessing a good command of forte and of medium register. (Score generally available)

CONCERT AIRS

TITLE	COMP.	TESS.	TYPE	REMARKS
Ah, lo previdi	d1-bb2	g1-g2	Soprano	Recitative and an allegro, andante, allegro air.
A questo seno deh vieni	eb1-bb2	g1-g2	Soprano	Recitative and a light animated rondo. Demands considerable flexibility.
Bella mia fiamma, addio!	d1-a2	g1-f2	Soprano	Recitative, andante, allegro. Demands considerable flexibility.
Ch'io me scordi di te	ab-bb2	eb1-eb2	Dramatic soprano	Recitative, andante, allegro. Demands considerable flexibility.
Ma che vi fece, o stelle	f1-f3	a1-g2	Coloratura soprano	Recitative, andante, allegro. Very florid.

TITLE	COMP.	TESS.	TYPE	REMARKS
Mia speranza adorata	c1-f3	bb1-g2	Coloratura soprano	Recitative, andante, allegro. Florid. Demands a rather unusual coloratura voice, commanding a good forte and having a well-developed medium register.
Misera, dove son!	f1-bb2	g1-g2	Soprano	Recitative, andante, allegro. Demands considerable flexibility.
Non più.Tutto ascoltavi	e1-bb2	bb-g2	Soprano	Recitative, andante, allegro. Has florid passages.

A collection of Concert Arias by Mozart is published by Peters and by Breitkopf & Härtel.

MEZZO-SOPRANO

Così fan Tutte
Recitative:

TITLE	COMP.	TESS.	TYPE	REMARKS
Ah, scostati! Air: Smanie implacabili	d1-ab2	eb1-eb2	Mezzo-soprano (dramatic soprano)	Recitative and a spirited, vigorous, dramatic air. (Score generally available)

Idomeneo
Recitative:

Estinto è Idomeneo Air: Tutte nel cor vi sento	c1-a2	a1-f2	High mezzo-soprano or dramatic soprano	An extended recitative and a spirited, vigorous dramatic air. (Score, Peters)

La Clemenza di Tito
Recitative:

Ecco il punto Air: Non più di fiori	c1-a2 (g)	f1-f2	Mezzo-soprano or dramatic soprano	Scena, andante, allegro. Demands some flexibility. (Schirmer, Operatic Anthology)

La Clemerza di Tito

Deh per questo instante solo	c#1-f#2	a1-e2	Mezzo-soprano or soprano	Demands some flexibility. (Score, Peters)

La Clemenza di Tito

Deh, se piacer mi vuoi	b-b2	g1-d2	High mezzo-soprano or dramatic soprano	An andante, allegro air. Quite florid. (Score, Peters)

La Clemenza di Tito

Parto, parto, ma tu, ben mio	c1-bb2	g1-eb2	Mezzo-soprano or soprano	An andante, allegro air. Has florid passages. (Score, Peters)

La Clemenza di Tito

Torna di Tito a lato	d1-g2	g1-d2	Mezzo-soprano or soprano	Graceful. Demands some flexibility. (Score, Peters)

Le Nozze di Figaro

Al desio	b-a2	f1-f2	Mezzo-soprano or soprano	An andante, allegro air. Has florid passages. An alternate air for the role of the Countess never used in stage performances of the opera now. (Score generally available)

TITLE	COMP.	TESS.	TYPE	REMARKS
Le Nozze di Figaro Il capro e la capretta	f#1-b2	b1-g2	Soprano or high mezzo-soprano	Originally intended for a high mezzo-soprano. A graceful minuet and a spirited allegro. In parts quite florid. (Score generally available)
Le Nozze di Figaro Non so più	eb1-g2	g1-eb2	Mezzo-soprano or soprano	Very rapid, light. Demands very facile articulation. (Generally available)
Le Nozze di Figaro Voi che sapete	c1-f2	f1-eb2	Mezzo-soprano or soprano	Graceful. Vocally not taxing. (Generally available)

TENOR

All the airs listed below are most suitable for rather light, flexible tenor voices, with the possible exception of the Idomeneo airs. It seemed therefore unnecessary to retain the Type of Voice column.

TITLE	COMP.	TESS.	REMARKS
Così fan Tutte Recitative: In qual fiero contrasto Air: Tradito, schernito, dal perfido cor	f-a1	a-g1	Recitative and a vigorous allegro. Demands some flexibility. (Score generally available)
Così fan Tutte Recitative: Non sperarlo Air: Ah, io veggio quella anima bella	f-bb1	bb-g1	Recitative and an animated air. Demands considerable flexibility and lightness of tone. The tessitura is uncommonly high, the bb1 occurring frequently. (Score generally available)
Così fan Tutte Un'aura amorosa	d-a1	a-f#1	Sustained. Demands considerable flexibility. (Generally available)
Die Entführung aus dem Serail Constanze! Dich wieder zu sehen (German text)	e-a1	a-e1	Slow. Quite florid. (Score generally available)
Die Entführung aus dem Serail Frisch zum kampfe (German text)	d-b1	a-f#	A spirited vigorous, mock-heroic air. (Score generally available)
Die Entführung aus dem Serail Hier soll ich dich denn sehen (German text)	g-a1	c-g1	Sustained. Demands some flexibility. (Score generally available)

TITLE	COMP.	TESS.	REMARKS
Die Entführung aus dem Serail			
Ich baue ganz auf deine Stärke (German text)	eb-bb1	bb-g1	Sustained. Quite florid. (Score generally available)
Die Entführung aus dem Serail			
Im Mohrenland (German text)	e#-d1	a-d1	A delicate, subdued serenade. Vocally not taxing. Demands good command of pianissimo. (Score generally available)
Die Entführung aus dem Serail			
Wenn der Freude Thränen spriessen (German text)	C-ab1	bb-f1	Andante, allegro. Has some florid passages. (Score generally available)
Don Giovanni			
Dalla sua pace	d-g1	b-g1	Very sustained. Demands some flexibility. (Generally available)
Don Giovanni			
Il mio tesoro	d-a1	bb-f1	Sustained. Has florid passages. (Generally available)
Idomeneo Recitative: Ah qual gelido orror m'ingombrai i sensi Air: Il padre adorato	e-g1	g-f1	A vigorous dramatic air. (Score, Peters)
Idomeneo Non ho colpa	e-a1	a-f1	Spirited. Demands some flexibility. (Score, Peters)
Idomeneo No la morte, la morte io non pavento	e-g1	g-e1	Spirited. Vigorous. Has a sustained middle section. Demands some flexibility. (Score, Peters)
Idomeneo Recitative: Popoli! a voi l'ultima legge impone Idomeneo Air: Torna la pace al core	f-g1	a-f1	A very extended recitative. The air is sustained, has a graceful allegretto for the middle section. Demands some flexibility. (Score, Peters)
Idomeneo Recitative: Qual mi contrubai sensi Air: Fuor del mar hò un mar in seno	d-g1	g-d1	A spirited, florid air. Somewhat long. Can be cut, easily, beginning with the recapitulation 'Fuor del mar" second time. (Score, Peters)
Idomeneo Se il tuo duol, se il mio desio	d-a1	g-e1	Spirited. In parts quite florid. (Score, Peters)
Idomeneo Recitative: Sventurata Sidon Air: Se colà nè fato è scritto	e-a1	g#-e1	Recitative and a sustained air. Has florid passages. (Score, Peters)

TITLE	COMP.	TESS.	REMARKS
Idomeneo			
Vedrommi intorno	e-g1	g-e1	Andante, allegro. Demands some flexibility. (Score, Peters)
La Clemenza di Tito			
Ah, se fosse intorno al trono	f#-a1	a-f#1	Animated. Demands some flexibility. (Score, Peters)
La Clemenza di Tito			
Del piu sublime soglio	e-a1	g-e1	Sustained. Demands some flexibility. (Score, Peters)
La Clemenza di Tito			
Se all'impero, amici Dei	f-bb1	a-f1	Allegro, andantino, allegro. In parts quite florid. (Score, Peters)
Le Nozze di Figaro			
In quegli'anni	eb-g1	a-f1	Andante, minuet, allegro. A comic air. Demands facile articulation. (Score generally available)
Zauberflöte			
Alles fühlt der Liebe Freuden (German text)	d-e1	g-d1	A rapid buffo verse song. Demands good command of p and very facile articulation. (Score generally available)
Zauberflöte			
Dies Bildnis ist bezaubernd schön (German text)	f1-ab1	bb-g1	Slow and sustained. Demands some flexibility. (Generally available)

CONCERT AIRS

Recitative: Misero! Air: O sogno, o son desto?	eb-ab1	bb-g1	Recitative, andante, and a brilliant allegro. (Peters; Breitkopf & Härtel)
Per pietà, non ricercare	c-ab1	g-g1	Andante, allegro. (Peters; Breitkopf & Härtel)

BASS AND BARITONE

TITLE	COMP.	TESS.	TYPE	REMARKS
Cosi fan Tutte				
Donne mie, la fatte a tanti	B-e1	g-d1	Bass or bass-baritone	A spirited buffo air. Demands facile articulation. (Score generally available)
Die Entführung aus dem Serail				
O! wie will ich triumphiren (German text)	D-e1	d-d1	Bass	Rapid, vigorous buffo air. Demands very facile articulation, some flexibility, and a good command of low D. (Score generally available)
Die Entführung aus dem Serail				
Solche hergelaufene Laffen (German text)	F-f1	c-c1	Bass	A spirited, vigorous buffo air. Demands some flexibility, and facile articulation. (Score generally available)
Die Entführung aus dem Serail				
Wer ein Liebchen hat gefunden (German text)	G-d1	d-bb	Bass	A sustained verse song with variated accompaniment. (Score generally available)

TITLE	COMP.	TESS.	TYPE	REMARKS
Don Giovanni Ah pietà, Signori miei	A-e1	d-c1	Bass or bass-baritone	Rapid. Demands facile articulation. (Score generally available)
Don Giovanni Deh vieni alla finestra	d-e1	a-d1	Bass-baritone or baritone	A graceful, light, animated serenade. (Generally available)
Don Giovanni Finchè han dal vino	d-eb1	f-d1	Bass-baritone or baritone	Extremely rapid. Demands very facile articulation. (Generally available)
Don Giovanni Ho capito, Signor, si	c-c1		Bass-baritone or baritone	A rapid buffo air. Demands facile articulation. (Score generally available)
Don Giovanni Madamina! Il catalogo è questo	A-e1	d-d1	Bass or bass-baritone	A rapid buffo air. Demands very facile articulation. (Generally available)
Don Giovanni Metà di voi quà vadano	c-e1	f-c1	Baritone or bass-baritone	Animated. Demands facile articulation. (Score generally available)
La Clemenza di Tito Tardi s'avvede	B-e1	f#-d1	Bass or baritone	Animated. Demands some flexibility. (Score, Peters)
Le Nozze di Figaro Recitative: Hai già vinta la causa Air: Vedrò mentr'io sospiro	A-f#1	d-d1	Baritone	An extended recitative and a vigorous, spirited air. (Score generally available)
Le Nozze di Figaro La vendetta, oh la vendetta	A-e1	d-d1	Bass	A vigorous, spirited buffo air. Demands facile articulation. (Score generally available)
Le Nozze di Figaro Non più andrai	c-e1	e-c1	Baritone	Spirited, vigorous, rhythmical. Demands facile articulation. (Generally available)
Le Nozze di Figaro Se vuol ballare	c-f1	f-c1	Baritone	A spirited allegretto and a presto which demands facile articulation. (Generally available)
Le Nozze di Figaro Recitative: Tutto è disposto Air: Aprite un po'quegli occhi	Bb-eb1	eb-c1	Bass-baritone or baritone	An extended recitative and a spirited, comic air. Demands facile articulation. (Score generally available)
Zauberflöte Der Vogelfänger bin ich ja (German text)	d-e1	g-c1	Baritone	A spirited, gay verse song. Demands some flexibility and facile articulation. (Score generally available)

TITLE	COMP.	TESS.	TYPE	REMARKS
Zauberflöte Ein Mädchen oder Weibchen (German text)	B-d1	f-c1	Baritone	A spirited, light verse song. Demands some flexibility. (Score generally available)
Zauberflöte In diesen heilgen Hallen (German text)	F#-c#1	b-b	Bass	Very slow, sustained, stately. (Generally available)
Zauberflöte O Isis und Osiris (German text)	F-c1	c-a	Bass	Slow, grave, very sustained. (Generally available)

CONCERT AIR

TITLE	COMP.	TESS.	TYPE	REMARKS
Mentre ti lascio	A-eb1	d-c1	Bass or bass-baritone	An andante, allegro air. Demands some flexibility. (Novello)

SOLO EXCERPTS FROM SACRED WORKS

TITLE	COMP.	TESS.	TYPE	REMARKS
Motet: Exsultate, Jubilate (Latin text)			Soprano	The very brilliant florid Alleluja is widely known and often performed separately. The two other movements, however, the somewhat florid, spirited "Exsultate, Jubilate" and the sustained "Tu Virginum Corona" deserve to be as widely known. The entire motet can form a most effective recital group. (Breitkopf & Härtel; Alleluja" generally available)
In three movements:				
(1) Exsultate Jubilate Recitative	d1-a2	g1-f2		
(2) Tu Virginum Corona	e1-a2	a1-e2		
(3) Alleluja	f1-a2 (c3)	a1-f2		
Mass in C Minor K.V.427 Et Incarnatus est (Latin text)	b-c3	g1-g2	Lyric soprano (dramatic soprano)	Not fast. In parts very florid, elaborate air. (Score, Breitkopf & Härtel)
Mass in C Minor K.V.427 Laudamus Te (Latin text)	a-a2	f1-f2	Mezzo-soprano or alto	Spirited. In parts quite florid. (Score, Breitkopf & Härtel)

SONGS

The songs of Mozart are for the most part simple, almost sketchlike occasional pieces, written perhaps primarily for home entertainment. Their very small number, if compared with Mozart's fantastically prodigious output in all other musical forms, is in itself significant as a possible indication of their relative unimportance among Mozart's vocal compositions, which are almost exclusively intended for either the operatic stage or the church.

Delightful as his songs are, their study could hardly assist one in forming an adequate idea of Mozart's unparalleled and miraculous genius as a composer of vocal music. His operatic airs are much more representative of his style of writing; curiously enough, a great number of them seem to be but little known or performed.

Editions: Peters reprinted by Kalmus
Breitkopf & Härtel
Universal
An excellent collection of songs and airs published by Novello.

TITLE	COMP.	TESS.	TYPE	REMARKS
Abendempfindung	e1-f2	g1-eb2	All voices	Slow and sustained.
Ah, spiegarti, oh Dio (Italian text)	d1-a2	f1-d2	Soprano	A concert arietta, sustained.
Als Louise die Briefe ihres ungetreuen Liebhabers verbrannte	a1-f2	g1-eb2	Women's voices, except a very light soprano	Dramatic, somewhat declamatory.
An Chloe	eb1-ab2	g1-eb2	Not too suitable for very heavy voices.	Light and delicate Note the time signature ¢. Often taken too slowly.
Dans un bois solitaire (French text)	eb1-ab2	g1-eb2	All voices	An animated arietta. Has a recitative passage in the middle section. Demands some flexibility.
Das Kinderspiel	e1-e2	g#1-d2	All voices	Light and gay. Demands some flexibility. Verses 2 and 3 could be omitted.
Das Veilchen	f1-g2	bb1-e2	Most suitable for high voices	A miniature cantata. Delicate, interpretatively not easy.
Die Alte	b-e2	e1-b1	Mezzo-soprano or alto	An amusing character song. Note Mozart's direction "to be sung a bit through the nose."
Die ihr des unermesslichen Weltalls	d1-a2	g1-g2	High voices, except a very light soprano	A solo cantata. Recitative and several short contrasting movements. Rather grave and declamatory.
Die kleine Spinnerin	e1-f2	g1-d2	Women's voices	Light and animated. Verse 2 or 3 could be omitted.
Gesellenreise	f1-g2	bb1-eb2	All voices	Sustained. A Masonic song.
Ich würd auf meinem Pfad	c#1-g2	a1-e2	All voices	Sustained. Verse 2, 3, or 4 could be omitted.
Oiseaux, si tous les ans (French text)	g1-g2	b1-g2	Most suitable for high voices	A delicate arietta.

TITLE	COMP.	TESS.	TYPE	REMARKS
Ridente la calma (Italian text)	c1-a2	a1-f2	Most suitable for high voices	A slow, sustained arietta. Demands some flexibility.
Sehnsucht nach dem Frühling	f1-f2	f1-c2	Not too suitable for very low heavy voices	Delicate and gay. Verses 3 and 4 could be omitted.
Verdankt sei es dem Glanz	c1-f2	g1-e2	Not too suitable for very light, high voices	Very sustained. Verses 2 or 3 could be omitted.
Warnung	c1-d2	f1-c2	All voices	A delightful, humorous song. Demands facile articulation.
Wiegenlied	f1-f2	f1-c2	Women's voices	This delicate little song has been attributed to Mozart for so long that it seemed best to list it here. The composer is B. Flies, Mozart's contemporary.

II

SONGS

NINETEENTH AND TWENTIETH CENTURIES

GERMAN

Many excellent songs by German and Austrian composers could not be included in the following list. Were one to try to list all the noteworthy German songs one could easily extend this list to the size at present allotted to the entire volume, since practically every German and Austrian composer of note has written a considerable number of songs. Moreover, practically every German and Austrian musician, including those who have been primarily performing artists, can boast at least a few songs of undeniable merit.

Confronted with this extraordinary wealth of material it seemed best to limit this list to the most famed songs of the outstanding German and Austrian composers.

The very great number of songs by mid- and late-nineteenth century composers of comparatively small stature, such as Marschner, Lassen, Raff, had to be omitted to provide space for the somewhat extended lists of songs by such towering figures as Schubert, Schumann, Brahms, and Hugo Wolf. The inclusion of a few songs of some minor composers, like Bohm, for instance, seemed justified in view of their great popularity.

As in the case of the French list, the contemporary German and Austrian composers, particularly those whose writing tends toward extremes in experimentation, are not represented here, with the exception of some songs of Hindemith, Schönberg and Berg. Historically, therefore, this list is admittedly in no way complete. For all practical purposes, however, it can be considered as representative of the German lied, for the extraordinary songs of Schubert, Schumann, Brahms and Wolf are as fully represented here as the scope of this volume can allow.

LUDWIG VAN BEETHOVEN
(1770-1827)

As a composer of songs, Beethoven does not occupy the same towering position he holds in the realm of instrumental music. Nevertheless, songs like "Adelaide" and "An die ferne Geliebte" can at the very least be considered equal to the best examples of the German lied, or any other type of song.

Beethoven wrote but sixty-six songs: fifty-nine to German texts and seven to texts in Italian, including the concert aria, "Ah, Perfido."

The songs intended for tenor or heavy voices present no extraordinary vocal difficulties. It is only in the treatment of the vocal line in the songs for a light soprano that Beethoven deviates somewhat from the usual procedure, whereby the entire or almost the entire range of the voice is as a rule utilized. Ordinarily, if a composer intends a song for a soprano possessing a range of approximately c1-e3, for example, he is almost certain to make use of the g2-e3 section of the voice. Thus the character of the voice intended is established beyond doubt and the singer is given a chance to display the high voice. Beethoven, not concerned in his songs with furnishing a singer with an opportunity of displaying the voice, abandons the usage. His soprano songs seem, at first glance, to demand a voice of limited range c1-a2. Yet for such a voice, the tessitura and the prosody seem cruelly high and demanding; the reason for this, of course, is simply that these songs are intended for a voice with a much wider range-approximately up to e3.

This curious discrepancy between the seemingly short total compass and the handling of the tessitura and prosody is perhaps responsible for the oft-repeated charge that Beethoven wrote badly for the voice.

Most of the soprano songs by Beethoven will gain if transposed down, should they be sung by a soprano of c1-c3 range. But many of his songs, in their original keys, would provide a most welcome addition to the concert repertoire of coloraturas. The following list ought to prove itself useful in the study of Beethoven songs.

TITLE	COMP.	TESS.	TYPE	REMARKS
Adelaide	eb1-a2	a1-g2	Most suitable for men's voices	Sustained. Has an animated final section. Interpretatively not easy. Demands an accomplished pianist.
Andenken	d1-g2	f#1-e2	High or medium voices	Graceful, sustained.
An die ferne Geliebte (A cycle of six connected songs)	eb1-g2	eb1-eb2	Most suitable for men's voices	Interpretatively not easy. Demands an accomplished pianist. Really a piece of chamber music.
An die Geliebte	e1-e2	f#1-d2	All voices except a very light soprano	Animated, not fast.
Aus Goethe's Faust	c1-d2	eb1-c2	Men's voices	Animated, rather vigorous. See Mussorgsky, "The Song of the Flea."
Busslied (From Sechs Geistliche Lieder, op. 48)	e1-g2	f#1-e2	Not suitable for light high voices	Sustained. Has a more animated final section.
Das Geheimnis	g1-e2		All voices	Sustained.
Der Kuss	e1-g#2	f#1-e2	Men's voices	An animated, humorous character song of no particular distinction.
Der Liebende	f#1-f#2	g1-e2	All voices	Animated
Die Ehre Gottes aus der Natur (From Sechs Geistliche Lieder, op. 48)	c1-g2	e1-e2	Heavy voices	Majestic, vigorous, sustained.
Die Trommel gerühret	f1-f2	g1-e2	Women's voices, except a light soprano	Vigorous, very animated, rhythmic.
Freudvoll und leidvoll	g#1-a2	a1-f#2	Women's voices except a very heavy alto	A song of contrasting moods and tempi. Interpretatively not easy. See Liszt; Schubert, "Die Liebe"; Rubinstein, "Clärchens Lied".
Ich liebe dich	d1-f2	g1-d2	All voices	Sustained, delicate.

TITLE	COMP.	TESS.	TYPE	REMARKS
In questa tomba	c1-e2	eb1-c2	Low or medium voices	Slow, somber. Beethoven has six songs and a concert air to Italian texts of which this song and "La Partenza" are best known. Somewhat of a curiosity is the "L'amanto impaziente" which Beethoven set to music twice, once in a buffo style and once in an exaggeratedly serious vein.
Lied aus der Ferne	e1-g2	f1-f2	Most suitable for rather light high voices	Animated, graceful. Demands lightness of tone, some flexibility, and an accomplished pianist.
Mailied	eb1-eb2		Not too suitable for very low voices	Animated, graceful. Demands facile articulation and some flexibility.
Marmotte	e1-e2	a1-d2	All voices	A very short, graceful, simple song undeservedly neglected.
Mignon (Kennst du das Land)	e1-f#2	g#1-e2	Women's voices	Sustained. Has contrasting animated sections. Interpretatively not easy. See Schubert, Schumann, Liszt, H. Wolf.
Mit einem gemalten Band	e1-a2	a1-f2	Most suitable for rather light high voices	Animated, graceful. Demands lightness of tone and some flexibility. The tessitura is higher than it may appear at first glance.
Neue Liebe, neues Leben	e1-a2	g1-f2	Not too suitable for very heavy low voices	Very animated, rhythmic. Demands facile articulation.
Resignation	e1-f#2	a1-e2	All voices	Not fast, somewhat declamatory.
Sehnsucht	e#1-f#2	f#1-d2	All voices	Animated, graceful. Demands facile articulation and an accomplished pianist.
Vom Tode (From Sechs Geistliche Lieder, op. 48)	c#1-g2	f#1-e2	Not suitable for light high voices	Sustained, somber.

TITLE	COMP.	TESS.	TYPE	REMARKS
Wonne der Wehmut	d#1-g2	f#1-d#2	All voices except a very light soprano	Slow. Interpretatively not easy. See Franz.
Ah, Perfido (concert air)	bb-bb2	eb1-f2	Dramatic soprano	A dramatic scena and a compound brilliant air. Has a very sustained slow movement. The final allegro demands in parts considerable flexibility.

ALBAN BERG
(1885-1936)

Alban Berg, the composer of <u>Wozzek</u>, one of the most stirring of contemporary operas, has written only a few songs; most of them belong to his earliest efforts. For the most part they are musically quite complex and are not recommended to inexperienced singers.

Edition: Universal

TITLE	COMP.	TESS.	TYPE	REMARKS
Im Zimmer (from Sieben frühe Lieder)	d1-g2	f1-d2	High voices	Delicate, sustained.
Liebesode (from Sieben frühe Lieder)	c1-f#2	e1-e2	Medium or high voices, except a very light soprano or tenor	Slow, sustained. Has very imposing climaxes. See Joseph Marx, "Selige Nacht".
Schilflied (from Sieben frühe Lieder)	eb1-f2	f1-e2	High voices	Sustained, rather subdued. Demands an accomplished pianist. See Charles Griffes, "By a Lonely Forest Pathway".

Vier Lieder: opus 2
"Der Glühende": three songs

TITLE	COMP.	TESS.	TYPE	REMARKS
(1) Schlafend trägt man mich	b-fb2	f-db2	Medium or low voices	Slow, short, rather sustained. Musically not easy.
(2) Nun ich der Riesen stärksten überwand	cb1-e2	eb1-c2	Medium or low	Somewhat declamatory. Musically not easy.
(3) Warm die Lüfte	a-g#2	e1-e2	Medium or low voices	Slow, somewhat declamatory. Has a very dramatic climax. Musically complex. Demands an accomplished pianist.

TITLE	COMP.	TESS.	TYPE	REMARKS
Schlafen, schlafen	a-f2	e1-b1	Medium or low voices	Slow, subdued, sustained. Musically not easy.

TITLE	COMP.	TESS.	TYPE	REMARKS

LEO BLECH
(1871-   )
Edition: Universal

TITLE	COMP.	TESS.	TYPE	REMARKS
Der Sandmann	d♯1-g♯2	b1-f♯2	High voices	Light. Demands good command of pp. and an excellent pianist. See Schumann. One of the series of thirty-two songs "to be sung for children."
Heimkehr vom Feste	b♭-g2	a1-f2	Most suitable for high or medium voices	Light and gently humorous. One of the series of thirty-two songs "to be sung for children."
Herr Hahn und Fräulein Huhn	b♭-a♭2		Most suitable for high or medium voices	A droll burlesque. One of the series of thirty-two songs "to be sung for children."

CARL BOHM
(1844-1920)

TITLE	COMP.	TESS.	TYPE	REMARKS
Still wie die Nacht	d1-a♭2	g1-e♭2 (H)	All voices	Very sustained. Effective. (Generally available)

JOHANNES BRAHMS
(1833-1897)

The manner in which Brahms sets a poem to music could be perhaps best understood if one would give serious consideration to the fact that he was earnestly and actively engaged in collecting, harmonizing and imitating folk songs of German, as well as of western Slavic, origin.

The attempt to combine the purely melodic expressiveness of a folk song with the more elaborate musicodramatic conception of a nineteenth century song seems to be one of the predominant characteristics of Brahms's vocal works.

Brahms never seems to sacrifice his melodic line for any consideration; often complex pianistically, harmonically and rhythmically in his accompaniments, he keeps the melodic line as simple and as expressive in itself as that of any folk song. This is not to be understood as meaning that Brahms lacked the dramatic sensitivity of a Hugo Wolf, for instance; even a cursory examination of his songs would make such a statement untenable; but he differs widely in his choice of methods of expression from the then fashionable manner of insisting upon the dramatic and poetic content of a song in preference to its purely musical content.

Thus a song of Brahms demands above all a melodically satisfactory manner of vocalization; there are hardly any instances of a demand for a parlato style, for even in his rapid songs, requiring a syllable on almost every note, as it sometimes happens, the melodic line is superbly in evidence.

Brahms has been popularly identified with writing songs suitable mostly for heavy, low voices. It is true that among his best songs one finds a great number intended for this type of voice; it is equally true, however, that among his best songs one finds an equal, if not a greater number of songs intended for light, high voices. A coloratura soprano, for instance, could easily sing several groups of Brahms songs without finding it necessary to transpose any of them to suit her voice. For some unknown reason this fact has never been sufficiently emphasized in popular discussions of Brahms songs.

For the most part Brahms demands an accomplished pianist for his songs, well versed in the art of adjusting the sonority of his instrument to that of the voice of the singer for whom he is playing. Often Brahms writes thickly for the piano, and although the resulting balance of sonorities must by all means be preserved, it can, if overstressed, overpower and distort the song.

Editions: 4 vols. Peters (reprinted by Kalmus, Scarsdale, N.Y.)
          (Original edition Simrock)
          Also Breitkopf & Härtel
          Good selections: Musicians Library, O. Ditson
          One-volume edition: G. Schirmer
          One-volume edition: C. Fischer
          Numerous reprints of single songs
          Zigeunerlieder reprinted by Associated Music Publishers

TITLE	COMP.	TESS.	TYPE	REMARKS
Ach wende diesen Blick	eb1-g2	ab1-f2	Not suitable for very light, high voices	Dramatic. Demands an accomplished pianist.
Agnes	g1-g2	bb1-f2	Women's voices, except a very light soprano	Animated, rhythmical, somber. See Wolf.
Alte Liebe	d1-f2	eb1-eb2	Not too suitable for very light high voices	Animated, somber.
Am Sonntag Morgen	e1-a2	a1-f#2	Not too suitable for very light high voices	Dramatic. Demands an accomplished pianist.
An den Mond	e#1-g2	a#1-f#2	Not too suitable for very heavy voices	Very sustained.
An die Nachtigall	d#1-g2	a1-f#2	All voices	Sustained.
An ein Veilchen	d#1-g#2	a1-f#2	All voices	Slow and sustained. Demands good command of high pp.
An eine Aeolsharfe	eb1-a2	ab1-f#2	Women's voices	Very sustained. Demands an accomplished pianist. Note the time signature ¢ Often sung too slowly. See Wolf.

TITLE	COMP.	TESS.	TYPE	REMARKS
Anklänge	e1-g2	a1-f2	All voices	Very sustained. Demands good command of pp.
Auf dem Kirchhofe	b-eb2	eb1-c2	Not too suitable for very light high voices	Grave and somber. Interpretatively not easy. Demands an accomplished pianist.
Auf dem Schiffe	g1-a2	b1-f#2	High voices	Rapid and light. Demands an excellent pianist.
Auf dem See (An dies Schifflein)	d#1-a2	g#1-f#2	Not too suitable for very heavy low voices	Graceful. Demands an accomplished pianist.
Auf dem See (Blauer Himmel)	d#1-f#2	g#1-e2	All voices	The vocal line is very sustained.
Bei dir sind meine Gedanken	e1-f#2	a1-f2	All voices	Animated, delicate. Demands an accomplished pianist.
Bittres zu sagen denkst du	e1-g2	a1-e2	All voices	Delicate
Blinde Kuh	g1-g2	bb1-f2	Not too suitable for very low voices	Rapid. Demands facile articulation and an excellent pianist.
Botschaft	f1-ab2	ab1-gb2	Not too suitable for very low voices	Light and spirited. Demands some flexibility and an excellent pianist. The tempo mark "grazioso" is often disregarded and the song taken at too fast a tempo. Sounds best in the original high key.
Dämmrung senkte sich von oben	g-e2	d1-d2	Low or medium voices	Slow and sustained. Demands an accomplished pianist. Sounds best in the original low key.
Das Mädchen	f#1-g#2	a1-f#2	Women's voices	Spirited. Interpretatively not easy.
Das Mädchen spricht	e1-f#2	a1-e2	Soprano or mezzo-soprano	Light, animated. Demands some flexibility, facile articulation, and an accomplished pianist.
Dein blaues Auge	bb-g2	g1-eb2	Not too suitable for very light high voices	Slow and sustained.

TITLE	COMP.	TESS.	TYPE	REMARKS
Der Gang zum Liebchen	b-e2	e1-c♯2	All voices	A delicate waltz song in folk vein. Demands an accomplished pianist.
Der Jäger	f1-f2	a1-f2	Women's voices	Light and rapid. In folk vein. Demands facile articulation.
Der Schmied	f1-f2	b♭-e♭2	Heavy soprano, mezzo or contralto	Spirited and very vigorous. Demands an accomplished pianist.
Der Tod das ist die kühle Nacht	c1-a2	f♯1-f♯2	All voices	Slow and sustained. Interpretatively and vocally not easy.
Der Überläufer	b-d2	e1-b1	Men's voices	Very sustained. In folk vein.
Des Liebsten Schwur	c1-f2	f1-d2	Soprano or mezzo-soprano	Rapid and light. In folk vein. Demands facile articulation, some flexibility, and an accomplished pianist.
Die Mainacht	b♭-f♭2	g1-e♭2	Not too suitable for very light high voices	Very sustained. Interpretatively and vocally not easy.
Dort in den Weiden	a1-a2	b1-f♯2	Soprano or mezzo-soprano	Spirited. In folk vein. Demands facile articulation.
Eine gute, gute Nacht	g1-a2	a1-f♯2	Most suitable for high voices	Delicate.
Erinnerung	e1-g2	g1-g2	All voices	Very sustained.
Es hing der Reif	d1-a2	a1-f2	Not too suitable for very heavy low voices	Very sustained.
Es liebt sich so lieblich im Lenze	d1-g2	a1-f♯2	Not too suitable for very heavy low voices	Animated. Interpretatively not easy. Demands an accomplished pianist. See R. Franz.
Es schauen die Blumen	f♯1-g♯2	b1-f♯2	Most suitable for high voices	Animated. Demands an accomplished pianist.
Es träumte mir	g1-f♯2	b1-f♯2	All voices	Slow and very sustained. Interpretatively not easy. Demands good command of high pp.
Feldeinsamkeit	c1-e♭2	e1-d♭2	All voices	Slow and very sustained.

TITLE	COMP.	TESS.	TYPE	REMARKS
Geheimnis	f#1-a2	c#2-g2	Not too suitable for very heavy low voices	Light and delicate. Demands good command of high pp.
Heimkehr	e1-g#2	b1-f#2	Most suitable for men's voices	Rapid and very vigorous.
Ich schleich umher betrübt	d1-d2	e1-bb1	Low or medium voices	Very sustained.
Immer leiser wird mein Schlummer	a-f2	c#1-d2	Women's voices	Slow and very sustained. Interpretatively not easy. Note the time signature ¢. Often sung too slowly.
In der Fremde	g#1-g2	b1-f#2	All voices	Sustained. See Schumann, "In der Fremde" ("Aus der Heimat").
In der Gasse	c#1-gb2	f1-eb2	Not too suitable for very light high voices	Dramatic.
In Waldeseinsamkeit	f#1-g2	b1-f#2	All voices	Slow and very sustained. Interpretatively not easy. Demands good command of high pp.
Juchhe!	d1-ab2	f1-c2	All voices	Spirited and gay. Demands facile articulation and an excellent pianist. The tessitura is curiously low, considering the frequent use of f2, g2, and ab2. Very suitable for medium or low voices if transposed down.
Klage (Aus dem Böhmischen)	d1-f#2	f#1-d2	All voices, except a very light soprano	Animated. In folk vein.
Komm bald	d#1-g2	g1-f2	All voices	Delicate, sustained.
Lerchengesang	f#1-g#2	b1-f#2	Not suitable for very heavy low voices	Very delicate and sustained. Demands good command of pp.
Liebe kam aus fernen Landen	db1-f2	eb1-db2	Men's voices	No. 4 of the "Romanzen aus Magelone" cycle of songs, opus 33. Sustained. Has an animated middle section Interpretatively not easy

TITLE	COMP.	TESS.	TYPE	REMARKS
Liebestreu	eb1-ab2	ab1-gb2	Women's voices, except a light soprano	Very slow and sustained. Dramatic.
Mädchenfluch	e1-a2	a1-e2	Women's voices	Dramatic. In folk vein. In parts very rapid. Demands an accomplished pianist.
Mädchenlied (Ach und du mein kühles Wasser)	a1-g2	c2-g2	Women's voices	Slow and sustained. In folk vein.
Mädchenlied (Am jüngsten Tag)	f1-f2	a1-f2	Women's voices	Delicate and gently humorous.
Mädchenlied (Auf die Nacht in der Spinnstub'n)	f#1-f#2	b1-e2	Women's voices	Sustained. Demands in parts considerable dramatic intensity. See Schumann, "Die Spinnerin".
Maienkätzchen	f1-g2	g1-eb2	All voices	Delicate, graceful.
Meerfahrt	e1-ab2	a1-f#2	All voices, except a very light soprano	Somber. Interpretatively and vocally not easy. Demands an accomplished pianist. See R. Franz; H. Wolf, "Mein Liebchen, wir sassen zusammen".
Meine Lieder	e#1-f#2	g#1-e2	All voices	Delicate, Animated.
Mein wundes Herz	e1-g2	g1-e2	Not too suitable for very light high voices	Animated.
Meine Liebe ist grün	e#1-a2	a#1-f#2	All voices, except a very light soprano	Spirited and vigorous. Demands an accomplished pianist.
Minnelied	d1-g2	g1-f2	Men's voices	Very sustained. See Mendelssohn.
Mit vierzig Jahren	f#-d2	b-b1	Low voices	Grave and sustained.
Mondenschein	d1-g2	f1-d2	All voices	Slow and sustained.
Muss es eine Trennung geben	f#1-f#2	g1-d2	All voices, except a very light soprano	Very sustained. No. 12 of the Romanzen aus Magelone, opus 33.
Nachklang	f#1-a2	b1-f#2	All voices	Delicate. Demands some flexibility. The melodic material of this song and of the "Regenlied" is employed in the first movement of the G major violin sonata.
Nachtigall	d1-a2	a1-g2	All voices	Slow and sustained. Interpretatively and vocally not easy.

TITLE	COMP.	TESS.	TYPE	REMARKS
Nachtigallen schwingen	f1-g2	bb1-f2	Not too suitable for very low voices	Animated. Demands lightness of tone and an excellent pianist. Interpretatively not easy. Sounds best in the original high key.
Nicht mehr zu dir zu gehen	c#1-eb2	d1-c2	Low or medium voices	Dramatic; somewhat declamatory. Interpretatively not easy. Sounds best in the original low key.
O komme, holde Sommernacht	c#1-f#2	f#1-e2	Most suitable for light high voices	Very rapid and light. Demands an excellent pianist. Sounds best in the original high key.
O kühler Wald	d1-eb2 (f2)	ab1-eb2	Not too suitable for very light high voices	Slow and very sustained.
O liebliche Wangen	f#1-a2	a1-f#2	All voices	Spirited. Demands facile articulation and good rhythmic sense.
O wüsst ich doch den Weg zurück	e1-f#2	g#1-e2	All voices	Slow and sustained. Demands an accomplished pianist.
Ruhe, Süssliebchen	eb1-f#2	g1-eb2	Men's voices	Slow and sustained. No. 9 of the Romanzen aus Magelone, opus 33. See R. Franz, "Schlummerlied".
Salome	g1-g2	b1-f#2	Women's voices	Spirited and vigorous. Demands good sense of rhythm. See Wolf, "Singt mein Schatz".
Sandmännchen	d1-e2	g1-d2	All voices	Delicate. In folk vein.
Sapphische Ode	a-d2	a-a1	Low voices	Very slow and sustained. Note the time signature ¢. Often sung too slowly and too loudly.
Schön war, das ich dir weihte	e1-g2	ab1-f2	All voices	Slow and sustained. A remarkably beautiful song, neglected for some unknown reason.
Schwermut	d1-f2	ab1-eb2	Not too suitable for very light high voices	Slow and very sustained.
Sehnsucht (Hinter jenen dichten Wäldern)	eb1-ab2	c2-gb2	Not suitable for light voices	Spirited and vigorous. The vocal line very sustained.
Serenate	f#1-g#2	b1-f#2	All voices	Delicate, sustained.

TITLE	COMP.	TESS.	TYPE	REMARKS
Sind es Schmerzen sind es Freuden	c1-g2	ab1-f2	Men's voices	No. 3 of the Romanzen aus Magelone, opus 33. A complex song of many moods. Interpretatively not easy. Demands an accomplished pianist. See Weber.
So willst du den Armen	eb1-g2	a1-f2	Men's voices	No. 5 of the Romanzen aus Magelone, opus 33. Spirited.
Sommerabend	d1-d2	f1-c2	Not too suitable for very light high voices	Slow and sustained.
Sonntag	c1-f2	f1-d2	All voices	Graceful. In folk vein.
Spanisches Lied	e1-f#2	a1-e2	Women's voices	Light and delicate. See Wolf, "In dem Schatten meiner Locken." Also Jensen.
Ständchen	d1-g#2	g1-f#2	All voices	Light. Demands facile articulation, good command of high pp. and an excellent pianist.
Steig auf, geliebter Schatten	bb-eb2	eb1-bb1	Medium or low voices	Very sustained.
Tambourliedchen	e1-a2	a1-f#2	All voices	Very spirited. Demands facile articulation and an accomplished pianist.
Therese	b-d2	f#1-b1	Women's voices	Delicate, sustained. Interpretatively not easy. See Wolf, "Du milch-junger Knabe."
Todessehnen	a#-d#2	c#1-a1	Not too suitable for light high voices	Slow and sustained.
Treue Liebe	d#1-e2	f#1-d2	Medium or low voices	Slow and sustained. In parts demands con-siderable dramatic intensity.
Über die Heide	d#1-f2	a1-e2	All voices	Somber. Interpre-tatively not easy.
Über die See	f#1-g2	g1-e2	Women's voices	Very sustained.
Vergebliches Ständchen	e1-f#2	a1-e2	All voices	Light, humorous. In folk vein. Demands facile articulation.
Verrat	F#-d#1	d-b	Bass or baritone	A dramatic narrative song (ballade). Could be sung by a dramatic tenor if transposed.

TITLE	COMP.	TESS.	TYPE	REMARKS
Verzagen	c#1-f#2	f#1-e2	Not suitable for light high voices	Somber. Has a sustained vocal line over an elaborate accompaniment. Demands an excellent pianist.

Vier Ernste Gesänge: opus 121, for bass or baritone

TITLE	COMP.	TESS.	TYPE	REMARKS
(1) Denn es gehet dem Menschen	A-f1	d-d1		Sustained, somber. Has animated sections. Demands an excellent pianist.
(2) Ich wandte mich	G-eb1	d-d1		Very sustained, grave.
(3) O Tod, wie bitter bist du	B-f#1	c#-c#1		Very sustained, grave.
(4) Wenn ich mit Menschen und mit Engelszungen	A-f1 (Ab) (g1)	c-c#1		Rather animated, vigorous. Has very sustained slow sections.
Von ewiger Liebe	a-f#2	e1-e2	Not suitable for light high voices	Dramatic. Vocally and interpretatively not east. Demands an excellent pianist.
Vorschneller Schwur	d1-a2	a1-f#2	All voices	Animated. Gently humorous. In folk vein.
Wenn du nur zuweilen lächelst	g1-g2	bb1-f2	All voices	Slow and sustained. Interpretatively not easy.
Wie bist du meine Königin	d1-f#2	ab1-f2	Men's voices	Slow and sustained.
Wie froh und frisch	d1-g2	g1-e2	Not suitable for very light voices	No. 14 of the Romanzen aus Magelone, opus 33. Spirited and vigorous. Demands an accomplished pianist.
Wie Melodien zieht es	a-e2	e1-d2	All voices	Very delicate. Interpretatively not easy. Note the time signature ¢. Often sung too slowly.
Wie schnell verschwindet so Licht als Glanz	c1-eb2	f1-c2	Not too suitable for very light high voices	No. 11 of the Romanzen aus Magelone, opus 33. Slow and sustained.
Wiegenlied	eb1-eb2	g1-eb2	All voices	Delicate, sustained.
Willst du dass ich geh?	d1-f#2 (a2)	a1-f#2	All but very light high voices	Rapid, dramatic. Demands facile articulation and an excellent pianist.
Wir müssten uns trennen	db1-g2	ab1-f2	Men's voices	No. 8 of the Romanzen aus Magelone, opus 33. A complex song, of many moods. Interpretatively not easy. Demands an accomplished pianist.

| Wir wandelten | e♭1-g♭2 | a♭1-f2 | All voices | Slow and very sustained. Demands an accomplished pianist. |

"Zigeunerlieder": eight songs, opus 103 (originally written for vocal quartet and pianoforte, arranged for solo voice by Brahms)

(1) He! Zigeuner	d♯1-g2	a1-e2 (H)	Not suitable for very light voices	Rapid and vigorous. Demands an accomplished pianist.
(2) Hochgetürmte Rimaflut	d1-g2	a1-e2 (H)	Not suitable for light voices	Very rapid. Vigorous.
(3) Wüsst ihr wann mein Kindchen	f♯1-g2	a1-d2 (H)	All voices	Light, spirited.
(4) Lieber Gott, du weisst	f1-f2	a1-e2 (H)	All voices	Light, spirited.
(5) Brauner Bursche	d1-g2	f♯1-d2 (H)	Not too suitable for very light voices	Spirited, rhythmical. Demands an accomplished pianist.
(6) Röslein dreie	e♭1-g2	a1-e2 (H)	All voices	Rapid, light. Demands facile articulation and an accomplished pianist.
(7) Kommt dir manchmal in den Sinn	d♯1-g♯2	g♯1-e2 (H)	All voices	Very sustained.
(8) Rote Abendwolken	e♭1-a♭2	a♭1-e♭2 (H)	Not suitable for very light voices	Spirited, vigorous.

See also the arrangements of German folk songs, "Deutsche Volkslieder" among them, the famous "Schwesterlein" and "Mein Mädel hat einen Rosenmund," the "Volkskinderlieder," the two songs for alto with viola obbligato opus 91.

PETER CORNELIUS
(1824-1874)

With the exception of a few, one rarely encounters songs by Cornelius on the present-day concert program. This neglect does not seem justified; Cornelius' songs deserve a permanent and esteemed place in every serious singer's repertoire. They are, apart from their poetic and musical qualities, well written for the voice. This consideration alone has too often brought a long life to much music immeasurably inferior to his.

Cornelius, like Wagner and in some instances Debussy and Mussorgsky, wrote for the most part his own texts. He had a remarkable poetic gift and would undoubtedly be still considered one of the important minor poets of his time had he not written anything but the texts to his songs.

Editions: Breitkopf & Härtel (complete ed. 2 vols.)
Weihnachtslieder, Boston Music Co.
A few reprints of single songs by Schirmer and others

TITLE	COMP.	TESS.	TYPE	REMARKS
Angedenken	c1-d2	d1-a1	Not too suitable for very light high voices	Very slow and somber. From "Trauer und Trost," a cycle of 6 songs.

"Brautlieder": a cycle of six songs; text by the composer

TITLE	COMP.	TESS.	TYPE	REMARKS
(1) Ein Myrtenreis	e1-f#2	g#1-e2	Women's voices	Sustained, delicate.
(2) Der Liebe Lohn	b-f#2	e1-c#2	Women's voices, except a very light soprano	Animated. Demands an accomplished pianist.
(3) Vorabend	c#1-g2	g1-d2	Women's voices	Sustained.
(4) Am Morgen	d1-g2	f#1-d2	Women's voices	Slow, somewhat declamatory.
(5) Aus dem hohen Liede	d1-a2	g1-e2	Women's voices, except a very light soprano	Spirited, vigorous.
(6) Märchenwunder	d#1-g#2	g#1-e2	Women's voices	Animated. Demands an accomplished pianist.

TITLE	COMP.	TESS.	TYPE	REMARKS
Ein Ton			All voices	This celebrated song, in which the voice part consists of one incessantly repeated note is originally written in e minor, the voice note being b1. From "Trauer und Trost," a cycle of 6 songs.
Komm, wir wandeln	f1-g#2	ab1-f2	All voices	Sustained. One of Cornelius' best known and very representative songs.

"Weihnachtslieder": a cycle of six songs; text by the composer

TITLE	COMP.	TESS.	TYPE	REMARKS
(1) Christbaum	d1-e2	g1-d2	All voices	Spirited.
(2) Die Hirten	c#1-eb2	e1-c#2	All voices	Sustained.
(3) Die Könige	b-e2	d1-b1	All voices	Slow. The accompaniment is an independent choral.
(4) Simeon	b-d2	e1-b1	All voices	A narrative song.
(5) Christus der Kinderfreund	c1-c2	eb1-bb1	All voices	Slow, rather delicate.
(6) Christkind	c1-eb2	eb1-c2	All voices	Spirited.

See also the following cycles: "Vater under," "Rheinische Lieder," "An Bertha."

ROBERT FRANZ
(1815-1892)

Practically none of the songs of Robert Franz make any unusual technical demands upon the singer or the pianist.

One of the outstanding characteristics of his manner of writing is its
unassuming, almost self-effacing simplicity. Although the harmonic
structure of his songs is by no means elementary, and although he is uncommonly inventive and extremely fastidious in regard to the part leading
(especially in the treatment of the inner parts of his accompaniments),
his reluctance to employ any violent harmonic or rhythmic effects makes
his songs appear utterly devoid of complexity. Even though his technical
demands upon the vocalist are moderate, his treatment of the vocal line
is such that his songs at first glance invariably appear even less exacting
than they are. Thus, it seems only natural that many of his songs have
been used extensively for teaching purposes; this has undoubtedly contributed to the undeserved neglect of most of his songs by many a concert
singer, branding Franz, in his eyes as a composer of "teaching songs."

Although it is true that a more or less adequate performance of many
of his songs may be within the powers of almost any competent vocalist,
a more satisfactory performance of a song by Franz requires a rare
poetic insight and a considerable musical sensitivity. The very outward
simplicity of his songs tends to emphasize any inadequacy of this kind on
the part of the singer, an inadequacy which may be much less apparent in
a more elaborate musical setting of a poem.

Out of nearly three hundred songs that Franz wrote, the following list
of fifty-six seemed adequate for the purpose of this volume, as his writing
is rather uniform in style and his choice of poetic material, though nearly
impeccable in taste, seems to be on the whole somewhat limited in scope.

It is claimed on good authority that Franz always had a mezzo-soprano
voice in his mind when composing his songs and resented any attempts
to transpose them to fit other voices, although, as one writer puts it, "he
did not object to having his songs sung by men."

> Editions: Peters
> Breitkopf & Härtel
> Schirmer
> Musicians Library, Oliver Ditson
> Numerous reprints of single songs

TITLE	COMP.	TESS.	TYPE	REMARKS
Abends	d#1-g2	g1-e2	All voices	Delicate, sustained.
Ach, wenn ich doch ein Immchen wär	e#1-f#2	a#1-d#2	Most suitable for light high voices	Light and delicate. Demands an accomplished pianist.
Altes Lied	b-f#2	g1-e2	Most suitable for medium or low voices	A rather curious poem. Interpretatively not easy.
Auf dem Teich, dem regungslosen	eb1-g2	bb1-f2	All voices	Delicate, sustained. Demands good command of p. See Mendelssohn, "Schilflied," and the setting of this Lenau poem by C. Griffes.

TITLE	COMP.	TESS.	TYPE	REMARKS
Auf dem Meere (Das Meer hat seine Perlen)	c#1-g#2	e1-d#2	Not too suitable for very light high voices	Slow and sustained.
Auf geheimem Waldespfade	gb1-gb2	bb1-eb2	All voices	Sustained. Demands good command of p. See C. Griffes, "By a Lonely Forest Pathway."
Aus meinen grossen Schmerzen	c#1-e2	f1-c2	All voices	Slow and sustained. See H. Wolf.
Bitte	db1-db2	f1-c2	Medium or low voices	Slow and very sustained.
Da die Stunde kam	d1-f2	g1-d2	All voices	Delicate.
Das Meer erstrahlt im Sonnenschein	c1-g2	g1-c2	Not too suitable for very light high voices	Slow and very sustained.
Denk ich dein	d1-g2	g1-e2	All voices	Delicate. Very sustained.
Der Fichtenbaum	db1-gb2	f1-db2	All voices	Slow and very sustained. See Liszt.
Der Schalk	e#1-f#2	a#1-e2	Not too suitable for very low voices	Light and delicate.
Die blauen Frühlingsaugen	c#1-g#2	f#1-d#2	All voices	Graceful, delicate. Demands lightness of tone and an accomplished pianist.
Die Lotosblume (Geibel)	f1-g2	bb1-f2	All voices	Sustained. Demands good command of pp.
Du liebes Augee	f#1-f#2	g#1-d#2	All voices	Very sustained.
Durch den Wald im Mondenscheine	c#1-f#2	g#1-e2	All voices	Rapid. Demands an accomplished pianist. See Mendelssohn, "Neue Liebe."
Ein Friedhof	c1-eb2	eb1-c2	Medium or low voices	Grave and very sustained. Demands good command of p.
Ein Stündlein wohl vor Tag	c1-g2	e1-c2	Women's voices	Delicate, graceful. Demands some flexivility. See Wolf.
Er ist gekommen	eb1-f2	ab1-eb2	Women's voices, except a very light soprano	Rapid, vigorous.
Es hat die Rose sich beklagt	db1-f2	eb1-bb1	All voices	Delicate, graceful. See Rubinstein.
Es ragt in's Meer der Runenstein	g-f2	c1-c2	Most suitable for medium or low voices	Grave, somewhat declamatory.

TITLE	COMP.	TESS.	TYPE	REMARKS
Frühling und Liebe	e1-f#2	a1-e2	Not suitable for very heavy low voices	Graceful, delicate.
Frühlingsgedränge	f1-ab2	ab1-f2	High voices	Light and animated. See R. Strauss.
Für Musik	gb1-ab2	bb1-eb2	All voices	Slow and sustained. See Rubinstein, "Nun die Schatten dunkeln." Also see Jensen.
Gute Nacht	e1-e2	a1-d2	All voices	Delicate, subdued.
Hör' ich das Liedchen klingen	e1-g2	b1-e2	Not too suitable for very heavy voices	Delicate. Demands some flexibility. See Schumann.
Ich hab' in deinem Auge	eb1-f2	ab1-eb2	All voices	Very sustained.
Im Herbst	c1-ab2	g1-eb2	Not suitable for light voices	Dramatic, somber.
Im Rhein, im heiligen Strome	c#1-e2	e1-c#2	All voices	Delicate, sustained. Demands good command of p. See Schumann and Liszt.
In meinen Armen wieg' ich dich	c1-eb2	ab1-eb2	All voices	Slow and very sustained. Interpretatively not easy.
Kommt feins Liebchen heut'	b#-f#2	f#1-c#2	Most suitable for men's voices	Very sustained, subdued. See Schumann, "Morgens steh' ich auf und frage."
Lieb Liebchen	a-e2	a1-d2	Most suitable for men's voices	Animated. Interpretatively not easy. See Schumann.
Lieber Schatz sei wieder gut mir	d1-f2	g1-d2	Women's voices	Delicate, graceful. In folk vein.
Mädchen mit dem roten Mündchen	eb1-gb2	ab1-eb2	All voices	Graceful, delicate.
Marie	d1-f2	f1-c2	All voices	Sustained, delicate. See Jensen.
Meerfahrt	c#1-d#2	f#1-c#2	All voices	Delicate. See Brahms, and H. Wolf, "Mein Liebchen, wir sassen beisammen."
Mein Schatz ist auf der Wanderschaft	eb1-g2	g1-eb2	Women's voices	Light and animated. Demands facile articulation.
Mit schwarzen Segeln	c1-f2	g1-eb2	Not suitable for light voices	Somber, animated and vigorous.
Mutter, o sing' mich zur Ruh'	e1-g2	a1-e2	Women's voices	Slow and sustained. Demands an accomplished pianist.
O Lüge nicht	e1-e2	g1-d2	Not too suitable for very light high voices	Very sustained.

TITLE	COMP.	TESS.	TYPE	REMARKS
O säh ich auf der Haide dort	f1-f2	g1-d2	Not suitable for very light voices	Rapid and vigorous. See also Mendelssohn's version of this Burns poem, (Duet for two soprani).
Sag mir	c1-a2	a1-e2	Most suitable for light voices	Gently humorous. Interpretatively not easy.
Schlummerlied	e1-f#2	g#1-d#2	All voices	Delicate, sustained. See Brahms, "Ruhe Süssliebchen."
Sie liebten sich beide	d#1-e#2	g#1-d#2	All voices	Delicate. Interpretatively not easy.
Sonnenuntergang: schwarze Wolken ziehn	c#1-f#2	f#1-d#2	Not suitable for light high voices	Somber, animated and vigorous.
Sterne mit den goldnen Füsschen	d#1-e2	g#2-e2	All voices	Graceful, delicate. Demands lightness of tone.
Stille Sicherheit	e1-f2	ab1-eb2	All voices	Delicate, sustained.
Umsonst	f1-e2	a1-d2	All voices	Slow, sustained and subdued.
Und die Rosen die prangen	c1-g2	g1-eb2	All voices	Delicate, sustained.
Waldfahrt	d1-g2	b1-e2	All voices	Spirited.
Wandl' ich in dem Wald	d#1-f#2	f#1-d#2	All voices	Delicate, sustained.
Widmung	eb1-f2	ab1-eb2	All voices	Slow and very sustained.
Wie des Mondes Abbild	gb1-f2	bb1-f2	Most suitable for light voices	Slow and very sustained. Demands good command of pp.
Wilkommen, mein Wald	c1-g2	g1-eb2	All voices, except a very light soprano	Spirited.
Wonne der Wehmut	f1-g2	ab1-db2	All voices	Slow and sustained. See Beethoven.

PAUL HINDEMITH
(1895-   )

Paul Hindemith, perhaps one of the outstanding composers of our time, has written only a comparatively small number of songs. The most remarkable among them are perhaps those contained in the "Marienleben" cycle, of which a few are listed below. Hindemith's songs may seem very complex and dissonant at first reading, but upon closer acquaintance one becomes aware of their extraordinary logic and simplicity. They are expertly written for the voice and can under no circumstances be considered vocally taxing. The short list here is primarily intended for those who are not at all familiar with his songs. It is sincerely hoped that they will stimulate the reader to acquaint himself more fully with songs by Hindemith.

TITLE	COMP.	TESS.	TYPE	REMARKS

Editions: Schott
Associated Music Publishers, New York

TITLE	COMP.	TESS.	TYPE	REMARKS
Argwohn Josephs (from "Marienleben" a cycle of 15 songs, opus 27)	c1-g2	f1-f2	Mezzo-soprano or soprano	Rapid. Musically not easy. Demands an accomplished pianist.
Auf der Treppe sitzen meine Öhrchen (8 songs, opus 18)	eb1-f2	ab1-d2	High or medium voices	Not fast. Subdued. Demands facile articulation. Musically and interpretatively not easy.
Geburt Marias (from "Marienleben" a cycle of 15 songs, opus 27)	e1-a2	a1-f#2	Soprano	Very delicate. Sustained.
Pietà. (from "Marienleben," a cycle of 15 songs, opus 27)	c1-e2		Mezzo-soprano or soprano	Slow and declamatory; grave. Musically and interpretatively not easy.
Trompeten (8 songs, opus 18)	b-ab2 (ab)	g1-eb2	Most suitable for high voices	Slow, somewhat declamatory. Demands good command of high pp. Musically and interpretatively not easy.

Eight English Songs

TITLE	COMP.	TESS.	TYPE	REMARKS
Sing on there in the swamp	c#1-g#2	f#1-f#2	High or medium voices	Very slow, subdued. Interpretatively not easy.
The moon	d#1-eb2	f#1-c#2	Not suitable for very light high voices	Very animated. Has a slow, rather declamatory and subdued ending. Interpretatively not easy. Demands an accomplished pianist.
The wild flower's song	e1-g2	f1-e2(H)	Not too suitable for very low voices	Sustained.
The whistling thief	e1-f2		High or medium voices	An animated comic song.

TITLE	COMP.	TESS.	TYPE	REMARKS
Envoy	eb1-f#2	f#1-e2	High or medium voices, except a very light soprano	Slow, sustained. In parts demands considerable dramatic intensity. Musically not easy.

See also "Die Junge Magd" 6 songs for mezzo-soprano and chamber orchestra.

ENGELBERT HUMPERDINCK
(1854-1921)

TITLE	COMP.	TESS.	TYPE	REMARKS
Am Rhein	c1-g2	f1-f2	Not too suitable for very light high voices	Sustained, effective. (Associated Music Publishers)
Wiegenlied	c1-f2	f1-d2	Women's voices	Sustained, subdued. (Associated Music Publishers)

ADOLF JENSEN
(1837-1879)

Jensen's songs, though very popular at the turn of the century, seem of but little importance or interest now, and have, perhaps justly, almost disappeared from the present-day repertoire. They are, however, expertly written, possess a certain not inconsiderable elegance and are, if well performed, quite effective.

Editions: Peters
   A very comprehensive collection by Ditson (Musician's Library)
   Numerous reprints of single songs

TITLE	COMP.	TESS.	TYPE	REMARKS
Am Ufer des Flusses, des Manzanares	d1-f#2	f#1-d2	Not too suitable for very heavy low voices	Spirited and light. Demands an accomplished pianist.
Barcarole	f1-f2	a1-e2	Not too suitable for very heavy low voices	Light and delicate.
Lehn' deine Wang'	c1-eb2	g1-d2	All voices	Very sustained. See Schumann.
Leis' rudern hier	f#1-g2	a1-e2	Men's voices	Light and delicate. See Schumann, "Venetianisches Lied."
Marie	f1-d2	a1-c2	All voices	Very sustained, delicate. See Franz.

TITLE	COMP.	TESS.	TYPE	REMARKS
Margreta	f1-f2	ab1-eb2	Men's voices	Light and spirited. Demands facile articul-ation. One of Jensen's best songs.
Mein Herz ist im Hochland	c#1-e2	e1-c#2	Not suit-able for very light voices	Best for baritone. Vigorous and spirited. The original words by Burns ("My heart's in the Highlands") can be substituted. One of Jensen's best songs.
Murmelndes Lüftchen	e1-ab2	db2-gb2	Most suit-able for high light voices	Very light and delicate. Demands good command of high pp.
Nun die Schatten dunkeln	f1-ab2	ab1-eb2	All voices	Very sustained. See Rubinstein, and Franz, "Fur Musik."
Süss und sacht	db1-gb2	g1-eb2	Women's voices	Delicate, sustained. The original words by Tennyson ("Sweet and low") can be sub-stituted.
Wenn durch die Piazzetta	e1-g2 (a2)	a1-f2	Most suit-able for men's voices	Light and delicate. Demands an accom-plished pianist. See Schumann, "Venetian-isches Lied," and Mendelssohn "Venetian-isches Gondellied."
Wie so bleich	d#1-e2	f#1-b1	Mezzo-soprano or alto	Grave and very sus-tained. (from Dolorosa cycle) One of Jensen's best songs.

ERICH WOLFGANG KORNGOLD
(1897-)
Edition: Associated Music Publishers.

TITLE	COMP.	TESS.	TYPE	REMARKS
Das Ständchen	c1-f#2	e1-e2	Not too suitable for very light high voices	Animated. Demands an accomplished pianist. See H. Wolf, "Standchen."
Liebesbriefchen	d#1-f#2	g#1-d#2	All voices	Sustained.
Nachtwanderer	c#1-f2	d1-d2	Most suit-able for medium or low voices	Dramatic. Interpre-tatively not easy.
Schneeglöckchen	c1-g2	f1-d2	All voices	Delicate, sustained.

ERNST KŘENEK
(1900-   )

Ernst Křenek, best known as the composer of the so-called "jazz opera" Johnny spielt auf, has written a considerable number of songs. Two cycles: "Fiedellieder," opus 64, 7 songs, most suitable for baritone or mezzo-soprano (ab-f#1) and "Reisebuch aus den Osterreichischen Alpen," opus 62, 20 songs for medium or high voices, are among the most representative of his manner of writing.

Edition: Universal

FRANZ LISZT
(1811-1886)

Some of Liszt's songs, not unlike some of his instrumental music, seem to have lost much of their former appeal, even though the historical significance of his music appears to be more generally recognized and appreciated now than ever before.

Yet songs like "Die drei Zigeuner," "Comment, disaient-ils," and "Oh, quand je dors" are masterpieces of such remarkable individuality and power that it seems strange to have to recommend them to the present-day singer.

Liszt's songs demand for the most part considerably developed vocal technic, as well as a highly developed dramatic instinct, and his accompaniments, like the piano part in "Die drei Zigeuner," often demand a pianist of soloist stature.

Editions: Breitkopf & Härtel
Universal
Excellent selection Musician's Library, Ditson
12 songs (2 vols.), Schirmer
Numerous reprints of single songs

TITLE	COMP.	TESS.	TYPE	REMARKS
Angiolin dal biondo crin (Italian text)	c1-eb2	f1-d2	Women's voices	Sustained, graceful.
Comment, disaient-ils (French text)	c#1-ab2 (b2)		Most suitable for light soprano	Rapid, delicate. Demands good command of high pp. and an accomplished pianist. See Lalo.
Das Veilchen	d1-eb2	g1-d2	All voices	Graceful, delicate.
Der Fischerknabe	d#1-ab2	ab1-f2	Soprano or mezzo-soprano	Delicate, sustained. Demands good command of high pp. and an accomplished pianist.
Der König von Thule	b-f2 (g#)	eb1-c2	Not suitable for light voices	A dramatic narrative song. See a simple setting by Schubert.
Der du von dem Himmel bist	e1-g#2	b1-f#2	All voices	Very slow, sustained. Somewhat declamatory. See Schubert and Löwe.

TITLE	COMP.	TESS.	TYPE	REMARKS
Die drei Zigeuner	b-g2	d1-d2	Not suitable for very light voices	Dramatic, descriptive. Interpretatively not easy. Demands an excellent pianist. One of Liszt's most remarkable songs.
Die Lorelei	b-g1 (bb2)	g1-e2	Heavy voices	A dramatic, narrative song. Demands an accomplished pianist.
Du bist wie eine Blume	e1-g2	a1-e2	All voices	Slow, very sustained. See Schumann, Rubinstein.
Ein Fichtenbaum steht einsam	d1-f2	ab1-eb2	All voices	Slow, very sustained. Demands good command of high pp. See R. Franz's version among many others.
Es muss ein Wunderbares sein	c1-eb2	f1-db2	All voices	Very sustained.
Freudvoll and leidvoll	eb1-g2 (ab2)	ab1-f2	Women's voices	Sustained. In parts demands considerable dramatic intensity. See Schubert, "Die Liebe"; and Rubinstein, "Clärchens Lied."
Kling leise mein Lied	e1-g#2	f#1-f#2	Not too suitable for very low heavy voices	Animated, delicate. Demands good command of sustained pp.
Lasst mich ruhen	d#1-eb2	f#1-c#2	All voices	Slow and sustained. Demands good command of pp.
Mignon's Lied (Kennst du das Land)	b#-f#2	f#1-d#2	Women's voices, except a very light soprano	Dramatic. Demands an excellent pianist. See Schubert, Beethoven, Schumann, H. Wolf.
Oh, quand je dors (French text)	d#1-a2	g#1-e2	Most suitable for high voices	Very sustained. In parts demands considerable dramatic intensity, also good command of high pp.
Schlüsselblümchen	eb1-f2	f1-eb2	All voices	Animated, graceful. Demands lightness of tone.
S'il est un charmant gazon (French text)	eb1-f2	ab1-eb2	All voices	Delicate, graceful. See G. Fauré, "Rêve d'amour."
Wanderers Nachtlied (Über allen Gipfeln)	b-e2	f1-d2	Not too suitable for very light high voices	Slow and very sustained. See Schubert, C. Löwe, and Schumann, "Nachtlied."

TITLE	COMP.	TESS.	TYPE	REMARKS
Jeanne D'Arc au bûcher (French text)	c1-g#2 (a2)	e1-e2	Dramatic soprano (mezzo-soprano)	A "dramatic scene" originally written for voice and orchestra. A declamatory adagio and a somewhat martial animato. (Schirmer, Album of Concert Arias)

CARL LÖWE
(1796-1869)

Most of the ballades (narrative songs) and songs of Löwe, with but few exceptions, are written for heavy dramatic voices.

Löwe's unerring dramatic instinct enabled him to create extraordinarily forceful effects with elementary harmonic and melodic devices. In performing his songs and ballades one should perhaps try to emulate this simplicity by avoiding as much as possible an overdramatization in the manner of delivery.

Editions: Schlesinger (complete)
Albums: Peters
Breitkopf & Härtel
Schirmer

TITLE	COMP.	TESS.	TYPE	REMARKS
Archibald Douglas	g-eb2	d1-d2	Not suitable for light voices; most suitable for baritone	A dramatic, narrative song of considerable length. Demands an accomplished pianist.
Canzonetta	b-a2	g#1-f#2	Most suitable for high voices	Slow and sustained. Demands considerable flexibility.
Der Heilige Franziskus	a-e2	e1-b1	Low or medium voices	Slow, sustained.
Die nächtliche Heerschau	bb-f2 (g)	d1-d2	Low or medium voices	An animated, march-like dramatic narrative song (ballade).
Der Mohrenfürst auf der Messe	b-g2	e1-e2	Not suitable for light high voices	A dramatic narrative song (ballade). Demands an excellent pianist. One of the best examples of Löwe's musicodramatic style. No. 3 of the trilogy, opus 97; "Der Mohrenfürst", "Die Mohrenfürstin", and "Der Mohrenfürst auf der Messe."

TITLE	COMP.	TESS.	TYPE	REMARKS
Der Mummelsee	a-g2	d1-d2	Mezzo-soprano or soprano; not suitable for very light high soprano	A narrative song (ballade). Very florid. Demands an accomplished pianist.
Der selt'ne Beter	a-e2	b-b1	Medium or low voices	A dramatic narrative song (ballade).
Der Zahn	c1-f2	e1-e2	All voices	A jolly song in praise of a baby's first tooth.
Des Glockenthürmers Töchterlein	c#1-a2	a1-f#2	Most suitable for high light voices	Light, gently humorous. Quite florid.
Die Uhr	b♭-f2	d1-d2	Not too suitable for light high voices	A simple narrative song.
Edward	b♭-g♭2 (a♭)	e♭1-e♭2	Not suitable for very light high voices	A dramatic narrative song (ballade). One of the best examples of Löwe's musicodramatic style. Demands an accomplished pianist.
Erlkönig	a1-g2	d1-d2	Not suitable for light voices	A dramatic, narrative song (ballade). One of the best examples of Löwe's musicodramatic style. See Schubert and an admirable essay on Löwe's "Erlkönig" by D. Tovey.
Mädchen sind wie der Wind	b-e2 (g)	d1-d2	Medium or low voices	Light and rapid. Demands an accomplished pianist.
Niemand hat's geseh'n	d#1-f#2 (a2)	e1-e2	Most suitable for light soprano	Very animated, light. Demands considerable flexibility.
Odins Meeres-Ritt	b-f#2	e1-e2	Not suitable for light high voices	A dramatic narrative song.
O Süsse Mutter	d1-g2	g1-e2	Women's voices	Animated. Demands facile articulation. See H. Wolf, "Die Spinnerin."
Süsses Begräbris	d#1-e2	g#1-d#2	All voices	Sustained.
Walpurgisnacht	g-g2	c1-c2	Women's voices, except a very light soprano	Very animated, dramatic. Demands facile articulation.

See also:
"Die Verfallene Mühle"
"Tom der Reimer"   all dramatic narrative songs.
"Der Nöck"

GUSTAV MAHLER
(1860-1911)

The songs of Gustav Mahler, as characteristic of his manner of writing
as are his symphonies, seem to possess a much wider popular appeal.
Of great melodic simplicity, they are nevertheless not too easy vocally
or interpretatively, being written for the most part for rather heavy
voices possessing a somewhat extensive range and capable of commanding
a great variety of dynamics. Practically all of them are written for voice
and orchestra; the pianoforte arrangements of the orchestral score are,
however, Mahler's own, in most cases.

The "Lieder eines fahrenden Gesellen," "Wer hat dies Liedlein erdacht,"
"Ich atmet' einen linden Duft," "Liebst du um Schönheit," "Ich bin der
Welt abhanden gekommen" are recommended to those not at all acquainted
with his manner of writing.

Editions: Universal.
Some reprints by Boosey.

TITLE	COMP.	TESS.	TYPE	REMARKS
Blicke mir nicht in die Lieder	c1-f2	c1-c2	All voices	Very animated. Demands an accomplished pianist.
Das irdische Leben	bb-gb2 (H)		Dramatic soprano or mezzo-soprano	Dramatic, animated. Demands an excellent pianist.
Der Tamboursg'sell	A-g1	c-c1	Most suitable for baritone	A marchlike, dramatic song. Interpretatively not easy.
Des Antonius von Padua Fischpredigt	d1-g2 (a) (H)		Not too suitable for very light high voices	Humorous. Demands some flexibility and an excellent pianist. A trifle long.
Erinnerung	d1-f2 (a2)	g1-eb2	All voices	Slow, sustained and subdued.
Frühlingsmorgen	d1-g2	g1-e2	Most suitable for high voices	Light, delicate. Demands some flexibility and an accomplished pianist.
Hans und Grethe	c1-f2 (c3)		Not too suitable for very low voices	A waltz. In folk vein.
Ich atmet einen Linden Duft	bb-f#2	f#1-d2	Not suitable for very low heavy voices	Slow, sustained, very delicate. Demands good command of high pp.

-201-

TITLE	COMP.	TESS.	TYPE	REMARKS
Ich bin der Welt abhanden gekommen	bb-f2	eb1-eb2	All voices	Slow, subdued. Interpretatively not easy. Demands some flexibility and good command of high pp.

"Kindertotenlieder": a cycle of five songs for low or medium voice and orchestra. (Intended to be sung without interruption as a unit)

TITLE	COMP.	TESS.	TYPE	REMARKS
(1) Nun will die Sonn' so hell aufgeh'n!	d1-eb2	e1-bb1		Slow, sustained, somber. Interpretatively not easy.
(2) Nun seh' ich wohl, warum so dunkel Flammen	a-f2	d1-d2		Sustained, somber. Demands good command of high pp. Interpretatively not easy.
(3) Wenn dein Mütterlein	g-f2	c1-c2		Sustained, somber. Demands in parts considerable dramatic intensity. Interpretatively not easy.
(4) Oft denk' ich, sie sind nur ausgegangen	bb-gb2	eb1-eb2		Not fast. Sustained, somber. In parts very dramatic. Demands good command of high pp. Interpretatively not easy.
(5) In diesem Wetter!	bb-f2	d1-d2		Animated, somewhat declamatory, dramatic. The final section sustained and delicate. Interpretatively not easy. Demands an accomplished pianist.

TITLE	COMP.	TESS.	TYPE	REMARKS
Liebst du um Schönheit	eb1-f2		Most suitable for women's voices	Sustained. Demands good command of high pp.

Leider eines fahrenden Gesellen

TITLE	COMP.	TESS.	TYPE	REMARKS
(1) Wenn mein Schatz Hochzeit macht	b-g2	a1-e2	High baritone or mezzo-soprano	Sustained. This magnificent cycle of four songs is originally written for voice and orchestra. The piano arrangement is by Mahler. The songs can be sung separately, but

TITLE	COMP.	TESS.	TYPE	REMARKS
Cont'd				
(1) Wenn mein Schatz Hochzeit macht				are best performed as a unit. They are interpretatively complex and demand an accomplished pianist.
(2) Gieng heut Morgen uber's Feld	a-f#2 (g2)	f#1-e2		Animated, delicate. Demands good command of high pp.
(3) Ich hab ein glühend Messer	bb-gb2 (g2)	f1-eb2		Very dramatic and rapid.
(4) Die zwei blauen Augen	a-g2	e1-c2		Very subdued, in march tempo. Demands good command of high pp.
Lob des hohen Verstandes	a-bb2	d1-d2	Not suitable for very light high voices	Humorous. Demands an excellent pianist. The bb2 is not sung, but is used in an imitation of a donkey's bray.
Phantasie	b-f#2	f#1-d2	All voices, except a very light soprano	Sustained, very subdued.
O Röschen rot (alto solo from Symphony No. 2)	db1-eb2	db1-db2	Alto	Sustained. In the manner of a choral.
Revelge	d-a1	f-eb1	Most suitable for dramatic tenor or high baritone	Marchlike, dramatic. Interpretatively not easy. Demands an accomplished pianist.
Rheinlegendchen	b-f#2	e1-e2	Soprano or mezzo-soprano	Light, gently humorous. Demands some flexibility and an accomplished pianist.
Serenade	e1-g2	f#1-d2	Most suitable for men's voices	Sustained, delicate.
Um Mitternacht	b-g2	e1-e2	Not too suitable for light voices	Very sustained. Demands in parts considerable dramatic intensity. Interpretatively not easy.
Wer hat dies Liedlein erdacht	c-f1 (a2)	f1-d2 (H)	All voices	Light, gently humorous. Demands considerable flexibility and an excellent pianist.
Wo die schönen Trompeten blasen	a-g2	f#1-f#2	Not too suitable for very light high voices	Very subdued. Interpretatively not easy. Demands good command of sustained pp.

See also nine early songs to texts from "Des Knaben Wunderhorn"; solo excerpts from symphonies Nos. 3, 4, 8, and "Das Klagende Lied", for soprano, alto, tenor, chorus and orchestra. See also "Das Lied von der Erde," 6 songs for tenor and alto (or baritone) and orchestra. (Not overly suitable for performance with piano.)

JOSEPH MARX
(1882-   )

Marx's many songs, effective and well written as they are, seem sometimes to suffer from a certain overornateness and overelaboration of the accompaniment. The extremely effective and well-known "Hat dich die Liebe berührt" and "Der Ton" are perhaps not so direct and moving as "Marienlied," "Selige Nacht," and "Nocturne," which can perhaps be classed among the outstanding examples of Marx's style at its best.

Edition: Universal
Associated Music Publishers

TITLE	COMP.	TESS.	TYPE	REMARKS
An einen Herbstwald	c#1-f#2	f#1-c#2	Not suitable for light high voices	Grave, vigorous. Demands an accomplished pianist.
Der bescheidene Schäfer	e1-a2	g1-e2	Soprano or mezzo-soprano	Humorous, light.
Der Rauch	c#1-f#2	f#1-c#2	All voices	Slow, sustained and subdued.
Der Ton	c1-f2	f1-db2	Medium or low voices	Very effective. Has a sustained vocal line over an elaborate accompaniment. Demands an excellent pianist.
Hat dich die Liebe berührt	eb1-g2 (bb2)	g1-eb2	Not suitable for light voices	Slow and sustained. Has very effective, dramatic climaxes. Demands an accomplished pianist.
Lied eines Mädchens	c#1-f#2	f#1-d#2	Women's voices	Slow, sustained, rather delicate.
Marienlied	d1-ab2	g1-eb2	Not too suitable very low voices	Delicate, sustained.
Nocturne	eb1-ab2	ab1-f2	High voices	Has a sustained vocal line over an elaborate accompaniment. Demands an excellent pianist. The extremely important piano part would lose too much of its sonority if transposed.
Selige Nacht	db1-gb2	gb1-eb2	All voices	Sustained, delicate.
Tuch der Tränen	c1-ab2	g1-eb2	All voices	Sustained, rather subdued, somber.

TITLE	COMP.	TESS.	TYPE	REMARKS
Und gestern hat er mir Rosen gebracht	e1-a2	a1-f#2	Soprano	Light, animated. Very effective. Demands an accomplished pianist.
Valse de Chopin	c#1-g#2	c#1-c#2	Not too suitable for very light high voices	Animated. Interpretatively not easy. Demands an excellent pianist.
Waldseligkeit	d#1-a2	a1-e2	All voices	Sustained, effective.
Wie einst	d1-g2	eb1-eb2	All voices	Slow, sustained, delicate.

FELIX MENDELSSOHN
(1809-1847)

Mendelssohn's songs are seldom encountered on concert programs today. The general reaction so prevalent during the past twenty or thirty years against their so-called "sentimentality" seems to have prejudiced many a singer against Mendelssohn; although it may be questioned how many of such singers have taken the pains to acquaint themselves with his songs. The curious fact is that Mendelssohn in his songs is perhaps less sentimental than, for instance, Schumann or Franz, and that most of his songs demand an almost Mozartean clarity, restraint and precision of execution, especially in regard to rhythm and phrasing. Songs like "Neue Liebe," "Jagdlied," "Lieblingsplätzchen," "Pagenlied," "Frühlingslied" (In Schwäbischer Mundart), "Erndtelied," to name but a few, are magnificent examples of the German lied at its best and it seems rather peculiar that any serious singer should have to be reminded of their existence.

Editions: Peters
Schirmer
Novello, and many others.

TITLE	COMP.	TESS.	TYPE	REMARKS
Altdeutsches Lied	e1-e2	a1-e2	All voices	Very sustained.
An die Entfernte	f1-f2	g1-d2	All voices	Delicate, light. Demands facile articulation.
Auf Flügeln des Gesanges	eb1-f2	bb1-eb2	All voices	Very sustained.
Bei der Wiege	f1-f2	f1-d2	Women's voices	Delicate. Demands lightness of tone.
Das erste Veilchen	f1-f2	a1-eb2	All voices	Graceful, sustained.
Das Waldschloss	e1-e2	g1-d2	Not too suitable very light high voices	Vigorous, dramatic.
Der Blumenstrauss	e1-f#2	a1-e2	All voices	Graceful.
Der Mond	e1-g#2	g#1-e2	All voices	Very sustained.
Erndtelied (Es ist ein Schnitter, der heisst Tod)	d1-d2	e1-b1	Not too suitable for very light high voices	A chorale-like setting of a beautiful old religious poem. Verses 2, 4 and 5 could be omitted. A little known, remarkable song.

TITLE	COMP.	TESS.	TYPE	REMARKS
Frühlingslied (In dem Walde)	e1-f♯2	a1-e2	All voices	Very sustained.
Frühlingslied (In Schwäbischer Mundart)	d♯1-g♯2	g♯1-e2	Most suitable for light soprano	Light and graceful. In dialect, but German words can be easily substituted. Demands some flexibility and an accomplished pianist.
Gruss	d♯1-f♯2	a1-d2	All voices	Sustained, delicate.
Hirtenlied	d1-g2	g1-e2	Most suitable for high voices	Sustained, graceful.
Im Grünen	c♯1-g♯2 (b2)	b1-f♯2	Most suitable for high voices	Rapid and gay. Demands facile articulation.
Jagdlied	b-e2	e1-b1	All voices	Spirited.
Lieblingsplätzchen	f♯1-e2	g1-d2	All voices	Delicate.
Maienlied	d1-f♯2	a1-e2	All voices	Animated, delicate.
Minnelied (Wie der Quell)	e1-f♯2	a1-e2	All voices	Very sustained.
Minnelied im Mai	f1-g2	a1-d2	Most suitable for men's voices	Graceful, sustained. See Brahms, "Minnelied."
Nachtlied	d1-ab2	g1-eb2	All voices	Slow. Interpretatively not easy.
Neue Liebe	c♯1-a2	a1-f♯2	Most suitable for high light voices	Very rapid and light. Demands facile articulation and an excellent pianist. One of the most remarkable of Mendelssohn's songs. See R. Franz, "In dem Mondenschein im Walde."
O Jugend, o schöne Rosenzeit	e1-a2	a1-f♯2	All voices	Animated, the vocal line sustained. In folk vein.
Pagenlied	e1-e2	g1-d2	All voices	Light and delicate.
Reiselied (Der Herbstwind rüttelt)	e1-g2	g1-e2	Not too suitable for very light high voices	Rapid, vigorous, dramatic. Demands an accomplished pianist.
Schilflied	c♯1-f♯2	g♯1-d2	All voices	Somber. In parts demands considerable dramatic intensity. See R. Franz, "Auf dem Teich dem regungslosem," and C. Griffes.
Sonntagslied	e1-f♯2	a1-e2	Women's voices	Animated. In folk vein.
Suleika (Was bedeutet die Bewegung)	e1-g♯2	g♯1-e2	Women's voices	Spirited. See Schubert.
Tröstung	d1-f♯2	f♯1-d2	All voices	Very sustained.

TITLE	COMP.	TESS.	TYPE	REMARKS
Venetianisches Gondellied	e1-f#2	b1-f#2	Most suitable for men's voices	Delicate. See Schumann and A. Jensen, "Wenn durch Piazzetta."
Wenn sich zwei Herzen scheiden	e1-f#2	g1-d2	All voices	Sustained.
Infelice! Già dal mio sguardo (concert air) (Italian text)	d1-bb2	f1-f2	Dramatic soprano (lyric soprano)	Recitative, andante, allegro. (Schirmer, Album of Concert Arias)

Solo Excerpts from English Oratorios

Note: The title of the Oratorio is placed above the title of the excerpt.

Soprano

Elijah

TITLE	COMP.	TESS.	TYPE	REMARKS
Hear ye, Israel	e1-a2	a1-f#2	Dramatic soprano (lyric soprano)	A very sustained, adagio and a spirited, vigorous, dramatic allegro maestoso.
Hear my prayer (Motet) O for the wings of a dove	d1-g2	g1-d2	Soprano	Sustained, rather delicate..

Lauda Sion

Caro cibus (Lord at all times)	d1-g2	f1-f2	Lyric soprano (dramatic soprano)	Sustained.

St. Paul

Recitative: So they being filled Air: I will sing of thy great mercies	e1-f2	g1-e2	Lyric soprano (dramatic soprano)	Sustained, graceful.

St. Paul

Jerusalem, thou that killest the prophets	f1-f2	bb1-f2	Lyric soprano (dramatic soprano)	Slow, very sustained.

All these excerpts are generally available.

Alto or Mezzo-soprano

Elijah

TITLE	COMP.	TESS.	TYPE	REMARKS
O rest in the Lord	b-d2	e1-c2		Slow, very sustained.

Elijah

Woe unto them	b-e2	d#1-b1		Slow, sustained.

St. Paul

Recitative: And he journeyed with companions Air: But the Lord is mindful of His own	a-d2	d1-a1		Slow, very sustained.

All these excerpts are generally available.

TITLE	COMP.	TESS.	TYPE	REMARKS

Tenor

TITLE	COMP.	TESS.	REMARKS
Elijah Then shall the righteous shine forth	e♭-a♭1	a♭-f1	Slow, sustained.
Elijah Recitative: Ye people, rend your hearts Air: If with all your hearts	f♯-a♭1	b♭-e♭1	Sustained.
Hymn of Praise Recitative: Sing ye praise Air: He counteth all your sorrows	d-g1	g-d1	Animated. The vocal line is very sustained.
Hymn of Praise The sorrows of death	c-a♭1	g-e1	Sustained. In parts demands considerable dramatic intensity. Not too suitable for separate performance.
St. Paul Be thou faithful unto death	d-g1	g-e1	Very sustained.

All these excerpts are generally available

Bass or Baritone

TITLE	COMP.	TESS.	REMARKS
Elijah Recitative: I go on my way Air: For the mountains shall depart	B-e1	e-d1	Slow, sustained.
Elijah Is not his word like a fire	B-f1	e-d1	Very animated, vigorous, dramatic. Demands some flexibility.
Elijah It is enough	A-e1	f♯-d1	Slow, very sustained. Has a very animated, dramatic, vigorous middle section.
Elijah Lord, God of Abraham	B♭-e♭1	d-b♭1	Sustained, majestic.
St. Paul Consume them all	B-d1	f♯-c♯1	Rapid, vigorous. The vocal line sustained.
St. Paul For know ye not	A-d1	d-d1	Very sustained, vigorous.
St. Paul O God, have mercy	B-d1	f♯-d1	A very sustained adagio; the middle section is a somewhat declamatory; vigorous allegro maestoso.

All these excerpts are generally available.

GIACOMO MEYERBEER
(1791-1864)

TITLE	COMP.	TESS.	TYPE	REMARKS
Der Mönch	F-e1	c-c1	Bass	Sustained, dramatic, effective. Has a vigorous, animated middle section. At one time one of the most popular bass songs. Demands good command of low f. (Generally available)
Du schönes Fishersmädchen	c1-f2	f1-c2	Most suitable for men's voices	Light, graceful. (Generally available)

MAX REGER
(1873-1916)

Reger's music has never become widely known outside of Germany. An extraordinarily prolific composer, he has written a startlingly large number of songs. The few examples listed here could be considered quite representative, since Reger's style is rather uniform.

Edition: Universal
Bote & Bock.

TITLE	COMP.	TESS.	TYPE	REMARKS
Aeolsharfe	c1-f2 (cb1)	f1-db2	All voices	Slow, sustained. Musically not easy.
Beim Schneewetter	b-e2	e1-c2(L)	All voices	Delicate, sustained.
Darum	d1-f#2	f#1-d2	Women's voices	Animated, gently humorous. Demands some flexibility and an accomplished pianist.
Des Kindes Gebet	f1-g2	a1-f2 (H)	All voices	Delicate. Demands good command of pp.
Es blüht ein Blümlein rosenrot	eb-abb2	ab1-f2 (H)	All voices	Slow and sustained. Demands good command of high pp.
Es schläft ein stiller Garten	a-e2	eb1-c2	Most suitable for low voices	Slow, very sustained. In parts demands considerable dramatic intensity.
Friede	eb1-g2	ab1-f2 (H)	All voices	Very sustained.
Frühlingsmorgen	eb1-f#2	g1-e2	High or medium voices	Very sustained. Demands in parts considerable dramatic intensity.
Mariä Wiegenlied	f1-f2	a1-d2	Women's voices	Sustained, delicate. Demands good command of high pp. (Generally available)

TITLE	COMP.	TESS.	TYPE	REMARKS
Mit Rosen bestreut	c#1-d2	f#1-d2 (L)	All Women's voices	Delicate, sustained.
Sommernacht	a#-e1	e1-b1	Most suitable for medium or low voices	Sustained. In parts demands considerable dramatic intensity.
Waldeinsamkeit	a-d2	d1-b1 (L)	All Women's voices	Graceful, gently humorous.

ARNOLD SCHÖNBERG
(1874-   )

The songs of Arnold Schönberg, a figure of immense importance in contemporary music, can be roughly classified as falling in two categories -- the early songs, which are highly chromatic, somewhat complex, but nevertheless adhere to the principles of tonality, and the songs of the later period, in which a definite break with the conventional system of tonality is attempted. The still controversial nature of Schönberg's later music makes the inclusion of examples of this latter style into this volume somewhat questionable. Anyone interested in acquainting himself with this facet of Schönberg's style of writing is referred to the catalogue of the Universal Edition which lists all his songs. The somewhat fragmentary list here is primarily designed for those who are not at all familiar with Schönberg's vocal music.

Edition: Universal

TITLE	COMP.	TESS.	TYPE	REMARKS
Das schöne Beet betracht' ich	c#1-e#2	e1-c2	All voices	Slow and sustained. Musically complex.
Der verlorene Haufen (opus 12)	Ab-g1	d-e1	Baritone	A vigorous, animated, dramatic ballade. Demands an accomplished pianist. Musically and interpretatively not easy.
Erhebung	e#1-a2	e#1-e2	High voices, except a very light soprano	Sustained. Demands in parts considerable dramatic intensity.
Geübtes Herz (opus 3, no. 5)	a#-f2	f#1-d#2	Most suitable for medium voices (preferably baritone)	Sustained.
Ghasel (opus 6)	c1-g#2	f1-e2	High voices except a light soprano	Sustained. Demands in parts considerable dramatic intensity.

TITLE	COMP.	TESS.	TYPE	REMARKS

Excerpts from "Gurrelieder" for soli, chorus and orchestra

TITLE	COMP.	TESS.	TYPE	REMARKS
Lied der Waldtaube: "Tauben von Gurre"	a-b♭2	d♭1-e♭2	Mezzo-soprano or alto	Dramatic. Interpretatively and musically not easy.
Tove: "Nun sag ich dir zum ersten mal"	b-f♯2	d♯1-d2	Dramatic soprano	Sustained.
Waldemar: "Du wunderliche Tove"	c♯-a1	f-f1	Tenor	Sustained. In parts demands considerable dramatic intensity.
Waldemar: "So tanzen die Engel"	c♯-g1	f♯-e♭1	Tenor	Sustained.
Hochzeitslied (opus 3, no. 4)	d1-f♯2	f♯1-d2	Not too suitable for very light high voices	Sustained, not slow.
Ich darf nicht dankend	a-f2	d1-e♭2	Medium or low voices	Slow, rather sustained.
In diesen Wintertagen	b-g2	d-e2	Not suitable for very light high voices	Not fast. Demands in parts considerable dramatic intensity.
Mädchenlied (opus 6)	d♯1-a2	f1-f2	Soprano	Rapid, dramatic. Musically not easy. Demands an accomplished pianist.
Verlassen (opus 6)	b-g♭2	e1-d2	Not suitable for very light high voices	Sustained, somber, dramatic. Musically not easy.
Warnung (opus 3, no. 3)	b♭-e♭2	d♭1-d♭2	Medium or low voices (preferably baritone)	Very animated, dramatic. Interpretatively and musically not easy. Demands an accomplished pianist.

FRANZ SCHREKER
(1878-1934)

TITLE	COMP.	TESS.	TYPE	REMARKS
Dass er ganz ein Engel werde	c♯1-e2	f♯1-c♯2	Women's voices, except a very light soprano	Slow and somber. Demands good command of pp. (Universal)
Einst gibt ein Tag mir alles Glückes eigen	b♭-e♭2	b♭-b♭1	Low voices	Slow, declamatory. Musically and interpretatively not easy. (Universal)
O Glocken, böse Glocken	b♭-g♭2	d1-d2	Women's voices, except a very light soprano	Sustained. Demands in parts considerable dramatic intensity. (Universal)

FRANZ SCHUBERT
(1797-1828)

So much has been written about Schubert that it seems best to dispense with anything in the nature of general remarks concerning his unequaled importance as a composer of songs, especially in a brief prefatory note.

Specifically, however, one observation in regard to the performance of his songs may be of some value. The considerable and probably only difficulty facing a present-day singer who is attempting to sing Schubert lies in the domain of style. By this is meant that in order to sing Schubert properly one must try to adjust one's attitude toward art in general, and toward music, poetry and singing in particular, to the attitude that was prevalent in the Vienna of Schubert's time and that influenced him to no small degree.

The problem of such an adjustment is of course ever present in the attempt to perform any music. Yet, in the case of Schubert songs it seems to be of special importance, due perhaps to the fact that the stylistic conventions of his time are not so obviously and unmistakably different from ours, as those, for instance, which governed Bach and Mozart's mode of musical expression.

The present-day singer is liable to forget that vocalization in Schubert's time had reached an almost unprecedented and probably never afterward equaled degree of elegance, that the musicodramatic conception, existing as it did since the time of Peri and Monteverde, was still subject to purely musico-theoretic considerations, that the poetic climate tended toward refined sentimentality, not yet fully released from the eighteenth century gallant and mythological patterns, and that Schubert, notwithstanding the fact that he was the possessor of a great and miraculous genius, was none the less a man living in the Vienna of that time.

I know of no easy and simple way of attaining stylistic sensitivity. One must first of all become familiar with the attitudes and standards of the period; this necessitates some familiarity with the poetry, literature, painting, and other arts of the period, with its aesthetic writings, social usages, and living conditions.

Then, if one possesses sufficient imagination, one may instinctively arrive at the attitude one is trying to establish.

Practically, the following advice may be of some slight help:

(1) Do not try to dramatize Schubert, in the Wagnerian sense of the word, that is, never sacrifice the phrase (sentence) to the single word.

(2) The melodic line should at all times be kept flowing smoothly and elegantly.

(3) The rhythm must at no time be allowed to become slack or vague.

(4) Do not try to use Schubert songs as vehicles for exhibition of vocal powers; remember that the size of a voice was not considered as important, even in opera, at Schubert's time, as a singer's elegance and the perfection of his vocalization. (Mozart and Rossini were the most admired composers of vocal music at that time.)

(5) Have a classical dictionary handy, for the number of mythological allusions in the poetry used by Schubert is very great.

Schubert's accompaniments, simple as they seem harmonically, are often pianistically complex demanding an instrumentalist of polish. In many of his songs the balance between the voice part and the piano is of the type more often encountered in the chamber music than in the songs of that period, though, of course, the piano part is hardly ever treated independently, even in songs like "Erlkönig," where it demands a virtuoso technic.

Editions: Complete: Breitkopf & Härtel (Mandyszewski)
Peters (Friedländer) 7 vols.; 2 vols.
(1 and 2) reprinted by Schirmer.
Selections: Kalmus
Three-volume selection-Universal
Augener
Two volumes, Musician's Library, Oliver Ditson
(The second volume, 50 additional songs, is especially valuable.)
One volume, Carl Fischer.
Numerous reprints of single songs.
The Oxford University Press has published some interesting English translations of Schubert's texts by A. H. Fox-Strangways and Stewart Wilson ("Schöne Müllerin," "Winterreise," and selected songs) that any singer not thoroughly familiar with the German language ought to welcome.

TITLE	COMP.	TESS.	TYPE	REMARKS
Abendbilder	e1-a2	b1-g2	Most suitable for high light voices	Delicate, animated. Demands lightness of tone and an accomplished pianist.
Abendstern	e1-g2	a1-e2	All voices	Sustained.
Abschied	d1-ab2	ab1-eb2	Men's voices	Animated, graceful. Demands lightness of tone and facile articulation. Verses 4 and 5 may be omitted.
Am Bach im Frühling	ab-db2	db1-bb1	Medium or low voices	Sustained. In parts declamatory.
Am Flusse	d1-f#2	a1-d2	All voices	Sustained.
Am Grabe Anselmo's	d1-g2	g1-fb2	Women's voices	Slow and sustained, somber.
Am Meer	d1-f2	g1-e2	All voices, except a very light soprano	Slow and sustained. In parts demands considerable dramatic intensity. Interpretatively not easy.
Am See	d1-f2	g1-eb2	All voices	Sustained, delicate. Demands some flexibility.
Am Strome	d#1-f#2	b1-e2	All voices	Sustained.
An den Mond (Geuss lieber Mond)	f1-gb2	ab1-eb2	All voices	Slow, sustained, delicate.
An den Tod	bb-c#2	d1-b1	Medium or low voices	Very sustained, majestic.
An die Entfernte	f#1-g2	c2-f2	All voices	The tessitura is somewhat high. Slow and sustained. In parts demands considerable dramatic intensity.

TITLE	COMP.	TESS.	TYPE	REMARKS
An die Laute	d1-f#2	a1-d2	All voices	Light and delicate.
An die Leyer	bb-f2	eb1-c2	Not suit-able for very light high voices	Very sustained. In parts declamatory. Interpretatively not easy.
An die Musik	c#1-f#2	f#1-d2	All voices	Note the tempo mark mässig, ¢. Sustained. Often sung too slowly.
An die Nachtigall	g1-g2	c2-f2	Most suit-able for light voices	Delicate, sustained.
An die Türen will ich schleichen	g#1-g2	b1-f2	Men's voices	Sustained. Demands good command of pp. See Schumann and H. Wolf.
An Schwager Kronos	a-f#2	f1-e2	Heavy voices	Dramatic, very vigor-ous. Demands an ex-cellent pianist. In-terpretatively not easy.
An Sylvia	e1-f#2	a1-e2	All voices	Delicate, sustained.
Auf dem Wasser zu singen	eb1-gb2	ab1-eb2	Not too suitable for very low voices	Animated, delicate. Demands lightness of tone, some flexibility and an excellent pianist.
Aufenthalt	b-g2	e1-e2	Heavy voices	Vigorous, sustained, somber.
Aus Heliopolis (Fels an Felsen)	g-d2	d1-c2	Heavy medium or low voices	Dramatic, vigorous.
Aus Heliopolis (Im kalten, rauhen Norden)	a-e2 (g#)	e1-c#2	Medium or low voices	Sustained.
Ave Maria	f1-f2	g1-eb2	Most suit-able for women's voices	Slow and very sustained. Care should be taken to sing the sixteenths evenly. The substi-tion of the Latin prayer text for the original poem is not recom-mended in view of the fact that the accents of the Latin text do not coincide with the ac-cents of the melodic line.
Blumenlied	e1-g#2	g#1-e2	Not too suitable for very low voices	Delicate. Demands some flexibility.
Das Fischermädchen	c1-gb2	ab1-eb2	Men's voices	Animated. Demands lightness of tone.

TITLE	COMP.	TESS.	TYPE	REMARKS
Das Lied im Grünen	e1-a2	a1-e2	All voices	Delicate. Demands lightness of tone and facile articulation. The song is somewhat long, but cuts are permissible and in some respects desirable.
Das Rosenband	f1-f2	ab1-eb2	All voices	Delicate and graceful.
Dass sie hier gewesen	g1-g2	c2-f2	All voices	Slow and very sustained. Demands good command of pp. The tessitura is somewhat high.
Dem Unendlichen (Third version)	c1-ab2	f1-eb2	Heavy voices	Majestic and declamatory. Interpretatively complex.
Der Alpenjäger	c1-f#2	f1-d2	Not suitable for light voices	Spirited and vigorous.
Der Atlas	d1-ab2	g1-e2	Heavy voices	Dramatic, very vigorous. Demands an accomplished pianist.
Der Doppelgänger	b1-g2	d1-d2	Not suitable for light voices	Dramatic, slow. Often sung and played slovenly in regard to time values, thus losing much of its dramatic impact.
Der Einsame	d1-g2	g1-e2	All voices	Delicate. Demands lightness of tone, facile articulation, and an accomplished pianist.
Der Erlkönig	c1-g2	a1-f2	Not suitable for very light voices	Dramatic narrative song. Demands a virtuoso pianist. Observe Schubert's MM ♪ = 152. See C. Löwe, "Erlkönig", and an admirable essay upon it by Donald Tovey.
Der Jüngling am Bache	eb1-f2	g1-eb2	All voices	Sustained. Demands some flexibility.
Der Jüngling an der Quelle	e1-a2	a1-g2	All voices	Slow and sustained Delicate.
Der Jüngling auf dem Hügel	c1-f2 (g)	g1-e2	Medium or low voices	Slow, sustained. Interpretatively not easy.
Der Knabe	a1-a2	c#2-g2	Light high voices	Delicate, graceful.
Der Liebliche Stern	d1-f2	g1-d2	Most suitable for light voices	Delicate. Demands lightness of tone and some flexibility.
Der Musensohn	f#1-g2	b1-e2	All voices	Light, graceful, very animated. Demands facile articulation and an excellent rhythmic sense.

TITLE	COMP.	TESS.	TYPE	REMARKS
Der Schiffer	bb-eb2	eb1-c2	Medium or low voices	Rapid and vigorous. Demands facile articulation and an accomplished pianist.
Der Schmetterling	e1-f2	f1-c2	Not too suitable for very heavy or very low voices	Delicate, graceful, animated.
Der Tod und das Mädchen	a-eb2 (d)	d1-a1	Mezzo-soprano or alto	This celebrated song has seemingly become an almost exclusive property of alti no doubt because of the optional final d, mostly used for exhibitionistic purposes, often without much success. However, should this one note be omitted and d1 taken instead, this song can be most effectively sung by a lighter voice, even a soprano, as the entire low passage is expressly marked pp., which is, incidentally, very rarely obeyed. The tempo, according to Schubert's own markings, is $\bar{d}$=54 about twice as fast as this song is often taken.
Der Wachtelschlag	d#1-f#2	a1-e2	Most suitable for light, high voices	Light and animated. Demands some flexibility and an accomplished pianist.
Der Wanderer	g#-e2 (e)	e1-c#2	Medium or low voices	Slow, somber. Interpretatively not easy.
Der Wanderer an den Mond	d1-f2	g1-d2	All voices	Demands lightness of tone and good sense of rhythm. Delicate, animated.
Der Winterabend	e1-f2	a1-e2	All voices	Delicate. Demands lightness of tone and an accomplished pianist A trifle long.
Der Zürnende Barde	a-e2	f1-c2	Bass, baritone or heroic tenor	Vigorous, animated. Demands facile articulation.
Der Zwerg	a-gb2	f#1-e2	Not suitable for light voices	A dramatic narrative song.

TITLE	COMP.	TESS.	TYPE	REMARKS
Des Mädchens Klage	c1-eb2	g1-c2	Women's voices	Slow and sustained.
Die Allmacht	c1-a2 (bb2)	bb1-g2	Heavy voices	Very sustained, majestic, vigorous. Vocally not easy.
Die Forelle	eb1-gb2	ab1-eb2	All voices	Demands facile articulation and an accomplished pianist. Light and animated.
Die junge Nonne	c1-gb2	ab1-e2	Women's voices, except a very light soprano	Not slow. Dramatic. Demands an accomplished pianist.
Die Liebe	g1-bb2	d2-g2	Soprano or mezzo-soprano	Slow and very sustained. Has a high tessitura. See "Freudvoll und Leidvoll" by Beethoven and by Liszt; and Rubinstein, "Clärchens Lied."
Die Liebe hat gelogen	g1-f2	bb1-eb2	All voices, except a very light soprano	In parts demands considerable dramatic intensity. Sustained.
Die Männer sind Mechant!	e1-f2	e1-c#2	Women's voices	Sustained. Somewhat humorous.
Die Rose	g1-g2	bb1-eb2	Most suitable for light high voices	Graceful and delicate.

"Die Schöne Müllerin": a cycle of 20 songs, opus 25, text by W. Müller

As in the case of some other song cycles, it seemed advisable to list these songs under one heading, and in their original order, instead of alphabetically. This cycle follows a definite plot; ideally, therefore, it is desirable to perform the whole as a unit, which of course is, to say the least, a rather ambitious undertaking.

The practice of performing these songs separately is widespread, however, and is by no means to be condemned, although one must admit that many a song loses thus some of its meaning. The cycle was originally intended for tenor, but, it can and has been performed by practically every type of voice, by men as well as women. Generally speaking, it seems to suit high voices best.

(1) Das Wandern	f1-f2	bb1-eb2	All voices	Spirited. Demands lightness of tone and excellent sense of rhythm.
(2) Wohin	d1-g2	f#1-e2	All voices	Light and animated. One of the best known songs in this cycle. Demands facile articulation, lightness of tone, and an accomplished pianist.

TITLE	COMP.	TESS.	TYPE	REMARKS
(2) Wohin cont'd.				Often taken at too fast a tempo.
(3) Halt	f1-g2	g1-e2	All voices	Animated.
(4) Danksagung an den Bach	f#1-g2	b1-f#2	All voices	Slow, very sustained. The tessitura is somewhat high. Demands good command of high p.
(5) Am Feierabend	c1-g2	a1-f2	Not too suitable for very light high voices	Rapid, dramatic. Demands facile articulation and an accomplished pianist.
(6) Der Neugierige	e#1-g2	b1-e2	All voices	Slow, sustained. One of the best known songs in this cycle. Observe the 3/8 rest before the "Sehr langsam" section.
(7) Ungeduld	e1-a2	a1-f#2	All voices	Rapid. One of the best known songs in this cycle. Demands very facile articulation, good command of high voice, and an excellent pianist. Often taken at too fast a tempo. Verse 3 may be omitted.
(8) Morgengruss	g1-f2	c1-e2	All voices	Sustained.
(9) Des Müllers Blumen	e1-f#2	a1-e2	All voices	Delicate and sustained. Demands lightness of tone.
(10) Thränenregen	d#1-e2	f#1-d2	All voices	Sustained. Interpretatively not easy.
(11) Mein	d1-f#2	f#1-d2	All voices	Spirited. Demands facile articulation and some flexibility. In some editions marked ¢.
(12) Pause	e1-f2	g1-eb2	All voices	Sustained. Interpretatively not easy.
(13) Mit dem grünen Lautenbande	e1-f2	bb1-eb2	All voices	Graceful. In folk vein.
(14) Der Jäger	c1-g2	g1-eb2	All voices	Very rapid. Demands exceptionally facile articulation. Seldom performed separately.
(15) Eifersucht und Stolz	d1-g2	g1-eb2	All voices	Very rapid. Demands facile articulation and an excellent pianist.
(16) Die liebe Farbe	f#1-f#2	b1-e2	All voices	Slow and very sustained.
(17) Die böse Farbe	d#1-g2	b1-f#2	Not too suitable for very light soprano	Dramatic, vigorous. Demands very facile articulation in parts and an excellent pianist.

TITLE	COMP.	TESS.	TYPE	REMARKS
(18) Trockne Blumen	f#1-g2	g1-e2	All voices	Slow and sustained. One of the best known songs in this cycle. Demands good command of pp., excellent rhythmic sense, and an accomplished pianist.
(19) Der Müller und der Bach	f#1-g2	g1-e2	All voices	Slow and very sustained.
(20) Des Baches Wiegenlied	g#1-g#2	b1-e2	All voices	Sustained. Seldom sung separately. Note the tempo mark, mässig ¢. Often sung too slowly.
Die Spinnerin	f#1-a2	b1-f#2	Light soprano	Delicate. Demands some flexibility. Verses 4, 5, 6 could be omitted.
Die Stadt	c1-g2	g1-eb2	All voices, except a very light soprano	Sustained, somber. Demands in parts considerable dramatic intensity. Interpretatively not easy. Demands an accomplished pianist. Often sung rather slovenly in regard to time values, thus losing much of its dramatic impact.
Die Taubenpost	f1-g2	a1-e2	All voices	Delicate, sustained. Demands lightness of tone.
Du bist die Ruh'	f1-ab2	bb1-f2	All voices	Slow and very sustained. Note the full bar rests.
Du liebst mich nicht	e1-f#2	a1-e2	All voices, except a very light soprano	Sustained. Demands in parts considerable dramatic intensity.
Ellens zweiter Gesang	eb1-eb2	bb1-eb2	Mezzo-soprano or alto	Animated. Demands good sense of rhythm.
Erlafsee	e1-g2	a1-f2	Most suitable for high light voices	Sustained, delicate. Demands lightness of tone and some flexibility.
Erster Verlust	c2-f2	e2-f2	All voices	Very slow and sustained. The tessitura is somewhat high. See Mendelssohn.
Fahrt zum Hades	a-d2 (f)	d1-bb1	Medium or low voices	Dramatic, somber, somewhat declamatory.
Fischerweise	d1-e2	f#1-d2	Medium or low voices	Spirited. Demands facile articulation.
Fragment aus dem Aeschylus	c1-gb2	f1-eb2	Heavy voices	Dramatic, declamatory. Interpretatively complex.

TITLE	COMP.	TESS.	TYPE	REMARKS
Frühlingsglaube	eb1-f2	g1-eb2	All voices	Slow and sustained.
Frühlingslied	e1-g2	g1-d2	All voices	Animated, light.
Frühlingssehnsucht	e1-g2	bb1-f2	All voices	Rapid and light. Demands facile articulation. The second verse may be omitted.
Ganymed	d#1-f2	ab1-e2	All voices	Sustained. Interpretatively not easy. Demands an accomplished pianist. See H. Wolf.
Gebet währed der Schlacht	c#1-e2	f1-d2	Bass, baritone, or heroic tenor	Dramatic; in parts declamatory.
Geheimes	eb1-ab2	ab1-f2	All voices	Graceful, delicate, light.
Gott im Frühling	e1-g#2	g#1-e2	Not too suitable for very low voices	Graceful, delicate.
Gretchen am Spinnrade	e1-a2	a1-f2	Women's voices, except a very light soprano	Sustained. Demands considerable dramatic intensity in parts, and an excellent pianist. Observe Schubert's MM mark ♩ =72.
Gretchens Bitte	b-g2	ab1-f2	Women's voices, except a very light soprano	Slow, sustained. In parts demands considerable dramatic intensity.
Grenzen der Menschheit	bb-ab2 (a)	f#1-e2	Heavy voices	Majestic, declamatory. Interpretatively complex. See H. Wolf.
Gruppe aus dem Tartarus	c1-eb2	e1-c2	Heavy voices	Dramatic. Interpretatively not easy. Demands an excellent pianist.
Heiden Röslein	g1-g2	d1-g2	All voices	Graceful, delicate.
Ihr Bild	f1-eb2	g1-d2	All voices	Slow and sustained. Interpretatively not easy.
Ihr Grab	d1-gb2	bb1-f2	Men's voices	Very slow and sustained.
Im Abendroth	eb1-f2	ab1-eb2	All voices	Slow and very sustained. Demands good command of pp.
Im Frühling	d1-f#2	g1-e2	Not too suitable for very heavy voices	Delicate. Interpretatively not easy. Demands an accomplished pianist.
Im Haine	c#1-g2	a1-f#2	Most suitable for light high voices	Very delicate, sustained. Demands some flexibility.

TITLE	COMP.	TESS.	TYPE	REMARKS
In der Ferne	b-g2	f♯1-e2	Heavy voices	Sustained, dramatic. Interpretatively not easy.
Jägers Abendlied	g1-g♭2	b♭1-e♭2	All voices	Very slow and sustained. Demands good command of pp.
Kriegers Ahnung	a-f2	g1-e2	Baritone or bass	Dramatic. Interpretatively not easy.
Lachen und Weinen	e♭1-f2	a♭1-e♭2	All voices	Delicate, graceful. Demands lightness of tone. Interpretatively not easy.
Liebesbotschaft	e1-g2	a1-e2	All voices	Delicate, graceful. Demands lightness of tone, facile articulation, and an accomplished pianist. Often taken at too fast a tempo.
Liebe schwärmt auf allen Wegen	g1-g2	g1-e2	Soprano	Delicate, animated, graceful.
Lied der Mignon (Heiss mich nicht reden)	c1-g2	g1-e2	Women's voices except a very light soprano	Sustained. Demands in parts considerable dramatic intensity.
Lied der Mignon (Nur wer die Sehnsucht kennt)	g1-f2	c2-f2	Women's voices	Slow and sustained. See Beethoven, Schumann, H. Wolf, Tchaikovsky, among many others.
Lied der Mignon (So lasst mich scheinen)	d♯1-f♯2	b1-e2	Women's voices, except a very light soprano	Sustained. Demands in parts considerable dramatic intensity. See Schumann and H. Wolf.
Lied eines Schiffers an die Dioskuren	c1-e♭2	f1-d♭2	Not too suitable for very high voices	Slow and very sustained.
Litaney	c1-e♭2	g1-d2	Not too suitable for very high light voices	Slow and very sustained. The poem has 9 verses, of which 7 are, as a rule, omitted.
Lob der Thränen	f♯1-f♯2	a1-e2	All voices	Slow and sustained.
Meeresstille	b-d2	d♯1-a1	Medium or low voices	Very slow and sustained. Demands good command of pp.
Memmon	a♭-f2	f1-d♭2	All voices, except a very light soprano	Slow and sustained. Interpretatively not easy. Demands an accomplished pianist.
Minnelied	d♯1-f♯2	g♯1-e2	Most suitable for men's voices	Delicate, sustained. See Brahms and Mendelssohn.

TITLE	COMP.	TESS.	TYPE	REMARKS
Nachtgesang	bb-eb2	c1-g1	Low or medium voices	Very slow and sustained.
Nacht und Träume	d#1-e2	f#1-d#2	Not too suitable for very high voices	Very slow and sustained. Demands good command of pp. Vocally not easy.
Nachtviolen	a1-a2	c1-f2	Most suitable for light voices	Slow and sustained. Demands good command of pp.
Nähe des Geliebten	f1-gb2	db1-gb2	All voices	Very slow and sustained. The tessitura is quite high.
Prometheus	cb1-f2	f1-eb2	Heavy voices, preferably heroic tenor or baritone	Majestic, declamatory, dramatic. Interpretatively complex. Demands an accomplished pianist. See H. Wolf.
Rastlose Liebe	d#1-a2	b1-g2	Not too suitable for very light voices	Rapid, vigorous. Demands an excellent pianist. See R. Franz.
Romanze (from Rosamunde)	c1-eb2	g1-db2	Most suitable for medium voices	Sustained.
Schäfers Klagelied	c1-fb2	g1-eb2	All voices	Sustained. Demands in parts considerable dramatic intensity.
Schlaflied (sometimes called Schlummerlied)	c1-f2	f1-d2	All voices	Delicate, sustained. Demands good command of pp.
Schwanengesang	eb1-g2	g1-eb2	All voices	Slow and very sustained.
Sei mir gegrüsst	g1-g2	bb1-f2	All voices	Slow and sustained.
Sprache der Liebe	d1-g#2	g#1-e2	Most suitable for high voices	Delicate.
Ständchen (Horch, horch die Lerch)	f1-g2	c2-f2	All voices	Delicate, animated, graceful.
Ständchen (Leise flehen)	d1-g2	a1-f2	All voices	Sustained. Demands lightness of tone. Note the tempo mark, "mässig." Often sung too slowly.
Suleika I (Was bedeutet die Bewegung)	d#1-g2	a1-f#2	Soprano or mezzo-soprano	Animated. Interpretatively not easy. Demands an accomplished pianist.
Suleika II (Ach um diese feuchten Schwingen)	f1-bb2	bb1-f2	Soprano or mezzo-soprano	Animated. Interpretatively and vocally not easy. Demands an accomplished pianist. See Mendelssohn.

TITLE	COMP.	TESS.	TYPE	REMARKS
Thekla	bb1-e2		Mezzo-soprano or alto	Very slow and sustained.
Todesmusik	d1-g2	g1-e2	All voices	Slow, sustained. Interpretatively not easy.
Totengräbers Heimweh	a-f2	f1-f2	Baritone	Dramatic, animated. Demands good command of pp. Interpretatively not easy.
Über Wildemann	c#1-g2	f1-e2	Men's voices	Rapid and vigorous. Demands facile articulation and an accomplished pianist.
Wanderers Nachtlied (Der du von dem Himmel bist)	eb1-g2	g1-eb2	All voices	Slow, sustained. See H. Wolf, Liszt, C. Löwe.
Wanderers Nachtlied (Über allen Gipfeln)	f1-f2	bb1-d2	All voices	Slow and sustained. Demands good command of pp. See Schumann, "Nachtlied," and "Wanderers Nachtlied" by Liszt and by C. Löwe.
Wehmut	d1-f2	a1-d2	All voices	Slow and very sustained.
Wer nie sein Brot	e1-g2	a1-e2	Men's voices, except a light tenor	Slow and sustained; in parts dramatic. See Schumann, Liszt and H. Wolf.
Wer sich der Einsamkeit ergibt	c1-fb2	a1-e2	Men's voices, except a light tenor	Slow and sustained; in parts dramatic. See Schumann and H. Wolf.
Wiegenlied	eb1-f2	bb1-eb2	Women's voices	Delicate, sustained. Demands lightness of tone.

Winterreise: a cycle of twenty-four songs, opus 89, text by W. Müller

As in the case of some other song cycles, it seemed advisable to list these songs under one heading, and in their original order instead of alphabetically.

Although the 24 songs comprising this cycle are somewhat more loosely connected than those in the "Schöne Müllerin" they should ideally be performed as a unit. Needless to say this is a formidable task. The practice of performing these songs separately is widespread, however, and is by no means to be condemned, although one must admit that many a song loses thus some of its poignancy and impact.

The cycle was originally intended for tenor, of a heavier, darker timbre than the one demanded by the "Schöne Müllerin." It can and has been performed by practically every type of voice, by men as well as women. Generally speaking it does not seem to suit high light voices too well.

TITLE	COMP.	TESS.	TYPE	REMARKS
(1) Gute Nacht	c1-f♯2	e1-d2	All voices	Sustained. Note the tempo mark, "mässig in gehender Bewegung." The second verse is sometimes omitted. Often sung too slowly.
(2) Die Wetterfahne	e1-g2	g♯1-e2	All voices	Animated. Interpretatively not easy. Demands some flexibility and an excellent pianist.
(3) Gefrorene Tränen	c1-f2	f1-eb2	Not too suitable for very high light voices	Sustained, somber. Note the tempo mark, "Nicht zu langsam" ¢. Often sung too slowly.
(4) Erstarrung	f1-ab2	g1-f2	All voices	Rapid and dramatic. Demands facile articulation and an excellent pianist.
(5) Der Lindenbaum	c1-e2	e1-b1	All voices	Very sustained. One of the best known songs in this cycle. Demands an excellent pianist.
(6) Wasserflut	b-g2	e1-e2	All voices	Very slow and sustained, somber.
(7) Auf dem Flusse	b-g2 (a♯)-(a2)	e1-e2	All voices	Slow. Interpretatively not easy. Demands in parts considerable dramatic intensity.
(8) Rückblick	d1-g2	g1-e2	All voices	Animated. Rhythmically not easy. Demands facile articulation and an excellent pianist.
(9) Irrlicht	b-g2	f♯1-f♯2	Not too suitable for very light voices	Slow and somber. Demands some flexibility.
(10) Rast	b-g2	g1-eb2	All voices	Sustained. Demands in parts considerable dramatic intensity. Demands some flexibility.
(11) Frühlingstraum	e1-f♯2	a1-e2	All voices	Delicate, graceful. One of the best known songs in this cycle. In parts dramatic. Interpretatively not easy.
(12) Einsamkeit	c♯1-f♯2	f♯1-eb2	Not too suitable for very light high voices	Very sustained. Demands in parts considerable dramatic intensity.

TITLE	COMP.	TESS.	TYPE	REMARKS
(13) Die Post	eb1-ab2	ab1-f2	All voices	Animated. One of the best known songs in this cycle. Demands facile articulation and an accomplished pianist.
(14) Der greise Kopf	c1-f2	eb1-eb2	All voices	Sustained; in parts dramatic.
(15) Die Krähe	c1-g2	f1-d2	Not too suitable for very light high voices	Very sustained. Demands in parts considerable dramatic intensity. Note the tempo mark, "Etwas langsam" 2/4. Often sung too slowly in 4/8.
(16) Letzte Hoffnung	bb-g2	g1-eb2	All voices	Sustained. In parts demands considerable dramatic intensity. Interpretatively not easy.
(17) Im Dorfe	d1-e2	f#1-d2	All voices	Sustained. Seldom sung separately. The accompaniment is not so easy as it may seem.
(18) Der stürmische Morgen	c#1-eb2	d1-bb1	Most suitable for heavy voices	Spirited, vigorous.
(19) Täuschung	d#1-e2	e1-c#2	All voices	Animated, delicate. Seldom sung separately.
(20) Der Wegweiser	f#1-g2	g1-e2	All voices, except a very light soprano	Sustained, somber. One of the best known songs in this cycle. Interpretatively not easy.
(21) Das Wirtshaus	e1-f2	f1-d2	All voices	Very slow and sustained, somber.
(22) Mut	bb-g2	d1-bb1	Most suitable for heavy voices	Spirited and vigorous.
(23) Die Nebensonnen	a1-f2	a1-d2	All voices	Very slow and sustained. One of the best known songs in this cycle.
(24) Der Leiermann	e1-f2	a1-e2	All voices	Slow. One of the best known songs in this cycle. Vocally and musically of utmost simplicity, this song is interpretatively very difficult.

ROBERT SCHUMANN
(1810-1856)

Schumann was perhaps more conscious and articulate in regard to his objectives as a composer than any composer before him, with the possible exception of Gluck, who stated his objectives so nobly and clearly in his short preface to Alceste.

The best way to acquaint oneself with Schumann's aesthetic theories is to read his writings on music, which are available in English translations. These writings are of course recommended not so much for their intrinsic value, which, considerable as it may be, has but little bearing on musical matters of today, as for the light they shed on his style and the objectives he tried to attain as a composer.

For any prospective performer of Schumann's music, even a casual acquaintance with Schumann the music critic and the aesthetic theorist ought to prove of great value.

The songs of Schumann, presenting as they do with few exceptions hardly any musical or vocal problems, demand a singer and a pianist of considerable poetic sensitivity. For the most part, they are best suited to voices possessing a well-controlled medium register. The greatest danger facing a present-day singer attempting to perform Schumann is the tendency to overlook the fact that sentiment is by no means synonymous with sentimentality, and that feelings can be expressed without violence.

In his songs Schumann demands considerable elegance in phrasing, a rubato that must stay within the frame of the rhythmic pulse, and a simplicity and sincerity of recitation almost naïve in its lack of artifice. Thus, it may be superfluous to add that, unless the singer can unreservedly and enthusiastically accept the poem of any particular song by Schumann, he would be wise not to sing it, even though it may seem musically and vocally to his liking, for under such circumstances he will not be able to achieve the synthesis between the poetry and the music so overwhelmingly important in Schumann's approach to the problem of setting a poem to music.

Schumann's accompaniments are almost always of great importance. He often uses the device of dividing the melodic line between the voice and the piano ("Der Nussbaum," for instance) thus achieving an effect more often associated with instrumental chamber music than with songs. Often his accompaniments are independently pianistic, and sometimes, as in "Aufträge," they demand an almost virtuoso technic.

Editions: 3 vols. Peters (reprinted by Kalmus)
3 vols. Universal
Breitkopf & Härtel
Fair selection: Ditson, Musician's Library
Schirmer
Fischer
Dichterliebe, complete, Fischer (somewhat overedited)
Numerous reprints of single songs.

TITLE	COMP.	TESS.	TYPE	REMARKS
An den Mond	e1-f2	g1-eb2	Most suitable for medium or low voices	Slow and sustained. See Mendelssohn, "Schlafloser Augen Leuchte," and H. Wolf, "Sonne der Schlummerlosen."
An die Türen will ich schleichen	c-eb1	g-c1	Baritone	Slow and sustained. Demands good command of pp. See Schubert and H. Wolf.
An den Sonnenschein	d1-g2	f1-d2	All voices	Sustained. In folk vein.
Auf einer Burg (Liederkreis, no.7)	c1-c2	e1-b1	Medium or low voices	Very slow and sustained.

TITLE	COMP.	TESS.	TYPE	REMARKS
Aufträge	e1-f♯2 (a2)	a1-e2	Not too suitable for very low voices	Light and rapid. Demands facile articulation and an excellent pianist. Sounds best in the original key, sung by a light high voice.
Aus den hebräischen Gesängen	a-f♯2	e1-c♯2	Heavy voices	Slow. Interpretatively not easy. Demands an accomplished pianist.
Aus den östlichen Rosen	d1-e♭2	g1-c2	All voices	Delicate, sustained.
Belsatzar	c1-g2	g1-e♭2	Not too suitable light voices	A dramatic, narrative song (ballade). Demands an accomplished pianist.
Da liegt der Feinde gestreckte Schaar	F-c1	c-a♭	Bass or bass-baritone	Grave, dramatic.
Das verlassene Mägdlein	d1-d2	f1-c2	Women's voices	Somber, slow and very sustained. See Wolf.
Dein Angesicht	d1-g♭2	b♭1-e♭2	All voices	Slow and very sustained.
Der Arme Peter	b-g2	g1-e2	Not too suitable for light high voices	Three poems by Heine, set as one continuous piece (in the manner of Beethoven's "An die ferne Geliebte"). Dramatic.
Der Contrabandiste	A-g1	f-d1	Baritone	A rapid character song. Demands facile articulation, some flexibility, and an excellent pianist.
Der Himmel hat eine Träne geweint	d1-f2	a♭1-d♭2	All voices	Slow and very sustained.
Der Husar, trara!	d-d1 (e♭1)	f-c1	Baritone	Vigorous and spirited.
Der Nussbaum	d1-f♯2	g1-e2	All voices	Delicate. Demands an accomplished pianist.
Der Sandmann	c1-f2	a1-e2	Not too suitable for very low voices	Light and delicate. Demands facile articulation and an accomplished pianist. See L. Blech.
Der schwere Abend	e♭1-g♭2	a♭1-e♭2	All voices	Slow and very sustained.
Der Soldat	c1-f2	a1-d2	Men's voices	Dramatic. Interpretatively not easy. Demands an accomplished pianist.
Der Zeisig	e1-g2	f1-d2	All voices	Light.

"Dichterliebe": a cycle of sixteen songs, opus 48, text by H. Heine.

As in the case of some other song cycles, it seemed advisable to list these songs under one heading, and in their original order instead of alphabetically.

Generally speaking, it is best to perform these songs as a unit. However, Nos. 1 to 7 inclusively are sometimes sung together, as a sort of abbreviated version of the cycle, and Nos. 10, 13 and 14 are sung separately occasionally, as well as Nos. 3, 4, 6 and 7.

Although the texts of these songs sound most convincing when sung by a man, this cycle has been much sung by women.

Like most of Schumann's songs, these songs present no obvious vocal difficulties. Yet a satisfactory performance of this cycle, considered by many to be one of the most notable examples of chamber music for voice and piano demands two accomplished artists in absolute command of their instruments.

These Heine poems, as well as most of his poetry, have been admirably translated into English by Louis Untermeyer.

TITLE	COMP.	TESS.	TYPE	REMARKS
(1) Im wunderschönen Monat Mai	f#1-g2	b1-e2	All voices	Delicate, sustained. This song and the following one are harmonically connected. Thus a separate performance of this song seems unadvisable; the second song, however, could be sung by itself if so desired. See R. Franz.
(2) Aus meinen Tränen spriesen	f#1-d2	a1-c#2	All voices	Very delicate.
(3) Die Rose, die Lilie	d1-e2	a1-d2	All voices	Spirited and light. Demands facile articulation. Often sung at too fast a tempo. Bar 10: Heine's original text, "Aller Liebe Bronne" instead of "Wonne," a mistake by Schumann, dutifully reprinted in most editions. See R. Franz.
(4) Wenn ich in deine Augen seh'	f#1-f2 (g2)	g1-d2	All voices	Slow. Interpretatively not easy.
(5) Ich will meine Seele tauchen	a#1-f#2	b1-e2	All voices	Animated, very delicate. Demands an accomplished pianist. Often sung too slowly.
(6) Im Rhein, im heiligen Strome	d1-f2	e1-c2	Not too suitable for very light high voices	Heavy, sustained. See R. Franz and Liszt.
(7) Ich grolle nicht	c1-e2 (a2)	e1-c2	Not too suitable for light voices	Very sustained, dramatic. The optional a2, g2, f2 in the final climax ought not be attempted if the recitation of the poem would be in any way impeded by the high tessitura of this passage.
(8) Und wüssten's die Blumen, die kleinen	g#1-f2	a1-e2	All voices	Animated. Demands an accomplished pianist. No tempo mark in the original. Approximately MM ♩ = 66.

TITLE	COMP.	TESS.	TYPE	REMARKS
(9) Das ist ein Flöten und Geigen	c1-f2	a1-e2	Not too suitable for very light high voices	Animated. Demands an excellent pianist.
(10) Hör' ich das Liedchen klingen	d1-d♭2	e♭1-b♭1	All voices	Slow, and sustained. The postlude for piano solo demands an accomplished pianist. See R. Franz.
(11) Ein Jüngling liebt ein Mädchen	b♭1-f2	f1-d2	Not too suitable for very high light voices	A spirited almost crudely satirical song. Demands facile articulation. In Ms. marked allegro.
(12) Am leuchtenden Sommermorgen	f1-d2	g1-c2	All voices	Delicate and sustained. The postlude for piano solo, utilized in the extended postlude to the cycle, demands an accomplished pianist.
(13) Ich hab' im Traum geweinet	d♭1-f♭2	e♭1-b♭1	Not too suitable for very light high voices	Slow. Interpretatively difficult. Often sung slovenly in regard to time values, thus losing much of its dramatic impact. See R. Franz, C. Löwe, and "J'ai pleuré en rêve" by G. Huë.
(14) Allnächtlich im Traume	a♯-d♯2	f♯1-c♯2	All voices	Delicate. See Mendelssohn.
(15) Aus alten Märchen	b-g♯2	g♯1-e2	All voices	Animated. Demands facile articulation and an accomplished pianist.
(16) Die alten, bösen Lieder	c♯1-g♯2	f♯1-c♯2	Not suitable for very light voices	Dramatic, vigorous. Demands an accomplished pianist. The extended postlude for piano solo makes a separate performance of this song seem unadvisable.
Dichters Genesung	c♯1-e2	e1-b1	Most suitable for medium or low voices	Animated. Interpretatively not easy. Demands an accomplished pianist.
Die beiden Grenadiere	b♭-d2 (a)	d1-b♭1	Men's voices, except a light tenor	A dramatic narrative song (ballade). See Wagner's setting of the French version of this Heine poem.
Die Kartenlegerin	b♭-e♭1	e♭1-b♭1	Mezzo-soprano or alto	An amusing, light character song. Demands facile articulation and an accomplished pianist.

TITLE	COMP.	TESS.	TYPE	REMARKS
Die Lotosblume	c1-g2	a1-e2	All voices	Delicate and sustained. See R. Franz.
Die Meerfee	c♯1-f♯2	a1-e2	Most suitable for high voices	Light and delicate.
Die Sennin	e♯1-f♯2	g♯1-e2	All voices	Delicate and sustained. Demands some flexibility.
Die Soldatenbraut	c1-f2 (b♭)	f1-d2	Women's voices	Rhythmic and delicate.
Die Spinnerin	c♯1-e2	f♯1-c♯2	Women's voices	Sustained. Demands an accomplished pianist. See Brahms, "Mädchenlied" (Auf die Nacht).
Die Stille (Liederkreis no.4)	d1-e2	g1-d2	Women's voices (if sung separately)	Delicate. Demands lightness of tone. See Mendelssohn, "Es weiss und rät es doch keiner."
Die Tochter Jephtha's	c1-g♭2	e♭1-e♭2	Women's voices, except a light soprano	Dramatic.
Du bist wie eine Blume	g1-f2	b♭1-e♭2	All voices	Slow and sustained. This Heine poem has been set to music innumerable times. See Liszt, Rubinstein, and many British and American composers (Chadwick, F. Bridge).
Einsamkeit	d1-e2	f1-b1	Most suitable for medium or low voices	Slow and sustained, somber.
Er ist's	e1-a2	b1-f♯2	Not too suitable for very low voices	Spirited. Sounds best in the original key. See H. Wolf.
Erstes Grün	d1-d2	g1-c1	All voices	Very delicate, sustained.
Es fiel ein Reif	e1-c2		All voices	Slow and somber, very subdued. Exceedingly simple musically. Interpretatively not easy. No. 2 of the cycle of two songs and a duet to the poems of Heine, entitled "Tragödie."
Es leuchtet meine Liebe	c1-g2	g1-e♭2	Not too suitable for very light voices	Animated. Interpretatively not easy. Demands an excellent pianist. Should not be transposed too low.

TITLE	COMP.	TESS.	TYPE	REMARKS
Es treibt mich hin	d1-f♯2 (a♯)(g2)	f♯1-d2	Men's voices, except a very light tenor	Rapid and dramatic.
Flügel, Flügel um zu fliegen	c♯1-a2	f♯1-f♯2	Not too suitable for very light voices	Dramatic, very animated. Demands an excellent pianist.
Frage	e♭1-a♭2	a♭1-e♭2	All voices	Slow and very sustained.

"Frauenliebe und Leben": a cycle of 8 songs, opus 42, text by A. Chamisso.

As in the case of some other song cycles it seemed best to list these songs under one heading and in their original order instead of alphabetically. All the songs in this cycle save No. 8 lend themselves well to the individual performance; however, it is best to sing these songs as a unit. These songs lend themselves best to a rather high mezzo-soprano voice; they have been, however, performed by practically every type of women's voices, save perhaps a coloratura soprano.

(1) Seit ich ihn gesehen	e♭1-e♭2	f1-b♭1	Women's voices	Slow and sustained.
(2) Er, der Herrlichste von Allen	c1-g♭2	g1-e♭2	Women's voices	Rhythmic and spirited. Demands good command of medium voice.
(3) Ich kann's nicht fassen, nicht glauben	c1-f2	g1-d2	Women's voices	Animated, dramatic. Demands facile articulation.
(4) Du Ring an meinem Finger	c1-f2	e♭1-c2	Women's voices	Slow and very sustained.
(5) Helft mir, ihr Schwestern	b♭-g2	f1-d2	Women's voices	Animated. Often sung at too fast a tempo.
(6) Süsser Freund du blickest	e1-e2	g1-d2	Women's voices	Slow. Interpretatively not easy.
(7) An meinem Herzen an meiner Brust	d1-f♯2	a1-d2	Women's voices	Spirited. Demands facile articulation.
(8) Nun hast du mir den ersten Schmerz getan	c♯1-d2	d1-a1	Women's voices	Grave and declamatory. The extended postlude for piano solo, utilizing the material employed in the first song of this cycle, makes a separate performance of this song seem unadvisable.
Frühlingsfahrt	c♯1-f♯2	a1-e2	Not too suitable for very light high voices	Narrative, vigorous. Interpretatively not easy.
Frühlingslust	d1-g2	f♯1-d2	Not too suitable for very low voices	Light and delicate.

TITLE	COMP.	TESS.	TYPE	REMARKS
Frühlingsnacht (Liederkreis No. 12)	d#1-f#2	e1-b1	All voices	Rapid. Demands facile articulation and an excellent pianist. See A. Jensen.
Geisternähe	e1-f#2 (a2)	a1-f#2	Most suitable for high voices	Animated. Interpretatively not too easy.
Geständnis	e1-g2	g1-e2	All voices	Animated, exuberant. Interpretatively not easy. Demands an accomplished pianist.
Heiss mich nicht reden	b-g2	f1-d2	Women's voices except a light soprano	Dramatic, declamatory. See Schubert, H. Wolf.
Hoch, hoch sind die Berge	a-f2	eb1-c2	Mezzosoprano or alto	Slow and very sustained.
Ich wandelte unter den Bäumen	d#1-g#2	f#1-d#2	All voices	Slow and very sustained.
Ihre Stimme	d1-g2	f1-eb2	All voices, except a very light soprano	Very sustained. Demands good command of medium voice.
Im Walde (Liederkreis No. 11)	c#1-d2 (a)	e1-b1	Most suitable for medium or low voices	Animated. Interpretatively not easy.
Im Westen	f1-f2	g1-e2	Women's voices	Very sustained.
In der Fremde (Liederkreis No. 1)	f#1-e2	a1-d2	Not too suitable for very light high voices	Very sustained. See Brahms.
In der Fremde (Liederkreis No. 8)	e1-f2	a1-e2	All voices	Delicate. Interpretatively not easy.
Intermezzo (Liederkreis No. 2)	e1-f#2	a1-d2	All voices	Delicate and sustained.
Jasminenstrauch	f#1-f#2	b1-e2	Most suitable for light high voices	Very delicate. Being extremely short it is sometimes sung twice without interruption.
Jemand	e1-g2	g1-e2	Women's voices	A short song of contrasting moods and tempi.
Jung Volkers Lied	c#1-e2	f#1-c#2	Men's voices	Spirited and vigorous.
Lieb Liebchen	b-e2	e1-b1	Men's voices	Interpretatively not easy. See R. Franz.
Liebster, deine Worte stehlen	d1-g2	e1-d2	Women's voices, except a very light soprano	Animated. Interpretatively not easy.
Lied der Suleika	e1-f#2	a1-e2	Women's voices	Sustained.

TITLE	COMP.	TESS.	TYPE	REMARKS
Lieder der Braut				
No. 1	d1-a2	a1-e2	Women's	These two songs ought
No. 2	e1-e2	a1-d2	voices	to be performed together. Very delicate and sustained.
Lorelei	e1-e2	g#1-d#2	All voices	Delicate, sustained.
Kommen und Scheiden	eb1-f#2	bb1-d2	All voices	Slow and subdued. Interpretatively not easy.
Marienwürmchen	f1-f2	g1-d2	Most suitable for women's voices	Light and delicate. A setting of an old rhyme (Lady bug, lady bug, fly away home). Must be sung very simply.
Märzveilchen	e1-e2	g1-d2	All voices	Very delicate. See Gade.
Meine Rose	db1-gb2	gb1-d2	All voices	Delicate and sustained. Interpretatively not easy. Demands an accomplished pianist.
Mein schöner Stern	eb1-g2	a1-f2	All voices	Written for tenor. Very sustained.
Meine Töne still und heiter	f#1-a2	a1-e2	Men's voices	Written for tenor. Light and delicate. Demands good sense of rhythm.
Melancholie	d1-g2	f1-d2	Not too suitable for very light high voices	Declamatory.
Mignon (Kennst du das Land)	f#1-g2 (a2)	bb1-f2	Women's voices, except a very light soprano	Dramatic, sustained. See Beethoven, Schubert, Liszt, and H. Wolf.
Mit Myrten und Rosen	d1-g2	a1-f#2	Not too suitable for very light high voices	Sustained. Demands in parts considerable dramatic intensity. Interpretatively not easy.
Mondnacht (Liederkreis No. 5)	e1-f#2	b1-e2	All voices	Slow. Very sustained. Demands good command of pp. and an accomplished pianist.
Morgens steh' ich auf und frage	d1-e2	e1-b1	Men's voices	Delicate, sustained. See R. Franz, "Kommt feins liebchen heut," and Liszt.
Muttertraum	a-eb2	e1-c2	Mezzo-soprano or alto	Somber and subdued. Interpretatively not easy.
Nachtlied	d1-f2	g1-e2	All voices	Slow and very sustained. See Schubert, "Wanderers Nachtlied" (Uber allen Gipfeln); Löwe, and Liszt.
Nur wer die Sehnsucht Kennt	d1-ab2	g1-eb2	Women's voices, except a very light soprano	Slow and sustained. In parts demands considerable dramatic intensity. See Beethoven, Schubert, H. Wolf, Tchaikovsky among many others.

TITLE	COMP.	TESS.	TYPE	REMARKS
O Freund, mein Schirm, mein Schutz	d1-eb2	g1-d2	Women's voices, except a very light soprano	Slow and sustained. Interpretatively not easy.
O wie lieblich ist das Mädchen	f1-bb2	bb1-g2	Most suitable for high voices	Light and delicate. Demands facile articulation. See Schumann, "Weh, wie zornig ist das Mädchen."
Provenzalisches Lied	e1-g2	a1-f2	Men's voices	Written for tenor. Spirited, graceful.
Requiem	eb1-g2	g1-eb2	All voices, except a light soprano	Slow and very sustained.
Romanze	d1-f#2	a1-d2	Men's voices	Sustained, graceful. Demands an accomplished pianist.
Röselein, Röselein	f#1-f#2	a1-e2	Not too suitable for very low voices	Delicate. Interpretatively not easy. Demands an accomplished pianist.
Schneeglöckchen (Der Schnee, der Gestern)	d1-g2	g1-eb2	All voices	Very delicate.
Schöne Fremde (Liederkreis No. 6)	f#1-g#2	g#1-e2	Not too suitable for very light high voices	Animated. Interpretatively not easy. Demands considerable dramatic intensity in parts and an accomplished pianist.
Schöne Wiege meiner Leiden	d#1-f2	e1-e2	Not too suitable for very light high voices	Animated. In parts dramatic. Demands an accomplished pianist.
Sehnsucht	c1-g2	f1-c2	Not too suitable for very light voices	Dramatic, animated.
Ständchen	d1-g2	d1-b1	Men's voices	Light and delicate.
So lasst mich scheinen	e1-a2	a1-f#2	Women's voices	Slow and sustained. Interpretatively not easy. In parts demands considerable dramatic intensity. See Schubert, H. Wolf.
Stille Liebe	eb1-ab2	g1-eb2	All voices	Very sustained.
Stille Tränen	g1-a2 (bb2)	c2-g2	All voices	Slow and very sustained. Vocally perhaps the most exacting song that Schumann wrote. Demands exceptionally good command of breath

TITLE	COMP.	TESS.	TYPE	REMARKS
Stille Tränen cont'd.				and of high voice. In the original key most suitable for a lyric soprano capable of singing a d♭3 or d3 with ease.
Stiller Vorwurf	d1-g2	a1-e2	All voices	Slow. Interpretatively not easy.
Talismane	b-d2 (g2)	e1-c2	Heavy voices	Vigorous and declamatory.
Tief im Herzen trag' ich Pein	f1-f2	g1-d2	All voices	Written for soprano. Slow and sustained.
Viel Glück zur Reise, Schwalbe	d1-f2	f1-d2	Not suitable for very low voices	Delicate and light. Demands facile articulation and an accomplished pianist. Being extremely short, it can be sung twice without interruption.
Venetianisches Lied No. 1 (Leis rudern hier)	d1-d2	g1-c2	Most suitable for men's voices	Light and gently humorous. Demands facile articulation. See A. Jensen.
Venetianisches Lied No. 2 (Wenn durch Piazzetta)	f♯1-e2	g1-d2	Most suitable for men's voices	Light and delicate. See Mendelssohn, "Venetianisches Gondollied," and A. Jensen, "Wenn durch Piazzetta."
Volksliedchen	d1-g2	a1-e2	Women's voices	Light and delicate. Demands facile articulation.
Waldesgespräch (Liederkreis No. 3)	e1-e2 (b)(g♯2)	g♯1-e2	Not too suitable for very light voices	Dramatic, animated.
Wanderlied	d1-a2 *	b♭1-f2	Men's voices	Spirited and vigorous.
Wanderung	e♭1-g2	f1-d2	Most suitable for men's voices	Spirited and light
Was will die einsame Träne	e1-f♯2	g1-e2	All voices	Slow and sustained. See R. Franz, P. Cornelius.
Weh, wie zornig ist das Mädchen	f1-g2	a1-e♭2	All voices	Light and gently humorous. Demands facile articulation. Often used as a companion piece to "O wie lieblich ist das Mädchen."
Wehmut (Liederkreis No. 9)	e1-e2	f♯1-c♯2	All voices	Slow and very sustained.
Wer nie sein Bro⁺	G-f1	g-d1	Bass or bass-baritone	Sustained. In parts demands considerable dramatic intensity.

TITLE	COMP.	TESS.	TYPE	REMARKS
Wer nie sein Brot cont'd.				See Schubert, Liszt, H. Wolf.
Wer machte dich so krank	eb1-eb2	eb1-bb1	All voices	Written for baritone. Sustained. Same melody with another set of words, also by J. Kerner, "Alte Laute."
Wer sich der Einsamkeit ergibt	eb-f1	g-eb1	Baritone	Slow and sustained. In parts demands considerable dramatic intensity. See Schubert and H. Wolf.
Widmung	b-gb2	ab1-eb2	All voices	Spirited. Demands good command of medium voice. Note the tempo mark "Innig, Lebhaft 3/2."Often sung too slowly.
Zum Schluss	f1-f2	ab1-db2	All voices	Very slow and sustained.
Zwielicht (Liederkreis No. 10)	a#-e2	g1-d2	Not too suitable for very high voices	Slow and sustained. Interpretatively not easy.

RICHARD STRAUSS
(1864-   )

In his songs, in contrast to his operas and orchestral works, Richard Strauss seems deliberately to avoid any attempts at experimentation. Many of the songs of Liszt, for instance, are fully as "modern" as some of Strauss' songs, written some fifty years later.

Strauss writes expertly for the voice. The vocal line in his songs is always magnificently effective, and contrary to the popular belief most considerate of the singer. But he often demands a voice of operatic dimensions, in both range and volume. Sometimes this is not realized, and many a singer with a voice of less imposing proportions, concludes, after vainly trying to master a Strauss song, not intended for his type of voice, that the fault lies with the composer.

Most of the well-known songs of Strauss are neither musically nor interpretatively complex, though they may present some vocal, dramatic and pianistic problems not likely to be encountered in Schubert or Brahms, for instance.

Strauss is very direct in his treatment of the poetic text, so direct sometimes that some critics have found him obvious. In his choice of text, he seems to prefer poetry that possesses an easily definable mood and thus lends itself well to either a naturalistically dramatic setting or to a purely lyrical, melodic interpretation.

Strauss' treatment of the piano part varies considerably. Often his accompaniments demand a purely orchestral approach, but fully as often they are superbly pianistic. Sometimes, again, he uses the piano only for the purpose of providing a harmonic background for the melodic line.

> Editions: Universal
> Breitkopf & Härtel
> Fürstner

Very comprehensive selection of 40 songs,
Musician's Library, Ditson.
Numerous reprints by Schirmer and others.

TITLE	COMP.	TESS.	TYPE	REMARKS
Ach, Lieb, ich muss nun scheiden	d1-g2	ab1-f2	All voices	Slow and sustained.
All' mein Gedanken, mein Herz und mein Sinn	e1-g#2	b1-f#2	Not too suitable for very low voices	Light and delicate. See Max Reger.
Allerseelen	d1-ab2	ab1-f2	All voices	Slow and sustained.
Am Ufer	a#-f#2	c#1-d2	Not too suitable for very light high voices	Very slow and sustained. Demands good command of pp.
Barkarolle	db1-bb2	bb1-gb2	Most suitable for high light voices	Animated, delicate. Demands good command of high pp. and an accomplished pianist.
Befreit	b-e#2	f#1-eb2	Not suitable for light voices	Slow, very sustained. Interpretatively not easy.
Blauer Sommer	c#1-g#2	f#1-f#2	All voices	Slow and very sustained. Demands an accomplished pianist.
Briet über mein Haupt	gb1-ab2	db1-ab2	All voices	Slow and very sustained, very effective. The tessitura is quite high.
Cäcilie	e1-b2	b1-g2	Heavy voices	Rapid, vigorous; very effective. Demands an excellent pianist.
Der Einsame	F-c1	Ab-f	Bass	Very slow, sustained. No. 2 of the two songs for bass and orchestra, opus 51.
Die Nacht	f1-g2	a1-f#2	All voices	Slow and sustained. Demands good command of p.
Die Zeitlose	c#1-g2	g1-e2	All voices	Slow and sustained. Interpretatively not easy.
Du meines Herzens Krönelein	db1-gb2	gb1-eb2	All voices	Slow and sustained. Demands good command of high pp. See Max Reger.
Freundliche Vision	d1-g2	f#1-f#2	All voices	Slow and sustained. Demands good command of pp. and an accomplished pianist.
Frühlingsgedränge	f#1-a2	b1-g#2	Not suitable for very low voices	Light, very rapid. Demands an excellent pianist. See R. Franz.

TITLE	COMP.	TESS.	TYPE	REMARKS
Für fünfzehn Pfennige	b–b2	g1–g2	Not too suitable for very low voices	Rapid. A comic character song. Demands facile articulation, some flexibility and an accomplished pianist. See Max Reger.
Glückes genug	c♯1–g♯2	f♯1–f♯2	All voices	Slow and sustained. Demands good command of p. See Max Reger.
Hat gesagt, bleibts nicht dabei	b–b2	f♯1–f♯2	Women's voices	A humorous character song. Demands some flexibility and an accomplished pianist.
Heimkehr	b–e2	e1–c♯2	All voices	Slow and sustained. Demands good command of high pp.
Heimliche Aufforderung	d♯1–a♭2	f1–f2	All voices	Rapid, brilliant and effective. Demands an excellent pianist.
Ich schwebe	e1–a♯2	a1–f♯2	Not suitable for very low voices	Animated, the vocal line sustained.
Ich trage meine Minne	c♯1–a♭2	g♭1–g♭2	All voices	Very sustained, subdued.
Im Spätboot	g♭–d♭2	c1–b♭1	Not suitable for light high voices	Slow and very sustained. Interpretatively not easy. Demands an accomplished pianist.
Kling!	g1–c3	c2–g2	Most suitable for high heavy voices	Very animated, has imposing climaxes.
Leise Lieder	c1–e♯2	g1–e2	All voices	Very sustained, subdued. Demands an accomplished pianist.
Liebeshumnus	f1–b♭2	b♭1–g♭2	All voices	Very sustained.
Madrigal	e♭1–g♭2	g1–e2	Men's voices	Slow and very sustained. Demands in parts considerable dramatic intensity.
Mein Auge	b♭–g2	d1–d2	Not too suitable for very low voices	Slow and very sustained. Interpretatively and musically not easy. Demands an accomplished pianist.
Mein Herz ist stumm	e♭1–a♭2	a♭1–g♭2	Most suitable for high voices	Slow and somber. Demands good command of pp. and an accomplished pianist.
Meinem Kinde	d1–g2	g1–f2	All voices	Very sustained. Demands good command of pp. and an accomplished pianist.
Mit deinen blauen Augen	c1–g♯2	a1–f♯2	All voices	Slow and sustained. Demands an accomplished pianist.

TITLE	COMP.	TESS.	TYPE	REMARKS
Morgen	f#1-g2	g1-e2	All voices	Slow. Interpretatively not easy. Demands an accomplished pianist.
Muttertändelei	b-f#2	e1-e2	Women's voices	Light and spirited. Demands considerable flexibility and an accomplished pianist.
Nachtgang	db1-gb2	eb1-eb2	All voices	Slow and sustained. Demands good command of pp. Interpretatively not easy.
Ruhe, ruhe, meine Seele	c1-f#2	f1-f2 (H)	Not suitable for very light voices	Slow, declamatory and dramatic.
Schlagende Herzen	d1-a2 (b2)	g1-g2	Most suitable for high voices	Animated, light, graceful. Demands an accomplished pianist.
Schlechtes Wetter	bb-bb2	f1-f2	Not too suitable for very low voices	Animated. A characteristic satirical song. Interpretatively not easy. Demands and excellent pianist.
Seitdem dein Aug' in meines schaute	c1-ab2	f1-f2	All voices	Slow, very sustained.
Ständchen	c#1-a#2	f#1-f#2	All voices	Rapid and light. Demands an excellent pianist. The last "hochglühen" on a#2 is traditionally held two bars.
Traum durch die Dämmerung	c#1-gb2	d#1-d#2	All voices	Slow and sustained, subdued. Demands good command of pp. See Christian Sinding.
Von dunklem Schleier umsponnen	eb1-g#2	gb1-eb2	Not too suitable for very low voices	Very slow and sustained. Demands good command of pp.
Weisser Jasmin	c#1-g#2	g#1-e2	Not too suitable for very low voices	Delicate. Demands an accomplished pianist.
Wer lieben muss, muss leiden	b-f#2	d1-d2	Women's voices, except a very light soprano	Sustained. In folk vein.
Wie sollten wir geheim sie halten	d1-a2	a1-g#2	All voices	Rapid, brilliant and effective. Demands an excellent pianist.
Wiegenlied	d1-g#2	f#1-e2	Women's voices	Very sustained vocal line over a rapid arpeggio accompaniment. Demands good command of pp.

TITLE	COMP.	TESS.	TYPE	REMARKS
Wiegenliedchen	a-f#2	d#1-d#2	Women's voices, except a very light soprano	Very delicate.
Winternacht	c1-f#2	g1-eb2	Not suitable for light voices	Rapid and vigorous. Demands an accomplished pianist.
Wozu noch, Mädchen	f#1-a2	c1-f#2	Men's voices	Light, animated. Demands facile articulation, good command of high p. and an accomplished pianist.
Zueignung	e1-a2	g1-f2	All voices, except a very light soprano	Animated, effective.

<h1 style="text-align:center">RICHARD TRUNK
(1879-   )</h1>

Trunk is chiefly known in this country for his charming and simple "In meiner Heimat". His many songs, which include such fine examples of lyric writing as "Die Stadt," "Wunsch,""Sommerfäden," are worthy of any serious singer's attention.

Editions: Breitkopf & Härtel
Otto Halbreiter (Munich)

TITLE	COMP.	TESS.	TYPE	REMARKS
Das Hemd	f#1-a2	g#1-e2	Women's voices	Very rapid and humorous. Demands facile articulation.
Der Feind	c1-eb2 (e#2)	e1-d2	Heavy voices	Dramatic. Demands an excellent pianist.
Die Stadt	c#1-f2	f1-d2	Not too suitable very light high voices	Slow. Interpretatively not easy. Demands an accomplished pianist.
In der Nacht	d#1-g#2	g#1-e#2	All voices	Slow and sustained.
In meiner Heimat	eb1-ab2 (H)	ab1-fb2	All voices	Delicate and sustained.
Meine Mutter hat's gewollt	d1-f2 (a2)	a1-f2	Women's voices, except a very light soprano	Dramatic.
Nachtgesang	db1-g2	f1-db2	All voices	Very sustained.
Schlafen, schlafen	b-d2	d1-b1	Most suitable for medium or low voices	Very slow and sustained.
Schmerz	c#1-g2	g#1-e2	Heavy voices	Dramatic.
Sommerfäden	d1-d2	f#1-c#2	All voices	Delicate.
Tanzlied	d1-f2	g1-eb2	All voices	Delicate and light.
Wunsch	d#1-fx2	f#1-d#2	All voices	Very delicate. Extremely short (13 bars).

The "Fünf Gedichte füreine Frauenstimme," containing the two celebrated studies for Tristan and Isolde (Träume and Im Treibhaus), are the
only songs that Wagner has written as a mature composer. The five other
songs - four of them to French text - were written between 1838 and 1840
and can hardly be considered representative, although one can by no means
dismiss them as mere "youthful efforts."

Editions: Schott
Fünf Gedichte - Schirmer and many
other publishers

TITLE	COMP.	TESS.	TYPE	REMARKS
Der Engel	c#1-g2	g1-e2	All voices	Originally written for soprano. Very sustained and subdued.
Dors, mon enfant (French text)	d1-f2	g1-e2	Women's voices	Sustained. Demands good command of pp.
Im Treibhaus	c#1-f#2	e1-d2	Most suitable for soprano	Very slow and sustained. Demands good command of high pp. Inter pretatively not easy. A study for Tristan.
Les deux grenadiers (French text)	A-e1	e-c#1	Bass-baritone or baritone	A dramatic narrative song. See Schumann, "Die beiden Grenadiere," written in 1839 and dedicated to H. Heine. It is curious to note that Schumann in his setting of this Heine poem also makes use of the "Marseillaise" in the final section.
Schmerzen	c1-ab2	f1-eb2	Not suitable for light voices	Originally written for soprano. Sustained. Demands in parts considerable dramatic intensity. Interpretatively not easy.
Stehe still	c1-g2	f1-e2	Not suitable for very light voices	Originally written for soprano. Animated. Interpretatively not easy. Demands an accomplished pianist.
Träume	c1-gb2	eb1-c2	Not suitable for very light voices	Originally written for soprano. Very sustained. Demands an accomplished pianist. Interpretatively not easy. A study for Tristan.

See also "Mignonne," "Attente," "Der Tannenbaum."

CARL MARIA von WEBER
(1786-1826)

Weber's operas and concert arias are by far more representative of his style of writing for the voice than most of his songs. His numerous settings of folk songs and his songs in folk vein are, however, most interesting and like "Die Zeit," "Elfenlied," "Das Mädchen und das erste Schneeglöckchen," to name but a few, deserve to be heard more often than they are.

Editions: Peters
Universal

TITLE	COMP.	TESS.	TYPE	REMARKS
Das Mädchen und das erste Schneeglöckchen	d1-g2	f♯1-eb2	Women's voices	Slow and sustained.
Die gefangenen Sänger	d1-g2	f1-d2	All voices	Sustained.
Die Zeit	c1-e2 (a)	e1-c2	Not suitable for light high voices	Very sustained, somber.
Elfenlied	e1-f♯2	a1-e2	Light soprano	Rapid and light. Demands some flexibility.
Heimlicher Liebe Pein (Mein Schatz,derist)	b-b1	e1-b1	Mezzo-soprano or alto	Slow, sustained and somber. In folk vein.
Herzchen, mein Schätzchen	e1-f♯2	f♯1-d2	Most suitable for men's voices	Animated. In folk vein.
Ich denke dein	e1-g2	f1-d2	All voices	Slow and sustained. In parts demands considerable dramatic intensity. See Beethoven.
Reigen	a-g2	d1-d2	High baritone	A lively, rollicking dance tune. In folk vein.
Sind es Schmerzen sind es Freuden	a-g2	c1-c2	Men's voices, except a very light tenor	Animated, dramatic. See Brahms.
Wiegenlied	c1-e2	e1-c2	Women's voices	Delicate, sustained. Verses 2 and 3 could be omitted.

See also the four solo songs from the "Leyer und Schwert" 10 songs, 6 for unaccompanied male chorus.

HUGO WOLF
(1860-1903)

Most of the songs of Hugo Wolf are so dominated by their texts that unless one approaches them from a musicodramatic standpoint their melodic line may often seem disjointed and their harmonic and rhythmic structure may even seem unmotivated. The singer who attempts to sing Hugo Wolf must above all and at all times be conscious of the relationship between the text and the music, in the same sense in which Wolf himself seems to regard this relationship; namely, that the music of a song must not merely be inspired by the poetic idea embodied in the text, but that it must follow, interpret and illustrate the poem, sentence by sentence, or even word by word. This approach to the relationship between the text and the music, although popularly considered "Wagnerian," is almost as old as the composed song itself. The "nuovi musici" of the Italian Renaissance have often tried to approach their texts in a like manner. To a greater or lesser degree, practically every composer writing for solo voice has at least in isolated instances followed the same procedure. In the songs of Wolf, however, this attitude is so prevalent and sometimes so extreme that, when one tries to describe the demands his songs make upon the singer, the demand for a definite and a sympathetic approach to his manner of setting the text to music seems to be of primary importance.

Most of his songs are musically not overcomplex; in some instances, however, his chromaticism and his use of certain rhythmic devices, designed to ensure the proper recitation of the poem, may make a song seem complex at first reading.

An adequate performance of a song by Wolf always demands a pianist uncommonly sensitive to the poem and Wolf's musical reaction to it. Often the piano part demands a technic of great brilliancy; sometimes almost the entire burden of musical illustration and interpretation of the text is left to the pianist; the instances where Wolf uses the piano for the purpose of merely providing a harmonic background for the melody are extremely rare.

Wolf wrote little outside of songs (one opera, <u>Corregidor</u>, a symphonic poem and a string quartet). Most of his 245 songs are written for the c1-a2 high voice and are vocally not taxing. However, a very light soprano (c1-e3) as well as a bass or bass-baritone can both find among his songs a great number that would prove most welcome additions to their concert repertoire.

Editions: Peters (complete)
          Peters (excellent selection by E. Gerhart (recently
            reprinted by Patelson, New York).
          Good selection Breitkopf & Härtel
          Good selection Musician's Library, Ditson
          Numerous reprints of single songs.

TITLE	COMP.	TESS.	TYPE	REMARKS
Ach des Knaben Augen	eb1-f2	bb1-f2	All voices	Sustained and subdued. Interpretatively not easy.
Ach im Maien	e1-g♯2	a1-e2	All voices	Animated, delicate. The vocal line is very sustained.
Agnes	f1-gb2	g1-db2	Women's voices	Slow and sustained. Interpretatively not easy. See Brahms.
Alle gingen, Herz, zur Ruh'	d1-f2	f1-d2	Not too suitable for very high light voices	Slow and sustained. Demands in parts considerable dramatic intensity.

TITLE	COMP.	TESS.	TYPE	REMARKS
Alles endet was entstehet	F#-c#1	B#-a	Bass	Slow and somber. Interpretatively not easy.
Anacreons Grab	d1-d2	f#1-d2	All voices	Slow and sustained.
An den Schlaf	f#1-f#2	ab1-f2	All voices	Slow and sustained. Demands good command of pp.
An die Geliebte	eb1-ab2	ab1-f2	All voices	Very slow, declamatory. Musically and interpretatively not easy. Demands good command of high pp.
An eine Aeolsharfe	c#1-g#2	g#1-e2	Women's voices	Very sustained. Interpretatively and musically complex. Demands an accomplished pianist. Sounds best in the original high key. See Brahms.
Auch kleine Dinge	e1-f#2	a1-e2	All voices	Very delicate and sustained.
Auf dem grünen Balkon	e1-f#2	a1-e2	All voices	Animated, light. Demands an accomplished pianist.
Auf ein altes Bild	f#1-e#2	b1-d2	All voices	Slow and sustained. Demands good command of pp.
Auf eine Christblume I	c-f2	f#1-d2	All voices	Slow and interpretatively complex. Demands an accomplished pianist.
Auf eine Christblume II	c#1-g2	e1-d#2	All voices	Slow and sustained. Demands good command of pp.
Auf einer Wanderung	b-g2	g1-eb2	Not too suitable for very light high voices	Animated. Musically and interpretatively complex. Demands an excellent pianist. The extremely important piano part loses much of its senority if transposed.
Bedeckt mich mit Blumen	d1-f2	g1-eb2	All voices	Slow and sustained. Musically not easy. Demands an accomplished pianist.
Begegnung	d1-gb2	g1-eb2	All voices	Animated. Interpretatively not easy.
Biterolf	d1-f1	f-d1	Bass or bass-baritone	Very slow and sustained.
Blumengruss	eb1-f2	g1-eb2	All voices	Delicate, sustained.
Citronenfalter im April	e1-a2	c2-f#2	Most suitable for light high voices	Very delicate. Demands an accomplished pianist.
Dank des Paria	c1-gb2	ab1-eb2	Heavy voices	Grave, declamatory.

TITLE	COMP.	TESS.	TYPE	REMARKS
Das Köhlerweib ist trunken	c1-g2	a1-f2	Not too suitable for very light voices	Very rapid, dramatic. Musically and interpretatively complex. Demands an excellent pianist.
Das Ständchen	c#1-gb2	f#1-eb1	All voices	Has a very sustained vocal line over an independent, somewhat complex accompaniment. See Korngold.
Das verlassene Mägdlein	e1-f2	a1-e2	Women's voices	Slow and sustained. See Schumann.
Das Vöglein	c#1-f#2	f#1-e2	High voices	Light and animated. Demands facile articulation and an excellent pianist.
Denk' es, o Seele	b#-d2	g1-c#2	All voices, except a very light soprano	Somber and sustained. Interpretatively not easy. Has a very dramatic climax. See Pfitzner.
Der Feuerreiter	c1-g2		Heavy voices	Rapid, dramatic. An uncommonly long, difficult song. Demands an excellent pianist.
Der Freund	c#1-f#2	e1-e2	Most suitable for heavy voices	Vigorous, dramatic. Demands an accomplished pianist.
Der Gärtner	a1-g2	b1-f#2	Most suitable for light high voices	Light and delicate. See Schumann.
Der Genesene an die Hoffnung	bb-ab2	f#1- e2	Not too suitable for very light voices	Grave and sustained. Musically and interpretatively not easy. Demands an accomplished pianist.
Der Knabe und das Immlein	c#1-a2	bb1-g2	Most suitable for light high voices	Delicate and gently humorous. Interpretatively not easy. Demands an excellent pianist.
Der Mond hat eine schwere Klag' erhoben	bb-db1	eb-bb1	Medium or low voices	Slow and very sustained.
Der Musikant	d#1-e2	e1-c#2	Most suitable for men's voices	Gently humorous. Interpretatively not easy.
Der Rattenfänger	c1-f2	e1-e2	Heavy voices, preferably baritone or dramatic tenor	Rapid and vigorous. Demands an excellent pianist.

TITLE	COMP.	TESS.	TYPE	REMARKS
Der Soldat I	e1-f♯2	g1-e2	Men's voices	Humorous, lively.
Der Soldat II	e♭1-a♭2	g♭1-f2	Men's voices	Very rapid and dramatic. Demands facile articulation and an excellent pianist.
Der Tambour	b♯-g♯2	g♯1-f♯2	Most suitable for men's voices	Humorous. Demands an accomplished pianist.
Die ihr schwebet	g1-g2	c♯2-f♯2	Women's voices, except a very light soprano	Animated. Demands considerable dramatic intensity in parts and an accomplished pianist. See "Geistliches Wiegenlied" by Brahms, opus 91 no. 2.
Die Geister am Mummelsee	a♯-g♯2		Heavy voices	Dramatic. A very difficult song. Demands an excellent pianist.
Die Spinnerin	d♯1-f♯2		Women's voices, except a light soprano	Very animated, dramatic. Interpretatively complex. Demands an excellent pianist. See C. Löwe.
Die Zigeunerin	c1-a2	f1-f2	Soprano or mezzo-soprano	Musically and interpretatively quite complex. Demands considerable flexibility and an excellent pianist.
Du denkst mit einem Fädchen mich zu fangen	e♭1-f2	g1-e♭2	Women's voices	Light and delicate. Interpretatively not easy.
Ein Ständchen euch zu bringen	c♯1-g2	g1-d2	Men's voices	Light and animated. Demands facile articulation and an excellent pianist.
Ein Stündlein wohl vor Tag	a♭1-g2	c2-f2	Women's voices	Slow and sustained. Interpretatively not easy. See R. Franz.
Elfenlied	d1-f2	f1-d2	Not too suitable for very heavy low voices	Light and gently humorous. Demands very facile articulation and and accomplished pianist.
Er ist's	d1-g2	b1-g2	All voices	Spirited and brilliant. Demands an excellent pianist. See Schumann.
Erstes Liebeslied eines Mädchens	e♭1-a♭2	a1-f2	Women's voices, except a very light soprano	Very rapid. Interpretatively complex. Demands an excellent pianist.

TITLE	COMP.	TESS.	TYPE	REMARKS
Epiphanias	d1-bb2	g1-eb2	Not too suitable for very light voices	Humorous, characteristic. Demands an excellent pianist.
Frage und Antwort	d1-ab2	bb1-f2	Most suitable for high voices	Sustained. Musically and interpretatively not easy. Demands good command of high pp.
Frühling übers Jahr	d#1-a2	a1-e2	High light voices	Very delicate and light. Demands an accomplished pianist.
Fühlt meine Seele	A-d1	e-c1	Bass or bass-baritone	Slow, declamatory. Musically and interpretatively not easy. Demands an accomplished pianist.
Fussreise	c#1-e2	f#1-c#2	All voices, except a very light soprano	Spirited. Demands good sense of rhythm.
Ganymed	f#1-g2	a1-f#2	All voices	Interpretatively and musically complex. Demands an accomplished pianist. Sounds best in the original high key. See Schubert.
Gebet	d1-f#2	f#1-d2	All voices, except a very light soprano	Slow and sustained.
Geh, Geliebter, geh jetzt	c#1-gb2	f#1-e2	Women's voices, except a very light soprano	Animated, dramatic. Musically and interpretatively complex. Demands an excellent pianist.
Gesang Weyla's	db1-f2	ab1-db2	Not too suitable for very high light voices	Slow and very sustained.
Gesegnet sei durch den die Welt entstund	d1-g2	f1-f2	All voices	Slow and declamatory.
Geselle, woll'n wir uns in Kutten hüllen	d1-f2	e1-d2	Men's voices	A humorous character song. Demands an accomplished pianist.
Gleich und Gleich	f#1-ab2	b1-f#2	Most suitable for high light voices	Delicate, light.
Grenzen der Menschheit	F-eb1	e-c1	Bass	Slow and sustained, declamatory. Interpretatively complex. See Schubert.

TITLE	COMP.	TESS.	TYPE	REMARKS
Harfenspieler I (Wer sich der Einsamkeit ergibt)	B-f1	f-d1	Baritone	Slow. Interpretatively not easy. See Schubert and Schumann.
Harfenspieler II (An die Türen will ich schleichen)	c-d1	g-c1	Bass or baritone	Very sustained. Demands good command of pp. See Schubert and Schumann.
Harfenspieler III (Wer nie sein Brot)	c-e1	f-db1	Bass or baritone	Slow. In parts demands considerable dramatic intensity. See Schubert, Schumann, Liszt.
Heb' auf dein blondes Haupt	f1-f2	ab1-eb2	Men's voices	Very sustained.
Heimweh (Anders wird die Welt)	cb1-f2	g1-eb2	All voices	Slow and sustained. Demands good command of pp.
Herr, was trägt der Boden hier	b-e2	a1-d2	All voices	Slow. Interpretatively not easy.
Heut Nacht erhòb' ich mich	c♯1-f2	f1-d2	All voices	Delicate. Interpretatively not easy.
Ich hab' in Penna	c1-a2	g1-d2	Women's voices	Very rapid, humorous. Demands facile articulation and an excellent pianist.
Im Frühling	b-g2	e1-e2	All voices	Sustained. Musically and interpretatively complex. Demands an accomplished pianist.
In dem Schatten meiner Locken	d1-f2	g1-eb2	Women's voices	Light and delicate. Interpretatively not easy. Demands an accomplished pianist. See Brahms, "Spanisches Lied," and A. Jensen.
In der Frühe	b-g2	e1-e2	Medium or low voices	Slow and grave.
Jägerlied	e1-a2	a1-e2	Men's voices	Light. Demands facile articulation and a good sense of rhythm.
Karwoche	b-ab2	ab1-f2	All voices	Slow. Musically and interpretatively not easy. Demands an accomplished pianist.
Klinge, klinge mein Pandero	db1-f2	g1-d2	All voices, except a very light soprano	Animated. Demands an excellent pianist. See A. Jensen.
Köpfchen, Köpfchen nicht gewimmert	f1-g2	c2-f2	Light soprano	Delicate and light. See Cornelius.
Lebe wohl	db1-ab2	ab1-f2	All voices	Slow. Demands in parts considerable dramatic intensity.
Liebe mir im Busen	e1-f♯2	a1-f2	Women's voices	Very rapid, dramatic. Demands an excellent pianist.

TITLE	COMP.	TESS.	TYPE	REMARKS
Lied vom Winde	c1-g2	a1-e2	High voices	Very animated. Musically and interpretatively not easy. Demands an excellent pianist. The extremely important piano part loses much in sonority if transposed.
Mansfallen-sprüchlein	db1-g2	a1-f2	Most suitable for women's voices	Light and delicate. Interpretatively not easy. Demands an accomplished pianist.
Mein Liebster hat zu Tische mich geladen	c1-g2	f1-e2	Women's voices	Light, gently humorous.
Mein Liebster singt am Haus	d1-f2	g1-eb2	Women's voices	Sustained. Demands an accomplished pianist.
Mignon (Kennst du das Land?)	bb-ab2	gb1-f2	Women's voices, except a very light soprano	Sustained, in parts very dramatic. Musically and interpretatively not easy. Demands an excellent pianist. See Beethoven, Schubert, Schumann, Liszt.
Mignon I (Heiss mich nicht reden)	c1-f2	f1-d2	Women's voices, except a very light soprano	Slow, declamatory. Demands in parts considerable dramatic intensity. See Schubert and Schumann.
Mignon II (Nur wer die Sehnsucht kennt)	d1-g2	g1-f2	Women's voices, except a very light soprano	Animated. Interpretatively not easy. See Beethoven, Schubert, Schumann, Tchaikovsky.
Mignon III (So lasst mich scheinen)	c#1-g2	g1-e2	Women's voices	Slow and sustained. Musically not easy. Demands good command of pp. See Schubert and Schumann.
Mögen alle bösen Zungen	f#1-f#2	a1-e2	Women's voices	Animated. Interpretatively not easy. Demands an accomplished pianist.
Morgenstimmung	b#-g#2	f#1-e2	Not suitable for very light voices	Slow and sustained. Demands an accomplished pianist and considerable dramatic intensity in the final climax. See "Morning Hymn" by Henschel.
Morgentau	e1-e2	a1-e2	All voices	Delicate, sustained.
Mühvoll komm' ich und beladen	d1-g2	ab1-e2	Not too suitable for very light voices	Slow and grave. Musically and interpretatively not easy.

TITLE	COMP.	TESS.	TYPE	REMARKS
Nachtzauber	c#1-f#2	f#1-d#2	All voices	Very sustained. Demands good command of pp. and an accomplished pianist. Musically not easy.
Nein, junger Herr	d1-f2	f#1-d2	Women's voices	Animated, graceful. Interpretatively not easy. Demands an accomplished pianist.
Neue Liebe	c1-ab2	g1-f2	Not suitable for very light voices	Slow, declamatory. Demands in parts considerable dramatic intensity.
Nicht Gelegenheit macht Diebe	c#1-g2	f1-d2	All voices	Animated. Demands an accomplished pianist.
Nimmersatte Liebe	eb1-ab2	ab1-eb2	All voices	Humorous. Interpretatively complex.
Nixe Binsefuss	e1-g2	b1-f#2	Light soprano	Rapid and light. Demands facile articulation and an excellent pianist.
Nun lass uns Frieden schliessen	eb1-eb2	bb1-eb2	All voices	Very sustained, delicate.
Nun wandre, Maria	g1-f#2	b1-e2	All voices	Slow and sustained. Interpretatively not easy. Demands an accomplished pianist.
Prometheus	B-e1	f-eb2	Bass or bass-baritone	Dramatic and declamatory. Demands an excellent pianist. A very difficult song. See Schubert.
Schafendes Jesuskind	c#1-ab2	a1-e2	All voices	Slow and very sustained. Demands good command of pp.
Schweig einmal still	e1-f2	a1-e2	Women's voices	An amusing, character song. Demands an accomplished pianist.
Seemann's Abschied	c#1-a2	c1-f2	Men's voices, except a very light tenor	Rapid, dramatic. Demands an excellent pianist.
Sonne der Schlummerlosen	c#1-e2	d1-b1	Medium or low voices	Slow. Interpretatively not easy. See Schumann, "An den Mond," and Mendelssohn, "Schlafloser Augen Leuchte."
St. Nepomuks Vorabend	d1-ab2	a1-f2	Most suitable for light high voices	Slow, very sustained and delicate. Demands good command of pp.
Storchenbotschaft	c1-bb2	g1-f2	Most suitable for high voices	A humorous, narrative song. Interpretatively not easy. Demands an excellent pianist.

TITLE	COMP.	TESS.	TYPE	REMARKS
Tief im Herzen trag' ich Pein	c1-eb2	eb1-c2	Not suitable for very light high voices	Slow, declamatory. Interpretatively not easy. See Schumann.
Treibe nun mit Lieben Spott	d1-f2	g1-eb2	Most suitable for men's voices	Light and delicate. Demands facile articulation. Interpretatively not easy.
Tretet ein hoher Krieger	c#1-g2	a1-e2	Women's voices	Gently humorous. Demands good sense of rhythm.
Trunken müssen wir alle sein	e#1-f#2	b1-f#2	Men's voices, except a very light tenor	Very vigorous and spirited. Demands an accomplished pianist.
Über Nacht	d1-g2	g1-eb2	Not suitable for very light high voices	A dramatic song in contrasting moods and tempi.
Um Mitternacht	g#-e2	c#1-c#2	Low voices	Very slow and sustained. See R. Franz.
Und willst du deinen Liebsten sterben sehen	eb1-fb2		Most suitable for men's voices	Very slow, sustained, delicate. Musically not easy.
Verborgenheit	d1-g2	bb1-eb2	All voices	Sustained. See R. Franz.
Verschwiegene Liebe	c#1-f#2	f#1-eb2	All voices	Delicate and very sustained. Demands good command of high pp.
Waldmädchen	e1-g#2	c1-g2	Soprano	Very rapid. Demands facile articulation and an excellent pianist.
Wanderers Nachtlied (Der du von dem Himmel bist)	d#1-g2	gb1-eb2	All voices	Very slow and sustained. See Schubert, C. Löwe, and Liszt.
Was für ein Lied soll dir gesungen werden	eb1-eb2		All voices	Slow and sustained.
Was soll der Zorn	db1-f2	f1-eb2	Not suitable for light voices	Dramatic.
Wenn du zu den Blumen gehst	d#1-g2	a1-f#2	All voices	Delicate and sustained. Musically not easy. Demands an accomplished pianist.
Wer rief dich denn?	db1-gb2	f1-f2	Women's voices	Dramatic. Interpretatively not easy.
Wie glänzt der helle Mond	b-e2	g1-eb2	Women's voices	Slow and very sustained. Demands good command of pp.
Wieviele Zeit verlor' ich	d1-eb2		All voices	Delicate and sustained.
Wir haben beide lange Zeit geschwiegen	bb-f2	f1-db2	All voices	Slow and sustained. Interpretatively not easy.

TITLE	COMP.	TESS.	TYPE	REMARKS
Wo find' ich Trost	d1-ab2	g1-f2	Not suitable for very light voices	Slow, declamatory. Musically and interpretatively not easy. Demands an accomplished pianist.
Wohl denk' ich oft	c-e1	e-c1	Bass or bass-baritone	Grave and declamatory.
Zum neuen Jahr	d1-b2	c#1-g#2	Very high light voices	Animated. The tessitura is uncommonly high.
Zur Ruh', zur Ruh'	b-ab2	eb1-eb2	Not suitable for very light voices	Grave and very sustained. Demands considerable dramatic intensity in the climax.

ERICH WOLFF
(1874-1913)

Erich Wolff, whose excellent "Alle Dinge haben Sprache" has become one of the very popular concert songs, has written a great number of most effective and distinguished songs. He is perhaps at his best in his least elaborate moments, for songs like, for instance, "Fäden," "Spaziergang," "Märchen" are in many ways sufficiently remarkable to be classed among the best examples of the post-Wagnerian German school.

Editions: Harmonie, Berlin
Bote & Bock, Berlin
Reprints by Harmonie Edition (with English titles), New York
and some songs by Schirmer

TITLE	COMP.	TESS.	TYPE	REMARKS
Alle Dinge haben Sprache	bb-gb2	f1-f2	Not suitable for very light high voices	Sustained. Has an imposing climax. Demands an accomplished pianist.
Aus der Ferne in die Nacht	c#1-f#2	f#1-d2	All voices	Delicate. Demands good command of high pp.
Das Gärtlein dicht verschlossen	c1-f2	g1-eb2	All voices	Slow and very sustained. Demands good command of pp.
Der Kuckuk ist ein braver Mann	b-g#2	e1-e2	All voices	Light and humorous.
Du bist so jung	a#-f#2	e1-e2	Most suitable for baritone	Slow, somewhat declamatory. Demands an accomplished pianist.
Einsamkeit	bb-f2	e1-b1	Medium or low voices	Slow and somber.
Ein Sonntag	e1-g2	b1-g2	Most suitable for light high voices	Very delicate. Demands good command of pp.
Ewig	bb-fb2	eb1-c2	Heavy voices	Sustained, majestic.
Fäden	c#1-f#2	a#1-e2	All voices	Very delicate, sustained.
Friedhof	c1-f#2	e1-e2	All voices	Somber. Interpretatively not easy. Demands an accomplished pianist.

TITLE	COMP.	TESS.	TYPE	REMARKS
Ich bin eine Harfe	b-f♯2	f♯1-d♯2	Not suitable for high light voices	Slow. Interpretatively not easy. Demands good command of p. and an accomplished pianist.
Immer wieder	d1-f♯2	f1-d2	All voices	Slow and sustained. Demands good command of p.
Knabe und Veilchen	d1-d2	a1-d2	All voices	Light and delicate.
Märchen	d1-e2		All voices	Very delicate, sustained. Demands good command of pp.
Mich tadelt der Fanatiker	d1-g2		Men's voices	Spirited and humorous. Demands an accomplished pianist.
Schlafe ruhig ein	c♯1-f♯2	f♯1-e♯2	Soprano or mezzo-soprano	Delicate, sustained.
Spaziergang	c♯1-g2	a♯1-f♯2	Most suitable for light high voices	Very delicate. Demands good command of high pp.

The list of French songs in this volume is primarily designed to be of some practical value to a present-day singer outside of France. Thus it is admittedly not as representative as it would be were it intended as a historical survey of French song.

Most of the examples of the nineteenth century "drawing-room" music, for instance, have little if any practical value for the present-day performer. Thus it seemed best to limit to a minimum the listing of songs of Chaminade, Godard, Thomas, and to include just a few of the many songs of Gounod, although historically they have no inconsiderable importance.

Extraordinarily popular some fifty years ago, these songs are almost forgotten today, particularly outside of France. It has seemed rather unnecessary to try to revive interest in them by listing them in this volume. Naturally, masters like Gounod and Thomas are represented in the section devoted to the operatic excerpts; their operas do not seem to have lost any of their validity on the stage of today, even if their songs seem to have lost much, if not all, of their former appeal.

Again, with the exception of some of the most representative examples of the most significant contemporary French composers, it seemed best not to try to list too many songs of avowedly experimental nature or of extraordinary complexity and difficulty. To list a great number of such songs in a volume, the purpose of which is primarily to provide the singer with a foundation upon which an individual repertoire could be built, seemed unwarranted.

The inclusion of some songs by such minor composers as Fourdrain, Bemberg, Poldowski, Sculc, etc., seemed warranted by the still rather powerful appeal they seem to possess for the performer as well as the public outside of France. The exclusion, however, of many fine examples of a number of French composers of equal stature seemed equally proper in view of the fact that their songs seem for one reason or another never to have attained sufficient popularity outside of France,

Songs by Duparc, Chausson, Fauré, Debussy and Ravel form the backbone of this list. It does not seem unreasonable to assume that any list of French songs which includes a sufficient number of examples of these five great masters could fail to represent, for all practical purposes, the most important and significant examples of French song literature.

Naturally, a multitude of fine and effective French songs, old and new, could easily be added. Yet such an amplification would hardly effect any change in the general complexion of this list; in so far as the present-day singer and public are concerned it would still be dominated by the work of these five composers, which rightfully seem to represent the French song to the world in general.

EVA DELL' ACQUA
(1860 -)

TITLE	COMP.	TESS.	TYPE	REMARKS
Chanson provençale	d-bb2 (bb)(c3)	g1-g2	Light soprano	Light, somewhat florid. Demands good command of high pp. (Schirmer)
Villanelle	eb1-d3	bb1-g2	Coloratura soprano	A very florid display piece. (Schirmer)

TITLE	COMP.	TESS.	TYPE	REMARKS

ADOLPHE ADAM
(1803-1856)

TITLE	COMP.	TESS.	TYPE	REMARKS
Cantique pour Noël	e♭1-g2	g1-e♭2 (H)	All voices	Sustained. Religious text. (Ditson)
Variations on: Ah, vous dirai-je, maman	b-e3	g1-b2	Coloratura soprano	A brilliant, florid display piece. Flute obbligato ad lib. (Edited by E. Liebling. Schirmer)

LOUIS AUBERT
(1877 -)
Edition: Durand

TITLE	COMP.	TESS.	TYPE	REMARKS
La lettre	e1-a2	g1-f2 (H)	All voices	Slow and subdued. Somewhat declamatory. Interpretatively not easy. Demands good command of pp.
Sérénade	e1-g2	f♯1-e2	All voices	Animated, rhythmical.
Si de mon premier rêve	e♭1-g2	g1-e♭2	All voices	Sustained. (From "Rimes Tendres," three songs)
Vieille chanson espagnole	e1-a2	a1-e2 (H)	All voices	A sustained habanera.

GEORGES AURIC
(1899 -)

TITLE	COMP.	TESS.	TYPE	REMARKS
Alphabet	c1-f2	f1-e2	High or medium voices	Seven short, amusing songs. Demand an accomplished pianist. Interpretatively not easy. (Eschig)
Printemps	e1-f♯2	a1-e2	Light soprano	An animated, delicate waltz song. Demands some flexibility. (Durand)

ALFRED BACHELET
(1864-1943)

TITLE	COMP.	TESS.	TYPE	REMARKS
Chère nuit	d1-b♭2	b♭1-g♭2	Most suitable for high light voices	Slow and very sustained. Demands an accomplished pianist. (Schirmer)
Vocalise	c1-b♭2	f1-f2	High voices	Sustained. (Hettich, Répertoire Moderne de Vocalises. Leduc, Paris)

HENRI BEMBERG
(1861 -)

TITLE	COMP.	TESS.	TYPE	REMARKS
Chant hindou	c#1-f#2	f#1-d2	Women's voices	Slow, sustained; effective. (Schirmer)
Il neige	f#1-g2	b1-f#2	Not too suitable for very low voices (H)	Light, animated. Demands facile articulation. (Grus)

HECTOR BERLIOZ
(1803-1869)

The very few songs of Berlioz are perhaps among his least representative compositions. The four songs listed below seem to be most representative of his manner of writing for the voice.

Edition: Costellat

TITLE	COMP.	TESS.	TYPE	REMARKS
L'absence	c#1-f#2	f#1-d#2	All voices	Slow, somewhat declamatory. Demands in parts considerable dramatic intensity, as well as a good command of high pp.
La captive	a-f#2	d1-d2	Mezzo-soprano or alto	Sustained. Demands some flexibility. (Originally for voice and orchestra.)
Le spectre de la rose	a-f2	d#1-d2	Women's voices, except a light soprano	Slow, sustained. In parts demands considerable dramatic intensity.
Villanelle	e1-f#2	a1-e2	Not too suitable for heavy low voices	Light and delicate. (Ditson)
L'Enfance du Christ (Part II,No.3) Le repos de la Sainte Famille	e-a1	a-e1	Tenor	Sustained, graceful. (Score, Costellat)
L'Enfance du Christ (Part I,No.3) Recitative: Toujours ce rêve Air: O misère des rois	F-eb1	c-c1	Bass	Grave, sustained. In parts dramatic. (Score, Costellat)

PAUL BERNARD
(1827-1879)

TITLE	COMP.	TESS.	TYPE	REMARKS
Ca fait peur aux oiseaux	g#1-f2	a1-e2	Soprano	Graceful, delicate. Demands facile articulation. (Schirmer)

Perhaps because of the extraordinary popularity of Carmen, the rest
of Bizet's music seems to have suffered comparative neglect. His songs,
for instance, among them such charming and individual things as "Chanson
d'avril," "Douce mer," "Après l'hiver," to name but a few, deserve an
esteemed place in any singer's French repertoire. Though by no means
of extraordinary importance, they undoubtedly belong among the few artistically still valid examples of the mid-nineteenth century French
"Romance."

Editions: Two vols. Schirmer
Choudens; Paris
Various reprints of single songs by many publishers

TITLE	COMP.	TESS.	TYPE	REMARKS
Adieux de l'hôtesse arabe	c1-g2 (bb)(ab2)	g1-f2	Women's voices	Sustained. Demands some flexibility, es- pecially in the final florid passage.
Après l'hiver	e1-g2	f1-eb2	All voices	Animated, delicate.
Chanson d'avril	e1-g2	f1-f2	All voices	Light, delicate. Demands facile articu- lation.
Douce mer	eb1-ab2	ab1-f2	Most suit- able for high voices	Delicate, sustained. Demands good com- mand of high pp. and some flexibility.
Ma vie a son secret	bb-g2	f1-eb2	All voices, except a very light soprano	Sustained.
Ouvre ton coeur	d#1-g#2 (b2)	b1-f#2	Most suit- able for women's voices	An effective, spirited serenade in Spanish style. Demands some flexibility and a good sense of rhythm.
Pastorale	d1-g2	g1-e2	Not too suitable for very heavy low voices	Light. Demands facile articulation.
Vieille chanson	eb1-ab2	ab1-f2	Most suit- able for light high voices	Delicate. Demands some flexibility.
Agnus Dei	d1-bb2	a1-f2 (H)	All voices	Very sustained. Has effective climaxes. Latin and English texts. (Schirmer)

ERNEST BLOCH
(1880 -)

The very remarkable songs of Ernest Bloch, while written in a most individual idiom, never seem obscure or experimental. Few in number,
they are for the most part written for voice and orchestra. Bloch's music
is in its essence Hebraic. He has achieved a peculiar and striking musi-

cal language of his own which could perhaps be termed nationalistic, but only in the widest sense of the word, since this language is hardly based on folk material.

The three Psalms and the four "Poèmes d'Automne" are among his most remarkable works. They are all written for rather heavy voices, and are musically and interpretatively fairly complex. The accompaniments, being originally scored for full orchestra, demand considerable ingenuity and a well-developed sense of dynamics from the pianist.

Edition: Schirmer

TITLE	COMP.	TESS.	TYPE	REMARKS
Invocation (Poèmes d'Automne)	c1-f2	g1-e2	Most suitable for medium voices	Slow, subdued, somewhat declamatory. Demands good command of p. Interpretatively not easy.
L'abri (Poèmes d'Automne)	c#1-g2	f#1-e2	Not too suitable for very light high voices	Slow, somewhat declamatory. In parts demands considerable dramatic intensity. Interpretatively not easy. Demands an accomplished pianist.
La vagabonde (Poèmes d'Automne)	e1-e2		Most suitable for medium voices	Slow, somber, somewhat declamatory. Interpretatively not easy. Demands an accomplished pianist.
Le déclin (Poèmes d'Automne)	c1-eb2	db1-db2	Most suitable for medium voices	Slow, somewhat declamatory, subdued. In parts demands considerable dramatic intensity. Interpretatively not easy. Demands an accomplished pianist.
Psaume 22	c#-f1	f-d1	Baritone	Dramatic, somewhat declamatory. Musically and interpretatively not easy. English version by Waldo Frank is very good.
Psaume 114	a1-a2	a1-f2	High voices	Dramatic, somewhat declamatory. Musically and interpretatively not easy. Demands an excellent pianist. English version by Waldo Frank is very good.
Psaume 137	gb1-a#2	bb1-g2	High voices, except a very light tenor or soprano	Dramatic, somewhat declamatory. Musically and interpretatively not easy. Demands an excellent pianist. The English version by Waldo Frank is very good.

See also: "Historiettes au crépuscule" four songs for medium voice
(Demets, Paris)

TITLE	COMP.	TESS.	TYPE	REMARKS

CHARLES BORDES
(1863-1909)

TITLE	COMP.	TESS.	TYPE	REMARKS
Danson la gigue	e1-e2		High or medium voices	Rapid. Demands an excellent pianist. See Poldowski, Carpenter. (Hamelle)
Promenade matinale	d#1-a2	g1-e2	Not too suitable for very low voices	Not slow, sustained. Interpretatively not easy. (Rouart, Lerolle)

NADIA BOULANGER
(1887 -)

TITLE	COMP.	TESS.	TYPE	REMARKS
Cantique	f1-f2	f1-d2	All voices	Sustained; for the most part, subdued. (Hamelle)

ALFRED BRUNEAU
(1857-1934)

TITLE	COMP.	TESS.	TYPE	REMARKS
La pavane (from "Chansons à danser")	d1-f#2	e1-d2	High or medium	Sustained, rather subdued. (Choudens)
La sarabande (from "Chansons à danser")	db1-f2	f1-d2	Not too suitable for very light voices	Animated. Interpretatively not easy. Demands in parts considerable dramatic intensity. (Choudens)
Le sabot de frêne (from "Les lieds de France")	d1-e2	a1-d2	Women's voices	Spirited and gay. Demands facile articulation. (Choudens)
L'heureux vagabond (from "Les lieds de France")	eb1-g2	g1-eb2 (H)	Men's voices	Vigorous. Interpretatively not easy. (Schirmer)

HENRI BÜSSER
(1872 -)

TITLE	COMP.	TESS.	TYPE	REMARKS
La meilleure pensée	f#1-a2	a1-e2	Not suitable for very low voices	Animated. The vocal line very sustained. (Durand)

ANDRÉ CAPLET
(1878-1925)

TITLE	COMP.	TESS.	TYPE	REMARKS
Forêt (from "Le Vieux Coffret" - four songs)	d1-gb2	f1-eb2	High or medium voices	Slow, somewhat declamatory. In parts demands considerable dramatic intensity. Musically not easy. Demands an accomplished pianist. (Durand)

TITLE	COMP.	TESS.	TYPE	REMARKS
La ronde (from "Cinq Ballades Françaises")	d1-f♯2	e1-e2	Most suitable for high voices	Rapid, light. Demands facile articulation and an accomplished pianist. Musically not easy. (Durand)
Le Corbeau et le Renard (from "Trois Fables de La Fontaine")	a♯-g2	c♯1-d♯2	High or medium voices	Humorous, somewhat declamatory, in the manner of a free recitative. Musically and interpretatively not easy. Demands an accomplished pianist. (Durand)
Les Prières: 1. Oraison Dominicale 2. Salutation Angélique 3. Symboles des Apôtres	d♯1-g2	d♯1-d♯2	High or. medium voices	Sustained. A setting of three prayers. The last one has an imposing final climax. Demands an accomplished pianist. (Durand)
Prière normande	d1-f♯2	e1-e2	Medium or high voices	Not fast, rather sustained. Musically not easy. (Durand)

See also "Le Pain Quotidien' - fifteen vocalises for soprano. Musically quite complex. (Durand)

EMMANUEL CHABRIER
(1841-1894)

The four delightful "animal songs" listed here could be considered as forerunners of Ravel's "Histoires Naturelles." Chabrier's wit, droll humor and originality in setting these texts to music are the more astonishing considering the fact that in his treatment of other texts (like "L'île heureuse" and "Romance de l'étoile") he does not seem to rise above the conventional pattern of the mid-nineteenth century French "Romance."

TITLE	COMP.	TESS.	TYPE	REMARKS
Ballade des gros dindons	b-f2	f1-b♭1	All voices	Humorous. Demands an accomplished pianist. (Schirmer)
Les cigales	c1-f♯2	f♯1-e2	Not too suitable for very low voices	Rapid and light. Demands facile articulation and an accomplished pianist. (Enoch, Paris)
L'île heureuse	b-f2	d1-d2	Medium or low voices	Animated. The vocal line sustained. Has effective climaxes. (Enoch, Paris)
Pastorale des cochons roses	c1-e2	d1-d2	Most suitable for medium voices	Humorous. Demands facile articulation. A trifle long. (Enoch, Paris)

TITLE	COMP.	TESS.	TYPE	REMARKS
Romance de l'étoile	c1-g2 (bb)	eb1-bb1	All voices	Delicate. Requires good command of high pp. (Enoch, Paris)
Villanelle des petits canards	b-e2	f1-d2	All voices	Very light, humorous. Demands facile articulation and a good sense of rhythm. (Homeyer, Boston)

CÉCILE CHAMINADE
(1861-1944)

TITLE	COMP.	TESS.	TYPE	REMARKS
Chant slave	c1-g2 (bb2)	d1-f2	Alto or mezzo-soprano	Sustained, effective. (Schirmer)
L'anneau d'argent	c1-g2	f1-d2	Women's voices	Delicate and sustained. (Schirmer)
L'été	e1-a2	f1-f2	Most suitable for soprano	Animated, effective. Demands considerable flexibility. (Schirmer)
Trahison	b-a2	e1-e2	Not too suitable for very light high voices	Animated, dramatic. Has effective climaxes. (Schirmer)

GUSTAVE CHARPENTIER
(1860 -)

TITLE	COMP.	TESS.	TYPE	REMARKS
Les chevaux de bois	e1-a2	a1-g2	High voices	Very animated, in parts quite vigorous. Demands an accomplished pianist. See Debussy. (Heugel)

ERNEST CHAUSSON
(1855-1899)

The songs of Chausson, with the exception of a few ("Les papillons," "Le temps des lilas," "Le colibri"), are infrequently performed. Such masterpieces as "La caravane," "Les heures," "La chanson bien douce," "Chanson perpétuelle," to name but a few, are for some unknown reason neglected by the great majority of singers, who are sufficiently well equipped to perform "Le temps des lilas" or "Les papillons."

Most of Chausson's songs are neither musically nor interpretatively easy. Although his harmonies and rhythms are never overcomplex, his use of them is so highly individual as to be almost startling at first acquaintance. "La dernière feuille," "Le charme," "Le colibri" and "Les morts" are perhaps the simplest of his songs and can be recommended to those who wish to acquaint themselves with his style of writing.

Editions: Rouart, Lerolle
Hamelle
A number of single songs reprinted by Boston Music Co.

TITLE	COMP.	TESS.	TYPE	REMARKS
Amour d'antan	d1-f#2	b1-e2	All voices	Sustained, somber. Interpretatively not easy.
Apaisement	eb1-g2	g1-e2	Most suitable for light, high voices	Very sustained. See "La lune blanche" by G. Fauré and "L'heure exquise" by R. Hahn and Poldowski. Demands good command of pp.
Cantique à l'épouse	c1-f2	f1-c2	Men's voices	Slow and sustained.
Chanson d'amour	e1-g2	a1-f2	All voices	A setting of "Take, o take, those lips away." In parts demands considerable dramatic intensity. Sustained.
Chanson de clown	d-eb1	gb-c1	Baritone	A setting of "Come away, come away, death." Grave.
Chanson d'Ophélie	c1-e2	e1-c2	Mezzo-soprano or alto	A setting of "He is dead and gone, lady." Slow.
Chanson perpétuelle	c#1-g#2	g#1-e2	Mezzo-soprano or dramatic soprano	Slow, somewhat declamatory. Interpretatively and musically not easy. In parts very dramatic.
Dans la forêt du charme et de l'enchantement	c1-g2	g1-d2	Not too suitable for very heavy or low voices	Not fast. Interpretatively not easy. Demands lightness of tone, facile articulation, and an accomplished pianist.
Fauves las (from "Serres Chaudes")	e1-gb2	f1-d2	All voices	Sustained. Interpretatively not easy.
L'aveu	f1-gb2	a1-eb2	Men's voices	A song of contrasting moods and tempi. In parts demands considerable dramatic intensity.
La caravane	c#1-a2	a1-f2	Not suitable for light voices	Dramatic. Interpretatively not easy. Demands an excellent pianist.
La chanson bien douce	d1-e2	f1-c2	All voices	Not fast. Interpretatively not easy. Demands facile articulation, lightness of tone, and an accomplished pianist.
La dernière feuille	b-d#2	f#1-b1	Most suitable for low or medium voices	Somber, sustained.

TITLE	COMP.	TESS.	TYPE	REMARKS
Lassitude (from "Serres Chaudes")	c#1-f#2	f#1-c#2	All voices	Slow and sustained. Interpretatively not easy.
Le charme	bb-eb2	eb1-c2	All voices, except a very light soprano	Sustained.
Le colibri	f1-f2	ab1-db2	All voices	Sustained.
Le temps des lilas	d1-g#2	a1-f2	All voices, except a very light soprano	Excerpt from "Poème de l'amour et de la mer" for high voice and orchestra. Sustained. In parts demands considerable dramatic intensity. Demands an accomplished pianist.
Les heures	d1-d2	f1-c2	Most suitable for low or medium voices	Grave and sustained.
Les morts	c#1-g2	e1-c#2	Not too suitable for very high light voices	Grave and sustained. (Ditson)
Les papillons	c1-f2	g1-e2	Not too suitable for very low voices	Rapid and light. Demands facile articulation and an excellent pianist.
Nanny	b-g2	g1-e2	All voices, except a very light soprano	Slow and sustained.
Nocturne	e1-g#2	b1-e2	All voices	Very sustained. Demands good command of p. and an accomplished pianist.
Nos souvenirs	d#1-e2	f#1-c#2	Most suitable for medium or low voices	Somber. Interpretatively not easy. Demands an accomplished pianist.
Oraison (from "Serres Chaudes")	eb1-g2	bb1-f2	All voices	Very sustained. Interpretatively not easy.
Sérénade	d1-a2	g#1-e2	Most suitable for high light voices	Very sustained.
Sérénade italienne	c1-e2	g1-d#2	Most suitable for medium or low voices	Sustained. Demands an accomplished pianist. Rhythmically not easy.

TITLE	COMP.	TESS.	TYPE	REMARKS
Serre chaude (from "Serres Chaudes')	d1-g2 (a2)	a1-f♯2	All voices	Animated. Musically and interpretatively complex. Demands an accomplished pianist.
Serre d'ennui (from "Serres Chaudes")	b-f2	a1-e2	All voices	Sustained. Interpretatively not easy. Demands good command of p.
Printemps triste	c1-g2	ab1-f2	Not too suitable for very light high voices	Somber and slow. Interpretatively not easy. Demands an accomplished pianist.

CLAUDE DEBUSSY
(1862-1918)

The importance of Debussy as a composer of songs can hardly be over-estimated. Although he wrote only some 60 songs (including his earliest, imitative efforts), his style of writing for the voice has had and is still having a most profound and pronounced influence on much, if not most, of contemporary vocal music. With the exception of a very few, his songs demand much musically and interpretatively from singer and pianist. Vocally they present few problems; one, and perhaps the most important of these, is the demand he makes upon the singer to find an exact and most delicately adjusted balance between the spoken word and the sung tone, so that neither dominates the other. Often, to ensure this effect, he deliberately uses the very edges of a voice's limits, writing, for instance, whole passages between c1 and e1 for a light high voice from which he may expect and an a2 a few bars later. The singer who would attempt to produce a cantilena tone in such passages would, of course, demand an impossible and artistically most undesirable effect from himself.

Three considerations must be kept in mind when approaching his songs: First, in the treatment of his poetic texts Debussy is as much of a musical dramatist as Liszt or Hugo Wolf, though in his own somewhat veiled and oblique manner, and unlike the two latter composers he is hardly an illustrative realist. Second, the fact that Debussy wrote most expertly for the voice and knew to the minutest detail every shade of sonority that the combination of the human voice and the piano could produce. And, third, that he was one of the most fastidious composers in so far as the notation of his songs is concerned. Everything is marked, every accent, every dynamic shading, every rubato, every shade of tempo change. It will also help to remember that a most exacting rhythmic precision is demanded at all times unless otherwise indicated. Generally speaking most of Debussy songs seem to lend themselves best to rather light voices, commanding a good pianissimo.

Editions: Durand, Paris
Some reprints Boston Music Co. and Oliver Ditson

TITLE	COMP.	TESS.	TYPE	REMARKS
Ballade de Villon à s'amye	c1-f2	d1-c♯2	Most suitable for medium voices	Slow. Musically and interpretatively not easy. Demands an accomplished pianist.

TITLE	COMP.	TESS.	TYPE	REMARKS
Ballade des femmes de Paris	b-e2	e1-c2	All voices, except a very light soprano	Rapid, humorous. Demands facile articulation and an excellent pianist. Musically not easy.
Ballade que Villon feit à la requestre de sa mère	bb-e2	d1-d2	Mezzo-soprano or alto	Slow. Interpretatively not easy. Demands facile articulation and and accomplished pianist.
Beau soir	c1-f#2	f#1-d#2	All voices	Slow, sustained.
C'est l'extase langoureuse	c#1-a2	f#1-d#2	Not suitable for very low voices	Slow, delicate. Has a dramatic climax. Demands an accomplished pianist. See Fauré.
Chevaux de bois	c1-g2	g1-e2	High or medium voices	Spirited. Interpretatively not easy. Demands facile articulation and an excellent pianist. See Charpentier.
Clair de lune	c#1-f#2	f#1-d#2	Most suitable for high voices	Delicate, very sustained. Demands good command of high pp. and an accomplished pianist. See Fauré, Szulc.
Colloque sentimental	a-fb2	e1-db2	All voices	Very slow, declamatory. Interpretatively quite complex. Demands in parts considerable dramatic intensity. Musically not easy.
Crois mon conseil, chère Climène	c1-f#2	c#1-d#2	Not too suitable for very low voices	Slow, very delicate. Demands good command of pp. and an accomplished pianist. Musically and interpretatively not easy.
Dans le jardin	c1-f#2 (g#2)	f1-c#2	Not too suitable for very low voices	Animated, delicate. Demands facile articulation, good command of pp. and an accomplished pianist. Interpretatively not easy.
En sourdine	c1-f#2	g#1-d#2	Not too suitable for very low voices	Slow, delicate. See Fauré, Hahn, Poldowski.
Eventail	d1-f#2	f1-c#2	Not too suitable for very low voices	Rapid, light. Demands very facile articulation, good command of pp. and an accomplished pianist. Musically and interpretatively quite complex.
Fleurs de blés	c#1-g2	a1-f2	Most suitable for high voices	Sustained, delicate.

TITLE	COMP.	TESS.	TYPE	REMARKS
Fantoches	d1-a2	g1-f2	Most suitable for high voices	Rapid, light. Demands very facile articulation, good command of high pp. and an accomplished pianist. Often taken at too fast a tempo.
Green	c1-ab2	ab1-f2	Not too suitable for very low voices	Animated, delicate. Demands good command of high pp. and an accomplished pianist. See Fauré and "Offrande" by Hahn.
Harmonie du soir	b-f#2	e1-e2	Most suitable for high voices	Slow. Interpretatively and musically not easy. Demands good command of high pp. and an accomplished pianist.
Ici-bas	e#1-f#2	f#1-d#2	All voices	Sustained, delicate. See Fauré. This song was composed by Paul and Lucien Hillemacher, published as by Debussy. Another song, "Chanson d'un fou", composed by Émile Pessard was also published under Debussy's name. (Schott)
Il pleure dans mon coeur	c#1-g#2	g#1-d#2	Not too suitable for very low voices	Sustained. Interpretatively not easy. Demands good command of pp. and an accomplished pianist.
Je tremble en voyant ton visage	ab-f2	db1-db2	Not too suitable for very high voices	Slow, sustained. Demands an accomplished pianist.
La chevelure (Chansons de Bilitis)	cb1-f#2	e1-c2	Women's voices, except a very light soprano	Slow, interpretatively not easy. Demands an accomplished pianist.
La flûte de Pan (Chansons de Bilitis)	b-b1	e1-b2	Women's voices	Slow, very delicate. Demands facile articulation and an accomplished pianist. Interpretatively not easy.
La grotte	b-d#2	d#1-b1	Medium or low voices	Slow and very subdued. Musically and interpretatively not easy.
La mer est plus belle	d1-g2	f#1-e2	All voices	Animated. Vocal line sustained. Demands good command of occasional high pp.

TITLE	COMP.	TESS.	TYPE	REMARKS
La mort des amants	bb-a2	gb1-f#2	Not too suitable for very low voices	Sustained. Musically and interpretatively not easy. Demands good command of high pp. and an accomplished pianist. See Charpentier.
Le balcon	b#-a2	g1-g2	Most suitable for high voices	Animated. A song of uncommon complexity, interpretatively. Musically and vocally not easy. Demands an excellent pianist.
L'échelonnement des haies	e#1-f#2	g#1-d#2	Most suitable for high voices	Animated, delicate. Demands facile articulation, good command of high pp., and an accomplished pianist.
Le faune	c1-c2	c1-a2	Medium or low voices	Animated. Interpretatively not easy. Demands an accomplished pianist.
Le jet d'eau	c1-g#2	e1-e2	Not too suitable for very low voices	Sustained. Musically and interpretatively not easy. Demands good command of p. and an accomplished pianist.
Le son du cor s'afflige	db1-e2		Medium or low voices	Slow, subdued, somewhat declamatory.
Le temps a laissié son manteau	b-f#2	e1-c#2	All voices	Spirited. Demands facile articulation.
Le tombeau des Naïades (Chansons de Bilitis)	c1-f#2	d1-a1	Women's voices	Slow and delicate. Musically and interpretatively not easy. Demands an accomplished pianist.
Les Angélus	c#1-f#2	f#1-d#2	Not too suitable for very low voices	Very sustained, delicate. Demands good command of pp.
Les cloches	d#1-g#2	f#1-d#2	All voices	Sustained, delicate.
Les ingénus	c1-f2	e1-db2	All voices	Delicate. Interpretatively and musically not easy.
L'ombre des arbres	d#1-a#2	e#1-d#2	Most suitable for high voices	Slow. Demands good command of high pp. Interpretatively not easy. See "Brûme" by Poldowski.
Mandoline	c1-g2	g1-e2	All voices	Rapid and light. Demands facile articulation and an accomplished pianist. See Fauré and "Fêtes galantes" by Hahn.

TITLE	COMP.	TESS.	TYPE	REMARKS
Noël des enfants qui n'ont plus de maisons	c1-g2	f1-e2	Not too suitable for very low voices	Animated, dramatic. Interpretatively not easy. The text (dealing with German aggression in the World War I) is by Debussy.
Nuit d'étoiles	d1-g2	g1-eb2	All voices	Very sustained. See Widor.
Placet futile	c1-g2		High or medium voices	Not fast. Demands very facile articulation. Interpretatively and musically quite complex. Demands an accomplished pianist. See Ravel.
Pour ce que plaisance est morte	c1-e2	e1-c2	All voices	Slow. Musically and interpretatively not easy.

Proses Lyriques - four songs; texts by the composer.

TITLE	COMP.	TESS.	TYPE	REMARKS
(1) De rêve	b-a2	e1-e2	High or medium voices	Musically and interpretatively quite complex. Demands an excellent pianist.
(2) De grève	c#1-a2	f#1-d#2	High or medium voices	Animated. Musically and interpretatively not easy. Demands an excellent pianist.
(3) De fleurs	c1-ab2	e1-e2	High or medium voices	Slow. Demands in parts considerable dramatic intensity. Musically and interpretatively quite complex. Demands an accomplished pianist.
(4) De soir	c#1-g#2	g#1-e2	High or medium voices	Animated. Interpretatively not easy. Demands an accomplished pianist.

TITLE	COMP.	TESS.	TYPE	REMARKS
Recueillement	c1-g#2	e1-d#2	Most suitable for high voices	Very slow. Musically and interpretatively not easy. Demands good command of high pp. and an accomplished pianist.
Rondeau	e1-a2	a1-f2	Most suitable for high voices	Sustained, delicate.
Romance	d1-f#2 (g#2)	f#1-d2	All voices	Sustained.
Soupir	c1-f2	g1-eb2	High or medium voices	Slow, very sustained. Demands good command of pp. and an accomplished pianist. Musically and interpretatively not easy.

TITLE	COMP.	TESS.	TYPE	REMARKS
Spleen	db1-bb2	e1-e2	Not too suitable for very light high voices	Slow, dramatic. Musically and interpretatively not easy.
Voici que le printemps	d1-g2 (c#1)	f#1-e2	High or medium voices	Very light and delicate. Demands facile articulation. Interpretatively not easy. In parts gently humorous.

"Trois chansons de Charles d'Orléans" - originally written for mixed chorus, transcribed for solo voice and pianoforte by Lucien Garbau

TITLE	COMP.	TESS.	TYPE	REMARKS
Dieu, qu'il la fait bon regarder	d#1-f#2	f#1-e2	High or medium voices	Slow, sustained, delicate. Demands good command of high pp.
Yver, vous n'estes qu'un villain	e1-f#2	f#1-d2	All voices	Rapid, rhythmic. Has an effective ending. Demands facile articulation.
Quand j'ai ouy le tabourin	d1-e2	e1-c#2	Not too suitable very light high voices	Originally alto solo, with choral accompaniment. Animated, delicate, gently humorous. Demands good command of pp. and facile articulation.

LÉO DÉLIBES
(1836-1891)

TITLE	COMP.	TESS.	TYPE	REMARKS
Bonjour Suzon	c1-f2	f1-d2 (H)	Men's voices	Light and rapid. Demands facile articulation. Of no particular distinction.
Chant de l'almée	d1-e3 (b)	a1-a2	Coloratura soprano	A very florid, bravura song.
Jours passés (also called Regrets)	f#1-ab2	a1-e2	Most suitable for high voices	Slow and sustained.
Les filles de Cadix	c#-c#2	f#1-e2	Coloratura or lyric soprano	Light and brilliant. Demands facile articulation and an accomplished pianist. See "Cadix" by Castelnuovo-Tedesco.
Le rossignol	b-c3 (a#)	d1-b1	Soprano or mezzo-soprano	Light. Has florid cadenzas.
Myrto	c1-a2	f1-d2	High or medium voices	Rather animated, rhythmical.

All the songs listed above are available in Schirmer reprints.

PAUL DUKAS
(1865-1935)

| Sonnet | db1-d2 | eb1-b1 | Most suit-
able for
men's
voices | Sustained, subdued.
Musically and interpre-
tatively not easy.
(Durand) |

HENRI DUPARC
(1848-1933)

Duparc songs occupy a position of such generally acknowledged emi-
nence that it seems unnecessary to discuss their excellence and importance
here.

All of his 13 songs are listed below. They are neither vocally not interpretatively easy and cannot be recommended to inexperience singers
or pianists, with the possible exception of "Lamento" or "Chanson triste."
Musically they present hardly any difficulties.

Editions: Rouart, Lerolle
Collection of Six Songs, Boston Music Co.

Au pays où se fait la guerre	c1-ab2	f1-eb2	Women's voices, except a very light soprano	Slow. Demands consid- erable dramatic inten- sity, in parts, and an accomplished pianist.
Chanson triste	c#1-a2	bb1-f2	All voices	Very sustained. In- terpretatively not easy. Demands an accom- plished pianist.
Elégie	c1-f2	f1-d2	All voices	Slow and sustained. In- terpretatively not easy.
Extase	g1-a2	a1-f#2	Most suit- able for high voices	Slow and sustained. Demands good command of high pp. Interpre- tatively not easy. See "Nocturne" by Hahn.
La vague et la cloche	b-e2 (ab)	e1-c#2	Not suit- able for light high voices	Dramatic. Interpre- tatively complex. Demands an excellent pianist.
La vie antérieure	eb1-ab2 (bb)	bb1-f2	Not suit- able for very light high voices	Slow and grave. Has a magnificent climax. In- terpretatively not easy. Demands an excellent pianist.
Lamento	d1-f2	f1-d2	All voices	Slow and somber. Demands an accom- plished pianist.
Le manoir de Rosemonde	d1-ab2	a1-f2	Not suit- able for very light high voices	Rapid, dramatic, some- what declamatory. Demands an accom- plished pianist.

TITLE	COMP.	TESS.	TYPE	REMARKS
L'invitation au voyage	f1-ab2	g1-f2	All voices	Very sustained. Interpretatively not easy. Demands an accomplished pianist. See Charpentier.
Phidylé	eb1-ab2	ab1-f2	All voices	Slow and sustained. Interpretatively complex. Has a magnificent climax. Demands an excellent pianist.
Sérénade florentine	eb1-f2	g1-eb2	All voices	Sustained, very delicate.
Soupir	e1-ab2	a1-f2	Most suitable for high voices	Slow. Interpretatively not easy.
Testament	c1-gb2	eb1-d2	Not suitable for very light high voices	Animated. In parts demands considerable dramatic intensity. Interpretatively not easy. Demands an excellent pianist.

GABRIEL DUPONT
(1878-1914)

TITLE	COMP.	TESS.	TYPE	REMARKS
Chanson des noisettes	e1-a2	g1-e2	High voices	Light, animated. Demands facile articulation. (Heugel)
Mandoline	eb1-a2	g1-eb2	Most suitable for high voices	Rapid, light. Demands an accomplished pianist. See Debussy, Fauré, Szulc, Poldowski and "Fêtes galantes" by Hahn. (Durand)
Les caresses	d1-g2	a1-e2	High voices	Sustained. (Heugel)

LOUIS DUREY
(1888 -)

TITLE	COMP.	TESS.	TYPE	REMARKS
La métampsychose (from "Trois Poèmes de Pétrone)	c#1-g#2	f#1-d2	High voices	Sustained, delicate. (Durand)
Le bestiaire	c1-ab2	e1-e2	Medium or high voices	Twenty-six very short, amusing songs about animals. Musically and interpretatively not easy. Demand an accomplished pianist. See seven of these texts set to music by Poulenc ("Le Bestiaire") and Auric. (Chester)

GABRIEL FAURÉ
(1845-1924)

The songs of Gabriel Fauré, with the exception of a very few, are but little known outside of France. The reason for this is hard to understand, for one could hardly imagine songs more deserving of greater popularity, on every conceivable ground.

Fauré's idiom cannot be considered experimental, yet it is never ordinary and always decidedly and unmistakably his own; his mastery as a musical craftsman is astonishing, his poetic and musical taste impeccable, and his manner of writing for the voice is perhaps the most graceful and cultivated among the late nineteenth century composers. In his songs he combines an extremely sensitive poetic perception with a remarkable melodic gift, an uncommonly pliable and individual harmonic construction, and a rare elegance of form. It seems incomprehensible that so many of his masterly songs are rarely performed. Vocally and musically his songs cannot be considered exacting. A competent performance of a song by Fauré is none the less not so easy as it may sometimes seem, for Fauré demands simplicity, elegance and clarity in execution as well as in intention from both the singer and the pianist, which necessitates an ensemble of considerable excellence.

Fauré's accompaniments are uncommonly transparent in their texture and demand excellent pedaling. Pianistically they are expertly handled and should be played with considerable attention to accuracy of detail.

Most of his songs are suitable for all types of voices, if performed by a singer possessing the requisite polish and simplicity.

Editions: **J.** Hamelle, Paris
Some songs, Durand, Paris
Reprints, Boston Music Co. (6 songs)
The 3 vol. collection by Hamelle is reprinted by Edward Marks, New York

TITLE	COMP.	TESS.	TYPE	REMARKS
Après un rêve	d1-g2	a1-f2	All voices	Very sustained.
Arpège	e1-f♯2	f♯1-e2	All voices	Delicate. Interpretatively not easy. Demands an accomplished pianist.
Au bord de l'eau	c♯1-f♯2	e1-e2	All voices	Delicate, sustained. Demands lightness of tone.
Au cimetière	d1-f2	f1-d2	Not suitable for light voices	Somber, slow. Interpretatively not easy. The middle section is very dramatic.
Automne	d1-f♯2	f♯1-d2	Not too suitable for very light voices	Sustained. Interpretatively not easy. Demands considerable dramatic intensity, in parts, and an accomplished pianist.
Aurore	c1-f2	f1-c2	All voices, except a very light soprano	Sustained.

TITLE	COMP.	TESS.	TYPE	REMARKS
C'est l'extase	c1-fb2	ab1-db2	All voices	Slow. Interpretatively and musically not easy. Demands an accomplished pianist. See Debussy.
Clair de lune	f1-f2	a1-db2	All voices	Delicate. Demands lightness of tone and an accomplished pianist. Interpretatively not easy. see Debussy and Szulc.
Dans les ruines d'une abbaye	e1-f#2	f#1-e2	Not too suitable for very low voices	Light, very delicate. Demands very facile articulation and great lightness of tone.
En prière	eb1-eb2	g1-eb2	All voices	Delicate, sustained.
En sourdine	c1-eb2	f1-db2	All voices	Slow. Interpretatively and musically not easy. See Debussy, Hahn, Poldowski.
Fleur jetée	db1-a2	f1-f2	Not suitable for very light high voices	Very rapid, dramatic. In some editions a curious misprint, MM ♩.- 172 instead of MM ♩. - 72 has caused many a singer and pianist to attempt the impossible. Demands an excellent pianist.
Green	d#1-ab2	ab1-f2	All voices	Animated. Interpretatively and musically not easy. See Debussy, and "Offrande" by Hahn.
Ici-bas	f#1-g2	g1-eb2	All voices	Slow, delicate. See Debussy.
La fleur qui va sur l'eau	b-e2	f#1-d2	Not suitable for very light high voices	Animated. Demands considerable dramatic intensity, in parts, and an accomplished pianist.
La lune blanche luit dans les bois (from "La Bonne Chanson" - 9 songs to text by Paul Verlaine)	d1-f#2	f#1-e2	Most suitable for high voices	Sustained, for the most part subdued. See Szulc, "Appaisement" by Chausson, "L'heure exquise" by Hahn and Poldowski.
Larmes	c#1-g#2	g#1-e2	Not too suitable for very light high voices	Somber, dramatic. Demands an accomplished pianist.
Le parfum impérissable	c#1-e2	e1-c#2	All voices	Slow, sustained. Interpretatively not easy.
Le plus doux chemin	eb1-eb2	g1-db2	All voices	Delicate.

TITLE	COMP.	TESS.	TYPE	REMARKS
Le secret ·	db1-eb2	ab1-db2	All voices	Very delicate, sustained. Demands lightness of tone.
Les berceaux	bb-f2 (ab)	f1-db2	Not suitable for very light high voices	Slow and very sustained.
Les roses d'Ispahan	d1-f#2	f#1-d2	All voices	Delicate, sustained.
L'hiver a cessé (from "La Bonne Chanson" - 9 songs to text by Paul Verlaine)	c#1-g2	g1-e2	High voices, except a very light soprano	Very animated. In parts demands considerable dramatic intensity. Requires an excellent pianist.
Lydia	g1-g2	a1-f#2	All voices	Delicate, very sustained.
Madrigal	f1-f2	a1-f2	Most suitable for men's voices	Delicate, sustained.
Mandoline	e#1-e2	g1-d2	Medium or high voices	Animated. Demands considerable flexibility, very facile articulation, and an excellent pianist. See Debussy, and "Fêtes galantes" by Hahn.
Nell	f#1-ab2	bb1-f2	Not too suitable for very low voices	Graceful, very delicate. Demands an accomplished pianist.
Nocturne	ab-c2	db1-ab1	Low or medium voices	Slow and sustained.
Noël	eb1-ab2	gb1-eb2 (H)	All voices	Animated. Has a vigorous and effective ending.
Notre amour	d#1-a2 (b2)	e1-e2	All voices	Light and animated. Demands facile articulation and an accomplished pianist.

"Poèmes d'un jour": Three songs

TITLE	COMP.	TESS.	TYPE	REMARKS
(1) Rencontre	c#1-f#2	f#1-d#2	All voices	Very sustained. Interpretatively not easy. Demands an accomplished pianist.
(2) Toujours	e1-g2	g1-e2	Not too suitable for very light high voices	Rapid, dramatic. Demands facile articulation and an accomplished pianist.
(3) Adieu	e1-e2	g#1-d#2	All voices	Very delicate, sustained. Demands lightness of tone. Interpretatively not easy.

TITLE	COMP.	TESS.	TYPE	REMARKS
Prison	eb1-f#2	g1-eb2	Not too suitable for very light high voices	Slow. In parts demands considerable dramatic intensity. See "d'une prison" by Hahn.
Puisque l'aube grandit (from "La Bonne Chanson" - 9 songs to text by Paul Verlaine)	c1-f#2	f#1-e2	Medium or high voices	Animated. Interpretatively not easy.
Rêve d'amour	d1-g2	f1-f2	Not too suitable for very low voices	Light and graceful. Demands facile articulation. See "S'il est un charment gazon" by Liszt.
Seule!	f#1-eb2	g1-d2	Not suitable for light, high voices	Grave, very sustained. See Hahn.
Soir	c1-f#2	f1-db2	All voices, except a very light soprano	Slow and sustained. Musically and interpretatively not easy. Demands an accomplished pianist.
Spleen	d1-e2		All voices, except a very light soprano	Delicate, sustained. Interpretatively not easy. See "Il pleure dans mon coeur" by Debussy.
Sylvie	g1-ab2	ab1-f2	Not too suitable for very low voices	Light and delicate. Demands facile articulation and an accomplished pianist.
Tristesse	d1-f2	a1-f2	Not too suitable for very low voices	Animated. Demands facile articulation. Interpretatively not easy.
Vocalise	b-g#2	e1-e2	High voices	Slow. Has some rather intricate florid passages. (Leduc)

See also: "La Chanson d'Eve" - 9 songs for mezzo-soprano or alto (Heugel)
"Le Jardin Clos" -   8 songs for medium voice (Durand)
"L'Horizon Chimérique" - 4 songs for medium voice (Durand)
"Mirages" -   4 songs for medium voice (Durand)

JEAN FAURE
(1830-1914)

| Alleluia d'ameur | e1-g#2 | g#1-e2 | All voices | Animated, effective. Demands some flexibility. (Schirmer) |

TITLE	COMP.	TESS.	TYPE	REMARKS
Les rameaux	e1-g2 (a2)	g1-e2	All voïces, except a very light soprano	A sustained, majestic religious song. Has effective climaxes. (Schirmer)

GUSTAVE FERRARI
(1872 -)

TITLE	COMP.	TESS.	TYPE	REMARKS
Le miroir	c#1-d2	e1-a2	All voices	Slow, delicate. (Edw. Marks)

HENRI FÉVRIER
(1875 -)

TITLE	COMP.	TESS.	TYPE	REMARKS
L'intruse	b-db2	c1-c2	Not too suitable for very light high voices	Dramatic, declamatory, very subdued. Interpretatively not easy. (Heugel)
Prière pour qu'un enfant ne meure pas	db1-g#2		Not suitable for very low voices	Not fast. Interpretatively not easy. In parts dramatic. Demands an accomplished pianist. (Leduc)

FÉLIX FOURDRAIN
(1880-1923)

Edition: Ricordi

TITLE	COMP.	TESS.	TYPE	REMARKS
Carnaval	c1-f2 (a2)	a1-e2	All voices	Very rapid, effective. Demands facile articulation.
Chanson norvégienne	e1-a2	g1-eb2	Women's voices, except a very light soprano	A dramatic, effective song. Animated.
Le long des saules	c1-a2	g1-d2	High voices	Rapid, light. In parts declamatory. Demands good command of high pp.
Mon jardin	eb1-f2	g1-d2	Medium or high voices, except a very light soprano	Sustained.

See also "Le papillon" and "Impression basque" - among a great number of other effective songs.

CÉSAR FRANCK
(1822-1890)

César Franck exercised an immense influence on the development of

French music in the late nineteenth century and especially on French song of that period. The contemporary French school may easily be considered as having received its impetus from Franck and his pupils, among whom were Duparc, Chausson, and d'Indy. His very few songs, however, with the exception of "La Procession" and "Nocturne," which are magnificent examples of French song at its best, can hardly be considered as representative of his style of writing and his genius.

Edition: Six Songs, Boston Music Co. (includes "La Procession")

TITLE	COMP.	TESS.	TYPE	REMARKS
La procession	e1-g♯2	g♯1-e2	Not suitable for very light high voices	Majestic, sustained. Demands an accomplished pianist. Interpretatively not easy. One of the most remarkable of Franck's songs.
Les cloches du soir	f1-a♭2	g1-e♭2	All voices	Sustained, for the most part subdued.
Le mariage des roses	e1-f♯2	f♯1-d♯2	All voices	Delicate.
Le vase brisé	d1-g2 (c1)	g1-e♭2	Not too suitable for very light voices	Sustained. In parts demands considerable dramatic intensity.
Lied	f♯1-f♯2	a1-e2	All voices	Delicate, sustained.
Ninon	e1-f♯2	a1-e2	All voices	Delicate, graceful.
Nocturne	d♯1-d♯2	e♯1-c♯2	Not too suitable for very light high voices	Slow and sustained. One of the most remarkable of Franck's songs. (Edward Marks)
Panis Angelicus (from "Messe Solennelle")	a1-f♯2	a1-e2	Tenor or soprano	Very sustained. (Latin and English texts. Schirmer)

ALEXANDRE GEORGES
(1850-1938)

TITLE	COMP.	TESS.	TYPE	REMARKS
Hymne au soleil	e1-a2	c♯2-g♯2	Dramatic soprano or mezzo-soprano	Declamatory, very effective. (Homeyer, Boston)
La pluie	e1-e2	a1-c♯2	Women's voices	Very delicate and light. Demands good command of pp. (Enoch)

BENJAMIN GODARD
(1849-1895)

TITLE	COMP.	TESS.	TYPE	REMARKS
Chanson de Florian	d1-f♯2	f♯1-d2	Women's voices	Light, in style of a bergerette. (Generally available)

CHARLES GOUNOD
(1818-1893)

Editions: Schir.ner
Ditson

TITLE	COMP.	TESS.	TYPE	REMARKS
Au printemps	db1-ab2	ab1-eb2	All voices	Animated, effective. At one time extremely popular.
Au rossignol	e1-g2	g1-d2	All voices	Sustained, delicate.
Envoi de fleurs	g1-g2	g1-e2	All voices, except bass	Graceful. Demands lightness of tone.
Le vallon	e1-g#2	g#1-e2	Not suitable for very light voices	Somewhat declamatory. In parts dramatic.
Medjé	g1-g2	g1-d2	Men's voices	Sustained, "Oriental" in character, effective.
Primavera	f1-g2	a1-e2	Not too suitable for very low voices	Animated, graceful.

See also "Chanson de la glu" and "Mignon."

GABRIEL GROVLEZ
(1879-1944)

TITLE	COMP.	TESS.	TYPE	REMARKS
Créole	f1-g2	g1-e2	High voices	A sustained, habanera-like song. Interpretatively not easy. Demands an accomplished pianist. (Gallet)
Guitares et mandolines	eb1-g#2	g#1-f#2	High voices	Brilliant and effective. Musically and interpretatively not easy. Demands an excellent pianist. See Saint-Saëns. (Durand)

REYNALDO HAHN
(1875 -)

Hardly any of Hahn's songs present any vocal or musical problems. Expertly and gracefully written, they seem to suit practically any type of voice and are musically anything but complex. None the less, most of his songs are not to be recommended to inexperienced singers. Hahn's songs demand considerable elegance and delicacy in phrasing and rhythm, a most sensitive delivery of the poem, effortless articulation, and a definite aptitude for the style of expression that he represents. Sung clumsily and ploddingly, these slight and charming songs lose too much of their substance to be enjoyed.

Editions: Heugel, Paris.
        A number of reprints of single songs: Ditson, Schirmer, Boston Music Co., Marks, New York.

TITLE	COMP.	TESS.	TYPE	REMARKS
A Chloris	d#1-f#2	g#1-e2	All voices	Slow and sustained.
Chanson au bord de la fontaine	a1-e2		All voices	Delicate.
D'une prison	bb-eb2	f1-d2	Not too suitable for very light high voices	'Sustained. Demands in parts considerable dramatic intensity. See "Prison" by G. Fauré.
Fêtes galantes	b-g#2	g1-d2	Most suitable for high voices	Rapid and light. Demands an excellent pianist. See "Mandoline" by Debussy and by G. Fauré.
Fumée	e1-e2	g1-c2	All voices	Very delicate. Demands good command of pp.
Infidélité	c1-eb2	f1-c2	All voices	Sustained. Interpretatively not easy. Demands good command of p.
L'heure exquise (from "Chansons grises")	b-d#2	d#1-d#2	All voices	Very delicate and sustained. Demands good command of pp. See "Apaisement" by Chausson, "La lune blanche" by Fauré, and "L'heure exquise" by Poldowski.
Le printemps	f#1-a2	b1-f#2	Most suitable for high voices	Spirited and effective. Demands an accomplished pianist.
Le rossignol des lilas	eb1-ab2	ab1-f2	Most suitable for high voices	Delicate and sustained.
Le souvenir d'avoir chanté	e1-f#2	f#1-d2	All voices	Very sustained. Interpretatively not easy.
Les cygnes	bb-f2	f1-eb2	All voices	Very sustained. Interpretatively not easy.
Nocturne	e1-f#2	a1-e2	All voices	Very delicate. Demands good command of pp. See "Extase" by Duparc.
Offrande	c1-c2	e1-a1	All voices	Subdued, somewhat declamatory. Interpretatively not easy. Demands good command of pp. See "Green" by Debussy and by G. Fauré.
Paysage	c1-e2	e1-c2	All voices	Sustained.
Quand je fus pris au pavillon	f#1-f#2	g#1-d#2	All voices	Rapid and light. Demands very facile articulation and an accomplished pianist.
Seule	b-e2	g#1-d#2	Most suitable for medium voices	Animated. Interpretatively not easy. See G. Fauré.

TITLE	COMP.	TESS.	TYPE	REMARKS
Si mes vers avaient des ailes	b-f#2	f#1-d2	Not too suitable for very heavy low voices	Delicate and sustained. Demands good command of high pp.
Sur l'eau	cb1-e2	fb1-cb2	All voices	Very delicate. Demands good command of pp.

AUGUSTA HOLMÈS
(1847-1903)

TITLE	COMP.	TESS.	TYPE	REMARKS
Noël d'Irlande	b-e2	d1-a1	All voices	Slow, somewhat declamatory. (Ditson)

ARTHUR HONEGGER
(1892 -)

The very remarkable songs of Honegger are to be most emphatically recommended to any one interested in contemporary music. One must be, however, sufficiently well equipped musically to be able to perform them.

Edition: M. Senart, Paris

TITLE	COMP.	TESS.	TYPE	REMARKS
Berceuse de la Sirène	cb1-eb2	gb1-db2	Mezzo-soprano or alto	Slow and sustained. Musically not easy.
Chanson de fol	d#1-f#2	f#1-d#2	High or medium voices	Light and rapid. Musically not easy.
Chanson (Ronsard)	a-e2	f1-d2	Low or medium voices	Slow and sustained. A rather simple song recommended as a splendid introduction to songs of Honegger.
Cloche du soir	b-f2	d1-d2	Medium or low voices	Sustained. Musically not easy.
Le chasseur perdu en forêt	c1-eb2	f1-db2	Medium or low voices	Animated, vigorous. Musically very complex. Demands an accomplished pianist.
Les cloches (from "Six Poèmes de G. Apollinaire")	c#1-f#2	f#1-d#2	Women's voices, except a very light soprano	Animated. In parts demands considerable dramatic intensity.

See also "Six Poésies de Jean Cocteau."

Solo excerpts from King David. English versions by Edward Agate. Vocal score published by E. C. Schirmer, Boston.

TITLE	COMP.	TESS.	TYPE	REMARKS
In the Lord I put my faith	c-f#1	e-e1	Tenor	Not fast. In parts declamatory. Short.

TITLE	COMP.	TESS.	TYPE	REMARKS
O had I wings like a dove	f♯1-a2	a1-e2	Soprano	Short, slow, sustained. In parts demands considerable dramatic intensity. Musically not easy.
O shall I raise mine eyes	d-g1	g-e1	Tenor	Short, slow, majestic; somewhat declamatory.
Pity me, Lord	d-a1	e-f♯1	Tenor	Short, slow, sustained. The second section is vigorous and animated. Demands some flexibility. Musically not easy.
Song of the Handmaid (Oh, my love, take my hand)	b♯-e♭2	e1-c2	Alto	Short, sustained, subdued. Musically not easy.
The Song of David (God shall be my shepherd)	b-e2	e1-c♯2	Alto	Short, sustained. Musically not easy.

GEORGES HUE
(1858 -)

Hüe, a somewhat conservatively inclined composer, has written a considerable number of tasteful and expertly executed songs. The short list here seems quite representative of his manner of writing, with the possible exception of the very popular, yet hardly deservedly so, "J'ai pleuré en rêve."

A des oiseaux	e1-g2	g1-d2·	Most suitable for light high voices	Light and delicate. Demands facile articulation and a good command of pp. (Boston Music Co.)

Chansons du Valet de Coeur - four songs

(1) Tête de femmes est légère	e1-g2	g1-d2	All voices	Spirited. Demands facile articulation and a good sense of rhythm. (Durand)
(2) Sur la tour de Montlhéry	d♭1-f2	g♭1-e♭2	All voices	Very rapid, dramatic. (Durand)
(3) A la croisée	d♭1-f♭2	g1-e♭2	Soprano or mezzo-soprano	Very sustained. Interpretatively not easy. (Durand)
(4) Le passant	d1-g2	g1-e2	Most suitable for men's voices	Light and rapid. Demands facile articulation. (Durand)

Il a neigé des fleurs	e♭1-a♭2	a♭1-e♭2	Most suitable for light, high voices	Light and delicate. (Baudoux)
J'ai pleuré en rêve	e1-f♯2 (a2)	a1-e2	All voices, except a	Dramatic, effective. See "Ich hab' im Traum

TITLE	COMP.	TESS.	TYPE	REMARKS
Cont'd				
J'ai pleuré en rêve			very light soprano	geweinet'' by Schumann, R. Franz, and C. Löwe. (Ditson)
La fille du roi de Chine	f#1-g#2	b1-e2	Most suitable for tenor	Rapid and brilliant. Demands an accomplished pianist. (Heugel)
L'âne blanc	eb1-g2	g1-eb2	Most suitable for light high voices	Light and delicate. Demands an accomplished pianist. (Heugel)
Les clochettes des muguets	e1-gb2	b1-e2	Most suitable for light high voices	Delicate and animated. (Baudoux)
Par la fenêtre grande ouverte	db1-f2	ab1-eb2	All voices	Slow and sustained. Requires good command of p. (Baudoux)
Sonnez les matines	f#1-g2	f#1-e2	All voices	Sustained. Demands in parts considerable dramatic intensity. (Heugel)

VINCENT d'INDY
(1851-1931)

TITLE	COMP.	TESS.	TYPE	REMARKS
Lied maritime	b-g2	g1-f2 (H)	Not too suitable for very light high voices	Sustained. Demands in parts considerable dramatic intensity. Interpretatively not easy. (Schirmer)
Madrigal dans le style ancien	e1-e2		All voices	Sustained. Has a severely contrapuntal accompaniment. (Ditson)
Mirage	c#1-e2	g1-d#2	Most suitable for men's voices	Somewhat declamatory. In parts demands considerable dramatic intensity. (Hamelle)

ÉMILE JACQUES-DALCROZE
(1865 -)

TITLE	COMP.	TESS.	TYPE	REMARKS
La chère maison	f1-g2	a1-f2	Most suitable for high voices	Graceful, delicate. (E. Marks)
Le coeur de ma mie	f#1-f#2	g1-d2	All voices	Delicate, light. (Schirmer)
L'oiseau bleu	e#1-a2	a1-f#2	Light soprano	Graceful, delicate. Demands facile articulation and some flexibility. (Fischer)

CHARLES KOECHLIN
(1867 -)

The songs of Charles Koechlin, a somewhat conservatively inclined composer, could easily be considered among his outstanding works. Tasteful,
distinctive and expertly written, they deserve an esteemed place in every
singer's French repertoire.

TITLE	COMP.	TESS.	TYPE	REMARKS
L'air	f1-f#2	a1-f2	High voices	Sustained, for the most part subdued, delicate. (Rouart, Lerolle)
La lune	c1-f2	f1-d2	High or medium voices	Very light, animated. Demands facile articulation. (Rouart, Lerolle)
La prière du mort	db1-e2	g-db2	Not suitable for very light high voices	Slow. In parts very dramatic. (Hachette)
Le thé	e1-g#2	g#1-d#2	Not suitable for very low voices	Animated, light. Demands an accomplished pianist. (Boston Music Co.)
L'hiver	e1-e2 (g2)		Not suitable for very low voices	Very delicate. Has a curious accompaniment in which a glissando figure, e2-b3 and b3-e2, is used incessantly. Interpretatively not easy. (Boston Music Co.)
Si tu le veux	f#1-e2	f#1-c#2	Most suitable for high voices	Animated, dleicate. The vocal line is sustained. Demands good command of high pp. (Edw. Marks)
Villanelle (Le temps, l'étendue et le nombre)	a-d#2	c1-a1	Low or medium voices	Rather slow, very subdued. (Hachette)
Vocalise	a-e2	c1-c2	Low or medium voices	Rather sustained. (Leduc)

EDOUARD LALO
(1823-1892)

TITLE	COMP.	TESS.	TYPE	REMARKS
Ballade à la lune	c1-d2 (g2)	f1-c2	All voices	Rapid, humorous. Demands facile articulation. (Hamelle)
Chant breton	e1-e2		Women's voices	Sustained, plaintive. (Hamelle)
Guitare	f#1-f#2	f#1-d2	All voices	Animated, light. See "Comment, disaient-ils" by Liszt. (Hamelle)
La chanson de l'alouette	eb1-b2	b1-g2	Light soprano	Rapid and light. (Schirmer)

TITLE	COMP.	TESS.	TYPE	REMARKS
L'esclave	e1-f#2	f1-d2 (H)	Women's voices, except a very light soprano	Slow and sustained. (Schirmer)
Marine	d#1-f#2	g#1-d#2	Most suitable for men's voices	Sustained, somewhat declamatory. In parts demands considerable dramatic intensity. (Hamelle)
Oh! quand je dors	e1-g2	a1-f2	All voices	Sustained. See Liszt. (Hamelle)

RAOUL LAPARRA
(1876-1943)

TITLE	COMP.	TESS.	TYPE	REMARKS
Les pas de sabots	d1-f2	e1-e2	Soprano	Rapid, delicate. Demands facile articulation. (Enoch)
Lettre à une Espagnole	eb1-f2	gb1-eb2	All voices	Animated, light, rhythmical. (Enoch)

GUILLAUME LEKEU
(1870-1894)

TITLE	COMP.	TESS.	TYPE	REMARKS
Ronde	d1-g#2	f#1-e2	High or medium voices	Animated. Interpretatively not easy. Demands an accomplished pianist. (Rouart, Lerolle)
Sur une tombe	d1-eb2 (g2)	f1-d2 (H)	Not too suitable for very light high voices	Slow and somber. (Schirmer)

RENÉ LENORMAND
(1846-1932)

TITLE	COMP.	TESS.	TYPE	REMARKS
Berceuse	c1-f2	f1-c2	Medium or high voices	Sustained, delicate. (Hamelle)
Le petit gardeur de chèvres	f1-db2		All voices	Sustained, delicate. (Hamelle)
Quelle souffrance	d1-g2 (bb1)	eb1-c2	Most suitable for men's voices	Very sustained, effective. Demands good command of sustained forte. (Hamelle)

XAVIER LEROUX
(1863-1919)

TITLE	COMP.	TESS.	TYPE	REMARKS
Le Nil	e1-a2	g1-e2	All voices	Sustained. (Schirmer)

JULES MASSENET
(1842-1912)

More widely known as one of the outstanding operatic composers of France, Massenet has written a great number of tasteful and charming songs, like "Bonne nuit," "Crépuscule," "Les femmes de Magdala," "Que l'heure est donc brève," to mention but a few, songs which seem to deserve to be as popular as some of the more famous excerpts from his operas.

Editions: Collection, 2 vols., Schirmer.
Numerous reprints of single songs by various publishers.

TITLE	COMP.	TESS.	TYPE	REMARKS
Bonne nuit	f1-g2	bb1-f2	All voices	Delicate, sustained.
Chant provençal	c1-f2 (a2)	f1-d2	All voices	Delicate, sustained.
Crépuscule	e1-f#2	f#1-d#2	All voices	Delicate, sustained.
Elégie	c1-f2	f1-c2 (H)	All voices	Very slow and sustained. Perhaps the most widely known, though by no means one of the best songs of Massenet.
Les femmes de Magdala	d1-f#2	g1-d2	All voices	Delicate, sustained.
Ouvre tes yeux bleus	e1-g2	f1-d2	All voices	Animated, effective.
Première danse	e1-g2	a1-e2	All voices	Light, rapid, effective. Demands facile articulation.
Que l'heure est donc brève	e1-e2	a1-d2	All voices	Very delicate.
Roses d'octobre	d1-g2	g1-d2	All voices	Sustained, very subdued.
Si tu veux, Mignonne	e1-f#2	g#1-e2	Most suitable for men's voices	Animated, delicate. The vocal line is very sustained.
Sonnet	e1-f#2	f#1-e2	All voices	Sustained. Demands in parts considerable dramatic intensity.

DARIUS MILHAUD
(1892 -)

One of the most remarkable of the contemporary French composers, Milhaud has written a very considerable number of songs, ranging from the rather inconsequential "Soirées de St.- Pétersbourg" to the extraordinarily forceful "Poèmes Juifs." As a rule his songs are musically quite complex, although vocally they present few difficulties. Anyone interested in contemporary vocal music would do well to acquaint himself thoroughly with Milhaud's songs.

Berceuse (from "Chants Populaires Hébraïques" - 6 songs)	e1-d2		All voices	Subdued, delicate. Demands somewhat facile articulation. (Heugel)

TITLE	COMP.	TESS.	TYPE	REMARKS
Catalogue de fleurs	c1-f2		Most suitable for medium voices	Six delightful, very short songs. Musically and interpretatively not easy. Demands an accomplished pianist. (Also orchestrated by the composer) (Durand)
Chant hassidique (from "Chants Populaires Hébraïques")	c1-d2		Medium or low voices	Animated. Interpretatively not easy. (Heugel)
La tourterelle ("Quatre poèmes Léo Latil")	b-g2	d#1-d2	All except very low voices	Animated. Demands facile articulation and an accomplished pianist. Musically not easy. (Durand)
L'aurore ("Trois poèmes de Lucile de Chateaubriand")	d#1-f2	f1-d#2	All voices	Delicate, subdued. Musically not easy. (Salabert)

Poèmes Juifs
(published by Eschig)

TITLE	COMP.	TESS.	TYPE	REMARKS
Chant d'amour	c1-gb2	eb1-db2	Not suitable for very low voices	Rapid. Demands an accomplished pianist. Musically somewhat complex.
Chant de forgeron	c1-f#2	c1-c2	Not suitable for light high voices	Very vigorous, rhythmic. Demands an accomplished pianist. Musically somewhat complex.
Chant de la pitie	c1-eb2	e1-c2	Medium or low voices	Sustained. Musically complex.
Chant de nourrice	c1-g2	e1-c#2	Soprano or mezzo-soprano	Delicate, slow. Musically very complex. Interpretatively not easy.
Chant de résignation	f1-d2		Medium or low voices	Very sustained, delicate. Musically somewhat complex.
Chant de Sion	eb1-eb2	ab1-db2	All voices	Sustained. Musically somewhat complex.
Chant du laboureur	b-f2	d1-d2	Not suitable for very light high voices	Animated. Has a vigorous and rapid ending. Musically somewhat complex.
Lamentation	a-e2	e1-c#2	Medium or low voices	Animated. Musically somewhat complex.

TITLE	COMP.	TESS.	TYPE	REMARKS
Tais-toi, babillarde (from "Chansons de Ronsard" - 4 songs for coloratura soprano and orchestra)	g1-c3 (e3)	c2-a2	Coloratura soprano	Animated, light, florid. Demands facile articulation and an accomplished pianist. (Boosey & Hawkes)

TITLE	COMP.	TESS.	TYPE	REMARKS

ERNEST MORET

TITLE	COMP.	TESS.	TYPE	REMARKS
Le Nélumbo	e1-db2 (gb2 or bb2)		Not suitable for very low voices	Slow, very subdued, delicate. Demands good command of pp. (Heugel)

ÉMILE PALADILHE
(1844-1926)

TITLE	COMP.	TESS.	TYPE	REMARKS
Lamento provençal	c#1-f#2	f#1-d2	Not too suitable for very light high voices	Slow, somewhat declamatory. Demands in parts considerable dramatic intensity. (Homeyer)
Le roitelet	d#1-g#2	g#1-e2	Light soprano	Rapid and light. Demands facile articulation. (Schirmer)
Les trois prières	db1-ab2 (H)	gb1-eb2	All voices	Slow and sustained. (Schirmer)
Psyché	bb-f2 (gb2)	gb1-eb2	All voices	Delicate, sustained. (Schirmer)

ÉMILE PESSARD
(1843-1917)

TITLE	COMP.	TESS.	TYPE	REMARKS
L'adieu du matin	d1-f#2	a1-e2	All voices	Delicate. Demands rather facile articulation. (Schirmer)
Requiem d'un coeur	d1-f2		Most suitable for men's voices	Not fast. In parts demands considerable dramatic intensity. Effective. (Leduc)

GABRIEL PIERNÉ
(1863-1937)

TITLE	COMP.	TESS.	TYPE	REMARKS
A Lucette	g#1-g2 (H)	a1-f2	Not too suitable for very heavy low voices	A song in antique style. Delicate and sustained. (Leduc)
Ils étaient trois petits chats blancs	e1-f#2	e1-e2	High or medium voices	Rapid, light, humorous. Demands facile articulation. (Marks)
La rieuse	c#1-f#2	e1-e2	All voices	A delicate narrative song. Interpretatively not easy. (Leduc)
Le moulin	d1-f#2	g1-e2	All voices	Animated. Demands an accomplished pianist. A little long. Perhaps one of Pierné's best songs. (Leduc)
L'oeillet rouge	c#1-d2	e1-bb1 (L)	All voices	Slow and sustained. (Leduc)

TITLE	COMP.	TESS.	TYPE	REMARKS
Villanelle	d1-e2	g1-d2 (L)	All voices	A light, delicate song in eighteenth century style. See also "Chanson de berger" by Pierné, set in the same style. (Leduc)

POLDOWSKI (Lady Dean Paul)
(1880-1932)

Editions: Chester, unless otherwise marked.

TITLE	COMP.	TESS.	TYPE	REMARKS
Colombine	d1-g♭2	g♭1-d2	Not too suitable for very light high voices	Rapid, very effective. Demands an accomplished pianist. Interpretatively not easy.
Cortège	d1-f♯2	e1-c2	Medium or high voices	Rapid. Demands facile articulation and an accomplished pianist. Interpretatively not easy.
Cythère	e1-e♭2	f♯1-c♯2	Medium or low voices	Rapid. Demands facile articulation.
Dansons la gigue	d1-g2	g1-d2	Not too suitable for low voices	Rapid, dramatic. Demands facile articulation. See Carpenter.
En sourdine	d1-a2	f♯1-d2	All voices	Sustained. Demands in parts considerable dramatic intensity. See Debussy, Fauré, Szulc.
Impression fausse	a-e2	d1-a1	Medium or low voices	Rapid, subdued. Demands facile articulation. The entire middle section is sustained and declamatory. Very effective, interpretatively not easy.
L'heure exquise	d♭1-a♭2	g♭1-d♭2	All voices	Slow, sustained. Demands in parts considerable dramatic intensity. See Hahn, "Apaisement" by Chausson, "La lune blanche" by Fauré, Szulc. (Durand)
Mandoline	f1-f2	g♯1-c♯2	All voices	Light and rapid. Demands facile articulation and an accomplished pianist. See Debussy, Fauré, and "Fêtes galantes" by Hahn.

FRANCIS POULENC
(1899 -)

It could be said that perhaps no outstanding contemporary French composer would seem to have achieved as complete a liberation from the influence of Debussy as Poulenc.

Poulenc's harmonic scheme varies considerably. Some of his songs, like the "Tel jour, tel nuit" series, are dissonant and rather complex experimentations; others, like the well-known "Airs chantés" are deliberately confined to the tonic, subdominant, dominant harmonic scheme, and are almost mocking in their simplicity.

His songs, as a rule, demand a great deal of vocal and stylistic elegance and are interpretatively rather complex.

Poulenc is a prolific composer, and this list is primarily intended for those who are not at all familiar with his manner of writing.

TITLE	COMP.	TESS.	TYPE	REMARKS
A sa guitare	d1-f#2	f#1-eb2	Not too suitable for very light high voices	Very sustained. (Durand)
Airs Chantés				
(1) Air romantique	c1-e2	e1-c2	Not suitable for very light high voices	Very rapid, spirited and vigorous. Demands an accomplished pianist. (Rouart, Lerolle)
(2) Air champêtre	c#1-b2	b1-g2	High light voices	Very animated, delicate. Demands an accomplished pianist. (Rouart, Lerolle)
(3) Air grave	e1-ab2	ab1-f2	High voices	Sustained. (Rouart, Lerolle)
(4) Air vif	c1-ab2	g1-d2	Not suitable for low voices	Very rapid. Demands some flexibility and an accomplished pianist. (Rouart, Lerolle)
Attributs (From "Cinq Poèmes de Ronsard" for mezzo-soprano)	c1-gb2	f1-eb2	Not too suitable for very low voices	Animated, amusing. Interpretatively not easy. Demands an accomplished pianist. (Heugel)
Bleuet	d#1-ab2	g1-e2	High voices	Sustained, in parts dramatic. Interpretatively not easy. (Rouart, Lerolle)
C (J'ai traversé les ponts de Cé)	eb1-ab2	ab1-f2	Most suitable for high voices	Sustained. Requires good command of high pp. Interpretatively not easy. (Rouart, Lerolle)
Chanson à boire	B-e1	c-ab	Bass or baritone	A slow, mock-solemn song. No. 2 of the "Chansons Gaillardes" for baritone. (Heugel)

TITLE	COMP.	TESS.	TYPE	REMARKS
Fleurs (from "Fiançailles pour rire")	db1-f2	f1-eb2	All voices	Slow, sustained, subdued. (Rouart, Lerolle)
Hier (from "Trois Poèmes de Louise Lalanne")	eb1-f2	g1-e2	Most suitable for high voices	Sustained, subdued. Requires good command of high pp. (Rouart, Lerolle)
Je n'ai plus que les os (from "Cinq Poèmes de Ronsard" for mezzo-soprano)	b-f2	e1-d2	Not too suitable for very light, high voices	Very slow, somber. Musically complex. Demands an accomplished pianist. (Heugel)
La belle jeunesse	d-f1	f-eb1	Baritone or a heavy tenor	A very animated, rowdy song. Demands facile articulation. No. 7 of the "Chansons Gaillardes" for Baritone. (Heugel)
Le bestiaire (6 short songs)	b-e2		Most suitable for medium or low voices	These six amusing, very short songs - "Le Dromadaire," "La Chèvre de Thibet,""La Sauterelle," "Le Dauphin," "L'Ecrevisse" and "La Carpe" are originally scored for string quartet, flute, clarinet and bassoon. Interpretatively not easy. See Durey. (Sirène Musicale)
Violon (from "Fiançailles pour rire")	c#1-gb2	eb1-e2	Most suitable for medium or high voices	Sustained. Interpretatively not easy. Demands an accomplished pianist. (Rouart, Lerolle)

HENRI RABAUD
(1873 -)

TITLE	COMP.	TESS.	TYPE	REMARKS
Instant	c1-e2		All voices	Somewhat declamatory, very subdued. (Heugel)

RENÉ RABEY

TITLE	COMP.	TESS.	TYPE	REMARKS
Tes yeux	eb1-g2	bb1-eb2	All voices	Very sustained, effective. (Durand)

MAURICE RAVEL
(1875-1937)

In his songs Ravel's extraordinary mastery is as apparent as it is in his instrumental and orchestral works. Precise to an astonishing degree in his notation, almost uncanny in his knowledge of the variety of unexpected sonorities that the combination of the human voice and the pianoforte or a group of instruments are able to produce, fastidiously exact in his treatment of French prosody, Ravel in his songs demands a most exacting precision on the part of the performer.

Always fully aware of the possibilities as well as of the limitations of the human voice, his treatment of the vocal line is extraordinarily effective, not perhaps from the traditional point of view of a vocalist who is in search of a suitable vehicle for the purpose of exhibiting his vocal equipment, but from the point of view of the composer. In other words, Ravel writes for the voice in a manner that unfailingly ensures the exact musical effect he desires, provided, of course, both singer and pianist follow his instructions.

Most of his songs are musically and interpretatively difficult, though vocally not exacting, and demand an extraordinarily sensitive ensemble.

Only a few could possibly be recommended to inexperienced singers, among them the delightful and ingenious arrangements of the five Greek songs, and the four "Chansons Populaires."

Chansons Populaires
Editions: Durand

TITLE	COMP.	TESS.	TYPE	REMARKS
Chanson espagnole	d1-bb1		Medium or low voices	An arrangement of a Spanish folk song. Animated, rhythmical.
Chanson francaise	g1-f2	g1-d2	All voices	Delicate. An arrangement of a French folk song.
Chanson hebraïque	e1-e2	e1-c2	Not too suitable for very light high voices	An arrangement of a Hebrew folk song. Has contrasting tempi and moods.
Chanson italienne	c1-f2	eb1-eb2	All voices	Slow, very sustained, plaintive. An arrangement of an Italian folk song.

Cinq Mélodies Populaires Grecques

(1) Chanson de la mariée	g1-eb2		Not suitable for very low voices	Rapid, delicate. Demands facile articulation, good command of pp., and an excellent pianist. The five Greek folk tunes arranged by Ravel are vocally quite simple. They are very short songs provided with extremely interesting accompaniments. They can be sung separately.
(2) Là-bas,vers l'église	g#1-e2		All voices	Slow and very sustained, plaintive.

TITLE	COMP.	TESS.	TYPE	REMARKS
(3) Quel galant m'est comparable	d1-f2	a1-d2	All voices	Spirited. If sung by itself, it should be preferably sung by a man.
(4) Chanson des cueilleuses de lentisques	a1-e2		All voices	Slow and very sustained.
(5) Tout gai!	eb1-f2	ab1-eb2	All voices	Animated, rhythmical. Demands an accomplished pianist.

D'Anne jouant de l'espinette	c#1-g#2 (b)	f#1-d#2	High voices	Delicate. Musically not easy. Demands an accomplished pianist.
D'Anne qui me jecta de la neige	c#1-f#2	f#1-d#2	High or medium voices	Very slow, delicate. Musically not easy.

Don Quichotte à Dulcinee

(1) Chanson romanesque	Bb-f	f-c1	Three songs for baritone and orchestra (also available in a transposed edition for tenor)	Not fast. Interpretatively and rhythmically not easy.
(2) Chanson épique	A-f1	c-c1		Very slow and sustained. Interpretatively not easy.
(3) Chanson à boire	B-f1	e-eb1		Very rapid and spirited. Musically and interpretatively complex. Demands some flexibility and an excellent pianist.

Histoires Naturelles

(1) Le paon	c1-f2		Most suitable for medium or high voices	Rather slow. Musically and interpretatively complex. Demands an accomplished pianist.
(2) Le grillon	db-f2		Most suitable for medium or high voices	Delicate. One of the simpler songs of this series.

TITLE	COMP.	TESS.	TYPE	REMARKS
(3) Le cygne	d♯1-e♯2		Most suitable for medium and high voices	Slow. Musically very complex. Demands an excellent pianist.
(4) Le martin-pêcheur	c♯1-e2		Most suitable for medium voices	Slow. Musically complex.
(5) La pintade	c♯1-f2		Most suitable for medium or high voices	Rapid. Musically and interpretatively very complex. Demands an excellent pianist.

Kaddisch	c1-g2	e♭1-e♭2	Not too suitable for very light high voices	A setting of the Hebrew prayer for the dead. Very sustained. Demands considerable flexibility. Musically not easy.

L'enfant et les Sortilèges

It seemed best to list the following three airs from "L'enfant et les Sortilèges" in this section instead of in that devoted to the operatic excerpts, as they are more frequently encountered on the concert programs than on the operatic stage and could hardly be classed as standard operatic material.

TITLE	COMP.	TESS.	TYPE	REMARKS
Air de l'enfant	e♭-d2	f1-b♭1	Mezzo-soprano or soprano	Sustained, delicate. Vocally not taxing.
Air de l'horloge	B♭-g1		Baritone or mezzo-soprano	Rapid, vigorous. Demands very facile articulation. Humorous. Musically and interpretatively not easy. Demands an accomplished pianist.
Air du feu	d1-c3	g1-g2	Coloratura soprano	Fast, rather vigorous, in parts very florid. Musically and interpretatively not easy. Demands an accomplished pianist.

Les grands vents venus d'outremer	c♯1-f♯2	d♯1-d♯2	Most suitable for medium voices	Musically complex. Demands an excellent pianist.

TITLE	COMP.	TESS.	TYPE	REMARKS
Manteau de fleurs	c#1-g#2 (a#)	d#1-d#2	Most suitable for high or medium voices	Animated, delicate. Demands facile articulation. Musically not easy. Demands an accomplished pianist.
Nicolette	b-f#2	f#1-d2	All voices	Animated. Demands facile articulation. Interpretatively not easy.
Noël des jouets	b#-f#2	d1-b1	All voices	Not fast. Musically and interpretatively not easy. Demands an accomplished pianist. Has an effective ending. (Mathot)
Rêves	d1-f2	d1-d2	All voices	Very sustained, subdued. Demands good command of pp. Has an uncommonly sparse accompaniment.
Ronde	c#1-a2	f#1-f#2	High voices	Rapid. Demands facile articulation.
Ronsard à son âme	c#1-e2	f#1-c#2	Medium or low voices	Sustained, subdued. Has an uncommonly sparse accompaniment.
Sainte	c1-g2	f1-d2	Not suitable for very low voices	Slow and sustained, very delicate. Demands good command of pp. and an accomplished pianist.

Shéhérazade

TITLE	COMP.	TESS.	TYPE	REMARKS
(1) Asie	db1-g2		Most suitable for medium or high voices	Three songs for voice and orchestra. "Asie" is the longest of the three, the most complex musically and interpretatively, and the least suitable for a performance with piano.
(2) La flûte enchantée	d#1-f#2	g#1-e2	Most suitable for high voices	Delicate. The most performed of the three songs. When sung separately one should remember that the text calls for a woman singer. Demands an accomplished pianist.
(3) L'indifférent	c#1-e2	d#1-b1	Most suitable for medium voices	Slow. Demands good command of pp. Interpretatively complex.

TITLE	COMP.	TESS.	TYPE	REMARKS
Sur l'herbe	c1-g2		Most suitable for medium or high voices	Musically and interpretatively very complex.

TITLE	COMP.	TESS.	TYPE	REMARKS
Trois beaux oiseaux du paradis	bb-g2	eb1-eb2	High or medium voices	Sustained, delicate.
Vocalise	bb-g2	eb1-eb2	High or medium voices	A vocalised habanera. Has some rather intricate florid passages. (Hettich, Répertoire moderne de vocalises, Leduc, Paris) Reprinted by Marks.

See also: "Trois Poèmes de Mallarmé" - medium voices
"Chansons Madécasses" - three songs for mezzo-soprano or soprano, flute, cello and piano.

RHENÉ-BATON
(1879-1940)

TITLE	COMP.	TESS.	TYPE	REMARKS
Berceuse	b-d2	d1-b1	Most suitable for medium or low voices	Delicate, sustained. (From Chansons Douces, 12 songs for medium or low voices, Durand)
L'âme des iris	d1-e2	a1-e2	All voices	Slow, sustained and subdued. (Durand)
Il pleut des pétales de fleurs	c#1-e2	e1-b1	Medium or low voices	Slow, somewhat declamatory. Demands in parts considerable dramatic intensity. (Durand)
Tendresse	b-f2	eb1-db2	All voices	Delicate, sustained. (Durand)

GUY ROPARTZ
(1864 -)

TITLE	COMP.	TESS.	TYPE	REMARKS
Berceuse	c1-e2	e1-c2	Women's voices	Very sustained. (Ditson)

MANUEL ROSENTHAL
(1904 -)

TITLE	COMP.	TESS.	TYPE	REMARKS
Le marabout	c1-eb2	ab1-db2	High or medium voices	An amusing, monotonous character song. Musically and interpretatively not easy. (No. 4 of the "Chansons de Bleu," a set of twelve children's songs, Eschig)
Le petit chat est mort	db1-f2	f1-eb2	High or medium voices	Slow. Musically and interpretatively not easy. (From "Chansons de Bleu," Eschig)

ALBERT ROUSSEL
(1869-1937)

TITLE	COMP.	TESS.	TYPE	REMARKS
Amoureux séparés	c1-gb2	g1-e2	High or medium voices	Rather animated. Has a vigorous middle section. (Rouart, Lerolle)
A un jeune gentilhomme	c1-g2	f1-d2	Soprano or mezzo-soprano	Rapid and light. Demands facile articulation and an accomplished pianist. See "Don't come in, sir, please" by J. A. Carpenter and Cyril Scott. (Rouart, Lerolle)
Le bachelier de Salamanque	c1-g2	g1-eb2	Medium or high voices, except a very light soprano	Animated. Demands facile articulation and an accomplished pianist. Musically not easy. (Durand)
Le jardin mouillé	c1-f#2	g1-eb2	All, except very low voices	Delicate. Musically not easy. Demands an accomplished pianist. (Rouart, Lerolle)
Nuit d'automne	db1-g2	f1-d2	Not suitable for very light high voices	Slow, somewhat declamatory. Musically not easy. (Rouart, Lerolle)
Réponse d'une épouse sage	d#1-a2	f#1-e2	Soprano	Sustained, somewhat declamatory. Interpretatively not easy. (Durand)

CAMILLE SAINT-SAËNS
(1835-1921)

Almost all of Saint-Saëns many songs are effective and masterfully written. "Danse macabre," "L'attente," "Tournoiement" and "Le bonheur est chose légère" are particularly recommended, being perhaps among his most characteristic songs.

Editions: Durand
Collection of 12 songs published by Schirmer.

TITLE	COMP.	TESS.	TYPE	REMARKS
Aimons-nous	gb1-ab2	c2-f2	All voices	Very sustained, effective.
Au cimetière (from "Mélodies Persanes")	e1-a2	a1-f2	Most suitable for high voices	Sustained. Requires good command of high pp.
Clair de lune	db1-eb2	eb1-bb1	Not too suitable for very high light voices	Delicate.

TITLE	COMP.	TESS.	TYPE	REMARKS
Danse macabre	bb-eb2	d1-bb1	Medium or low voices	Very rapid and dramatic. Demands facile articulation and an excellent pianist.
Guitares et mandolines	g1-g2	a1-e2	Not too suitable for very heavy low voices	Light and rapid. Demands flexibility and an accomplished pianist. See G. Grovlez.
La cloche	dbb1-ab2	ab1-f2	All voices	Very sustained. Has an effective climax.
La feuille de peuplier	b-e2	g1-e2	All voices	Delicate and animated. Requires good command of pp.
La libellule	c1-d3 (e3)	f#1-f#2	Coloratura soprano or light soprano	An effective waltz song. Somewhat florid.
La sérénité	c1-f2	f1-d2	All voices	Very sustained.
La solitaire	d1-g#2	f#1-d#2	Women's voices, except a very light soprano	Rapid. Demands facile articulation and some flexibility. Effective.
L'attente	e1-g2	a1-f2	All women's voices, except a light soprano	Rapid and dramatic. Demands facile articulation.
Le bonheur est chose légère	c1-a2	f1-f2	Most suitable for high voices	Animated, light, delicate.
Le lever de la lune	b-f#2	f#1-d#2	Not too suitable for very light high voices	The vocal line is very sustained.
Mai	g1-f#2 (a2)	a1-e2	Medium or high voices	Light and rapid. Demands facile articulation and an excellent pianist.
Tournoiement (Songe d'opium) (from "Poésies Persanes")	d1-g2	f1-f2	Not too suitable for very low voices	Very rapid. Demands facile articulation and an excellent pianist. Interpretatively not easy.
Tristesse	c1-g2	e1-c2	Not suitable for very light high voices	Slow. Demands in parts considerable dramatic intensity.
Vocalise (The nightingale and the rose)	d1-d3	g1-g2	Coloratura soprano	Slow, florid. Demands good command of high pp. (Fischer)
Domine, ego credidi (Christmas Oratorio)	f-a1	g-f1	Tenor	Solo with chorus. Sustained. (Score, Schirmer)

TITLE	COMP.	TESS.	TYPE	REMARKS
Expectans Dominum (Christmas Ortario)	b–f#2	e1–c#2	Alto or mezzo-soprano	Sustained. (Score, Schirmer)

ERIK SATIE
(1866-1925)

TITLE	COMP.	TESS.	TYPE	REMARKS
Daphénéo	d1–d2	f#1–b1	All voices	An amusing delicate song. Interpretatively not easy. (Rouart, Lerolle)
La statue de bronze	bb–f2	d1–d2	Not suitable for very light high voices	An amusing song. Interpretatively not easy. (Rouart, Lerolle)
Le chapelier	a–a2	f#1–e2	All voices	A parody on Gounod to the words from Alice in Wonderland. (Rouart, Lerolle)

FLORENT SCHMITT
(1870 -)

TITLE	COMP.	TESS.	TYPE	REMARKS
Il pleure dans mon coeur	c#1–f#2	f#1–d2	High or medium voices	Sustained, subdued. See Debussy, Fauré, Carpenter. (Durand)
Lied	c#1–e2	d#1–c#2	Medium or low voices	Slow, subdued, delicate. (Durand)
Nature morte	c#1–f#2	f1–d2	High or medium voices	Sustained, somewhat declamatory, subdued. (Baudoux)

DÉODAT DE SÉVERAC
(1873-1921)

TITLE	COMP.	TESS.	TYPE	REMARKS
Chanson de Blaisine	c1–g2	e1–c2	High voices	Sustained, delicate. (Demets)
Chanson pour le petit cheval	d1–g2 (b)		All voices	Animated. Demands facile articulation and an accomplished pianist. In parts dramatic. (Rouart, Lerolle)
L'aube dans la montagne	d1–g2	f1–e2	High voices	Slow, subdued. Has a very effective final climax. Demands an accomplished pianist. (Rouart, Lerolle)
Le ciel est par-dessus le toit	eb1–gb2	gb1–eb2	High voices	Slow, somewhat declamatory. See "Prison" by Fauré, "D'une prison" by Hahn. (Rouart, Lerolle)

TITLE	COMP.	TESS.	TYPE	REMARKS
Ma poupée chérie	d1-f#2	f#1-d2	Women's voices	Sustained, delicate, subdued. (Rouart, Lerolle)
Temps de neige	d1-g2	e1-d2 (H)	All voices	Delicate, subdued. (Rouart, Lerolle)
Les hiboux	c1-g2	g1-d2 (H)	Most suitable for men's voices	Slow, somber, sustained. (Rouart, Lerolle)

VICTOR STAUB

L'heure silencieuse	eb1-g2	ab1-eb2	Most suitable for light high voices	Delicate, sustained. Demands good command of pp. (Durand)

JOSEPH SZULC
(1874-1935)

Clair de lune	db1-gb2	bb1-f2	Not too suitable for very low heavy voices	Slow, sustained. Demands good command of pp. See Debussy and Fauré. (Schirmer)
En sourdine	c1-f2 (ab2)	eb1-eb2	Not too suitable for very low voices	Slow, sustained, subdued. Demands in parts considerable dramatic intensity as well as a good command of high pp. See Debussy, Fauré, Poldowski. (Durand)
La lune blanche	db1-g2	gb1-e2	All voices	Sustained, very subdued. Demands good command of high pp. See Fauré, "L'heure exquise" by Hahn and Poldowski, and "Apaisement" by Chausson. (Durand)
Mandoline	d1-a2 (b2)	g#1-e2	Soprano	Rapid, light. Demands some flexibility and an accomplished pianist. See Debussy, Fauré, Poldowski, and "Fêtes galantes" by Hahn. (Rouart, Lerolle)
Menuet	c1-g2	g1-d2	Not too suitable for very low voices	Delicate, rhythmically somewhat complex. (Ricordi)

AMBROISE THOMAS
(1811-1896)

Le Soir	d1-ab2	ab1-f2	All voices	Delicate, sustained. (Ditson)

TITLE	COMP.	TESS.	TYPE	REMARKS

CHARLES MARIE WIDOR
(1845-1937)

TITLE	COMP.	TESS.	TYPE	REMARKS
Je ne veux pas autre chose	d1-f2	f1-d2	All voices	Sustained, subdued. (Hamelle)
L'aurore	d#1-f#2	f#1-d#2	All voices	Sustained. The pianoforte part is animated. (Hamelle)
Le plongeur	c#1-f#2	f#1-d2	Most suitable for men's voices	Very animated, rhythmical. Vigorous narrative song. Demands facile articulation and an accomplished pianist. (Hamelle)
Nuit d'étoiles	db1-gb2	ab1-f2	Not too suitable for very heavy low voices	Delicate and sustained. Demands good command of high pp. See Debussy. (Schirmer)

BRITISH AND AMERICAN

The selection of British and American songs for this volume presented a not inconsiderable problem. British and American composers of the nineteenth century, the century in which the song experienced its greatest growth as a form of musical expression, produced few songs that were accorded a more than fleeting and local success. This is a fact which cannot be denied, no matter what interpretation one attaches to it or to what causes one attributes it. Yet, since the beginning of the twentieth century British and American composers seem to have produced a vertiable avalanche of songs. These songs, like songs in all countries and at all times, seem to fall into three categories: (1) Purely imitative songs, well made, flattering to the voice and effective, but as a rule of little musical value. (2) Purely experimental songs: as a rule somewhat awkardly written and often overly insistent on being "modern" at any cost. (3) Songs of undeniable individuality and musical merit, even though not necessarily on the same level of inspiration as, for instance, Schubert or Debussy.

The songs belonging to the first category naturally outweigh all others in numbers, in so far as the published material is concerned. Their success is often considerable at the moment, but after a few years they seem to appear less and less frequently on concert programs and soon seem to disappear into the limbo of forgotten music, to be supplanted by more recent productions of the same kind. They fulfill a certain definite need, especially as teaching material, and, though often excellent in their own way, cannot be classed as anything of a more permanent nature. It seemed only fair to include many such songs in this list, though no doubt in a few years a considerable number of them will be justly forgotten. Only a few songs of purely experimental nature have been included. Musical experimentation, necessary and welcome as it is, can hardly command general attention, unless the emotional and technical persuasivness of the composer makes the fact that such experimentation has been attempted seem of small import in comparison with the impact it carries as an emotionally satisfying or stimulating work.

Thus, the majority of the songs listed below are chosen from the first and third categories. This selection like any other, can and will no doubt be criticized on many grounds, and even if accepted will seem incomplete, for admittedly many a song of merit has not been listed. This, however, is only natural in view of the fact that it is an inhumanly arduous task to examine, even superficially, all the British and American songs published in the past forty-five years, for their number is startlingly large.

Many, if not most, of the prominent American composers of the present generation seem to be apparently more interested in symphonic, choral and instrumental music than in songs. Their published songs are so few in number and seem for the most part to be so much less representative of their manner of writing than their orchestral, choral and instrumental works that it seemed best not to try to list such material. Those particularly interested in this phase of contemporary American music are referred to the catalogues of the Arrow Press, the Associated Music Publishers, and Delkas Co. of Philadelphia, among others which list much of the available published material of composers like George Antheil, Aaron Copland, Henry Cowell, Roy Harris, Roger Sessions, Virgil Thomson, etc.

It seems only fair to add that in the opinion of this writer American popular music abounds in songs written in a much more indigenous idiom and often immeasurably superior in content as well as in workmanship to some of the examples of the so-called concert and teaching songs listed below.

It seems a pity that songs from the musical comedies by composers like George Gershwin, Cole Porter and Jerome Kern are, for some unknown reason, not as yet considered serious music, while many an imitative, empty, bombastic and poorly executed ballad is still charitably referred to as an "art song."

NOTE: (Br.) indicates a British composer.

TITLE	COMP.	TESS.	TYPE	REMARKS

CREIGHTON ALLEN

TITLE	COMP.	TESS.	TYPE	REMARKS
Eldorado	bb-eb2 (g2)	d1-d2	Most suitable for baritone	An animated, effective ballad. (Schirmer)

ERNST BACON

TITLE	COMP.	TESS.	TYPE	REMARKS
A clear midnight	G#-c#1	B-g#	Bass or alto	Slow, very sustained, subdued. See V. Williams' "Nocturne". (New Music)
Ancient Christmas carol	b#-e2		Medium or low voices	Slow, subdued, sustained. (New Music)
Five poems by Emily Dickinson	c1-g2 (a2)	e1-e2	High voices	Five short, delicate songs. Interpretatively not easy. (Schirmer)
Is there such a thing as day?	d#1-f#2	g#1-d#2	Most suitable for high light voices	Sustained, very delicate. (Associated Music Publishers)
Omaha	c1-f2 (ab2)	e1-c2	Not suitable for light voices	Vigorous. Musically not easy. Demands an accomplished pianist. (New Music)
The grass	c1-f#2 (a2)	d1-d2	Most suitable for light soprano	Very delicate, graceful. (Associated Music Publishers)

See also "Along Unpaved Roads," arrangements of American folk songs published by Delkas.

EDGAR L. BAINTON (Br.)

TITLE	COMP.	TESS.	TYPE	REMARKS
Ring out, wild bells	d1-f2	f1-d2	All voices, except a very light soprano	Vigorous, majestic. (Oxford)
The nightingale near the house	db1-bb2	eb1-f2	Soprano	Not fast. Demands in parts considerable dramatic intensity as well as considerable flexibility and a good command of high pp. (Curwen)

TITLE	COMP.	TESS.	TYPE	REMARKS

GRANVILLE BANTOCK (Br.)

TITLE	COMP.	TESS.	TYPE	REMARKS
A dream of spring	e1-g2	e1-d1 (H)	All voices	Delicate, somewhat declamatory. (Chester)
A feast of lanterns	f#1-a2	a1-f#2	All voices	Rapid. Demands facile articulation and an accomplished pianist. (Elkin)
Land of promise	c1-g2	e1-e2	All voices	Sustained. (Elkin)
Silent strings	f1-g2	g1-eb2 (H)	All voices, except a very light soprano	Sustained, somewhat declamatory. Has an effective final climax. (Boosey)
The boat song of the Isles	f1-g2		High or medium voices	Sustained. In folk vein. (Elkin)
The celestial weaver	b#-f#2	e1-e2	Medium or low voices	Slow, declamatory. (Chester)
Yung-Yang	e1-g2	f1-e2	All voices	Animated, graceful. (Elkin)

SAMUEL BARBER

Samuel Barber, one of the outstanding of the younger American composers, has written a considerable number of excellent songs which ought to be welcomed by every serious singer as valuable additions to his repertoire.
A complete list of his songs may be obtained from his publishers, Schirmer.

TITLE	COMP.	TESS.	TYPE	REMARKS
A nun takes a veil	g1-g2 (H)		Women's voices	Slow, somewhat declamatory.
I hear an army	db1-ab2	g1-eb2	Not too suitable for very light high voices	Animated, vigorous, dramatic. Demands an accomplished pianist.
Rain has fallen	d1-e2			Sustained, delicate. In parts demands considerable dramatic intensity. Musically not easy. Demands an accomplished pianist.
Sleep now	c1-f2		Not too suitable for very low voices	Delicate. Demands some flexibility. Musically and interpretatively not easy.
Sure on this shining hour	b-e2	e1-d2	All voices	Sustained.
With rue my heart is laden	e1-f2	f#1-e2 (H)	All voices	Sustained, subdued.

See also "Dover Beach" for medium voice and string quartet.

ARNOLD BAX (Br.)

The songs of Arnold Bax belong undoubtedly among the most significant and interesting songs of contemporary composers written to English texts. The fourteen songs listed below are sufficiently characteristic of his manner of writing to suit the purposes of this volume. "I heard a piper piping," "Cradle song," and "The pigeons" are most highly recommended to those who wish to acquaint themselves with his songs.

Editions: Chester
Murdoch & Murdoch

TITLE	COMP.	TESS.	TYPE	REMARKS
A Christmas carol	d1-a2	f1-d2	Not too suitable for very light high voices	Very sustained, majestic.
A lullaby	b-f#2	e1-e2	Soprano or mezzo-soprano	Delicate. Demands some flexibility and an accomplished pianist.
Across the door	c1-f2	eb1-cb2	Women's voices	Musically and interpretatively not easy. Demands an excellent pianist.
A milking sian	d1-g2	e1-e2	Soprano	Slow and delicate. Demands an accomplished pianist.
As I came over the grey, grey hills	bb-gb2	eb1-eb2	Most suitable for medium or low voices	A solemn, marchlike song. Demands an accomplished pianist.
Beg Innish	c1-g2	e1-e2	Most suitable for men's voices	Spirited and rhythmical. Demands facile articulation and an accomplished pianist.
Cradle song	db1-gb2	eb1-eb2	Soprano or mezzo-soprano	Subdued, delicate. Demands good command of high pp. and an accomplished pianist.
I heard a piper piping	b-e2	e1-d2	All voices	Slow. Demands good command of pp. and an accomplished pianist. See Norman Peterkin.
In the morning	e1-f2		High or medium voices	Sustained, subdued. (Oxford)
Rann of exile	d1-g2	e1-d2	Not too suitable for very light high voices	Somber, sustained. Demands in parts considerable dramatic intensity.
Rann of wandering	bb-f2	eb1-eb2	Not suitable for light high voices	Vigorous.
Shieling song	c#1-a2	d1-d2	Soprano	Light, animated. Demands some flexibility.

TITLE	COMP.	TESS.	TYPE	REMARKS
The enchanted fiddle	c1-a2	d1-d2	Most suitable for men's voices	Very rapid and gay. Demands facile articulation and an accomplished pianist.
The pigeons	b-d2	f1-db2	Women's voices	Slow and subdued. Interpretatively and musically not easy.
The white peace	eb1-gb2	g1-eb2	All voices	Very slow and sustained.
To Eire	c1- f2	f1-eb2	All voices, except a very light soprano	Sustained, grave. Demands an accomplished pianist.

See also a Celtic song cycle - five songs. (Chester)

MRS. H. H. A. BEACH

TITLE	COMP.	TESS.	TYPE	REMARKS
Ah, love but a day	eb1-a2 (H)	ab1-f2	All voices	Sustained. Has effective climaxes. (Schmidt)
Fairy lullaby	e1-f2 (a2)	f1-f2	High voices	Delicate, demands some flexibility. Text by Shakespeare. (Schmidt)
The year's at the spring	ab1-ab2 (H)	ab1-f2	All voices	Rapid, has an effective final climax. (Schmidt)

ARTHUR BENJAMIN (Br.)

TITLE	COMP.	TESS.	TYPE	REMARKS
Before dawn	e1-f2	f1-d2	High voices	Animated, subdued. Demands facile articulation. Christmas song. (Curwen)
Calm sea and mist	c1-f2	c1-c2	High or medium voices	Subdued and sustained. (Curwen)
Hedgerow	d#1-f2	f1-c2	High or medium voices	Very animated, subdued. (Curwen)
The piper	e1-a2	f#1-e2	Most suitable for high voices	Rapid. Demands facile articulation and an accomplished pianist. See M. Head. (Boosey)
The wasp	c1-f2	e1-e2	High or medium voices	Animated, delicate. Demands an accomplished pianist. (Curwen)

LORD BERNERS (Br.)

TITLE	COMP.	TESS.	TYPE	REMARKS
Theodore or the pirate king	c#1-f#2	eb1-eb2	Medium voices	A short, amusing song. (Chester)

MAURICE BESLEY (Br.)

TITLE	COMP.	TESS.	TYPE	REMARKS
An epitaph	cb1-eb2 (ab)	eb1-c2	Low or medium voices	Sustained. See Ivor Gurney. (Curwen)

TITLE	COMP.	TESS.	TYPE	REMARKS
Listening	e1-a2 (b2)	g1-g2	High voices	Animated. Demands some flexibility and, in parts, some dramatic intensity. (Curwen)
Three little fairy songs	db1-f2	eb1-eb2	Most suitable for soprano	Three short, animated, light songs. Demand some flexibility. (Chappell)

ARTHUR BLISS (Br.)

TITLE	COMP.	TESS.	TYPE	REMARKS
A child's prayer	f1-f2	a1-d2	Most suitable for soprano	Sustained, delicate. (Curwen)
Lovelocks (Three Romantic Songs)	d1-f2	eb1-d2	High voices	Sustained, delicate. Demands good command of high pp. (Goodwin & Tabb)
Rich or poor	e1-f2	e1-d2	Most suitable for tenor or high baritone	Sustained and for the most part subdued. (Curwen)
The buckle	b-f#2	e1-e2	Women's voices	Rapid and light, gently humorous. Demands an accomplished pianist. (Curwen)
The hare (Three Romantic Songs)	e1-g#2	g1-e2	Soprano	Delicate. Demands good command of high pp. and an accomplished pianist. (Goodwin & Tabb)
Three jolly gentlemen	eb1-gb2	f1-f2	High voices	Rapid, amusing. Demands some flexibility and an accomplished pianist. (Composers' Music Corp., N. Y.)

CARRIE JACOBS BOND

TITLE	COMP.	TESS.	TYPE	REMARKS
A perfect day	g1-f2 (H)		All voices	Sustained, effective. (Boston Music Co.)
I love you truly	f1-eb2 (H)		All voices	Sustained, effective. (Boston Music Co.)

PAUL BOWLES

TITLE	COMP.	TESS.	TYPE	REMARKS
Letter to Freddy	eb1-eb2		Women's voices	A setting of a Gertrude Stein text. Interpretatively not easy. (New Music)

TITLE	COMP.	TESS.	TYPE	REMARKS

A HERBERT BREWER (Br.)

TITLE	COMP.	TESS.	TYPE	REMARKS
The fairy pipers	f1-g2	a1-g2 (H)	Women's voices	Rapid, light. Demands facile articulation and good command of high pp. (Boosey)

FRANK BRIDGE (Br.)

TITLE	COMP.	TESS.	TYPE	REMARKS
Adoration	c1-g2	f1-eb2	Most suitable for high voices	Slow, sustained, subdued. Has an effective final climax. (Winthrop Rogers)
Come To me In my Dreams		—		
Fair daffodils	c1-d2	e1-c2	All voices	Animated, graceful. (Winthrop Rogers)
Into her keeping	e1-g#2	f1-f2	All voices	Sustained. Demands in parts considerable dramatic intensity. (Winthrop Rogers)
Love went a-riding	f1-g2	bb1-f2	Not too suitable for very light voices	Animated, vigorous, effective. Demands an accomplished pianist. (Winthrop Rogers)
Mantle of blue	d1-f2	g1-d2	Most suitable for women's voices	Sustained, subdued. See "Cradle Song" by Arnold Bax. (Winthrop Rogers)
O that it were so	d1-g2 (b2)	a1-f#2 (H)	All voices	Sustained. Has an effective climax. (Chappell)
Thy hand in mine	f#1-g2	g1-e2	All voices	Sustained. Has an effective climax. (Winthrop Rogers)
Tis but a week	g#1-g#2 (H)	c#1-f#2	Most suitable for men's voices	Vigorous, rhythmical, animated. (Winthrop Rogers)
When you are old	d1-g2	e1-e2	High or medium voices	Sustained. Demands in parts considerable dramatic intensity as well as a good command of high pp. (Chappell)

H. T. BURLEIGH

TITLE	COMP.	TESS.	TYPE	REMARKS
By the pool at the Third Rosses	f1-bb2	ab1-f2	Not too suitable for very low voices	Very sustained. Has an effective climax. (Ricordi)
Jean	eb1-g2	g1-eb2 (H)	Men's voices	Delicate, sustained. (Ricordi)

See many admirable arrangements of Negro spirituals by H. T. Burleigh, published by Ricordi.

TITLE	COMP.	TESS.	TYPE	REMARKS

CHARLES S. BURNHAM

TITLE	COMP.	TESS.	TYPE	REMARKS
Sing me a song of a lad that is gone	d1-f2	g1-d2	Men's voices	Not slow. In folk vein. (Schirmer)

GEORGE BUTTERWORTH (Br.)
(1885-1916)

TITLE	COMP.	TESS.	TYPE	REMARKS
Is my team plowing? (Shropshire Lad)	eb1-eb2		Men's voices	Sustained, somewhat declamatory. (Augener)
Loveliest of trees (from "Six Songs to Shropshire Lad")	c#1-e2	e1-e2	High or medium voices	Sustained. See John Duke. (Augener)
Requiescat	d1-g2	g1-e2	High or medium voices	Delicate, subdued. (Augener)
The lads in their hundreds	c#1-e2	e-c#2	High or medium voices	Graceful, subdued. (Augener)
Think no more, lad (Shropshire Lad)	c#1-f2	e1-d2	Men's voices	Vigorous, spirited. Demands facile articulation. (Augener)
When I was one-and-twenty (Shropshire Lad)	d1-e2		High or medium voices	Animated. In folk vein. See Arthur Bliss. (Augener)
With rue my heart is laden (from "Bredon Hill and Other Songs")	c#1-e2	e1-c#2		Sustained, somber. (Augener)

CHARLES WAKEFIELD CADMAN

TITLE	COMP.	TESS.	TYPE	REMARKS
At dawning	eb1-g2	f1-eb2 (H)	All voices	Sustained. Effective. (Ditson)
From the land of the sky blue water (from "Four American Indian Songs")	f1-f2 (H)		All voices	Sustained. Effective. (E. H. Morris Co.)

LOUIS CAMPBELL-TIPTON

TITLE	COMP.	TESS.	TYPE	REMARKS
A spirit flower	db1-a2	f#1-gb2 (H)	All voices	Sustained. Has effective climaxes. Demands good command of high pp. (Schirmer)
The crying of water	f#1-g#2	b1-f#2 (H)	All voices	Sustained. In parts demands considerable dramatic intensity as well as a good command of pp. (Schirmer)

JOHN ALDEN CARPENTER

The songs of John Alden Carpenter are too well known to need any introduction. With the exception of the "Gitanjaly" cycle, however, few of his songs seem to have attained the popularity they deserve. The following list, though not complete, would seem sufficiently representative for the purposes of the volume.

Editions: Schirmer
A few songs published by Ditson.

TITLE	COMP.	TESS.	TYPE	REMARKS
A cradle song	c1-eb2	eb1-c2	Women's voices, except a very light soprano	Slow, very sustained, subdued.
Berceuse de guerre (French text)	c1-g2	c1-bb1	Women's voices, except a very light soprano	Dramatic. Interpretatively not easy.
Bid me to live	bb-d2	db1-bb1	Medium or low voices	Slow and sustained.
Chanson d'automne (French text)	b-c#2	b-a1	Low voices	Slow, sustained, somewhat declamatory. See Hahn, "Les sanglots longs."
Dansons la gigue (French text)	b-e2	f#1-d2	Medium or low voices	Rapid. See Poldowski.
Don't ceare	c1-d2		Medium or low voices	An amusing, light Dorsetshire dialect song in folk vein. Demands facile articulation. Can be sung in English.
Go, lovely rose	c#1-eb2	f1-db2	Most suitable for medium voices	Graceful, delicate. See Roger Quilter.

Gitanjali, a cycle of six songs

(1) I am like a remnant of a cloud in autumn	bb-f2	eb1-eb2	Not suitable for light high voices	Dramatic and declamatory.
(2) Light, my light	c1-g2	g1-e2	Not suitable for very light voices	Very animated, effective The vocal line very sustained.
(3) On the day when death will knock at thy door	c1-f2	eb1-eb2	Not suitable for very high light voices	Dramatic and declamatory.
(4) On the seashore of endless worlds	c1-f#2	eb1-c2	Not too suitable for very light high voices	Musically and interpretatively not easy. Demands an accomplished pianist.
(5) The sleep that flits on baby's eyes	b-f#2	f#1-d2	High or medium voices	Slow, very delicate. Demands good command of high pp.

TITLE	COMP.	TESS.	TYPE	REMARKS
(6) When I bring to you colour'd toys	c#1-f#2	f#1-c#2	High or medium voices	Light and animated. Demands an accomplished pianist.

TITLE	COMP.	TESS.	TYPE	REMARKS
If	d1-e2	g1-d2	All voices	Light and humorous.
Il pleure dans mon coeur (French text)	d1-d2	g1-c2	All voices	Delicate, very subdued. See Debussy, and "Spleen" by Fauré.
Le ciel (French text)	c#1-f#2	g#1-d#2	High or medium voices, except a very light soprano	Slow. In parts demands considerable dramatic intensity. See "Prison" by Fauré and "D'une prison" by Hahn
Les silhouettes (English text)	c1-g2	f1-d2	Most suitable for high voices	Slow, somewhat declamatory. Demands good command of high p.
Looking-glass river	b-d2 (a)	d1-b1	Medium or low voices	Slow and sustained.
May the maiden	d1-g2	g1-d2	All voices	Slow, subdued, sustained.
Rest	c1-g2	e1-d2	Not too suitable for very low voices	Slow, sustained, very subdued. Demands good command of high pp.
Serenade	eb1-a2 (c3)	f1-f2 (H)	Not too suitable for very low voices	Animated. Interpretatively not easy. Demands an accomplished pianist. Published also in a low key, which is quite suitable for high voices (c1-a2).
Slumber song	b-g#2	e1-e2	All voices	Slow, sustained. In parts demands considerable dramatic intensity. Musically and interpretatively not easy.
The cock shall crow	b-e2	e1-d2	Medium or low voices	Animated and light. Demands facile articulation.
The day is no more	g#-d#2	d#1-d#2	Low voices	Slow, subdued, sustained. Interpretatively not easy.
The green river	b-e2	f#1-b1	Medium or low voices	Sustained, slow, somewhat declamatory. In parts demands considerable dramatic intensity.
The player queen	bb-eb2 (gb2)	eb1-bb1	Mezzo-soprano or alto	Sustained.
The pools of peace	d1-f2	f1-d2	Not too suitable for very low voices	Slow, sustained, delicate.

TITLE	COMP.	TESS.	TYPE	REMARKS
To one unknown	a-d#2	b-b1	Low or medium voices	Sustained. Has an imposing climax in the middle section.

Watercolors - four Chinese tone poems

TITLE	COMP.	TESS.	TYPE	REMARKS
(1) On a screen	bb-db2	db1-c2	Medium or low voices	Slow, sustained, very subdued.
(2) The odalisque	eb1-eb2		All voices	Light, delicate.
(3) Highwaymen	c1-f2	d1-d2	All voices, except a very light soprano	Slow, somewhat declamatory.
(4) To a young gentleman	c1-f2	eb1-db2		Animated, light, humorous. See also Cyril Scott.

GEORGE W. CHADWICK
(1854-1931)

TITLE	COMP.	TESS.	TYPE	REMARKS
A ballad of trees and the master	G-eb1	c-c1	Baritone	A marchlike narrative song. Religious text. (Ditson)
Allah	c#1-g#2	e1-c#2 (H)	Not too suitable for very high light voices	Slow and sustained. (Schmidt)
In my beloved eyes	bb-f2	f1-c2	Medium or low voices	Slow, sustained. (Schirmer)
Oh let night speak of me	d1-g2	g1-e2 (H)	All voices	Sustained. (Schmidt)
Thou art so like a flower	e1-g#2	g#1-e2 (H)	All voices	Sustained. See "Du bist wie eine Blume," Schumann, Rubinstein, Liszt. (Schmidt)

THEODORE CHANLER

TITLE	COMP.	TESS.	TYPE	REMARKS
Eight epitaphs	b-f2	d1-d2	High or medium voices	Eight short songs to poems by Walter De la Mare. Musically and interpretatively not easy. (Arrow Press)
✓ I rise when you enter	c#-g1	e-e1	Tenor or high baritone	Very animated, light, effective. (Schirmer)

See also:
"The Children" a cycle of nine songs for high or medium voices. (Schirmer)

TITLE	COMP.	TESS.	TYPE	REMARKS

ERNEST CHARLES

TITLE	COMP.	TESS.	TYPE	REMARKS
Clouds	f1-ab2	ab1-db2 (H)	All voices	Sustained. Has an effective climax. (Schirmer)
My lady walks in loveliness	e1-g2 (a2)	a1-eb2	Most suitable for men's voices	Sustained. Has an effective climax. (Schirmer)
When I have sung my songs *Youth –*	d1-g2	f1-d2	All voices	Sustained. Effective encore song. (Schirmer)

REBECCA CLARKE (Br.)

TITLE	COMP.	TESS.	TYPE	REMARKS
Down by the Salley Gardens	d1-e2		Most suitable for men's voices	Delicate, sustained. In folk vein. (Winthrop Rogers)
Eight o'clock	db1-f2	f1-bb1	Not too suitable for very light high voices	Slow, somewhat declamatory. Has a very dramatic final climax. (Winthrop Rogers)
June twilight	c1-f#2	f1-c2	High or medium voices	Sustained, for the most part subdued. (Winthrop Rogers)
Shy one	c1-a2	g1-d2	Not too suitable for very low voices	Delicate, graceful. (Boosey)
The seal man	c1-g2	c1-c2	High or medium voices	Declamatory in the manner of a free recitative. Interpretatively and musically not easy. Has dramatic climaxes. Demands an accomplished pianist. (Winthrop Rogers)

H. CLOUGH-LEIGHTER

TITLE	COMP.	TESS.	TYPE	REMARKS
My lover, he comes on the skee	f1-ab2	ab1-f2	Women's voices	Animated. Effective. Demands an accomplished pianist. (Schirmer)
Who knows?	d1-f2	g1-d2	High or medium voices	Sustained, rather subdued. (Schirmer)

SAMUEL COLERIDGE-TAYLOR (Br.)

TITLE	COMP.	TESS.	TYPE	REMARKS
Life and death	e1-ab2	ab1-f2 (H)	All voices	Very sustained. Has effective climaxes. (Schmidt)
She rested by the broken brook	bb-eb2	g1-d2	All voices	Sustained, subdued. Demands good command of high pp. (Winthrop Rogers)

TITLE	COMP.	TESS.	TYPE	REMARKS
Scenes from the Song of Hiawatha Onaway! Awake, beloved	f-bb1	ab-f1	Tenor	Sustained. Has effective climaxes. Demands good command of high pp. (Score, Novello)
Scenes from The Song of Hiawatha Spring had come with all its splendour	f#1-a2	a1-f#2	Lyric soprano (dramatic soprano)	Animated. Has effective climaxes. (Score, Novello)
Scenes from The Song of Hiawatha True is all Iagoo tells us	Bb-f1	d-eb1	Baritone	Declamatory, sustained. Has effective climaxes. (Score, Novello)

R. L. COTTENET

TITLE	COMP.	TESS.	TYPE	REMARKS
Red, red rose	d1-bb2	g1-g2 (H)	Most suitable for soprano	Animated, light. Demands some flexibility and an accomplished pianist. (Fischer)

BAINBRIDGE CRIST

TITLE	COMP.	TESS.	TYPE	REMARKS
Chinese Mother Goose rhymes	c1-g2	e1-e2	Mezzo-soprano or soprano	Seven short, amusing songs. (Fischer)
Evening	c1-g2 (a2)	f1-d2	High voices	Sustained, subdued. Demands good command of high pp. (Schirmer)
O come hither	d1-b2 (d3)	g1-g2	Coloratura soprano	Animated, light, quite florid. In the style of an eighteenth century pastorale. (Fischer)
White hours like snow	c#1-bb2	e1-e2	High voices	Sustained, subdued. Has an effective climax in the middle section. (Fischer)

PEARL G. CURRAN

TITLE	COMP.	TESS.	TYPE	REMARKS
Nocturne	eb1-g2 (bb2)	g1-eb2 (H)	All voices	Sustained. Effective. (Schirmer)

WALTER DAMROSCH

TITLE	COMP.	TESS.	TYPE	REMARKS
Danny Deever	A-eb1 (f1)	d-c1	Baritone	An effective narrative song. (J. Church Co.)

TITLE	COMP.	TESS.	TYPE	REMARKS

CARL DEIS

Come down to Kew	d1-f#2 (a2)	g1-e2	All voices	Animated, gay. Demands facile articulation. In folk vein. (Schirmer)

VAUGHN DE LEATH

Wild geese	c1-f2 (g2)	g1-d2	Soprano or mezzo-soprano	Animated. In folk vein. (Schirmer)

FREDERICK DELIUS (Br.)
(1862-1934)

The songs of Delius seem to be much more rarely performed in Great Britain and the United States than his symphonic and choral works. It is possible that the fact that in his choice of texts Delius did not limit himself to poetry in English is somewhat responsible for this. He set to music a considerable number of German translations of Scandinavian poems as well as of original German and French texts; their available English translations, for the most part, leave much to be desired.

Delius's harmonic scheme is not orthodox, though it is by no means experimental. Some of his songs are neither musically nor vocally easy. The short list below is primarily designed for those who are not at all acquainted with his style of writing.

I-Brasil	c1-f2	d1-d2	Medium or high voices	Slow, rhythmical. In parts demands good command of pp. (Oxford)
Indian love song (I arise from dreams of thee)	eb1-bb2	g1-f2	Most suitable for high dramatic voices	Sustained, delicate. The middle section is rapid and has an effective climax. (Oxford)
Le ciel est pardessus le toit (French text - from "Three Poems by Paul Verlains")	db1-gb2	f1-eb2	High voices	Slow. In parts demands considerable dramatic intensity. See Séverac, "D'une prison" by R. Hahn, and "Prison" by G. Fauré.
Longing	cb1-f#2 (a)	e1-d2	Heavy voices	Very animated, vigorous. (Augener)
Lullaby (for a modern baby)	c#1-g2	e1-e2	Soprano	A sustained, subdued vocalise. (Universal)
So white, so soft, so sweet is she	b-f#1 (H)	g1-e2	All voices	Delicate, sustained. From "Four Old English Lyrics." See "Have you seen but a white lily grow" (Anon). (Winthrop Rogers)

TITLE	COMP.	TESS.	TYPE	REMARKS
The homeward journey (Heimkehr)	eb1-f2	eb1-c2	Not too suitable for very light high voices	Sustained, somewhat declamatory. English translation by F. S. Copeland good. (Oxford)
The nightingale	d1-g2	f#1-e2	Not too suitable for very low voices	Sustained. Requires good command of high pp. (Augener)
To daffodils	c#1-g#2	e1-e2 (H)	All voices	Slow, sustained. Has effective climaxes. (Winthrop Rogers)
To the queen of my heart	d#1-a#2	f#1-f#2	Most suitable for heavy tenor	Very animated. Has very imposing climaxes. (Oxford)
Twilight fancies (Abendstimmung)	d1-f#2	g1-d2	Not too suitable for very high light voices	Subdued, somewhat declamatory. Demands in parts some dramatic intensity. See Grieg, Kjerulf. English translation by F. S. Copeland is good. (Oxford)

TERESA DEL RIEGO (Br.)

TITLE	COMP.	TESS.	TYPE	REMARKS
Homing	d1-ab2	g1-e2 (H)	All voices	Sustained. Effective encore song. (Chappell)

J. AIRLIE DIX (Br.)

TITLE	COMP.	TESS.	TYPE	REMARKS
The trumpeter	e-g1	g-e1	Men's voices	Dramatic. Effective ballad. (Boosey)

TOM DOBSON

TITLE	COMP.	TESS.	TYPE	REMARKS
Cargoes	d1-f2	a1-e2	All voices, except a very light soprano	Lively. Effective. An amusing poem. (Schirmer)

JOHN DUKE

TITLE	COMP.	TESS.	TYPE	REMARKS
February twilight	f#1-f#2		All voices	Very sustained, subdued. (Schirmer)
I've dreamed of sunsets	c1-g2	f1-d2	High or medium voices, except a very light soprano	Sustained. (Schirmer)
Loveliest of trees	c1-d2	f1-c2	All voices, except a very light soprano	Graceful, delicate. (Schirmer)
Lullaby	b-d2		Alto or mezzo-soprano	Sustained, delicate. (Schirmer)

TITLE	COMP.	TESS.	TYPE	REMARKS

THOMAS F. DUNHILL (Br.)

TITLE	COMP.	TESS.	TYPE	REMARKS
To the queen of heaven	c1-g2	f1-d2	Not too suitable for very light high voices	Very sustained, majestic. (Curwen)
The cloths of heaven	eb1-g2	g1-eb2 (H)	All voices	Very delicate, sustained. Demands good command of high pp. See Rebecca Clarke. (Stainer & Bell)

JAMES P. DUNN

TITLE	COMP.	TESS.	TYPE	REMARKS
The bitterness of love	d#1-ab2	g#1-eb2 (H)	All voices	Sustained. Has an effective climax. (Fischer)

ROBERT EDEN (Br.)

TITLE	COMP.	TESS.	TYPE	REMARKS
What's in the air today	e1-g2 (a2)	f1-f2	Not too suitable for very low voices	Rapid. The vocal line sustained. An effective encore song. (Elkin)

CLARA EDWARDS

TITLE	COMP.	TESS.	TYPE	REMARKS
By the bend of the river	gb1-ab2 (bb2)	gb1-eb2 (H)	All voices	Sustained. In popular vein. (Schirmer)
Into the night	e1-f2 (g2)	g1-e2	All voices	Sustained. Effective. (Schirmer)

SIR EDWARD ELGAR (Br.)
(1857-1934)

Edition: Novello

TITLE	COMP.	TESS.	TYPE	REMARKS
Pleading	d1-f#2	e1-e2	All voices	Sustained. Effective.
The pipes of Pan	d1-f#2	f#1-d#2	All voices	Spirited. Effective.
Sea Pictures (A cycle of 5 songs)				
(1) Sea slumber song	b-d2 (g)	e1-b1	Alto	Sustained.
(2) In haven	c1-c2	e1-c2	Alto	Delicate, animated.
(3) Sabbath morning at sea	b-f2 (g2)	e1-c2	Alto	Sustained, somewhat declamatory, solemn.
(4) Where corals lie	d1-d2 (a#)	d1-d2	Alto	Light, delicate. Demands good command of pp. and facile articulation.
(5) The swimmer	a-f2 (g)(a2)	e1-e2	Alto	Very animated, vigorous, somewhat declamatory.

TITLE	COMP.	TESS.	TYPE	REMARKS

Airs from Oratorios

TITLE	COMP.	TESS.	TYPE	REMARKS
King Olaf And King Olaf heard the cry	eb-a1 (bb1)	f1-f2	Dramatic tenor	A vigorous, animated, dramatic narrative solo.
The Light of Life As a spirit didst Thou pass before mine eyes	eb-a1 (bb1)	ab-f1	Tenor	Sustained, rather animated. Has a short slow middle section. Has effective climaxes.
The Light of Life Be not extreme, o Lord	c1-ab2	f1-f2	Dramatic soprano or lyric soprano	Animated, in parts dramatic. The vocal line sustained.
The Light of Life I am the good shepherd	c-eb1	f-db1	Baritone	Sustained.
The Light of Life Thou only hast the words of life	c1-d2 (a)	e1-b1	Alto or mezzo-soprano	Sustained, rather subdued.

NOTE: "The Dream of Gerontius," "The Apostles," and "Caractacus" although abounding in solo passages, do not seem to have soli suitable for separate performance, since the numerous solo passages are for the most part only sections of larger musical forms.

HERBERT ELWELL

TITLE	COMP.	TESS.	TYPE	REMARKS
In the mountains	db1-f2	gb1-eb2	High voices	Sustained, rather subdued. (Broadcast Music)
The road not taken	b-f#2	c#1-c#2	Medium or high voices	Animated, somewhat declamatory. (Schirmer)

CARL ENGEL

TITLE	COMP.	TESS.	TYPE	REMARKS
A sprig of rosemary	eb1-f2	g1-eb2	All voices	Sustained, somewhat declamatory. Demands good command of high p. (Schirmer)
Sea shell	eb1-eb2	gb1-db2	Most suitable for women's voices	Delicate. (Schirmer)
The trout	g1-g2	g1-e2	Soprano	Light, gently humorous. (Schirmer)

BLAIR FAIRCHILD

TITLE	COMP.	TESS.	TYPE	REMARKS
A memory	c1-eb2	eb1-bb1	All voices	Very delicate, sustained, subdued. (Boston Music Co.)

ARTHUR FARWELL

TITLE	COMP.	TESS.	TYPE	REMARKS
Afternoon on a hill	d1-e2	g1-d2	Women's voices	Graceful. (Galaxy)

TITLE	COMP.	TESS.	TYPE	REMARKS
Summer shower	c1-e2 (g#2)	g1-e2	Soprano	Somewhat declamatory, not fast. (Schirmer)
These saw visions	c1-e2	d1-ab1	Low or medium voices	Slow, subdued, somewhat declamatory. (Galaxy)

GEORGE FERGUSSON

TITLE	COMP.	TESS.	TYPE	REMARKS
Sonnet	c1-g2	f1-d2	Most suitable for men's voices	Sustained, delicate. (Fischer)

ARTHUR FOOTE
(1853-1937)

TITLE	COMP.	TESS.	TYPE	REMARKS
An Irish folksong	d1-g2	g1-e2	All voices	Sustained. In folk vein. Demands some flexibility. (Schmidt)
Constancy	eb1-ab2 (H)	f1-f2	All voices	Animated. See "I cannot help loving thee" by Clayton Johns. (Schmidt)
I'm wearing away	db1-f2	f1-db2	Most suitable for men's voices	Sustained. In folk vein. (Schmidt)
The lake isle of Innisfree	eb1-a2	g1-e2	High voices	Sustained. (Schmidt)
On the way to Kew	c1-e2	e1-c2	Not suitable for very light high voices	Sustained. (Schmidt)

CECIL FORSYTH

TITLE	COMP.	TESS.	TYPE	REMARKS
From the hills of dream	c1-d2	d1-c2	Low or medium voices	Sustained, subdued. Demands good command of pp. (Ditson)
June	b-d2 (f#2)	f#1-c#2	All voices, except a light soprano	Sustained, delicate. Has an effective final climax. (Schirmer)
The bell man	c1-eb2	eb1-c2	Most suitable for men's voices	Sustained, subdued. Demands good command of high pp. (Ditson)

STEPHEN FOSTER
(1826-1864)

All songs generally available

TITLE	COMP.	TESS.	TYPE	REMARKS
Ah! May the red rose live alway!	c#1-f#2	e1-d2	All voices	Sustained.
Come where my love lies dreaming	e1-a2	f1-f2 (H)	All voices	Sustained.

TITLE	COMP.	TESS.	TYPE	REMARKS
Jeannie with the light brown hair	c1-f2	f1-d2	Most suitable for tenor	Sustained, graceful.
Katy Bell	c1-f2	e1-e2	All voices	Sustained.
Little Belle Blair	c1-e2	e1-e2	All voices	Sustained.
Nell and I	c1-e2	c1-c2	All voices	Sustained.
Open thy lattice, love	d1-f#2	e1-d2	All voices	Graceful.
Sweetly she sleeps, my Alice fair	d1-f2	f1-d2	All voices	Sustained.
The old folks at home	d1-e2	d1-d2	All voices	Sustained.

J. BERTRAM FOX

TITLE	COMP.	TESS.	TYPE	REMARKS
Wonder	g1-g2	g1-eb2 (H)	All voices	Sustained, rather subdued. (Fischer)

RUDOLF GANZ

TITLE	COMP.	TESS.	TYPE	REMARKS
Memory	e1-g2	g1-d2	All voices	Very delicate, sustained. (Schirmer)

EDWARD GERMAN (Br.)

TITLE	COMP.	TESS.	TYPE	REMARKS
Charming Chloe	d1-g2	f1-f2 (H)	All voices	Animated, graceful. Demands facile articulation. (Novello)
My song is of the sturdy North	d1-f2	g1-e2	Men's voices	Vigorous, spirited, effective. (Cramer)
Rolling down to Rio	A-e1	d-d1	Bass or baritone	A vigorous, spirited ballad. Demands some flexibility. (Novello)

VITTORIO GIANNINI
Edition: Ricordi

TITLE	COMP.	TESS.	TYPE	REMARKS
Far above the purple hills	c#1-a2	f#1-e2	High voices, except a very light	Sustained. In parts demands considerable dramatic intensity.
Heart cry	eb1-bb2	eb1-eb2	High voices	Somewhat declamatory. Dramatic, effective.
If I had known	e1-a2	g#1-d#2	High voices, except a very light soprano	Sustained. Has effective climaxes.
I shall think of you	d1-g2	g1-e2	Most suitable for men's voices	A free recitative-like song.
Tell me, oh blue, blue sky!	f#1-g#2 (c#1)	g#1-d#2	High voices	Sustained. In parts dramatic. Demands good command of high pp. Effective.

See also Giannini's arrangements of Italian and Neapolitan folk songs published by Ricordi, among them the very effective "Zompa llari lira."

C. ARMSTRONG GIBBS (Br.)

TITLE	COMP.	TESS.	TYPE	REMARKS
Five eyes	f1-f2	f1-db2 (H)	All voices	A rapid, amusing song. Demands facile articulation. (Winthrop Rogers)
	d1-e2	f1-e2	Soprano	Sustained, delicate. (Stainer & Bell)
On Duncton hill	f#1-f#2	f#-d2	High voices	Sustained and subdued. (Curwen)
Padraic the fidiler	e1-f2	g1-d2	High or medium voices	Animated. In folk vein. Poem in dialect. (Curwen)
Silver	c#1-f#2	f#1-d2	All voices	Slow, sustained, very subdued. (Winthrop Rogers)
Sweet sounds, begone	d1-f#2	f1-e2	High voices	Sustained. (Winthrop Rogers)
Take heed, young heart	e1-g2	e1-e2	High voices	Sustained and for the most part subdued. (Curwen)
The market	a-e2	e1-c2	Most suitable for baritone	Animated, humorous. (Curwen)
To one who passed whistling through the night	f1-g2	g1-eb2	Most suitable for light high voices	Somewhat declamatory, subdued. Demands some flexibility. (Curwen)

HENRY F. GILBERT

TITLE	COMP.	TESS.	TYPE	REMARKS
Pirate song	c-g1	eb-d1	Men's voices, except a light tenor	Vigorous. Effective. (Novello)

EUGENE GOOSSENS (Br.)

TITLE	COMP.	TESS.	TYPE	REMARKS
Melancholy	d1-fb2	f#1-c#2	Medium or low voices	Sustained, somber. Musically not easy. (Chester)
The curse	f#1-g2	b#1-e2	High voices, except a very light soprano	A short, amusing song. (Chester)
When thou art dead	f#1-eb2		All voices	Sustained. (Curwen)

GUY GRAHAM (Br.)

TITLE	COMP.	TESS.	TYPE	REMARKS
Callao	c1-f2	f1-d2	Men's voices	Vigorous, spirited. Effective. (Boosey)

CHARLES T. GRIFFES
(1884-1920)

Griffes, perhaps one of America's outstanding composers, has written twenty-eight songs to English and German texts. No American singer can afford to neglect Griffes and would profit greatly by a closer acquaintance with songs other than the well-known "By a lonely forest pathway."

Edition: Schirmer

TITLE	COMP.	TESS.	TYPE	REMARKS
An old song resung	eb1-f2	eb1-eb2 (H)	Most suitable for men's voices	A vigorous narrative song.
Auf dem Teich dem regungslosen (O'er the tarn's unruffled mirror)	b-g#2	e1-c#2	High voices except a very light soprano	Very sustained, subdued. Demands good command of high pp. English translation by H. G. Chapman fairly good.
Auf geheimem Waldespfade (By a lonely forest pathway)	eb1-ab2	g1-eb2 (H)	All voices	Slow and sustained. See Robert Franz. English translation by H. G. Chapman good.
Auf ihrem Grab (Upon their grave)	c1-g2	f1-eb2	Not too suitable for very low voices	Sustained. Demands good command of high p. Excellent English translation by Louis Untermeyer.
Der träumende See (The dreamy lake)	b#-g#2	d#1-c#2	High voices, except a very light soprano	Very sustained, subdued. English translation by Dole very good.
Elfe (Elves)	f-ab2	ab1-f2	High voices	Rapid, light. Demands facile articulation and an accomplished pianist. Excellent English translation by Louis Untermeyer.
Evening song	d#1-g#2	g#1-e2	High voices	Sustained. Demands in parts considerable dramatic intensity. Demands an accomplished pianist.
In a myrtle shade	f#1-a2	g#1-f#2	Most suitable for high light voices	Slow, sustained. Demands good command of high pp.
Könnt ich mit dir (If I could go with you)	e1-g#2	g#1-e2	Most suitable for high voices	Sustained, delicate. Excellent English translation by Louis Untermeyer.
La fuite de la lune (To outer senses there is peace)	c#1-f2	eb1-db2	All voices, except a bass or a very light soprano	Slow. Interpretatively not easy.

TITLE	COMP.	TESS.	TYPE	REMARKS
Phantoms	bb-f2	eb1-d2	Not suitable for light high voices	Dramatic, somewhat declamatory. Musically not easy.
Sorrow of Mydath	b-f#2	g1-eb2	Not suitable for light high voices	Dramatic. Musically and interpretatively not easy. Demands an accomplished pianist.
Symphony in yellow	d#1-gb2	f#1-eb2	Not too suitable for very low voices	Slow and very subdued. Demands good command of high pp.
The first snowfall	d1-f2	a1-e2	Not too suitable for very low voices	Slow, very delicate. Demands good command of high pp.
The half-ring moon	d#1-e2		Women's voices, except a light soprano	Rapid, the vocal line very sustained. Demands considerable dramatic intensity.
The lament of Ian the Proud	d#1-a#2	f#1-f#2	Most suitable for tenor	Slow, somewhat declamatory. Demands in parts considerable dramatic intensity. Musically and interpretatively not easy. Demands an accomplished pianist.
The rose of the night	c#1-a2	g#1-e2	Most suitable for high voices	Sustained. In parts demands considerable dramatic intensity. Musically and interpretatively not easy. Demands an excellent pianist.
This book of hours	c#1-f#2	e1-c#2	Not too suitable for very low voices	Slow and very sustained. Demands good command of pp.
Thy dark eyes to mine	eb1-ab2	ab1-f2	High voices	Sustained. Musically not easy. Demands in parts considerable dramatic intensity as well as good command of high pp. Demands an accomplished pianist. See Arnold Bax.
Wai Kiki	d#1-g#2	e1-e2	Most suitable for high voices	Musically and interpretatively not easy. Demands considerable dramatic intensity, in parts, and an accomplished pianist.

TITLE	COMP.	TESS.	TYPE	REMARKS
We'll to the woods and gather May	db1-f2	f1-db2	Women's voices, except a light soprano	Rapid and vigorous. Of no particular distinction.
Wohl lag ich einst in Gram und Schmerz (Time was when I in anguish lay)	e1-g#2	f#1-d#2	Not suitable for light high voices	Rapid, vigorous. English translation by Chapman very good.
Zwei Könige sassen auf Orkadal (Two kings sat together in Orkadal)	bb-e2	b-b1	Low voices	A dramatic narrative song. The English translation is fair.

See also "Five Poems of the Ancient Far East" for medium voice and piano.

LOUIS GRUENBERG

TITLE	COMP.	TESS.	TYPE	REMARKS
Animals and insects	a-a2		Most suitable for soprano	Seven short songs to very amusing words by Vachel Lindsay. Musically quite complex. Demand an excellent pianist. (Universal)

DAVID W. GUION

TITLE	COMP.	TESS.	TYPE	REMARKS
At the cry of the first bird	d1-g2	f#1-d2	High or medium voices	Sustained, effective. Religious text. (Schirmer)
Mam'selle Marie	d1-e2	e1-b1	Women's voices	Sustained, subdued dialect song. (Schirmer)

IVOR GURNEY (Br.)
(1890-1937)

The songs of Ivor Gurney, whom some critics consider one of the most gifted of contemporary British song composers, are practically unknown outside of Great Britain. This short list is primarily designed for those who are not familiar with his songs.

TITLE	COMP.	TESS.	TYPE	REMARKS
All night under the moon	d#1-f#2	d#1-d#2	Most suitable for high voices	Slow, sustained, subdued. (Oxford)
An epitaph	d1-e2	e1-d2	All voices	Slow, very sustained, subdued. (Oxford)
Bread and cherries	e1-f#2	g1-e2	Not too suitable for very low voices	Animated, light. (Oxford)
Down by the Salley gardens	db1-f2	eb1-c2	Most suitable for men's voices	Sustained. (Oxford)

TITLE	COMP.	TESS.	TYPE	REMARKS
Hawk and Buckle	d1-eb2	d1-d2	Men's voices	Spirited, rhythmical. Demands facile articulation. (Oxford)
Last hours	bb-e2	e1-d2	Medium or low voices	Slow, sustained, subdued, somber. (Oxford)
The scribe	bb-e2	e1-c2	Not too suitable for very light high voices	Not slow, sustained. (Oxford)
Under the green-wood tree	c1-f#2	e1-d2	Medium or high voices	Graceful. (Winthrop Rogers)
The folly of being comforted	c#1-f#2 (g#2)	e1-e2	Most suitable for high voices	Rather slow, somewhat declamatory. Interpretatively not easy. Demands in parts considerable dramatic intensity. (Oxford)

See also: "Ludlow and Teme" - seven poems by A. E. Housman for voice, string quartet and pianoforte (Stainer & Bell)

HENRY K. HADLEY

TITLE	COMP.	TESS.	TYPE	REMARKS
My shadow	d1-e2		All voices	Animated, gently humorous. Demands facile articulation. (Schmidt)
The time of parting	e#1-g#2		High or medium voices	Sustained, rather subdued. (Fischer)

The Night Wind —

PATRICK HADLEY (Br.)

TITLE	COMP.	TESS.	TYPE	REMARKS
The sheep	c#1-f2	e1-d2	Medium or high voices	Sustained and for the most part subdued. (Oxford)

RICHARD HAGEMAN

TITLE	COMP.	TESS.	TYPE	REMARKS
At the well	db1-ab2 (cb3)	gb1-gb2	Not too suitable for very low voices	An effective light song. Demands an excellent pianist. (Schirmer)
Christ went up into the hills	eb1-gb2 (ab2)	gb1-eb2	All voices	Slow, sustained. Has effective climaxes. Religious text. (Fischer)
Do not go, my love	d#1-g2	f#1-d2 (H)	All voices	Slow, sustained. In parts demands considerable dramatic intensity as well as a good command of high pp. (Schirmer)
Me company along	f1-bb2	a1-f2	Most suitable for high voices	Animated, effective. Demands an excellent pianist. (Fischer)

TITLE	COMP.	TESS.	TYPE	REMARKS
Miranda	e1-a2	a1-e2 (H)	All voices	A rapid, effective song. Demands an accomplished pianist. See an excellent setting of this Belloc poem, "The Inn", by Francis Toye (baritone). (Galaxy)
Music I heard with you	f1-a2	a1-e2 (H)	All voices	Sustained. Has effective climaxes. (Galaxy)

VICTOR HARRIS

TITLE	COMP.	TESS.	TYPE	REMARKS
A man's song	F#-c1	c-c1	Men's voices	Effective, vigorous. (Schirmer)
The hills o'Skye	d1-g2	a1-f2	All voices	In Scottish folk song vein. Rhythmical, sustained. (Ditson)

SIDNEY HARRISON (Br.)

TITLE	COMP.	TESS.	TYPE	REMARKS
I hear an army	b-d2	d1-c2	Low voices	Animated. Has dramatic climaxes. See Barber. (Cramer)

HERBERT HAMILTON HARTY (Br.)

TITLE	COMP.	TESS.	TYPE	REMARKS
Across the door	b-f2	d1-d2	Women's voices, except a very light soprano	Animated. Interpretatively not easy. Demands an accomplished pianist. See A. Bax. (Novello)
Homeward	C-e1	c-c1	Bass or baritone	A vigorous, spirited sailor's song. In folk vein. (Novello)
My Lagan love (from "Three Traditional Ulster Airs")	d1-g2	e1-e2	All voices	Sustained. In folk vein. (Boosey)
Sea wrack	c1-f2	e1-e2	Women's voices, except a light soprano	Sustained. Has dramatic climaxes. (Boosey)

See also "Three Irish Folksongs" arranged by Hamilton Harty. (Oxford University Press)

MICHAEL HEAD (Br.)

TITLE	COMP.	TESS.	TYPE	REMARKS
A piper	eb1-g2	f1-eb2	All voices	Animated. Demands facile articulation and an accomplished pianist. (Boosey)
Money, O!	b-f#2	f#1-e2	Men's voices	An animated, effective ballad. (Boosey)

TITLE	COMP.	TESS.	TYPE	REMARKS
Nocturne (from "Over the rim of the moon")	e1-g♯2	g1-d2	All voices	Somewhat declamatory. In parts dramatic. Demands good command of high pp. (Boosey)
The sea gipsy	e1-g♯2	g1-e2 (H)	Men's voices	An effective, vigorous ballad. (Boosey)
The ships of Arcady	d1-g2	a1-f♯2 (H)	All voices	Sustained, for the most part delicate and subdued. (Boosey)
When I think upon the maidens	d1-g2	g1-eb2 (H)	Men's voices	A very rapid, humorous character song. Demands facile articulation. (Boosey)
You shall not go a-Maying	eb1-g2	g1-eb2	All voices	Sustained, effective. (Boosey)

V. HELY-HUTCHINSON (Br.)

TITLE	COMP.	TESS.	TYPE	REMARKS
Old Mother Hubbard	d1-g2	g1-eb2 (H)	All voices	A parody on Handel. Demands some flexibility. (Fischer)
Three nonsense songs: (1) The owl and the pussy cat (2) The table and the chair (3) The duck and the kangaroo	c1-f2	d1-d2	High or medium voices	Three settings of Edward Lear's nonsense poems. Light and humorous. (Paterson)

SIR GEORGE HENSCHEL (Br.)
(1850-1934)

TITLE	COMP.	TESS.	TYPE	REMARKS
Morgen-Hymne (Morning Hymn)	d♯1-g♯2	g♯1-d♯2	Not suitable for light high voices	Slow. Has a very effective climax. English translation by Th. Baker fairly good. See H. Wolf. (Schirmer)
There was an ancient king	a-f♯2	c1-d2	Alto or baritone	Sustained, grave. (Schmidt)

JOSEF HOLBROOKE (Br.)

TITLE	COMP.	TESS.	TYPE	REMARKS
Come not, when I am dead	d1-ab2	f1-f2 (H)	Not suitable for light high voices	Grave, somber. Has dramatic climaxes. (Enoch)
If birds can soar	eb1-g2	eb1-eb2	High or medium voices	Sustained. Demands in parts considerable dramatic intensity. (Curwen)

JOHN C. HOLLIDAY (Br.)

TITLE	COMP.	TESS.	TYPE	REMARKS
Chumleigh fair	c1-d2		Men's voices	Animated, gently humorous. In folk vein.

TITLE	COMP.	TESS.	TYPE	REMARKS
Chumleigh fair (cont'd)				Demands facile articulation. (Boosey)

GUSTAV HOLST (Br)
(1874-1934)

TITLE	COMP.	TESS.	TYPE	REMARKS
A little music	d1-g2	f1-f2	High voices	Animated. Demands facile articulation. (Augener)
Journey's end	c1-gb2	g1-e2	High or medium voices	Sustained, somewhat declamatory. (Augener)
Now in these fairylands	d1-f2	f1-d2	High and medium voices	Very sustained, rather subdued. (Augener)
✓The heart's worship	c1-e2	e1-b1 (H)	Not suitable for very light high voices	Slow, sustained, somewhat declamatory. (Stainer & Bell)
The sergeant's song	A-e1	e-e1	Baritone or bass	A vigorous, spirited ballad. (Ashdown)
The thought	c#1-f#2		Medium or high voices	Sustained, declamatory in manner of a recitative. (Augener)

See also: "Hymns from the Rig Veda," medium or high voices. (Chester)

SIDNEY HOMER
(1864 -)

The songs of Sidney Homer (over a hundred in number) need no introduction, as they are sufficiently well known to every American singer. The scant selection listed here, though in some ways representative of his style of writing, is admittedly in no way complete. It is hoped that this short list may serve as a point of departure for those who do not happen to be familiar with his songs.

Edition: Schirmer

TITLE	COMP.	TESS.	TYPE	REMARKS
A banjo song	e1-f2	g1-e2	Most suitable for men's voices	Sustained. Effective, tuneful song in popular vein.
Dearest	eb1-ab2	eb1-eb2	All voices	Sustained. Demands in parts considerable dramatic intensity.
General William Booth enters into heaven	c1-eb2	eb1-c2	Low or medium voices	A vigorous narrative song. See Ives.
Lullaby, oh lullaby	eb1-eb2	bb1-eb2	Women's voices	Very delicate and sustained. See C. Scott.
Mary's baby	e1-f2	g#1-e2	All voices	Slow and subdued.
Requiem	eb1-db2	f1-cb2	Men's voices	Slow, sustained, and rather vigorous.

TITLE	COMP.	TESS.	TYPE	REMARKS
Sheep and lambs	eb1-e2	eb1-bb1	Not too suitable for very high light voices	Very sustained. In parts demands considerable dramatic intensity.
Sweet and low	c1-c2	db1-ab1	Women's voices	Sustained, delicate.
The fiddler of Dooney	d1-g2	d1-d2	Most suitable for men's voices	Rapid and spirited.
This is the house that Jack built	a-f2	bb-bb1	All voices	An amusing setting of the old nursery rhyme. Very animated. Demands very facile articulation. (J. Church Co.)
When death to either shall come	e1-e2	g#1-e2	All voices	Slow and sustained.

EDWARD HORSMAN

In the yellow dusk	f#1-ab2	f#1-e2	Not too suitable for very low voices	Sustained. (Schirmer)
The bird of the wilderness	db1-ab2 (bb2)	ab1-eb2	Not too suitable for very light voices	Sustained. Has effective climaxes. (Schirmer)
The dream	f1-g2	g1-e2	High voices	Sustained. Has effective climaxes. (Schirmer)

MARY HOWE

Berceuse	eb1-f2	g1-d2	Soprano or mezzo-soprano	Delicate, sustained. (Schirmer)
To the unknown soldier	d1-g2	g1-g2	High voices, except a light soprano	Sustained, grave. Has dramatic climaxes. (Schirmer)

HERBERT HOWELLS (Br.)

Gavotte	d1-g2	d1-d2	High or medium voices	Animated, graceful. (Oxford)

CHARLES HUERTER

Pirate dreams	eb1-ab2	ab1-eb2	Most suitable for soprano	Sustained, subdued. Demands good command of high pp. (Ditson)

TITLE	COMP.	TESS.	TYPE	REMARKS

BRUNO HUHN

TITLE	COMP.	TESS.	TYPE	REMARKS
Cato's advice	G-c1 (d1)	c-a	Bass	A vigorous, spirited drinking song in eighteenth century style. (Schirmer)
Invictus	bb-db2	f1-c2	Not suitable for light voices	Very vigorous, somewhat declamatory. (Schirmer)

JOHN IRELAND
(1879 -)

Among contemporary British songs those of John Ireland, in the opinion of this writer, occupy a highly honored position. Tastefully and skillfully written, neither experimental nor tritely effective, yet possessing an idiom of their own, they present no particular performance problems.

TITLE	COMP.	TESS.	TYPE	REMARKS
A report song	eb1-eb2		All voices	Animated, graceful. Demands facile articulation. (Winthrop Rogers)
Bed in summer	eb1-f2 (H)		All voices	Animated, graceful. Poem is from Child's Garden of Verses by Stevenson. (Curwen)
Epilogue	f1-ab2 (H)	g1-g2	High or medium voices	Sustained. (Augener)
Great things	d-f#1 (H)	d-d1	Men's voices	Animated, vigorous. (Augener)
Hope the hornblower	e1-e2 (f#2)	e1-e2	Men's voices	Vigorous, animated. (Boosey)
I have twelve oxen	d1-f#2	e1-d2	Most suitable for men's voices	Animated. In folk vein. See Warlock. (Winthrop Rogers)
I was not sorrowful	eb1-gb2 (H)	g1-c2	Most suitable for men's voices	Sustained, for the most part subdued, somber. (Boosey)
If there were dreams to sell	d1-g2 (H)	f1-f2	All voices	Sustained. (Boston Music Co.)
In boyhood	c#1-f2	d1-d2	High or medium voices	Sustained and somewhat declamatory. (Oxford)
Ladslove (from "The land of lost content" - 6 songs to poems of A. E. Housman)	f1-ab2 (H)	f1-f2	High or medium voices	Sustained. (Augener)
Remember	d#1-g2 (H)	f#1-e2	All voices	Sustained. Demands considerable dramatic intensity. (Winthrop Rogers)
Sea fever	e1-g2 (H)	a1-e2	Men's voices	Somewhat declamatory. Perhaps the best setting of this famous Masefield poem. (Augener)

TITLE	COMP.	TESS.	TYPE	REMARKS
Spring sorrow	eb1-f2	f1-eb2	All voices	Sustained. (Winthrop Rogers)
The bells of San Marie	f1-g2	g1-f2	Most suitable for men's voices	Sustained. (Augener)
The heart's desire	f1-ab2	f1-f2 (H)	All voices	Sustained. Demands in parts considerable dramatic intensity. (Winthrop Rogers)
The lent Lily (from "The land of lost content" - 6 song to the poems of A. E. Housman)	g1-f♯2 (H)		All voices	Sustained, delicate. (Augener)
The Salley gardens (from "Songs sacred and profane")	d1-d2 (H)		All voices	Sustained, graceful. (Schott)
Vagabond	f1-f2	g1-d2 (H)	Men's voices	Rather slow, declamatory, subdued. (Augener)
We'll to the woods no more	d1-f2	f1-d2	Medium or high voices	Slow, somewhat declamatory. (Oxford)

See also "Five Poems by Thomas Hardy" - for baritone.

CHARLES IVES

One of America's most individualistic composers, Ives had begun to experiment with unorthodox harmonies and sonorities long before such experimentation was fashionable among American composers. Although he has written over a hundred songs, most of them have been printed privately and only a few are generally available (in the New Music "Cos Cob Press" edition). Of these only two have been listed below, since most of Ives's mature songs are extraordinarily complex and do not seem, as yet, to be generally acceptable to the majority of singers or music lovers.

Charlie Rutlage	d1-d2		Men's voices	A narrative song, much of which is spoken. Demands an accomplished pianist. Some of the piano part is supposed to be played with fist. Musically complex. (Cos Cob Press)
Evening	c♯1-d2	e1-b1	Medium or low voices	Slow, sustained, subdued. Musically not easy. (Cos Cob Press)

FREDERICK JACOBI

TITLE	COMP.	TESS.	TYPE	REMARKS
Two poems by Chaucer				
(1) Roundel	d1-eb2	g1-eb2	Medium voices	Sustained, delicate. (Schirmer)
(2) Ballade	c#1-a2	f#1-f#2	High voices	Rapid, light. (Schirmer)
Circé (Vocalise-Etude)	c1-b2	eb1-f#2	Soprano	Slow, sustained. Has a more animated and dramatic middle section. (A.L. Hettich, Répertoire Moderne de Vocalise. Leduc)
Aria (Vocalise-Etude)	e1-g2	e1-e2	High or medium voices	Sustained. (A. L. Hettich, Répertoire Moderne de Vocalise. Leduc)

CLAYTON JOHNS

TITLE	COMP.	TESS.	TYPE	REMARKS
I cannot help loving thee	e1-g#2	e1-e2	Not suitable for low voices	Light, very animated. See "Constancy" by Arthur Foote. (Schirmer)

WERNER JOSTEN

TITLE	COMP.	TESS.	TYPE	REMARKS
Cupid's counsel	eb1-ab2	g1-f2	Soprano	Light, animated, humorous song. Demands facile articulation. (Schirmer)
Summer night	c1-g2	g1-f2	Soprano	Animated, effective. (Schirmer)

FREDERICK KEEL (Br.)

TITLE	COMP.	TESS.	TYPE	REMARKS
Trade winds	bb-eb2	eb1-bb1	Men's voices	Gently animated, sustained. (Boosey)

WENDELL KEENEY

TITLE	COMP.	TESS.	TYPE	REMARKS
The aspen	d1-f#2 (g2)	e1-d2	Not suitable for very light high voices	Slow, somber. Demands an accomplished pianist. (Schirmer)

MARSHALL KERNOCHAN

TITLE	COMP.	TESS.	TYPE	REMARKS
Lilacs	e1-g#2	f#1-c#2	High voices	Very delicate, subdued. (Galaxy)
Smuggler's song	c#-eb1	e-c#1	Baritone	An effective character song. Demands facile articulation. (Galaxy)
We two together	e1-ab2	f1-db2	All voices, except a very light soprano	Sustained, somewhat declamatory. Has a very effective final climax. (Galaxy)

TITLE	COMP.	TESS.	TYPE	REMARKS

CHARLES KINGSFORD

Wallpaper for a little girl's room	b♭-f2	e♭1-e♭2	Most suitable for women's voices	Delicate, somewhat declamatory. (Schirmer)

RICHARD KOUNTZ

The sleigh	f1-f2 (a♭2)		All voices	A rapid encore song. (Schirmer)

A. WALTER KRAMER

✓ For a dream's sake	d1-g2	g1-d2 (H)	All voices	Slow, somewhat declamatory, effective. (J. Fischer)
Swans	e♭1-b♭2	a♭1-f2	Most suitable for high light voices	Sustained. Demands good command of high pp. (Ricordi)
The faltering dusk	e♭1-g♭2	e♭1-c2	Women's voices	Dramatic, effective. (Ditson)
The last hour	e1-g♯2	g1-e2	All voices	Somewhat declamatory, effective. (J. Church Co.)

FRANK LA FORGE

Come unto these yellow sands	f♯1-b2 (d3)	b1-a2	Coloratura soprano	Animated, light. Has florid passages. (Schirmer)
Hills	e1-g2 (b2)	g1-e2	Not suitable for very light voices	Animated, effective. (Ricordi)
I came with a song	e1-b♭2	g♭1-g♭2	All voices, except bass	Sustained. Has an effective final climax. (Schirmer)
Retreat (Schlupfwinkel)	e1-g2	g♯1-f2	All voices	Slow and sustained. (Schirmer)
Song of the open	e♭1-a♭2 (c3)	f1-f2	Not suitable for very light voices	Very animated, effective. Demands an accomplished pianist. (Ditson)

LIZA LEHMANN (Br.)
(1862-1918)

In a Persian garden (A song cycle for four solo voices - soprano, alto, tenor, bass). The solo excerpts of this cycle have been much used for

TITLE	COMP.	TESS.	TYPE	REMARKS

teaching purposes and still enjoy considerable popularity. Expertly written for the respective voices, they are melodious and effective. (Schirmer)

Mother sleep	e1-g2 (b)	e1-e2	All voices	Not slow, very subdued, the vocal line sustained. (Schirmer)

THURLOW LIEURANCE

By the waters of Minnetonka	e1-f♯2	e1-e2	All voices	Sustained. Effective imitation of an Indian song. (Presser)

CHARLES MARTIN LOEFFLER
(1861-1935)

Les paons (French text)	d1-f2	g1-e2	High or medium voices	Slow. Interpretatively not easy. Demands good command of pp. and an accomplished pianist. (Schirmer)
To Helen	d♭1-f2	f♯1-e2	Medium or high voices	Sustained. In parts demands considerable dramatic intensity. Demands an accomplished pianist. (Schirmer)
Sonnet	d♭1-f2	f1-e♭2	Medium or high voices	Sustained. Demands in parts considerable dramatic intensity. Demands an excellent pianist. Musically not easy. (Schirmer)

HERMANN LÖHR

The ringers	e♭1-e♭2	e♭1-c2	Men's voices	An effective, humorous ballad. Demands facile articulation. (Chappell)

ERNEST LUBIN

A cradle song	d1-g2	e1-c2	Soprano	Sustained, for the most part subdued. (Schirmer)
The piper	c1-a2	f♯1-e2	Most suitable for light soprano	Animated, graceful. Demands some flexibility. (Schirmer)

EDWARD MacDOWELL
(1861-1908)

The songs of Edward MacDowell have not attained the popularity of his pianoforte works. Unpretentiously melodic in character, they possess all the qualities which would seem to ensure a lasting popularity, were it not for the fact that, for the most part, his songs are vocally somewhat awkward. The almost uninterrupted vocal line seldom allows the singer a breathing space, and thus makes rather severe demands upon the singer's technique and endurance.

Editions: Arthur Schmidt
Schirmer
Breitkopf & Härtel

TITLE	COMP.	TESS.	TYPE	REMARKS
A maid sings light	e1-g2	ab1-f2	All voices	Light and animated. Demands facile articulation.
As the gloaming shadows creep	e1-g2	g1-d2	All voices	Very sustained. Demands good command of high pp.
Cradle hymn	e1-d2 (f♯2)	a1-d2	Women's voices	Delicate and sustained. Demands good command of pp.
Deserted (Ye banks and braes)	f1-f2	a1-e2	All voices	Slow and sustained.
Fair springtide	c♯1-f♯2	d1-d2	All voices	Very slow and sustained.
Long ago	d1-g2	f1-f2	All voices	Very sustained. Demands good command of pp.
Menie	d1-f2	f1-d2	All voices	Sustained. Demands good command of pp.
The sea	d1-d2	d1-bb1	Not suitable for very light high voices	Sustained. In parts demands considerable dramatic intensity.
The swan bent low to the lily	d1-f2	g1-e2	All voices, except a very light soprano	Very sustained.
Thy beaming eyes	c1-f2		All voices; not suitable for very light soprano	Sustained.
To a wild rose	db1-gb2	gb1-f2	All voices	Very sustained.

ROBERT MacGIMSEY

Shadrack	d-g1 (a1)	g-d1 (H)	Most suitable for men's voices	Vigorous ballad in the manner of a Negro spiritual. A considerable number of effective spiritual-like songs have been written by MacGimsey, of which this is among the most popular. (Fischer)

DERMOT MacMURROUGH (Br.)

The shepherdess	e1-f2	f1-e2 (H)	All voices	Sustained, delicate. Demands good command of high pp. (Enoch)

TITLE	COMP.	TESS.	TYPE	REMARKS

HARL McDONALD

TITLE	COMP.	TESS.	TYPE	REMARKS
Daybreak	e1-g2	a1-f#2	Most suitable for heavy high voices	Sustained, very effective. (Elkan-Vogel)

MANA-ZUCCA

TITLE	COMP.	TESS.	TYPE	REMARKS
I love life	f1-f2 (a2)	a1-f2 (H)	All voices	Animated, effective. (J. Church Co.)

KATHLEEN LOCKHART MANNING

TITLE	COMP.	TESS.	TYPE	REMARKS
Shoes	f1-g2	f1-f2 (H)	All voices	Light encore song. (Schirmer)
White clouds	d1-g2	g1-e2	All voices	Very subdued, delicate. (Ditson)

EASTHOPE MARTIN (Br.)

TITLE	COMP.	TESS.	TYPE	REMARKS
Come to the fair	g1-g2 (H)		All voices	Gay, spirited ballad. (Enoch)

DANIEL GREGORY MASON

TITLE	COMP.	TESS.	TYPE	REMARKS
A grain of salt	A-d1	c-bb	Bass or baritone	Animated, humorous. (Schirmer)
A sea dirge	d1-eb2	g1-c2	Medium or low voices	Animated, vigorous. (Witmark)
I ain't afeared o' the admiral	A-e1	c-c1	Bass or baritone	Humorous character song. (Schirmer)
Take, o take those lips away	d1-f2	e1-e2	Medium or high voices	Sustained. Demands in parts considerable dramatic intensity. (Witmark)
The constant cannibal maiden	c-f#1	e-c#1	Baritone	Humorous. Demands in parts considerable dramatic intensity. (Witmark)

ROBIN MILFORD (Br.)

TITLE	COMP.	TESS.	TYPE	REMARKS
If it's ever spring again (from "Four Hardy Songs")	d1-g2	g1-e2	High voices	Animated, light. (Oxford)
The colour (from "Four Hardy Songs")	e1-g2	g1-e2	High voices	Sustained. In folk vein. Demands in parts considerable dramatic intensity. (Oxford)

E. J. MOERAN (Br.)

"Seven Poems" by James Joyce (one is omitted here). (Publisher: Oxford)

TITLE	COMP.	TESS.	TYPE	REMARKS
Bright cap	d1-e2	e1-d2	Medium or high voices	Animated. Demands some flexibility.
Donnycarney	eb1-f2	f1-eb2	Men's voices	Sustained, delicate.
Rain has fallen	c#1-f#2	e1-d#2	High or medium voices	Slow, sustained, subdued.
Strings in the earth and air	d1-f2	f1-d2	Medium or high voices	Sustained and delicate.
The merry green wood	e1-e2		Most suitable for men's voices	Animated, rather vigorous.
The pleasant valley	c1-f2	f1-d2	Medium or high voices	Sustained.

JAMES L. MALLOY (Br.)
(1837 - 1909)

Love's old sweet song	d1-f2 (ab2)	eb1-eb2	All voices	Sustained, tuneful encore song. (Schirmer)
The Kerry dance	c1-g2	f1-d2	All voices	Animated, rhythmical. Demands facile articulation. In folk vein. Has attained the popularity of a folk song. (Generally available)

DOUGLAS MOORE

Adam was my grandfather	c1-f#2	eb1-db2	Men's voices	Vigorous, spirited, somewhat humorous. (Galaxy)
Sigh no more, ladies	d1-e2	e1-c2	Medium voices	Sustained. (Boosey)

CHARLES NAGINSKI
(1909 - 1940)

Among the young American composers, few have shown such remarkable promise, especially in the field of vocal music, as Charles Naginski, who died so tragically at the very outset of his career. The few songs listed below are unfortunately almost all of the vocal music he had completed before his death, except the "Nonsense Alphabet" for soprano and pianoforte (later orchestrated) and another three or four songs as yet unpublished. It is hoped that his songs will find as wide a public as, in the opinion of this writer, they seem to deserve.

Edition: Schirmer

Look down, fair moon	d1-e2	g1-d2	Not too suitable for very light high voices	Slow, very sustained, somber.

TITLE	COMP.	TESS.	TYPE	REMARKS
Mia Carlotta	c1-f2	d1-d2	Men's voices	A comic dialect song. Demands very facile articulation.
Night song at Amalfi	d1-eb2	f#1-d2	Women's voices	Slow, somewhat declamatory and subdued. See H. H. A. Beach.
Richard Cory	a-e2 (g2)	c1-c2	Not suitable for light high voices	A somber, satirical narrative song. Demands facile articulation.
The pasture	bb-eb1	eb1-bb1	Most suitable for women's voices	Light, very delicate.
The ship starting	bb-bb1		Medium or low voices	Sustained, somewhat declamatory. Demands an accomplished pianist.
Under the harvest moon	d1-e2	e1-b1	Most suitable for medium or high voices	Sustained, rather delicate.

ETHELBERT NEVIN
(1862-1901)

TITLE	COMP.	TESS.	TYPE	REMARKS
At twilight	d1-e2		All voices	Sustained, subdued, effective. (Schirmer)
The rosary	d1-e2	e1-bb1	All voices	Sustained, effective. At one time very popular. (Schirmer)

PAUL NORDOFF

TITLE	COMP.	TESS.	TYPE	REMARKS
Fair Anette's song	c1-f2	f-f2	Soprano	Animated, delicate. (Associated Music Publishers)
Serenade	c#1-f#2	f#1-f#2	Soprano	Delicate, demands good command of high pp. (Associated Music Publishers)
There shall be more joy	c#1-f#2	f#1-eb2	High voices	Animated. Demands some flexibility and an accomplished pianist. (Associated Music Publishers)
White nocturne	e1-e2		All voices	Sustained, very subdued. (Ditson)

GEOFFREY O'HARA

TITLE	COMP.	TESS.	TYPE	REMARKS
Give a man a horse he can ride	d-a1	g-e1 (H)	Men's voices	Vigorous and effective. (Huntzinger)
There is no death	eb1-ab2	bb1-g2	Most suitable for men's voices	Effective, dramatic. (Chappell)

TITLE	COMP.	TESS.	TYPE	REMARKS
The wreck of the "Julie Plante"	d-g1	g-g1 (H)	Men's voices	Effective, dramatic ballad in French-Canadian dialect. (Ditson)

HORATIO PARKER
(1863-1919)

Excerpts from Hora Novissima, an Oratorio (Latin text)

(Score published by Novello)

TITLE	COMP.	TESS.	TYPE	REMARKS
Gens duce splendida	c1-e2	c1-c2	Alto or mezzo-soprano	Vigorous. In parts demands considerable dramatic intensity.
O bona patria	eb1-ab2	ab1-f2	Dramatic soprano (lyric soprano)	Sustained. In parts demands considerable dramatic intensity as well as command of high pp.
Spe modo vivitur	A-e1	e-d1	Bass or baritone	Sustained, vigorous. In parts demands considerable dramatic intensity.
Urbis Syon aurea	d-a1	g-e1	Tenor	Very sustained. In parts demands considerable dramatic intensity.

See also "Six Old English Songs" (J. Church Co.), among them the well-known "The lark now leaves his wat'ry nest."

C. HUBERT PARRY (Br.)
(1848-1918)

TITLE	COMP.	TESS.	TYPE	REMARKS
A Welsh lullaby	f1-f2	a1-f2	Most suitable for soprano	Sustained, delicate. (Novello)
Love is a bauble	c1-eb2	eb1-bb1	Medium or low voices	Rapid, vigorous, humorous. Demands some flexibility. (Novello)
Under the greenwood tree	c1-e2	e1-d2	Most suitable for men's voices	Spirited, vigorous (Novello)
Why so pale and wan	c#1-e2	d1-d2	All voices, except a very light soprano	Animated, humorous. (Novello)

NORMAN PETERKIN (Br.)

TITLE	COMP.	TESS.	TYPE	REMARKS
I heard a piper piping	g1-f2	g1-d2	All voices	Somber, subdued. See Arnold Bax. (Oxford)

TITLE	COMP.	TESS.	TYPE	REMARKS
So, we'll go no more a-roving	db1-d2		Medium or low voices	Sustained, rather subdued. (Oxford)
The fiddler	f1-f2 (ab2)	f1-eb2	High or medium voices	Animated, rhythmical. (Oxford)
The galliass	c1-e2	e1-b1	Medium or low voices	Slow, somewhat dra-matic. Interpretatively not easy. (Oxford)
The garden of bamboos	eb1-f2	f1-eb2	Women's voices, except a heavy alto	Delicate, sustained. (Oxford)

EDWARD PURCELL (Br.)

TITLE	COMP.	TESS.	TYPE	REMARKS
Passing by	f#1-f#2	a1-e2 (H)	Most suit-able for men's voices	Sustained, graceful. (Ditson) This pleasant, tuneful little song is, curiously enough, often attributed to the pen of the great Henry Purcell and is even sometimes programmed as such.

ROGER QUILTER (Br.)

The songs of Roger Quilter have attained a wide popularity in the United States as well as in Great Britain. Effective, well written and possessing excellent texts, they need little introduction.

TITLE	COMP.	TESS.	TYPE	REMARKS
Blow, blow, thou winter wind	e1-g#2	g#1-e2	All voices, except a very light soprano	Vigorous. (Boosey)
Come away, death	e1-g2	g1-e2	All voices	Sustained. (Boosey)
Dream valley (from "Three Songs of William Blake")	eb1-gb2	gb1-eb2	Most suit-able for high or medium voices	Sustained, delicate. (Winthrop Rogers)
Fair house of joy (from "Seven Elizabethan Lyrics")	f1-ab2	ab1-f2 (H)	All voices, except bass or alto	Sustained. Has effective climaxes. (Boosey)
Fill a glass with golden wine	e1-g#2	g#1-e2 (H)	Most suit-able for men's voices	Very vigorous. (Boosey)
Go lovely rose	f1-gb2	gb1-eb2 (H)	All voices	Sustained. See J. A. Carpenter. (Chappell)
It was a lover and his lass	f1-ab2	ab1-f2	All voices	Animated, light. (Boosey)
I will go with my father a-ploughing	d1-f2 (g2)	g1-d2 (H)	Men's voices	Not slow. In folk vein. (Elkin)

TITLE	COMP.	TESS.	TYPE	REMARKS
Love's philosophy	d1-a2	a1-f2 (H)	All voices	Very animated, effective Demands an accomplished pianist. (Boosey)
Music when soft voices die	f1-g2	bb1-f2 (H)	All voices	Sustained. (Winthrop Rogers)
Now sleeps the crimson petal	eb1-gb2	gb1-eb2 (H)	All voices	Slow, very delicate. (Boosey)
O mistress mine	d1-g2	g1-e2	All voices	Animated, light. (Boosey)
Song of the blackbird	e1-g2	g1-e2 (H)	Not suitable for very low voices	Very animated, effective. See "The Nightingale has a Lyre of Gold" by Whelpley. (Boosey)
The fuchsia tree	c#1-g#2	g#1-e2	All voices	Graceful. (Winthrop Rogers)
To daisies	eb1-ab2	ab1-f2	Not too suitable for very low voices	Sustained, delicate. (Boosey)

OSCAR RASBACH

Trees	c1-g#2	e1-c#2 (H)	All voices	Sustained, effective. (Schirmer)

JAMES H. ROGERS

At parting	c#1-f#2	g#1-d#2	All voices	A sustained, graceful encore song. (Schirmer)
Cloud shadows	c1-e2	f1-db2	High or medium voices	Sustained, delicate, subdued. (Schirmer)
The last song	e1-ab2	a1-e2	All voices, except a light soprano	Vigorous, effective. (Schirmer)
The star	c1-ab2	ab1-f2 (H)	All voices	Sustained, effective. (Schirmer)

LANDON RONALD (Br.)

Down in the forest (from "A Cycle of Life")	e1-a2	g1-f#2	All voices	Sustained, for the most part subdued, effective. (Ricordi)
O lovely night	eb1-g2 (bb2)	f1-eb2	All voices	Sustained, effective. (Enoch)
The dove	c1-g2	f1-f2	Most suitable for women's voices	Sustained. (Enoch)

ALEC ROWLEY (Br.)

Pretty Betty	db1-eb2		Men's voices	Sustained, rather delicate. (Oxford)
The toll-gate house	c1-e2	e1-b1	All voices	Very animated, for the most part very subdued (Winthrop Rogers)

EDMUND RUBBRA (Br.)

TITLE	COMP.	TESS.	TYPE	REMARKS
A widow bird sat mourning	e1-g2	g1-e2	Most suitable for high voices	Slow, sustained, subdued. (Oxford)
In dark weather	b-g2 (b2)	e1-e2	Not suitable for very light high voices	Slow, somber. Demands in parts considerable dramatic intensity, especially in the final climax. (Augener)

WALTER M. RUMMEL

TITLE	COMP.	TESS.	TYPE	REMARKS
Ecstasy	gb1-ab2 (H)	ab1-f2	All voices	Very animated, the vocal line sustained, effective. (Schirmer)
June	d1-g2 (H)	g1-e2	All voices	Sustained. Has an effective final climax. (Schirmer)

LOUIS V. SAAR

TITLE	COMP.	TESS.	TYPE	REMARKS
The little gray dove	d1-bb2	bb1-f2	Most suitable for light soprano	An animated, light encore song. (Schirmer)

JOHN SACCO

TITLE	COMP.	TESS.	TYPE	REMARKS
Mexican serenade	f1-gb2	a1-f2	All voices	Animated, light, humorous. Demands facile articulation. (Boston Music Co.)
Never the nightingale	eb1-gb2	f1-f2	High voices	Sustained. Demands in parts considerable dramatic intensity. (Galaxy)
Rapunzel	f#1-bb2	bb1-f#2	Women's voices	Animated, effective, the vocal line sustained. (Schirmer)
Strictly germ-proof	d1-f2	a1-e2	High or medium voices	Animated, light, humorous. Demands facile articulation and some flexibility. (Schirmer)

MARY TURNER SALTER

TITLE	COMP.	TESS.	TYPE	REMARKS
Cry of Rachel	c1-ab2	f1-f2	Women's voices, except very light soprano	Animated, dramatic, effective. (Schirmer)
The pine tree	f#1-f#2	g#1-d#2	All voices	Sustained. (Schirmer)

TITLE	COMP.	TESS.	TYPE	REMARKS

WILFRED SANDERSON (Br.)

TITLE	COMP.	TESS.	TYPE	REMARKS
Captain Mac'	A-f#1	d-d1	Men's voices	Spirited, effective, humorous ballad. (Boosey)

EDWIN SCHNEIDER

TITLE	COMP.	TESS.	TYPE	REMARKS
Flower rain	d1-a2	f1-f2 (H)	Light soprano	Animated, light. Demands an accomplished pianist Effective encore song. (Clayton F. Summy)
The cave	d1-f2 (a2)	f1-d2	All voices	Sustained. Has an effective climax. (Boosey)

WILLIAM SCHUMAN

TITLE	COMP.	TESS.	TYPE	REMARKS
Orpheus with his lute	c1-f#2	f1-e2	High or medium voices	Sustained, subdued. See Vaughan Williams. (Schirmer)

ALICIA ANN SCOTT (PERRENOT)

TITLE	COMP.	TESS.	TYPE	REMARKS
Think on me	f#1-g2	a1-d2 (H)	All voices	Very sustained encore song. (Galaxy)

CYRIL SCOTT (Br.)

Cyril Scott, a prolific British composer, has written a great number of songs, many of which have attained wide popularity. His harmonic scheme is mildly influenced by Debussy, but his vocal line is always conventionally singable and effective.

TITLE	COMP.	TESS.	TYPE	REMARKS
Blackbird's song	d1-g2	f1-f2	Most suitable for high voices	Animated, effective. Demands some flexibility. (Elkin)
Lullaby	d1-f2 (g#2)	f1-d2 (H)	Women's voices	Very sustained, graceful, very subdued. (Galaxy)
Night song	c1-f2	eb1-d2	All voices	Delicate, not fast. (Elkin)
Rain	d#1-f#2	f#1-d2 (H)	Not too suitable for very low voices	Very delicate. Demands good command of high pp. (Elkin)
Songs without words (1) Tranquillity (2) Pastorale	d1-c3	f1-f2	Soprano	Two vocalises for soprano. (Ricordi)
Time of day	e1-g2	a1-e2 (H)	Men's voices	Rapid, rhythmical. Demands some flexibility and facile articulation. (Elkin)
The sands of Dee	eb1-g2	eb1-eb2 (H)	All voices	A short narrative song. (Elkin)

TITLE	COMP.	TESS.	TYPE	REMARKS
The unforeseen	d1-a2	f#1-e2 (H)	All voices	Sustained. Has an effective climax. (Elkin)
Water-lilies	eb1-g2	f1-d2 (H)	All voices	Sustained, delicate. Demands good command of high pp. (Elkin)

JOHN PRINDLE SCOTT

TITLE	COMP.	TESS.	TYPE	REMARKS
The wind's in the south	d1-c3	g1-g2	Soprano	Animated, light, effective. (R. L. Huntzinger)

EARL CRANSTON SHARP

TITLE	COMP.	TESS.	TYPE	REMARKS
Japanese death song	b-e2	c1-g1	All voices	Sustained, somber. (Ditson)

MARTIN SHAW (Br.)

Martin Shaw, perhaps one of the most skillful among the contemporary British song writers, has written a considerable number of distinctive songs, many of which have attained a well-deserved popularity.

TITLE	COMP.	TESS.	TYPE	REMARKS
Cuckoo	f-f2		All voices	Light, delicate. (Curwen)
Down by the Salley gardens	b-d1	e1-b1	Most suitable for men's voices	Sustained, subdued and delicate. See Rebecca Clarke, and the Hughes arrangement of an old Irish folk tune with these words added. (Curwen)
Heffle cuckoo fair	e1-e2 (a2)		Not suitable for very low voices	Animated, light. Demands facile articulation. (Curwen)
Lullaby	c1-d2	e1-c2	Women's voices	Sustained, delicate. See Cyril Scott. (Curwen)
O Falmouth is a fine town	c1-e2	e1-c#2	Most suitable for baritone	Animated. Demands facile articulation. (Curwen)
Over the sea	d1-f2	f1-d2	All voices	Sustained. (Curwen)
Song of the palanquin bearers	e1-f2	b1-e2	Most suitable for high light voices	Light and animated. Demands good sense of rhythm and facile articulation. (Curwen)
The cavalier's escape	Bb-d1 (f1)	d-d1	Baritone	A spirited, vigorous ballad. Demands facile articulation. (Curwen)
The land of heart's desire	c1-e2 (g2)	e1-b1	Most suitable for medium or low voices	Sustained, subdued, somewhat declamatory. (Curwen)

TITLE	COMP.	TESS.	TYPE	REMARKS

OLEY SPEAKS

TITLE	COMP.	TESS.	TYPE	REMARKS
Morning	c#1-g2 (a2)	a1-f2 (H)	All voices	A slow introduction and an animated, effective main section. (Schirmer)
On the road to Mandalay	B♭-e♭1 (f1)	e♭-e♭1	Baritone	A vigorous, spirited ballad. (Schirmer)
Sylvia	d1-g2	d1-d2 (H)	All voices	Sustained, effective. (Schirmer)

SIR ARTHUR SULLIVAN (Br.)
(1842-1900)

TITLE	COMP.	TESS.	TYPE	REMARKS
Orpheus with his lute	d1-g2 (b♭2)	f1-f2	All voices	Spirited. Demands occasionally good command of high pp. (Generally available)
Sigh no more, ladies	e1-g2 (a2)	f#1-e2	Not too suitable for very low voices	Not fast. Demands some flexibility. (Generally available)
The lost chord	e♭1-a♭2	g1-d♭2	Not too suitable for very light high voices	Sustained. Has a very effective final climax. (Generally available)
The willow song	b-e2	b-b1	Most suitable for alto	Slow, subdued. (Generally available)

COLIN TAYLOR (Br.)

TITLE	COMP.	TESS.	TYPE	REMARKS
The windmill	d1-c2		All voices	A gently humorous character song. (Oxford)

DEEMS TAYLOR

TITLE	COMP.	TESS.	TYPE	REMARKS
A song for lovers	d1-f2	g1-e♭2	All voices	Sustained, very subdued. (Fischer)
Captain Stratton's fancy	B♭-f1	d-d1	Bass or baritone	Vigorous, spirited, humorous. (Fischer)
The rivals	e1-g2	g1-e2	Not too suitable for very low voices	Animated, light. (Fischer)

RANDALL THOMPSON

TITLE	COMP.	TESS.	TYPE	REMARKS
⌐My master hath a garden	e♭1-e♭2	f1-c2	All voices	Sustained, graceful. (E. C. Schirmer, Boston)
Velvet shoes	c1-e2	f1-c2	All voices	Delicate. Demands good sense of rhythm and an accomplished pianist. (E. C. Schirmer, Boston)

TITLE	COMP.	TESS.	TYPE	REMARKS

DAVID CLEGHORN THOMSON (Br.)

TITLE	COMP.	TESS.	TYPE	REMARKS
Epitaph	b-d2	d1-d2	Most suitable for medium or low voices	Sustained, subdued. See Ivor Gurney. (Cramer)
The birds	c1-e2 (a)	e1-c2	Not too suitable for very light high voices	Sustained. In the manner of a chorale. See Alec Rowley, Vera Buck. (Cramer)
The knight of Bethlehem	eb1-g2	eb1-c2	All voices	Sustained. Interpretatively not easy. (Novello)

FRANCIS TOYE (Br.)

TITLE	COMP.	TESS.	TYPE	REMARKS
In Dorset	b-e2	e1-d2	Medium or low voices	Not slow, somber, sustained. (Curwen)
The inn	Bb-e1	d-d1	Baritone	Very animated, rhythmical. Interpretatively not easy. Has a somber sustained final section. Demands an accomplished pianist. (Curwen)

BRYCESON TREHEARNE

TITLE	COMP.	TESS.	TYPE	REMARKS
A little song for sleep	eb1-g2	g1-eb2	Soprano	Sustained, delicate. (Schirmer)
A widow bird sat mourning	f#1-ab2	g1-f2	Most suitable for light soprano	Not fast. Demands some flexibility and a good command of high pp. See Edmund Rubbra. (Schirmer)
Anthony Crundle	c1-e2	f1-d2	Medium or high voices	Animated. Demands facile articulation. (Boston Music Co.)
Corals	f1-f2 (f#2)		Most suitable for women's voices	Sustained, delicate. (Schirmer)
My lady sleep	e1-g2	g1-e2	High voices	Sustained, delicate. (Boston Music Co.)
The booted hens	d1-f#2	f1-e2	High voices	Animated. Demands facile articulation. Has an effective final climax. (Schirmer)

CHARLES VALE (Br.)

TITLE	COMP.	TESS.	TYPE	REMARKS
Devotion	db1-gb2	gb1-eb2	All voices, except a very light soprano	Sustained. See "Fair House of Joy" by Roger Quilter. (Asherberg, Hopwood & Crew)

RALPH VAUGHAN WILLIAMS
(1872-   )

In his songs Vaughan Williams, one of the foremost contemporary British composers, attempts to fuse the melodic and rhythmic patterns of the folk songs of the British Isles with contemporary harmonic and poetic material. Since most of his songs do not demand an extensive range, are nearly impeccable in prosody, and are excellently written for the voice, they present hardly any vocal problems. Some of his songs, however, like the admirable "Water Mill" may prove interpretatively somewhat complex, because of the purely descriptive and rather impersonal character of the text.

Vaughan Williams has made admirable arrangements of a great number of English folk songs, most of which are published in the Novello collection of English folk songs. The five English folk songs containing the well-known arrangement of "Rolling in the Dew" are published by the Oxford University Press.

TITLE	COMP.	TESS.	TYPE	REMARKS
Bright is the ring of words (Songs of Travel)	db1-gb2	f1-d2 (H)	All voices, except a very light soprano	Very sustained. (Boosey)
Linden Lea	e1-f#2	a1-e2 (H)	All voices	Sustained. In folk vein. (Boosey)
On Wenlock edge	d-a1		Tenor	A cycle of six songs (text by A. E. Housman) for tenor and pianoforte and string quartet. (Boosey)
Orpheus with his lute	d1-g2	g1-f#2	All voices	Very sustained, subdued. Perhaps one of the most beautiful contemporary settings of this Shakespeare poem. (Keith Prowse)
Silent noon	c1-eb2	g1-d2	All voices	Slow and sustained. See Wilfred Sanderson. (Ashdown)
The roadside fire (Songs of Travel)	eb1-ab2	ab1-f2 (H)	Most suitable for men's voices	Animated, delicate. The vocal line is sustained.
The vagabond (Songs of Travel)	d#1-g2	e1-e2 (H)	Men's voices	Vigorous, rhythmical.
The water mill	c1-d2		All voices	A descriptive tranquil narrative song. Demands facile articulation and an accomplished pianist. (Oxford)

Three Poems by Walt Whitman

(1) Nocturne	b-f2	f#1-d2	Not suitable for light high	Not fast, somewhat declamatory, very subdued. Demands good

TITLE	COMP.	TESS.	TYPE	REMARKS
(1) Nocturne cont'd			voices	command of high pp. Interpretatively not easy. See Ernst Bacon's, "This is thy hour, o soul." (Oxford)
(2) A clear midnight	e1-f2	g1-d2	All voices	Slow, very sustained, subdued. (Oxford)
(3) Joy, shipmate, joy!	e1-f2	g1-e2	Not suitable for light voices	Vigorous, animated. (Oxford)

Two Poems by Seumas O'Sullivan

TITLE	COMP.	TESS.	TYPE	REMARKS
(1) The twilight people	c1-f2	c1-c2	Medium or low voices	Subdued, somewhat declamatory. (Oxford)
(2) A piper	c1-eb2	d1-d2	Medium or low voices	Rapid and light. Demands facile articulation. See M. Head and A. Benjamin. (Oxford)

RUGGERO VENÉ

TITLE	COMP.	TESS.	TYPE	REMARKS
The rats	e1-a2	a1-f2	High voices	Animated, humorous encore song. (Ricordi)

BERNARD WAGENAAR

TITLE	COMP.	TESS.	TYPE	REMARKS
From a very little sphinx	c1-f2		Most suitable for women's voices	Seven short, amusing poems by Edna St. Vincent Milley. Interpretatively not easy. (Schirmer)
May night	c1-e2 (g2)	e1-db2	All voices, except a very light soprano	Slow, sustained. (Schirmer)

HARRIET WARE

TITLE	COMP.	TESS.	TYPE	REMARKS
By the fountain	f1-c3	g1-f2	Coloratura soprano	A delicate encore song. (Flammer)

PETER WARLOCK (Philip Heseltine) (Br.)
(1894-1930)

In his songs Peter Warlock seems to attempt a fusion of Elizabethan poetry, English folk melos and a contemporary harmonic idiom. Well written for the voice, impeccable in prosody, his settings of old English poems have become very popular since his death. They present no particular performance problem except that of style, which involves the suc-

TITLE	COMP.	TESS.	TYPE	REMARKS

cessful blending of the three elements mentioned above, and which may not always be instantly achieved.

TITLE	COMP.	TESS.	TYPE	REMARKS
As ever I saw	db1-gb2	f1-db2	Most suitable for men's voices	Spirited. The melody of the first verse is inverted (backwards) in the second verse. (Winthrop Rogers)
Captain Stratton's fancy	c-f1	c-d1	Men's voices	Vigorous, spirited ballad. See version by Deems Taylor. (Augener)
Consider	c1-g2	f1-d2	Not too suitable for very light high voices	Very animated, effective. Demands an accomplished pianist. (Oxford)
Cradle song	d1-f2	f1-d2	Women's voices	Delicate, sustained. (Oxford)
Good ale	c-f1	d-d1	Men's voices	A rapid, rollicking drinking song, very effective. Demands facile articulation and a good sense of rhythm. (Augener)
In an arbour green	d1-g2	e1-e2	Men's voices	Fast and gay. Demands an accomplished pianist. (Paterson)
Jillian of Berry	d1-f2	f1-d2	Most suitable for men's voices	A short jolly song. Rhythmically difficult. Demands an accomplished pianist. (Oxford)
Passing by	d1-g2	g1-e2	Most suitable for men's voices	Sustained. See the famous setting of this poem by Edward Purcell. (Oxford)
Pretty ring time	d1-g2	eb1-eb2	All voices	Light and spirited setting of Shakespeare's "It Was a Lover and His Lass." (Oxford)
Rest sweet nymphs	f-f2	g1-eb2	Most suitable for men's voices	Delicate, sustained. (Oxford)
Sleep	d1-eb2	g1-d2	All voices, except a very light soprano	Slow and very sustained. Musically and interpretatively not easy. (Oxford)
The passionate shepherd	d1-g2	f#1-e2	High or medium voices	Very animated, light. (Elkin)
The toper's song	B-e1	e-b	Baritone	A vigorous, amusing drinking song. (Winthrop Rogers)

TITLE	COMP.	TESS.	TYPE	REMARKS

ELINOR REMICK WARREN

TITLE	COMP.	TESS.	TYPE	REMARKS
White horses of the sea	f1-g2	bb1-f2	Not suitable for very light high voices	Animated, effective. (Schirmer)

WINTTER WATTS

TITLE	COMP.	TESS.	TYPE	REMARKS
Blue are her eyes	f#1-f#2	a1-e2	Not suitable for very low voices	Sustained. (Ditson)
Little shepherd's song	g1-bb2	g1-e2	Most suitable for soprano	Light, effective. (Ricordi)
Stresa (from "Vignettes of Italy")	d1-bb2	ab1-f#2 (H)	Women's voices	Sustained. Demands in parts considerable dramatic intensity. (Ditson)
The poet sings	eb1-ab2	ab1-f2	Not too suitable for very low voices	Sustained. (Ditson)
Wings of night	c#1-g2	f#1-f#2	Most suitable for high voices	Subdued, sustained. Demands good command of high pp. (Schirmer)

POWELL WEAVER

TITLE	COMP.	TESS.	TYPE	REMARKS
Moon-marketing	e1-g2	g1-e2	All voices	Light, sprightly encore song. (Schirmer)
The abbot of Derry	b-g2	g1-e2 (H)	Most suitable for men's voices	Rapid, humorous. Demands facile articulation. (Schirmer)

BENJAMIN WHELPLEY

TITLE	COMP.	TESS.	TYPE	REMARKS
I know a hill	f1-f2		All voices	Sustained. (Boston Music Co.)
The nightingale has a lyre of gold	f#1-g#2	g#1-e2	All voices	Animated, effective. See Delius. (Boston Music Co.)

JACQUES WOLFE

TITLE	COMP.	TESS.	TYPE	REMARKS
De glory road	A-f1	d-d1	Medium or low men's voices	Effective ballad in Negro dialect. (Schirmer)
Gwine to hebb'n	B-e1	e-e1	Medium or low men's voices	Effective ballad in Negro dialect. (Schirmer)
The janitor's boy	eb1-f2 (H)		Women's voices	A sprightly encore song. (Schirmer)

TITLE	COMP.	TESS.	TYPE	REMARKS

R. HUNTINGTON WOODMAN

TITLE	COMP.	TESS.	TYPE	REMARKS
A birthday	f1-b♭2	a♭1-f2 (H)	High or medium voices	Animated, effective. (Schirmer)
I am thy harp	a♭-e♭2	f1-d♭2	Low voices	Sustained, effective. (Schirmer)
My heart is a lute	d1-f♯2	g1-d2	All voices	Sustained. (Schirmer)

AMY WORTH

TITLE	COMP.	TESS.	TYPE	REMARKS
Midsummer	e1-a2	a1-f♯2 (H)	All voices	An effective encore song. (Schirmer)

ITALIAN

The song literature of Italy is comparatively small, most of the vocal music having been written for the stage. Only a few Italian composers, mostly contemporary, have written songs more than occasionally. The foremost among them are perhaps Respighi, Pizzetti, and Castelnuovo-Tedesco.

Very few songs of the nineteenth century are included in this list as most of them seem to possess only historical interest at the present time. The few songs of Rossini and Donizetti, still used as display pieces, are listed below; songs of Verdi are perhaps among his most unrepresentative compositions; songs of Sgambati, Martucci and Bossi, historically of no inconsiderable importance, can be highly recommended to those who are interested in tracing the emergence of contemporary song in Italy, but are otherwise of little practical value in so far as the present-day singer and the public outside of Italy are concerned. The inclusion of some songs by Tosti, musically no doubt inferior to the former, seemed warranted, however, in view of the fact that they are extraordinarily singable and effective, and can be used to great advantage as teaching material.

Only a few songs of Malipiero and Casella, two of the foremost contemporary Italian composers, have been included in this list, as they are for the most part very complex and of obviously experimental nature.

Those who are particularly interested in the development of the Italian song literature may be interested in acquainting themselves with songs by Alaleona, Alfano, Davico, Rocca and Tommasini among the contemporary composers, and with songs and arrangements of folk songs of Wolf-Ferrari, Pick-Mangiagalli, Pierraccini and Sinigaglia among the Italian composers of the late nineteenth and early twentieth century.

LUIGI ARDITI
(1822-1903)

TITLE	COMP.	TESS.	TYPE	REMARKS
Il bacio	c#1-b2 (d3)	f#1-f#2	Light soprano	A somewhat florid waltz song. (Schirmer)
Parla	c#1-b2 (d3)	g1-g2	Coloratura soprano	A florid waltz song. (Schirmer)

ALBERTO BIMBONI

Sospiri miei	e1-eb2	f1-d2	All voices	Sustained. (Ricordi)

GAETANO BRAGA
(1829-1907)

O quali mi risvegliano (Angel's serenade)	d1-g2	g1-e2	All voices	Sustained, effective. (Generally available)

RENATO BROGI
(1873-1924)

Gotine gialle	d1-g2	g1-e2	Most suitable for women's voices,	Sustained, very delicate. Demands good command of high pp. (Homeyer)

TITLE	COMP.	TESS.	TYPE	REMARKS
Gotine gialle cont'd.			except a very heavy contralto	

ALFREDO CASELLA
(1883 -)

TITLE	COMP.	TESS.	TYPE	REMARKS
Il bove	db1-f2	d1-d2	Medium or low voices	A robust, vigorous, sustained hymn in praise of an ox. Musically not easy. (Ricordi)
Sonnet (French text)	b-g2	e1-e2	All voices	Slow, for the most part subdued, sustained. (Mathot, Paris)

Tre Canzone Trecentesche
(Ricordi)

TITLE	COMP.	TESS.	TYPE	REMARKS
(1) Giovane bella, luce del mio core	c1-g#2	e1-e2	High voices	Delicate, sustained. Demands some flexibility.
(2) Fuor de la bella gaiba	c#1-a2	a1-f#2	Light soprano	Slow, delicate, subdued. Demands considerable flexibility and a good command of high pp. Musically not easy. Demands an accomplished pianist.
(3) Amante sono, vaghiccia di voi	d#1-g2	f#1-e2	High voices, except a very light soprano	Animated, declamatory, vigorous. Musically and interpretatively not easy. Demands an accomplished pianist.

MARIO CASTELNUOVO-TEDESCO
(1895 -)

Castelnuovo-Tedesco, one of the most noteworthy of contemporary Italian composers, has written a considerable number of very excellent songs to English, French, Spanish, as well as, of course, to Italian texts. His harmonic idiom is somewhat more complex than that of Respighi and Pizzetti, yet hardly as frankly experimental as that of Casella or Malipiero. "Ninna Nanna," "L'infinito," "Tamburino," and the delightfully humorous "La ermita de San Simon" are particularly recommended to those who wish to acquaint themselves with his style of writing.

Editions: Ricordi
Forlivesi

TITLE	COMP.	TESS.	TYPE	REMARKS
Ballatella	d1-g2	e1-e2	Most suitable for high voices	Light, animated. Demands very facile articulation and an accomplished pianist. Interpretatively not easy.

TITLE	COMP.	TESS.	TYPE	REMARKS
Cadix (French text)	c1-g2	g1-eb2	Soprano or mezzo-soprano	Spirited. Demands some flexibility. Musically not easy. See "Les filles de Cadix by Délibes.

Coplas

Out of the eleven "coplas," traditional Spanish folk poems, that Castelnuovo-Tedesco has set to music, only three are listed, selected almost at random. Any singer interested in contemporary music and able to cope with some of its difficulties will find these songs very worthy of his attention.

See also "Stelle cadenti" (twelve traditional Tuscan Folk poems) set to music in somewhat similar manner.

TITLE	COMP.	TESS.	TYPE	REMARKS
En medio de lo mar	f1-g2	g#1-f2	High voices	Slow. Musically not easy. Demands considerable dramatic intensity in parts and an accomplished pianist.
Gitano, porque vas preso	e#1-g2	g#1-d#2	High voices, except a very light soprano	Declamatory, dramatic Musically and interpretatively not easy. Demands an accomplished pianist.
Hermosa blanca	c#1-f2	g1-e2	All voices	Slow. Has a characteristic rhythm of a Spanish folk song. Musically not easy. Demands an accomplished pianist.

TITLE	COMP.	TESS.	TYPE	REMARKS
Il passo delle Nazarene (from "Bricciole")	c1-e2	e1-c2	All voices	Slow, subdued, somewhat declamatory. Demands facile articulation.
Leggenda	d1-f2	f1-d2	Soprano or mezzo-soprano	Interpretatively and musically not easy.
La ermita de San Simon	eb1-g2	f1-f2	Most suitable for high voices	Light and humorous. Demands some flexibility. Interpretatively not easy. Demands an accomplished pianist.
L'infinito	c1-f2 (g2)	eb1-c2	Not too suitable for very light high voices	Slow, subdued. Musically and interpretatively not easy.
Ninna Nanna	d1-f2	g1-e2	Soprano or mezzo-soprano	Sustained, delicate.
Recuerdo (English text)	d1-g2	a1-f2	Most suitable for high voices	Rather animated. Demands an accomplished pianist.

TITLE	COMP.	TESS.	TYPE	REMARKS
Tamburino	d1-f2	d1-d2	Not suitable for very light high voices	Very rapid, rhythmic. Demands very facile articulation and an accomplished pianist. Musically not easy.

Twelve Shakespeare Songs

(Chester)

TITLE	COMP.	TESS.	TYPE	REMARKS
Old song (Come away, come away, Death)	e1-f2	f#2-d2	Most suitable for medium voices	Slow and sustained.
O mistress mine	e1-g2	g1-e2	Most suitable for tenor	Animated. Demands an excellent pianist.
Orpheus	c#1-a2	g1-e2	Most suitable for light soprano	Slow and sustained. See "Orpheus with his Lute" by Vaughan Williams among many other settings of this poem.

PIETRO CIMARA
(1887 -)

Pietro Cimara, chiefly known in this country for his charming "Fiocca la neve" has written a great number of very effective songs. Among those listed below, the "Non più" and the "Scherzo" are perhaps musically most rewarding.

Editions: Forlivesi
Ricordi
Some reprints by Schirmer

TITLE	COMP.	TESS.	TYPE	REMARKS
A una rosa	eb1-g2	f1-d2	All voices	Sustained.
Canto di primavera	d1-g2 (a2)	a1-f2	Not too suitable for very light voices	A spirited, very effective song. Demands an accomplished pianist.
Fiocca la neve	g1-g2	a1-e2	All voices	Sustained, delicate.
Melodia autumnale	eb1-g2	g1-e2	All voices	Sustained.
Non più	e1-f#2	f#1-d#2	All voices	Sustained, subdued. Interpretatively not easy.
Ondina	d#1-a2	b1-g2	Not too suitable for low voices	Light and delicate.
Paesaggio	db1-f2	gb1-eb2	All voices	Sustained. Demands good command of high pp. and an accomplished pianist.

TITLE	COMP.	TESS.	TYPE	REMARKS
Scherzo	d1-g2	g1-d2	Women's voices	Light and animated. See Respighi
Stornellata marinara	d1-g2	bb1-f2	All voices	An effective barcarole.
Vecchia chitarra	c#1-f#2	f#1-d2	Most suitable for medium voices	Sustained. Demands an accomplished pianist.

VINCENZO DAVICO
(1889 -)

TITLE	COMP.	TESS.	TYPE	REMARKS
Come un cipresso notturno (No. 3 of "Tre Liriche")	db1-c2		Most suitable for low or medium voices	Slow, very subdued. (Ricordi)

STEPHANO DONAUDY
(1879-1925)

The charming imitations of the eighteenth century Italian airs and canzoni by Donaudy have long been popular among teachers and singers. Unpretentious, well written for the voice and expertly made they fully deserve their popularity.

The question why one should not prefer the genuine examples of this style, of which so many are now available, to even the most successful imitation of it, is one that only the individual singer can seem to answer.

Editions: Ricordi
Schirmer

TITLE	COMP.	TESS.	TYPE	REMARKS
Ah mai non cessate	eb1-ab2	g1-eb2	High voices	Rapid. Demands considerable flexibility and facile articulation.
Amorosi miei giorni	c1-g2	f1-d2	All voices	Slow and sustained. Demands some flexibility.
Cuor mio, cuor mio non vedi	c1-g2	f1-d2	All voices	Light and animated.
Freschi luoghi	db1-ab2	ab1-f2	Most suitable for high voices	Delicate, graceful. Demands some flexibility.
O bei nidi d'amore	db1-ab2	ab1-f2	All voices	Slow, very sustained.
O del mio amato ben	eb1-f2	ab1-eb2	All voices	Slow and sustained.
Perduto ho la speranza	d1-bb2	g1-eb2	All voices	Very sustained.
Quando ti rivedrò	d1-f#2	f#1-d2	Not too suitable for very light high voices	Very slow and sustained.
Se tra l'erba	d#1-f#2	e1-c#2	All voices	Light and animated.
Spirate pur, spirate	eb1-g2	g1-eb2	All voices	Animated. Demands considerable flexibility.

TITLE	COMP.	TESS.	TYPE	REMARKS
Vaghissima sembianza	e1-a2	a1-f#2	All voices	Slow and sustained.

GAETANO DONIZETTI
(1797-1848)

TITLE	COMP.	TESS.	TYPE	REMARKS
La Zingara	d#1-a2	a1-f2	Light soprano	Rapid, florid, brilliant. (Schirmer)

RUGGIERO LEONCAVALLO
(1858-1919)

TITLE	COMP.	TESS.	TYPE	REMARKS
Mattinata	c1-ab2	g1-f2 (H)	All voices	Animated, very effective. (Generally available)

FRANCESCO MALIPIERO
(1882 -)

TITLE	COMP.	TESS.	TYPE	REMARKS
Ballata	d1-g2	f#-e2	High or medium voices	Declamatory, not fast. Demands facile articulation. (Chester)
Inno a Maria nostra donna	eb1-f2	f#1-eb2	All voices	Slow, declamatory, grave. (Chester)
La madre folle (from "Sette Canzoni")	d1-ab2	g1-f2	Soprano	Dramatic, declamatory. Vocally, musically, and interpretatively quite complex. (Chester)
L'eco	e1-g2	a1-f#2	Most suitable for high, light voices	Delicate, animated. Demands good command of high pp. and an accomplished pianist. (Chester)

Quattro Sonetti del Burchiello
(Pizzi & Co., Bologna)

TITLE	COMP.	TESS.	TYPE	REMARKS
(1) Cacio stillato	d1-e2	f#-d#2	Soprano; not suitable for very light high soprano	Interpretatively and musically not easy. Demands facile articulation.
(2) Va in mercato, Giorgin	e1-g2	a1-e2	Soprano; not suitable for very light high soprano	Rapid, rhythmical. Demands facile articulation. Musically not easy. Demands an accomplished pianist
(3) Andando a uccellare	c#1-g2	f#1-d#2	Soprano; not suitable for very light high soprano	Interpretatively and musically not easy.
(4) Rose spinose	d1-e2	f#1-d#2	Soprano; not suitable	Very rhythmical, vigorous. Musically not easy.

TITLE	COMP.	TESS.	TYPE	REMARKS
(4) Rose spinose cont'd			for very light high soprano	Demands facile articulation.
Se tu m'ami (No. 2 of "I Tre Canti di Filomela)	d1-g2	g1-e2	Light soprano	Delicate, light. Demands some flexibility and an accomplished pianist. See "Se tu m'ami" by Pergolesi. (Universal)

ILDEBRANDO PIZZETTI
(1880 -)

TITLE	COMP.	TESS.	TYPE	REMARKS
Il Clefta prigione	c1-g2	eb1-c2	Not suitable for light voices	Vigorous, dramatic, somewhat declamatory. Musically and interpretatively not easy. Demands an accomplished pianist. (Forlivesi)
I pastori	d1-g2	e1-e2	Most suitable for high voices	Slow, subdued. Interpretatively not easy. Demands good command of high pp. and an accomplished pianist. (Forlivesi)
La madre al figlio lontano	d1-g2	e1-bb1	Women's voices, except a light soprano	Sustained, somewhat declamatory. Demands in parts considerable dramatic intensity. Musically and interpretatively not easy. (Forlivesi)
La vita fugge e non s'arresta un'ora	b-e2	e1-c#2	Most suitable for medium or low voices	Slow, somber, somewhat declamatory. Interpretatively not easy. (Ricordi)
Levommi il mio pensier	c1-g2	g1-f2	Most suitable for high voices	Slow, somewhat declamatory. Interpretatively not easy. (Ricordi)
Passeggiata	d1-a2	g1-e2	High voices, except a very light soprano	Somewhat declamatory. Demands in parts considerable dramatic intensity. Musically and interpretatively not easy. Demands an accomplished pianist. (Ricordi)
Quel rosignuol che si soave piagne	b#-a2	f#1-e2	Most suitable for high voices	Slow, sustained and subdued. Musically and interpretatively not easy. Demands an accomplished pianist. (Ricordi)

TITLE	COMP.	TESS.	TYPE	REMARKS
San Basilio	d1-g2	a1-e2	Not too suitable for very light high voices	Vigorous. Demands some flexibility and an accomplished pianist. (Ricordi)

OTTORINO RESPIGHI
(1879-1936)

Respighi, perhaps one of the most important contemporary Italian composers, has written a great number of excellent songs. "Nebbie" is, of course, one of the most famous and popular.

Among those listed below, "Abbandono," "Canto funebre," "E se un giorno tornasse," "Io sono la madre," "Mattino de luce," "Notte," "Pioggia" and "In alto mare" deserve, in my opinion, an equal popularity. Hardly any of his songs are musically difficult, though his harmonic and melodic idiom is contemporary. They are beautifully written for the voice and demand for the most part an accomplished pianist. His five "Canti all'antica," although written in old style, are by no means outright imitations of old masters in the Donaudy manner and are excellently suited for teaching purposes.

Edition: Ricordi

TITLE	COMP.	TESS.	TYPE	REMARKS
Abbandono	f1-g2	ab1-f2	All voices	Slow and sustained.
Au milieu du jardin (French text)	d1-f#2	a1-f#2	Most suitable for high light voices	Slow and sustained. Demands good command of high pp. Respighi has a number of songs to French texts. Another one listed here is "Le repos en Egypte."
Ballata	d1-f2	g1-d2	All voices	Slow. (from "Cinque canti all'antica," 5 simple songs in old style).
Bella porta di rubini	e1-g2	g1-e2	All voices	Sustained, graceful ("Cinque canti all'antica").
Canto funebre	b#-gb2	f#1-d#2	Heavy voices	Animated, somber and dramatic. Demands an accomplished pianist.
Canzone di Re Enzo	e1-g2	a1-d2	Men's voices	Sustained, rhythmical.
Contrasto	eb1-f2	f1-d2	All voices	Very sustained, delicate.
E se un giorno tornasse	c1-f2	f1-db2	Women's voices	A free recitative. Interpretatively not easy.
In alto mare	c#1-g#2	b1-e2	Not suitable for light voices	Dramatic, animated.
Invito alla danza	eb1-ab2	ab1-f2	Most suitable for men's voices	A light, graceful waltz song.

TITLE	COMP.	TESS.	TYPE	REMARKS
Io sono la madre	e1-e2	f#1-d2	Mezzo-soprano or alto	Slow, dramatic (from Quattro liriche su poemi Armeni'').
La najade	c#1-f#2	f#1-d#2	Most suitable for high voices	Delicate. Musically not easy.
L'udir tal volto	d1-g2	g1-d2	All voices	Sustained (''Cinque canti all'antica'').
Le repos en Egypte (French text)	c#1-g2	f#1-eb2	All voices	Sustained and subdued. Demands good command of high pp. Interpretatively not easy.
Ma come potrei	f1-f2	g1-d2	All voices	Slow, sustained (''Cinque canti all'antica'').
Mattinata	c1-ab2	d#1-d#2	Not too suitable for very light voices	Animated.
Mattino di luce	c1-gb2	f1-d2	Not too suitable for light voices	A solemn, very sustained prayer.
Nebbie	d#1-g#2	g#1-e2 (H)	Not too suitable for light voices	Slow and very sustained, dramatic. (Generally available)
Nevicata	eb1-g#2	eb1-c2	All voices	Slow and sustained.
Notte	db1-e2	f1-db2	Soprano or mezzo-soprano	Slow and sustained. Demands good command of pp.
Pioggia	f1-g2	a1-e2 (H)	Women's voices	Rapid. Demands an accomplished pianist.
Razzolan, sopra a l'aja, le galline	d1-g2	bb1-f2	Soprano	Rapid, gently humorous. Demands some flexibility and an accomplished pianist.
Scherzo	eb1-db2	g1-db2	Women's voices	Light. See Cimara.
Stornellatrice	eb1-ab2	ab1-eb2	All voices	A free, recitative-like song.
Venitelo a vedere	e1-g2	bb1-g2	Soprano	Sustained. Demands good command of high pp.
Viene di là lontan, lontan	c1-g2 (a2)	ab1-f2	Soprano	Very delicate, animated. Demands an accomplished pianist.

See also ''Il tramonto,'' a cycle of songs for mezzo-soprano and string quartet.

GIOACCHINO ROSSINI
(1792-1868)

La danza	e1-a2	a1-f2	Most suitable for	A bravura tarantella. Demands very rapid

TITLE	COMP.	TESS.	TYPE	REMARKS
La danza cont'd.			tenor	articulation and a good sense of rhythm. Note Rossini's metronome mark of ♪. -152, often taken at too fast a tempo. (Generally available)
La pastorella	e1-c3	g1-g2	Coloratura soprano or lyric soprano	Animated, light. Demands flexibility. (Arr. by La Forge, Fischer)
Stabat Mater Cujus animam	eb-db2	ab-f1	Tenor	Dramatic, majestic. The db2 is touched only once, so that the compass is really eb-bbb1.
Stabat Mater Fac ut portem	b-g#2	e1-e2	Alto or mezzo-soprano	Sustained. Demands some flexibility.
✓ Stabat Mater Inflammatus et accensus	c1-c3	g1-g2	Dramatic soprano (lyric soprano)	Solo with chorus. Majestic, dramatic. Demands some flexibility.
Stabat Mater Pro peccatis	A-e1	e-c#1	Bass	Majestic. Demands some flexibility and, in parts, considerable dramatic intensity.

The "Stabat Mater" score is generally available

FRANCESCO SANTOLIQUIDO
(1883 -)

Santoliguido's very effective songs are musically not difficult, although contemporary in feeling and idiom. The three "Poesie Persiane" to the Italian translations of Omar Khayyam seem perhaps most individual and representative of his songs.

Editions: Forlivesi

TITLE	COMP.	TESS.	TYPE	REMARKS
Alba di luna sul bosco	c#1-e2 (g#2)	f#1-d#2	All voices	Delicate and sustained. Has an effective ending (from "Canti della Sera").
Melancolie (French text)	c-eb2	g1-eb2	Women's voices, except a very light soprano	Slow and subdued. Interpretatively not easy.
Nel giardino	c1-f2	a1-e2	All voices, except a very light soprano	Sustained (from "7 poemi del Sole").

TITLE	COMP.	TESS.	TYPE	REMARKS
Poesia Persiana:				
1.	f1-f♯2	f♯1-eb2	All voices, except a very light soprano	Grave, declamatory.
2.	c1-g2	g1-eb2	All voices, except a very light soprano	Grave, declamatory, very effective. Demands an accomplished pianist.
3.	e1-g♯2	e1-e2	All voices, except a very light soprano	Sustained, declamatory.
Riflessi	e1-g♯2	b1-f♯2	High voices	Spirited, effective (from "7 poemi del Sole").
Tristezza crepuscolare	c1-gb2	db1-db2	Not too suitable for very light high voices	Slow and sustained (from "Canti della Sera").

FRANCESCO PAOLO TOSTI
(1846-1916)

TITLE	COMP.	TESS.	TYPE	REMARKS
Aprile	eb1-eb2		All voices, except a very light soprano	Sustained, effective. (Ricordi)
Good-bye (English text)	eb1-ab2	ab1-eb2	All voices	Sustained, very effective. At one time extraordinarily popular. (Generally available)
L'ultima canzone	d1-f2	f1-d2	All voices	Animated. Vocal line sustained. Effective. (Ricordi)
Mattinata	d1-f2	e1-d2	All voices	Sustained, effective. (Ricordi)
Non m'ama più	e1-f♯2	g♯1-d♯2	All voices	An effective, melodious drawing-room song. (Ricordi)

Note: See also other songs by Tosti, equally effective, among them: "Lamento d'amore," "Verrei morire," "Ninon," etc.

GIUSEPPE VERDI
(1813-1901)

TITLE	COMP.	TESS.	TYPE	REMARKS
Requiem Confutatis maledictis	A-e1	e-c♯1	Bass or baritone	Dramatic, in parts very sustained. (Score, Schirmer)
Requiem Ingemisco	f-bb1	bb-f1	Tenor	Sustained. In parts requires a good com-

-361-

TITLE	COMP.	TESS.	TYPE	REMARKS
Ingemisco (cont'd.)				mand of high pp. (Score, Schirmer)
Requiem Liber scriptus	b-ab2	d1-f2	Alto or mezzo-soprano	Dramatic, sustained. (Score, Schirmer)
Requiem Libera me	b-ab2	eb1-eb2	Dramatic soprano (lyric soprano)	Dramatic, somewhat declamatory. (Score, Schirmer)

SPANISH

The following list of songs by Spanish composers is admittedly a sketchy one. Contemporary Spanish composers seem to be so influenced by and so steeped in their native folklore that, as a consequence, a great number of their songs could be easily considered modernized concert transcriptions of Spanish folk songs and popular airs. It seems almost impossible, especially for one who is not an authority on Spanish folk music, to draw the line between the original compositions in folk vein, on the one hand, and the conscious transcriptions of folk songs and old popular airs, on the other. Because of this, as well as because of the decision to exclude folk songs in languages other than English (the reasons for this decision are obvious, and have been discussed in the preface) it seemed best to list the examples of the most prominent Spanish composers not in detail, as has been done in other instances, but in a broader manner, which could be termed primarily bibliographical.

The composers represented below include:

Albéniz (who curiously enough does not seem to have written any songs to Spanish texts)

Da Falla (whose most famous songs are his transcriptions of Spanish folk songs)

Granados

Nin (who apparently devoted his energies almost entirely to transcribing old Spanish music and folk songs)

Turina

Obradors (whose remarable "Canciones Clásicas seem to be based for the most part on Spanish folk songs and old popular airs)

In closing I would like to remark that no South and Central American composers are represented in this book. For those who would like to become acquainted with the vocal music of South and Central America the following list of composers may be of some help.

Chavez	Lecuona	Pedrell	Rivueltas
Grever	Longas	Plaza	Villa Lobos
Guarnieri	Mignone	Ponce	(Portuguese texts)

ISAAC ALBÉNIZ
(1860-1909)

TITLE	COMP.	TESS.	TYPE	REMARKS
Crépuscule (French text)	eb1-gb2	eb1-eb2	Most suitable for high voices	Sustained, subdued. Demands good command of high pp. (Rouart, Lerolle)
Il en est de l'amour (French text)	d1-f2	f1-db2	High or medium voices	Sustained, subdued. (Rouart, Lerolle)
Pepita Jiménez Romance de Pepita: Hélas! Soir parfumé (French text)	eb1-ab2	ab1-fb2	Lyric soprano (coloratura soprano)	Sustained. Demands Demands good command of high pp. (Eschig)
The caterpillar (English text)	e1-f♯2	g1-d2	Most suitable for high voices	Sustained, delicate. See also "Four Melodies," text by F. M. Coutts. (Rouart, Lerolle; Boston Music Co.)

TITLE	COMP.	TESS.	TYPE	REMARKS

MANUEL DE FALLA
(1876 -)

El Amor Brujo
(Chanson du Feu Follet:)

Lo mismo que er fuego	b-b1	f♯1-b1	Alto	Rapid, light. In folk vein. Demands facile articulation. Demands an accomplished pianist. (Chester)

El Amor Brujo
(Canción del amor dolido:)

Yo no sé qué siento	c1-c2	c1-g1	Alto	Rapid, rhythmical, vigorous. In folk vein. Demands facile articulation and some flexibility. Demands an accomplished pianist. (Chester)

La Vida Breve
(Air de Salud:)

Vivian los que rien!	b-a2	f♯1-f2	Soprano (dramatic, possibly lyric)	In folk vein. Slow. Has many florid embellishments. For the most part sustained. Demands an accomplished pianist. (Eschig)
Les colombes (French text)	cx1-g♯2	f♯1-e2	High voices	Not fast, somewhat declamatory, for the most part subdued, somber. Musically not easy. Demands an excellent pianist. (Rouart, Lerolle)
Seguidille (French text)	c1-g♯2	e1-e2	High or medium voices	Animated, rhythmical. In folk vein. Demands an excellent pianist. (Rouart, Lerolle; Edward Marks, New York)
Soneto a Córdoba	d1-a2	f♯1-e2	High voices except a light soprano or tenor	Sustained, majestic. The accompaniment is either pianoforte or harp. (Oxford University Press)
Tus ojillos negros	d1-g2	a1-e2	Most suitable for high voices	Animated. Demands very facile articulation. (Schirmer)

See also "Seven Popular Spanish Songs." Not too suitable for very light high voices. Demand an excellent pianist. (Reprinted by Associated Music Publishers, New York)

ENRIQUE GRANADOS
(1867-1916)

Callejeo (from Colección de Tonadillas, 12 songs)	c♯1-f2	e1-e2	Women's voices, except a	Animated. Demands some flexibility. (Unión Musical Española)

TITLE	COMP.	TESS.	TYPE	REMARKS
Callejeo cont'd.			very light soprano	
Canción del Postillón	d-g1	f-eb1	Baritone	Spirited, vigorous. (Schirmer)
Cantar	c#1-a2	f#1-e2	High voices	Animated. Demands some flexibility and an accomplished pianist. (Schirmer)
Descúbrase el pensamiento	d#1-b2	f#1-f#2	High light voices	Sustained. Demands considerable flexibility. The tessitura is quite high. (Schirmer)
El majo discreto (from "Colección de Tonadillas" 12 songs)	e1-a2 (c#1)	e1-e2	Most suitable for high voices	Animated, light. Demands some flexibility. (Unión Musical Española)
La maja dolorosa No.1 (O muerte cruel) (from "Colección de Tonadillas"-12 songs)	g-ab2		Mezzo-soprano or dramatic soprano	Dramatic, sustained. (Unión Musical Española)
La maja y el ruiseñor (Porqué entre sombras el ruiseñor) (from "Goyescas")	b#1-a2	f#1-e2	Soprano or tenor	Very sustained. Demands some flexibility and an accomplished pianist. (Schirmer)
Mañanica era	d1-f#2 (a2)	a1-e2	High voices	Delicate, sustained. (Schirmer)

ERNESTO HALFTER
(1905 -)

TITLE	COMP.	TESS.	TYPE	REMARKS
La corza blanca	f1-f2	bb1-eb2	High or medium voices	Sustained. In the manner of a free arioso. (Eschig)
La niña que se va al mar	d1-a2	g#1-e2	Most suitable for soprano	Animated. Has florid passages. Demands an excellent pianist. (Eschig)

JOAQUIN NIN
(1879-)

Is represented here in the capacity of an editor and arranger of some excellent songs and airs of eighteenth century Spanish composers, seemingly not otherwise available in modern reprints. All are published by Eschig in two volumes.

TITLE	COMP.	TESS.	TYPE	REMARKS
José Bassa (1670-1730?)				
Minué cantado	fx1-e2		All voices	A delicate minuet.
Sebastian Duron (1645-1716?)				
Cloris hermosa	d#1-f#2	e1-c2	Most suitable for men's voices	Sustained, not slow, rather delicate.

TITLE	COMP.	TESS.	TYPE	REMARKS
Pablo Esteve (1730-1792?)				
Alma sinatmos	a1-gb2	bb1-eb2	High voices, except a very light soprano	Very sustained, somber.
Blas de Laserna (1751-1816)				
El jilguerito con pico de oro (Los Amantes Chasquesados)	f#1-a2	g1-e2	High voices	An animated, graceful brilliant minuet air. Demands considerable flexibility and an accomplished pianist.
Antonio Literes (1680-1755?) Aria de Acis y Galatea				
"Si de rama en rama"	c1-g2	g1-d2	Soprano	Recitative and an animated, somewhat florid air. See also "Confiado Jilguerillo," an arrangement by Obradors of the same air for coloratura soprano.
José Marin (1619-1699)				
Corazón que en prisión	c1-f2	eb1-eb2	Not suitable for very light high voices	Slow, very sustained, somber.
José Marin				
Desengañémonos ya	d1-gb2	gb1-eb2	High voices, except a very light soprano	Very sustained.

See also:
  Nin, "Dix Noëls Espagnols" - medium or high voices. (Transcriptions of ten old Spanish Christmas carols) (Eschig)
  Nin, "Vingt Chants Populaires Espagnol" - not too suitable for very light high voices. Demand an accomplished pianist. (Transcriptions of Spanish folksongs) (2 vols. Eschig)

FERNANDO J. OBRADORS

"Canciones Clásicas Españolas" twenty-three songs for high voices Demand an excellent pianist. (Pulbished by Unión Musical Espanola)

JOAQUIN TURINA
(1882 -)
Poema en Forma de Canciónes

(Four songs and an introductory piece for pianoforte)
(published by Union Musical Espanola)

TITLE	COMP.	TESS.	TYPE	REMARKS
(3) Cantares	d1-a2	a1-f2	High voices	Rapid, brilliant. In folk vein. Has florid passages. Demands an accomplished pianist.
(5) Las locas por amor	e1-a2	g1-e2	High voices	Very animated, brilliant. Demands an accomplished pianist.
Rima (Yo soy ardiente)	e1-a2	a1-e2	Soprano	Animated, has brilliant climaxes and a slower, somewhat declamatory middle section. Demands an accomplished pianist. (Demets, Paris)

Triptico

(Unión Musical Española)

TITLE	COMP.	TESS.	TYPE	REMARKS
(1) Farruca	a-f2	d1-eb2	Alto or mezzo-soprano	Animated, rhythmical, in parts very florid.
(2) Cantilena	c1-eb3	a1-a2	Coloratura soprano	Delicate, graceful. Has florid passages. Demands an accomplished pianist.
(3) Madrigal	d1-bb2	a1-f2	Soprano or high tenor	Animated. The vocal line for the most part sustained. Has a brilliant final climax.

RUSSIAN
(in English)

The listing of songs by the Russian composers available in English translations presented a number of not inconsiderable problems. To begin with
only an infinitesimally small part of the extraordinarily varied and rich
song literature of Russia is available in English translations. Thus, a
great number of representative and significant Russian songs of great importance had to be omitted. Then the available English translations has to
be considered. The rhythmical differences between the two languages make
the problem of translating a Russian poem into English a difficult one. A
virtuoso versifier can sometimes retain the original metric pattern, but
even a most well-intentioned and erudite translator will find a number of
seemingly insoluble problems when this metric structure is accentuated
by the rhythmic pattern of the melodic line of a song. The use of extraordinarily colorful folk idioms and folk metaphors encountered in Russian
poetry complicates the matter still further. If translated literally, such
metaphors become almost meaningless in English, or at least very obscure,
especially during the performance of a song, where the listener does not
have time to consult footnotes or to accustom himself to the strange and
peculiar imagery of the text; such a translation may have a disturbing effect upon the listener, or even appear senseless and ridiculous. The subject matter of the poems themselves may often seem strangely unfitting
as song texts for an English-speaking audience, accustomed as it is to an
entirely different poetic climate. In view of all this, and in view of the fact
that, at least in so far as I know, no British or American poet of distinction
has ever tried to collaborate with a musician in translating the texts of the
Russian songs, it seemed very gratifying to have been able to list even the
few songs given here, the English versions of which are usable and can be
sung without embarrassment. It seemed utterly ridiculous to try to list
these songs in French or German translations, which are for the most part
as clumsy and inaccurate as their English counterparts, especially as this
volume is primarily designed for the use of English-speaking singers. A
performance of a Russian song by a British or an American singer in a
clumsy and inaccurate French or German translation for the benefit of an
English-speaking audience seems to border on a farce, to which even a
vocalised or instrumental version of the song would seem preferable.

Whenever a song happens to be originally written to a German or French
poem (as is often the case with songs of Rubinstein, and sometimes of
Tchaikovsky and Borodin) the title of the poem in the original language and
not in English has been given.

The very extensive and musically most valuable field of solo excerpts
from the Russian operas (Glinka, Serov, Dargomijsky, Tchaikovsky,
Mussorgsky, Rimsky-Korsakov) has had to be most regretfully omitted
from this volume almost in its entirety, since the available English versions are for the most part too inadequate to be recommended, and since
with the exception of the two examples by Tchaikovsky the listing of such
excerpts in translations other than English seemed inadvisable for reasons
discussed above. The few excerpts listed are to be found appended to the
song lists of the respective composers.

ANTON STEPANOVICH ARENSKY
(1861-1906)

Out of a great number of charming and effective songs of Arensky, only six seem to be available in fairly good English translations. The most remarkable of those is undoubtedly the "Valse," which is also one of Arensky's most well-known songs.

TITLE	COMP.	TESS.	TYPE	REMARKS
Autumn	c#1-g#2	f#1-e2	High or medium voices	Very sustained. English version by George Harris is fairly good. (Schirmer)
Deep hidden in my heart	d1-e2	e1-b1	All voices	Sustained, rather delicate. The English version by Constance Purdy is fairly good. (Ditson)
Revery	d#1-f#2	f#1-d#2	All voices	Slow, sustained, subdued. The English version by Constance Purdy is good. (Ditson)
The eagle	ab-f#2	db1-db2	Not suitable for light high voices	Slow, in parts very sustained, dramatic, effective. The English version by H. G. Chapman is fairly good. (Schirmer) The English version by F. H. Martens is fairly good. (Ditson)
The little fish's song	d1-a2	a1-f#2	Most suitable for light soprano	Light, graceful, sustained. The English version by R. H. Hamilton is good. (Ditson)
Valse	db1-gb2	eb1-eb2	Most suitable for high voices	Sustained, subdued. Interpretatively not easy. The English version by Carl Engel is good. (Arr. by Nina Koschetz Schirmer)

MILI BALAKIREV
(1837-1910)

Most of Balakirev's great number of remarkable songs are not available in English versions. This is a great pity, since practically all of them deserve to be much more widely known than many an inferior, effective song by some otherwise undistinguished Russian composer, which through sheer accident of having been adequately translated and properly distributed represents "Russian vocal music" outside of Russia.

TITLE	COMP.	TESS.	TYPE	REMARKS
A rose in autumn	eb1-f2	f1-db2	All voices	Sustained. The English version by Rosa Newmarch is good. (Six Russian Songs, Novello)
Burning out is the sunset's red flame	a#-d#2	d#1-c#2	Not suitable for light high voices	Sustained. The English version by Constance Purdy is fairly good. (Ditson)

TITLE	COMP.	TESS.	TYPE	REMARKS
Invocation (To Russia)	e1-a2 (b)	f#1-d2	All voices, except a very light soprano	A rather free recitative-like sustained song in folk vein. The English version by George Harris, Jr., is good. (Schirmer)
The pine tree	c#1-f#2	c#1-c#2	Not too suitable for very light high voices	Slow, somewhat declamatory. The English version by Constance Purdy is good. (Ditson)

ALEXANDER PORPHYRIEVITCH BORODIN
(1833-1887)

The most important works of Borodin are his orchestral compositions and his one opera, Prince Igor.

He has written only a few songs, out of which only a handful is available In English translations. One of his most striking songs, "On the shores of distant homeland," justly famous in Russia, had to be omitted from this list as it does not seem to have been translated into English.

TITLE	COMP.	TESS.	TYPE	REMARKS
A dissonance	eb1-f2	f1-db2	All voices	Sustained. In part demands considerable dramatic intensity. English version by K. Schindler is fair. (Schirmer) English version by F. H. Martens is fair. (Ditson)
Fleurs d' amour (French text)	e1-f#2	f#1-d2	All voices	Graceful, sustained. The poem is a French version of Heine's "Aus meine Tränen spriessen." See Schumann's "Dichterliebe." The English version by H. G. Chapman is good. (Schirmer)
La reine de la mer (French text)	e1-a2	a1-e2	Women's voices	Animated. The vocal line is sustained. The English version by H.G. Chapman is fairly good. (Schirmer)
My songs are envenomed and bitter	bb-f#2	eb1-eb2	Not too suitable for very light high voices	Sustained, dramatic, somewhat declamatory. The English version by Charles F. Manney is good. (Ditson)
Song of the dark forest	b-f2	e1-c#2	Heavy voices	Vigorous, somber, in parts dramatic. In folk vein. Has very interesting 7/4, 5/4, 3/4 rhythm. The English version by H. G. Chapman is good. (Schirmer)

TITLE	COMP.	TESS.	TYPE	REMARKS
The sea	d#1-g#2	f#1-eb2	Not suitable for light voices	A very animated, vigorous, dramatic narrative song. Demands and accomplished pianist. The English version by Grace Hall is fairly good. (Ditson)
The sleeping princess	db1-f2	eb1-db2	Most suitable for women's voices, except a very light soprano	A delicate narrative song. The English version by H. G. Chapman is good. (Schirmer)

CÉSAR CUI
(1835-1918)

TITLE	COMP.	TESS.	TYPE	REMARKS
Dusk fallen	b#-e2	d#1-c#2	Most suitable for men's voices	Sustained, subdued. The English version by Constance Purdy is good. (Ditson)
The statue at Tsarskoe Selo	db1-eb2	f1-c2	All voices	Delicate, sustained. The unidentified English version is fair. (Schirmer)

ALEXANDER DARGOMIJSKY
(1813-1869)

Most of Dargomijsky's, nearly one hundred, remarkable songs are as yet unavailable in English versions. A composer of extraordinary power and individuality Dargomijsky has influenced the vocal music of Russia to a degree hardly appreciated in Western Europe or America. Those who are familiar with Mussorgsky's vocal music and admire it ought to acquaint themselves with the vocal music of Dargomijsky, who has perhaps influenced this great master to a greater degree than is often assumed.

TITLE	COMP.	TESS.	TYPE	REMARKS
An Eastern song	c#1-d2	f#1-b1	Most suitable for men's voices	Slow, somewhat declamatory, sustained. The English version by Rose Newmarch is good. (Six Russian Songs, Novello)
Heavenly clouds	a#-f#2	d1-d2	All voices	Sustained; in parts, however, quite florid. Has a spirited, somewhat florid final section. The English version by H. G. Chapman is fairly good. (Schirmer)
O thou rose maiden	e1-g2	a1-e2	Most suitable for tenor	Sustained, delicate. Demands some flexibility. The English version by Constance Purdy is fair. (Ditson)

TITLE	COMP.	TESS.	TYPE	REMARKS
Silent sorrow	c#1-f#2	e1-c#2	All voices, except a very light soprano	Sustained, not slow. The English version by Rosa Newmarch is good. (Six Russian Songs, Novello)
Ye dear, fleeting hours	c1-f2	eb1-c2	All voices, except a very light soprano	Slow, very sustained. Has effective climaxes. The English version by H. G. Chapman is good. (Schirmer)

REINHOLD GLIÈRE
(1875 -)

TITLE	COMP.	TESS.	TYPE	REMARKS
Ah, twine no blossoms	d1-ab2	f1-db2	Not too suitable for light high voices	Sustained, effective, in parts dramatic. The English version by Deems Taylor is fairly good. (Ditson)
Over the depths of the sea	b-a2	f#1-e2	High voices, except a very light soprano	Sustained. Has effective climaxes. Demands an accomplished pianist. The English version by Constance Purdy is fairly good. (Schirmer)

MICHAEL GLINKA
(1804-1857)

Since no adequate English versions of Glinka's songs and operatic excerpts seem to be available it seemed best not to try to list any examples of the great Russian master.

ALEXANDER GLAZUNOV
(1865-1936)

TITLE	COMP.	TESS.	TYPE	REMARKS
The Nereid	f#1-a2	a1-e2	High voices	Sustained, effective. The English version by H. G. Chapman is good. (Schirmer)

ALEXANDER TICHONOVICH GRETCHANINOV
(1864 -)

The songs of Gretchaninov enjoy a well-deserved popularity everywhere. The eight songs listed below are among his most representative ones. They also happen to be available in good English versions. All of them are beautifully written for the voice and are neither musically nor interpretatively complex.

TITLE	COMP.	TESS.	TYPE	REMARKS
Hushed the song of the nightingale	db1-f2	d1-c2	All voices	Very sustained, delicate. The English version by Constance Purdy is good. (Ditson) See "In silent woods" by Rimsky-Korsakov.

TITLE	COMP.	TESS.	TYPE	REMARKS
My native land	e1-g2	g1-e2	Not suitable for light high voices	A free recitative-like short song in folk vein. Most effective. The English version by Deems Taylor and Kurt Schindler is good. (Schirmer)
Over the steppe	c1-g2	d1-b1	Not too suitable for light high voices	Slow, declamatory. In parts demands considerable dramatic intensity. The English version by Deems Taylor and Kurt Schindler is good. (Schirmer)
Slumber song	d1-f2 (bb)	g1-eb2 (g2)	Women's voices	Sustained, subdued. English version by L. Baum is good. (Schirmer)
The captive	b♯-f♯2	e1-c♯2	Heavy voices	Slow, sustained, in parts dramatic. Has an effective final climax. The English version by Grace Hall is fairly good. (Ditson)
The skylark	bb-gb2	g♯1-eb2	Not too suitable for very low voices	Very animated. Has effective climaxes. Demands an accomplished pianist. The English version by A. M. von Blomberg is fairly good. (Ditson)
The snowdrop	bb-f2	eb1-bb	All voices, except bass	Very animated, graceful. The English version by A. M. von Blomberg is good. (Ditson)
The wounded birch	d♯1-g2	a1-e2	All voices	Sustained, somewhat declamatory. The English version by Deems Taylor and Kurt Schindler is good. (Schirmer)

VASSILY KALINNIKOV
(1866-1901)

TITLE	COMP.	TESS.	TYPE	REMARKS
On a lone, ancient grave-mound	e1-f2	f1-e2	Medium or low voices	Sustained. Demands in parts considerable dramatic intensity. The English version by Isabel Hapgood is good. (Schirmer)

THEODOR KOENEMAN

TITLE	COMP.	TESS.	TYPE	REMARKS
When the king went forth to war	A-e1	c♯-c♯1	Bass or bass-baritone	A vigorous, spirited ballad. The English version by Rosa New-

TITLE	COMP.	TESS.	TYPE	REMARKS
When the king went forth to war (Cont'd.)				march is good. (E. Marks)

LEONID MALASHKIN
(1842-1902)

TITLE	COMP.	TESS.	TYPE	REMARKS
O could I but express in song	d1-g2 (b2)	e1-e2 (H)	All voices	Sustained. Has effective climaxes. The English version by Rosa Newmarch is good. (Chester)

NICOLAI MEDNIKOFF

TITLE	COMP.	TESS.	TYPE	REMARKS
The hills of Gruzia	d1-a2	a1-e2 (H)	Not too suitable for very light high voices	Dramatic, declamatory, effective. The English version by Alice Mattulath is good. (Fischer)

NICOLAI MEDTNER
(1880 -)

The songs of Medtner, one of the least nationalistically inclined Russian composers, are at this writing almost totally unavailable in English versions. A few of his German songs are included in the Newman Anthology of the Modern Russian Song (Ditson). The remainder of his very considerable output of songs being published by the Edition Russe de Musique is at this writing impossible to procure, especially the copies provided with English versions. Since G. Schirmer, Inc., is preparing a comprehensive collection of his songs with English translations by Henry Drinker, which will probably appear before this volume does, it seemed best to refer the reader to this collection and not to list the few early songs mentioned above. His very unusual "Sonate Vocalise" is listed below:

TITLE	COMP.	TESS.	TYPE	REMARKS
Sonate vocalise	c1-ab2		Most suitable for lyric soprano	The setting of a poem by Goethe "Geweihter Platz" serves as an introductory "Motto" (d1-a2) to the "Sonata" which is sung on vowels only. A difficult piece of vocal chamber music. Demands an excellent pianist.

MODEST PETROVICH MUSSORGSKY
(1839-1881)

Mussorgsky's genius as a composer of vocal music is of a stature that has perhaps no equal among his contemporaries, Russian or otherwise. His manner of setting a text to music is unique, and even now almost shocking in its utter lack of conventionality and the disdain for any facile formula. He is perhaps the only composer who has ever succeeded in welding the native folk melos with a seemingly utterly uninhibited and musically unbridled manner of dramatic recitation. In his choice of texts, many of which stem from his own pen, he is perhaps as remarkable as he is in his musical treatment of them. None of Mussorgsky's contemporaries seem to have dared to choose such unconventional texts for their songs. No composer of his time seems to have aimed at and attained the variety of Mussorgsky's expression ranging from starkly objective realism and mordant social satire to naïve, childlike humor, an almost mystically introspective lyricism, and fantasy.

Mussorgsky's extraordinary songs are as yet not fully appreciated or widely known in the English-speaking countries. One of the primary reasons for this neglect is undoubtedly the lack of adequate English translations of his texts. It is a great pity that perhaps the most adequate English versions of his songs, those by Edward Agate, are but little known to the English-speaking singers, being available only in the Bessel-Breitkopf & Härtel edition. The texts that Mussorgsky uses are so direct and simple that it would seem not at all impossible to translate them into idiomatically correct English. In the original Russian, the texts are for the most part almost crude in their lack of traditional poetic flights of fancy. Their verbal material is simple and everyday. In the available English translations, however, including even those by Mr. Agate, this quality is unfortunately too often lacking, so that the mood of the music seems not to be quite in accord with the elaborate, almost bookish English of the texts. It seems obvious that in songs of a composer like Mussorgsky, who is a musical dramatist above everything else, such a discrepancy between the text and the music is bound to produce a most incongruous effect. It is sincerely to be hoped that some enterprising British or American publisher will soon find it possible to make all of Mussorgsky's songs available to the English-speaking public, translated into idiomatically normal English.

Vocally, Mussorgsky's songs present no problems, being written for the most part within a limited range most suitable for medium voices. Interpretatively, of course, they demand a great deal from both the vocalist and the pianist. An acquaintance with Russian literature would undoubtedly benefit any singer attempting to perform these songs.

Editions: Bessel-Breitkopf & Härtel (complete) (English texts).
          Schirmer Masters of Russian Song, vol. I, and A Century of
          Russian Song, both edited by Kurt Schindler.
          Ditson (Modern Russian Song edited by Ernest Newman)
          Songs published by Carl Fischer, Chester, Augener, and many
          other publishers.

TITLE	COMP.	TESS.	TYPE	REMARKS
A child's song	c#1-f#2	g#1-d#2	Most suitable for light voices	Delicate, graceful. The English version by Edward Agate is fairly good. (Bessel-Breitkopf & Härtel)
After the battle	bb-eb2	eb1-bb1	Medium or low voices	Grave, dramatic. The English version by George Harris, Jr., and Kurt Schindler is good. (Schirmer)
A vision	g-db2	eb1-cb2	Low or medium voices	Somewhat declamatory, subdued, not fast. The English version by Edward Agate is good. (Bessel-Breitkopf & Härtel)

TITLE	COMP.	TESS.	TYPE	REMARKS
By the river Don	c-f1	f-c1	Men's voices	Graceful. In folk vein. The English version by Edward Agate is fairly good. (Bessel-Breitkopf & Härtel)
Cradle song of the poor	b-d♯2	e1-b1	Women's voices, except a light soprano	Slow. Interpretatively not easy. The English version by Rosa Newmarch is fairly good. (Bessel-Breitkopf & Härtel)
Hopak	c♯1-f♯2	f♯1-c♯2	Women's voices, except a light soprano	Vigorous, grim, spirited dance song. Interpretatively not easy. Demands an accomplished pianist. The English version by Constance Purdy is fair. (Ditson)
I fain would pour forth all my sorrow	d1-e2 (a)	f♯1-d2	All voices, except a very light soprano	Sustained, delicate. The English version by Edward Agate is good. (Bessel-Breitkopf & Härtel) The original German words by Heine, "Ich wollt' meine Schmerzen ergössen," can be substituted.
Joyless	c1-f2	eb1-c2	Not suitable for light high voices	Not fast, somber, somewhat declamatory. The English version by Edward Agate is fairly good. (Bessel-Breitkopf & Härtel)
King Saul	e1-g2	a1-e2	Most suitable for men's voices	Vigorous, martial. The English version by Edward Agate is good. (Bessel-Breitkopf & Härtel)
Little star, where art thou?	d1-f♯2	f♯1-d2	All voices	Sustained. In folk vein. Demands some flexibility; slow. The English version by Constance Purdy is good. (Ditson)
Master Haughty	c1-d2	f1-c2	Not suitable for light high voices	Not fast, somewhat declamatory. Interpretatively not easy. The English version by Edward Agate is good. (Bessel-Breitkopf & Härtel)
Misfortune	d1-f2	a1-d2	Not suitable for	Somber, rather slow, somewhat declamatory.

TITLE	COMP.	TESS.	TYPE	REMARKS
Misfortune (Cont'd.)			light high voices	The English version by Edward Agate is good. (Bessel-Breitkopf & Härtel)
Night	c♯1-g2	f♯1-d♯2	High or medium voices	Slow. A free recitative-like song. Demands good command of high pp. The English version by Edward Agate is good. (Bessel-Breitkopf & Härtel)
On the river Dnyéper	c1-g♭2	f1-d♭2	Most suitable for men's voices, except a very light tenor	Sustained, vigorous. In folk vein. The English version by George Harris, Jr., is good. (Schirmer)
Oriental chant (from the cantata, Josua Navine) Hear ye Amorea's daughters	b♭-e2	f♯1-d2	Alto or baritone	Slow, sustained. In parts quite florid. The English version by H. G. Chapman is good. (Schirmer)
Peasant cradle song	b♭-f2	f1-d♭2	Not suitable for light high voices	Slow, somber. The English version by H. G. Chapman is fairly good. (Schirmer) The English version by Edward Agate is fairly good. (Bessel)
Silently floated a spirit	d♭1-e♭2	e♭1-c♭2	Medium or low voices	Sustained, somewhat declamatory, subdued. The English version by George Harris, Jr., is fairly good. (Schirmer)
Song of the flea	A♯-g1	f♯-d1	Men's voices, except a very light tenor	A sardonic narrative song. Interpretatively not easy. The English version by M. C. N. Collet is good. (Chester, Ltd) See Beethoven, "Aus Goethe's Faust."
Song of the harp-player	e♭-e♭1		Baritone	Slow, sustained. The English version by Edward Agate is good. (Bessel-Breitkopf & Härtel) See "An die Türen will ich schleichen" Schubert, Schumann, Hugo Wolf.

Songs and Dances of Death

TITLE	COMP.	TESS.	TYPE	REMARKS
(1) Death and the peasant	d1-f2	e♭1-d2	Not suitable for light voices	Dramatic. Interpretatively not easy. Demands an excellent

TITLE	COMP.	TESS.	TYPE	REMARKS
(1) Death and the peasant (Cont'd.)				pianist. The English version by Kurt Schindler and H. G. Chapman is fairly good. (Schirmer)
(2) Death's lullaby	a-f#2	c#1-c#2	Low or medium voices, preferably alto or mezzo-soprano	Slow, dramatic, somewhat declamatory. Interpretatively not easy. The English version by Deems Taylor and Kurt Schindler is fairly good. (Schirmer)
(3) Serenade	c1-f2	f1-eb2	All voices, except a very light soprano	Sustained. Interpretatively not easy. Demands an accomplished pianist. The English version by Constance Purdy is fairly good. (Ditson)
(4) Death the commander	d#1-g2	g1-e2	Heavy voices	Very dramatic. Interpretatively not easy. Demands an excellent pianist. The English version by George Harris, Jr., is good. (Schirmer)

TITLE	COMP.	TESS.	TYPE	REMARKS
Sphinx	b-e2	e1-c#2	Medium or low voices	Slow, declamatory. Interpretatively not easy. The English version by Edward Agate is fairly good. (Bessel-Breitkopf & Härtel)
The classic	b-d2	g1-db2	Medium or low voices	A satirical character song. The English version by Edward Agate is fairly good. (Bessel-Breitkopf & Härtel)
The goat	b#-e2	c#1-c#2	Most suitable for men's voices	Satirical. Interpretatively not easy. The English version by George Harris, Jr., is good. (Fischer)
The grave	c-c1	f-bb	Baritone or bass	Slow, sustained, somber. Demands an accomplished pianist. The English version by Edward Agate is good. (Bessel-Breitkopf & Härtel)
The magpie	c1-f#2	f1-d2	Medium or high voices	Light and animated. Demands facile articulation. The English version by Edward Agate

TITLE	COMP.	TESS.	TYPE	REMARKS

The magpie (Cont'd.)
        is good. (Bessel-Breitkopf & Härtel)

The Nursery

Also published by Augener as "Chansons Enfantines" with English translations by E. M. Lockwood.

TITLE	COMP.	TESS.	TYPE	REMARKS
(1) With nursery	c#1-f2	eb1-db2	Most suitable for soprano or high mezzo	Animated. Musically and interpretatively not easy. Demands an accomplished pianist. The English version by Edward Agate is good. (Bessel-Breitkopf & Härtel)
(2) In the corner	c1-f2	f1-d2	Most suitable for soprano or high mezzo	Rapid. Interpretatively not easy. Demands an excellent pianist. The English version by Edward Agate good. (Bessel-Breitkopf & Härtel)
(3) The beetle	db1-f2	a1-e2	Most suitable for soprano or high mezzo	Animated. Demands facile articulation and an accomplished pianist. Interpretatively not easy. The English version by Edward Agate is good. (Bessel-Breitkopf & Härtel)
(4) With the doll	eb1-eb2	g1-db2	Most suitable for soprano or high mezzo	Sustained, subdued. The English version by Edward Agate is good. (Bessel-Breitkopf & Härtel)
(5) Evening prayer	c1-e2	eb1-c2	All voices, except bass	Not fast. Demands facile articulation. Interpretatively not easy. The English version by Edward Agate is good. (Bessel-Breitkopf & Härtel)
(6) The hobby horse	c#1-g2	ab1-eb2	Most suitable for soprano or high mezzo	Rapid. Interpretatively not easy. Demands facile articulation and an excellent pianist. The English version by Edward Agate is good. (Bessel-Breitkopf & Härtel)
(7) The naughty puss	c#1-g#2	a1-f#2	Most suitable for soprano	Rapid, light. Demands facile articulation and an accomplished pianist.

TITLE	COMP.	TESS.	TYPE	REMARKS
The naughty puss (Cont'd.)				Interpretatively not easy. The English version by Edward Agate is good. (Bessel-Breitkopf & Härtel)
The orphan	c1-f2	g1-d♭2	Women's voices, except a very light soprano	Somewhat declamatory. In parts demands considerable dramatic intensity. The English version by Edward Agate is fairly good. (Bessel-Breitkopf & Härtel)
The seminarian	B-e1	f♯-c♯1	Men's voices	A comic character song. Demands in parts facile articulation. The English version by Deems Taylor and Kurt Schindler is good. (Schirmer)
The tempest	A-e1	d♯-c♯1	Baritone	Dramatic, animated, vigorous. Demands an accomplished pianist. The English version by Edward Agate is fairly good. (Bessel-Breitkopf & Härtel)
The wanderer	f♯1-f♯2	a1-e2	All voices	Slow, sustained. The English version by Edward Agate is good. (Bessel-Breitkopf & Härtel)

Without Sunlight

TITLE	COMP.	TESS.	TYPE	REMARKS
(1) In my attic	c♯1-d2	d1-b♭1	Most suitable for medium or low voices	Sustained, subdued, somewhat declamatory. The English version by Deems Taylor and Kurt Schindler is good. (Schirmer)
(2) After years	a-e♭2	c♯1-b♭1	Low or medium voices	Somewhat declamatory, not fast. The English version by Deems Taylor and Kurt Schindler is good. (Schirmer)
(3) Retrospect	b-e2	c1-c2	Most suitable for baritone	Sustained, somewhat declamatory. In parts demands considerable dramatic intensity. Interpretatively not easy. The English version by

TITLE	COMP.	TESS.	TYPE	REMARKS
Retrospect (Cont'd.)				Deems Taylor and Kurt Schindler is good. (Schirmer)
(4) Resignation	b-d#2	e1-c2	Medium or low voices	Rather slow, somewhat declamatory, somber. The English version by Deems Taylor and Kurt Schindler is fair. (Schirmer)
(5) Elegy	c#1-f2	f#1-c#2	Medium or low voices	Dramatic. Interpretatively not easy. Demands an accomplished pianist. The English version by Deems Taylor and Kurt Schindler is good. (Schirmer)
(6) By the water	c#1-d2	e1-c#2	Medium or low voices	Slow, sustained, subdued, somber. Interpretatively not easy. The English version by Kurt Schindler is good. (Schirmer)

See also the following important songs, the available English version of which seemed inadequate: "The Ragamuffin," "Darling Savishna" (Love song of an idiot), "Calistratus," "The musical peep show," "Minstrel's song," "The country feast," "Gathering mushrooms."

Operatic Excerpts

TITLE	COMP.	TESS.	TYPE	REMARKS
Boris Godunov Boris's Monologue: I have attained to power (Act II)	Bb-gb1	eb-eb1	Bass-baritone	A dramatic, somewhat declamatory scena. In parts very sustained. Unidentified English version in the Bessel-Breitkopf & Härtel vocal score is good.
Boris Godunov Farewell, my son, I am dying (Boris - Act IV, Scene 2)	eb-e1	eb-c1	Bass-baritone	A dramatic, declamatory scena. Unidentified English version is good. (Bessel-Breitkopf & Härtel)
Boris Godunov Pimen's narrative: One evening, as daylight faded (Act IV, Scene 2)	c-e1	d-d1	Bass or bass-baritone	Sustained, somewhat declamatory. Unidentified English version is good. (Bessel-Breitkopf & Härtel)
Boris Godunov The siege of Kazan: When I stopped at Kazan	f-e1	f-c1	Bass or bass-baritone	Vigorous, spirited, dramatic narrative song. English version

TITLE	COMP.	TESS.	TYPE	REMARKS
When I stopped at Kazan (Cont'd.)				by H. G. Chapman is good. (Schirmer)
Khovanstchina Divination by water: "Spirits of nether worlds"	g#-f#2	e1-c#2	Alto or mezzo-soprano	Dramatic, declamatory. The final section sustained. In folk vein. English version by Kurt Schindler is fairly good. (Schirmer)
Khovanstchina Martha's song: "And by day and by night"	b-d2	d1-c2	Alto or mezzo-soprano	Sustained. In folk vein. Demands in parts considerable dramatic intensity. English version by G. Chapman is fair. (Schirmer)

SERGEI PROKOFIEFF
(1891 -)

The songs of Prokofieff, one of the foremost Russian composers of today, are unfortunately almost totally unavailable in English translations. Prokofieff has written a considerable number of remarkable songs and it is hoped that at least some of them will be soon published in Great Britain or America provided with adequate English versions.

TITLE	COMP.	TESS.	TYPE	REMARKS
Five vocalises, (op. 35)				
(1) Andante	eb1-a2	g1-g2		
(2) Lento, ma non troppo	b#-a2	e1-e2		
(3) Animato, ma non allegro	c1-bb2	gb1-gb2		
(4) Andantino, un poco scherzando	b#-a2	f#1-f#2		
(5) Andante non troppo	b-b2	f#1-g#2	Soprano	Vocally and musically not easy. Demand an accomplished pianist.
The ugly duckling, (op. 18)	b-a2	e1-e2	High voices	A setting of Andersen's fairy tale for voice and pianoforte (29 pages long). Interpretatively not easy. Demands an accomplished pianist. The English version by Robert Burness is good. (Gutheil-Breitkopf & Härtel)

SERGEI VASSILIEVITCH RACHMANINOFF
(1873-1943)

Rachmaninoff's songs as well as his pianoforte pieces are perhaps among his best known as well as representative and appealing compositions.

Beautifully written for both voice and pianoforte, they seem to be nearer to Tchaikovsky's manner of writing than to that of Mussorgsky. For the most part, they are written for rather heavy voices and demand an accomplished pianist.

The nineteen songs listed below seem to be sufficiently representative of his style of writing. Most of them are available in good English versions.

Editions: Gutheil-Breitkopf & Härtel, 2 vol. (71 songs), Russian and
      English texts
      Schirmer
      Ditson
      Carl Fischer
      Boston Music Co. (6 songs)

TITLE	COMP.	TESS.	TYPE	REMARKS
As fair is she as noonday light	A-f1	d-d1	Baritone	Slow, sustained. In parts demands considerable dramatic intensity. The English version by George Harris, Jr., and Deems Taylor is fairly good. (Schirmer)
Before my window	e1-a2 (b2)	a1-e2	Most suitable for high voices	Slow, subdued. Demands good command of high pp. The English version by Constance Purdy is good. (Ditson) Also the English version by H. G. Chapman is good. (Schirmer)
By a new made grave	c1-e2	e1-c2	All voices	Slow, in parts dramatic, somewhat declamatory. The English version by Constance Purdy is good. (Ditson)
Christ is risen	d1-f2	a1-eb2	Not suitable for light voices	Sustained, dramatic. The English version by Rosa Newmarch is good. (Galaxy)
Daisies	f1-ab2	a1-f2	Most suitable for high voices	Slow, rather delicate. Demands an accomplished pianist. The English version by Kurt Schindler is good. (Gutheil-Breitkopf & Härtel)
Floods of spring	db1-g#2 (ab)	db1-db2	Not suitable for light voices	Very animated. Has imposing climaxes. Demands an excellent pianist. The English version by Constance Purdy is good. (Ditson)
God took from me mine all	f#1-e2		Not suitable for light high voices	Animated, dramatic, very effective. The English version by Deems Taylor and Kurt Schindler is good. (Schirmer)

TITLE	COMP.	TESS.	TYPE	REMARKS
Here beauty dwells	d1-b2	g1-e2	All voices	Sustained. Demands occasionally good command of high pp. Vocally not easy. The English version by Geraldine Farrar is good. (Fischer)
In the silence of the night	e1-a2	a1-f2	Not too suitable for very light high voices	Sustained. Has very effective climaxes. Demands good command of high p. and an accomplished pianist. The English version by Carl Engel is good. (Schirmer)
Lilacs	eb1-g2	g1-eb2	Most suitable for women's voices	Animated, very delicate. The English version by H. G. Chapman is good. (Schirmer)
O, do not grieve!	bb-ab2	db1-c2	Not suitable for light high voices	Sustained. Has dramatic climaxes. The English version by Rosa Newmarch is good. (Gutheil-Breitkopf & Härtel)
Oh, no, I pray, do not depart	a#-e2	c#1-b1	Not suitable for very light high voices	Animated, dramatic. The English version by Constance Purdy is fairly good. (Ditson)
Sorrow in spring	d1-bb2	g1-eb2	Most suitable for high voices	Animated, dramatic. Demands an accomplished pianist. The English version by Arthur Westbrook is good. (Ditson)
The harvest of sorrow	g1-bb2	a1-f2	High or medium voices	Slow, sustained. In folk vein. In parts demands considerable dramatic intensity. The English version by Rosa Newmarch is good. (Gutheil-Breitkopf & Härtel) Also available in Schirmer edition ("O thou billowy Harvest Field") in a fair translation.
The island	db1-f2		All voices	Delicate, sustained. The English version by Carl Engel is good. (Schirmer)
The raising of Lazarus	c1-f2	eb1-c2	Low voices	Grave, somewhat declamatory. The English version by Edward Ágate is good. (Gutheil-Breitkopf & Härtel)
The soldier's bride	f#1-g2	g1-d2	Women's voices,	Very slow, sustained. In folk vein. Demands

TITLE	COMP.	TESS.	TYPE	REMARKS
The soldier's bride (Cont'd.)			except a very light soprano	considerable dramatic intensity. The English version by Deems Taylor and George Harris, Jr., is good. (Schirmer)
The songs of Grusia	e1-a2	a1-f2	High voices	Sustained. In parts demands considerable dramatic intensity and some flexibility. Demands an accomplished pianist. The English version by Deems Taylor and Kurt Schindler is good. (Schirmer)
To the children	e1-f2	f1-c2	All voices	Slow, somewhat declamatory. Demands in parts considerable dramatic intensity. The English version by Rosa Newmarch is good. (Ditson)
Vocalise	c♯1-a2 (c♯3)	g♯1-e2	Not suitable for very low voices	Slow, very sustained. (Schirmer) Also published in a transposed edition (a-f2).

NICOLAI RIMSKY-KORSAKOV
(1844-1908)

The songs of Rimsky-Korsakov are for the most part much less representative of his manner of writing than his operas. He has written a considerable number of songs of which only a few seem to equal his operatic excerpts in content as well as in workmanship.

TITLE	COMP.	TESS.	TYPE	REMARKS
Hebrew love song	c♯1-e2	f♯1-c♯2	Women's voices	Slow, sustained, subdued. Demands some flexibility. The English version by H. G. Chapman is good. (Schirmer)
In silent woods	f1-f2	ab1-eb2	All voices	Sustained, very subdued. See Gretchaninov, "Hushed the Song of the Nightingale." The English version by George Harris, Jr., and Kurt Schindler is very good. (Schirmer)
Like mountains the waves	d1-g2	g1-e2	Not suitable for very light high voices	Animated. In parts demands considerable dramatic intensity. Demands an accomplished pianist. The English version by Constance Purdy is fairly good. (Ditson)

TITLE	COMP.	TESS.	TYPE	REMARKS
On the Georgian hills	d#1-f#2	f#1-c#2	All voices, except a very light soprano	Sustained. Demands in parts considerable dramatic intensity. The English version by H. G. Chapman is fairly good. (Schirmer) See Mednikoff, "On Hills of Gruzia."
The cloud and the mountain	b-g1		All voices	Sustained, subdued. The English version by Deems Taylor is fairly good. (Schirmer)
The maid and the sun	c#1-a2	a1-e2	Women's voices	Sustained. Demands some flexibility. The English version by Charles F. Manney is fairly good. (Ditson)
The nightingale and the rose	f#1-f#2	a1-d2	All voices	Very sustained. The English version by Deems Taylor is good. (Ditson)
The octave	e1-a2	f1-e2	All voices	Sustained. The English version by Constance Purdy is good. (Ditson)

Operatic Excerpts

TITLE	COMP.	TESS.	TYPE	REMARKS
Golden Cockerel				
Hymn to the sun (To me give answer)	f#1-b2	a1-f#2	Coloratura soprano (lyric soprano)	Sustained. Has rather intricate florid passages. The English version by George Harris, Jr., and Deems Taylor is fairly good. (Masters of Russian Song). (Schirmer)
Sadko				
Song of Glorification (Blue is the ocean)	e-a1	g#-f#1	Tenor	Sustained. The English version by George Harris, Jr., and Deems Taylor is fairly good. (Schirmer)
Sadko				
Song of India (Unnumbered diamonds)	d-g1	g-d1	Tenor	Sustained. Demands some flexibility and a good command of pp. The English version by Constance Purdy is fairly good. (Ditson)
Snow Maiden (Snegourotchka)				
Song of the Shepherd Lehl	eb1-f2	f1-eb2	Mezzo-soprano or alto	Light, animated. In folk vein. The English version by H. G. Chapman is fairly good. (Schirmer)

ANTON RUBINSTEIN
(1830-1894)

Rubinstein's songs, with the exception of a very few like "Der Asra" and

"Es blinkt der Tau," have been for the most part forgotten outside of Russia.

All his songs are effective and are well written for the voice. As his style is rather uniform and as a great number of his songs have been written to the original German texts, it seemed best to list below only his German songs, especially in view of the fact that the available English versions of his Russian songs seem, as a rule, rather poor.

Editions: Schirmer, 2 vols.
Novello
Many single songs published by most publishers.

TITLE	COMP.	TESS.	TYPE	REMARKS
Clärchens lied	c1-f2	ab1-eb2	Women's voices	Sustained. See "Freudvoll und Leidvoll" by Beethoven and Liszt, and "Die Liebe" by Schubert.
Der Asra	d1-ab2	g1-d2	Most suitable for men's voices	Sustained. In parts demands considerable dramatic intensity.
Die Lerche	eb1-g2	f1-eb2	All voices	Animated. The vocal line is very sustained.
Die Rose (Persian songs, op. 34)	c1-f2	g1-c2	All voices	Sustained, delicate. Demands some flexibility. See "Es hat die Rose sich beklagt" by Robert Franz.
Du bist wie eine Blume	e1-g2	g1-d2	All voices	Sustained, subdued. See Schumann, Liszt.
Es blinkt der Tau	eb1-gb2	a1-f2	All voices	Sustained, effective.
Frühlingslied (Die blauen Frühlings-Augen)	d#1-g#2	f#1-d#2	All voices	Delicate. See Robert Franz.
Gelb rollt mir zu Füssen (Persian songs, op.34)	d1-g2	f1-eb2	All voices	Very sustained. Demands some flexibility.
Lied (Es war ein alter König)	d1-g2	g1-d2	All voices	Sustained, somewhat declamatory.
Nicht mit Engeln (Persian songs, op.34)	eb1-f2	ab1-db2	Most suitable for men's voices	Very sustained. Demands some flexibility.
Nun die Schatten dunkeln	db1-f2	f1-eb2	All voices	Sustained. See A. Jensen, and "Für Musik" by Robert Franz.

IGOR STRAVINSKY
(1882 -)

Stravinsky, one of the foremost composers of our time, has written very few songs. With the exception of his earliest efforts ("A song of the dew," "The Cloister," "Pastorale") most of his songs are of great complexity and are not recommended to inexperienced singers.

TITLE	COMP.	TESS.	TYPE	REMARKS
A song of the dew	c#1-f#2	a1-e2	Mezzo-soprano or soprano	Dramatic. Interpretatively quite complex. Demands an accomplished pianist. The English version by M. D. Calvocoressi is fair. The French version by Calvocoressi, available in the same copy, is fairly good. (Jurgenson)
Con queste paroline (Italian text)	G-e1	d-d1	Bass, bass-baritone	A very animated arietta after Pergolesi. Demands some flexibility. (Chester)
The cloister	d#1-fx2	a1-f#2 (H)	Women's voices	Animated. In parts demands some flexibility and considerable dramatic intensity. Interpretatively not easy. Demands an accomplished pianist. The English version by M. D. Calvocoressi is fairly good. (Ditson)
Three Japanese lyrics	g#1-bbb2	g#1-g2	Light soprano	Three short songs of considerable musical complexity. Originally scored for voice and chamber orchestra. The piano arrangement is by the composer. Demands an excellent pianist. The English versions by Robert Burness is good. (Edition Russe de Musique)
Vocalise (Pastorale)	c#1-f#2	d#1-d#2	High voices	Graceful and delicate. (Schirmer)

PETER ILIYTCH TCHAIKOVSKY
(1840-1893)

One could hardly consider most of Tchaikovsky's many songs as being among his most representative and important compositions. As a rule, they tend to follow a rather facile formula; at present many of them seem to have lost much of the appeal that made them so popular at one time. Yet no matter how insignificant some of his songs may seem when compared with his symphonic music, one cannot help but admit that they could not have been written by anyone but a great master. Any composer of a smaller stature would have undoubtedly earned a world-wide renown with songs like "Nur wer die Sehnsucht kennt," "The pilgrim's song," "A ball room meeting," "Don Juan's serenade," "The legend," and "Was I not a blade of grass?" to name but a very few.

The available English versions of Tchaikovsky's songs are for the most part rather poor. This seems strange in view of the fact that neither his texts nor his treatment of them seems to demand any extraordinary rhythmic virtuosity on the part of the translator.

Tchaikovsky's songs present hardly any problems, vocally, musically, or interpretatively, being extraordinarily well written for the voice and for the most part purely melodic in character.

Editions: Ditson (Fifty Songs, Musicians Library)
Schirmer (Twelve Songs)
Novello (Twenty-five Songs)
Many single songs published by Carl Fischer, Augener, and other publishers.

TITLE	COMP.	TESS.	TYPE	REMARKS
A ball room meeting	b-e2	f#1-d2	All voices	A delicate, subdued waltz song. One of the most appealing of Tchaikovsky's songs. English version by Rosa Newmarch is good. (6 Russian songs, Novello)
A legend	d1-e2	e1-b1	All voices	Sustained. The English version by H. G. Chapman is fairly good. (Schirmer)
By the window	e1-g2	a1-e2	Most suitable for high voices	Animated, very effective. The English version by Deems Taylor and Kurt Schindler is good. (Schirmer)
Cradle song	d1-g2	g1-d2	Women's voices	Sustained. Demands good command of high pp. The English version by Charles F. Manney is fair. (Ditson)
Death	d1-g2	f1-d2	Not suitable for very light high voices	Sustained, grave. The English version by Isidora Martinez is fairly good. (Ditson)
Don Juan's serenade	A-d1 (e1)	e-c1	Bass or baritone	Animated. The vocal line sustained. Has very effective climaxes. Demands an accomplished pianist. The unidentified French version is good. The English version by N. H. Dole is rather poor. (Schirmer)
Evening	c1-f2	d1-c2	All voices	Sustained, somewhat declamatory, rather delicate. The English version by Kurt Schindler is good. (Schirmer)
Farewell	c1-a2	d1-c2	Not suitable for	Sustained, somewhat declamatory, in parts

TITLE	COMP.	TESS.	TYPE	REMARKS
Farewell (Cont'd.)			light high voices	dramatic. The English version by F. H. Martens is fairly good. (Ditson)
Linger yet	d♯1-f♯2	f♯1-eb2	All voices	Sustained, subdued. The English version by A. Westbrook is good. (Ditson)
No tidings came from thee	c-f1	g-d1	Baritone	Sustained. In parts demands considerable dramatic intensity. The English version by Lady Macfarren is fairly good. (Novello)
Nur wer die Sehnsucht kennt (German text)	c1-f2	eb1-c2	All voices	Sustained. In parts demands considerable dramatic intensity. See Beethoven, Schubert, Schumann, and H. Wolf.
O child, in the silence of night	d1-a2	e1-e2	Most suitable for men's voices	Animated, rather delicate serenade. The English version by F. H. Martens is good. (Ditson)
Oh, could you but for one short hour	c♯-eb1	f♯-c♯1	Baritone	Very animated. Demands considerable dramatic intensity in parts and an accomplished pianist. The English version by Lady Macfarren is good. (Novello)
✓Pilgrim's song	B-e1	g♯-c♯1	Bass or baritone	Sustained. Has a very imposing final climax. The English version by Paul England is good. (Schirmer)
Regret	e1-g♯2	e1-e2	All voices	Sustained. Demands in parts considerable dramatic intensity. English version by Rosa Newmarch is good. (6 Russian Songs, Novello)
Sérénade (French text)	b-f♯2	e1-c♯2	Not too suitable for very light high voices	Animated, delicate. (Ditson)
Song of a Gipsy girl	d1-f2	e1-c2	Women's voices	Sustained. The English version by F. H. Martens is good. (Ditson)
Tears	d1-e2	d1-c2	Medium or low voices	Sustained. In parts demands considerable dramatic intensity. The

TITLE	COMP.	TESS.	TYPE	REMARKS
Tears (Cont'd.)				English version by Charles F. Manney is good. (Ditson)
To sleep	bb-f2	f1-db2	Not suitable for very light high voices	Sustained. In parts demands considerable dramatic intensity. The English version by Isidora Martinez is fair. (Ditson)
'Twas you alone	c1-a2	g1-eb2	All voices	Sustained, somewhat declamatory. Demands in parts considerable dramatic intensity. The English version by F. H. Martens is fairly good. (Ditson)
Was I not a blade of grass	b-b2	f#1-e2	Women's voices, except a very light soprano	Sustained, in parts dramatic. Perhaps one of Tchaikovsky's most characteristic songs. The English version by Charles F. Manney is rather poor. (Ditson)
Whether day dawns	d#1-a2	g#1-d#2	Not suitable for light voices	Very animated, effective. Demands an excellent pianist. The English version by Charles F. Manney is fairly good. (Ditson)
Wherefore?	d1-g2 (a2)	g1-d2	Most suitable for men's voices	Sustained. In parts demands considerable dramatic intensity. The English version by Charles F. Manney is fairly good. (Ditson)
Why?	d1-a2	a1-d2	All voices, except a very light soprano	Sustained. Demands considerable dramatic intensity. The English version by A. Westbrook is fair. (Ditson)

Two operatic airs in French translations (for soprano and alto or mezzo-soprano) are listed in the "Operatic Excerpts" Section.

ALEXANDER TCHEREPNIN
(1899 -)

TITLE	COMP.	TESS.	TYPE	REMARKS
Cradle song	f1-g2	bb1-eb2	Most suitable for soprano	Slow, sustained, subdued. The English version by Constance Purdy is fairly good. (Ditson) See Gretchaninov.
Quiet night	eb1-ab2	ab1-f2	Not too suitable	Sustained, subdued, delicate. The English

TITLE	COMP.	TESS.	TYPE	REMARKS
Quiet night (Cont'd.)			for very low voices	version by Constance Purdy is good. (Ditson)

SERGEI VASSILENKO
(1872 -)

TITLE	COMP.	TESS.	TYPE	REMARKS
A maiden sang	d♯1-g2	e1-e2	Most suitable for high voices	Sustained, delicate. The English version by Constance Purdy is good. (Ditson)
Longing	e1-a2	a1-f♯2	Most suitable for soprano	Slow, sustained. Demands some flexibility and good command of high pp. The English version by Deems Taylor is good. (Ditson)

The following list of songs by Scandinavian composers is pitifully small, since apparently only a few of their songs have been published with adequate English translations.

It is possible that after a most exhaustive research more material could have been listed. However, since much of that material would undoubtedly be almost totally unavailable now, it seemed best to limit this list to songs available in the United States, although this decision was made with great reluctance and much regret, for the song literature of Norway, Sweden, Denmark and Finland is rich and musically very significant.

TITLE	COMP.	TESS.	TYPE	REMARKS

AGATHE BACKER-GRÖNDAHL
(1847-1907)

TITLE	COMP.	TESS.	TYPE	REMARKS
At sea (Tilsjös)	bb-eb2	f1-c2	Medium or low voices	Vigorous and spirited. English version by C. Purdy is good. (Werrenrath, Modern Scandinavian Songs. Ditson)
In dance you met me	c1-gb2	f1-db2	High or medium voices	A delicate, graceful waltz song. Demands an accomplished pianist. English version by G. Sundelius is fairly good. (Homeyer)
When the linden's in flower (Lind)	d#1-f#2	f#1-d#2	Not too suitable for very low voices	Delicate, sustained. English version by A. Forestier is fairly good. (Stub, Songs from the North. Ditson)

I. A. BERG

TITLE	COMP.	TESS.	TYPE	REMARKS
The herdsman's song (Herdegossen)	c#1-a2	f#1-c#2	All voices	Slow and very sustained. English version by A. Forestier is good. (Stub, Songs from the North. Ditson)

EDVARD GRIEG
(1843-1907)

Grieg's mode of musical expression, predominantly melodic in character, seems perhaps best suited to the smaller forms in which he excelled. His songs could be easily considered among his most characteristic and remarkable compositions.

Grieg's idiom, greatly influenced by the Norwegian folk melos, is always peculiarly and unmistakably his own. All of his songs are beautifully written for the voice and can hardly be considered either musically or vocally taxing. An acquaintance with Scandinavian folklore and literature, however, would be helpful to any singer seeking to establish a stylistically satisfactory mode of their interpretation. It is a great pity that most of Grieg's songs have been known in English-speaking countries practically exclusively in German versions, and that the available English versions are for the most part rather poor. The following list, therefore, can by no means be considered representative, omitting as it does many of Grieg's most remarkable songs because of the lack of available English versions, among them the celebrated cycle "Haugtussa."

Editions: Peters (German texts only)
Ditson (Musicians' Library - German and English texts)
Schirmer (German and English texts)
Many reprints of single songs by various publishers.

TITLE	COMP.	TESS.	TYPE	REMARKS
A swan (En Svane)	d1-f2	f1-d2	All voices	Slow, sustained. In parts demands considerable dramatic intensity. I have found no satisfactory English translation of this celebrated song. (Generally available)
Cradle song	b-d#1	b-g#1	Most suitable for medium or low voices	Animated, somber. English version by N. H. Dole is fair. (Ditson)
Die verschwiegene Nachtigall (German text)	d1-e2	g1-e2	Women's voices	Light and delicate, sustained. (Ditson)
Ein Traum (German text)	c1-ab2	ab1-f2	Not too suitable for very light soprano	Sustained. Ends in an effective climax. (Generally available)
Eros	c1-f2	e1-c2	Not too suitable for very light voices	Declamatory and effective. English version by N. H. Dole is fairly good. (Ditson)
Good morning (God morgen)	d1-f#2	a1-e2	All voices	Rapid and rhythmical. English versions by A. Forestier and N. H. Dole are fair. (Ditson)
I love thee (Jeg elsker dig)	e1-f2	g1-e2	All voices	Very sustained. Demands in parts considerable dramatic intensity. English version by R. Werrenrath is good. (Werrenrath, Modern Scandinavian Songs. Ditson)
In the boat	d1-e#2	g1-d2	All voices	Light and delicate. English version by N. H. Dole is fair. (Ditson)
Lauf der Welt (German text)	d1-f#2	f#1-e2	Most suitable for men's voices	Light and animated. Demands facile articulation. (Ditson)

TITLE	COMP.	TESS.	TYPE	REMARKS
Love's first meeting (Det förste Möde)	c1-ab2	f1-f2	All voices	Slow, sustained. English version by A. Forestier is fairly good. (Stub, Songs from the North. Ditson)
Margaret's cradle song	c1-f2	e1-c2	Women's voices	Slow and subdued. English version by A. Westbrook is good. (Ditson)
My dear old mother (Gamif mor)	d1-f#2	f#1-d2	Not too suitable for very light high voices	Sustained. English version by A. Forestier is fairly good. (Stub, Songs from the North. Ditson)
Solveig's song (Solvejgs sang)	e1-a2	a1-e2	Women's voices	Sustained. Demands in parts considerable flexibility and good command of high pp. English version by A. Westbrook is good. (Ditson)
Springtide	d#1-f#2	f#1-d#2	All voices	Slow and sustained. English version by N. H. Dole is fair. (Ditson)
Thanks for thy counsel (Tak for dit råd)	c1-a2	a1-f#2	Most suitable for men's voices	Rapid and vigorous, very effective. English version by R. Werrenrath is good. (Werrenrath, Modern Scandinavian Songs. Ditson)
The mother sings (Moderen synger)	db1-eb2	f1-db2	Women's voices	Slow and somber. English version by N. H. Dole is good. See Sinding. (Ditson)
The princess	d1-g2	f#1-eb2	All voices	Somewhat declamatory. Demands in parts considerable dramatic intensity. English version by N. H. Dole is rather poor. The Forestier translation used in the Kjerulf setting could be successfully substituted. See "Twilight Fancies" by Delius and "Twilight Musing" by Kjerulf. (Ditson)
To Norway (Til Norge)	e1-f2	f1-d2	All voices	Slow and sustained. English version by A. Forestier is good. (Stub, Songs from the North. Ditson)
'Twas on a lovely eve in June	c#1-f#2	f#1-d2	All voices	Delicate. English version by C. F. Manney is fair. (Ditson)

TITLE	COMP.	TESS.	TYPE	REMARKS
With a water lily	d#1-f2	e1-c#2	All voices	Delicate, animated. Demands an accomplished pianist. I have found no satisfactory English translation of this, perhaps one of the best songs of Grieg. (Generally available)

See also "Seven Children's Songs," op. 61. (Boston Music Co.)

SVERRE JORDAN
(1889-)

Finland	d1-g2	f1-d2	All voices	Sustained. English version by C. Purdy is good. (Werrenrath, Modern Scandinavian Songs. Ditson)

YRJÖ KILPINEN
(1892-)

The songs of Kilpinen, a Finnish composer, comparatively unknown outside of Scandinavia, England and Germany, should, in the opinion of this writer, occupy one of the foremost places in any singer's contemporary repertoire. Extraordinarily individual in their musical structure, yet hardly ever musically or vocally complex, terse, precise, and almost overpoweringly direct in their dramatic impact, Kilpinen's songs seem to be never subject to any intellectually conceived formula and thus avoid the pitfalls of experimentalism as well as of triteness.

Kilpinen's choice of poetic material as well as his treatment of it seems to be well-nigh impeccable. None of his songs make any extraordinary demands upon the singer, except of course the demand for extreme sensitiveness for the poetic text. For the most part, Kilpinen seems to write for medium voices, within a short compass seldom exceeding c1-g2.

His accompaniments are perhaps among the most transparent and sparse of the contemporary composers, although harmonically bold and by no means elementary. Never afraid of dissonance, Kilpinen is sparing in its use, relying primarily on the melodic line and not on the harmonic effect for his expression.

For the list below only songs written originally in German (texts by Morgenstern, Sergel and V. Zwehl) have been considered. Kilpinen has written a great number of magnificent songs to Finnish and Swedish texts.

Editions: Bote & Bock, Berlin
Associated Music Publishers, New York

Lieder der Liebe I
Opus 60
(Christian Morgenstern)

(1) Mein Herz is leer	c1-e2	f#1-c#2	Medium or low voices	Slow, somewhat declamatory. Musically and interpretatively not easy.

TITLE	COMP.	TESS.	TYPE	REMARKS
(2) Es ist Nacht	g1-f2	bb1-f2	High or medium voices	Animated, somber. The final section slow and sustained. Interpretatively not easy. Demands an accomplished pianist.
(3) Unsere Liebe	f1-fb2	ab1-eb2	Medium or low voices	Sustained. Musically and interpretatively not easy.
(4) Wir sitzen im Dunkeln	c1-f2	g1-eb2	Medium or low voices	Sustained, subdued, very short.
(5) Schicksal der Liebe	d1-f#2	g1-d#2	High or medium voices	Animated, for the most part subdued. The final section slow and sustained. Interpretatively not easy. Demands an accomplished pianist.

Lieder der Liebe II
Opus 60
(Christian Morgenstern)

TITLE	COMP.	TESS.	TYPE	REMARKS
(1) Heimat	f#1-d#2		All voices	Slow, sustained, subdued.
(2) Kleines Lied	d1-e2		All voices	Sustained, delicate, very simple.
(3) Deine Rosen an der Brust	eb1-f2	f1-db2	Soprano or mezzo-soprano	Delicate, animated.
(4) Über die tausend Berge	f#1-f#2	f#1-d#2	High or medium voices	Animated. Has a brilliant final climax.
(5) Anmutiger Vertrag	d#1-f#2	f#1-e#2	Not too suitable for very heavy low voices	Rapid, light, gently humorous. Demands facile articulation and an accomplished pianist.

Lieder nach Gedichten von Albert Sergel
Opus 75

TITLE	COMP.	TESS.	TYPE	REMARKS
(1) Im Walde liegt ein Stiller See	eb1-eb2		High or medium voices	Very sustained, subdued, delicate.
(2) Tausend stille weisse Blumen	eb1-gb2	g1-d2	High or medium	Animated, delicate. The vocal line sustained.
(3) Heiligendamm	f#1-f#2	g#1-d2	Women's voices, except a heavy alto	Sustained, for the most part subdued. Demands good command of high pp.

TITLE	COMP.	TESS.	TYPE	REMARKS
(4) Mein Herz der wilde Rosen- strauch	c#1-f#2	f#1-c#2	High or medium voices	Animated, delicate.
(5) Sommersegen	c1-g2	g1-eb2	High or medium voices	Very sustained, for the most part subdued.
(6) Unter Blüten	c#1-f#2	f#1-d#2	High or medium voices	Very sustained.

Lieder um den Tod
Opus 62
(Christian Morgenstern)

TITLE	COMP.	TESS.	TYPE	REMARKS
(1) Vöglein Schwermut	c1-f2	f#1-d2	Medium or high voices	Sustained, subdued, somber. Interpre- tatively not easy.
(2) Auf einem verfallenen Kirchhof	c#1-fb2	eb1-db2	Medium or low voices	Very sustained, somber. Demands in parts some flexibility. Musically and interpretatively not easy.
(3) Der Tod und der einsame Trinker	c1-f2	f1-e2	Medium or low voices	A dramatic dialogue. Interpretatively quite complex.
(4) Winternacht	eb1-f2	f1-d2	Medium or high voices	Sustained, subdued, somber.
(5) Der Säemann	f1-f2	f1-c2	Medium or low voices	Very animated, dramatic, rather vigorous. Demands an accom- plished pianist.
(6) Unverlierbare Gewähr	c#1-e2	f1-c#2	Low or medium voices	Slow, sustained, for the most part subdued. Musically and interpre- tatively not easy.

TITLE	COMP.	TESS.	TYPE	REMARKS
Nachts am Posten (op. 79, no. 6)	c1-f2	eb1-eb2	Most suit- able for men's voices, except a very light tenor	Sustained, grave. Has a more animated, lyrical middle section.
Siehe, auch ich-lebe (op. 59, no. 5)	f#1-f#2	a1-d2	Medium or high voices	Very animated. Has vigorous climaxes.
Thalatta! (op. 59, no. 6)	d#1-f#2	f#1-d#2	Heavy voices	Very vigorous, animated.
Von zwei Rosen (op. 59, no. 3)	eb1-g2	ab1-eb2	Most suit- able for high voices	Animated, for the most part delicate. The vocal line sustained.

TITLE	COMP.	TESS.	TYPE	REMARKS
Vorfrühling (op. 79, no. 3)	d1-f♯2	f♯1-e2	Most suitable for high voices	Animated, delicate, graceful.

See also "Spielmannslieder," op. 77 - eight songs most suitable for men's voices (c♯1-f♯2)

HALFDAN KJERULF
(1815-1868)

TITLE	COMP.	TESS.	TYPE	REMARKS
In days of yore (Det var då)	d1-f♯2	a1-e2	Not too suitable for very light high voices	Grave, somewhat declamatory. English version by A. Forestier is fairly good. (Stub, Songs from the North. Ditson)
Ingrid's song (Ingrids Vise)	c1-f2	f1-d2	Women's voices	Light, rhythmical folk dance tune. English version by C. Purdy is fairly good. (Werrenrath, Modern Scandinavian Songs. Ditson)
Longing (Last night the nightingale woke me) (Laengsel)	eb-g2	eb1-eb2	All voices	Sustained, delicate. English version by A. Forestier is good. (Stub, Songs from the North, Ditson)
My heart and lute (Mit Hjerte og min Lyre)	e1-f♯2 (a2)	g♯1-e2	All voices	Slow and sustained. English version by A. Forestier is good. (Stub, Songs from the North. Ditson)
Sing! sing, nightingale, sing! (Syng, Syng)	e1-f♯2	g1-e2	All voices	Sustained. English version by A. Forestier is good. (Stub, Songs from the North. Ditson)
Synnöve's song	c1-f2	f1-c2	Women's voices	Slow and sustained. English version by A. Forestier is fairly good. (Stub, Songs from the North. Ditson)
Twilight musing	d1-f2	a1-d2	All voices	Sustained. English version by A. Forestier is good. (Stub, Songs from the North. Ditson) See "Twilight Fancies" by Delius and Grieg.

PETER E. LANGE-MÜLLER
(1850-1926)

TITLE	COMP.	TESS.	TYPE	REMARKS
Autumn (Efteraar)	d1-b1		All voices	A free recitative-like song. English version by C. Purdy is fairly good. (Werrenrath, Modern Scandinavian Songs. Ditson)

TITLE	COMP.	TESS.	TYPE	REMARKS
Shine bright and clear (Skin ud, du klare solskin)	a-e2	e1-c2	All voices	Animated, rhythmical. English version by C. Purdy is good. (Werrenrath, Modern Scandinavian Songs. Ditson)

SIGURD LIE
(1871-1904)

TITLE	COMP.	TESS.	TYPE	REMARKS
Snow (Sne)	db1-eb2	eb1-c2	All voices	Sustained and very subdued. Demands good command of pp. English version by Westbrook is good. (Werrenrath, Modern Scandinavian Songs. Ditson)

LILLJEBJORN

TITLE	COMP.	TESS.	TYPE	REMARKS
When I was seventeen (Arranged by A. W. Kramer)	c#1-b2	f#1-g#2	Light soprano	Sustained, graceful. Has some florid passages. (Ricordi)

SELIM PALMGREN
(1878-)

TITLE	COMP.	TESS.	TYPE	REMARKS
In the willows (Ivassen)	c1-eb2	e1-c2	All voices	Delicate. C. Purdy translation is good. (Werrenrath, Modern Scandinavian Songs. Ditson)

See also a collection of six songs published by Boston Music Co. with English texts by Carl Engel.

JEAN SIBELIUS
(1865-)

Although Sibelius has written a great number of songs to Swedish and Finnish texts and although many of them have been published by Breitkopf & Härtel provided with English translations, most of such copies are now unavailable and his songs are but rarely heard in America or Great Britain, notwithstanding the fact that his symphonic music has found a large public in both countries.

It seemed therefore best to list the few of his songs which are at present available in English translations reprinted by American publishers, and to list the few very famous songs published abroad, although such an exceedingly scant list can in no way be considered representative of the foremost Finnish composer of our time.

TITLE	COMP.	TESS.	TYPE	REMARKS
A maiden yonder sings (Tuol laulaa Neitonen)	d#1-d#2		All voices	Slow, very sustained and subdued. English version by C. Purdy is good. (Werrenrath, Modern Scandinavian Songs. Ditson)

TITLE	COMP.	TESS.	TYPE	REMARKS
Black roses (of- 36) (Svarta Rosor)	c1-g#2	e1-e2	Not suitable for light high voices	Sustained. Has a very dramatic final climax. Unidentified English version in the Breitkopf & Härtel edition is poor.
Die Stille Stadt (German text)	db1-d2	f1-e2	All voices	Sustained and very subdued. (Werrenrath, Modern Scandinavian Songs. Ditson)
From the North	d#1-g2	a1-f2	High voices	Sustained. Demands some flexibility. English version by Dr. Th. Baker is fair. (Schirmer)
Longings vain are my heritage (Längtan heter min arfvedel)	d1-g2	g1-e2	High voices	Sustained. English version by Elizabeth E. Lockwood is fairly good. (Associated Music Publishers)
The first kiss	bb-g#2	e1-e2	High or medium voices	Not fast, rather sustained. Unidentified English version is fair. (Breitkopf & Härtel)
The tryst (Flickan kom)	c#1-g#2	f1-db2	Women's voices, except a light soprano	A dramatic narrative song. English version by W. Wallace is fairly good. (Breitkopf & Härtel)
Was it a dream?	b-g#2	f#1-e2	High or medium voices	Sustained. Has effective climaxes. Demands an accomplished pianist. Unidentified English version is fair. (Breitkopf & Härtel)

CHRISTIAN SINDING
(1856-)

TITLE	COMP.	TESS.	TYPE	REMARKS
Alb (German text)	eb1-f2	ab1-db2	Not too suitable for very light high voices	Slow, somber, sustained. (Schirmer)
Amber (Rav)	c1-f2	f1-e2	All voices	Animated, somber. English version by A. Forestier is good. (Stub, Songs from the North. Ditson)
A May night (Majnat)	d1-f2	f1-d2	All voices	Sustained. English version by A. Forestier is good. (Stub, Songs from the North. Ditson)
Ein Weib (German text)	b-g#2	c#1-d2	Not suitable for very high light voices	Dramatic. Demands in part some flexibility, and an accomplished pianist. (Hansen)

TITLE	COMP.	TESS.	TYPE	REMARKS
Schmied Schmerz (German text)	d1-f2 (a)	d1-d2	Not suitable for light high voices	Vigorous, somber. (Schirmer)
Sylvelin	e1-e2	a1-e2	All voices	Sustained, rather subdued. English version by F. H. Martens is fairly good. (Schirmer)
The mother sings (Moderen Synger)	d1-f2	g1-d2	Women's voices	Sustained, somber. English version by A. Forestier is fairly good. (Stub, Songs from the North. Ditson) See Grieg.
There cried a bird (Der Skreg en Fugl)	bb-f2	c1-c2	Not suitable for very light high voices	Sustained. Unidentified English translation is good. (Schirmer)

WILHELM T. SÖDERBERG
(1845-1939)

TITLE	COMP.	TESS.	TYPE	REMARKS
Cradle song (Vaggvisa)	d1-e2	g1-d2	Women's voices	Slow and sustained. English version by A. Forestier is good. (Stub, Songs from the North. Ditson)
The bird's song (Fågelns Visa)	d1-f#2	e1-c#2	Most suitable for women's voices	Delicate, sustained. English version by A. Forestier is fair. (Stub, Songs from the North. Ditson)

VALDEMAR THRANE
(1790-1828)

TITLE	COMP.	TESS.	TYPE	REMARKS
The Norwegian echo song	d1-b2	a1-f#2	Soprano	Animated. Has florid passages. One of Jenny Lind's famous songs. Best for coloratura soprano. English version by A. Forestier is fair. (Schirmer)

MISCELLANEOUS
(in English)

FRÉDÉRIC CHOPIN
(1810-1849)

Chopin's seventeen songs (to Polish texts) although generally available are provided with English versions which seem too poor to be recommended. The German versions seem almost equally clumsy. French versions are for the most part fair.

Editions: Schirmer (German and English texts)
Durand (French texts)

ANTONIN DVOŘÁK
(1841-1904)

Dvořák is perhaps the only Czech composer whose songs are widely known in English-speaking countries. Among his many songs the two sets, "Gipsy Songs" (Op. 55) and "Biblical Songs" (Op. 99), are perhaps the most remarkable. It is fortunate that the texts of at least these two sets of songs are available in adequate English versions.

In texture his songs remind one of Brahms, although Dvořák has of course an idiom unmistakably his own, and the point of similarity is primarily confined to the marked influence which folk melos and folk rhythms exercised upon the formation of the vocal line in the songs of both composers. All of Dvořák's songs are beautifully written for the voice. For the most part they seem to suit rather heavy voices best, and they are predominantly melodic in their conception.

Editions: Simrock
Novello
Associated Music Publishers

Gipsy Songs
A Cycle of Seven Songs, Opus 55
(Simrock Edition)

TITLE	COMP.	TESS.	TYPE	REMARKS
(1) I chant my lay	d1-g2	bb1-f2	Not too suitable for very light voices	Sustained, vigorous. Demands an accomplished pianist and occasionally good command of high pp. The English version is good.
(2) Hark, how my triangle	g1-a2	bb1-f2	All voices	Rapid, rhythmical. Demands an accomplished pianist. The English version is good.
(3) Silent and lone	d1-g2	f#1-eb2	Not too suitable for very light voices	Very sustained and subdued. The English version is fair.
(4) Songs my mother taught me	f#1-g2	b1-g2	All voices	Very sustained. The English version is fair-

-403-

TITLE	COMP.	TESS.	TYPE	REMARKS
(4) Songs my mother taught me (Cont'd.)				ly good. The accompaniment is rhythmically complex.
(5) Tune thy strings	a1-a2	a1-f2	All voices	Animated, rhythmical. Demands an accomplished pianist. The English version is fairly good.
(6) In his wide and ample	e1-g2	a1-e2	All voices	Light and animated, rhythmical. Demands an accomplished pianist. The English version is fair.
(7) Cloudy heights of Tatra	f1-g2 (bb2)	f1-f2	Not too suitable for light voices	Animated, vigorous. Demands an accomplished pianist. The English version is fairly good.

TITLE	COMP.	TESS.	TYPE	REMARKS
Goin' home	c1-g2	g1-eb2 (H)	All voices	Slow and very sustained. Adapted from the Largo of the "New World Symphony" and supplied with text by W. A. Fisher. (Ditson)

Ten Biblical Songs, Opus 99 (Simrock Edition)

TITLE	COMP.	TESS.	TYPE	REMARKS
(1) Clouds and darkness are round Him	d#1-f#2	f#1-d#2 (H)	Not too suitable for very light high voices	Sustained, somewhat declamatory. Demands in parts considerable dramatic intensity. The English version is good.
(2) Lord, thou art my refuge	e1-f2	g#1-e2 (H)	All voices	Sustained. The English version is good.
(3) Hear my prayer	eb1-a2	g1-eb2 (H)	All voices, except a very light soprano	Sustained. Demands in parts considerable dramatic intensity. The English version is good.
(4) God is my shepherd	e1-f#2	f#1-d#2 (H)	All voices	Very sustained for the most part, subdued. The English version is good.
(5) I will sing new songs of gladness	g1-g2	g1-e2	All voices, except a very light soprano	Animated, majestic, vigorous. The English version is good.
(6) Hear my prayer, o Lord	e1-g2	g1-e2 (H)	All voices	Sustained. The English version is good.
(7) By the waters of Babylon	d#1-g2	g1-e2	All voices	Sustained. In parts demands considerable dramatic intensity. The Eng-version is good.

TITLE	COMP.	TESS.	TYPE	REMARKS
(8) Turn thee to me	f1-f2	g1-e2 (H)	All voices	Sustained, grave. The English version is good.
(9) I will lift mine eyes	f#1-g2	a1-e2 (H)	All voices	Not fast, subdued, somewhat declamatory. The English version is good.
(10) Sing ye a joyful song	f1-g2	g1-d2 (H)	All voices	Animated, gay. The English version is good.
Stabat Mater				
Inflammatus et accensus (Latin text)	a-eb2	c1-c2	Alto	Sustained, in parts dramatic. Demands in parts some flexibility. (Novello)

LEO JANÁČEK
(1854-1928)

No songs of Janacek, one of Czechoslovakia's greatest composers, seem to be available in English translations.

JAROSLAV KŘIČKA
(1882-)

An outstanding Czech composer who has written a considerable number of remarkable songs is unfortunately represented by one song only, since "The albatross" seems to be the only one available in English version.

The albatross	b-f#2	e1-c#2	All voices, except a very light soprano or tenor	Sustained. Demands in parts considerable dramary intensity. Interpretatively not easy. English version by Fr. McAllister is good. (Homeyer)

BEDŘICH SMETANA
(1824-1884)

No English versions of Smetana's songs seem to be available. The piano score of The Bartered Bride provided with an English translation is published by the Gamble Hinge Co., Chicago.

KAROL SZYMANOWSKI
(1883-1937)

Since no adequate English versions of the very remarkable songs of Szymanowski seem to be available, it seemed best not to try to list any of the examples of this outstanding Polish composer. Most of his songs with Polish and German texts are published by Universal edition.

MISCELLANEOUS FLORID DISPLAY PIECES
and arrangements for coloratura soprano not otherwise listed.

For other similar material see the Song Lists of Adam, Dell' Acqua, Arditi, Bishop, Delibes, Saint-Saens among others, as well as Operatic Excerpts for Soprano.

ALABIEFF				
"The nightingale"	c1-ab2 (c3)	g1-g2		(Generally available)
BENEDICT				
"Carnival of Venice"	d1-eb3	g1-g2		Arr. by E. Liebling (Schirmer)

TITLE	COMP.	TESS.	TYPE	REMARKS
BENEDICT				
"The Gipsy and the bird"	d1-d3 (e3)	g1-g2		Arr. by E. Liebling (Schirmer)
DELIBES				
"Passepied"	d♯1-c♯3	g♯1-g♯2		Arr. by A. Aslanoff (Schirmer)
ECKERT				
"Swiss echo song"	d1-b♭2 (a) (d3)	a1-a2		Arr. by E. Liebling (Schirmer)
GLAZUNOV				
"La primavera d'or"	d1-b♭2	g1-g2		Arr. by F. La Forge (Schirmer) A waltz.
HAYDN				
"Già la notte"	c1-a2	f1-f2		Arr. by Viardot-Garcia. An arrangement of a serenade from one of Haydn's string quartets. Suitable for lyric soprano. (Generally available)
LIADOV				
"The musical snuffbox"	c♯1-d3	f♯1-g2		Arr. by A. Aslanoff (Schirmer)
PROCH				
Theme and variations (Deh torna mio bene)	b♭-e♭3	f1-g♭2		(Generally available)
RODE				
Theme and variations (Al dolce canto)	b♭-c3	g1-g2		(Marchesi, "Coloratur Arien." Peters)
STRAUSS				
"Voci di primavera"	e1-c3	g1-f2		A florid waltz (Schirmer)

For cadenzas for the principal operatic airs for coloratura soprano see:
Estelle Liebling, "Coloratura Digest" (Schirmer)
Mathilda Marchesi, "Variantes et Points d'Orgue" (Heugel; reprinted by E. Marks, New York)

III

FOLK SONGS

FOLK SONGS

Folk songs, in the form in which they are available to the performer of today, fall in three categories:

1. The true folk song, the words and the melody of which have been faithfully recorded and provided with a piano accompaniment.

2. The folk tune, in which the melody of a folk song has been retained but which melody a different set of words has been added. As an example of this type of arrangement see any number of Irish songs arranged by Hughes, Irish Melodies by Moore and Balfe, and Songs of the Hebrides arranged by Kennedy-Fraser.

3. A song in folk style or the traditional air, which, because of its similarity to the true folk song, is popularly considered such. ("Killarney" by Balfe or "Down by the Swanee River" by Stephen Foster, for instance.)

It has been my endeavor to concentrate mainly on the first two categories while preparing this list.

A complete or comprehensive list of American, English, Scottish and Irish folk songs would no doubt comprise several thousand entries. The list below does in no way claim to be complete or even very representative. It is primarily based on admittedly personal and no doubt somewhat arbitrary decision to list only such material as this writer considers of practical value to the singer or the vocal student.

Thus this list will not be of much value to those who are primarily interested in the study of folklore and secondarily in concert and teaching material which happens to be of folk origin. Judged by musicological and historical standards, this list is pitifully inadequate and no doubt amateurish. Yet, having been prepared for the use of performers, the selection has to be primarily based on the practical artistic value of the text and music and not on the historical, anthropological and linguistic factors which so often make an artistically insignificant folk song a culturally most valuable, elucidating and interesting example.

The American list is perhaps more adequately treated than any of the others. British singers have long been appreciative of their folk-song heritage, while American singers have as yet paid comparatively slight attention to their native folk music. It seemed therefore advisable to list the American examples more adequately.

As most of the songs listed rarely exceed a compass of a tenth it seemed advisable to dispense with the naming of the tessituras.

No Welsh folk songs have been listed, since in the opinion of this writer it seems preferable to sing them in their original language.

Since many of the American folk songs stem from England, a great number of duplications and slightly different versions of the same tune and the same text exist. In case of such duplication this writer has favored the American version. Thus many a famous ballad and song not found in the English list (such as "Lord Randal" or "Barbara Allen") will be found in the American list.

An excellent list of collections of folk songs of Great Britain and America is published by the American Academy of Teachers of Singing and may be obtained by applying to Walter L. Bogert, Secretary, 25 Claremont Ave., New York, N. Y.

The performance of folk songs in a present-day concert hall presents a number of problems. In the opinion of this writer it seems most advisable to treat the folk songs primarily as music and not as some "quaint examples" of folklore. In other words, unless the singer can wholeheartedly accept the text and the music of a folk song as such, and unless this text and its musical expression can produce within him an emotional reaction sufficiently strong to warrant a performance, it would be better not to try to perform such songs. Utmost simplicity, understatement rather than a so-called "dramatic projection," clear, unaffected diction not marred by any attempt to imitate a dialect, and a clear delivery of the melodic line seem imperative to a dignified and satisfactory performance of a folk song in a concert hall. Any conscious attempt to inject the so-called "native flavor" into a folk song or to imitate the mannerisms of an untrained singer is almost invariably bound to result in an exaggerated, carricature-like performance, embarrassing alike in its crudeness and insincerity, which are bound to be accentuated by the stage, footlights, grand piano, and the dress of the performers. Folk songs are best accompanied on a guitar or other such instrument, since in its nature the instrumental accompaniment of a folk song is confined to a simple harmonic background accentuating the rhythmic structure of the melody. The accompanist using the modern piano should make his part as inconspicuous as possible.

TITLE	ARR. & PUB.	COMP.	TYPE	REMARKS
AMERICAN				
As I walked out (Kentucky)	McGill, Folk Songs of the Kentucky Mountains, Boosey	d1-f2	All voices	Sustained, graceful.
Barbara Allen (Kentucky)	Brockway and Wyman, Lonesome Tunes, Gray	b-d2	All voices	Sustained narrative song.
Barbary Ellen (Kentucky)	Niles, American Folk Song Series, Set 18, Schirmer	b-e2	All voices	Sustained narrative song.
Billie boy (Kentucky)	Brockway and Wyman, Lonesome Tunes, Gray	eb1-eb2	All voices	Gently humorous, graceful.
Bird's courting song (Vermont)	Sturgis and Hughes, Songs from the Hills of Vermont, Schirmer	c1-eb2	All voices	Animated, gently humorous, rhythmical.
Black is the color of my true love's hair (Kentucky)	Niles, Seven Kentucky Mountain Songs, Schirmer	b-e2	Most suitable for men's voices	Sustained, plaintive.
Bury me not on the lone prairie	Siegmeister, A Treasury of American Song, Knopf	b-d2	Most suitable for men's voices	Sustained, somber.
Careless love	Bacon, Along Unpaved Roads, Delkas	e1-f#2	All voices	Sustained, plaintive.
Come, all you young and handsome girls (Kentucky)	Brockway and Wyman, Twenty Kentucky Mountain Songs, Ditson	d1-d2	Women's voices	Sustained, plaintive.

TITLE	ARR. & PUB.	COMP.	TYPE	REMARKS
Come o my love (North Carolina)	Matteson, American Folk Song Series, Set 15, Schirmer	c1-c2	All voices	Sustained, plaintive.
Common Bill	Bacon, Along Unpaved Roads, Delkas	b-f2	Women's voices	Gently humorous, graceful.
Daily growing (Vermont)	Sturgis and Hughes, Songs from the Hills of Vermont, Schirmer	d1-d2	Women's voices	Sustained, plaintive.
Down in that valley (Kentucky)	Niles, American Folk Song Series, Set 18, Schirmer	e1-e2	All voices	Sustained.
Ef I had a ribbon bow (Kentucky)	Niles, Seven Kentucky Mountain Songs, Schirmer	g1-f2	Women's voices	Sustained.
Father Grumble (Ohio)	Niles, American Folk Song Series, Set 18, Schirmer	c1-d2	All voices	Animated, humorous narrative song.
Foggy, foggy dew	Sandburg, The American Song Bag, Harcourt, Brace	eb1-db2	Men's voices	Sustained.
Frog went a-courting	Brockway and Wyman, Lonesome Tunes, Gray	d1-d2	All voices	Rapid, humorous. Demands facile articulation and an accomplished pianist. See "Toad's Courtship."
He's gone away	Siegmeister, A Treasury of American Song, Knopf	c1-e2	All voices	Sustained, plaintive.
I'm sad and I'm lonely	Siegmeister, A Treasury of American Song, Knopf	d1-e2	Women's voices	Sustained, plaintive.
I wash my face in a golden vase (Kentucky)	Niles, American Folk Song Series, Set 18, Schirmer	d1-d2	Women's voices	A sustained, delicate Christmas carol.
I wish I was single (Nebraska)	Sandburg, The American Song Bag, Harcourt, Brace	db1-c2	Men's voices	Humorous. Demands facile articulation.
I wonder as I wander (North Carolina)	Niles, American Folk Song Series, Set 14, Schirmer	c1-e2	All voices	Sustained, plaintive, subdued. Religious theme.
John Riley (Kentucky)	Brockway and Wyman, Lonesome Tunes, Gray	c1-c2	All voices	Sustained, graceful narrative.

TITLE	ARR. & PUB.	COMP.	TYPE	REMARKS
Lady Ishbel and the elfin knight (North Carolina)	Niles, American Folk Song Series, Set 20, Schirmer	c1-d2	All voices	Sustained narrative song.
Little brown jug	Siegmeister, A Treasury of American Song, Knopf	e1-e2	Men's voices	Animated, humorous.
Little rosewood casket (Kentucky)	Thomas, Devil's Ditties, Hatfield, Chicago	e1-f2	Women's voices	Sustained, delicate.
Little sparrow (Kentucky)	Brockway and Wyman, Lonesome Tunes, Gray	e1-e2	Women's voices	Sustained.
Liza Jane (Kentucky)	Thomas, Devil's Ditties, Hatfield, Chicago	b-e2	Men's voices	Animated, comic.
Lonesome road (Indiana, Texas)	Sandburg, The American Song Bag, Harcourt, Brace	d1-c2	All voices	Sustained.
Lord Randal (Kentucky)	McGill, Folk Songs of the Kentucky Mountains, Boosey	eb1-f2	All voices, except a light soprano	Dramatic narrative.
Lord Thomas (Kentucky)	McGill, Folk Songs of the Kentucky Mountains, Boosey	c1-eb	All voices, except a very light soprano	Dramatic narrative song
Madam, I have come a-court-ing (Maine)	Ring, Folk Songs, Ballads, etc., Set IV, E. C. Schirmer, Boston	c1-c2	All voices	Animated, humorous.
My horses ain't hungry (Kentucky)	Niles, American Folk Song Series, Set 14, Schirmer	b-e2	All voices	Gently humorous, graceful.
Night-herding song	Siegmeister, A Treasury of American Song, Knopf	c1-c2	All voices	Sustained, graceful, subdued.
O death (Southern Mountains)	Siegmeister, A Treasury of American Song, Knopf	b-d2	Not too suitable for light high voices	Sustained, somber.
Oh, who's goin' to shoe your pretty little foot (North Carolina)	Niles, American Folk Song Series, Set 18, Schirmer	b-c2	Men's voices	Graceful.
Poor way faring stranger (Southern Mountains)	Siegmeister, A Treasury of American Song, Knopf	c1-e2	Men's voices	Sustained, plaintive.

TITLE	ARR. & PUB.	COMP.	TYPE	REMARKS
See - Jesus the saviour (Kentucky)	Niles, American Folk Song Series, Set 16, Schirmer	e1-c2	Most suitable for light voices	A sustained, delicate Christmas carol.
Sinful shoe	Bacon, Along Unpaved Roads, Delkas	c1-eb2	Not too suitable for very light high voices	Sustained. Demands in parts considerable dramatic intensity.
Sourwood mountain (Kentucky)	Brockway and Wymay, Lonesome Tunes, Gray	b-c#2	All voices	Vigorous, animated.
Sweet Betsy from Pike (Kentucky)	Thomas, Devil's Ditties, Hatfield, Chicago	c#1-e2	All voices	Animated, humorous.
The barnyard song (Kentucky)	Brockway and Wyman, Lonesome Tunes, Gray	eb1-eb2	All voices	Animated, humorous nursery rhyme.
The bee (New England)	Siegmeister, A Treasury of American Song, Knopf	d1-d2	All voices	Graceful, humorous.
The bed-time song (Kentucky)	Brockway and Wymay, Lonesome Tunes, Gray	c#1-d2	All voices	Graceful, delicate.
The blue-eyed boy (North Carolina)	Matteson, American Folk Song Series, Set 15 Schirmer	c1-c2	Women's voices	Sustained.
The cherry tree (Kentucky)	Niles, Seven Kentucky Mountain Songs, Schirmer	a1-e2	All voices	A sustained, graceful Christmas carol.
The daemon lover (Kentucky)	Brockway and Wymay, Twenty Kentucky Mountain Songs, Ditson	c1-eb2	All voices	Sustained narrative song.
The deaf woman's courtship (Virginia)	Powell, Five Virginian Songs, Fischer	b-f#2	All voices	Animated, humorous.
The dear companion (North Carolina)	Sharp, American Folk Song Series, Set 21, Schirmer	e1-c2	Women's voices	Sustained, plaintive.
The false young man (Tennessee)	Sharp, American Folk Song Series, Set 21, Schirmer	b-d2	Women's voices	Sustained, plaintive.
The farmer's curst wife (Kentucky)	Niles, American Folk Song Series, Set 20, Schirmer	e1-e2	All voices	A rapid, comic narrative. Demands facile articulation.
The lass from the low country (North Carolina)	Niles, American Folk Song Series, Set 20, Schirmer	b-d2	All voices	Sustained, somber.

TITLE	ARR. & PUB.	COMP.	TYPE	REMARKS
The little Mohee (Kentucky)	Brockway and Wymay, Lonesome Tunes, Gray	c#1-d2	Most suitable for men's voices	Sustained narrative song.
The nightingale (Kentucky)	Brockway and Wymay, Lonesome Tunes, Gray	db1-f2	Not too suitable for very low voices	Graceful, sustained.
The old maid (Kentucky)	Brockway and Wyman, Twenty Kentucky Mountain Songs, Ditson	eb1-eb2	Women's voices	Animated, humorous.
The old maid's song (Kentucky)	Brockway and Wymay, Lonesome Tunes, Gray	eb1-f2	Women's voices	Rhythmical, humorous.
The rich old lady (Virginia)	Powell, Five Virginian Songs, Fischer	d1-e2	All voices	Animated, comic narrative song.
The rich old miser courted me (Maine)	Ring, Folk Songs, Ballads, etc., Set IV, E. C. Schirmer, Boston	c1-d2	Women's voices	Animated, humorous.
The riddle song (Kentucky)	Sharp, American Folk Song Series, Set 21, Schirmer	e1-e2	All voices	Sustained, delicate.
The single girl	Siegmeister, A Treasury of American Song, Knopf	d1-e2	Women's voices	Sustained, graceful, humorous.
The swapping song (Kentucky)	Brockway and Wymay, Twenty Kentucky Mountain Songs, Ditson	f1-d2	Most suitable for men's voices	Animated, comic.
The toad's courtship (Kentucky)	Brockway and Wymay, Twenty Kentucky Mountain Songs, Ditson	d1-e2	All voices	Animated, humorous narrative song. See "Frog Went A-Courting."
The twa corbies (Kentucky)	Niles, American Folk Song Series, Set 18, Schirmer	b-f2	Women's voices	Sustained, somber.
The warranty deed (Vermont)	Sturgis and Hughes, Songs from the Hills of Vermont, Schirmer	eb1-eb2	All voices	Animated comic song.
The watercresses (Kentucky)	Niles, American Folk Song Series, Set 20, Schirmer	c1-f2	All voices	Graceful, delicate, rhythmical.
Tom Bolynn (New England)	Siegmeister, A Treasury of American Song, Knopf	d1-d2	All voices	An animated, humorous narrative.
Wanderin' (New York)	Sandburg, The American Song Bag, Harcourt, Brace	d1-d2	Most suitable for men's voices	Sustained, subdued.

AMERICAN NEGRO

TITLE	ARR. & PUB.	COMP.	TYPE	REMARKS
Ain't goin to study war no mo'	Burleigh, Negro Spirituals, Ricordi	f1-eb2	All voices	Rhythmical, graceful.
Blind man	Seigmeister, A Treasury of American Song, Knopf	c1-c2	All voices	Sustained, somber.
By and by	Johnson, The Book of American Negro Spirituals, Viking	e1-f#2	All voices	Sustained.
City called heaven	Hall Johnson, Robbins Music Corporation	c1-f2	All voices	Slow, sustained.
Crucifixion	John Payne, Schirmer	b1-b2	Low voices	Slow, very sustained, tragic.
Deep river	Burleigh, Negro Spirituals, Ricordi	ab-f2	Most suitable for medium or low voices	Very sustained. Demands in parts considerable dramatic intensity.
De gospel train	Burleigh, Negro Spirituals, Ricordi	f1-d2	All voices	Spirited, rhythmical.
De ol' ark's a-moverin' an I'm goin home	Johnson, The Second Book of Negro Spirituals, Viking	d1-g2	All voices	Animated, rhythmical.
Dere's no hidin' place down dere	Johnson, The Book of American Negro Spirituals, Viking	f1-d2	All voices	Rhythmical, animated.
Don't you weep when I'm gone	Burleigh, Negro Spirituals, Ricordi	db1-eb2	All voices	Sustained.
Go down, death	Kennedy, Mellows, A. and C. Boni	bb-eb2	All voices	Majestic, sustained.
Go down, Moses	Burleigh, Negro Spirituals, Ricordi	f#1-f#2	Not suitable for very light voices	Vigorous, dramatic.
Grumbellin' people	Kennedy, Mellows, A. and C. Boni	d1-e2	All voices	Animated, rhythmical, gently humorous.
Heav'n, heav'n	Burleigh, Negro Spirituals, Ricordi	f1-d2	All voices, except a very light soprano	Spirited, rhythmical, vigorous.
Hold on	Hall Johnson, Robbins Music Corporation	e1-e2	Not suitable for very light voices	Rhythmical and dramatic. See also "Sinful Shoe," arranged by Ernest Bacon.
Honor! honor!	Hall Johnson, Fischer	eb1-g2	All voices	Very spirited.
I cannot stay here by myself (A slave's lament)	Hall Johnson, Fischer	c1-e2	Most suitable for low voices	Very somber.

TITLE	ARR. & PUB.	COMP.	TYPE	REMARKS
I got a home in a dat rock	Burleigh, Ricordi	d1-f2	All voices	Rhythmical.
I'm troubled in mind	Johnson, The Book of American Negro Spirituals, Viking	c1-c2	Not too suitable for very light high voices	Slow, sustained.
I'm goin' to thank God	R. Nathaniel Dett, J. Fisher and Bros.	d1-g2	Most suitable for high voices	Sustained.
I stood on the river of Jerdon	Burleigh, Ricordi	c1-c2	All voices	Sustained.
John Henry (Negro work song)	Hall Johnson, Fischer	c1-eb2	Men's voices	Rhythmical.
Joshua fit de battle ob Jericho	Burleigh, Ricordi	d#1-e2	Not suitable for very light voices	Vigorous.
Lis'en to de lam's	Johnson, The Book of American Negro Spirituals, Viking	e1-g2	All voices	Sustained, delicate.
Lit'le David, play on yo' harp	Johnson, The Book of American Negro Spirituals, Viking	d1-g2	All voices, except a very light soprano	Spirited, rhythmical, vigorous.
My baby in a guinea-blue gown	Kennedy, Mellons, A. and C. Boni	b-e2	Most suitable for men's voices	Animated, rhythmical, humorous.
My soul's been anchored in the Lord	Florence Price, Gamble Hinged Music Co., Chicago	e1-f2 (a2)	Not suitable for very light voices	Sustained. Demands considerable dramatic intensity.
Nobody knows de trouble I've seen	Burleigh, Negro Spirituals, Ricordi	eb1-eb2	Not too suitable for very light high voices	Very sustained, somber.
Oh Peter go ring-a dem bells	Burleigh, Negro Spirituals, Ricordi	eb1-ab2	All voices	Spirited, rhythmical.
On ma journey	Edward Boatner, Ricordi	c1-c2	All voices	Spirited, rhythmical.
Sit down, servant, sit down	R. Nathaniel Dett Schirmer	c1-db2	All voices	Rhythmical.
Sometimes I feel like a motherless chile	Burleigh, Negro Spirituals, Ricordi	e1-e2	All voices	Very sustained, subdued.
Sometimes I feel like I wanna go home	J. Fisher and Bros., Seventy Negro Spirituals, Ditson	f1-c2	Most suitable for low voices	Sustained, subdued.
Steal away	Burleigh, Negro Spirituals, Ricordi	ab1-f2	All voices	Very sustained, subdued.

TITLE	ARR. & PUB.	COMP.	TYPE	REMARKS
Swing low, sweet chariot	Burleigh, Negro Spirituals, Ricordi	eb1-f2	All voices	Very sustained, slow.
The whale got Jonah down	Dan Lewis, Plantation Songs, White, Smith and Co.	f1-f2	All voices	A spirited, comic character song.
This is a sin-tryin' world	Siegmeister, A Treasury of American Song, Knopf	e1-b1	All voices	Animated, rhythmical.
'Tis me, o Lord	Burleigh, Negro Spirituals, Ricordi	ab1-eb2	All voices	Rhythmical, plaintive.
Trampin'	Edward H. Boatner, Galaxy Music Corp.	f1-d2	Most suitable for medium or low voices	Slow, rhythmical.
Troubles was hard	Kennedy, Mellons, A. and C. Boni	e1-e2	All voices, except a very light soprano	Animated, gently humorous narrative song about Biblical characters.
Water boy (a Negro convict song)	Avery Robinson, Boston Music Co.	d1-d2	Men's voices	Sustained.
Were you there	Burleigh, Negro Spirituals, Ricordi	c1-f2	All voices	Very sustained, subdued.
You may bury me in de Eas'	Burleigh, Negro Spirituals, Ricordi	f1-f2	All voices	Sustained, somber.

ENGLISH

TITLE	ARR. & PUB.	COMP.	TYPE	REMARKS
As down in the meadows	Moffat, Minstrelsy of England, Bailey & Ferguson	c1-f2	Most suitable for high voices	Graceful.
As I walked out through the meadows	Sharp, One-Hundred English Folk-Songs, Ditson	c1-d2	Men's voices	Sustained, graceful.
Botany bay	Sharp, One-Hundred English Folk-Songs, Ditson	e1-e2	Men's voices	Sustained narrative song.
Cross purposes	Moffat, Minstrelsy of England, Bailey & Ferguson	c1-f2	All voices	Graceful, humorous.
Early one morning	Moffat, Minstrelsy of England, Bailey & Ferguson	c1-f2	All voices	Sustained, graceful.
Gently, Johnny my jingalo	Sharp, One-Hundred English Folk-Songs, Ditson	d1-d2	Men's voices	Graceful, gently humorous.
Henry Martin	Sharp, One-Hundred English Folk-Songs, Ditson	d1-e2	Most suitable for men's voices	Sustained narrative song.
I'm seventeen come Sunday	Farnsworth and Sharp, Folk-Songs, Chanteys and Singing Games, H.W. Gray & Co.	d1-e2	All voices	Graceful, animated.

TITLE	ARR. & PUB.	COMP.	TYPE	REMARKS
In Bibberley town	Sharp, Songs of the West (Baring-Gould collector), Methuen & Co., London	d1-d2	All voices	Animated, humorous narrative song.
In search of a wife	Moffat, Minstrelsy of England, Bailey & Ferguson	d1-e2	Men's voices	Sustained, humorous.
I saw three ships	Arranged by Eric Thiman, Augener	d1-d2	Not too suitable for light high voices	A vigorous, spirited Christmas carol.
May day carol	Arranged by Deems Taylor, Fischer	d1-g2	Most suitable for men's voices	Sustained. The accompaniment is somewhat elaborate harmonically.
Mowing the barley	Farnsworth and Sharp, Folk-Songs, Chanteys and Singing Games, H. W. Gray & Co.	c1-e2	All voices	Graceful, humorous.
My mother did so before me	Sharp, Songs of the West (Baring-Gould collector), Methuen & Co., London	d1-f2	Women's voices	Spirited, humorous.
O no, John!	Farnsworth and Sharp, Folk-Songs, Chanteys and Singing Games, H. W. Gray & Co.	d1-d2	All voices	Animated.
O Sally, my dear	Sharp, One-Hundred English Folk-Songs, Ditson	c1-e2	Men's voices	Graceful, gently humorous.
O waly waly	Farnsworth and Sharp, Folk-Songs, Chanteys, and Singing Games, H. W. Gray & Co.	d1-d2	All voices	Sustained, plaintive.
Rolling in the dew	Vaughan Williams, Six English Folk-Songs, Oxford University Press	d1-e2	All voices	Animated, light, humorous, rhythmical.
Some rival has stolen my true love away	Arranged by Lucy E. Broadwood, Boosey	d1-e2	Most suitable for men's voices	Animated, vigorous.
Sweet nightingale	Sharp, Songs of the West (Baring-Gould collector), Methuen & Co., London	d1-d2	Not too suitable for very low voices	Sustained, delicate.
The brisk young bachelor	Sharp, One-Hundred English Folk-Songs, Ditson	c1-d2	Men's voices	Very animated, humorous. Demands facile articulation.

TITLE	ARR. & PUB.	COMP.	TYPE	REMARKS
The blue flame	Sharp, Songs of the West (Baring-Gould collector), Methuen & Co., London	c1-e2	Women's voices	Sustained, somber, subdued.
The golden vanity	Broadwood, English County Songs, Schuberth & Co., London	a-d2	Not too suitable for very light high voices	A dramatic narrative song.
The loyal lover	Maitland, English County Songs, Schuberth & Co., London	d1-e2		Sustained, graceful.
The mole-catcher	Sharp, Songs of the West (Baring-Gould collector), Methuen & Co., London	d1-d2	Most suitable for men's voices	A comic, parlato song.
The three ravens	Moffat, Minstrelsy of England, Bailey & Ferguson	d1-f2	All voices	Sustained, subdued, graceful narrative.
The tythe pig	Sharp, Songs of the West, Methuen & Co., London	c1-d2	All voices	Animated, comic narrative song.
Tobacco is an Indian weed	Sharp, Songs of the West, Methuen & Co., London	d1-d2	All voices	A mock-serious song.
Whistle, daughter, whistle	Sharp, One-Hundred English Folk-Songs, Ditson	a-d2	Women's voices	Sustained, gently humorous.
Yarmouth fair	Arranged by P. Warlock, Oxford University Press	d1-g2	Men's voices	Rapid, humorous. Demands facile articulation.

SCOTTISH

TITLE	ARR. & PUB.	COMP.	TYPE	REMARKS
An Eriskay love lilt	Kennedy-Fraser, Songs of the Hebrides, Boosey	d1-e2	All voices	Delicate.
Annie Laurie	Hopekirk, Seventy Scottish Songs, Ditson	c1-e2	All voices	Very sustained.
Benbecula bridal procession	Kennedy-Fraser, Songs, of the Hebrides, Boosey	f♯1-f♯2	All voices	Delicate, sustained.
Come, all ye jolly shepherds	Hopekirk, Seventy Scottish Songs, Ditson	c1-e2	Most suitable for men's voices	Animated, rhythmical.
Coming through the rye	Hopekirk, Seventy Scottish Songs, Ditson	c1-f♯	Most suitable for women's voices	Sustained, graceful. A Robert Burns poem.

TITLE	ARR. & PUB.	COMP.	TYPE	REMARKS
Flora Macdonald's love song	Kennedy-Fraser, Songs of the Hebrides, Boosey	c1-f2	Women's voices, except a very light soprano	Sustained. In parts demands considerable dramatic intensity.
Flow gently, sweet Afton	Hopekirk, Seventy Scottish Songs Ditson	d1-g2	All voices	Sustained.
Get up and bar the door	Pittman, Songs of Scotland, Boosey; Reid, Songs of Scotland, Boosey	d1-f2	All voices	Animated, humorous.
Heart o' fire-love	Kennedy-Fraser, Songs of the Hebrides, Boosey	g1-a2	All voices	Vigorous.
Here's to thy health	Somervell, Songs of the Four Nations Cramer, London	c1-f2	Most suitable for men's voices	Animated. The poem is by Robert Burns.
Isle of my heart	Kennedy-Fraser, Songs of the Hebrides, Boosey	c1-ab2	All voices	Graceful, delicate.
Land of heart's desire	Kennedy-Fraser, Songs of the Hebrides, Boosey	d1-g2	Not too suitable for low voices	Very sustained. Demands good command of high pp.
Loch Lomond	Hopekirk, Seventy Scottish Songs, Ditson	d1-e2	All voices	Sustained.
My boy Tammy	Reid, Songs of Scotland, Boosey	a-d2	All voices	Sustained, graceful.
My love, she's but a lassie yet	Hopekirk, Seventy Scottish Songs, Ditson	c1-g2	Men's voices	Spirited, delicate, gently humorous. Demands facile articulation.
My nannie's awa	Reid, Songs of Scotland, Boosey	c1-eb2	Most suitable for men's voices	Sustained, graceful.
O can ye sew cushions?	Arranged by Colin Taylor, Oxford University Press	g1-g2	Soprano	Very sustained. Demands good command of high pp.
Robin Adair	Pittman, Songs of Scotland, Boosey	f1-f2	Women's voices	Sustained.
Speed, bonny boat	Arranged by Malcolm Lawson, Ditson	d1-d2	All voices	Sustained.
The bens of Jura	Kennedy-Fraser, Songs of the Hebrides, Boosey	e1-g2	All voices, except a very light soprano	Very sustained. In parts demands considerable dramatic intensity.
The death farewell	Kennedy-Fraser Songs of the Hebrides, Boosey	c1-f2	All voices, except a very light soprano	Very sustained, somber.

TITLE	ARR. & PUB.	COMP.	TYPE	REMARKS
The hundred pipers	Arranged by Mac-Pherson and Stuart, Ditson	c1-f2	Men's voices	An animated marching song.
The laird o' Cockpen	Hopekirk, Seventy Scottish Songs, Ditson	c1-f2	All voices	Animated, humorous narrative song.
The mermaid's croon	Kennedy-Fraser, Songs of the Hebrides, Boosey	e1-e2	Women's voices	Sustained.
The seagull of the land-under-waves	Kennedy-Fraser, Songs of the Hebrides, Boosey	d1-d2	All voices, except a very light soprano	Sustained.
The troutling of the sacred well	Kennedy-Fraser, Songs of the Hebrides, Boosey	g1-g2	Women's voices, except a very heavy alto	Graceful, very delicate. Demands lightness of tone.
The wild swan	Kennedy-Fraser, Songs of the Hebrides, Boosey	e1-g2	All voices	Very sustained.
To people who who have gardens	Kennedy-Fraser, Songs of the Hebrides, Boosey	f1-c2	All voices	Animated, delicate. Demands facile articulation.
Turn ye to me	Reid, Songs of Scotland, Boosey	a-d2	Not too suitable for very light high voices	Sustained.
Weaving lilt	Fraser and Mac-lead, Songs of the Hebrides, Boosey	d1-e2	Women's voices	Graceful, gently humorous, delicate.
Whar' hae' ye been a' the day	Hopekirk, Seventy Scottish Songs, Ditson	c1-f2	Men's voices	Sustained, rhythmical.
Young Jamie lo'ed me weel	Hopekirk, Seventy Scottish Songs, Ditson	d1-g2	Women's voices	A sustained, personal narrative song.
Young Lochinvar	Reid, Songs of Scotland, Boosey	a-d2	Not too suitable for light high voices	Vigorous. Poem is by Sir Walter Scott.

IRISH

TITLE	ARR. & PUB.	COMP.	TYPE	REMARKS
A Ballynure ballad	H. Hughes, Irish Country Songs, Boosey	b-d2	Most suitable for men's voices	Animated, rhythmical, gently humorous.
Barney O'Hea	Page, Irish Songs Ditson	d1-eb2	Women's voices	Animated, humorous.
Believe me if all those endearing young charms	Generally available	eb1-eb2	All voices	Sustained.

TITLE	ARR. & PUB.	COMP.	TYPE	REMARKS
(otherwise known as: My lodging is on the cold, cold ground)				
Bendemeer's stream	Arranged by Gatty, Boosey	g1-g2	All voices	Sustained.
Down by the Sally gardens	H. Hughes, Irish Country Songs, Boosey	db1-eb2	All voices	Sustained, delicate.
I have a bonnet trimmed with blue	Hughes, Irish Country Songs, Boosey	f1-d2	Women's voices	Graceful, delicate.
I know my love	Hughes, Irish Country Songs, Boosey	c1-f2	Women's voices	A rapid comic song. Demands facile articulation.
I know where I'm goin'	Hughes, Irish Country Songs, Boosey	ab1-eb2	Women's voices	Graceful, delicate.
I'm not myself at all	Hughes, Irish Country Songs, Boosey	d#1-f#2	All voices	Animated, humorous. Demands facile articulation.
In Dublin's fair city	Page, Irish Songs, Ditson	d1-e2	Men's voices	Sustained, graceful.
I will walk with my love	Hughes, Irish Country Songs, Boosey	eb1-f2	Women's voices	Sustained, subdued.
Johnny, I hardly knew ye	Hughes, Irish Country Songs, Boosey	e1-e2	Women's voices	Animated. Demands facile articulation.
Katey's letter	Page, Irish Songs, Ditson	b-g2	Women's voices	Humorous, graceful.
Kathleen Mavourneen	Hatton and Molloy, The Songs of Ireland, Boosey	b-f2	Men's voices	Sustained.
Kathleen O'More	Hughes, Irish Country Songs, Boosey	f1-e2	Men's voices	Sustained, graceful.
Kitty my love will you marry me	Hughes, Irish Country Songs, Boosey	c1-f2	Men's voices	Rapid, gently humorous. Demands very facile articulation.
Lady, be tranquil	Hughes, Old Irish Melodies, Boosey	d1-d2	Men's voices	Humorous. Demands facile articulation.
Little boats	Hughes, Old Irish Melodies, Boosey	eb1-eb2	Most suitable for women's voices	Sustained, graceful lullaby.
Loving dark maid	Hughes, Old Irish Melodies, Boosey	bb-f2	Men's voices	Sustained, subdued.
Londonderry air	Generally available	b1-g2	All voices	Very sustained.

TITLE	ARR. & PUB.	COMP.	TYPE	REMARKS
(Would God I were a tender apple blossom; Danny boy)				
Love is cruel, love is sweet	Fischer, Sixty Irish Songs, Ditson	d1-g2	All voices	Graceful.
Must I go bound?	Hughes, Irish Country Songs, Boosey	c1-d2	Most suitable for men's voices	Sustained.
Reynardine	Hughes, Irish Country Songs, Boosey	c#1-f#2	Not too suitable for very low voices	Graceful, delicate.
She moved thro' the fair	Hughes, Irish Country Songs, Boosey	db1-eb2	Men's voices	Sustained.
Shule agra	Somervell, Songs of the Four Nations Cramer, London	c1-e2	Women's voices, except a very light soprano	Sustained. Demands in parts considerable dramatic intensity.
The banks of the daisies	Page, Irish Songs, Ditson	eb1-eb2	Men's voices	Sustained, graceful.
The blatherskite	Fischer, Sixty Irish Songs, Ditson	d1-f2	Men's voices	Animated, humorous.
The cork leg	Hughes, Irish Country Songs, Boosey	b-d2	Not too suitable for very light voices	Animated, vigorous, humorous.
The Fanaid grove	Hughes, Irish Country Songs, Boosey	b-d2	Not too suitable for very light high voices	Sustained, narrative, plaintive.
The fairy king's courtship	Hamilton Harty, Three Irish Folk Songs, Oxford University Press	eb1-f2	All voices	Sustained narrative song. Demands an accomplished pianist.
The foggy dew	Page, Irish Songs, Ditson	c1-f2	All voices	Sustained.
The game played in Erin-Go-Bragh	Hamilton Harty, Three Irish Folk Songs, Oxford University Press	c1-eb2	Men's voices, except a very light tenor	A rapid character song. Demands facile articulation.
The Gartan mother's lullaby	Hughes, Irish Country Songs, Boosey	d1-e2	Women's voices	Sustained, subdued.
The gentle maiden	Somervell, Songs of the Four Nations, Cramer, London	bb-eb2	Most suitable for men's voices	Sustained.
The harp that once through Tara's halls	Page, Irish Songs, Ditson	db1-eb2	All voices	Very sustained.

TITLE	ARR. & PUB.	COMP.	TYPE	REMARKS
'Tis the last rose of summer	Fischer, Sixty Irish Songs, Ditson	f1-f2	All voices	Sustained.
The leprehaun	Hughes, Irish Country Songs, Boosey	d1-g2	All voices	Graceful.
The light of the moon	Hughes, Irish Country Songs, Boosey	c1-f2	All voices	Animated, gently humorous.
The lover's curse	Hughes, Irish Country Songs, Boosey	bb-eb2	Women's voices, except a very light soprano	Vigorous, in parts dramatic.
The minstrel boy	Hatton and Molloy The Songs of Ireland, Boosey	c1-f2	Men's voices	Sustained.
The next market day	Hughes, Irish Country Songs, Boosey	a-c2	All voices	Rapid, gently humorous. Demands facile articulation.
The lowlands of Holland	Hamilton Harty, Three Irish Folk Songs, Oxford University Press	d1-e2	Women's voices, except a very light soprano	Very animated, dramatic. Demands an accomplished pianist.
The meeting of the waters	Page, Irish Songs, Ditson	d1-d2	All voices	Sustained.

See also Irish Melodies, words by Thomas Moore, airs arranged by M. W. Balfe, 87 songs, Novello. Among them are such famous songs as "Believe me if all those endearing young charms," "The harp that once thro' Tara's halls," "The meeting of the waters," " 'Tis the last rose of summer," etc.

IV

OPERATIC EXCERPTS

OPERATIC EXCERPTS

As already mentioned in the preface, the section devoted to nineteenth and twentieth century operatic airs and excerpts is very limited in scope.

One of the considerations which prompted the exclusion from these lists of all but the most celebrated operatic airs was the relative difficulty of obtaining in separate form at the present time any but the most widely used so-called "standard material." It seemed unfair and unnecessary to recommend much rather inconsequential music which could be obtained only in the complete piano score form, and then only with much difficulty and at a great expense. Even some of the airs listed below, celebrated as they are, are at present rather difficult to obtain. Most of them are, however, listed in the catalogues of various American publishers and since, if some of them are at present out of print, it is hoped that they are only temporarily unavailable, the major percentage of the airs listed below are, or will be shortly, easily obtainable.

There is a great number of collections of operatic airs in their original languages. Some of the most comprehensive anthologies are listed below:

Operatic Songs, published in 4 vols. by J. Church Co.

Krehbiel, Songs from the Operas, published by Schirmer.

Operas, 5 vols. published by Ditson.

Prima Donna Album for soprano, 1 vol., published by Schirmer.

Spicker, Operatic Anthology, 5 vols., published by Schirmer.

Opera Arias, 4 vols., published by Ricordi.

In addition see: Arien Album, published by Peters.
Arien Album, published by Breitkopf & Härtel (many in German translation only)
Arien Album, published by Universal and the Novello Collection (the latter only with Italian texts, often translations)

For opera airs of Gluck, Handel, Mozart, Haydn, see separate sections.

For concert airs see the song lists of respective composers.

On Accompanying Operatic Excerpts.

The playing of a nineteenth century orchestral accompaniment on the pianoforte presents a number of problems not encountered in the ordinary pursuit of pianistic studies. The problems are mainly those of sonority and omission of unimportant details, which details, if performed adequately in a pianistically correct manner, may often obscure and nullify the much more important features of an orchestrally conceived piece of music. Any pianist interested in doing justice to music of this nature will profit greatly by comparing the available pianoforte reduction with the orchestral score, so that he may establish the necessary distinction between the relatively unimportant figuration and the main trend of the musical thought (not always clearly discernible in an average pianoforte arrangement.) Listening to orchestral accompaniments in their original form (now made possible by the multitude of available records) will sometimes be even more profitable for the pianist, since the successful comparison of an orchestral score with its pianoforte counterpart does in its very nature demand an ability to imagine orchestral sonorities.

Purely mechanical pianistic problems of some complexity are almost invariably present in any letter-perfect but realistically ill-considered pianoforte reduction. The pianist should by no means feel bound always to retain the sometimes awkward doublings, the often still more clumsy spacing and rapid figuration of some of the available pianoforte reductions.

A clear delineation of the bass line, a full sonority of the harmonic background, a proportionately prominent treatment of the melodic line, when such line is contained in the accompaniment, and a very firm rhythm should be his primary aims. In such an attempt to approximate the outstanding musical features of the orchestral part, the pianist may sometimes be forced to omit many passages which may seem pianistically important to him at the moment. Such deletions and simplifications, totally inadmissable in a song accompaniment where the pianoforte part is conceived as such, is, in the opinion of this writer, not in the least reprehensible in playing orchestrally conceived accompaniments, as long as the general pattern of the music is not thereby adversely affected.

Some of the pianoforte reductions of accompaniments of songs for voice and orchestra, however, when made by the composer himself are often admirably executed and are best played as written.

VINCENZO BELLINI
(1801-1834)

TITLE	COMP.	TESS.	TYPE	REMARKS
Beatrice di Tenda Ah! non pensar che pieno Recitative:	f1-g2 (bb2)	f1-f2	Soprano	Slow, sustained. Demands some flexibility. (Ricordi)
Oh! Miei fedeli Air: Ma la sola, ohímé!	eb1-c3	g1-g2	Lyric soprano (coloratura soprano)	Recitative, andante, allegro; quite florid. (Schirmer, Prima Donna Album)
I Capuleti ed i Montecchi Ascolta, se Romeo t'uccise un figlio **I Capuletti ed i Montecchi**	g-b2	d1-g2	Dramatic soprano or mezzo-soprano	An andante, allegro air. Demands some flexibility. (Ditson, Songs from the Operas)
Recitative: Eccomi in lieta vesta Air: Oh! Quante volte	d1-c3	g1-f2	Soprano	Scena and a sustained air. Has florid passages. (Ricordi)
I Puritani Recitative: O rendetemi la speme Air: Qui la voce	eb1-db3	g1-f2	Coloratura soprano (lyric soprano)	Andante, allegro, florid. (Schirmer, Prima Donna Album)
I Puritani Son vergin vezzosa	b-b2	a1-f#2	Coloratura soprano	An animated, florid polonaise. (Schirmer, Prima Donna Album)
La Sonnambula Recitative: Ah! Non credea mirarti Air: Ah, non giunge	d1-eb3	f1-g2	Coloratura soprano (lyric soprano)	Andante, allegro, quite florid. (Schirmer, Prima Donna Album)
La Sonnambula Recitative: Care compagne Air: Come per me sereno Sovra il sen	d1-db3	ab1-ab2	Coloratura soprano	Recitative, andante, allegro, florid. The recitative, "Care compagne," may be easily omitted and the "Come pér me sereno" as well as "Sovra il sen" sung separately. (Schirmer, Prima Donna Album)
La Sonnambula Come per me sereno oggi renaque il di	d1-db3	ab1-g2	Coloratura soprano	An andante, allegro air, very florid. (Ricordi)
La Sonnambula De' lieti auguri a voi son grata	f1-c3	bb1-g2	Coloratura soprano	Animated, quite florid. (Ricordi)

OPERA & TITLE	COMP.	TESS.	TYPE	REMARKS
La Sonnambula				
Tutto è gioia, tutto è festo	eb1-c3	ab1-f2	Coloratura soprano (light soprano)	Animated, quite florid. (Ricordi)
Norma				
Casta Diva	e1-c3	a1-a2	Dramatic soprano (lyric soprano)	A very sustained andante and a brilliant allegro. Demands considerable flexibility. (Schirmer, Prima Donna Album)

ARRIGO BOITO
(1842-1918)

OPERA & TITLE	COMP.	TESS.	TYPE	REMARKS
Mefistofelé				
L'altra notte il fondo al mare	d1-b2	e1-e2	Dramatic soprano (lyric soprano)	Slow, dramatic, somber. In parts demands considerable flexibility. (J. Church Co., Opera Songs)
Nerone				
A notte cupa	c#1-bb2	f1-f2	Dramatic soprano	Somewhat declamatory. Has dramatic climaxes. (Ricordi)
Nerone				
Invan mi danni	b-c3	a1ᵣf2	Dramatic soprano	Very sustained, very dramatic. (Ricordi)

ALFREDO CATALANI
(1854-1893)

OPERA & TITLE	COMP.	TESS.	TYPE	REMARKS
La Wally				
Ebben? Ne andrò lontano	e1-b2	b1-e2	Dramatic soprano (lyric soprano)	Sustained. Has dramatic climaxes. (Ricordi)
Loreley				
Amor celesto ebbrezza (Act II)	d1-c3	g1-g2	Lyric soprano	Sustained, graceful. Requires good command of high pp. (Ricordi)
Loreley				
Da che tutta mi son data	d1-ab2	g1-eb2	Lyric soprano (dramatic soprano)	Animated, graceful. Demands some flexibility. (Ricordi)
Loreley				
Recitative: Dove son? D'onde vengo? Air: Ma..forse è un orrido sogno (Act I)	d1-c3	f#1-f#2	Dramatic soprano	A dramatic scena and a compound, dramatic air. Has many sustained sections. (Ricordi)
Loreley				
O forze recondite	d1-c3	f1-g2	Dramatic soprano	Animated, vigorous. Demands flexibility. (Ricordi)

FRANCESCO CILÈA
(1866)

OPERA & TITLE	COMP. TESS.	TYPE	REMARKS
Adriana Lecouvreur Io sono l'umile ancella (Act I)	c1-ab2 f1-f2	Dramatic soprano (lyric soprano)	Sustained. Has dramatic climaxes. (Score, Sonzogno)
Adriana Lecouvreur Poveri fiori	d1-a2 g1-g2	Dramatic soprano (lyric soprano)	Sustained. Demands considerable dramatic intensity. (Sonzogno)

GAETANO DONIZETTI
(1797-1848)

OPERA & TITLE	COMP. TESS.	TYPE	REMARKS
Anna Bolena Al dolce guidami	d1-g2 eb1-eb2	Soprano or mezzo- soprano	Sustained, in parts quite florid. (Schirmer)
Don Pasquale Recitative: Quel guardo il cavaliere Air: So anch'io la virtù magica	d1-db3 f1-f2	Lyric soprano (coloratura soprano)	Andante, allegro, quite florid. (Ricordi)
Il Castello di Kenilworth Par che mi dica ancora	c#1-a2 (b2) a1-f#2	All Soprano	Andante, allegro, quite florid. (Schirmer, Prima Donna Album)
La Favorita Recitative: Fia dunque vero Air: O mio Fernando	b-a2 e1-e2	Dramatic soprano (mezzo- soprano)	Recitative, andante, allegro. Has dramatic climaxes. (Generally available)
La Figlia del Reggimento Ciascun lo dice	c1-a2 g1-f2	Lyric soprano (coloratura soprano)	Light, graceful. Demands some flexi- bility. (Ricordi)
La Figlia del Reggimento Convien partir!	e1-a2 ab1-f2	Lyric soprano (coloratura soprano)	Sustained. Demands some flexibility. (Schirmer, Prima Donna Album)
La Regina di Golconda Che val ricchezza e trono	c1-c3 g1-e2	Soprano or mezzo- soprano	An andante, allegro air. Demands some flexi- bility. (Ricordi)
L'Elisir d'Amore Prendi, per me sei libero	c1-c3 a1-f2	Lyric soprano (coloratura soprano)	Andante, allegro, quite florid. (Score, Ricordi)

OPERA & TITLE	COMP.	TESS.	TYPE	REMARKS

Linda di Chamounix
 Recitative:
 Ah, tardai troppo
 Air:
   O luce di quest'
   anima
	c1-c3	a1-g2	Coloratura soprano (lyric soprano)	Recitative and a light, rather florid animated air. (Schirmer, Prima Donna Album)

Lucia di Lammermoor Il dolce suono mi colpĭ di sua voce (The mad scene)	eb1-bb2 (eb3)	g1-g2	Coloratura soprano (lyric soprano)	A florid scena. As a rule sung with many added cadenzas. See cadenzas - Marchesi and Liebling. (Generally available)
Lucia di Lammermoor Que n'avons-nous des ailes (Per che non ho del vento)	c#1-d3	g1-a2	Coloratura soprano	A very florid andante, allegro air. From the French edition of Lucia di Lammermoor edited by La Forge. (Fischer)
Lucia di Lammermoor Regnava nel silenzio	c1-c3	g1-f#2	Coloratura soprano (lyric soprano)	Andante, allegro, florid. For cadenzas see Marchesi and Liebling. (Generally available)
Lucrezia Borgia Come è bello quale incanto	bb-c3	g1-g2	Soprano	An andante, allegro air, very florid. (Ricordi)
Lucrezia Borgia M'odi, ah m'odi	d1-c3 (bb)	eb1-f2	Soprano	An andante, allegro air, quite florid. (Ricordi)

Maria di Rohan
 Recitative:
 Havvi un Dio
 Air:
   Benigno il cielo
   arridere
	c1-c3	ab1-g2	Coloratura soprano	A florid compound air. Larghetto, recitative, moderato, allegro. (Ricordi)

FRANCO FACCIO
(1841-1891)

OPERA & TITLE	COMP.	TESS.	TYPE	REMARKS

Amleto
 Recitative:
   Principe Amleto
 Air:
   Dubita pur che
   brillino
	d1-c3	g1-g2	Soprano	Sustained. Has an effective climax. Demands good command of high pp. (Schirmer)

UMBERTO GIORDANO
(1867-)

OPERA & TITLE	COMP.	TESS.	TYPE	REMARKS
Andrea Chenier La Mamma morta	c#1-b2	g1-e2	Dramatic soprano	Scena and a sustained air. Has many dramatic

OPERA & TITLE	COMP.	TESS.	TYPE	REMARKS
La Mamma morta (Cont'd.)			(lyric soprano)	climaxes. (Sonzogno)
Fedora Dio di giustizia (Act III)	c1-a2	f1-f2	Dramatic soprano (lyric soprano)	Very sustained, grave air. Demands in parts considerable dramatic intensity. (Sonzogno)
Fedora O grandi occhi (Act I)	e1-a2	g#1-e2	Soprano	Sustained, graceful air. (Sonzogno)
Fedora Se amor ti allena	f#1-b2	b1-g#2	Light soprano	Animated, graceful. (Sonzogno)

RUGGIERO LEONCAVALLO
(1858-1919)

Pagliacci Recitative: Qual fiamma avea nel guardo; Air: Stridono lassù	c#1-a2 (a#2,b2)	g#1-f#2	Lyric soprano (dramatic soprano)	Scena and a sustained air. Has dramatic climaxes. (Generally available)

EUSEBIO LILLO
(1826-1910)

Osteria Domani, o me felice	c#1-a2	e1-e2	Soprano	An animated, graceful bolero. Demands some flexibility. (J. Church Co., Opera Songs)

PIETRO MASCAGNI
(1863-   )

Cavalleria Rusticana Voi lo sapete o mamma	b-a2	a1-f#2	Dramatic soprano (high mezzo- soprano)	Sustained. Has dramatic climaxes. (Generally available)
Iris Un dì ero piccina	d1-b2	e1-e2	Dramatic soprano	Sustained. Has dramatic climaxes. (Ricordi)
L'Amico Fritz Son pochi fiori (Act I)	d1-g2	eb1-eb2	Dramatic soprano (lyric soprano)	Sustained. Has dramatic climaxes. (Score, Sonzogno)

AMILCARE PONCHIELLI
(1834-1886)

OPERA & TITLE	COMP.	TESS.	TYPE	REMARKS
La Gioconda				
Suicidio	c#1-b2	f#1-f#2	Dramatic soprano	Sustained. Has dramatic climaxes. (Generally available)

GIACOMO PUCCINI
(1858-1924)

OPERA & TITLE	COMP.	TESS.	TYPE	REMARKS
Gianni Schicchi				
O mio babbino caro	eb1-ab2	ab1-f2	Lyric soprano	Sustained, rather delicate. Demands good command of high p. (Ricordi)
La Bohème (Act III)				
Donde lieta uscì	d1-a2	f#1-e2	Lyric soprano (dramatic soprano)	Sustained, has effective climaxes. (J. Church Co., Opera Songs)
La Bohème (Act II)				
Quando me'n vo	f1-bb2 (db3)	bb1-gb2	Lyric soprano (dramatic soprano)	Sustained. Has effective climaxes. (Ricordi)
La Bohème (Act I)				
Si, mi chiamano Mimì	db1-bb2	ab1-eb2	Lyric soprano (Dramatic soprano)	Sustained, delicate. Demands in parts considerable dramatic intensity. (Ricordi)
La Fanciulla del West (Act II)				
Oh se sapeste	e1-b2	g#1-e2	Lyric soprano	A brilliant, sustained waltz song. (Ricordi)
Le Villi				
Se come voi piccina io fossi	d1-a2	a1-e2	Lyric soprano (dramatic soprano)	Sustained. Has effective climaxes. (Ricordi)
Madama Butterfly (Act I)				
Ancora un passo, or via	c#1-b2	f#1-f#2	Lyric soprano (dramatic soprano)	Animated. Demands some flexibility. Has an effective final climax. (Ricordi)
Madama Butterfly (Act II)				
Che tua madre dovrà prenderti in braccio	db1-ab2 (bb2)	gb1-eb2	Dramatic soprano (lyric soprano)	Sustained. Has dramatic climaxes. (Ricordi)
Madama Butterfly (Act II)				
Un bel dì vedremo	db1-bb2	f1-f2	Dramatic soprano (lyric soprano)	Sustained. Has dramatic climaxes. (Ricordi)
Manon Lescaut (Act II)				
In quelle trine morbide	db1-bb2	f1-f2	Lyric soprano (dramatic soprano)	Very sustained. Has dramatic climaxes. (Ricordi)

OPERA & TITLE	COMP.	TESS.	TYPE	REMARKS
Manon Lescaut (Act II) L'ora, o Tirsi, è vaga e bella	d1-a2 (c3)	g1-g2	Lyric soprano (coloratura soprano)	Graceful, light. Demands considerable flexibility. (Ricordi)
Manon Lescaut (Act III) Sola.......perduta, abbandonata	c1-bb2	ab1-f2	Lyric soprano (dramatic soprano)	Sustained, somewhat declamatory. Has dramatic climaxes. (Ricordi)
Tosca (Act I) Non la sospiri la nostra casetta	f1-bb2	ab1-f2	Dramatic soprano (lyric soprano)	Sustained, rather animated. Has effective climaxes. (Ricordi)
Tosca (Act II) Vissi d'arte	eb1-bb2	gb1-eb2	Dramatic soprano (lyric soprano)	Very sustained. Has dramatic climaxes. (Ricordi)
Turandot (Act II) In questa reggia	c#1-c3	a1-f#2	Dramatic soprano	Declamatory, sustained. Has dramatic climaxes. (Ricordi)
Turandot (Act I) Signore, ascolta	db1-bb2	bb1-gb2	Lyric soprano (dramatic soprano)	Slow, sustained, rather subdued. (Ricordi)
Turandot (Act III) Tu che di gel sei cinta	eb1-bb2	ab1-f2	Lyric soprano (dramatic soprano)	Sustained. Has dramatic climaxes. (Ricordi)

GIOACCHINO ROSSINI
(1792-1868)

OPERA & TITLE	COMP.	TESS.	TYPE	REMARKS
Bianca e Falliero Recitative: Come sereno è il di Air: Della rosa il bel vermiglio	b-b2	e1-e2	Soprano or mezzo-soprano	Scena, andante, allegro, very florid. (Schirmer, Prima Donna Album)
Guillaume Tell Recitative: Ils s'éloignent enfin Air: Sombre forêt (French text)	d1-ab2	ab1-f2	Lyric soprano	Recitative and a sustained, somewhat florid romanza. (Breitkopf & Härtel, Soprano Arias)
La Donna del Lago Oh mattutini albori!	b-g2	g1-d2	Soprano or mezzo-soprano	Sustained. Demands some flexibility. (Schirmer, Prima Donna Album)
La Gazza Ladra Di piacer me balza il cor	b-a2	f#1-f#2	Soprano or mezzo-soprano	An andante, allegro air. Demands considerable flexibility. (Schirmer, Prima Donna Album)

Il Barbiere di Siviglia

OPERA & TITLE	COMP.	TESS.	TYPE	REMARKS
Una voce poco fa	g#-g#2 (b2)	e1-e2	Coloratura soprano	Andante, allegro, very florid. In the original key (E major) this air was intended for a very flexible mezzo-soprano or alto. It is now traditionally sung in F major and provided with cadenzas suitable for a light soprano voice. For the traditional versions see the edition by Liebling published by Schirmer.

Mosè

OPERA & TITLE	COMP.	TESS.	TYPE	REMARKS
Ah! d'un' afflitta il duolo	b-b2	e1-g#2	Soprano or high mezzo-soprano	An andante, allegro air, very florid. (Ricordi)

Otello

OPERA & TITLE	COMP.	TESS.	TYPE	REMARKS
Assisa a piè d'un salice	c1-g2	g1-d2	Soprano or mezzo-soprano	Sustained. Has florid passages. (Schirmer, Prima Donna Album)

Otello

OPERA & TITLE	COMP.	TESS.	TYPE	REMARKS
Deh calma o ciel	c1-f2	eb1-eb2	Soprano or mezzo-soprano	Sustained, short. Vocally not taxing. Demands some flexibility. (Schirmer, Prima Donna Album)

Semiramide

OPERA & TITLE	COMP.	TESS.	TYPE	REMARKS
Recitative: Bel raggio lusinghier Air: Dolce pensiero	c#1-a2	e1-e2	Soprano or mezzo-soprano	An andante, allegro air, very florid. (Schirmer, Prima Donna Album)

Zelmira

OPERA & TITLE	COMP.	TESS.	TYPE	REMARKS
Recitative: Eccolo, a voi l'affido Air: Ciel pietoso, ciel clemente	c1-bb2	f1-f2	Soprano or mezzo-soprano	Recitative, andante, allegro, very florid. (Schirmer, Prima Donna Album)

GIUSEPPE VERDI
(1813-1901)

Aida

OPERA & TITLE	COMP.	TESS.	TYPE	REMARKS
Recitative: Qui Radamès verrà Air: O cieli azzurri	b1-c3	a1-f2	Dramatic soprano (lyric soprano)	Scena and a very sustained air. Demands good command of high pp. The tessitura is quite high. (Generally available)

Aida

OPERA & TITLE	COMP.	TESS.	TYPE	REMARKS
Recitative: Ritorna vincitor Air: L'insana parola	c1-bb2	ab1-f2	Dramatic soprano (lyric soprano)	Scena and a compound air. In parts very dramatic. (Generally available)

OPERA & TITLE	COMP.	TESS.	TYPE	REMARKS
Don Carlo Nel giardin dell bello saracin ostello	c#1-a2	e1-e2	Soprano or mezzo-soprano	Animated, brilliant, rather florid. (Ricordi)
Don Carlo Non pianger, mia compagna	b-b♭2	a♭1-f2	Dramatic soprano	Sustained. Demands in parts considerable dramatic intensity. (Ricordi)
Don Carlo ⌐O don fatale	c♭1-c♭3	e♭1-e♭2	Dramatic soprano (mezzo-soprano)	Scena, andante and allegro. In parts very dramatic. Often sung transposed a third lower. (Schirmer, Operatic Anthology)
Don Carlo Tu che le vanità conoscesti	a#-a#2	f#1-f#2	Dramatic soprano	Scena and a sustained air. Has dramatic climaxes. (Ricordi)
Ernani Ernani involami	b♭-c3	f1-f2	Dramatic soprano (lyric soprano)	Recitative, andante, allegro. Demands considerable flexibility. (Schirmer, Prima Donna Album)
Falstaff Sul fil d'un soffio etesio	d#1-a2	a1-f#2	Lyric soprano	Light, very delicate. Demands good command of high pp. (Ricordi)
I due Foscari Recitative: No, mi lasciate Air: Tu al cui sguardo onni possente	b-c3	g1-g2	Dramatic soprano (lyric soprano)	Recitative and a brilliant, rather florid, andante, allegro air. (Ricordi)
I Lombardi O madre dal cielo	d1-d♭3	a♭1-a♭2	Lyric soprano (coloratura soprano)	Sustained. Has a very florid final section. (Ricordi)
I Lombardi Preghiera: Te Vergin santa, invoco! Salve Maria!	c#1-b♭2	f#1-f#2	Dramatic soprano (lyric soprano)	Sustained. Demands in parts considerable dramatic intensity. For the most part subdued. (Ricordi)
Il Trovatore (Act I, No. 4) Tacea la notte placida	e♭1-d♭3 (a♭)	f1-f2	Dramatic soprano (lyric soprano)	Andante and a florid allegro. (Generally available)
Il Trovatore (Act IV, No. 19) Recitative: Timor di me Air: D'amor sull' ali rose	c1-d♭3	f1-f2	Dramatic soprano (lyric soprano)	The adagio from the "Miserere" scene. Slow, rather sustained. Has florid passages. The allegro "Tu vedrai" can be sung separately. (Score generally available)

Opera & Title	Comp.	Tess.	Type	Remarks
Il Trovatore (Act IV, No. 19) Tu vedrai che amor in terra	c1-c3	f1-f2	Dramatic soprano (lyric soprano)	The allegro from the "Miserere" scene. Spirited. Has florid passages. In parts quite dramatic. (Score generally available)
I Masnadieri Lo squardo avea degli angeli	d1-c3	g1-g2	Lyric soprano (coloratura soprano)	Graceful. Demands considerable flexibility and a good command of high pp. (Ricordi)
I Masnadieri Tu del mio Carlo al seno	f1-c3	g1-g2	Dramatic soprano (lyric soprano)	Sustained. Demands some flexibility. (Ricordi)
I vespri Siciliani Mercè, dilette amiche	a-c#3	e1-e2	Dramatic soprano (lyric soprano)	Very animated, florid. (Schirmer, Prima Donna Album)
La Forza del Destino Me pellegrina ed orfana	c1-bb2	f1-f2	Dramatic soprano	Sustained. Has dramatic climaxes. (Ricordi)
La Forza del Destino Pace, pace mio Dio	eb1-bb2	f1-f2	Dramatic soprano (lyric soprano)	Sustained. The final section is very animated. Demands in parts considerable dramatic intensity. (Generally available)
La Forza del Destino Recitative: Son siunta Air: Madre, pietosa Vergine	b-b2	f#1-e2	Dramatic soprano	Scena and a compound aria. Demands in parts considerable dramatic intensity. (Schirmer, Operatic Anthology)
La Traviata Addio del passato	e1-a2	a1-f2	Lyric soprano (coloratura soprano)	Delicate, subdued. Demands some flexibility and a good command of high pp. (Generally available)
La Traviata Recitative: È strano Air: Ah, forse lui	d1-db3	f1-f2	Lyric soprano (coloratura soprano)	Scena and an andante, allegro air with interpolated recitative passages. In parts quite florid. (Generally available)
Luisa Miller Lo vidi, e'l primo palpito	f#1-c3	b-g2	Lyric soprano (coloratura soprano)	Animated, graceful. Demands considerable flexibility. (Ricordi)
Luisa Miller Tu puniscimi, o Signore	c#1-b2	f#1-e2	Lyric soprano (dramatic soprano)	Animated, rather dramatic. Has a florid final cadenza. (Ricordi)

OPERA & TITLE	COMP.	TESS.	TYPE	REMARKS
Macbeth Un macchia è qui tuttora (Mad Scene)	cb1-db3	f1-f2	Dramatic soprano (lyric soprano)	Sustained, somewhat declamatory, dramatic air. (Ricordi)
Otello Ave Maria	eb1-ab2	eb1-eb2	Dramatic soprano (lyric soprano)	Slow, very sustained, subdued. Demands good command of high pp. (Schirmer, Operatic Anthology)
Otello Piangea cantando nell' ermalanda (Canzone del Salice)	c#1-a#2	f#1-f#2	Dramatic soprano (lyric soprano)	Sustained, delicate. Demands good command of high pp. The folk-songlike theme is often interrupted by recitative passages. (Ricordi)

Rigoletto
Recitative:
  Gualtier Maldè
Air:
  Caro Nome
	b-c#3	g#1-g#2	Coloratura soprano (lyric soprano)	Sustained. In parts very florid. (Generally available)

Simon Beccanegra Come in quest' ora bruna	db1-bb2	f1-f2	Lyric soprano (dramatic soprano)	Sustained. (Ricordi)

Un Ballo in Maschera
Recitative:
  Ecco l'orrido campo
Air:
  Ma dall'arido stelo divulsa
	b-c3 (a)	f1-f2	Dramatic soprano (lyric soprano)	Recitative and a sustained, dramatic air. Has animated, somewhat declamatory middle section. Demands some flexibility. (Ricordi)

Un Ballo in Maschera Morrò,ma prima in grazia	a-cb3	eb1-eb2	Dramatic soprano (lyric soprano)	Sustained. Demands some flexibility. Has dramatic climaxes. (Ricordi)
Un Ballo in Maschera Volta la terra	d1-c3	f1-f2	Lyric soprano (coloratura soprano)	Animated, graceful. Demands considerable flexibility. (Schirmer, Prima Donna Album)
Un Ballo in Maschera Saper vorresti	d1-b2	g1-e2	Lyric soprano (coloratura soprano)	Very animated. Demands facile articulation. (Schirmer, Prima Donna Album)

FRENCH

ADOLPHE ADAM
(1803-1856)

Le Postillon de Longjumeau Je vais donc le revoir	d1-c3 (c#3)	a1-a2	Coloratura soprano	Sustained recitative and a very florid display air. (Brandus et Dufours)

Opera & Title	Comp.	Tess.	Type	Remarks
Le Postillon de Longjumeau				
Mon petit mari	d1-bb2	g1-g2	Lyric soprano (coloratura soprano)	Graceful, animated and delicate. Demands flexibility. (Brandus et Dufours)
Si J'étais Roi				
De vos nobles aïeux	g-b2	f1-f2	Soprano (high mezzo-soprano)	A very florid display air; spirited, with sustained passages, and a complete vocalise at close. (Leduc)

DANIEL F. E. AUBER
(1782-1871)

Opera & Title	Comp.	Tess.	Type	Remarks
Fra Diavolo				
Recitative: Ne craignez rien,, my lord Air: Quel bonheur, je respire	d1-c3	g1-g2	Lyric soprano (coloratura soprano)	Recitative and a spirited, graceful air, somewhat florid. (Brandus et Dufours)
Fra Diavolo				
Voyez sur cette roche	d1-g2	g1-e2	Lyric soprano (mezzo-soprano)	Graceful, light soubrette air. (Brandus et Dufours)
Le Domino Noir				
Aragonaise: La belle Inès	db1-ab2	eb1-eb2	Soprano (mezzo-soprano)	Animated, dancelike song. Has some florid passages. (Brandus et Dufours)
Le Domino Noir				
Rondeau: Je l'ai sauvée en fin	b-b2	e1-f2	Coloratura soprano	Very animated air interrupted by recitative passages; the second half very florid. (Brandus et Dufours)
Le Domino Noir				
Recitative: Mais je suis, grâce au ciel Air: Flamme vengeresse	b-b2	d1-f#2	Lyric soprano (coloratura soprano)	Recitative and an animated, light, very florid air. (Ditson, Songs from the Operas)
Manon Lescaut				
C'est l'histoire amoureuse (The laughing song)	d1-d3	a1-f#2	Soprano	Bright, animated soubrette air. Demands facile articulation. Schirmer edition transposed one tone lower.

ADRIEN BARTHE

Opera & Title	Comp.	Tess.	Type	Remarks
La Fiancée d'Abydos O nuit qui me couvre	eb1-c3	g1-g2	Lyric soprano (coloratura soprano)	Very sustained. Demands some flexibility and a good command of high pp. (Schirmer, Operatic Anthology)

HECTOR BERLIOZ
(1803-1869)

Opera & Title	Comp.	Tess.	Type	Remarks
La Damnation de Faust Autrefois un roi de Thulé (Part III)	c1-f2	f1-d2	Soprano (mezzo-soprano)	Not fast, rather sustained. See "Es war ein König in Thule" - Schubert and Liszt. See also the Jewel Song "Je voudrais bien savoir" from Gounod's Faust. (Costellat)
La Damnation de Faust D'amour ardente flamme	c1-a2	g1-f2	Dramatic soprano (lyric soprano)	Sustained. Has a dramatic middle section. (Costellat)

GEORGES BIZET
(1838-1875)

Opera & Title	Comp.	Tess.	Type	Remarks
Carmen Recitative: C'est des contre-bandiers le refuge ordinaire Air: Je dis que rien ne m'épouvante	d1-b2	g1-g2	Lyric soprano (dramatic soprano)	Recitative and a very sustained air. Has dramatic climaxes. (Generally available)
Les Pêcheurs de Perles Recitative: Me voilà seule dans la nuit Air: Comme autrefois	c1-c3	f1-f2	Lyric soprano (coloratura soprano)	Recitative and a sustained air. Has a florid final cadenza. (Schirmer, Operatic Anthology)
Les Pêcheurs de Perles O Dieu Brahma	f1-b2 (b) (d3)	b1-g2	Lyric soprano (coloratura soprano)	A sustained andante and a light, florid allegro. (Schirmer, Operatic Anthology)

EMMANUEL CHABRIER
(1841-1894)

Gwendoline

Blonde aux yeaux de pervenche (Fileuse) (from Duet, Act I)	c#1-a2	f#1-e2	Lyric soprano (coloratura soprano)	Graceful, animated. Demands good command of high pp. (Enoch, Paris)

GUSTAVE CHARPENTIER
(1860-)

Louise

Depuis le jour	d1-b2	b1-f#2	Lyric soprano (dramatic soprano)	Sustained. Demands good command of high pp. (Heugel)

FÉLICIEN DAVID
(1810-1876)

Lalla Roukh

Si vous ne savez plus charmer	eb1-c3	f1-f2	Coloratura soprano	Spirited, animated, graceful soubrette air. Has florid passages. (Girod)

La Perle du Brésil

Charmant oiseau	d1-e3	g1-g2	Coloratura soprano	Delicate, graceful. Has florid cadenzas. (Generally available)

CLAUDE DEBUSSY
(1862-1918)

L'Enfant Prodigue

L'année en vain chasse l'année (Air de Lia)	c1-a2	f#1-e2	Lyric soprano (dramatic soprano)	Recitative and a compound air. Demands in parts considerable dramatic intensity. (Durand)

LÉO DÉLIBES
(1836-1891)

Lakmé
Recitative:

Les fleurs me paraissent plus belles Air: Pourquoi dans les les grands bois	e1-ab2	a1-e2	Coloratura soprano (light lyric soprano)	Recitative and a sustained air. (Score, Heugel)

Lakmé

Où va la jeune Indoue (Bell song)	e1-e3	b1-g2	Coloratura soprano	A very florid display piece. (Generally available)

OPERA & TITLE	COMP.	TESS.	TYPE	REMARKS
Lakmé Sous le ciel tout étoilé (Berceuse)	g1-g2 (c3)	c2-g2	Coloratura soprano (light lyric soprano)	Sustained. Demands good command of high pp. (Score, Heugel)

PAUL DUKAS
(1865-1935)

OPERA & TITLE	COMP.	TESS.	TYPE	REMARKS
Ariane et Barbe Bleue O, mes clairs diamants (Act I)	f#1-a#2	a#1-f#2	Dramatic soprano (lyric soprano)	A dramatic monologue. Sustained. Has many effective climaxes. (Durand)

BENJAMIN GODARD
(1849-1895)

OPERA & TITLE	COMP.	TESS.	TYPE	REMARKS
La Vivandière Viens avec nous petit	c1-g2	f1-e2	Soprano (mezzo-soprano)	An animated, martial verse song. Demands facile articulation. (Choudens)
Le Tasse Il m'est doux de revoir la place	eb1-bb2	bb1-gb2	Lyric soprano (dramatic soprano)	Sustained. Has dramatic climaxes. (Heugel)

CHARLES GOUNOD
(1818-1893)

OPERA & TITLE	COMP.	TESS.	TYPE	REMARKS
Faust Recitative: Elles se cachaient! Air: Il ne revient pas	d#1-a#2 (b2)	g1-f#2	Dramatic soprano (lyric soprano)	Scena and a sustained air. Has dramatic climaxes. Omitted in most stage performances. (Score generally available)
Faust Recitative: Je voudrais bien savoir Air: Ah! Je ris de me voir si belle (The Jewel Song)	c#1-b2	e1-e2	Lyric soprano (dramatic soprano)	A scena into which are incorporated a sustained ballad and a brilliant animated waltz air. Demands some flexibility. (Generally available)
La Reine de Saba Recitative: Me voilà seule Air: Plus grand dans son obscurité	c1-b2 (a)	f#1-f#2	Dramatic soprano	Recitative and a sustained air. Has many dramatic climaxes. (Generally available)
Mireille Heureux petit berger	g1-a2	g1-e2	Lyric soprano (coloratura soprano)	Sustained, delicate. (Choudens)

OPERA & TITLE	COMP.	TESS.	TYPE	REMARKS
Mireille Le jour se lève	d1-g2	g1-e2	Soprano or mezzo- soprano	Delicate, graceful. (Choudens)
Mireille O légères hirondelles	f#1-d3	b-a2	Coloratura soprano	A florid animated waltz song. (Ed. by La Forge, Fischer)
Mireille Recitative: Trahir Vincent Air: Mon coeur ne peut changer	d1-c#3 (f3)	g1-g2	Lyric soprano (coloratura soprano)	Recitative, andante, al- legro. Has florid pas- sages. (Schirmer, Operatic Anthology)
Philémon et Baucis Ah! Si je redevenais belle!	e1-a2	a1-f2	Lyric soprano (dramatic soprano)	Very sustained, rather delicate. (Schirmer, Operatic Anthology)
Philémon et Baucis Recitative: Il a perdu ma trace Air: O riante nature	e1-d3	a1-a2	Coloratura soprano	Andante, allegro air, very florid. (Choudens)
Philémon et Baucis Philémon m'aime- rait encore	d1-b2	a1-g2	Soprano	Animated, graceful. Has a recitative and a slow sustained middle section. (Choudens)
Polyeucte A vesta portez vos offrandes	g1-c3	bb1-f2	Lyric soprano (dramatic soprano)	Sustained. Has dramatic climaxes. (Schirmer)
Roméo et Juliette Recitative: Depuis hier je cherche en vain mon maître Air: Que fais-tu blanche tourterelle	f1-a2 (c3)	f1-eb2	Soprano or mezzo- soprano	Animated, light. Demands considerable flexibility. Usually as- signed to a high mezzo- soprano in stage per- formances. (J. Church Co., Opera Songs)
Roméo et Juliette Recitative: Dieu! Quel frisson court dans mes veines? Air: Amour, ranime mon courage	c1-c3	g1-g2	Lyric soprano (coloratura soprano)	A dramatic scena. Demands considerable flexibility. (Score generally available)
Roméo et Juliette Je veux vivre dans ce rêve	c1-d3	a1-f2	Lyric soprano (coloratura soprano)	An animated, light, rather florid waltz song. (Generally available)

JACQUES HALÉVY
(1799-1862)

La Fée aux Roses En dormant c'est à moi	c1-c3	a1-f2	Lyric soprano	Very sustained. Has

OPERA & TITLE	COMP.	TESS.	TYPE	REMARKS
La Fée aux Roses (Cont'd.)				florid passages. (Schirmer, Operatic Anthology)
La Juive Il va venir	d1-c♭3	b♭1-g♭2	Dramatic soprano (lyric soprano)	Sustained. Has dramatic climaxes. (Generally available)

LOUIS J. F. HÉROLD
(1791-1833)

OPERA & TITLE	COMP.	TESS.	TYPE	REMARKS
Le Pré aux Clercs Air de Nicette: A la fleur du bel âge	e1-a2	e1-e2	Lyric soprano (coloratura soprano)	Light, animated, graceful. (Score, Brandus et Cie)
Le Pré aux Clercs Jours de mon enfance	b-b2	e1-g2	Coloratura soprano	Compound, florid air. Demands in parts considerable dramatic intensity and a good command of low voice. (Score, Brandus et Cie)
Le Pré aux Clercs Oui Marguerite en qui j'espère	b-b2	e1-f♯2	Soprano	A rather dramatic, florid air. Requires good command of low voice. (Score, Brandus et Cie)
Le Pré aux Clercs Souvenir de jeune âge	e♭1-a♭2	a♭1-f2	Soprano	A graceful verse song. (Score, Brandus et Cie)

VICTORIN de JONCIÈRES
(1839-1903)

OPERA & TITLE	COMP.	TESS.	TYPE	REMARKS
Dimitri Pâles étoiles	e♭1-a♭2	b♭1-f2	Soprano	Very sustained. Demands good command of high pp. (Schirmer, Operatic Anthology)

EDOUARD LALO
(1823-1892)

OPERA & TITLE	COMP.	TESS.	TYPE	REMARKS
Le Roi d'Ys Recitative: De tous côtés j'aperçois dans la plaine Air: Lorsque je t'ai vu soudain	e♭1-g2	f1-f2	Dramatic soprano (mezzo-soprano)	Very animated, dramatic. (Heugel)

|---|---|---|---|---|
| **Le Roi d'Ys**
Vainement j'ai parlé de l'absence | d1-b2 | g1-eb2 | Dramatic soprano (lyric soprano) | Very animated, dramatic. (Heugel) |

VICTOR MASSÉ
(1822-1884)

OPERA & TITLE	COMP.	TESS.	TYPE	REMARKS
Galathée Recitative: Que dis-tu? Je t'écoute Air: Fleur parfumée	c#1-d3	f#1-f#2	Coloratura soprano	Recitative and a graceful, florid andante, allegro air. (Score, Léon Grus)
Galathée Sa couleur est blonde	b-b2 (d3)	e1-e2	Soprano (mezzo-soprano)	Spirited. Has florid cadenzas. (J. Church Co., Opera Songs)
Les Noces de Jeannette Au bord du chemin (Air du Rossignol)	eb1-db3	ab1-g2	Coloratura soprano	A very florid, graceful display piece. (Ditson)

JULES MASSENET
(1842-1912)

OPERA & TITLE	COMP.	TESS.	TYPE	REMARKS
Hérodiade Charmes des jours passés	d1-c3	g1-g2	Dramatic soprano (lyric soprano)	Generally sustained air with an extremely dramatic closing section. (Heugel)
Hérodiade Il est doux, il est bon	eb1-bb2	f1-eb2	Dramatic soprano (lyric soprano)	Sustained. Has dramatic climaxes. (Schirmer, Operatic Anthology)
La Navaraise Recitative: Une dot! Et combien? Air: Ah, mariez donc son coeur	c#1-a#2	f#1-f#2	Dramatic soprano	Declamatory, dramatic, effective. (Heugel)
Le Cid Recitative: De cet affreux combat Air: Pleurez! pleurez, mes yeux!	c#1-b2	b1-f#2	Dramatic soprano (lyric soprano)	Recitative and a very sustained air. Has dramatic climaxes. (Schirmer, Operatic Anthology)
Le Cid Plus de tourments	f1-bb2	g1-g2	Lyric soprano (dramatic soprano)	Sustained. Demands good command of high pp. (Schirmer, Operatic Anthology)
Manon Adieu notre petite table	d1-f2	g1-d2	Soprano	Sustained, graceful, subdued. (Score, Schirmer)

OPERA & TITLE	COMP.	TESS.	TYPE	REMARKS
Manon Recitative: Je marche sur tous les chemins Air: Obéissons quand leur voix appelle (Gavotte)	e1-c3 (e3)	g1-g2	Lyric soprano (coloratura soprano)	A brilliant scena and a graceful light air often sung separately (e1-b2) (d3). Has some optional florid cadenzas. (Generally available)
Manon Je suis encor tout étourdie	d1-bb2 (e3)	f1-f2	Lyric soprano (coloratura soprano)	Graceful, sustained, delicate. Has optional florid cadenzas. (Score, Schirmer)
Manon Oui dans les bois et dans la plaine (Fabliau)	d1-c#3 (d3)	g1-g2	Lyric soprano (coloratura soprano)	An alternate air for the gavotte. Animated, light. Demands considerable flexibility. (Score, Schirmer)
Manon Voyons, Manon, plus de chimères	f#1-a2		Lyric soprano (coloratura soprano)	Graceful. Has effective climaxes. (Score, Schirmer)
Marie Magdeleine Recitative: Aux pieds de l'innocent Air: O bien-aimé	c1-bb2	eb1-eb2	Dramatic soprano (lyric soprano)	Sustained. Has effective dramatic climaxes. Demands some flexibility. (Heugel)
Sapho Recitative: Ces gens que je connais Air: Pendant un an je fus ta femme	f1-bb2	f#1-e2	Dramatic soprano (lyric soprano)	Sustained. Has effective climaxes. Demands good command of high pp. (Heugel)
Thaïs Recitative: Ah je suis fatiguée Air: Dis-moi que je suis belle	d1-bb2 (d3)	g1-g2	Dramatic soprano (lyric soprano)	A declamatory, effective scena and air. Demands in parts considerable dramatic intensity. (Heugel)
Thaïs Recitative: Je ne veux rien garder Air: L'amour est une vertu rare	db1-bb2	f1-f2	Dramatic soprano (lyric soprano)	Sustained. Has effective climaxes. (Heugel)

ANDRÉ MESSAGER
(1853-1929)

OPERA & TITLE	COMP.	TESS.	TYPE	REMARKS
Fortunio La maison grise	e1-f2	g1-d2	Soprano	Sustained. Vocally not taxing; suitable for all voices. Often used as a song. (Choudens)

OPERA & TITLE	COMP.	TESS.	TYPE	REMARKS
Fortunio				
Chanson de Fortunio	e1-a2	a1-f#2	Soprano	Sustained. Has effective climaxes. Originally written for tenor. (Choudens)

GIACOMO MEYERBEER
(1791-1864)

OPERA & TITLE	COMP.	TESS.	TYPE	REMARKS
Dinorah				
Ombra leggiera (Italian text)	db1-db3 (eb3)	f1-f2	Coloratura soprano	Animated, very florid, compound air. (Generally available)
L'Africaine Recitative: Adieu, mon doux rivage Air: Pour celle qui m'est chère	c#1-c3	g1-eb2	Lyric soprano (coloratura soprano)	Animated, graceful, somewhat florid. Has a florid final cadenza. (Score, Breitkopf & Härtel)
L'Africaine D'ici je vois la mer	ab-b2	f1-f2	Dramatic soprano (lyric soprano)	Demands some flexibility. An extended scena. (Score, Breitkopf & Härtel)
L'Africaine Sur mes genoux, fils du soleil	b-b2	e1-e2	Dramatic soprano (lyric soprano)	Animated, quite florid. (Score, Breitkopf & Härtel)
Le Prophète Mon coeur s'élance et palpite	bb-c3	f1-f2	Coloratura soprano	Animated, brilliant, in parts very florid. Has a short, sustained middle section. (Score, Breitkopf & Härtel)
Les Hugueonts Nobles seigneurs, salut!	c1-c3	g1-f2	Lyric soprano (coloratura soprano)	Graceful, light, florid. Sometimes sung by high mezzo-soprani. (Generally available)
Les Huguenots O beau pays de la Touraine	d1-b2	g1-g2	Lyric soprano (dramatic soprano)	Sustained, in parts quite florid. (Score, Breitkopf & Härtel)
Les Huguenots Recitative: Un autre avait mon coeur Air: Parmi les pleurs	db1-c3	f1-f2	Soprano	Graceful. Demands considerable flexibility. (Score, Breitkopf & Härtel)
L'Etoile du Nord La, la, la, air chéri	c#1-c#3 (a)	a1-g2	Coloratura soprano	A once-famous display piece, very florid. Two flutes obbligato. (Score, Brandus et Cie)
Roberto il Diavolo Nel lasciar la Normandia (Italian text)	d1-c3	f1-f2	Lyric soprano (coloratura soprano)	Animated, in parts quite florid. (Schirmer, Prima Donna Album)

OPERA & TITLE	COMP.	TESS.	TYPE	REMARKS
Roberto il Diavolo Roberto, o tu che adoro (Italian text)	c1-bb2	f1-f2	Dramatic soprano (lyric soprano)	Sustained. Has dramatic climaxes and florid pas- sages. (Schirmer, Prima Donna Album)

JACQUES OFFENBACH
(1819-1880)

OPERA & TITLE	COMP.	TESS.	TYPE	REMARKS
Les Contes **d'Hoffman** Elle a fui, la tourterelle	d1-a2	f1-f2	Lyric soprano (dramatic soprano)	Recitative and a sus- tained "romance." (Score, Schirmer)
Les Contes **d'Hoffman** Les oiseaux dans la charmille	eb1-eb3	ab1-f2	Coloratura soprano	A very florid display piece. (Generally available)

MAURICE RAVEL
(1875-1937)

OPERA & TITLE	COMP.	TESS.	TYPE	REMARKS
L'Heure Espagnole Oh! La pitoyable aventure (Scene 17)	c#1-a2	e1-e2	Lyric soprano (dramatic soprano)	Not fast; declamatory. Demands in parts con- siderable dramatic in- tensity. Musically not easy. (Durand)

CAMILLE SAINT - SAËNS
(1835-1921)

OPERA & TITLE	COMP.	TESS.	TYPE	REMARKS
Etienne Marcel O beaux rêves évanouis	eb1-ab2	ab1-f2	Lyric soprano	Very sustained. Demands good command of high pp. (Schirmer, Operatic Anthology)

PETER I. TCHAIKOVSKY
(1840-1893)

OPERA & TITLE	COMP.	TESS.	TYPE	REMARKS

Jeanne d'Arc
Recitative:
  Oui, Dieu le veut
Air:
  Adieu, forêts
	db1-a2	f#1-eb2	Dramatic
			soprano
			(mezzo-
			soprano)
				Recitative and a sus-
				tained air. Has dramatic
				climaxes. Often sung by
				mezzo-soprani or alti
				a minor third lower than
				the original. (Schirmer)

AMBROISE THOMAS
(1811-1896)

OPERA & TITLE	COMP.	TESS.	TYPE	REMARKS
Hamlet Recitative: A vos jeux, mes amis Air: Pâle et blonde	e1-e3	f#1-f#2	Coloratura soprano	A florid scena and a very florid display air in several section. (Heugel)
Hamlet Recitative: Sa main depuis hier n'a pas touché ma main! Air: Les serments ont des ailes	c#1-c#3	f#1-e2	Lyric soprano (coloratura soprano)	Scena and an animated air. Demands some flexibility. (Heugel)
Mignon Recitative: A merveille! J'en ris d'avance Air: J'avais fait un plus doux rêve!	d1-c3 (d3)	g1-g2	Coloratura soprano	Animated, light, very florid. An alternate air for Filina. The middle section more sustained. (Score generally available)
Mignon Recitative: Ah! pour ce soir Air: Je suis Titania	c1-eb3	g1-g2	Coloratura soprano	Recitative and a brilliant, very florid polonaise. (Generally available)
Mignon Je connais un pauvre enfant	c#1-a2 (e3)	a1-f#2	Lyric soprano (coloratura soprano)	An animated "styrienne," quite florid. (Score generally available)
Psyché Ah! si j'avais jusqu' à ce soir	c1-c3	gb1-f2	Lyric soprano (coloratura soprano)	An andante, allegro air, rather florid. (Lévy Frères)
Psyché O toi, qu'on dit plus belle	c#1-g#2 (b)	f#1-c#2	Soprano or mezzo-soprano	Sustained. (Lévy Frères)

GERMAN

LUDWIG VAN BEETHOVEN
(1770-1827)

OPERA & TITLE	COMP.	TESS.	TYPE	REMARKS
Fidelio Recitative: Abscheulicher, wo eilst du hin? Air: Komm, Hoffnung	b-b2	e1-e2	Dramatic soprano	Recitative, andante, allegro. Demands some flexibility and considerable dramatic intensity. (Generally available)

Fidelio

O wär ich schon mit dir vereint	g1-a2	g1-f2	Lyric soprano (coloratura soprano)	Graceful. Demands lightness of tone and some flexibility. (Score generally available)

MAX BRUCH
(1838-1920)

Das Feuerkreuz·

Ave Maria	d1-bb2	f1-g2	Dramatic soprano (lyric soprano)	Dramatic, for the most part sustained. Has a recitative for a middle section. (Simrock)

FRIEDRICH VON FLOTOW
(1812-1883)

Martha

Den Theuren zu versöhnen	bb-d3	g1-g2	Lyric soprano (coloratura soprano)	Delicate, in parts quite florid. (Score generally available)

ERICH WOLFGANG KORNGOLD
(1897 -)

Die Tote Stadt

Glück das mir verblieb (Marietta's Lied)	f1-bb2	bb1-g2	Dramatic soprano (lyric soprano)	Slow, very sustained. Demands good command of high pp. (Associated Music Publishers)

KONRADIN KREUTZER
(1780-1849)

Das Nachtlager in Granada
Recitative:

Da mir alles nun entrissen Air: Seine fromme Liebesgabe	d1-b2	f1-f#2	Lyric soprano (dramatic soprano)	Recitative, andante, allegro. Demands some flexibility. (Breitkopf & Härtel, Arias for Soprano)

Das Nachtlager in Granada

Leise wehet, leise wallet rings der Tau	c#1-a2	e1-e2	Lyric soprano (dramatic soprano)	Graceful. Vocally not too taxing. (Breitkopf & Härtel, Arias for Soprano)

OTTO NICOLAI
(1810-1849)

Die Lustigen Weiber· von Windsor
Recitative:

Nun eilt herbei, Witz, heitre Laune Air: Verführer! Warum stellt ihr so	c1-bb2	f1-f2	Lyric soprano (dramatic soprano)	Recitative, andante, allegro, quite florid. (Score, Peters, Breitkopf & Härtel)

Die Lustigen Weiber
von Windsor
Recitative:

Opera & Title	Comp.	Tess.	Type	Remarks
Wohl denn! Gefasst ist der Entschluss	d1-b2	f#1-f#2	Dramatic soprano (lyric soprano)	Recitative, andante, allegro. Demands considerable flexibility. (Score, Peters, Breitkopf & Härtel)

FRANZ SCHUBERT
(1797-1828)

Fierrabras

Die Brust gebeugt von Sorgen	f#1-g2	a#1-f#2	Dramatic soprano	Very animated, vigorous. (Breitkopf & Härtel, Soprano Arias)

ROBERT SCHUMANN
(1810-1856)

Genoveva
Recitative:

Dort schleichen über'n Hof sie sacht	eb1-g2	g1-eb2	Lyric soprano (dramatic soprano)	An animated, recitative-like introduction and a slow, very sustained aria. (Breitkopf & Härtel, Soprano Arias)
Air: O du der über Alle wacht				

LOUIS SPOHR
(1784-1859)

Faust
Recitative:

La notte fugge ormai	bb-bb2	f1-f2	Lyric soprano (dramatic soprano)	Scena, larghetto, and a rather florid allegro. (Peters, Soprano Arias)
Air: Si lo sento (Italian text)				

Jessonda
Recitative:

Als in mitternächtger Stunde	e1-bb2	g1-f2	Lyric soprano (dramatic soprano)	Recitative, vigorous allegro and a sustained, somewhat florid larghetto. (Peters, Soprano Arias)
Air: Die ihr Fühlende betrübet				

Jessonda

Hohe Götter	e1-bb2	g1-f2	Lyric soprano (coloratura soprano)	Larghetto and a florid allegro. (Peters, Soprano Arias)

Zemire und Azor

Die Rose (Rose softly blooming)	e1-f#2 (a)	f#1-d2	Lyric soprano (coloratura soprano)	Slow, delicate. Demands some flexibility. Generally sung in English. (Generally available)

JOHANN STRAUSS
(1825-1899)

OPERA & TITLE	COMP.	TESS.	TYPE	REMARKS
Fledermaus. Mein Herr Marquis (Laughing song)	d1-b2 (d3)	g1-g2	Coloratura soprano (lyric soprano)	Animated, light waltz song. Has florid passages. (Schirmer)
Zigeunerbaron So elend und treu	c#1-b2	f1-f2	Soprano	A "gypsy song." Rather vigorous, the final part quite animated. (Score, A. Cranz)
Zigeunerbaron Ein Mädchen hat es gar nicht gut	d1-a2	g1-e2	Light soprano	Graceful, light, animated and humorous. Demands facile articulation. (Score, A. Cranz)

RICHARD STRAUSS
(1864 -)

OPERA & TITLE	COMP.	TESS.	TYPE	REMARKS
Ariadne auf Naxos Recitative: Grossmächtige Prinzessin; Air: Als ein Gott kam jeder gegangen	db-e3	f1-a2	Coloratura soprano	A strict form recitative, andante, allegro aria. In parts very florid. Musically not easy. (Score, Fürstner)
Der Rosenkavalier Da geht er hin, der aufgeblasne, schlechte Kerl (Monologue of Marschallin) (Act I, score mark 269)	c1-f2		Dramatic soprano	Declamatory. Interpretatively not easy. (Score, Fürstner)

RICHARD WAGNER
(1813-1883)

Soprano Excerpts from Wagner's Music Dramas

*None of these excerpts are suitable for light soprano voices. In the instances where "lyric soprano" is indicated as a second choice in the Type of Voice column, a rather heavy type of lyric voice is meant.

OPERA & TITLE	COMP.	TESS.	TYPE	REMARKS
Der Fliegende **Holländer** (Act II, Scene 3) Jo-ho-hoe! Traft ihr das Schiff?	bb-g2	d1-d2	Dramatic soprano (high mezzosoprano)	A vigorous "ballade." The second section of each verse is sustained and rather subdued. (Generally available)
Die Götterdämmerung (Act III, Scene 3) Starke Scheite schichtet mir dort	b-b2	e1-f#2	Dramatic soprano	An imposing, declamatory dramatic scene. (Score generally available)

OPERA & TITLE	COMP.	TESS.	TYPE	REMARKS
Die Götterdämme-rung (Prologue)				
Zu neuen Thaten, theurer Helde	c1-g2	eb1-eb2	Dramatic soprano	Sustained, majestic, declamatory. (Score generally available)
Die Walküre (Act I, Scene 3)				
Du bist der Lenz	db1-ab2	ab1-f2	Dramatic soprano	Animated, sustained. Has an imposing final climax. (Score gener-ally available)
Die Walküre (Act II, Scene 1)				
Hojoto-ho!	d#1-c3	g1-b2	Dramatic soprano	Very animated, extreme-ly vigorous. Demands very facile articulation in the middle section.
Die Walküre (Act III, Scene 3)				(Score generally avail-able)
War es so schmah-lich, was ich verbrach	a-g#2	e1-e2	Dramatic soprano	Slow, sustained, some-what declamatory. (Score generally avail-able)
Lohengrin (Act I, Scene 2)				
Einsam in trüben Tagen	eb1-ab2	eb1-eb2	Dramatic soprano (lyric soprano)	Sustained. Demands in parts considerable dra-matic intensity. (Generally available)
Lohengrin (Act II, Scene 2)				
Euch Lüften die mein Klagen	e1-f2	f1-eb2	Dramatic soprano (lyric soprano)	Slow, very sustained. Demands good command of high pp. (Score generally available)
Parsifal (Act II, Scene 2)				
Ich sah das Kind (Kundry's Erzählung)	c1-a#2	e1-d2	Dramatic soprano (mezzo-soprano)	Rather slow, somewhat sustained. Has dra-matic climaxes. (Score generally available)
Rienzi (Act II, Scene 1)				
Ich sah die Stadte	bb-a2	e1-e2	Dramatic soprano (lyric soprano or high mezzo-soprano)	Sustained. Demands in parts some flexibility. (Score generally avail-able)
Siegfried (Act III, Scene 3)				
Ewig war ich, ewig bin ich	e1-c3	f#1-e2	Dramatic soprano	Slow and very sustained. Has very imposing cli-maxes. (Score gener-ally available)
Tannhäuser (Act III, Scene 1)				
Allmächtge Jungfrau	db1-gb2	gb1-eb2	Dramatic soprano (lyric soprano)	Slow, very sustained, majestic. (Generally available)
Tannhäuser (Act II, Scene 2)				
Dich, theure Halle	d#1-a2 (b2)	g1-e2	Dramatic soprano (lyric soprano)	Animated, vigorous. (Generally available)

OPERA & TITLE	COMP.	TESS.	TYPE	REMARKS
Tristan und Isolde Act III, Scene 3) Mild und leise (Isolde's Liebestod)	d♯1-a♭2	f♯1-f♯2	Dramatic soprano	Very sustained. (Generally available)

CARL MARIA von WEBER
(1786-1826)

OPERA & TITLE	COMP.	TESS.	TYPE	REMARKS
Abu Hassan Wird Philomele trauern	d1-a2	g1-f2	Light soprano	A graceful, in parts quite florid andante, al- legro air. Rather short. (Score, Peters)
Der Freischütz Recitative: Einst träumte meiner sel'gen Base Air: Trübe Augen	d1-b♭2	g1-g2	Lyric soprano (coloratura soprano)	A comic recitative and a graceful, spirited, somewhat florid air. In concert performance the recitative may be omitted. (Score, Peters or Schirmer)
Der Freischütz Kommt ein schlan- ker Bursch	c1-b2	g1-g2	Lyric soprano (coloratura soprano)	Spirited, humorous. Demands some flexi- bility. (Generally available)
Der Freischütz Wie nahte mir der Schlummer	b-b2	f♯1-f♯2	Dramatic soprano (lyric soprano)	Scena and a very spirited allegro. Demands some flexi- bility. (Generally available)
Der Freischütz Und ob die Wolke	e♭1-a♭2	a♭1-f2	Lyric soprano (dramatic soprano)	Slow, very sustained. (Generally available)
Euryanthe Bethörte! Die an meine Liebe glaubt	a♯-c3	f♯1-g♯2	Dramatic soprano (high mezzo- soprano)	A dramatic scena and a very animated, vigor- ous air. Has florid passages. (Ditson)
Euryanthe Glöcklein im Tale	e1-a2	g1-e2	Soprano	Graceful, sustained. (Score, Peters)
Euryanthe O mein Leid ist unermessen	d♯1-g2		Dramatic soprano	Animated, vigorous. Demands some flexi- bility. (Score, Peters)
Euryanthe Recitative: So bin ich nun verlassen Air: Hier dicht am Quell	c1-f♯2	f♯1-d2	Soprano or mezzo- soprano	A scena and a slow declamatory, subdued air. (Score, Peters)
Oberon Recitative: Eil' edler Held Air: Ja, o Herr, mein Heil mein Leben	d1-b2	g1-e2	Dramatic soprano	Animated, vigorous. Demands some flexi- bility. (Score, Peters)

OPERA & TITLE	COMP.	TESS.	TYPE	REMARKS
Oberon				
Ozean! Du Ungeheuer	c1-c3 (b♭)	g1-g2	Dramatic soprano	Scena and a very vigorous, dramatic compound air. (Schirmer, Operatic Anthology)
Oberon				
Traure, mein Herz	b-f2	g1-d♭2	Dramatic soprano (mezzo-soprano)	Sustained. Demands some flexibility. (Score, Peters)
Preciosa				
Einsam bin ich nicht allein	d1-f♯2	g1-e2	Soprano	Sustained. Demands some flexibility. Vocally not taxing. (Score, Peters)

MISCELLANEOUS

MICHAEL W. BALFE
(1808-1870)

OPERA & TITLE	COMP.	TESS.	TYPE	REMARKS
The Bohemian Girl				
I dreamt that I dwelt in marble halls	e♭1-g2	g1-e♭2	Soprano or mezzo-soprano	Sustained, graceful. (Generally available)

FOR MEZZO-SOPRANO OR ALTO
ITALIAN

VINCENZO BELLINI
(1801-1835)

OPERA & TITLE	COMP.	TESS.	TYPE	REMARKS
I Capuletti ed i Montecchi				
Ascolta, se Romeo t'uccise un figlio	g-b2	d1-g2	Mezzo-soprano or dramatic soprano	An andante, allegro air. Demands some flexibility. (Ditson)
Norma				
Recitative: Scombra è la sacra selva	bb-gb2	f1-eb2	Mezzo-soprano or soprano	An extended recitative and a short, very sustained, slow air. Demands some flexibility. (Ricordi)
Air: Deh! Proteggimi, o Dio				

ARRIGO BOITO
(1842-1918)

Nerone (Act IV)				
Fanuèl....Morirò?	c1-eb2		Mezzo-soprano or alto	Slow, declamatory. (Ricordi)
Nerone (Act I)				
Padre nostro che sei ne' cieli	c1-c2		Mezzo-soprano or alto	Sustained. A setting of the Lord's prayer. (Ricordi)

GAETANO DONIZETTI
(1797-1848)

Anna Bolena				
Al dolce guidami	d1-ab2	eb1-eb2	Mezzo-soprano or soprano	Sustained, in parts quite florid. (Schirmer)
Anna Bolena				
Deh! non voler costringere	g-g2	eb1-eb2	Mezzo-soprano or alto	Not fast, rather sustained. Demands some flexibility. (Schirmer, Operatic Anthology)
Anna Bolena				
Recitative: È sgombro il loco	ab-g2	eb1-db2	Mezzo-soprano or alto	Scena and an animated rather florid air. (Schirmer, Operatic Anthology)
Air: Ah! Parea che per incanto				
Don Sebastiano				
Recitative: Ove celare, oh Dio	b-f2	d1-d2	Mezzo-soprano or alto	Recitative and a slow air. Demands some flexibility. (Schirmer, Operatic Anthology)
Air: Terra adorata de' padri miei				
La Favorita				
Recitative: Fia dunque vero	b-a2	e1-e2	Mezzo-soprano or alto	Recitative, andante, allegro. In parts demands considerable dramatic intensity. (Generally àvailable)
Air: O mio Fernando				

OPERA & TITLE	COMP.	TESS.	TYPE	REMARKS
Lucrezia Borgia				
Il segreto per esser felici	c1-f2	e1-c2	Mezzo-soprano or alto	Animated, light. Demands facile articulation. (Generally available)
Maria di Rohan				
Per non istare in ozio	g-g2	e1-c2	Mezzo-soprano or alto	Rather vigorous, not slow. Demands some flexibility. (Schirmer, Operatic Anthology)
Roberto Devereux				
All' afflitto è dolce il pianto	b-a2	d1-e2	Mezzo-soprano or alto	Slow, sustained. Has florid cadenzas. (Ricordi)

UMBERTO GIORDANO
(1867 -)

Andrea Chenier				
Temer? Perche?	f1-g2	g1-e2	Mezzo-soprano or dramatic soprano	Very animated, dramatic. (Sonzogno)

RUGGIERO LEONCAVALLO
(1858-1919)

La Bohème				
Da quel suon soavemento (Act II)	a-a2	e1-e2	Mezzo-soprano	An animated, brilliant waltz. Demands in parts facile articulation. (Sonzogno)

PIETRO MASCAGNI
(1863 -)

L'Amico Fritz				
Recitative: Povero amico Air: O pallida, che un giorno mi guardasti	e1-g2	g1-d2	Mezzo-soprano	Sustained. Has dramatic climaxes. (J. Church Co., Opera Songs)

SAVERIO MERCADANTE
(1795-1870)

Il Giuramento				
Recitative: La Dea di tutti i cor Air: Bella, adorata, incognita	b-e2	g1-d2	Alto or mezzo-soprano	Recitative and a sustained vigorous air. Demands in parts considerable dramatic intensity. (Schirmer, Operatic Anthology)
Medea				
Chi m'arresta?	b-e2	d1-b1	Alto or mezzo-soprano	Sustained. (Schirmer, Operatic Anthology)

AMILCARE PONCHIELLI
(1834-1886)

OPERA & TITLE	COMP.	TESS.	TYPE	REMARKS
I Promessi Sposi				
È questo della misera	c1-f2	eb1-eb2	Mezzo-soprano	A dramatic, animated air. Demands considerable flexibility. (Ricordi)
I Promessi Sposi				
Recitative:				
In questo loco solitario e mesto	c1-g2	e1-e2	Mezzo-soprano	Scena and a sustained air. Demands some flexibility. Has dramatic climaxes. (Ricordi)
Air:				
Involontaria vittima				
La Gioconda				
Recitative:				
E il tuo nocchier or la fuga t'appresta	a♯-a2	e1-e2	Mezzo-soprano	Animated. Has dramatic climaxes. (Ricordi)
Air:				
Stella del marinar				
La Gioconda				
Voce di donna	a-g2	g1-eb2	Mezzo-soprano or alto	Slow, sustained. Demands in parts considerable dramatic intensity. (Schirmer, Operatic Anthology)

GIOACCHINO ROSSINI
(1792-1868)

OPERA & TITLE	COMP.	TESS.	TYPE	REMARKS
Bianca e Falliero				
Recitative:				
Come sereno è il di	b-b2	e1-e2	High mezzo-soprano or soprano	Scena, andante, allegro, very florid. (Schirmer, Prima Donna Album)
Air:				
Della rosa il bel vermiglio				
Il Barbiere di Siviglia				
Recitative:				
Che vecchio sospettoso	c♯1-a2	f♯1-e2	Mezzo-soprano or alto	Recitative and a spirited comic air. Demands facile articulation and some flexibility. (Score, Schirmer)
Air:				
Il vecchiotto cerca moglie				
Il Barbiere di Siviglia				
Una voce poco fa	g♯-g♯2 (b2)	e1-e2	Mezzo-soprano or alto	An andante, allegro air, very florid. (See this entry in the soprano section)
La Cenerentola				
Recitative:				
Nacqui all' affanno	g♯-b2	e1-e2	Mezzo-soprano or alto	A very florid andante, and a light, florid allegro. (Schirmer, Operatic Anthology)
Air:				
Non piu mesta				

OPERA & TITLE	COMP.	TESS.	TYPE	REMARKS
La Donna del Lago Recitative: Mura felici Air: Oh quante lagrime	g#-f#2	e1-c#2	Mezzo- soprano or alto	An extended recitative, a florid andantino, and a florid, light allegro. (Schirmer, Operatic Anthology)
La Donna del Lago Oh mattutini albori	b-g2	g1-d2	Mezzo- soprano or soprano	Sustained. Demands some flexibility. (Schirmer, Prima Donna Album)
La Gazza Ladra Di piacer mi balza il cor	b-a2	f#1-f#2	Mezzo- soprano or soprano	An andante, allegro air. Demands considerable flexibility. (Schirmer, Prima Donna Album)
La Gazza Ladra Recitative: Ora mi par che il core Air: A questo seno	c#1-e2	d1-d2	Mezzo- soprano or alto	Recitative and a florid andante, allegro air. (Ricordi)
L'Italiana in Algeri Recitative: Amici, in ogni evento Air: Pensa alla patria	a-b2	b-e2	Mezzo- soprano or alto	Animated, florid air. (Ricordi)
Mosè Ah! d'un' afflitta il duolo	b-b2	e1-g#2	High mezzo- soprano or soprano	An andante, allegro air, very florid. (Ricordi)
Otello Assisa a piè d'un salice	c1-g2	g1-d2	Mezzo- soprano or soprano	Sustained. Has florid passages. (Schirmer, Prima Donna Album)
Otello Deh calma o ciel	c1-f2	eb1-eb2	Mezzo- soprano or soprano	Short, sustained. Vocally not taxing. Demands some flexi- bility. (Schirmer, Prima Donna Album)
Semiramide Recitative: Bel raggio lusingh- ier Air: Dolce pensiero	c#1-a2	e1-e2	Mezzo- soprano or soprano	An andante, allegro air, very florid. (Schirmer, Prima Donna Album)
Semiramide Recitative: Ecco come al fine in Babilonia Air: Ah quel giorno	g-g#2	e1-e2	Alto or mezzo- soprano	Scena, andante, allegro. Very florid. (J. Church Co., Opera Songs)
Semiramide In si barbara	g-g2	eb1-c2	Alto or mezzo- soprano	A very florid andante and a brilliant, florid allegro. (Schirmer, Operatic Anthology)

OPERA & TITLE	COMP.	TESS.	TYPE	REMARKS
Tancredi Recitative: O patria dolce Air: Di tanti palpiti	b♭-f2	f1-c2	Alto or mezzo- soprano	An extended recitative and a rather florid ani- mated air. (Schirmer, Operatic Anthology)
Zelmira Recitative: Eccolo, a voi l'affido Air: Ciel pietoso, ciel clemente	c1-b♭2	f1-f2	Mezzo- soprano or soprano	Recitative, andante, al- legro. Very florid. (Schirmer, Prima Donna Album)

THÉOPHILE SEMET
(1824-1888)

OPERA & TITLE	COMP.	TESS.	TYPE	REMARKS
Gil Blas Sotto il bel ciel delle Spagne	a♯-d2	f♯1-d2	Alto or mezzo- soprano	Animated. Demands facile articulation. (Generally available)

NICOLA VACCAI
(1790-1848)

OPERA & TITLE	COMP.	TESS.	TYPE	REMARKS
Giulietta e Romeo Recitative: O! vista è dessa Air: Ah! se tu dormi	b♭-f2	e♭1-e♭2	Alto or mezzo- soprano	A sustained air. Has a recitative passage for the middle section. Demands some flexi- bility. (Schirmer, Operatic Anthology)

GIUSEPPE VERDI
(1813-1901)

OPERA & TITLE	COMP.	TESS.	TYPE	REMARKS
Don Carlo Nel giardin del bello saracin ostello	c♯1-a2	e1-e2	Mezzo- soprano or soprano	Animated, brilliant, rather florid. (Ricordi)
Don Carlo O Don fatale	c♭1-c♭3	e♭1-e♭2	Mezzo- soprano or dramatic soprano	Scena, andante, allegro, in parts very dramatic. Often sung transposed a third lower. (Gener- ally available)
Il Trovatore (Act II, No. 10) Condotta ell' era in' ceppi **Il Trovatore** (Act II, No. 8)	a-b♭2	e1-e2	Alto or mezzo- soprano	A dramatic scena, sus- tained andante, and a declamatory allegro. (Score, Schirmer)
Stride la vampa	b-g2	f♯1-b1	Alto or mezzo- soprano	Animated, vigorous. Demands some flexi- bility. (Generally available)
Un Ballo in Maschera È lui! Ne palpiti come risento adesso	g-a♭2	f♯1-e♭2	Alto or mezzo- soprano	Not fast, somewhat de- clamatory. Has dra- matic climaxes. (Ricordi)

OPERA & TITLE	COMP.	TESS.	TYPE	REMARKS
Un Ballo in Maschera				
Re dell' abisso, affrettati	c1-g2	c1-c2	Alto or mezzo-soprano	Very sustained, somber. Has dramatic climaxes. (Ricordi)

FRENCH

DANIEL F. E. AUBER
(1782-1871)

OPERA & TITLE	COMP.	TESS.	TYPE	REMARKS
Le Domino Noir				
Aragonaise:				
La belle Inès	db1-ab2	eb1-eb2	Mezzo-soprano or soprano	Animated. Has some florid passages. (Brandus et Dufour)

HENRI BEMBERG
(1861 -)

OPERA & TITLE	COMP.	TESS.	TYPE	REMARKS
La Mort de Jeanne d'Arc				
Du Christ avec ardeur	db1-ab2	f1-eb2	Dramatic soprano or mezzo-soprano or alto	Sustained, effective. In parts demands considerable dramatic intensity. (Generally available)

HECTOR BERLIOZ
(1803-1869)

OPERA & TITLE	COMP.	TESS.	TYPE	REMARKS
Les Troyens à Carthage				
Monologue de Didon:				
Ah, je vais mourir	d1-f2	eb1-e2	Mezzo-soprano or dramatic soprano	A dramatic scena and a slow, subdued sustained air. (Choudens)

GEORGES BIZET
(1838-1875)

OPERA & TITLE	COMP.	TESS.	TYPE	REMARKS
Carmen				
L'amour est un oiseau rebelle	d1-f#2	d1-d2	Mezzo-soprano or alto	A habanera. Demands very facile articulation. (Generally available)
Carmen				
Près des remparts de Séville	b-f#2 (b2)	d1-d2	Mezzo-soprano or alto	A very animated seguidilla. Demands very facile articulation and some flexibility. (Generally available)
Carmen (Act III, No. 20)				
Recitative:				
Voyons que j'essaie à mon tour	b-f2	f1-db2	Alto or mezzo-soprano	Sustained, somber. Has dramatic climaxes. (Score, Schirmer)
Air: En vain pour éviter				
Djamileh				
Sans doute l'heure est prochaine (Lamento)	e1-f2	e1-d2	Mezzo-soprano	Slow and sustained. (Choudens)

ALFRED BRUNEAU
(1857-1934)

OPERA & TITLE	COMP.	TESS.	TYPE	REMARKS
L'Attaque du Moulin La guerre c'est le châtiment	e1-a2	g1-e2	Alto	Spirited, dramatic air. (Choudens)

CLAUDE DEBUSSY
(1862-1918)

Pelléas et Mélisande (Act I, Scene 2) Voici ce qu'il écrit à son frère Pelléas	a-d2	d1-a1	Alto or mezzo- soprano	A recitative-like solo. Not fast, declamatory. Interpretatively not easy. (Durand)

LÉO DÉLIBES
(1836-1891)

Jean de Nivelle Tant que le jour dure	c#1-f#2	f#1-c#2	Mezzo- soprano or alto	Graceful, rather light. (J. Church Co., Opera Songs)

THÉODORE DUBOIS
(1837-1924)

Aben Hamet Recitative: Oui, c'est lui Air: Va! Grenade enfin t'appelle	b-e2	e1-c#2	Alto or mezzo- soprano	Sustained. (J. Church Co., Opera Songs)

BENJAMIN GODARD
(1848-1895)

La Vivandière Viens avec nous petit	c1-g2	f1-e2	Mezzo- soprano or soprano	An animated, martial verse song. Demands facile articulation. (Choudens)

CHARLES GOUNOD
(1818-1893)

Cinq-Mars Recitative: Par quel trouble profond Air: Nuit resplendis- sante	d1-g2	f#1-e2	Mezzo- soprano or alto	Very sustained. Has effective climaxes. (Generally available)
Faust Faites-lui mes aveux	d1-g2	g1-e2	Mezzo- soprano or soprano	An animated, graceful air with a recitative for a middle section. Demands facile articu- lation. (Generally available)

OPERA & TITLE	COMP.	TESS.	TYPE	REMARKS
Faust				
Si le bonheur	c#1-e2	e1-c#2	Mezzo-soprano or alto	A short, sustained romance. Omitted in most stage performances. (Schirmer, Operatic Anthology)
Mireille				
Le jour se lève	d1-g2	g1-e2	High mezzo-soprano or soprano	Delicate, graceful. (Choudens)
Roméo et Juliette Recitative:				
Depuis hier je cherche en vain mon maître	f1-a2 (c3)	f1-eb2	Mezzo-soprano or soprano	Animated, light. Demands considerable flexibility. (J. Church Co., Opera Songs)
Air: Que fais-tu blanche tourterelle				
Sappho Recitative:				
Où suis-je?	cb1-gb2 (bb2)	f1-f2	Mezzo-soprano or alto	Very sustained. Has dramatic climaxes. (Generally available)
Air: O ma lyre immortelle				

JACQUES HALÉVY
(1799-1862)

OPERA & TITLE	COMP.	TESS.	TYPE	REMARKS
Charles VI Recitative:				
Sous leur sceptre de fer	g#-g#2	e1-e2	Mezzo-soprano or alto	A very dramatic scena and an andante, allegro aria. Demands considerable dramatic intensity. (Schirmer, Operatic Anthology)
Air: Humble fille des champs				
La Reine de Chypre				
Le gondolier dans sa pauvre nacelle	a-ab2	eb1-eb2	Mezzo-soprano or alto	A sustained andante, recitative, and a vigorous, dramatic allegro. (Schirmer, Operatic Anthology)

VICTORIN de JONCIÈRES
(1839-1903)

OPERA & TITLE	COMP.	TESS.	TYPE	REMARKS
Le Chevalier Jean				
Tu souris à la tourterelle	c1-g2	eb1-eb2	Soprano or mezzo-soprano	A rather florid air of contrasting moods and tempi. (Grus)

EDOUARD LALO
(1823-1892)

OPERA & TITLE	COMP.	TESS.	TYPE	REMARKS
Le Roi D'Ys Recitative:				
De tous côtés j'aperçois dans la plaine	eb1-g2	f1-f2	Mezzo-soprano or dramatic soprano	Very animated, dramatic. (Heugel)
Air: Lorsque je t'ai vu soudain				

VICTOR MASSÉ
(1822-1884)

Opera & Title	Comp.	Tess.	Type	Remarks
Galatée				
Sa couleur est blonde	b-b2 (d3)	e1-e2	Mezzo-soprano, soprano	Spirited. Has florid cadenzas. (J. Church Co., Opera Songs)
Galatée				
Tristes amours	g-f2	c2-c2	Alto or mezzo-soprano	Sustained andante and a vigorous allegro.(Grus)
Paul et Virginie				
Dans le bois à ma voix tout s'éveille	b-f♯2	e1-e2	Mezzo-soprano	Graceful, in parts rather florid. (J. Church Co., Opera Songs)
Paul et Virginie				
Parmi les lianes	c1-b♭2	d1-e♭2	Soprano or mezzo-soprano	Animated, rather dramatic. Demands considerable flexibility. (Ditson)

JULES MASSENET
(1842-1912)

Opera & Title	Comp.	Tess.	Type	Remarks
Don César de Bazan				
Dors, ami (Berceuse)	b♭-g♭2	d1-d2	Mezzo-soprano or alto	Sustained, subdued. Demands some flexibility. (Heugel)
Hérodiade (Act I)				
Hérode! Hérode! Ne me refuse pas	b♭-a2	f1-f2	Mezzo-soprano or alto	Sustained air with many effective dramatic climaxes. (Heugel)
Le Roi de Lahore Recitative: Repose, ô belle amoureuse Air: Ferme les yeux, ô belle maîtresse	b-b♭2	f1-f2	Mezzo-soprano	A sustained andante, and a light allegretto. Demands some flexibility. Has some dramatic climaxes. (Schirmer)
Werther				
Va! Laisse couler mes larmes	c1-f2	f1-d2	Mezzo-soprano; alto	Slow, sustained. Has effective climaxes. (Heugel)
Werther				
Werther...qui m'aurait dit la place que dans mon coeur	c1-g♭2	e1-e2	Mezzo-soprano or alto	An extended scena. Has dramatic climaxes. (Heugel)

GIACOMO MEYERBEER
(1791-1864)

Opera & Title	Comp.	Tess.	Type	Remarks
Dinorah Recitative: Ditemi buona gente Air: Da quel di che a lei narrate (Italian text)	a-a2 (b♭2)	f1-e♭2	Alto or mezzo-soprano	Light, animated, quite florid. (J. Church Co., Opera Songs)
Le Prophète				
Ah! Mon fils	b-a♯2	f♯1-d♯2	Mezzo-soprano or alto	Slow, sustained. Demands in parts considerable dramatic intensity and some flexibility. (Generally available)

OPERA & TITLE	COMP.	TESS.	TYPE	REMARKS
Le Prophète				
Donnez, donnez	b-g2	e1-e2	Mezzo-soprano or alto	Sustained, in parts dramatic. (Schirmer, Operatic Anthology)
Le Prophète				
Recitative:				
O prêtres de Baal	ab-ab2	db1-eb2	Mezzo-soprano or alto	Scena and a florid display air. (Score, Breitkopf & Härtel)
Air:	(c3)			
O toi qui m'abandonne				
Le Prophète				
Recitative:				
Qui je suis? Moi?	ab-ab2	eb1-eb2	Mezzo-soprano or alto	Animated, dramatic. Has florid cadenzas. (Score, Breitkopf & Härtel)
Air:	(bb2)			
Je suis, hélas, la pauvre femme				
Les Huguenots				
Non, non, non, vous n'avez jamais, je gage	g-bb2 (f)	eb1-eb2	Mezzo-soprano	Animated, graceful, very florid. (Score, Breitkopf & Härtel)

CAMILLE SAINT-SAËNS
(1835-1921)

OPERA & TITLE	COMP.	TESS.	TYPE	REMARKS
Samson et Dalila				
Mon coeur s'ouvre à ta voix	bb-gb2	f1-eb2	Mezzo-soprano or alto	Sustained. (Generally available)
Samson et Dalila				
Printemps qui commence	b-e2	e1-c#2	Mezzo-soprano or alto	Sustained. (J. Church Co., Opera Songs)
Samson et Dalila				
Recitative:				
Samson recherchant ma présence	ab-g2 (bb2)	eb1-db2	Mezzo-soprano or alto	Sustained. Has dramatic climaxes. (Schirmer, Operatic Anthology)
Air:				
Amour, viens aider				

PETER I. TCHAIKOVSKY
(1840-1893)

OPERA & TITLE	COMP.	TESS.	TYPE	REMARKS
La Dame de Pique				
Romance de Pauline: Oh! Jeunes filles!	a-ab2	eb1-cb2	Alto or mezzo. soprano	Sustained, somber. Has dramatic climaxes. (Noël, Paris)

AMBROISE THOMAS
(1811-1896)

OPERA & TITLE	COMP.	TESS.	TYPE	REMARKS
Hamlet				
Recitative:				
Toi, partir! Non, il t'aime	c1-ab2	f1-eb2	Alto or mezzo-soprano	Sustained. Has effective climaxes. (Heugel)
Air:				
Dans son regard plus sombre				

TITLE	COMP.	TESS.	TYPE	REMARKS
Mignon Recitative: C'est moi, j'ai tout brisé, n'importe Air: Me voici dans son boudoir	bb-f2	eb1-db2	Mezzo-soprano or alto	A graceful, light gavotte. Demands facile articulation. (Generally available)
Mignon Connais-tu le pays	c1-f2	eb1-c2	Mezzo-soprano	Very sustained. (Generally available)
Psyché Recitative: Non, ne la suivons pas Air: Sommeil, ami des dieux	bb-f2	f1-d2	Mezzo-soprano; alto	Sustained. Has a short cadenza. (Lévy Frères)
Psyché Recitative: Salut! Divinités des champs Air: O nymphes! En ces lieux	a#-a2 (b2)	e1-e2	Mezzo-soprano	Sustained. Demands in parts considerable flexibility. (Lévy Frères)

GERMAN

MAX BRUCH
(1838-1920)

TITLE	COMP.	TESS.	TYPE	REMARKS
Odysseus Penelope ein Gewand wirkend (Ich wob dies Gewand)	c1-f2	e1-c2	Mezzo-soprano or alto	Sustained. Demands in parts considerable dramatic intensity. (Schirmer)
Odysseus Penelope's Trauer Recitative: Hell strahlender Tag Air: O, Atryone	c1-f#2	f1-d2	Mezzo-soprano or alto	An extended recitative and a very sustained prayer. (Simrock)

FRIEDRICH VON FLOTOW
(1812-1883)

TITLE	COMP.	TESS.	TYPE	REMARKS
Martha Esser mesto il mio cor (Italian text)	g#-b2	f#1-f#2	Mezzo-soprano	An andante, allegro air, the latter "Jäerin, schlau im Sinn." A rather pretentious display piece, very effective. Demands considerable flexibility. Not suitable for voices limited in range. (Score, Schirmer)

Martha
| Jägerin, schlau im Sinn | c1-a2 | e1-c2 | Mezzo-soprano or alto | Light, animated. Demands facile articulation. A very elaborate version of this little air written as a display piece for Madame Nautier-Didiée, is usually appended to scores of Martha. (Score, Schirmer) |

RICHARD WAGNER
(1813-1883)

Alto and Mezzo-Soprano Excerpts from Wagner's Music Dramas

Das Rheingold
(Scene 4)
| Weiche Wotan, weiche | b♯-e2 | c♯1-c♯2 | Alto | Sustained, somber, declamatory, vigorous. (Score, Schirmer) |

Die Götterdämmerung
(Act I, Scene 3)
| Höre mit Sinn, was ich dir sage | g-g2 | e♭1-e♭2 | Alto or mezzo-soprano | Declamatory. Has dramatic climaxes. (Score, Peters) |

Die Walküre
(Act II, Scene 1)
| So ist es denn aus mit den ewigen Göttern | cx1-g♯2 | e1-e2 | Mezzo-soprano or dramatic soprano | Very animated, vigorous, dramatic. Demands facile articulation. (Score, Schirmer) |

Lohengrin
(Act II, Scene 2)
| Entweihte Götter! Helft jetzt meiner Rache! | f♯1-a♯2 | c♯1-f♯2 | Mezzo-soprano or dramatic soprano | An extremely vigorous, dramatic incantation. (Score, Schirmer) |

Rienzi
| Gerechter Gott | c1-a2 | g1-g2 | Dramatic soprano or mezzo-soprano | An extended, dramatic recitative, a very sustained andante, and a dramatic allegro. Demands some flexibility. In the Schirmer Operatic Anthology transposed a major third lower. (Available in the original key in the J. Church Co., Opera Songs) |

Tannhäuser
(Act I, Scene 2)
| Geliebter, komm', sieh' dort die Grotte | f1-a2 | f1-f2 | Mezzo-soprano or dramatic soprano | Sustained. Has an imposing final climax. (Score, Peters) |

OPERA & TITLE	COMP.	TESS.	TYPE	REMARKS
Tristan und Isolde (Act II, Scene 2) Einsam wachend in der Nacht	f#1-f#2	g#1-d#2	Alto or mezzo- soprano	Very sustained, rather subdued. (Score, Peters)

CARL MARIA von WEBER
(1786-1826)

OPERA & TITLE	COMP.	TESS.	TYPE	REMARKS
Eurianthe Recitative: So bin ich nun verlassen Air: Hier dicht am Quell	c1-f#2	f#1-d2	Mezzo- soprano or soprano	A scena and a slow, declamatory, subdued air. (Score, Peters)
Oberon Arabien mein Heimatland	a-f2	d1-d2	Mezzo- soprano or alto	A short, sustained an- dante and a short, grace- ful allegro. Demands some flexibility. (Score, Peters)
Oberon Arabiens einsam Kind	d#1-e2	e1-c#2	Mezzo- soprano or alto	Sustained. Demands some flexibility. (Score, Peters)
Oberon Traure mein Herz	b-f2	g1-db2	Mezzo- soprano or dramatic soprano	Sustained. Demands some flexibility. (Score, Peters)

MISCELLANEOUS

A. GORING THOMAS
(1850-1892)

OPERA & TITLE	COMP.	TESS.	TYPE	REMARKS
Nadeschda Recitative: What means Ivan! Air: My heart is weary	g#-ab2	db1-db2	Mezzo- soprano or alto	Sustained, effective. Has dramatic climaxes. (Schirmer, Operatic Anthology)

VINCENZO BELLINI
(1801-1835)

OPERA & TITLE	COMP.	TESS.	TYPE	REMARKS
Norma Meco all'altar di Venere	d-c2	g-e1	Tenor	A sustained andante and a vigorous allegro. (Ricordi)

ARRIGO BOITO
(1842-1918)

Mefistofele Dai campi, dai prati	f-bb1	a-f1	Tenor	Sustained. Has effective final climax. (J. Church Co., Opera Songs)
Mefistofele Giunto sul passo estremo (Epilogue)	f-ab1	bb-f1	Tenor	Sustained. Has effective climaxes. (Ricordi)

ALFREDO CATALANI
(1854-1893)

Loreley Recitative: Io resto Air: In franto ogni altro vincolo	e-b1	g#-e1	Tenor	Sustained, has dramatic climaxes. (Ricordi)
Loreley Nel verde Maggio, un·di	e-a1	a-e1	Tenor	Sustained. (Ricordi)

FRANCESCO CILÈA
(1866)

Adriana Lecouvreur (Act I) La dolcissima effigie	f-ab1	g-f1	Tenor	Sustained, has effective climaxes. (Sonzogno)
Adriana Lecouvreur (Act II) L'anima ho stanca	e-a1	a#-f#1	Tenor	Sustained, has effective climaxes. (Sonzogno)
L'Arlesiana Recitative: È la solita storia Air: Anch'io vorrei	e-a1	a-f1	Tenor	Sustained. Has dramatic climaxes. (Sonzogno)

GAETANO DONIZETTI
(1797-1848)

Anna Bolena
Recitative:

Vivi tu, te non scongioro Air: Nel veder la tua costanza	e-a1	g-g1	Tenor	An andante, allegro air. Demands some flexibility. (Schirmer)

Betly

E fia ver	g-bb1	bb-g1	Lyric tenor	A rather florid andante, allegro air. (Ricordi)

Don Pasquale

Com' è gentil	g#-a1	a-f#1	Lyric tenor	A sustained, graceful serenade. (Schirmer, Operatic Anthology)

Don Pasquale
Recitative:

Povero Ernesto Air: Cercherò, cercherò lontana terra	ab-bb1	c-ab1	Lyric tenor	An andante, allegro air. The tessitura is very high. (Ricordi)

Don Sebastiano

Deserto in terra	f-db2	bb-gb1	Lyric tenor	Sustained. Very high tessitura. (Ricordi)

La Favorita

Una vergine, un angel di Dio	e-a1 (c#2)	a-f#1	Tenor	Sustained. Demands some flexibility. (Ricordi)

La Favorita

Spirto gentil	g-c2	c-f1	Tenor	Sustained. (Generally available)

La Favorita
Recitative:

Gran Dio! Che degno io ne divenga or vuol Air: Si, che un tuo solo accento	e-a1	a-f#1	Tenor	Scena and vigorous air. (Ricordi)

La Regina di Golconda
Recitative:

Adorata regina Air: Se valor, rispetto e fede	f-g1	g-f1	Tenor	Sustained. (Ricordi)

L'Elisir d' Amore

Una furtiva lagrima	f-ab1	bb-f1	Tenor	Sustained, rather delicate. Demands some flexibility. (Generally available)

L'Elisir d'Amore

Quanto è bella	e-g1	g-e1	Lyric tenor	Slow, sustained. (Ricordi)

Linda di Chamounix
Recitative:

Linda! Si ritirò, povera Linda Air: Se tanto in ira	f#-ab1	ab-f1	Lyric tenor	Recitative and a sustained air. (Ricordi)

Lucia di Lammer-
moor
Recitative:

Tombe degl' avi miei Air: Fra poco a me ricovero	f-a1 (bb1)	a-f#1	Tenor	A dramatic scena and a sustained air. (Ricordi)

Maria di Rohan
Recitative:

Nel fragor della festa Air: Alma soave e cara	e-a1	a-e1	Tenor	A scena and a sustained air. (Schirmer)

Poliuto
Recitative:

Io piego la fronte nella polve Air: D'un' alma troppo fervida	ab-ab1	ab-f1	Tenor	Sustained. (Ricordi)

FRANCO FACCIO
(1841-1891)

Amleto

Essere o non essere	d-bb1	g-g1	Tenor	Scena and a sustained air. Has dramatic climaxes. A setting of the famous soliloquy from the Shakespeare play. (Schirmer)

UMBERTO GIORDANO
(1867 -)

Andrea Chenier

Come un bel dì	e-ab1 (bb1)	a-eb1	Tenor	Sustained, somewhat declamatory. Has dramatic climaxes. (Sonzogno)

Andrea Chenier

Si, fui soldato	f-ab1	g-e1	Tenor	Declamatory, dramatic. (Sonzogno)

Andrea Chenier

Un dì all'azzuro spazio	f-bb1	a-eb1	Tenor	Sustained, declamatory. Has dramatic climaxes. (Sonzogno)

Fedora

Amor ti vieta	b-a1	c-f1	Tenor	Sustained. Has effective climaxes. (Sonzogno)

Fedora

Mia madre la mia vecchia madre	d-g1	a-e1	Tenor	Animated. The vocal line is sustained. Demands in parts considerable dramatic intensity. (Sonzogno)

Fedora

Vedi io piango	g-ab1	a-f1	Tenor	Sustained, subdued. Demands in parts considerable dramatic intensity. (Sonzogno)

RUGGIERO LEONCAVALLO
(1858-1919)

OPERA & TITLE	COMP.	TESS.	TYPE	REMARKS
La Bohème Io non ho che una povera stanzetta (Act II)	eb-bb1	ab-f1	Tenor	Sustained. Has effective climaxes. (Sonzogno)
La Bohème Testa adorata (Act III)	f-bb1	gb-f1	Tenor	Sustained. Has dramatic climaxes. (Sonzogno)
Pagliacci O, Colombina	e-a1	g#-f1	Lyric tenor	Animated, light. Demands in parts very facile articulation. (Schirmer)
Pagliacci Recitative: Recitar! Mentre preso dal delirio Air: Vesti la giubba	e-a1 (d)	g-g1	Dramatic tenor	Very sustained. Has dramatic climaxes. (Generally available)

PIETRO MASCAGNI
(1863 -)

OPERA & TITLE	COMP.	TESS.	TYPE	REMARKS
Cavalleria Rusticana Mamma, quel vino è generoso (Final solo in the opera)	f-bb1	bb-f1	Most suitable for dramatic tenor	A declamatory, dramatic scena. Has very sustained passages. (Score, Schirmer)
Cavalleria Rusticana O Lola, bianca come fior	ab-ab1	c1-g1	Tenor	Very sustained. The tessitura is quite high. (Generally available)
Cavelleria Rusticana Viva il vino spumeggiante	g-g1	b-g1	Tenor	A spirited, animated drinking song. Demands facile articulation. (Score, Schirmer)
Iris Apri la tua finestra	e-a1	a-f1	Tenor	An effective serenade. (Ricordi)
L'Amico Fritz Ed anche Beppe amò	gb-bb1	bb-gb1	Tenor	Sustained. In parts demands considerable dramatic intensity. (J. Church Co., Opera Songs)
L'Amico Fritz O amore, o bella Lace	gb-bb1	ab-f1	Tenor	Very sustained. Has dramatic climaxes. (Sonzogno)

AMILCARE PONCHIELLI
(1834-1886)

OPERA & TITLE	COMP.	TESS.	TYPE	REMARKS
La Gioconda Cielo e mar	d-bb1	g-f1	Tenor	Sustained. Has dramatic climaxes. (Generally available)

GIACOMO PUCCINI
(1858-1924)

All these excerpts, with the exception of one, "Tra voi belle" from Manon Lescaut, are sustained, somewhat declamatory, and have most effective moments. None of them seem too suitable for a very light lyric voice. Available only in Ricordi edition, except the air from "Le Villi" which is included in the J. Church Co. Opera Songs volume.

OPERA & TITLE	COMP.	TESS.	REMARKS
Il Tabarro			
Hai ben ragione	eb-bb1	g-f1	
La Bohème			
(Act I)			
Che gelida manina	eb-bb1 (c2)	ab-f2	
La Fanciulla del West			
(Act III)			
Ch' ella mi creda	eb-bb1	gb-eb1	
La Fanciulla del West			
(Act II)			
Or son sei mesi	e-bb1	bb-g1	
Le Villi			
(Act II)			
Torna ai felici dî	f-bb1	bb-gb1	
Madama Butterfly			
(Act II, Part 2)			
Addio, fiorito asil	f-bb1	ab-eb1	
Madame Butterfly			
(Act I)			
Amore o grillo	f-bb1	gb-eb1	
Manon Lescaut			
(Act II)			
Ah! Manon, mi tradisce	e-bb1	a-f1	
Manon Lescaut			
(Act I)			
Donna non vidi mai	e-bb1	bb-f1	
Manon Lescaut			
(Act III)			
Pazzo son! Guardate, come io piango	e-a1 (b1)	b-g1	
Manon Lescaut			
(Act I)			
Tra voi belle, brune e bionde	f-a1	a-f1	Animated, light. Demands facile articulation.
Tosca			
(Act III)			
E lucevan le stelle	f#-a1	b-f#1	
Tosca			
(Act I)			
Recondita armonia	f-bb1	c-f1	

Opera & Title	Comp.	Tess.	Type	Remarks
Turandot (Act III) Nessun dorma	d-b1	a-f♯1		
Turandot (Act II) Non piangere Liù!	g♭-b♭1	b♭-f1		

GIOACCHINO ROSSINI
(1792-1868)

Opera & Title	Comp.	Tess.	Type	Remarks
Il Barbiere di Siviglia Cessa di più resistere	d♭-b♭1	f-f1	Lyric tenor	A florid maestoso, very florid andante, and a spirited, very florid moderato which can be sung as a separate piece: "Ah il più lieto." (Score, Schirmer)
Il Barbiere di Siviglia Ecco ridente	f♯-b1	g-g1	Lyric tenor	Graceful andante, allegro air, very florid. (Generally available)
Il Barbiere di Siviglia Se il mio nome	e-g1	g-f1	Lyric tenor	Sustained, delicate serenade. Has florid passages. (Generally available)
Guilliaume Tell Recitative: Ne m'abandonne point Air: Asile héreditaire (French text)	c♯-a1	a-e1	Tenor	Scena and andante, allegro air. Demands some flexibility. (Ditson)

GIUSEPPE VERDI
(1813-1901)

Opera & Title	Comp.	Tess.	Type	Remarks
Aida Recitative: Se quel guerrier io fossi Air: Celeste Aida	d-b♭1	f-f1	Dramatic tenor	Very sustained. In parts demands considerable dramatic intensity. (Generally available)
Aroldo Sotto il sol di Siria	d-b♭1	a♭-g♭1	Tenor	Recitative and an andante, allegro air. Has dramatic climaxes and a high tessitura. (Schirmer)

OPERA & TITLE	COMP.	TESS.	TYPE	REMARKS
Attila Recitative: Infida! il di che brami è questo Air: Oh dolore ed io vivea	ab-bbb1	ab-f1	Tenor	Sustained. Demands in parts considerable dramatic intensity. (J. Church Co., Opera Songs)
Don Carlo Recitative: Fontainebleau! Foresta immensa Air: Io la vidi, e al suo sorriso	f-b1	g-f1	Tenor	Recitative and a sustained air. Demands some flexibility. (Ricordi)
Ernani Recitative: Mercè, diletti amici Air: Come ruggiada al cespite	g-ab1	g-f1	Dramatic tenor	Recitative and a sustained air. Demands some flexibility. Has dramatic climaxes. (Ricordi)
Falstaff (Act III) Dal labbro il canto estasiato	d#-bb1	ab-f#1	Tenor	Sustained. Demands good command of high pp. Has effective climaxes. (Ricordi)
I Due Foscari All' infelice veglio	eb-bb1	ab-f1	Tenor	Sustained. Has dramatic climaxes. (Ricordi)
I Due Foscari Recitative: Notte! Perpetua notte Air: Non maledirmi, o prode	e-bb1	b-f1	Dramatic tenor	A dramatic scena and an animated, vigorous air. Has a sustained vocal line. (Ricordi)
I Due Foscari Recitative: Brezza del suol natìo Air: Dal più remoto esilio	eb-bb1	ab-f1	Tenor	An andante, allegro air, in parts very vigorous. (Schirmer, Operatic Anthology)
I Lombardi La mia letizia infondere	f#-a1	a-f#1	Tenor	Sustained. Demands good command of high pp. (J. Church Co., Opera Songs)
Il Trovatore (Act IV, No. 19) Ah! che la morte ognora	g-ab1	c-ab1	Dramatic tenor	Sustained. Has dramatic climaxes. (Ricordi)
Il Trovatore (Act III, No. 18) Ah sì, ben mio, coll' essere	f-ab1	ab-f1	Dramatic tenor	Sustained. Has dramatic climaxes. (Generally available)
Il Trovatore (Act I, No. 5) Deserto sulla terra	bb-ab1	cb1-gb1	Tenor	A sustained, short serenade. Introduction to trio finale, Act I. (Ricordi)

OPERA & TITLE	COMP.	TESS.	TYPE	REMARKS
Il Trovatore (Act III, No. 18) Di quella pira	g-b1 (c2)	c-g1	Dramatic tenor	Animated, vigorous. (Generally available)
I Masnadieri Recitative: Son gli ebbri inverecondi Air: O mio castel paterno	ab-bb1	ab-gb1	Tenor	Sustained. Demands some flexibility. (Ricordi)
I Vespri Siciliani Recitative: È di Monforte il cenno Air: Giorno di pianto, di fier dolore	eb-b1	a-f#1	Dramatic tenor	Scena, andante, allegro. Has very dramatic climaxes. (Ricordi)
La Forza del Destino Recitative: La vita è inferno all' infelice (Della natal sua terra) Air: O tu che in seno agli angeli	db-bb1	ab-f1	Tenor	Recitative, allegro moderato, and a very sustained andante. Has dramatic climaxes. (J. Church Co., Opera Songs)
La Traviata Recitative: Lunge da lei Air: De' miei bollenti spiriti	e-ab1	g-f1	Tenor	Scena and a sustained air. (Generally available)
Luisa Miller Quando le sere al placido	d-ab1	ab-eb1	Tenor	Sustained. Has dramatic climaxes. (Ricordi)
Macbeth Recitative: O figli miei Air: Ah la paterna mano	eb-bbb1	ab-f1	Tenor	Recitative, andante, allegro, in parts very vigorous. (Schirmer, Operatic Anthology)
Otello (Act III) Dio! Mi potevi scagliar tutti i mali	eb-bb1	eb-f1	Dramatic tenor	A dramatic scena, declamatory. (Ricordi)
Otello Recitative: Tu? Indietro! Fuggi Air: Ora e per sempre addio	e-bb1	g-eb1	Dramatic tenor	A dramatic scena and sustained dramatic air. (J. Church Co., Opera Songs)
Rigoletto Recitative: Ella mi fu rapita Air: Parmi veder le lagrime	d-bbb1	b-g1	Tenor	A scena and a very sustained air. Demands some flexibility. (Score, Schirmer)

OPERA & TITLE	COMP.	TESS.	TYPE	REMARKS
Rigoletto La donna è mobile	f#-a#1	b-f#1	Tenor	Animated, brilliant verse song. Has a florid cadenza. (Generally available)
Rigoletto Recitative: Ma dove or trovasi Air: Passente amor mi chiama	f#-a1	a-f#1	Tenor	Very animated, brilliant. Demands some flexibility. Very short. (Score, Schirmer)
Rigoletto Questa o quella	eb-ab1	ab-f1	Tenor	Rapid. Demands facile articulation and lightness of tone. (Generally available)
Simon Boccanegra Recitative: O inferno! Amelia qui Air: Sento avvampar nell'anima	e-a1	a-f#1	Dramatic tenor	Recitative, a dramatic allegro, and a sustained largo. (Ricordi)
Un Ballo in Maschera Di' tu se fedele il flutto	c-ab1	eb-eb1	Tenor	Animated. Demands facile articulation. (Ricordi)

ERMANNO WOLF-FARRARI
(1876 -)

OPERA & TITLE	COMP.	TESS.	TYPE	REMARKS
Gioielli della Madonna Benedici mi tu, madre mia	ab-ab1	ab-f1	Tenor	Very sustained. Has an effective final climax. (Schirmer)

RICCARDO ZANDONAI
(1883 -)

OPERA & TITLE	COMP.	TESS.	TYPE	REMARKS
Giuliano (Act I) Occhi soavi	f#-g#1	a-d#1	Tenor	A short, sustained air. Has effective climaxes. (Ricordi)

FRENCH

ADOLPHE ADAM
(1803-1856)

OPERA & TITLE	COMP.	TESS.	TYPE	REMARKS
Si j'étais Roi Romance: J'ignore son nom	f-ab1	ab-f1	Tenor	Sustained. (Leduc)
Si j'étais Roi Elle est princesse	f-c2	bb-f1	Tenor	Recitative and a sustained air. In parts demands considerable dramatic intensity. (Leduc)

OPERA & TITLE	COMP.	TESS.	TYPE	REMARKS
Le Postillon Romance du Postillon	B-d2	f-f1	Tenor	A difficult display piece. Demands great flexibility and range. (Brandus et Cie)
Le Postillon Mes amis écoutez l'histoire	d-b1	g-e1	Tenor	Sustained. (Brandus et Cie)

DANIEL F. E. AUBER
(1782-1871)

OPERA & TITLE	COMP.	TESS.	TYPE	REMARKS
La Muette de Portici Du pauvre seul ami fidèle	g-b1	a-f#1	Most suitable for lyric tenor	Animated, delicate. Demands good command of high pp. (Schirmer, Operatic Anthology)
Fra Diavolo (Act II) Agnès la jouvencelle (Barcarolle)	c#-a1	f#-e1	Most suitable for lyric tenor	Graceful. Demands some flexibility. (Brandus et Dufours)
Fra Diavolo (Act III) Pour toujours disait- elle je suis à tois	d-a1	g-f1	Most suitable for lyric tenor	Sustained and graceful. (Brandus et Dufours)

HECTOR BERLIOZ
(1803-1869)

OPERA & TITLE	COMP.	TESS.	TYPE	REMARKS
La Damnation de Faust (Part 3) Merci, doux crépuscule	e-ab1	g-f1	Tenor	Sustained. Demands in parts a good command of high pp. (Costellat)
La Damnation de Faust (Part 4) Nature immense	f#-a1	g#-e1	Tenor	Slow, sustained, declamatory. Has imposing climaxes. (Costellat)

GEORGES BIZET
(1838-1875)

OPERA & TITLE	COMP.	TESS.	TYPE	REMARKS
La Jolie Fille de Perth A la voix d'un amant fidèle	e-a1	a-f1	Tenor	Animated, graceful, sustained air. (Choudens)

OPERA & TITLE	COMP.	TESS.	TYPE	REMARKS
Les Pêcheurs de Perles				
Je crois entendre encore	e-b1	a-f1	Tenor	Very sustained, subdued. Demands good command of high pp. (Choudens)
Les Pêcheurs de Perles				
De savanes et des forêts	eb-ab1	ab-f1	Tenor	Short, animated. The vocal line is sustained. (Choudens)
Carmen				
La fleur que tu m'avais jetée	fb-fb1	ab-eb1	Tenor	Sustained. Demands in parts considerable dramatic intensity. (Generally availalbe)

ALFRED BRUNEAU
(1857-1934)

L'Attaque du Moulin				
Les adieux à la forêt	e-a1	a-f#1	Tenor	Sustained. (Choudens)

GUSTAVE CHARPENTIER
(1860 -)

Louise (Act II, Part 2, Scene 2)				
Dans la cité lointaine	f#-g#1	g#-e1	Tenor	A sustained serenade. (Heugel)

FÉLICIEN DAVID
(1810-1876)

Lalla Roukh				
Ma maîtresse a quitté la tente	e-a1	a-e1	Tenor	Sustained, graceful air. (Girod)

CLAUDE DEBUSSY
(1862-1918)

L'Enfant Prodigue Recitative: Ces airs joyeux Air:				
O temps à jamais effacé	d-a1	f#-f#1	Tenor	Sustained, somewhat declamatory. Demands considerable dramatic intensity. (Durand)

LÉO DÉLIBES
(1836-1891)

Lakmé Recitative: Je me souviens Air:				
Lakmé, dans la forêt profonde	f#-b1	a#-f#1	Tenor	Sustained. (Heugel)

Lakmé
Recitative:
Prendre le dessin
d'un bijou
Air:
Fantaisie aux divins mensonges — COMP. f-a1, TESS. ab-ab1, TYPE Tenor, REMARKS: Sustained. (Schirmer, Operatic Anthology)

BENJAMIN GODARD
(1849-1895)

Jocelyn
Recitative:
Cachés dans cet asile
Air:
Oh! Ne t'éveille pas (Berceuse) — f-a1, a-f1, Lyric tenor, Very sustained. Demands good command of high pp. (Generally available)

CHARLES GOUNOD
(1818-1893)

Faust
Recitative:
Quel trouble inconnu — eb-c2, ab-f1, Tenor — Very sustained. (Generally available)
Air:
Salut! Demeure chaste et pure

La Reine de Saba
Recitative:
Faiblesse de la race humaine — f-a1, g-g1, Dramatic tenor — A scena and a sustained vigorous air. Has dramatic climaxes. (Schirmer, Operatic Anthology)
Air:
Inspirez-moi

Mireille
Recitative:
Mon coeur est plein d'un noir souci — g-ab1, c-g1, Tenor — Very sustained. Has effective climaxes. (Schirmer, Operatic Anthology)
Air:
Anges du paradis

Polyeucte
Nymphes attentives — f-bb1, a-f1, Lyric tenor — A sustained barcarolle. (Schirmer, Operatic Anthology)

Polyeucte
Source délicieuse — f-a1 (bb1), bb-f1, Tenor — Very sustained. The final section more animated and demands considerable dramatic intensity. (Schirmer, Operatic Anthology)

Roméo et Juliette
Recitative:
L'amour! Oui son ardeur — f-bb1, a-f1, Tenor — Sustained. Has effective climaxes. (Generally available)
Air:
Ah, lève toi, soleil

Sapho
Recitative:
 J'arrive le premier eb-bb1   ab-f1   Lyric tenor Sustained. The optional
Air: (db2)   db1 is contained in the
 O jours heureux   final cadenza. (Schirmer,
  Operatic Anthology)

JACQUES HALÉVY
(1799-1862)

La Juive
Rachel, quand du   eb-c2   ab-g1   Tenor   Sustained. In parts
 Seigneur   very dramatic. Usually
  sung a tone lower.
  (Fischer)
L'Eclair
Quand de la nuit   b-g1   e-e1   Tenor   Sustained. (Schirmer)

LOUIS J. F. HÉROLD
(1791-1833)

Le Pré aux Clercs
Recitative:
 Ce soir j'arrive
  donc
Air:
 O ma tendre amie   f-c2   g-g1   Tenor   Short recitative and
  sustained air which
  has some very florid
  passages. (Brandus
  et Cie)

EDOUARD LALO
(1823-1892)

Le Roi d'Ys
 (Aubade)
Recitative:
 Puisqu'on ne peut
  fléchir
Air:
 Vainement, ma   eb-a1   a-e1   Lyric tenor Light, graceful.
  bien - aimée   Demands good command
  of high pp. (Generally
  available)

JULES MASSENET
(1842-1912)

Hérodiade
Recitative:
 Ne pouvant réprimer d-bb1   a-f1   Tenor   Recitative and a com-
  les élans   pound, dramatic mono-
Air: logue. Has many sus-
 Adieux donc vains   tained sections. (Schirmer,
  objets   Operatic Anthology)

OPERA & TITLE	COMP.	TESS.	TYPE	REMARKS
Le Cid O souverain, ô juge, ô père	eb-bb1	ab-f1	Tenor	Sustained. Has dramatic climaxes. (Schirmer, Operatic Anthology)

Le Roi de Lahore
Recitative:
  Aux troupes du
  Sultan
Air:
  Promesse de mon
  avenir
	eb-ab1	gb-eb1	Tenor	Sustained. Demands in parts considerable dramatic intensity. (J. Church Co., Opera Songs)

Manon
Recitative:
  Instant charmant
Air:
  En fermant les yeux
	e-a1	a-e1	Most suitable for lyric tenor	Sustained, delicate. Demands good command of high pp. (Generally available)

Manon
Recitative:
  Je suis seul
Air:
  Ah! fuyez
  douce image
	f-bb1	g-g1	Tenor	Sustained. Has very dramatic climaxes. (J. Church Co., Opera Songs)

Werther
Recitative:
  Je ne sais si je
  veille
Air:
  O nature pleine de
  grâce
	f#-a1	a-f#1	Tenor	Sustained. Has effective climaxes. (Heugel)

Werther
Recitative:
  Oui! Ce qu'elle
  m'ordonne
Air:
  Lorsque l'enfant
  revient d'un voyage
	f#-g#1
	(b1)
		b-f#1	Tenor	Sustained. Has effective climaxes. (Heugel)

Werther
Recitative:
  Traduire! Ah! Bien
  souvent mon rêve
Air:
  Pourquoi me
  réveiller
	f#-a#1	g#-d#1	Tenor	Sustained. Has effective climaxes. (Heugel)

Werther
Recitative:
  Un autre est son
  époux
Air:
  J'aurais sur ma
  poitrine
	g-bbb1	bb-f1	Tenor	Scena and an animated air. The vocal line is sustained. Has effective climaxes. (Heugel)

ANDRÉ MESSAGER
(1853-1929)

Opera & Title	Comp.	Tess.	Type	Remarks
Fortunio La maison grise	e-f1	g-d1	Tenor	Sustained. Vocally not taxing. Suitable for all voices; often used as a song. (Choudens)
Fortunio Chanson de Fortunio	e-a1	a-f#1	Tenor	Sustained. Has effective climaxes. Sometimes sung by soprani. (Choudens)

GIACOMO MEYERBEER
(1791-1864)

Opera & Title	Comp.	Tess.	Type	Remarks
L'Africaine Recitative: Pays merveilleux Air: O paradis	f-bb1	bb-gb1	Tenor*	An andante, allegro air with interpolated recitative passages. (Generally available)
Les Huguenots Recitative: Ah! Quel spectacle enchanteur Air: Plus blanche que la blanche hermine	e-b1	a-f#1	Lyric tenor	Sustained. In parts demands considerable flexibility. (Schirmer, Operatic Anthology)
Les Huguenots Recitative: Aux armes, mes amis Air: A la lueur de leurs torches funèbres	e-a1 (c2)	a-f1	Tenor	Recitative, andante, allegro. (Score, Breitkopf & Härtel)

JACQUES OFFENBACH
(1819-1880)

Opera & Title	Comp.	Tess.	Type	Remarks
Les Contes d'Hoffman (Act II) Recitative: Allons! Courage et confiance Air: Ah, vivre deux	e-g1	bb-f1	Tenor	Recitative and a sustained air. Has effective climaxes. (Score, Schirmer)

*Many tenor arias by Meyerbeer do not seem to be suitable for any but exceptionally high voices possessing the db2 and the d2.

AMBROISE THOMAS
(1811-1896)

Opera & Title	Comp.	Tess.	Type	Remarks
Hamlet Pour mon pays	f-b♭1	a♭-f1	Tenor	Sustained. Has effective climaxes. (Heugel)
Mignon Elle ne croyait pas	g-a1	a-e1	Lyric tenor	Sustained. In parts demands considerable dramatic intensity. (Generally available)

GERMAN

LUDWIG VAN BEETHOVEN
(1770-1827)

Opera & Title	Comp.	Tess.	Type	Remarks
Fidelio Recitative: Gott! Welch Dunkel hier Air: In des Lebens Frühlingstagen	e♭-b♭1	a♭-g1	Tenor	An extended recitative followed by an andante, allegro air. The tessitura in the allegro is very high. In parts very dramatic. (Generally available)

PETER CORNELIUS
(1824-1874)

Opera & Title	Comp.	Tess.	Type	Remarks
Der Barbier von Bagdad (Act I, Scene 2) Recitative: So leb' ich noch Air: Vor deinem Fenster die Blumen	f♯-a1	a-f1	Tenor	A scena and sustained air. Has effective climaxes. (Breitkopf & Härtel)

FRIEDRICH VON FLOTOW
(1812-1883)

Opera & Title	Comp.	Tess.	Type	Remarks
Martha Ach, so fromm, ach, so traut (or, as usually sung in the Italian version): M'appari	f-b♭1	a-f1	Tenor	Sustained. The tessitura is somewhat high. (Generally available)

OTTO NICOLAI
(1810-1849)

**Die Lustigen Weiber
von Windsor**

Opera & Title	Comp.	Tess.	Type	Remarks
Horch, die Lerche singt im Hain	g-g#1	b-e1	Lyric tenor	Sustained, rather delicate. (Score, Peters)

RICHARD WAGNER
(1813-1883)

Tenor Excerpts from Wagner's Music Dramas

*All these excerpts are most suitable for the heavy, dramatic type of voice, with the exception of the excerpts from Die Meistersinger and Lohengrin, which are not too unsuitable for less robust voices.

Opera & Title	Comp.	Tess.	Remarks
Der Fliegende Holländer (Act III, Scene 4)			
Willst jenes Tag's	f-bb1	a-f1	Sustained. Demands in parts considerable dramatic intensity. (J. Church Co., Opera Songs)
Die Meistersinger von Nürnberg (Act I, Scene 3)			
Am stillen Herd	d-a1	g-e1	Sustained. Has vigorous climaxes. (Schirmer, Operatic Anthology)
Die Meistersinger von Nürnberg (Act I, Scene 3)			
Fanget an! So rief der Lenz	f-a1	g-g1	Animated, vigorous. (Score, Peters)
Die Meistersinger von Nürnberg (Act III, Scene 5)			
Morgentlich leuchtend (Preislied)	d#-a1	b-g1	Has vigorous climaxes. (Generally available)
Die Walküre (Act I, Scene 3)			
Ein Schwert verhiess mir der Vater	c-g1	f-f1	Majestic, vigorous, somewhat declamatory. (Score, Peters)
Die Walküre (Act I, Scene 3)			
Winterstürme wichen dem Wonnemond	c-g1	f-f1	Sustained. Demands in parts considerable dramatic intensity. (Generally available)
Lohengrin (Act III, Scene 2)			
Atmest du nicht mit mir die süssen Düfte	g-ab1	g-f1	Very sustained. (Score, Peters)
Lohengrin (Act III, Scene 3)			
In Fernem Land	e-a1	a-e1	Slow, somewhat declamatory. (Generally available)

OPERA & TITLE	COMP.	TESS.	TYPE	REMARKS
Lohengrin (Act III, Scene 3) Mein Lieber Schwan	f♯-a1	b-g1		Sustained. Has dramatic climaxes. (Generally available)
Rienzi (Act V, Scene 1) Allmächt'ger Vater	f-ab1	bb-f1		Very sustained, majestic. Has dramatic climaxes. (Schirmer, Operatic Anthology)
Rienzi (Act IV, Scene 2) Ihr nicht beim Feste?	f-ab1	g-f1		Animated, vigorous. (Score, Peters)
Siegfried (Act I, Scene 3) Nothung! Nothung! Neidliches Schwert	d-a1	f-f1		Very vigorous. (Score, Peters)
Siegfried (Act I, Scene 3) Schmiede mein Hammer, ein hartes Schwert	g-a1	a-g1		Very vigorous. (Score, Peters)
Tannhäuser (Act I, Scene 2) Dir töne Lob! Die Wunder sein gepriesen	e♯-g1	a-f♯1		Animated, vigorous. In the opera the three verses of this song are respectively in the keys of db, d, and eb. The arrangement listed is by Carl Armbruster. (Wagner Lyrics for Tenor, Ditson)
Tristan und Isolde (Act III, Scene 1) Wie sie selig hehr und milde wandelt durch des Meer's Gefilde	d♯-f♯1	g♯-e1		Sustained. (Score, Peters)

CARL MARIA von WEBER
(1786-1826)

OPERA & TITLE	COMP.	TESS.	TYPE	REMARKS
Abu Hassan Recitative: Was nun zu machen? Air: Ich gebe Gastereien	c-g1	e-e1	Tenor	Very spirited, gay compound air. The middle section is sustained and delicate. Demands some flexibility. (Score, Peters)
Der Freischütz Recitative: Nein, länger trag' ich nicht die Qual Air: Durch die Wälder	d-a1 (c)	g-f1	Tenor	Recitative, andante, allegro. In parts dramatic and vigorous. (Schirmer, Operatic Anthology)
Euryanthe Unter blühenden Mandelbämen	f-bb1	a-f1	Tenor	Sustained. Demands some flexibility. (Generally available)
Euryanthe Wehen mir Lüfte	eb-ab1	ab-f1	Tenor	An andante, allegro air. In parts quite vigorous. Demands some flexibility. (Score, Peters)

OPERA & TITLE	COMP.	TESS.	TYPE	REMARKS
Oberon Ich jub'le in Glück und Hoffnungen	c-g1	g-f1	Tenor	Very animated, vigorous. Demands considerable flexibility. (Score, Peters)
Oberon Recitative: Ja selbst die Liebe weicht dem Ruhm Air: Klag' du Tochter des Morgenlands	d♯-a1	f-e1	Tenor	Scena, andante, allegro. In parts very vigorous. Demands some flexibility. (Score, Peters)
Oberon Schreckensschwur!	c-g1	f-d1	Dramatic tenor	Very vigorous, animated, dramatic. (Score, Peters)
Oberon Vater, hör'mich flehn zu dir	e-g1	g-e1	Tenor	Slow, sustained, very short. (Score, Peters)
Oberon Von Jugend auf in dem Kampfgefild'	d-b1	b-f♯1	Tenor	Very vigorous, animated. Démands considerable flexibility. (Ditson)

MISCELLANEOUS

MICHAEL W. BALFE
(1808-1870)

| The Bohemian Girl
Then you'll
remember me | g-ab1 | ab1-gb1 | Tenor | Sustained. (Generally available) |

FOR BASS AND BARITONE
ITALIAN

GIOVANNI APOLLONI
(1822-1889)

OPERA & TITLE	COMP.	TESS.	TYPE	REMARKS
L'Ebreo Recitative: Si, guerrieri Air: Fu Dio, che dissi	Ab-f	f-db1	Bass or bass-baritone	Sustained. Has dramatic climaxes. (Schirmer, Operatic Anthology)

VINCENZO BELLINI
(1801-1835)

OPERA & TITLE	COMP.	TESS.	TYPE	REMARKS
Beatrice di Tenda O divina Agnese	d-f1	f#-d1	Baritone	An andante, allegro air. Demands some flexibility. (Ricordi)
Beatrice di Tenda Qui m'accolse	d-f1	f-eb1	Baritone	An andante, allegro air. (Ricordi)
La Sonnambula Vi ravviso o luoghi ameni	G-eb1	eb-c1	Bass	An andante, allegro air. Demands some flexibility. (Ditson)

ARRIGO BOITO
(1842-1918)

OPERA & TITLE	COMP.	TESS.	TYPE	REMARKS
Mefistofele Ave Signor	Bb-eb1 (f1)	f-d1	Baritone or bass-baritone	Animated, satirical song. Demands facile articulation. In parts very vigorous. (Score, Ricordi)
Mefistofele Sono lo spirito che nega	G-e1	c-c1	Bass or bass-baritone	A dramatic monologue. In parts demands facile articulation. (J. Church Co., Opera Songs)

EUGÈNE DIAZ
(1837-1901)

OPERA & TITLE	COMP.	TESS.	TYPE	REMARKS
Benvenuto Recitative: Quante volte alla notte Air: O splendore infinito	A-f1	f-d1	Baritone	Recitative and a sustained, effective air. (L. Grus, Paris)

GAETANO DONIZETTI
(1797-1848)

OPERA & TITLE	COMP.	TESS.	TYPE	REMARKS
Don Pasquale				
Ah! un foco insolito	c-e1	g-c1	Bass	A rapid buffo air. Demands facile articulation. (Ricordi)
Don Pasquale				
Bella siccome un angelo	Ab-f1	f-db1	Baritone	Slow, sustained. In parts demands considerable flexibility. (Ricordi)
Don Sebastiano				
Recitative: Sente il cielo pietade Air: O Lisbona, alfin ti miro	d-f1	g-d1	Baritone	Recitative and a sustained larghetto. Demands some flexibility. (Schirmer, Operatic Anthology)
La Favorita				
Recitative: Alcun gli fea Air: Vien, Leonora	c-f1	f-d1	Baritone	Scena and a compound aria. Has dramatic climaxes. (Ricordi)
La Favorita				
Recitative: Fernando, ei del suo cor la brama Air: A tanto amor	c#-e1	f#-c#1	Bass or bass-baritone	Recitative and a sustained air. (Schirmer, Operatic Anthology)
L'Elisir d'Amore				
Udite, udite, o rustici	A-e1	e-c#1	Bass	An andante, allegro buffo air. Demands facile articulation. (Ricordi)
Le Rénégat				
Recitative: J'ai renié ma foi Air: Ange adoré (French text)	G-d1	d-b	Bass	Recitative, a short larghetto, and a very vigorous spirited allegro. (Peters, Arias for Bass)
Linda di Chamounix				
Ambo nati in questa valle	c#-e1	g-d1	Baritone	Sustained. (Ricordi)
Lucia di Lammermoor				
Cruda, funesta smania	c#-f#1 (g1)	g-e1	Baritone	A sustained larghetto and a spirited allegro. Demands some flexibility. (Schirmer, Operatic Anthology)
Lucrezia Borgia				
Vieni la mia vendetta	Ab-eb1	eb-db1	Bass	An andante, allegro air. Vigorous. Demands some flexibility. Has dramatic climaxes. (Schirmer, Operatic Anthology)
Marie di Rohan				
Voce fatal di morte	f-f1 (g1)	a-e1	High baritone	Sustained air for very high baritone. (Ricordi)

OPERA & TITLE	COMP.	TESS.	TYPE	REMARKS
Maria di Rådenz				
Recitative:				
Egli ancora non giunge	e-g1	g-eb1	Baritone	Sustained. Demands some flexibility. (Schirmer, Operatic Anthology)
Air:				
Ah, non avea più lagrime				
Poliuto				
Di tua beltade immagine	c-fb1	eb-db1	Baritone	An andante, allegro air. Demands some flexibility. (Ricordi)

UMBERTO GIORDANO
(1867 -)

OPERA & TITLE	COMP.	TESS.	TYPE	REMARKS
Andrea Chenier				
Compiacente a' colloquii	c#-f#1	f#-c#1	Baritone	Sustained, declamatory. The final section is very animated, the vocal line sustained. Has dramatic climaxes. (Sonzogno)
Andrea Chenier				
Nemico della patria?	c#-f#1	f#-d1	Baritone	A dramatic scena and a sustained air. Has dramatic climaxes. (Sonzogno)
Fedora				
(Act II)				
La donna Russa	eb-f1	g-eb1	Baritone	Spirited, brilliant. Has some florid passages. (Sonzogno)

ANTONIO C. GOMEZ
(1839-1896)

OPERA & TITLE	COMP.	TESS.	TYPE	REMARKS
Il Guarany				
Senza tetto, senza cuna	d-g1	g-e1	Baritone	Rapid, brilliant. Demands some flexibility. (Generally available)

RUGGIERO LEONCAVALLO
(1858-1919)

OPERA & TITLE	COMP.	TESS.	TYPE	REMARKS
Pagliacci				
Si può? Signore!				
(Prologue)	B-f1 (ab1)	e-eb1	High baritone	A dramatic scena followed by a very sustained andante. (Schirmer)
Zazà				
Zazà, piccola zingara	f-gb1	ab-f1	High baritone	Sustained, has effective climaxes. (Sonzogno)

OPERA & TITLE	COMP.	TESS.	TYPE	REMARKS

PIETRO MASCAGNI
(1863 -)

L'Amico Fritz

Per voi ghiottoni inutili (Song of the Rabbi)	d-f1	g-eb1	Baritone	Sustained, vigorous, dramatic. (J. Church Co., Opera Songs)

Cavalleria
Rusticana

Il cavallo scalpita	eb-f♯1	g-eb1	Baritone	Vigorous, animated. Demands facile articulation. (Schirmer, Operatic Anthology)

FILIPPO MARCHETTI
(1831-1902)

Ruy Blas

Ai miei rivali cedere	d-f♯1	a-e1	Baritone	Recitative and a sustained dramatic air. (Schirmer)

ITALO MONTEMEZZI
(1875 -)

L'Amore dei Tre Re

Italia, è tutto il mio ricordo	A-f1	f-d1	Bass-baritone or baritone	Dramatic, declamatory. Has an imposing final climax. (Ricordi)

AMILCARE PONCHIELLI
(1834-1886)

La Gioconda

Ah! Pescator	eb-f1	g-eb1	Baritone	Spirited, demands some flexibility. (Schirmer, Operatic Anthology)

La Gioconda

O monumento!	d-g1	g-d1	Baritone	A dramatic scena, declamatory and grave. (Ricordi)

La Gioconda
Recitative:
 Si, morir ella de'
Air:

Ombre di mia prosapia	G-eb1 (f1)	c-c1	Bass	A dramatic scena and a compound dramatic air. (Schirmer, Operatic Anthology)

GIACOMO PUCCINI
(1858-1924)

Il Tabarro

Scorri fiume eterno	Bb-g1	eb-eb1	Baritone	Sustained, declamatory. Has dramatic climaxes. (Ricordi)

-492-

OPERA & TITLE	COMP.	TESS.	TYPE	REMARKS
La Tosca				
Act 2				
Se la giurata fede	db-gb1	f-eb1	Baritone	Sustained. Has dramatic climaxes. (Ricordi)
Le Villi				
Recitative:				
No! Possibil non è				
Air:				
Anima santa della figlia mia	Bb-f1 (g1)	f-eb1	High baritone	A dramatic scena and a sustained air. Has dramatic climaxes. (J. Church Co., Opera Songs)

GIOACCHINO ROSSINI
(1792-1868)

OPERA & TITLE	COMP.	TESS.	TYPE	REMARKS
Guillaume Tell				
Sois immobile (French text)	c-f1	f-db1	Baritone	Very sustained. (Schirmer, Operatic Anthology)
Il Barbiere di Siviglia				
A un dottore	Bb-f1	eb-eb1	Bass	A spirited buffo air. Demands very facile articulation and considerable flexibility. Rather high tessitura. Usually omitted in stage performances of the opera, when an air by Pietro Romani, "Manca un foglio," is substituted. For Romani's air see Schirmer edition of Il Barbiere, page 319.
Il Barbiere di Siviglia				
La calunnia	c#-f#1	d-d1	Bass or bass-baritone	A spirited, comic air. Interpretatively not easy. Demands facile articulation. (Generally available)
Il Barbiere di Siviglia				
Largo al factotum	d-g1 (a1)	g-e1	High baritone	Very rapid. Demands very facile articulation. (Generally available)
La Cenerentola				
Recitative:				
Miei rampolli femminini	c-f1	e-d1	Bass or baritone	A spirited buffo air. Demands facile articulation. (Ricordi)
Air:				
Mi sognai fra il fosco e il chiaro				
La Gazza Ladra				
Il mio piano è preparato	A-e1	c#-c#1	Bass or bass-baritone	A florid andante, allegro buffo air. Demands facile articulation. (Ricordi)

OPERA & TITLE	COMP.	TESS.	TYPE	REMARKS
Le Siège de Corinthe Recitative: Qu'à ma voix la victoire s'arrête Air: La gloire et la fortune (French text)	Bb-f1	c-c1	Baritone	Recitative, andante, allegro. Demands some flexibility. (Schirmer, Operatic Anthology)
Robert Bruce Recitative: Le roi someille Air: Que ton âme si noble (French text)	Bb-eb1	eb-c1	Bass or bass-baritone	Animated. Demands some flexibility. (Schirmer, Operatic Anthology)

GIUSEPPE VERDI
(1813-1901)

OPERA & TITLE	COMP.	TESS.	TYPE	REMARKS
Attila Recitative: Tregua è cogl' uni Air: Dagli immortali vertici	c-g1	eb-eb1	Baritone	An extended recitative, a very sustained andante, and a vigorous allegro. (Schirmer, Operatic Anthology)
Don Carlo Recitative: Convien qui dirci addio Air: Per me giunto è il di supremo	c-gb1	f-d1	Baritone	For the most part sustained. In parts declamatory. Has dramatic climaxes. (Schirmer, Operatic Anthology)
Don Carlo Recitative: Ella giammai m'amò! Air: Dormirò sol nel manto mio regal	G-eb1	d-bb	Bass	Scena and a sustained air. Has dramatic climaxes. (Schirmer, Operatic Anthology)
Don Carlo Recitative: Son io mio Carlo Air: Per me giunto	c-gb1	g-e1	Baritone	Recitative, a very sustained andante, a dramatic declamatory middle section, and a broad, sustained final moderato. (Schirmer, Operatic Anthology)
Ernani Recitative: Che mai vegg'io Air: Infelice! E tuo credevi	G-eb1	eb-c1	Bass or bass-baritone	Recitative and a sustained air. Demands some flexibility. Has dramatic climaxes. (Schirmer, Operatic Anthology)

OPERA & TITLE	COMP.	TESS.	TYPE	REMARKS
Ernani				
Recitative:				
Gran Dio	c-gb1	f-eb1	Baritone	Recitative and a sustained air. Demands flexibility. Has dramatic climaxes. (Ricordi)
Air:				
Oh de verd' anni miei				
Ernani				
Lo vedremo, veglio audace	d-f#1	a-e1	Baritone	Animated. Has dramatic climaxes. Demands some flexibility. (Ricordi)
Falstaff				
(Act II, Scene 1)				
(Monologo di Ford)				
È sogno? O realtà?	c-gb1	eb-eb1	Baritone	A dramatic, declamatory scena. (Ricordi)
Falstaff				
(Act I, Scene 1)				
L'onore! Ladri!	Ab-g1	e-e1	Baritone	A declamatory scena. Interpretatively not easy. (Ricordi)
I due Foscari				
Recitative:				
Eccomi solo al fino	eb-f1	f-eb1	Baritone	Sustained. Demands some flexibility. Has dramatic climaxes. (Ricordi)
Air:				
O vecchio cor che batti				
Il Trovatore				
(Act I, No. 2)				
Di due figli vivea	B-e1	c#-c#1	Bass or bass-baritone	An andante, allegretto narrative song. For the most part subdued. Has dramatic climaxes. Demands some flexibility. (Score, Schirmer)
Il Trovatore				
Recitative:				
Tutto è deserto	A-f1 (g1)	f-eb1	Baritone	An extended recitative, and a very sustained largo. Demands some flexibility. (Generally available)
Air:				
Il balen del suo sorriso				
I Masnadieri				
Recitative:				
Tradimento! Risorgono i defunti	Bb-f1	f-eb1	Baritone	A very dramatic scena and a vigorous, dramatic, animated air. (Ricordi)
Air:				
Pareami che sorto da lauto convito				
I Vespri Siciliani				
In braccio alle dovizie	c#-f#1	f#-d#1	Baritone	A vigorous, dramatic allegro and a sustained meno mosso. (Ricordi)
I Vespri Siciliani				
Recitative:				
O patria, o cara patria	A-eb1	db-db	Bass or bass-baritone	Recitative and a sustained air. Has dramatic climaxes. Demands some flexibility. (Schirmer, Operatic Anthology)
Air:				
O, tu Palermo				
La Forza del Destino				
Recitative:				
Morir! Tremenda cosa	c-g1	f-eb1	Baritone	Scena and a sustained air. Demands some flexibility. Has dramatic climaxes. (Ricordi)
Air:				
Urna fatale				

OPERA & TITLE	COMP.	TESS.	TYPE	REMARKS
La Traviata Recitative: Mio figlio! Air: Di Provenza il mar, il suol	db-gb1	ab-eb1	Baritone	Very sustained. (J. Church Co., Opera Songs)
Luisa Miller Il mio sangue, la vita darei	Bb-gb1	eb-db1	Baritone	A dramatic, vigorous andante, allegro air. Has a florid final cadenza. (Ricordi)
Luisa Miller Sacra la scelta è d'un consorte	d-gb1	f-f1	High baritone	A dramatic andante, allegro air. Demands some flexibility. (Ricordi)
Macbeth Recitative: Perfidi! All'Anglo contro me v'unite Air: Pietà, rispetto, onore	c-f1	f-db1	Baritone	Recitative and a sustained air. Demands in parts considerable dramatic intensity. (Schirmer, Operatic Anthology)
Macbeth Recitative: Studia il passo, o mio figlio! Air: Come dal ciel precipita	A-e1	b-b	Bass or bass baritone	Recitative and a sustained air. Has dramatic climaxes. (Schirmer, Operatic Anthology)
Nabucodonosor (Nabucco) Chi mi toglie il regio scettro?(Finale II)	c-f1	f-eb1	Baritone	Animated, vigorous, dramatic. (Ricordi)
Nabucodonosor (Nabucco) Recitative: Vieni, o Levita Air: Tu sul labbro de'veggenti	G-e1	d-c1	Bass	Recitative and a sustained air. (Schirmer, Operatic Anthology)
Otello Recitative: Vanne, la tua meta gia vedo Air: Credo in un dio crudel	A#-f#	f-eb1	Baritone	A very dramatic declamatory scena. (J. Church Co., Opera Songs)
Rigoletto Recitative: Si, la mia figlia Air: Cortigiani, vil razza	c-f1	f-db1	Baritone	Recitative, a dramatic declamatory andante agitato, and a final very sustained andante. (Schirmer, Operatic Anthology)

OPERA & TITLE	COMP.	TESS.	TYPE	REMARKS
Simon Boccanegra				
Recitative:				
A te l'estremo addio	F#-d1	c#-b	Bass or bass-baritone	Slow, grave, sustained. (Schirmer, Operatic Anthology)
Air:				
Il lacerato spirito				
Simon Boccanegra				
Fratricidi! Plebe! Patrizi!	eb-f#1	ab-eb1	Baritone	Sustained, short. Has a dramatic opening section. (Ricordi)
Un Ballo in Maschera				
Recitative:				
Alzati! Là tuo figlio	c-g1	f-e1	Baritone	Scena and a dramatic, vigorous, sustained air. (Generally available)
Air:				
Eri tu che macchiavi				

ERMANNO WOLF-FERRARI
(1876 -)

OPERA & TITLE	COMP.	TESS.	TYPE	REMARKS
Gioielli della Madonna				
(Act II)				
Apri la bella (Serenade)	f#-f#1	g-e1	High baritone	Animated, brilliant serenade. (Schirmer)

FRENCH

ADOLPHE ADAM
(1803-1856)

OPERA & TITLE	COMP.	TESS.	TYPE	REMARKS
Le Chalet				
Recitative:				
Arrêtons-nous ici				
Air:				
Vallons de l'Helvétie	Bb-eb1	eb-c1	Bass-baritone	A scena and sustained, dramatic air. Has very florid passages. (Schirmer, Operatic Anthology)
Si j'étais Roi				
Dans le sommeil	eb-ab1	ab-eb1	High baritone	Sustained. (Leduc)

HECTOR BERLIOZ
(1803-1869)

OPERA & TITLE	COMP.	TESS.	TYPE	REMARKS
La Damnation de Faust				
(Part 2)				
Certain rat, dans une cuisine	A-d1	c-c1	Bass	A spirited, vigorous, satirical song. (Costellat)
La Damnation de Faust				
(Part 3)				
Recitative:				
Maintenant, chantons à cette belle				

Air:

Opera & Title	Comp.	Tess.	Type	Remarks
Devant la maison (Sérénade de Méphisto)	B-d♯1	e-c♯1	Baritone or bass-baritone	A satirical, animated serenade in waltz tempo. Demands some flexibility. (Ditson)

La Damnation de
Faust
(Part 2)

Une puce gentille (Chanson de la Puce)	d-f1	f-d1	Baritone	A spirited, satirical verse song. See "Song of the Flea" by Mussorgsky and "Aus Goethe's Faust" by Beethoven. (Costellat)

La Damnation de
Faust
(Part 2)

Voici des roses	c♯-e1	e-c♯1	Baritone	Sustained, subdued. (Costellat)

GEORGES BIZET
(1838-1875)

Carmen
Votre toast

(Song of the Toreador)	B♭-f1	f-d♭1	Baritone	Vigorous, spirited. (Generally available)

La Jolie Fille de
Perth

Quand la flamme de l'amour	B-e1	e-d1	Bass or bass-baritone	Animated, vigorous. (Schirmer, Operatic Anthology)

Les Pêcheurs de
Perles
Recitative:
L'orage s'est calmé
Air:

O Nadir, tendre ami	B-f♯	d-d1	Baritone	Recitative and a sustained air. Has effective climaxes. (Choudens)

GUSTAVE CHARPENTIER
(1860 -)

Louise
(Act IV, Scene 1)
Recitative:
Les pauvres gens
Air:

Voir naître un enfant	A♯-f1	f-d1	Baritone	A dramatic monologue. (Heugel)

CLAUDE DEBUSSY
(1862-1918)

OPERA & TITLE	COMP.	TESS.	TYPE	REMARKS
L'Enfant Prodigue Faites silence! Écoutez tous!	Bb-f1	f-d1	Baritone	Sustained, majestic. (Durand)

LÉO DÉLIBES
(1836-1891)

Lakmé Lakmé, ton doux regard se voile	eb-f1	f-db1	Bass or bass- baritone	Sustained. (Heugel)

CHARLES GOUNOD
(1818-1893)

Faust Avant de quitter ces lieux	c-g1	eb-eb1	Baritone	Sustained. In some editions transposed a whole tone lower. (Generally available)
Faust Écoute-moi bien, Marguerite (The Death of Valentine)	c-f1	f-d1	Baritone	Dramatic, declamatory. (Score, Schirmer)
Faust Recitative: Il était temps Air: O nuit étends sur eux ton ombre	G-c1 (db1)	g-c1	Bass	Slow and very sustained. (Score, Schirmer)
Faust Le veau d'or	c-eb1	eb-d1	Bass	A spirited, vigorous verse song. (Generally available)
Faust Souviens-toi du passé	G-d1	c-c1	Bass	Very sustained, somber. Omitted in most stage performances. (Score, Schirmer)
Faust Vous qui faites l'endormie	G-g1 (A)	d-d1	Bass or bass- baritone	A spirited, satirical serenade. Demands facile articulation and some flexibility. (Generally available)
La Reine de Saba Recitative: Oui, depuis quatre jours Air: Sous les pieds d'une femme	E-d1	B-b	Bass	Sustained. Demands some flexibility. (Schirmer, Operatic Anthology)
Mireille Si les filles d'Arles	c-f1	e-d1	Baritone	An animated, rather vigorous verse song. (Choudens)

OPERA & TITLE	COMP.	TESS.	TYPE	REMARKS
Philémon et Baucis Au bruit des lourds marteaux	A♭-e♭1	d-d♭1	Bass	Spirited, vigorous. Demands some flexibility. (Generally available)
Philémon et Baucis Que les songes heureux	E-c♯1	e-b	Bass	Very subdued, sustained. (Schirmer, Operatic Anthology)
Roméo et Juliette Recitative: Buvez donc ce breuvage Air: C'est là qu'après un jour	G-d1	e♭-b♭	Bass	Sustained, somber. The final section more animated, the vocal line sustained. (Score, Schirmer)
Roméo et Juliette Mab, la reine des mensonges	d-f♯1	f♯-c♯1	Baritone	Very animated, light. Demands facile articulation. (J. Church Co., Opera Songs)

JACQUES HALÉVY
(1799-1862)

OPERA & TITLE	COMP.	TESS.	TYPE	REMARKS
La Juive Si la rigueur	E-c1	c-b♭	Bass	Very sustained. (Generally available)
La Juive Vous qui du Dieu vivant outragez la puissance	G-e♭1	d-d1	Bass	Grave, majestic, somber. (Brandus et Cie)

JULES MASSENET
(1842-1912)

OPERA & TITLE	COMP.	TESS.	TYPE	REMARKS
Hérodiade Recitative: Ce breuvage pourrait me donner un tel rêve Air: Vision fugitive	c-g♭1	f-d♭1	Baritone	An extended recitative and a very sustained air. Has dramatic climaxes. (Schirmer, Operatic Anthology)
Hérodiade (Act III, Scene 1) Recitative: Dors, ô cité perverse Air: Astres étincilants	c-f1	e♭-d1	Bass or baritone	A dramatic monologue. Has many sustained sections. (Heugel)
Hérodiade Recitative: Elle a fui le palais Air: Salomé, Salomé	d♭-f1	g-e♭1	Baritone	Recitative and a sustained in parts very dramatic air. (Schirmer, Operatic Anthology)
Manon Recitative: Les grand mots que voilà!	c-f1	e-d1	Bass or baritone	Sustained. Has effective climaxes. (Score, Schirmer)

OPERA & TITLE	COMP.	TESS.	TYPE	REMARKS
Manon Air; Regardez-moi bien dans les yeux	c-e1	e-c#1	Baritone	Rather vigorous, rhythmical. (Score, Schirmer)
Le Jongleur de Notre Dame (Act II) Légende de la Sauge (Marie avec l'Enfant Jésus)	c#-f1	f-d1	Baritone	A sustained, narrative air. (Heugel)
Le Roi de Lahore Recitative: Aux troupes du Sultan Air: Promesse de mon avenir	db-gb1	f-eb1	Baritone	An extended recitative and a sustained air. Has dramatic climaxes. (Schirmer, Operatic Anthology)
Thaïs Voilà donc la terrible cité	B-f1	e-c#1	Baritone	An animated, dramatic monologue. The vocal line is quite sustained. (Heugel)

GIACOMO MEYERBEER
(1791-1864)

OPERA & TITLE	COMP.	TESS.	TYPE	REMARKS
L'Africaine Adamastor, roi des vagues profondes	A#-e1 (f#1)	e-e1	Baritone	Vigorous, spirited. Demands facile articu- lation and some flexi- bility. (Schirmer, Operatic Anthology)
L'Africaine Fille des rois	d-f1 (g1)	f#-eb1	Baritone	A very sustained an- dante and a spirited, vigorous allegro. (Schirmer, Operatic Anthology)
Le Pardon de Ploërmel Recitative: En chasse! Air: Le jour est levé	B-e1	d-d1	Bass or bass- baritone	Spirited. Demands facile articulation and some flexibility. (Schirmer, Operatic Anthology)
Le Pardon de Ploërmel Ah, mon remords te venge	db-gb1	gb-eb1	High baritone	Sustained. Has effective climaxes. The gb1 is very frequently employed. (Schirmer, Operatic Anthology)
Le Prophète Aussi nombreux que les étoiles	G#-e1	e-c#1	Bass or bass- baritone	An animated verse song. Demands facile articu- lation and considerable flexibility. (Score, Breitkopf & Härtel)

OPERA & TITLE	COMP.	TESS.	TYPE	REMARKS
Les Huguenots Chanson Huguenotte: Recitative: Piff, paff Air: Pour les couvents. c'est fini!	F#-e1	c-c1	Bass	An animated verse song. Demands some flexi- bility and facile articu- lation. (Score, Breitkopf & Härtel)
L'Etoile du Nord Recitative: Pour fuir son souvenir Air: O jours heureux	Gb-eb1 (Eb)	eb-c1	Bass	Demands some flexibi- bility. Sustained. (Schirmer, Operatic Anthology)
Robert Le Diable Recitative: Voici donc le débris du monastère antique Air: Nonnes qui reposez	B-d#1	b-b	Bass or bass- baritone	Dramatic, vigorous, declamatory. (Schirmer, Operatic Anthology)

JACQUES OFFENBACH
(1819-1880)

OPERA & TITLE	COMP.	TESS.	TYPE	REMARKS
Les Contes d'Hoffman Scintille diamant	Bb-f#1 (g#1)	e-c#1	Baritone	Sustained. Has effective climaxes. (Schirmer)

CAMILLE SAINT-SAËNS
(1835-1921)

OPERA & TITLE	COMP.	TESS.	TYPE	REMARKS
Henry VIII Qui donc commande quand il aime!	d#-f#1	f#-d#1	Baritone	A sustained larghetto. The middle section is a vigorous allegro. (Schirmer, Operatic Anthology)

AMBROISE THOMAS
(1811-1896)

OPERA & TITLE	COMP.	TESS.	TYPE	REMARKS
Le Caïd (Act I) Le Tambour-Major tout galonné d'or	A-e1	d-d1	Bass or bass- baritone	Spirited, robust and florid air. Demands facile articulation. (Ditson)
Hamlet O vin, dissipe la tristesse	c-f1 (g1)	f-d1	Baritone	A vigorous, spirited drinking song. (Schirmer, Operatic Anthology)
Hamlet Recitative: J'ai pu frapper le misérable				

OPERA & TITLE	COMP.	TESS.	TYPE	REMARKS
Hamlet (Cont'd.) Air: Etre ou ne pas être	c#-d#1	e-c#1	Baritone	A dramatic scena (a setting of the famous monologue). (Heugel)
Hamlet Je t'implore	Eb-eb1 (f1)	c-c1	Bass	Sustained, has dramatic climaxes. (Heugel)
Hamlet Comme une pâle fleur	Bb-f#1	f#-d#1	Baritone	Sustained, has dramatic climaxes. (Heugel)
Mignon De son coeur j'ai calmé la fièvre	A-d1	e-b	Bass	Sustained, very subdued. (Schirmer, Operatic Anthology)

GERMAN

LUDWIG VAN BEETHOVEN
(1770-1827)

Fidelio Ha! Welch ein Augenblick	Ab-e1	d-d1	Bass or bass-baritone	Very animated, vigorous, dramatic. (Score generally available)
Fidelio Hat man nicht auch Gold beineben	Bb-d1	d-bb1	Bass	Animated, in parts quite rapid. Demands in parts facile articulation. (Score generally available)

FRIEDRICH VON FLOTOW
(1812-1883)

Martha Lasst mich euch fragen	G-f1	c-c1	Bass	A spirited drinking song. (Schirmer, Operatic Anthology)

ALBERT LORTZING
(1801-1851)

Undine Es wohnt am Seegestade	A-e1	g-d1	Bass or bass-baritone	A sustained verse song. Demands some flexibility. (Peters, Arias for Bass)
Zar und Zimmerman O sancta justitia	G-e1	d-d1	Bass-baritone	An animated buffo air. Demands facile articulation. Has florid passages. Rather long. (Peters, Arias for Bass)

Zar und Zimmerman

Sonst spielt' ich mit Scepter	d-f1	g-d1	Bass-baritone or baritone	A sustained verse song. (Schirmer)

HEINRICH MARSCHNER
(1795-1861)

Hans Heiling

An jenem Tag	c#-f#1	g#-e1	Baritone	A sustained allegro, andante, and a vigorous final allegro. (Schirmer, Operatic Anthology)

FELIX MENDELSSOHN
(1809-1847)

Die Heimkehr aus der Fremde

Ich bin ein viel-gereïster Mann	G-f#1	d-d1	High baritone	A rapid comic air. Demands very facile articulation. (Ditson)

VICTOR NESSLER
(1841-1890)

Der Trompeter von Säkkingen

Es hat nicht sollen sein	c-e1	g-d1	Baritone or bass-baritone	Very sustained. (Schirmer, Operatic Anthology)

OTTO NICOLAI
(1810-1849)

Die Lustigen Weiber von Windsor

Als Büblein klein	E-e1	c#-c#1	Bass	A vigorous drinking song. (Schirmer, Operatic Anthology)

LOUIS SPOHR
(1784-1859)

Faust

Recitative:
  Che l'orco dia
  giustitia
Air:

Tu che sei quel dolce fiore (Italian text)	A-d1 (G)	d-d1 (f1)	Bass or baritone	Recitative and a compound air. Demands considerable flexibility. Peters, Arias for Bass)

OPERA & TITLE	COMP.	TESS.	TYPE	REMARKS
Jessonda Der Kriegeslust ergeben	c-f1	d-d1	Bass or baritone	Animated, vigorous. Demands considerable flexibility. (Peters, Arias for Bass)

RICHARD WAGNER
(1813-1883)

Bass and Baritone Excerpts from Wagner's Music Dramas

OPERA & TITLE	COMP.	TESS.	TYPE	REMARKS
Das Rheingold (Scene 4) Abendlich strahlt der Sonne Auge	B-f1	db-db1	Bass- baritone	Majestic, sustained. (Score generally avail- able)
Der Fliegende **Holländer** (Act I, Scene 3) Die Frist ist um	G-f1	d-d1	Baritone	An extended recitative and a dramatic, vigor- ous compound air. (Generally available)
Der Fliegende **Holländer** (Act II, Scene 6) Mögst du mein Kind	A-d1	e-d1	Bass- baritone or bass	Animated, rather vigor- ous. The vocal line is sustained. (Score, generally available)
Die Meistersinger **von Nürnberg** (Act II, Scene 5) Recitative: Jerum! Jerum! Air: Als Eva aus dem Paradies	c-f1	d-d1	Bass- baritone	Vigorous, in parts sus- tained, gently humorous. (Generally available)
Die Meistersinger **von Nürnberg** (Act I, Scene 3) Nun hört und versteht mich recht! (Pogner's Address)	A-f1	e-c1	Bass- baritone or bass	Animated, vigorous. (Generally available)
Die Meistersinger **von Nürnberg** (Act III, Scene 1) Wahn! Wahn! (Hans Sachs' Monologue)	A-e1	d-c1	Bass- baritone	Declamatory, in parts vigorous, sustained. (Generally available)

OPERA & TITLE	COMP.	TESS.	TYPE	REMARKS
Die Meistersinger von Nürnberg (Act II, Scene 3)				
Was duftet doch der Flieder (Hans Sachs' Monologue)	A–e1	e–d1	Bass-baritone	Sustained, somewhat declamatory. (Generally available)
Die Walküre (Act III, Scene 3)				
Leb' wohl, du kühnes, herrliches Kind (Wotan's Abshied)	B♭–e1	e–c#1	Bass-baritone	Declamatory, majestic, vigorous, sustained. (Generally available)
Die Walküre (Act III, Scene 2)				
Nicht send' ich dich mehr aus Walhall	c–f1	f–d♭1	Bass-baritone	Animated, majestic. The vocal line is sustained. (Score generally available)
Götterdämmerung (Act I, Scene 2)				
Hier sitz' ich zur Wacht	B♭–d#1	c–c1	Bass	Slow, somber, declamatory. (Score generally available)
Lohengrin (Act I, Scene 2)				
Mein Herr und Gott nun ruf' ich dich	F–e♭1	e♭–c1	Bass	Majestic, very sustained. (Score generally available)
Parsifal (Act III, Scene 2)				
Mein Vater! (Gebet des Amfortas)	A–e♭1	e♭–c1	Bass-baritone or baritone	Slow, declamatory, grave. (Generally available)
Siegfried (Act I, Scene 2)				
Auf wolkigen Höhn	c–f1	d♭–d♭1	Bass-baritone	Sustained, majestic. (Score generally available)
Tannhäuser (Act I, Scene 4)				
Als du in kühnem Sange uns bestrittest	d–e1	f#–d1	Baritone	Very sustained. (Score generally available)
Tannhäuser (Act II, Scene 4)				
Blick' ich umher	B–e♭1	d–d1	Baritone	Very sustained. (Score generally available)
Tannhäuser (Act III, Scene 2) Recitative: Wie Todesahnung Air: O du mein holder Abendstern	B♭–e♭1	d–d1	Baritone	An extended sustained recitative and a very sustained, rather subdued air. (Generally available)

Tannhäuser
 (Act II, Scene 4)
Recitative:
 O Himmel lass'
  dich jetzt erflehen
Air:

| Dir, hohe Liebe | eb-f1 | f#-eb1 | Baritone | Very animated, the vocal line sustained. (Score generally available) |

Tristan und Isolde
 (Act I, Scene 2)

| Darf ich die Antwort sagen | A-f1 | d-d1 | Baritone | Vigorous, animated. (Score generally available) |

CARL MARIA von WEBER
(1786-1826)

Der Freischütz

| Hier im ird'schen Jammertal | d-f#1 | f#-d1 | Baritone or bass-baritone | A vigorous verse song. Demands some flexibility. (Generally available) |

Der Freischütz

| Schweig, damit dich niemand warnt | F#-e1 | d-d1 | Baritone or bass-baritone | A vigorous dramatic air. Has florid passages. (Generally available) |

Euryanthe
Recitative:
 Wo berg' ich mich
Air:
 So weih' ich mich

| Wo berg' ich mich ... So weih' ich mich | G-f1 | d-d1 | Baritone or bass-baritone | A very extended recitative, a sustained vigorous andante, and a dramatic final allegro. Has florid passages. (Schirmer) |

MISCELLANEOUS

MICHAEL W. BALFE
(1808-1870)

The Bohemian Girl

| The heart bowed down | B-e1 | g-d1 | Baritone | Sustained. (Generally available) |